OPTIONS, FUTURES, & OTHER DERIVATIVES

Fourth Edition

John C. Hull

Joseph L. Rotman School of Management
University of Toronto

PRENTICE HALL, Upper Saddle River, NJ 07458

Acquisitions Editor: Paul Donnelly
Editorial Assistant: Cheryl Clayton
Editor-in-Chief: PJ Boardman
Marketing Editor: Lori Braumberger
Production Editor: Richard DeLorenzo
Permissions Coordinator: Monica Stipanov
Associate Managing Editor: Cynthia Regan
Manufacturing Buyer: Lisa DiMaulo
Manufacturing Supervisor: Paul Smolenski
Manufacturing Manager: Vincent Scelta
Designer: Kevin Kall
Design Manager: Patricia Smythe
Cover Design: Bruce Kenselaar
Cover Illustration: "Global Bull Market"/Beth Phillips Photography
Composition/Illustrator (Interior):   Publication Services

LIBRARY OF CONGRESS CATALOGING-IN-PUBLICATION DATA

Hull, John, 1946-
    Options, futures, and other derivatives / John C. Hull.—4th ed.
      p.   cm.
    Includes bibliographical references and index.
    ISBN 0-13-022444-8
    1. Futures.   2. Stock options.   3. Derivative securities.
    I. Title.
    HG6024.A3H85   1999
    332.63'2—dc21   99-26609
                                    CIP

Prentice-Hall International (UK) Limited, *London*
Prentice-Hall of Australia Pty. Limited, *Sydney*
Prentice-Hall Canada, Inc., *Toronto*
Prentice-Hall Hispanoamerica, S.A., *Mexico*
Prentice-Hall of India Private Limited, *New Delhi*
Prentice-Hall of Japan, Inc., *Tokyo*
Prentice-Hall (Singapore) Pte. Ltd.
Editora Prentice-Hall do Brasil, Ltda., *Rio de Janeiro*

Printed in the United States of America

10   9   8   7   6   5   4   3   2   1

To
My Family

Contents

Preface

This book is appropriate for graduate and advanced undergraduate elective courses in business, economics, and financial engineering. It is also suitable for practitioners who want to acquire a working knowledge of how derivatives can be analyzed.

One of the key decisions that must be made by an author who is writing in the area of derivatives concerns the use of mathematics. If the level of mathematical sophistication is too high, the material is likely to be inaccessible to many students and practitioners. If it is too low, some important issues will inevitably be treated in a rather superficial way. In this book, great care has been taken in the use of mathematics. Nonessential mathematical material has been either eliminated or included in end-of-chapter appendices. Concepts that are likely to be new to many readers have been explained carefully, and many numerical examples have been included.

This book provides a unifying approach to the valuation of all derivatives — not just futures and options. The book assumes that the reader has taken an introductory course in finance and an introductory course in probability and statistics. No prior knowledge of options, futures contracts, swaps, and so on is assumed. It is not therefore necessary for students to take an elective course in investments prior to taking a course based on this book.

Changes in This Edition

This edition contains more material than the third edition. The material in the third edition has been updated and its presentation has been improved in a number of places. The major changes include:

1. A new chapter (chapter 14) has been included on value at risk.
2. A new chapter (chapter 15) has been included on estimating volatilities and correlations. GARCH models are covered in much more detail than in the third edition.
3. Chapter 19 contains much new material and explains the role played by martingales and measures in the valuation of derivatives.
4. Chapter 20 on the standard market models for valuing interest rate derivatives has been revised. It now uses the material in chapter 19 to provide a more complete discussion of the models for valuing bond options, caps, and swap options.

5. There are now two chapters on equilibrium and no-arbitrage models of the term structure (chapters 21 and 22). Chapter 21 covers equilibrium models and one-factor no-arbitrage models of the short rate. Chapter 22 covers two-factor models of the short rate, the HJM model, and the LIBOR market (BGM) model.

6. Chapter 4 on Interest Rates and Duration has been rewritten to make the material clearer and more relevant.

7. Chapter 23 on Credit Risk has been rewritten to reflect developments in this important area.

8. More material has been added on volatility smiles and volatility skews (chapter 17).

9. The sequencing of the material has been changed slightly. Volatility smiles and alternatives to Black–Scholes now appear before the chapter on exotic options, which in turn appears before the material on interest rate derivatives.

10. The notation has been improved and simplified. S_0 and F_0 are used to denote the asset price and the forward price today (that is, at time zero) and the cumbersome "$T - t$" no longer appears in most parts of the book.

11. A glossary of terms has been included.

12. Many new problems and questions have been added.

Software

New Excel-based software, DerivaGem, is included with the book. This software is a big improvement over the software included with previous editions. It has been carefully designed to complement the material in the text. Users can calculate options prices, imply volatilities, and calculate Greek letters for European options, American options, exotic options, and interest rate derivatives. Interest rate derivatives can be valued either using Black's model or a no-arbitrage model. The software can be used to display binomial trees (see for example Figure 16.3 and Figure 21.11) and provide many different charts showing the impact of different variables on either option prices or the Greek letters.

The software is described more fully at the end of the book. Updates to the software can be downloaded from my Web site

http://www.mgmt.utoronto.ca/~hull

Slides

Several hundred PowerPoint slides can be downloaded from my Web site. The slides now use only standard fonts. Instructors can adapt the slides to meet their own needs.

Answers to Questions

Solutions to the end-of-chapter problems in the first three editions were available only in the Instructor's Manual. Over the years many people have asked me to make the solutions more generally available. I have hesitated to do this because it would prevent instructors from using the problems as assignment questions.

In this edition I have dealt with this issue by dividing the end-of-chapter problems into two groups: "Questions and Problems" and "Assignment Questions". There are over 450 Questions and Problems and solutions to these are in a book *Options, Futures, & Other Derivatives: Solutions Manual,* which is published by Prentice Hall. There are about 80 Assignment Questions. Solutions to these are available only in the Instructor's Manual.

Acknowledgments

Many people have played a part in the production of this book. The academics and practitioners who have made excellent and useful suggestions include Farhang Aslani, Jas Badyal, Emilio Barone, Giovanni Barone-Adesi, Alex Bergier, George Blazenko, Laurence Booth, Phelim Boyle, Peter Carr, Don Chance, J.-P. Chateau, Ren-Raw Chen, George Constantinides, Michel Crouhy, Emanuel Derman, Brian Donaldson, Dieter Dorp, Scott Drabin, Jerome Duncan, Steinar Ekern, David Fowler, Louis Gagnon, Dajiang Guo, Jörgen Hallbeck, Ian Hawkins, Michael Hemler, Steve Heston, Bernie Hildebrandt, Kiyoshi Kato, Kevin Kneafsy, Bill Margrabe, Izzy Nelkin, Neil Pearson, Paul Potvin, Shailendra Pandit, Eric Reiner, Richard Rendleman, Gordon Roberts, Chris Robinson, Cheryl Rosen, John Rumsey, Ani Sanyal, Klaus Schurger, Eduardo Schwartz, Michael Selby, Piet Sercu, Duane Stock, Edward Thorpe, Yisong Tian, P.V. Viswanath, George Wang, Jason Wei, Bob Whaley, Alan White, Hailiang Yang, and Victor Zak. I am particularly grateful to Eduardo Schwartz, who read the original manuscript for the first edition and made many comments that led to significant improvements, and to Richard Rendleman and George Constantinides, who made specific suggestions that led to improvements in this edition.

The first three editions of this book were very popular with practitioners and much of the material in the book has been greatly influenced by the informal contacts I have had with practitioners. The students in my elective courses on derivatives at the University of Toronto have also influenced the evolution of the book.

Alan White, a colleague at the University of Toronto (formerly a colleague at York University), deserves a special acknowledgment. Alan and I have been carrying out joint research in the area of derivatives for over 15 years. During that time we have spent countless hours discussing different issues concerning derivatives. Many of the new ideas in this book, and many of the new ways used to explain old ideas, are as much Alan's as mine. Alan read the original version of this book very carefully and made many excellent suggestions for improvement.

The staff at Prentice Hall have been a continual source of encouragement to me as this project has progressed. I would particularly like to thank Paul Donnelly, my editor, who has always shown a keen interest in the development of this book.

I welcome comments on the book from readers. My e-mail address is

hull@mgmt.utoronto.ca

John C. Hull
University of Toronto

CHAPTER 1

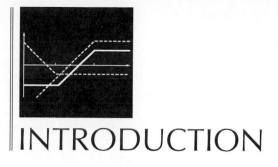

INTRODUCTION

A *derivative* (or *derivative security*) is a financial instrument whose value depends on the values of other, more basic underlying variables. In recent years, derivatives have become increasingly important in the world of finance. Futures and options are now traded actively on many exchanges. Forward contracts, swaps, and many different types of options are regularly traded outside exchanges by financial institutions, fund managers, and corporations in what is termed the *over-the-counter* market. Derivatives also often form part of a bond or stock issue.

Very often the variables underlying derivatives are the prices of traded assets. A stock option, for example, is a derivative whose value is dependent on the price of a stock. However, as we shall see, derivatives can be dependent on almost any variable, from the price of hogs to the amount of snow falling at a certain ski resort.

This book has two objectives. The first is to explore the properties of those derivatives that are commonly encountered in practice; the second is to provide a general framework within which all derivatives can be valued and hedged. In this opening chapter, we take a first look at forward contracts, futures contracts, and options. In later chapters, these instruments and the way they are traded are discussed in more detail.

1.1 FORWARD CONTRACTS

A *forward contract* is a particularly simple derivative. It is an agreement to buy or sell an asset at a certain future time for a certain price. It can be contrasted with a *spot contract*, which is an agreement to buy or sell an asset today. A forward contract is traded in the over-the-counter market—usually between two financial institutions or between a financial institution and one of its clients.

One of the parties to a forward contract assumes a *long position* and agrees to buy the underlying asset on a certain specified future date for a certain specified price. The other party assumes a *short position* and agrees to sell the asset on the same date for the same price. The price in a forward contract is known as the *delivery price*. At the time the contract is entered into, the delivery price is chosen so that the value of the forward contract to both sides is zero.[1] This means that it costs nothing to take either a long or a short position.

---

[1]In chapter 3 we explain the way this delivery price can be calculated.

Forward contracts are commonly used to hedge foreign currency risk. Suppose it is April 5 of a certain year and the treasurer of a U.S. corporation knows that the corporation will receive 1 million pounds sterling in three months (on July 5) and wants to hedge against exchange rate moves. The treasurer could contact a bank, find out that the exchange rate for a three-month forward contract on sterling is 1.6000, and agree to sell 1 million pounds. The corporation then has a short forward contract on sterling. It has agreed that on July 5 it will sell 1 million pounds sterling to the bank for $1.6 million. The bank has a long forward contract on sterling. It has agreed that on July 5 it will buy 1 million pounds sterling for $1.6 million. Both sides have made a binding commitment.

Forward Price

The *forward price* for a particular forward contract at a particular time is the delivery price that would apply if the contract were entered into at that time. Thus, on April 5 in our example, 1.6000 is the forward price for a forward contract that involves the delivery of sterling on July 5.

It is important to distinguish between the forward price and the delivery price. The two are the same when the contract is first entered into but are likely to be different at later times. In our foreign exchange example, the forward price and the delivery price are both 1.6000 on April 5 for a contract with a delivery date of July 5. However, consider the situation on May 5 when the forward contract has been in existence for one month. The delivery price in the forward contract is still 1.6000. The forward price is the price of sterling on May 5 for a (two-month) forward contract with a delivery date of July 5. In general, this will not be 1.6000. If the sterling exchange rate has increased between April 5 and May 5, it will be tend to be greater than 1.6000; if the sterling exchange rate has decreased between April 5 and May 5, it will tend to be less than 1.6000.

The forward price of a contract usually depends on maturity. Table 1.1 gives actual quotes for the sterling–U.S. dollar exchange rate on January 20, 1998. The first quote indicates that, ignoring bid–offer spreads, sterling can be bought or sold in the spot market (i.e., for virtually immediate delivery) at the rate of $1.6273 per pound; the second quote indicates that the forward price for a contract to buy or sell sterling in one month is $1.6246 per pound; the third quote indicates that the forward price for a contract to buy or sell sterling in two months is $1.6222 per pound; and so on.

Table 1.1	Spot and Forward Foreign Exchange Quotes on Sterling, January 20, 1998		
Spot	1.6273	3-month forward	1.6196
1-month forward	1.6246	6-month forward	1.6117
2-month forward	1.6222	1-year forward	1.5973

Payoffs from Forward Contracts

Consider a trader who enters into a long forward contract on January 20, 1998, to buy £1 million in three months at an exchange rate of 1.6196. What are the possible outcomes? The contract would obligate the trader to buy £1 million for U.S. $1,619,600. If the spot exchange rate rose to, say, 1.6500, at the end of the three months, the trader would gain $30,400 ($= \$1,650,000 - \$1,619,600$) because the pounds, as soon as they have been purchased, can be sold for $1,650,000. Similarly, if the spot exchange rate fell to 1.5500 at the end of the 90 days, the trader would lose $69,600 because the forward contract would lead to the trader paying U.S. $69,600 more than the market price for the sterling.

In general, the payoff from a long position in a forward contract on one unit of an asset is

$$S_T - K$$

where K is the delivery price and S_T is the spot price of the asset at maturity of the contract. This is because the holder of the contract is obligated to buy an asset worth S_T for K. Similarly, the payoff from a short position in a forward contract on one unit of an asset is

$$K - S_T$$

These payoffs can be positive or negative. They are illustrated in Figure 1.1. Because it costs nothing to enter into a forward contract, the payoff from the contract is also the trader's total gain or loss from the contract.

Forward Prices and Spot Prices

We will be discussing in some detail the relationship between spot and forward prices in chapter 3. In this section we illustrate the reason why the two are related by considering forward contracts on gold. We assume that there are no storage costs associated with gold.

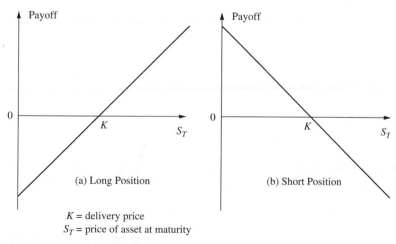

K = delivery price
S_T = price of asset at maturity

Figure 1.1 Payoffs from forward contracts.

Suppose that the spot price of gold is $300 per ounce and the risk-free interest rate for investments lasting one year is 5% per annum. What is a reasonable value for the one-year forward price of gold?

Suppose first that the one-year forward price is $340 per ounce. A trader can immediately take the following actions:

1. Borrow $300 at 5% for one year.
2. Buy one ounce of gold.
3. Enter into a short forward contract to sell the gold for $340 in one year.

The interest on the $300 that is borrowed (assuming annual compounding) is $15. The trader can, therefore, use $315 of the $340 that is obtained for the gold in one year to repay the loan. The remaining $25 is profit. Any one-year forward price greater than $315 will lead to this arbitrage trading strategy being profitable.

Suppose next that the forward price is $300. An investor who has a portfolio that includes gold can

1. Sell the gold for $300 per ounce.
2. Invest the proceeds at 5%.
3. Enter into a long forward contract to repurchase the gold in one year for $300 per ounce.

When this strategy is compared with the alternative strategy of keeping the gold in the portfolio for one year we see that the investor is better off by $15 per ounce. In any situation where the forward price is less than $315, investors holding gold have an incentive to sell the gold and enter into a long forward contract in the way that has been described.

The first strategy is profitable when the one-year forward price of gold is greater than $315. As more traders attempt to take advantage of this strategy, the demand for short forward contracts will increase and the one-year forward price of gold will fall. The second strategy is profitable for all investors who hold gold in their portfolios when the one-year forward price of gold is less than $315. As these investors attempt to take advantage of this strategy, the demand for long forward contracts will increase and the one-year forward price of gold will rise. Assuming that individuals are always willing to take advantage of arbitrage opportunities when they arise, we can conclude that the activities of traders should cause the one-year forward price of gold to be exactly $315. Any other price leads to an arbitrage opportunity.[2]

1.2 FUTURES CONTRACTS

Like a forward contract, a futures contract is an agreement between two parties to buy or sell an asset at a certain time in the future for a certain price. Unlike forward contracts, futures contracts are normally traded on an exchange. To make trading

---

[2]Our arguments make the simplifying assumption that the rate of interest on borrowed funds is the same as the rate of interest on invested funds.

possible, the exchange specifies certain standardized features of the contract. As the two parties to the contract do not necessarily know each other, the exchange also provides a mechanism that gives the two parties a guarantee that the contract will be honored.

The largest exchanges on which futures contracts are traded are the Chicago Board of Trade (CBOT) and the Chicago Mercantile Exchange (CME). On these and other exchanges, a very wide range of commodities and financial assets form the underlying assets in the various contracts. The commodities include pork bellies, live cattle, sugar, wool, lumber, copper, aluminum, gold, and tin. The financial assets include stock indices, currencies, and Treasury bonds.

One way in which a futures contract is different from a forward contract is that an exact delivery date is usually not specified. The contract is referred to by its delivery month, and the exchange specifies the period during the month when delivery must be made. For commodities, the delivery period is often the entire month. The holder of the short position has the right to choose the time during the delivery period when it will make delivery. Usually, contracts with several different delivery months are traded at any one time. The exchange specifies the amount of the asset to be delivered for one contract and how the futures price is to be quoted. In the case of a commodity, the exchange also specifies the product quality and the delivery location. Consider, for example, the wheat futures contract currently traded on the Chicago Board of Trade. The size of the contract is 5,000 bushels. Contracts for five delivery months (March, May, July, September, and December) are available for up to 18 months into the future. The exchange specifies the grades of wheat that can be delivered and the places where delivery can be made.

Futures prices are regularly reported in the financial press. Suppose that on September 1, the December futures price of gold is quoted as $300. This is the price, exclusive of commissions, at which traders can agree to buy or sell gold for December delivery. It is determined on the floor of the exchange in the same way as other prices (i.e., by the laws of supply and demand). If more traders want to go long than to go short, the price goes up; if the reverse is true, the price goes down.[3]

Further details on issues such as margin requirements, daily settlement procedures, delivery procedures, bid–ask spreads, and the role of the exchange clearinghouse are given in chapter 2.

1.3 OPTIONS

Options on stocks were first traded on an organized exchange in 1973. Since then there has been a dramatic growth in options markets. Options are now traded on many exchanges throughout the world. Huge volumes of options are also traded over the counter by banks and other financial institutions. The underlying assets include

---

[3]In chapter 3 we discuss the relationship between a futures price and the spot price of the underlying asset (gold, in this case).

stocks, stock indices, foreign currencies, debt instruments, commodities, and futures contracts.

There are two basic types of options. A *call option* gives the holder the right to buy the underlying asset by a certain date for a certain price. A *put option* gives the holder the right to sell the underlying asset by a certain date for a certain price. The price in the contract is known as the *exercise price* or *strike price*; the date in the contract is known as the *expiration date* or *maturity*. *American options* can be exercised at any time up to the expiration date. *European options* can be exercised only on the expiration date itself.[4] Most of the options that are traded on exchanges are American, and one contract is usually an agreement to buy or sell 100 shares. European options are generally easier to analyze than American options, and some of the properties of an American option are frequently deduced from those of its European counterpart.

It should be emphasized that an option gives the holder the right to do something. The holder does not have to exercise this right. This fact distinguishes options from forwards and futures, where the holder is obligated to buy or sell the underlying asset. Note that whereas it costs nothing to enter into a forward or futures contract, there is a cost to acquiring an option.

Examples

Consider the situation of a trader who buys one European call option contract on IBM stock with a strike price of $100 (that is, the trader purchases the right to buy 100 IBM shares for $100 each). Suppose that the current stock price is $98, the expiration date of the option is in two months, and the option price is $5. Because the options are European, the trader can exercise only on the expiration date. If the stock price on this date is less than $100, the trader will clearly choose not to exercise. (There is no point in buying for $100 a stock that has a market value of less than $100.) In these circumstances the trader loses the entire initial investment of $500. If the stock price is above $100 on the expiration date, the options will be exercised. Suppose, for example, that the stock price is $115. By exercising the options, the trader is able to buy 100 shares for $100 per share. If the shares are sold immediately, the trader makes a gain of $15 per share, or $1,500, ignoring transactions costs. When the initial cost of the options is taken into account, the net profit to the trader is $10 per option, or $1,000. (This calculation ignores the time value of money.) Figure 1.2 shows the way in which the trader's net profit or loss per option varies with the terminal stock price. Note that, in some cases, the trader exercises the options but takes a loss overall. Consider the situation when the stock price is $103 on the expiration date. The trader exercises the options but takes a loss of $200 overall. This is better than the loss of $500 that would be incurred if the options were not exercised.

---

[4]Note that the terms *American* and *European* do not refer to the location of the option or the exchange. Some options trading on North American exchanges are European.

Whereas the purchaser of a call option is hoping that the stock price will increase, the purchaser of a put option is hoping that it will decrease. Consider a trader who buys one European put option contract on Exxon with a strike price of $70 (that is, the trader buys the right to sell 100 Exxon shares for $70 each). Suppose that the current stock price is $66, the expiration date of the option is in three months, and the option price is $7. Because the options are European, they will be exercised only if the stock price is below $70 at the expiration date. Suppose that the stock price is $50 on this date. The trader can buy 100 shares for $50 per share and, under the terms of the put option, sell the same shares for $70, to realize a gain of $20 per share, or $2,000. (Again, transactions costs are ignored.) When the initial cost of the option is taken into account, the trader's net profit is $13 per option, or $1,300. Of course, if the final stock price is above $70, the put option expires worthless and the trader loses $7 per option, or $700. Figure 1.3 shows

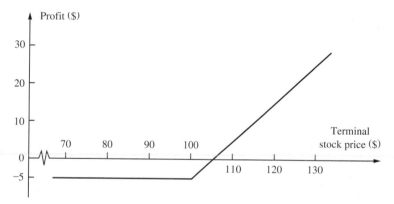

Figure 1.2   Profit from buying an IBM European call option: option price = $5, strike price = $100.

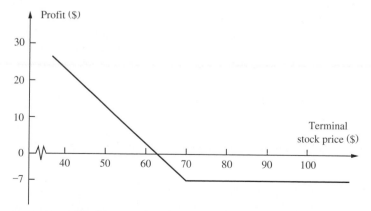

Figure 1.3   Profit from buying an Exxon European put option: option price = $7, strike price = $70.

the way in which the trader's profit or loss per option varies with the terminal stock price.

As already mentioned, stock options are often American rather than European. This means that the traders in the examples just given do not have to wait until the expiration date before exercising the options. We will see in later chapters that there are some circumstances under which it is optimal to exercise American options prior to maturity.

Option Positions

There are two sides to every option contract. On one side is the trader who has taken the long position (i.e., has bought the option). On the other side is the trader who has taken a short position (i.e., has sold or *written* the option). The writer of an option receives cash up front but has potential liabilities later. The writer's profit or loss is the

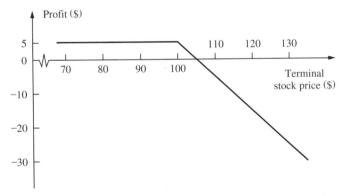

Figure 1.4 Profit from writing an IBM European call option: option price = $5, strike price = $100.

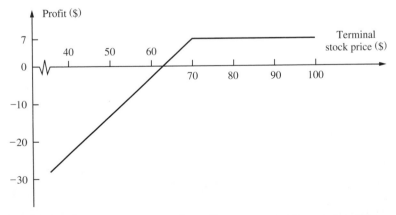

Figure 1.5 Profit from writing an Exxon European put option: option price = $7, strike price = $70.

reverse of that for the purchaser of the option. Figures 1.4 and 1.5 show the variation of the profit and loss with the final stock price for writers of the options considered in Figures 1.2 and 1.3.

Payoffs

Four basic option positions are possible:

1. A long position in a call option.
2. A long position in a put option.
3. A short position in a call option.
4. A short position in a put option.

It is often useful to characterize European option positions in terms of the payoff to the trader at maturity. The initial cost of the option is then not included in the calculation. If X is the strike price and S_T is the final price of the underlying asset, the payoff from a long position in a European call option is

$$\max(S_T - X, 0)$$

This reflects the fact that the option will be exercised if $S_T > X$ and will not be exercised if $S_T \leq X$. The payoff to the holder of a short position in the European call option is

$$-\max(S_T - X, 0)$$

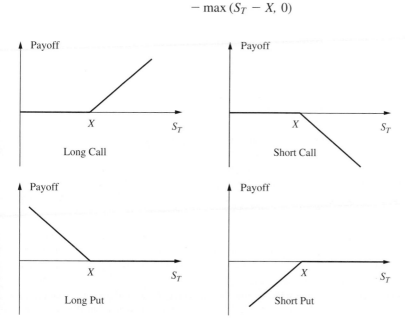

X = Strike price
S_T = Price of asset at maturity

Figure 1.6   Payoffs from positions in European options.

or

$$\min (X - S_T, 0)$$

The payoff to the holder of a long position in a European put option is

$$\max (X - S_T, 0)$$

and the payoff from a short position in a European put option is

$$- \max (X - S_T, 0)$$

or

$$\min (S_T - X, 0)$$

Figure 1.6 illustrates these payoffs graphically.

1.4   OTHER DERIVATIVES

The call and put options described in section 1.3 are sometimes termed "plain vanilla" or "standard" derivatives. Since the early 1980s, banks and other financial institutions have been very imaginative in designing nonstandard derivatives to meet the needs of clients. Sometimes these are sold by financial institutions to their corporate clients. On other occasions, they are added to bond or stock issues to make these issues more attractive to investors. Some nonstandard derivatives are simply portfolios of two or more "plain vanilla" call and put options. Others are far more complex. The possibilities for designing new interesting nonstandard derivatives seem to be almost limitless. Nonstandard derivatives are sometimes termed *exotic options* or just *exotics*. In chapter 18 we discuss different types of exotics and consider how they can be valued.

We now give examples of three derivatives that, although they appear to be complex, can be decomposed into portfolios of plain vanilla call and put options.[5]

Example 1.1: Standard Oil's Bond Issue   In 1986 Standard Oil issued some bonds from which the holder received no interest. At the bond's maturity the company promised to pay $1,000 plus an additional amount based on the price of oil at that time. The additional amount was equal to the product of 170 and the excess (if any) of the price of a barrel of oil at maturity over $25. The maximum additional amount paid was $2,550 (which corresponds to a price of $40 per barrel). These bonds provided holders with a stake in a commodity that was critically important to the fortunes of the company. If the price of the commodity went up, the company was in a good position to provide the bondholder with the additional payment.

Example 1.2: ICON   In 1985, Bankers Trust developed *index currency option notes* (ICONs). These are bonds in which the amount received by the holder at maturity varies with a foreign exchange rate. Two exchange rates, X_1 and X_2, are specified with $X_1 > X_2$. If the exchange rate at the bond's maturity is above X_1, the bondholder receives the full face value. If it is less than X_2, the bondholder receives nothing. Between X_2 and X_1, a portion of the full face value is received. Bankers Trust's first issue of an ICON was for

---

[5] See Problems 1.25, 1.26, and 1.31 at the end of this chapter for how the decomposition is accomplished.

the Long Term Credit Bank of Japan. The ICON specified that if the yen–U.S. dollar exchange rate, S_T, is greater than 169 yen per dollar at maturity (in 1995), the holder of the bond receives \$1,000. If it is less than 169 yen per dollar, the amount received by the holder of the bond is

$$1,000 - \max \left[0, \ 1,000 \left(\frac{169}{S_T} - 1 \right) \right]$$

When the exchange rate is below 84.5, nothing is received by the holder at maturity.

Example 1.3: Range Forward Contract *Range forward contracts* or *flexible forwards* are popular in foreign exchange markets. Suppose that on January 20, 1998, a U.S. company finds that it will require sterling in three months and faces the exchange rates shown in Table 1.1. It could enter into a three-month forward contract to buy at 1.6196. A range forward contract is an alternative. Under this contract an exchange rate band straddling 1.6196 is set. Suppose that the chosen band runs from 1.6000 to 1.6400. The range forward contract is then designed to ensure that if the spot rate in three months is less than 1.6000, the company pays 1.6000; if it is between 1.6000 and 1.6400, the company pays the spot rate; if it is greater than 1.6400, the company pays 1.6400.

Other, More Complex Examples

As mentioned earlier, there is virtually no limit to the innovations that are possible in the derivatives area. Some of the options traded over the counter have payoffs dependent on maximum value attained by a variable during a period of time; some have payoffs dependent on the average value of a variable during a period of time; some have exercise prices that are functions of time; some have features where exercising one option automatically gives the holder another option; some have payoffs dependent on the square of some future interest rate; and so on.

Traditionally, the variables underlying options and other derivatives have been stock prices, stock indices, interest rates, exchange rates, and commodity prices. However, other underlying variables are becoming increasingly common. For example, the payoffs from *credit derivatives*, which are discussed in chapter 23, depend on the creditworthiness of one or more companies; *weather derivatives* have payoffs dependent on the average temperature at particular locations; *insurance derivatives* have payoffs dependent on the dollar amount of insurance claims of a specified type made during a specified period; *electricity derivatives* have payoffs dependent on the spot price of electricity; and so on.

1.5 TYPES OF TRADERS

Derivatives attract three types of traders: hedgers, speculators, and arbitrageurs. We now review the activities of each of these.

Hedgers

We have already looked at one example of the way in which a forward contract can be used for hedging in section 1.1. A treasurer who knows that a certain amount of foreign currency will be received at a certain time in the future can hedge the foreign exchange risk by taking a short position in a forward contract. Similarly, a treasurer who knows that a certain amount of foreign currency will have to be purchased at a certain future time can hedge by taking a long position in a forward contract.

Options can also be used for hedging. Consider an investor who, in August, owns 500 IBM shares. The current share price is $102 per share. The investor is concerned that the share price may decline sharply in the next two months and wants protection. The investor could buy October put options on the Chicago Board Options Exchange (CBOE) to sell 500 shares for a strike price of $100. Because each put contract on the CBOE is for the sale of 100 shares, a total of five contracts would be purchased. If the quoted option price is $4, each option contract would cost $100 \times \$4 = \$400$, and the total cost of the hedging strategy would be $5 \times \$400 = \$2,000$.

The strategy costs $2,000 but guarantees that the shares can be sold for at least $100 per share during the life of the option. If the market price of IBM stock falls below $100, the options can be exercised so that $50,000 is realized for the whole holding. When the cost of the options is taken into account, the amount realized is $48,000. If the market price stays above $100, the options are not exercised and expire worthless. However, in this case the value of the holding is always above $50,000 (or above $48,000 when the cost of the options is taken into account).

There is a fundamental difference between the use of forward contracts and options for hedging. Forward contracts are designed to neutralize risk by fixing the price that the hedger will pay or receive for the underlying asset. Options contracts, by contrast, provide insurance. They offer a way for investors to protect themselves against adverse price movements in the future while still allowing them to benefit from favorable price movements. Unlike forward contracts, options involve the payment of an up-front fee.

Speculators

We now move on to consider how forward contracts and options can be used by speculators. Whereas hedgers want to avoid an exposure to adverse movements in the price of an asset, speculators wish to take a position in the market. Either they are betting that the price will go up or they are betting that it will go down.

Consider a treasurer who, on January 20, 1998, thinks that the pound sterling will strengthen relative to the U.S. dollar over the next two months and is prepared to back that hunch to the tune of £250,000. The treasurer can take a long position in a forward contract on £250,000. From Table 1.1, the forward foreign exchange rate is 1.6222. If the exchange rate turns out to be 1.7000 on March 20, the treasurer is able to buy for $1.6222 an asset worth $1.7000, so that a profit of $(1.7000 - 1.6222) \times 250,000 = \$19,450$ is realized.

Next we consider an example of how a speculator could use options. Suppose that in September, a speculator wants to go long in Exxon stock. In other words, the speculator wants to be in a position to gain if the stock price increases. Suppose that the stock price is currently $78 and that a December call with an $80 strike price is

Table 1.2	Comparison of Profits (Losses) from Two Alternative Strategies for Using $7,800 to Speculate on Exxon Stock

	December Stock Price	
Strategy	**$70**	**$90**
Buy shares	($800)	$1,200
Buy call options	($7,800)	$18,200

currently selling for $3. Table 1.2 illustrates two possible alternatives, assuming that the speculator is willing to invest $7,800. The first alternative involves the purchase of 100 shares. The second involves the purchase of 2,600 call options (i.e., 26 call option contracts) on Exxon.

Suppose that the speculator's hunch is correct and the price of Exxon's shares rises to $90 by December. The first alternative of buying the stock yields a profit of

$$100 \times (\$90 - \$78) = \$1,200$$

However, the second alternative is far more profitable. A call option on Exxon with a strike price of $80 gives a payoff of $10, because the option enables something worth $90 to be bought for $80. The total payoff from all the options that have been purchased is

$$2,600 \times \$10 = \$26,000$$

Subtracting the original cost of the options yields a net profit of

$$\$26,000 - \$7,800 = \$18,200$$

The options strategy is, therefore, over 15 times more profitable than the strategy of buying the stock.

Options also give rise to a greater potential loss. Suppose the stock price falls to $70 by December. The first alternative of buying stock yields a loss of

$$100 \times (\$78 - \$70) = \$800$$

Because the call options expire without being exercised, the options strategy would lead to a loss of $7,800—the original amount paid for the options.

It is clear from Table 1.2 that options provide a form of leverage. For a given investment, the use of options magnifies the financial consequences. Good outcomes become very good and bad outcomes become very bad.

Forward contracts and options are similar instruments for speculators in that they both provide a way that a type of leverage can be obtained. However, there is an important difference between the two. With a forward contract, the speculator's potential loss as well as the potential gain is very large. With a long position in options, no matter how bad things get, the speculator's loss is limited to the amount paid for the options.

Arbitrageurs

Arbitrageurs are a third important group of traders. Arbitrage involves locking in a profit by simultaneously entering into transactions in two or more markets. Earlier in this chapter we saw how arbitrage is possible when the forward price of gold is out of line with the spot price. In the rest of this book, we will see many other examples of arbitrage. This section illustrates the concept of arbitrage with a very simple example.

Consider a stock that is traded on both the New York Stock Exchange and the London Stock Exchange. Suppose that the stock price is $172 in New York and £100 in London at a time when the exchange rate is $1.7500 per pound. An arbitrageur could simultaneously buy 100 shares of the stock in New York and sell them in London to obtain a risk-free profit of

$$100 \times [(\$1.75 \times 100) - \$172]$$

or $300 in the absence of transactions costs. Transactions costs would probably eliminate the profit for a small trader. However, a large investment house faces very low transactions costs in both the stock market and the foreign exchange market. It would find the arbitrage opportunity very attractive and would try to take as much advantage of it as possible.

Arbitrage opportunities such as the one just described cannot last for long. As arbitrageurs buy the stock in New York, the forces of supply and demand will cause the dollar price of the stock to rise. Similarly, as they sell the stock in London, the sterling price of the stock will be driven down. Very quickly, the two prices will become equivalent at the current exchange rate. Indeed, the existence of profit-hungry arbitrageurs makes it unlikely that a major disparity between the sterling price and the dollar price could ever exist in the first place. Generalizing from this example, we can say that the very existence of arbitrageurs means that, in practice, only very small arbitrage opportunities are observed in the prices that are quoted in most financial markets. In this book, most of the arguments concerning the valuation of derivatives will be based on the assumption that there are no arbitrage opportunities.

1.6 THOSE BIG LOSSES

In the early 1990s organizations such as Gibson Greetings, Procter & Gamble, Kidder Peabody, Orange County, and Barings experienced huge losses from trading derivatives. The losses received a great deal of publicity and made many people very wary of derivatives. Some nonfinancial corporations announced plans to reduce their use of derivatives. The level of interest in some of the more exotic products offered by financial institutions declined, at least temporarily.

The stories behind the losses emphasize the point made in section 1.5 that derivatives can be used for either hedging or speculation; that is, they can be used either to reduce risks or to take risks. The losses occurred because derivatives were used inappropriately. Employees who had an implicit or explicit mandate to hedge their company's risks decided instead to speculate.

The lesson to be learned from the losses is the importance of *internal controls*. Senior management within a company should issue a clear and unambiguous policy statement about how derivatives are to be used, and the extent to which it is permissible for employees to take positions on movements in market variables. Management should then institute controls to ensure that the policy is carried out. It is a recipe for disaster to give one or two people complete authority to trade derivatives without a close monitoring of the risks being taken.

SUMMARY

One of the exciting developments in finance over the last 20 years has been the growth of derivatives markets. In many situations, both hedgers and speculators find it more attractive to trade a derivative on an asset than to trade the asset itself. Some derivatives are traded on exchanges. Others are traded by financial institutions, fund managers, and corporations in the over-the-counter market, or added to new issues of debt and equity securities. Much of this book is concerned with the valuation of derivatives. The aim is to present a unifying framework within which all derivatives—not just options or futures—can be valued.

In this chapter we have taken a first look at forward, futures, and options contracts. A forward or futures contract involves an obligation to buy or sell an asset at a certain time in the future for a certain price. There are two types of options: calls and puts. A call option gives the holder the right to buy an asset by a certain date for a certain price. A put option gives the holder the right to sell an asset by a certain date for a certain price. Forwards, futures, and options trade on a wide range of different underlying assets.

Derivatives have been very successful innovations in capital markets. Three main types of traders can be identified: hedgers, speculators, and arbitrageurs. Hedgers are in the position where they face risk associated with the price of an asset. They use derivatives to reduce or eliminate this risk. Speculators wish to bet on future movements in the price of an asset. They use derivatives to get extra leverage. Arbitrageurs are in business to take advantage of a discrepancy between prices in two different markets. If, for example, they see the futures price of an asset getting out of line with the cash price, they will take offsetting positions in the two markets to lock in a profit.

QUESTIONS AND PROBLEMS
(ANSWERS IN SOLUTIONS MANUAL)

1.1. What is the difference between a long forward position and a short forward position?

1.2. Explain carefully the difference between hedging, speculation, and arbitrage.

1.3. What is the difference between entering into a long forward contract when the forward price is $50 and taking a long position in a call option with a strike price of $50?

1.4. Explain carefully the difference between writing a call option and buying a put option.

1.5. A trader enters into a short forward contract on 100 million yen. The forward exchange rate is $0.0080 per yen. How much does the trader gain or lose if the exchange rate at the end of the contract is (a) $0.0074 per yen; (b) $0.0091 per yen?

1.6. A trader enters into a short cotton futures contract when the futures price is 50 cents per pound. The contract is for the delivery of 50,000 pounds. How much does the trader gain or lose if the cotton price at the end of the contract is (a) 48.20 cents per pound; (b) 51.30 cents per pound?

1.7. Suppose that you write a put option contract on 100 IBM shares with a strike price of $120 and an expiration date in three months. The current price of IBM stock is $121. What have you committed yourself to? How much could you gain or lose?

1.8. You would like to speculate on a rise in the price of a certain stock. The current stock price is $29, and a three-month call with a strike of $30 costs $2.90. You have $5,800 to invest. Identify two alternative strategies, one involving an investment in the stock and the other involving investment in the option. What are the potential gains and losses from each?

1.9. Suppose that you own 5,000 shares worth $25 each. How can put options be used to provide you with insurance against a decline in the value of your holding over the next four months?

1.10. A trader buys a European put on a share for $3. The stock price is $42 and the strike price is $40. Under what circumstances does the trader make a profit? Under what circumstances will the option be exercised? Draw a diagram showing the variation of the trader's profit with the stock price at the maturity of the option.

1.11. A trader sells a European call on a share for $4. The stock price is $47 and the strike price is $50. Under what circumstances does the trader make a profit? Under what circumstances will the option be exercised? Draw a diagram showing the variation of the trader's profit with the stock price at the maturity of the option.

1.12. A trader buys a call option with a strike price of $45 and a put option with a strike price of $40. Both options have the same maturity. The call costs $3 and the put costs $4. Draw a diagram showing the variation of the trader's profit with the asset price.

1.13. When first issued, a stock provides funds for a company. Is the same true of a stock option? Discuss.

1.14. Explain why a forward contract can be used for either speculation or hedging.

1.15. Suppose that a European call option to buy a share for $50 costs $2.50 and is held until maturity. Under what circumstances will the holder of the option make a profit? Under what circumstances will the option be exercised? Draw a diagram illustrating how the profit from a long position in the option depends on the stock price at maturity of the option.

1.16. Suppose that a European put option to sell a share for $60 costs $4 and is held until maturity. Under what circumstances will the seller of the option (i.e., the party with the short position) make a profit? Under what circumstances will the option be exercised? Draw a diagram illustrating how the profit from a short position in the option depends on the stock price at maturity of the option.

1.17. A trader writes a European-style call option maturing in September with a strike price of $20. It is now May; the stock price is $18, and the option price is $2. Describe the trader's cash flows if the option is held until September and the stock price is $25 at that time.

1.18. A trader writes a European-style put option maturing in December with a strike price of $30. The price of the option is $4. Under what circumstances does the trader make a gain?

1.19. A company knows that it is due to receive a certain amount of a foreign currency in four months. What type of option contract is appropriate for hedging?

1.20. A United States company expects to have to pay 1 million Canadian dollars in six months. Explain how the exchange rate risk can be hedged using (a) a forward contract; (b) an option.

1.21. The price of gold is currently $500 per ounce. The forward price for delivery in one year is $700. An arbitrageur can borrow money at 10% per annum. What should the arbitrageur do? Assume that the cost of storing gold is zero.

1.22. The Chicago Board of Trade offers a futures contract on long-term Treasury bonds. Characterize the traders likely to use this contract.

1.23. "Options and futures are zero-sum games." What do you think is meant by this statement?

1.24. Describe the profit from the following portfolio: a long forward contract on an asset and a long European put option on the asset with the same maturity as the forward contract and a strike price that is equal to the forward price of the asset at the time the portfolio is set up.

1.25. Show that an ICON such as the one described in section 1.4 is a combination of a regular bond and two options.

1.26. Show that a range forward contract such as the one described in section 1.4 is a combination of two options. How can a range forward contract be constructed so that it has zero value?

1.27. On July 1, 1999, a company enters into a forward contract to buy 10 million Japanese yen on January 1, 2000. On September 1, 1999, it enters into a forward contract to sell 10 million Japanese yen on January 1, 2000. Describe the payoff from this strategy.

1.28. Suppose that sterling–U.S. dollar spot and forward exchange rates are as follows:

Spot	1.6080
90-day forward	1.6056
180-day forward	1.6018

What opportunities are open to an arbitrageur in the following situations?

a. A 180-day European call option to buy £1 for $1.57 costs 2 cents.

b. A 90-day European put option to sell £1 for $1.64 costs 2 cents.

ASSIGNMENT QUESTIONS

1.29. The current price of a stock is $94, and three-month call options with a strike price of $95 currently sell for $4.70. An investor who feels that the price of the stock will increase is trying to decide between buying 100 shares and buying 2,000 call options (20 contracts). Both strategies involve an investment of $9,400. What advice would you give? How high does the stock price have to rise for the option strategy to be more profitable?

1.30. A trader buys a European call option and sells a European put option. The options have the same underlying asset, strike price, and maturity date. Describe the trader's position. Under what circumstances does the price of the call equal the price of the put?

1.31. Show that the Standard Oil bond described in section 1.4 is a combination of a regular bond, a long position in call options on oil with a strike price of $25, and a short position in call options on oil with a strike price of $40.

1.32. Use the DerivaGem software to calculate the value of the range forward contract considered in section 1.4 on the assumption that the exchange rate volatility is 15% per annum. Adjust the upper end of the band so that the contract has zero value initially. Assume that the dollar and sterling risk-free interest rates are 5.0% and 6.9% per annum, respectively.

1.33. A trader owns gold as part of a long-term investment portfolio. The trader can buy gold for $250 per ounce and sell gold for $249 per ounce. The trader can borrow funds at 6% per year and invest funds at 5.5% per year. (Both interest rates are expressed with annual compounding.) For what range of one-year forward prices of gold does the trader have no arbitage opportunities? Assume there is no bid-offer spread for forward prices.

CHAPTER

2

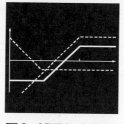

FUTURES MARKETS AND THE USE OF FUTURES FOR HEDGING

Futures contracts were introduced in chapter 1. They are exchange-traded instruments where one party agrees to buy an asset at a future time for a certain price and the other party agrees to sell the asset at the same time for the same price. In this chapter we explain the way in which exchanges organize the trading of futures contracts. We discuss issues such as the specification of contracts, the operation of margin accounts, and the way that quotes are made. We also discuss the accounting and tax treatment of futures contracts and the way in which they are used for hedging purposes.

2.1 TRADING FUTURES CONTRACTS

We examine how a futures contract comes into existence by considering the corn futures contract traded on the Chicago Board of Trade (CBOT). On March 5, an investor in New York might call a broker with instructions to buy 5,000 bushels of corn for delivery in July of the same year. The broker would immediately pass these instructions on to a trader on the floor of the CBOT. The broker would request a long position in one contract because each corn contract on the CBOT is for the delivery of exactly 5,000 bushels. At about the same time, another investor in Kansas might instruct a broker to sell 5,000 bushels of corn for July delivery. This broker would then pass instructions to short one contract to a trader on the floor of the CBOT. The two floor traders would meet, agree on a price to be paid for the corn in July, and the deal would be done.

The investor in New York who agreed to buy has a *long futures position* in one contract; the investor in Kansas who agreed to sell has a *short futures position* in one contract. The price agreed to on the floor of the exchange is the current *futures price* for July corn. We will suppose the price is 170 cents per bushel. This price, like any other price, is determined by the laws of supply and demand. If at a particular time more traders wish to sell July corn than buy July corn, the price will go down. New buyers then enter the market so that a balance between buyers and sellers is maintained. If more traders wish to buy July corn than to sell July corn, the price goes up.

Closing Out Positions

The vast majority of futures contracts do not lead to delivery. The reason is that most traders choose to close out their positions prior to the delivery period specified in the contract. Closing out a position means entering into the opposite type of trade from the original one. For example, the New York investor who bought a July corn futures contract on March 5 can close out the position by selling (i.e., shorting) one July corn futures contract on April 20. The Kansas investor who sold (i.e., shorted) a July contract on March 5 can close out the position by buying one July contract on April 20. In each case, the investor's total gain or loss is determined by the change in the futures price between March 5 and April 20.

It is important to realize that there is no particular significance to the party on the other side of a trade in a futures transaction. Consider trader A who initiates a long futures position by trading one contract. Suppose that trader B is on the other side of the transaction. At a later stage, trader A might close out the position by entering into a short contract. The trader on the other side of this second transaction does not have to be, and usually is not, trader B.

Types of Traders on Floor of Exchange

There are two types of traders on the floor of the exchange. *Commission brokers* earn a fee for executing trades for other people, and *locals* trade for their own account. There are many different types of trades that can be passed to a commission broker. In the example just given, we assumed that the New York and Kansas investors are prepared to trade at the current market price. This means they each place a *market order* with their broker and that these market orders are passed on to commission brokers representing the two sides. Another popular type of order is a *limit order*. This specifies a certain price and requests that the transaction be executed only if that price or a better one is obtained.

2.2   SPECIFICATION OF THE FUTURES CONTRACT

When developing a new contract, an exchange must specify in some detail the exact nature of the agreement between the two parties. In particular, it must specify the asset, the contract size (i.e., exactly how much of the asset will be delivered under one contract), how prices will be quoted, where delivery will be made, when delivery will be made, and how the price paid will be determined. Sometimes alternatives are specified for the asset that will be delivered and for the delivery arrangements. It is the party with the short position (the party that has agreed to sell) that chooses between these alternatives.

The Asset

When the asset is a commodity, there may be quite a variation in the quality of what is available in the marketplace. When specifying the asset, it is, therefore, important that the exchange stipulate the grade or grades of the commodity that are acceptable. The New York Cotton Exchange has specified the asset in its orange juice futures contract as

> US Grade A, with Brix value of not less than 57 degrees, having a Brix value to acid ratio of not less than 13 to 1 nor more than 19 to 1, with factors of color and flavor each scoring 37 points or higher and 19 for defects, with a minimum score of 94.

The Chicago Mercantile Exchange in its random-length lumber futures contract has specified that

> Each delivery unit shall consist of nominal 2×4s of random lengths from 8 feet to 20 feet, grade-stamped Construction and Standard, Standard and better, or #1 and #2; however, in no case may the quantity of Standard grade or #2 exceed 50 percent. Each delivery unit shall be manufactured in California, Idaho, Montana, Nevada, Oregon, Washington, Wyoming, or Alberta or British Columbia, Canada, and contain lumber produced from and grade-stamped Alpine fir, Englemann spruce, hem-fir, lodgepole pine and/or spruce pine fir.

In the case of some commodities, a range of grades can be delivered, but the price received is adjusted depending on the grade chosen. For example, in the Chicago Board of Trade corn futures contract, the standard grade is "No. 2 Yellow," but substitutions are allowed with price adjustments being made in a way specified by the exchange.

The financial assets in futures contracts are generally well defined and unambiguous. For example, there is no need to specify the grade of a Japanese yen. However, there are some interesting features of the Treasury bond and Treasury note futures contracts traded on the Chicago Board of Trade. The underlying asset in the Treasury bond contract is any long-term U.S. Treasury bond that has a maturity of greater than 15 years and is not callable within 15 years. In the Treasury note futures contract, the underlying asset is any long-term Treasury note with a maturity no less than 6.5 years and not greater than 10 years. In both of these cases, the exchange has a formula for adjusting the price received according to the coupon and maturity date of the bond delivered. This is discussed in chapter 4.

Contract Size

The contract size specifies the amount of the asset that has to be delivered under one contract. This is an important decision for the exchange. If the contract size is too large, many traders who wish to hedge relatively small exposures or who wish to take relatively small speculative positions will be unable to use the exchange. On the other hand, if the contract size is too small, trading may be expensive because there is a cost associated with each contract traded.

The correct size for a contract clearly depends on the likely user. Whereas the value of what is delivered under a futures contract on an agricultural product might be

$10,000 to $20,000, it is much higher for some financial futures. For example, under the Treasury bond futures contract traded on the Chicago Board of Trade, instruments with a face value of $100,000 are delivered.

Delivery Arrangements

As already mentioned, the vast majority of the futures contracts that are initiated do not lead to delivery of the underlying asset. They are closed out prior to maturity. The delivery arrangements are nevertheless important in understanding the relationship between the futures price and the spot price of the asset.

The place where delivery will be made must be specified by the exchange. This is particularly important for commodities where there may be significant transportation costs. In the case of the Chicago Mercantile Exchange random-length lumber contract, the delivery location is specified as

> On track and shall either be unitized in double-door boxcars or, at no additional cost to the buyer, each unit shall be individually paper-wrapped and loaded on flatcars. Par delivery of hem-fir in California, Idaho, Montana, Nevada, Oregon, and Washington, and in the province of British Columbia.

When alternative delivery locations are specified, the price received by the party with the short position is sometimes adjusted according to the location chosen by that party. For example, in the case of the corn futures contract traded by the Chicago Board of Trade, delivery can be made at Chicago, Burns Harbor, Toledo, or St. Louis. Deliveries at Toledo and St. Louis are made at a discount of 4 cents per bushel from the Chicago contract price.

Delivery Months

A futures contract is referred to by its delivery month. The exchange must specify the precise period during the month when delivery can be made. For many futures contracts, the delivery period is the entire month.

The delivery months vary from contract to contract and are chosen by the exchange to meet the needs of market participants. For example, currency futures on the Chicago Mercantile Exchange have delivery months of March, June, September, and December; corn futures traded on the Chicago Board of Trade have delivery months of March, May, July, September, and December. At any given time, contracts trade for the closest delivery month and a number of subsequent delivery months. The exchange specifies when trading in a particular month's contract will begin. The exchange also specifies the last day on which trading can take place for a given contract. This is generally a few days before the last day on which delivery can be made.

Price Quotes

The futures price is quoted in a way that is convenient and easy to understand. For example, crude oil futures prices on the New York Mercantile Exchange (NYMEX) are quoted in dollars per barrel to two decimal places (i.e., to the nearest cent). Treasury bond and Treasury note futures prices on the Chicago Board of Trade are quoted in dollars and 32nds of a dollar. The minimum price movement that can occur in trading is consistent with the way in which the price is quoted. Thus it is $0.01 (or 1 cent per barrel) for the oil futures and one-32nd of a dollar for the Treasury bond and Treasury note futures.

Daily Price Movement Limits

For most contracts, daily price movement limits are specified by the exchange. For example, at the time of writing, the daily price movement limit for oil futures is $1. If the price moves down by an amount equal to the daily price limit, the contract is said to be *limit down*. If it moves up by the limit, it is said to be *limit up*. A *limit move* is a move in either direction equal to the daily price limit. Normally, trading on a contract ceases for the day once the contract is limit up or limit down, but in some instances, the exchange has the authority to step in and change the limits.

The purpose of daily price limits is to prevent large price movements from occurring because of speculative excesses. However, these limits can become an artificial barrier to trading when the price of the underlying commodity is advancing or declining rapidly. Whether price limits are, on balance, good for futures markets is controversial.

Position Limits

Position limits are the maximum number of contracts that a speculator may hold. In the Chicago Mercantile Exchange random-length lumber contract, for example, the position limit at the time of writing is 1,000 contracts, with no more than 300 in any one delivery month. Bona fide hedgers are not affected by position limits. The purpose of the limits is to prevent speculators from exercising undue influence on the market.

2.3   OPERATION OF MARGINS

If two people get in touch with each other directly and agree to trade an asset in the future for a certain price, there are obvious risks. One of them may regret the deal and try to back out. It is also possible that one of them may not have the financial resources to honor the agreement. One of the key roles of the exchange is to organize trading so that contract defaults are minimized. This is where margins come in.

Marking to Market

To illustrate how margins work, consider a trader who contacts a broker on Monday, June 3, to buy two December gold futures contracts on the New York Commodity Exchange (COMEX). We suppose that the current futures price is $400 per ounce. Because the contract size is 100 ounces, the trader has contracted to buy a total of 200 ounces at this price. The broker will require the trader to deposit funds in what is termed a *margin account*. The amount that must be deposited at the time the contract is entered into is known as the *initial margin*. We will suppose this is $2,000 per contract, or $4,000 in total. At the end of each trading day, the margin account is adjusted to reflect the trader's gain or loss. This is known as *marking to market* the account.

Suppose, for example, that by the end of June 3, the futures price has dropped from $400 to $397. The trader has a loss of 200 × $3, or $600. This is because the 200 ounces of December gold, which the trader contracted to buy at $400, can now be sold for only $397. The balance in the margin account would therefore be reduced by $600 to $3,400. Similarly, if the price of December gold rose to $403 by the end of the first day, the balance in the margin account would be increased by $600 to $4,600. A trade is first marked to market at the close of the day on which it takes place. It is then marked to market at the close of trading on each subsequent day.

Note that marking to market is not merely an arrangement between broker and client. When there is a $3 decrease in the futures price so that the margin account of the trader is reduced by $600, the trader's broker has to pay the exchange $600 and the exchange passes the money on to the broker of a trader with a short position. Similarly, when there is an increase in the futures price, brokers for parties with short positions pay money to the exchange, and brokers for parties with long positions receive money from the exchange. We give more details of the mechanism by which this happens later in this section.

Maintenance Margin

A trader is entitled to withdraw any balance in the margin account in excess of the initial margin. To ensure that the balance in the margin account never becomes negative, a *maintenance margin*, which is somewhat lower than the initial margin, is set. If the balance in the margin account falls below the maintenance margin, the trader receives a *margin call* and is requested to top up the margin account to the initial margin level within a very short period of time. The extra funds deposited are known as a *variation margin*. If the trader does not provide the variation margin, the broker closes out the position by selling the contract. In the case of the trader in the preceding example, the broker would close out the position by selling on behalf of the investor 200 ounces of gold for delivery in December.

Table 2.1 illustrates the operation of the margin account for one possible sequence of futures prices in the case of the trader considered here. The maintenance margin is assumed for the purpose of the illustration to be $1,500 per contract, or $3,000 total. On June 11 the balance in the margin account falls $340 below the maintenance margin level. This triggers a margin call from the broker for an additional margin of $1,340. The table assumes that the trader does in fact provide this margin by close of trading on June 12. On June 17, the balance in the margin account again falls below the maintenance margin level and a margin call for $1,260 is sent out. The trader provides this margin by close of trading on the next business day, June 18. On June 24, the trader decides to close out the position by shorting the two contracts. The futures price on that day is $392.30, and the trader has taken a cumulative loss of

Table 2.1	Operation of Margins for a Long Position in Two Gold Futures Contracts

The initial margin is $2,000 per contract, or $4,000 total; the maintenance margin is $1,500 per contract, or $3,000 total. The contract is entered into on Monday, June 3, at $400 and closed out on June 24 at $392.3. The numbers in the second column, except for the first and last numbers, are the futures prices at the close of the trading.

Day	Futures Price (dollars)	Daily Gain (Loss) (dollars)	Cumulative Gain (Loss) (dollars)	Margin Account Balance (dollars)	Margin Call (dollars)
	400.00			4,000	
June 3	397.00	(600)	(600)	3,400	
June 4	396.10	(180)	(780)	3,220	
June 5	398.20	420	(360)	3,640	
June 6	397.10	(220)	(580)	3,420	
June 7	396.70	(80)	(660)	3,340	
June 10	395.40	(260)	(920)	3,080	
June 11	393.30	(420)	(1,340)	2,660	1,340
June 12	393.60	60	(1,280)	4,060	
June 13	391.80	(360)	(1,640)	3,700	
June 14	392.70	180	(1,460)	3,880	
June 17	387.00	(1,140)	(2,600)	2,740	1,260
June 18	387.00	0	(2,600)	4,000	
June 19	388.10	220	(2,380)	4,220	
June 20	388.70	120	(2,260)	4,340	
June 21	391.00	460	(1,800)	4,800	
June 24	392.30	260	(1,540)	5,060	

$1,540. Note that the trader has excess margin on June 12, 19, 20, and 21. The table assumes that this is not withdrawn.

Further Details

Some brokers allow their clients to earn interest on the balance in their margin accounts. The balance in a margin account does not, therefore, represent a true cost, provided that the interest rate is competitive with that which could be earned elsewhere. To satisfy the initial margin requirements (but not subsequent margin calls), a trader can sometimes deposit securities with the broker. Treasury bills are usually accepted in lieu of cash, at about 90% of their face value. Shares are also sometimes accepted in lieu of cash—but at about 50% of their face value.

The effect of the marking to market is that a futures contract is settled daily rather than at the end of its life. At the end of each day, the trader's gain (loss) is added to (subtracted from) the margin account. This brings the value of the contract back to zero. A futures contract is, in effect, closed out and rewritten at a new price each day.

Minimum levels for initial and maintenance margins are set by the exchange. Individual brokers may require greater margins from their clients than those specified by the exchange. However, brokers cannot require lower margins than those specified by the exchange. Margin levels are determined by the variability of the price of the underlying asset. The higher this variability, the higher the margin levels. The maintenance margin is usually about 75% of the initial margin.

Margin requirements may depend on the objectives of the trader. A bona fide hedger, such as a company that produces the commodity on which the futures contract is written, is often subject to lower margin requirements than a speculator. This is because there is deemed to be less risk of default. What are known as day trades and spread transactions often give rise to lower margin requirements than hedge transactions. A *day trade* is a trade where the trader announces to the broker that the position will be closed out in the same day. Thus, if the trader has taken a long position, the plan is to take an offsetting short position later in the day; if the trader has taken a short position, the plan is to take an offsetting long position later in the day. A *spread transaction* is one where the trader simultaneously takes a long position in a contract with one delivery month and a short position in a contract on the same underlying asset with another delivery month.

Note that margin requirements are the same on short futures positions as they are on long futures positions. It is just as easy to take a short futures position as it is to take a long futures position. The cash market does not have this symmetry. Taking a long position in the cash market involves buying the asset and presents no problems. Taking a short position involves selling an asset that you do not own. This is a more complex transaction that may or may not be possible in a particular market. It is discussed further in chapter 3.

Clearinghouse and Clearing Margins

The *exchange clearinghouse* is an adjunct of the exchange and acts as an intermediary or middleman in futures transactions. It guarantees the performance of the parties to each transaction. The clearinghouse has a number of members all with offices close to the clearinghouse. Brokers who are not clearinghouse members themselves must channel their business through a member. The main task of the clearinghouse is to keep track of all the transactions that take place during a day so that it can calculate the net position of each of its members.

Just as a trader is required to maintain a margin account with a broker, a clearinghouse member is required to maintain a margin account with the clearinghouse. This is known as a *clearing margin*. The margin accounts for clearinghouse members are adjusted for gains and losses at the end of each trading day in the same way as the margin accounts that individual traders keep with their brokers. However, in the case of the clearinghouse member, there is an original margin but no maintenance margin. Every day, the account balance for each contract must be maintained at an amount equal to the original margin times the number of contracts outstanding. Thus, depending on transactions during the day and price movements, the clearinghouse member may have to add funds to its margin account at the end of the day. Alternatively, it may find that it can remove funds from the account at this time. Brokers who are not clearinghouse members must maintain a margin account with a clearinghouse member.

In the calculation of clearing margins, the exchange clearinghouse calculates the number of contracts outstanding on either a gross or a net basis. The *gross basis* adds the total of all long positions entered into by clients to the total of all the short positions entered into by clients. The *net basis* allows these to be offset against each other. Suppose a clearinghouse member has two clients, one with a long position in 20 contracts and the other with a short position in 15 contracts. Gross margining would calculate the clearing margin on the basis of 35 contracts; net margining would calculate the clearing margin on the basis of 5 contracts. Most exchanges currently use net margining.

It should be stressed that the purpose of the margining system is to reduce the possibility of market participants sustaining losses because of defaults. Overall, the system has been very successful. Losses arising from defaults on major exchanges have been virtually nonexistent.

2.4 NEWSPAPER QUOTES

Many newspapers carry futures quotations. In *The Wall Street Journal*, futures quotations can currently be found in the Money and Investing section. Table 2.2 shows the quotations for commodities as they appeared in *The Wall Street Journal* on Wednesday, August 5, 1998. These refer to the trading that took place on the preceding day (Tuesday, August 4, 1998). The quotations for index futures and currency futures are given in chapter 3. The quotations for interest rate futures are given in chapter 4.

The asset underlying the futures contract, the exchange it is traded on, the contract size, and how the price is quoted are all shown at the top of each section. The first asset in Table 2.2 is corn, traded on the Chicago Board of Trade. The contract size is 5,000 bushels and the price is quoted in cents per bushel. The months in which particular contracts are traded are shown in the first column. Corn contracts with maturities in September 1998, December 1998, March 1999, May 1999, July 1999, September 1999, December 1999, and December 2000 were traded on August 4, 1998.

Prices

The first three numbers in each row show the opening price, the highest price achieved in trading during the day, and the lowest price achieved in trading during the day. The opening price is representative of the prices at which contracts were trading immediately after the opening bell. For December corn on August 4, 1998, the opening price was $220\frac{1}{2}$ cents per bushel; during the day, the price traded between $222\frac{1}{2}$ cents and $220\frac{1}{4}$ cents.

Table 2.2 Commodity Futures Quotes from *The Wall Street Journal,* August 5, 1998

FUTURES PRICES

Tuesday, August 4, 1998

Open Interest Reflects Previous Trading Day.

GRAINS AND OILSEEDS

	Open	High	Low	Settle	Change	Lifetime High	Lifetime Low	Open Interest
CORN (CBT) 5,000 bu.; cents per bu.								
Sept	213	215	212¾	213½	....	301	212¾	87,790
Dec	220½	222½	220¼	221¼	+ ¾	299½	220	157,619
Mr99	231¼	233¼	231¼	232	+ ¾	305	231	37,320
May	239½	240¼	238¾	239½	+ ¾	299	238½	11,108
July	244	245½	244	244½	+ ½	312	243¾	16,114
Sept	249	249½	248½	248½	....	280	248½	1,503
Dec	254	254	252¾	253½	....	291½	252¾	6,316
Dc00	265	265	264	264	− ½	279½	260	165
Est vol 50,000; vol Mon 64,988; open int 317,935, +4,674.								
OATS (CBT) 5,000 bu.; cents per bu.								
Sept	106	106½	104¾	105¼	− ½	177	104½	3,782
Dec	115	115½	113½	114	− ½	177½	113½	8,815
Mr99	124	124	122¾	122¾	− ½	166½	122½	1,852
Est vol 800; vol Mon 1,356; open int 14,552, +370.								
SOYBEANS (CBT) 5,000 bu.; cents per bu.								
Aug	571¼	574½	564	564½	− 8¾	745	564	9,466
Sept	552¾	568½	551	551½	− 4¼	723	551	16,805
Nov	552	555½	547	547¾	− 4¼	717	547	79,185
Ja99	560½	564½	557½	557¾	− 4½	701½	557½	10,761
Mar	572	573	561¾	567¾	− 4½	694	561¾	8,588
May	580	582	575	575	− 3½	671	575	2,422
July	588	588	583	583	− 3½	728	583	4,470
Nov	594	595½	591	591½	− 1½	680	591	2,403
Est vol 40,000; vol Mon 48,570; open int 134,152, −439.								
SOYBEAN MEAL (CBT) 100 tons; $ per ton.								
Aug	146.50	147.70	144.50	144.80	− 1.60	231.50	144.50	11,444
Sept	142.50	143.70	140.50	140.70	− 1.50	231.50	140.50	24,291
Oct	141.00	141.60	139.50	139.60	− .70	226.00	139.50	19,462
Dec	143.00	144.50	142.40	142.50	− .90	231.00	142.10	59,567
Ja99	146.50	146.70	144.60	144.80	− .50	215.50	144.60	9,868
Mar	151.00	151.00	149.40	149.60	− .70	195.00	149.40	8,454
May	154.00	154.80	144.00	152.00	− 1.00	192.50	144.00	2,761
July	158.00	158.00	156.20	156.40	− .40	188.00	156.20	2,243
Aug	159.00	159.00	158.00	158.50	+ 1.00	178.90	157.50	285
Est vol 20,000; vol Mon 31,371; open int 138,601, +1,964.								
SOYBEAN OIL (CBT) 60,000 lbs.; cents per lb.								
Aug	23.98	24.20	23.75	23.79	− .15	29.88	23.69	5,493
Sept	24.10	24.33	23.85	23.88	− .17	29.85	23.82	28,622
Oct	24.20	24.40	23.96	23.98	− .19	29.55	23.95	14,370
Dec	24.28	24.53	24.05	24.08	− .18	29.30	24.00	43,601
Ja99	24.60	24.60	24.15	24.16	− .20	29.05	24.15	4,548
Mar	24.70	24.70	24.24	24.35	− .20	28.80	24.24	7,814
May	24.50	24.50	24.25	24.38	− .10	28.30	24.25	2,353
July	24.55	24.55	24.28	24.38	− .18	27.50	24.28	1,760
Est vol 22,000; vol Mon 28,460; open int 108,850, −1,765.								
WHEAT (CBT) 5,000 bu.; cents per bu.								
Sept	250½	253	247	247¼	− 3½	403	247	47,674
Dec	266½	269½	263	263¼	− 3¼	417	263	51,611
Mr99	281	284	278¼	278¾	− 3	384½	278¼	18,892
May	291	293	288	288	− 2	355	288	3,257
July	301¼	303	298	299	− 1½	389	298	6,988
Est vol 17,000; vol Mon 14,360; open int 317,935, +4,674.								
WHEAT (KC) 5,000 bu., cents per bu.								
Sept	275½	276½	272¼	273	− 1¼	410	272	20,708
Dec	288½	290	286	286½	− 1	418½	286	28,585
Mr99	301½	302½	299	300¼	− ½	410½	299	10,728
May	308	308	306	306	....	370	306	2,073
July	314½	317	313	313	− 1	370	313	1,045
Est vol 8,644; vol Mon 9,798; open int 63,139, +210.								
WHEAT (MPLS) 5,000 bu.; cents per bu.								
Sept	308	309½	304	307½	− ½	418	304	11,611
Dec	318	318	311½	312½	− 3	422	311½	10,571
Mr99	326	326½	319	320¼	− 4¼	398	319	3,956
Est vol 5,788; vol Mon 4,825; open int 26,733, +876.								
CANOLA (WPG) 20 metric tons; Can. $ per ton								
Aug	357.70	358.00	355.00	355.00	− 6.00	415.50	355.00	1,759
Sept		....	....	357.30	− 4.80	397.00	361.30	3,834
Nov	364.60	365.00	361.20	362.00	− 4.60	397.50	361.20	35,669
Ja99	369.20	369.90	366.10	366.80	− 4.50	401.00	366.10	9,530
Mar	370.70	371.80	370.70	371.80	− 4.70	403.50	370.70	3,167
May		....	....	377.40	− 4.10	405.00	382.80	225
Est vol 7,010; vol Fr 7,170; open int 54,184, +995.								
WHEAT (WPG) 20 metric tons; Can. $ per ton								
Oct	140.00	140.00	135.90	136.00	− 4.90	180.50	135.90	2,448
Dec	139.50	139.60	138.10	138.30	− 4.50	170.00	138.10	4,202
Mr99	141.30	141.60	141.30	141.60	− 4.40	164.00	141.30	1,018
May		....	....	143.00	− 4.50	167.00	148.90	2,275
Est vol 250; vol Fr 373; open int 9,953, +595.								
BARLEY-WESTERN (WPG) 20 metric tons; Can. $ per ton								
Oct	117.00	117.00	115.00	115.00	− 3.40	158.00	115.00	4,581
Dec	119.00	119.50	117.00	117.50	− 3.00	151.50	117.00	5,006
Mr99		....	....	119.90	− 2.10	142.50	122.00	596
May		....	....	123.00	....	134.20	133.80	151
Est vol 750; vol Fr 774; open int 10,364, +104.								
LIVESTOCK AND MEAT								
CATTLE-FEEDER (CME) 50,000 lbs.; cents per lb.								
Aug	66.50	67.92	66.42	67.92	+ 1.50	83.25	65.77	7,528
Sept	66.10	67.55	66.10	67.55	+ 1.50	83.05	65.60	3,741
Oct	66.22	67.70	66.22	67.70	+ 1.50	83.00	65.77	5,327
Nov	68.10	69.55	68.10	69.55	+ 1.50	83.60	67.60	2,408
Ja99	69.25	70.75	69.25	70.70	+ 1.45	81.75	68.60	1,149
Est vol 3,945; vol Mon 5,511; open int 20,575, +1,176.								
CATTLE-LIVE (CME) 40,000 lbs.; cents per lb.								
Aug	58.35	59.82	58.35	59.82	+ 1.50	72.15	57.82	21,099
Oct	58.95	60.47	58.95	60.47	+ 1.50	74.05	58.42	40,292
Dec	60.30	61.85	60.22	61.85	+ 1.50	74.20	59.80	16,203
Fb99	62.32	63.82	62.25	63.82	+ 1.50	73.50	61.95	9,214
Apr	64.20	65.82	64.15	65.75	+ 1.40	73.25	63.77	3,631
June	62.82	64.30	62.77	64.00	+ 1.20	70.20	62.50	920
Est vol 15,732; vol Mon 23,728; open int 91,426, +2,667								
HOGS-LEAN (CME) 40,000 lbs.; cents per lb.								
Aug	49.65	50.60	49.35	50.40	+ .75	69.70	47.60	10,171
Oct	42.60	43.07	41.70	42.90	+ .35	66.00	40.60	11,828
Dec	42.70	43.17	41.95	42.92	+ .35	58.50	41.50	8,071
Fb99	47.00	47.20	46.45	46.87	− .02	59.50	46.30	2,192
Apr	46.27	46.40	46.00	46.32	+ .05	58.20	45.40	566
June	54.00	54.40	53.55	54.40	+ .45	65.50	53.40	340
Est vol 13,235; vol Mon 8,381; open int 33,339, +738.								
PORK BELLIES (CME) 40,000 lbs.; cents per lb.								
Aug	58.10	59.70	56.40	59.60	+ 2.70	75.00	39.05	2,731
Fb99	55.90	56.57	54.50	56.25	+ .90	58.70	50.00	1,086
Est vol 3,851; vol Mon 1,943; open int 3,824, +442.								

Settlement Price

The fourth number in the row is the *settlement price*. This is the average of the prices at which the contract traded immediately before the bell signaling the end of trading for the day. The fifth number is the change in the settlement price from the preceding day. In the case of the December 1998 corn futures contract, the settlement price was $221\frac{1}{4}$ cents on August 4, 1998, up $\frac{3}{4}$ cents from the previous day.

Table 2.2 Commodity Futures Quotes from *The Wall Street Journal*, August 5, 1998 (*Continued*)

FUTURES PRICES

FOOD AND FIBER

COCOA (CSCE)-10 metric tons; $ per ton.

Sept	1,541	1,560	1,541	1,554 +	19	1,836	1,456	23,051
Dec	1,578	1,599	1,578	1,592 +	17	1,863	1,510	25,006
Mr99	1,618	1,640	1,618	1,632 +	16	1,901	1,605	13,353
May	1,658	1,662	1,658	1,659 +	16	1,911	1,653	5,353
July	....	....		1,686 +	16	1,850	1,675	1,748
Sept	....	....		1,712 +	16	1,858	1,695	1,677
Dec	....	....		1,740 +	16	1,885	1,740	4,750
Mr00				1,768 +	16	1,910	1,747	2,099

Est vol 9,234; vol Mn 7,982; open int 77,037, −353.

COFFEE (CSCE)-37,500 lbs.; cents per lb.

Sept	129.50	129.80	127.30	129.00 −	1.90	186.00	105.00	15,762
Dec	121.50	123.00	121.00	122.65 −	1.00	157.50	106.00	9,897
Mr99	117.00	118.25	117.00	118.10 −	.90	154.00	107.10	5,443
May	117.50	118.00	117.50	118.25 −	1.25	151.50	109.00	2,269
July	117.50	117.75	117.50	118.35 −	1.30	131.00	110.50	1,065
Sept	....	....		118.75 −	1.65	123.00	111.00	444
Dec				119.75 −	1.65	123.00	114.00	149

Est vol 7,809; vol Mn 11,490; open int 36,029, −60.

SUGAR-WORLD (CSCE)-112,000 lbs.; cents per lb.

Oct	8.66	8.73	8.63	8.71 −	.02	11.97	7.50	86,298
Mr99	9.05	9.08	9.02	9.07 −	.03	11.87	8.15	39,818
May	9.07	9.10	9.04	9.10 −	.03	11.68	8.31	6,309
July	9.07	9.09	9.03	9.09 −	.05	11.68	8.47	5,187
Oct	9.24	9.28	9.24	9.24 −	.01	11.58	8.52	5,997
Mr00	9.39	9.40	9.34	9.34 −	.04	10.00	8.26	5,657
May	....	....		9.39	....	9.05	8.93	231

Est vol 10,489; vol Mn 8,501; open int 149,497, −479.

SUGAR-DOMESTIC (CSCE)-112,000 lbs.; cents per lb.

Sept	22.55	22.55	22.50	22.51 −	.04	23.00	21.95	2,504
Nov	22.36	22.39	22.36	22.39 +	.01	22.51	22.00	3,309
Ja99	22.26	22.27	22.26	22.27 +	.01	22.44	22.10	2,178
Mar	22.18	22.19	22.18	22.19 +	.02	22.42	22.10	2,199
May	22.31	22.32	22.31	22.32 +	.02	22.37	22.10	1,256
July	22.45	22.46	22.45	22.46	....	22.46	22.10	1,498
Sept	22.47	22.47	22.47	22.47	....	22.47	22.28	894

Est vol 963; vol Mn 951; open int 13,909, −207.

COTTON (CTN)-50,000 lbs.; cents per lb.

Oct	70.30	71.30	70.25	70.45 +	.05	81.20	65.60	8,317
Dec	70.00	70.59	69.84	70.17 +	.09	78.10	66.90	38,826
Mr99	70.73	71.10	70.50	70.79 +	.06	77.25	68.50	15,101
May	71.22	71.30	70.95	71.30	....	76.80	69.50	8,076
July	71.80	71.95	71.65	71.90 +	.10	77.31	69.80	4,313
Oct	71.65	71.75	71.65	71.70 +	.07	77.05	70.80	799
Dec	71.15	71.15	71.05	71.10 +	.05	74.10	70.10	5,484

Est vol 12,900; vol Mn 19,109; open int 78,742, +1,409.

ORANGE JUICE (CTN)-15,000 lbs.; cents per lb.

Sept	107.00	108.50	106.25	108.35 +	.55	119.50	78.25	13,979
Nov	110.50	111.75	109.80	111.75 +	.60	120.90	80.95	5,205
Ja99	113.00	113.25	113.00	114.50 +	.60	122.00	83.40	2,330
Mar	115.50	116.00	115.50	117.25 +	.60	123.75	86.05	1,525
May	....	....		120.00 +	.60	125.75	90.80	1,298
July	121.90	121.90	121.90	121.90	....	126.00	109.00	3,109

Est vol 1,800; vol Mn 1,021; open int 24,051, −63,317.

METALS AND PETROLEUM

COPPER-HIGH (Cmx.Div.NYM)-25,000 lbs.; cents per lb.

Aug	74.50	74.50	73.30	73.40 −	1.10	102.00	71.35	1,760
Sept	74.90	75.50	73.60	73.90 −	1.10	102.10	71.20	22,024
Oct	74.70	74.70	74.10	74.10 −	1.10	99.40	72.00	2,102
Nov	75.20	75.20	74.85	74.30 −	1.10	98.80	72.85	1,566
Dec	75.50	76.10	74.40	74.60 −	1.10	102.00	72.30	13,341
Ja99	75.40	75.40	74.80	74.80 −	1.10	96.80	73.40	1,828
Feb	75.60	75.60	75.60	74.95 −	1.10	94.60	73.60	918
Mar	76.00	76.10	75.20	75.20 −	1.05	98.20	73.30	3,709
Apr	....	....		75.40 −	1.05	96.00	73.80	902
May	76.40	76.40	75.60	75.55 −	1.05	98.50	73.70	2,002
June	....	....		75.65 −	1.15	91.00	74.40	744
July	76.50	76.50	76.00	75.75 −	1.05	95.75	74.20	1,987
Aug	....	....		75.80 −	1.00	90.50	74.25	583
Sept	76.50	76.60	76.40	75.85 −	.95	94.60	74.35	1,508
Oct	....	....		75.90 −	.95	90.00	74.75	381
Nov	....	....		75.95 −	.90	86.90	75.00	383
Dec	76.70	76.70	76.70	76.00 −	.90	86.00	74.70	1,641

Est vol 11,000; vol Mn 11,008; open int 57,459, −1,073.

GOLD (Cmx.Div.NYM)-100 troy oz.; $ per troy oz.

Aug	285.00	290.00	285.00	288.80 +	4.80	403.80	284.50	3,532
Oct	285.00	291.50	285.00	290.40 +	4.60	367.80	285.00	11,452
Dec	287.60	293.50	286.80	292.50 +	4.60	505.00	286.80	96,868
Fb99	290.80	293.00	290.80	294.30 +	4.60	349.50	290.80	13,816
Apr	292.00	296.70	292.00	296.30 +	4.60	351.20	291.50	8,960
June	294.50	295.80	294.50	298.20 +	4.60	520.00	294.50	12,361
Aug	....	....		300.00 +	4.60	327.00	298.80	1,997
Oct	....	....		301.80 +	4.60	304.70	301.50	218
Dec	300.80	304.50	300.80	303.50 +	4.60	506.00	299.50	6,899
Fb00	....	....		305.20 +	4.60	312.00	-310.60	315
Apr	....	....		307.00 +	4.60	307.00	307.00	490
June	....	....		308.70 +	4.60	473.50	309.50	7,341
Dec	311.50	311.50	311.50	313.90 +	4.60	474.50	311.50	4,882
Ju01	....	....		319.00 +	4.60	447.00	347.00	2,212
Dec	....	....		324.00 +	4.60	429.50	320.00	4,672
Ju02	....	....		329.30 +	4.60	385.00	335.00	1,460
Dec	....	....		334.60 +	4.60	....	....	215

Est vol 38,000; vol Mn 45,144, open int 177,691, +12,420.

PLATINUM (NYM)-50 troy oz.; $ per troy oz.

Oct	371.20	378.80	370.20	377.00 −	5.80	425.00	343.00	8,477
Ja99	374.00	374.00	374.00	375.00 −	5.80	418.00	349.50	848

Est vol 1,284; vol Mn 2,336; open int 9,350, −431.

SILVER (Cmx.Div.NYM)-5,000 troy oz.; cnts per troy oz.

Aug	....	....		544.3 +	9.3	536.0	529.0	0
Sept	536.5	548.0	535.0	545.3 +	9.3	728.0	453.0	39,404
Dec	540.0	551.5	538.0	548.7 +	9.5	734.0	448.5	26,536
Mr99	541.0	550.0	541.0	550.5 +	9.5	690.0	473.0	4,764
May	546.0	550.0	546.0	552.1 +	9.5	656.0	493.0	1,701
July	....	....		553.6 +	9.5	680.0	472.0	2,520
Sept	....	....		554.4 +	9.5	698.0	527.0	173
Dec	552.0	558.0	552.0	555.4 +	9.5	720.0	484.0	2,857
Mr00	....	....		555.4 +	9.5	555.0	537.0	104
July	....	....		555.9 +	9.5	590.0	510.0	1,006
Dec	....	....		555.9 +	9.5	685.0	530.0	779
Dc01	....	....		555.9 +	9.5	680.0	529.0	211
Dc02	....	....		556.9 +	9.5	613.0	533.0	196

Est vol 12,000; vol Mn 13,040; open int 80,282, −862.

Table 2.2 Commodity Futures Quotes from *The Wall Street Journal,* August 5, 1998 (*Continued*)

FUTURES PRICES

CRUDE OIL, Light Sweet (NYM) 1,000 bbls.; $ per bbl.

Sept	13.67	13.88	13.67	13.75	+	0.05	20.82	13.55	128,034
Oct	14.06	14.25	14.06	14.10	+	0.04	20.75	13.91	65,671
Nov	14.36	14.53	14.36	14.42	+	0.04	20.63	14.35	37,357
Dec	14.71	14.83	14.66	14.72	+	0.04	20.74	14.65	49,109
Ja99	15.03	15.10	14.95	14.98	+	0.03	20.30	14.95	30,445
Feb	15.26	15.30	15.21	15.23	+	0.02	20.32	15.20	17,731
Mar	15.43	15.54	15.41	15.45	+	0.04	20.20	15.41	12,659
Apr	....	....	....	15.63	+	0.06	20.27	15.64	9,882
May	15.81	15.90	15.77	15.77	+	0.06	20.29	15.75	4,755
June	15.99	16.00	15.99	15.90	+	0.06	20.47	15.90	17,276
July	16.04	16.04	16.04	16.02	+	0.06	20.14	15.98	7,635
Aug	....	....	....	16.14	+	0.06	19.47	16.14	7,877
Sept	....	....	....	16.26	+	0.07	20.10	16.29	4,604
Oct	....	....	....	16.37	+	0.07	20.14	16.40	4,801
Nov	....	....	....	16.47	+	0.08	19.90	16.62	1,994
Dec	16.60	16.60	16.58	16.56	+	0.09	20.75	16.58	29,968
Dc00	17.28	17.30	17.28	17.20	+	0.09	20.75	17.00	10,772
Jan	....	....	....	16.64	+	0.09	19.15	17.00	3,854
Feb	....	....	....	16.72	+	0.09	20.16	17.45	1,543
Mar	....	....	....	16.78	+	0.09	20.10	17.28	8,975
Apr	....	....	....	16.82	+	0.09	19.16	17.33	350
May	....	....	....	16.86	+	0.09	19.16	17.85	472
June	16.95	17.00	16.95	16.90	+	0.09	20.10	16.90	5,856
July	....	....	....	16.95	+	0.09	17.88	17.74	722
Aug	....	....	....	17.00	+	0.09	....	....	355
Sept	....	....	....	17.05	+	0.09	17.70	17.48	1,627
Dec	17.28	17.30	17.28	17.20	+	0.09	20.75	17.00	10,772
Dc01	....	....	....	17.54	+	0.11	20.98	17.00	8,724
Dc02	....	....	....	17.80	+	0.12	21.38	17.15	6,009
Dc03	....	....	....	18.05	+	0.13	22.00	16.95	3,940
Dc04	....	....	....	18.29	+	0.13	19.07	17.20	5,845

Est vol 68,900; vol Mon 107,354; open int 489,643, +9,223.

HEATING OIL NO. 2 (NYM) 42,000 gal.; $ per gal.

Sept	.3581	.3660	.3581	.3624	+	.0043	.5840	.3580	58,251
Oct	.3755	.3820	.3755	.3784	+	.0035	.5850	.3745	20,116
Nov	.3960	.3970	.3945	.3944	+	.0025	.5905	.3915	15,523
Dec	.4130	.4135	.4105	.4109	+	.0025	.5900	.4080	24,618
Ja99	.4240	.4250	.4220	.4229	+	.0025	.5950	.4210	23,659
Feb	.4345	.4345	.4325	.4314	+	.0025	.5850	.4280	14,676
Mar	.4390	.4390	.4350	.4354	+	.0025	.5830	.4340	15,393
Apr	.4380	.4390	.4380	.4369	+	.0025	.5900	.4365	5,642
May	.4400	.4400	.4390	.4374	+	.0020	.5330	.4380	3,887
June	.4430	.4400	.4400	.4399	+	.0015	.5300	.4400	5,996
July	.4475	.4475	.4475	.4429	+	.0015	.5290	.4450	2,514
Aug	.4550	.4550	.4550	.4499	+	.0010	.5120	.4550	3,145
Sept	.4640	.4640	.4640	.4584	+	.0005	.5200	.4640	635
Oct	....	....	....	.4669		....	.5200	.4730	580
Nov	....	....	....	.4759		....	.5235	.4760	340
Dec	.4875	.4875	.4875	.4849		....	.5275	.4875	665
Ja00	.4945	.4945	.4945	.4924		....	.5170	.4945	551

Est vol 33,501; vol Mon 23,648; open int 199,688, +155.

GASOLINE-NY Unleaded (NYM)) 42,000 gal.; $ per gal.

Sept	.4200	.4275	.4175	.4229	+	.0041	.6150	.4145	49,065
Oct	.4240	.4270	.4235	.4241	+	.0021	.5780	.4180	14,666
Nov	.4310	.4335	.4300	.4306	+	.0014	.5585	.4270	4,428
Dec	.4370	.4405	.4370	.4381	+	.0014	.5450	.4340	6,113
Ja99	.4460	.4460	.4460	.4456	+	.0014	.5350	.4460	3,048
Feb	....	....	....	.4531	+	.0009	.5275	.4520	1,211
Mar	....	....	....	.4616	+	.0009	.5230	.4700	1,155
Apr	.4930	.4950	.4930	.4936	+	.0009	.5500	.4930	1,033
May	....	....	....	.5011	+	.0004	.5500	.5030	1,299
June	....	....	....	.5056	−	.0001	.5210	.5080	677

Est vol 27,811; vol Mon 14,360; open int 84,390, +1,045.

NATURAL GAS, (NYM) 10,000 MMBtu.; $ per MMBtu's

Sept	1.880	1.915	1.860	1.895	+	.026	2.740	1.810	52,720
Oct	1.935	1.970	1.920	1.947	+	.021	2.750	1.840	29,654
Nov	2.210	2.240	2.205	2.224	+	.027	2.830	1.915	23,736
Dec	2.481	2.515	2.480	2.504	+	.027	2.940	1.950	25,225
Ja99	2.595	2.605	2.580	2.599	+	.027	2.950	2.085	24,039
Feb	2.485	2.515	2.485	2.504	+	.022	2.770	2.025	15,537
Mar	2.405	2.410	2.400	2.404	+	.017	2.600	1.945	13,732
Apr	2.310	2.315	2.300	2.309	+	.012	2.440	1.910	7,149
May	2.285	2.300	2.275	2.282	+	.007	2.380	1.960	6,717
June	2.305	2.305	2.275	2.281	+	.004	2.384	1.860	6,366
July	2.300	2.300	2.270	2.280	+	.004	2.390	1.960	4,893
Aug	2.280	2.305	2.275	2.280	+	.005	2.390	1.975	4,648
Sept	2.310	2.310	2.290	2.295	+	.005	2.380	1.970	4,196
Oct	2.335	2.335	2.315	2.323	+	.005	2.415	2.042	3,305
Nov	2.457	2.457	2.457	2.461	+	.004	2.535	2.140	2,986
Dec	2.600	2.600	2.600	2.586		....	2.680	2.213	5,315
Ja00	2.635	2.635	2.615	2.620		....	2.680	2.295	6,209
Feb	2.520	2.520	2.520	2.520		....	2.565	2.242	2,715
Mar	....	....	....	2.400		....	2.475	2.119	2,055
Apr	....	....	....	2.290		....	2.360	2.015	2,005
May	....	....	....	2.267		....	2.339	1.960	1,717
June	2.267	2.267	2.267	2.267		....	2.320	2.001	1,958
July	....	....	....	2.271		....	2.325	2.005	1,261
Aug	....	....	....	2.284		....	2.320	2.005	1,018
Sept	....	....	....	2.289		....	2.370	2.150	1,133
Oct	2.314	2.314	2.314	2.314		....	2.346	2.100	1,074
Nov	....	....	....	2.442		....	2.469	2.240	841
Dec	....	....	....	2.579		....	2.620	2.380	1,501
Ja01	2.599	2.599	2.599	2.599		....	2.675	2.480	1,750
Feb	....	....	....	2.486		....	2.522	2.400	973
Mar	2.387	2.387	2.387	2.392		....	2.420	2.300	745
Apr	2.291	2.291	2.291	2.291		....	2.315	2.192	970
May	2.278	2.278	2.278	2.278		....	2.305	2.218	560
June	....	....	....	2.278		....	2.301	2.228	187
July	....	....	....	2.278		....	2.310	2.250	787

Est vol 36,644; vol Mon 36,919; open int 259,690, +1,585.

BRENT CRUDE (IPE) 1,000 net bbls.; $ per bbl.

Sept	12.72	12.79	12.56	12.70	+	.14	19.36	12.25	67,815
Oct	13.00	13.08	12.86	12.93	+	.05	19.34	12.67	42,528
Nov	13.32	13.41	13.20	13.25	+	.05	19.15	13.06	17,825
Dec	13.65	13.66	13.48	13.52	+	.03	18.53	13.39	35,024
Ja99	13.82	13.82	13.68	13.70	+	.03	17.95	13.60	28,773
Feb	13.93	13.98	13.90	13.88	+	.04	17.35	13.91	18,293
Mar	14.11	14.14	14.04	14.06	+	.05	17.80	14.01	11,402
Apr	....	....	....	14.23	+	.07	16.15	14.26	6,630
May	14.49	14.49	14.42	14.39	+	.08	16.17	14.42	3,691
June	14.70	14.70	14.70	14.53	+	.08	17.30	14.61	5,850
July	....	....	....	14.66	+	.08	15.15	14.79	1,650
Aug	14.79	14.82	14.79	14.78	+	.08	15.13	14.79	1,000
Sept	....	....	....	15.01	+	.20	16.79	15.80	2,183
Dec	15.28	15.29	15.20	15.24	+	.11	17.80	15.20	13,070
Ju00	....	....	....	15.60	+	.11	16.58	16.23	1,000
Dec	15.95	15.95	15.95	15.95	+	.11	17.63	15.85	2,408

Est vol 60,000; vol Mn 49,318 ; open int 259,245, +4,497.

Table 2.2   Commodity Futures Quotes from *The Wall Street Journal,* **August 5, 1998** (*Continued*)

FUTURES PRICES

GAS OIL (IPE) 100 metric tons; $ per ton								
Aug	108.75	110.00	108.25	109.00	+	.50	182.00 108.25	26,803
Sept	113.25	113.50	112.25	112.75	+	.25	184.00 112.00	24,134
Oct	118.00	118.00	116.25	117.00	+	.25	179.75 116.25	20,810
Nov	121.75	121.75	120.50	121.25	+	.25	175.00 120.50	14,009
Dec	125.00	125.25	123.75	124.25	+	.25	162.00 123.75	35,865
Ja99	128.25	128.25	126.75	127.00		....	160.50 126.75	12,280
Feb	130.50	130.50	129.50	129.50		....	186.00 129.50	9,579
Mar	132.00	132.00	131.75	131.25		....	148.75 131.50	6,178
Apr	133.25	133.50	133.25	133.00		....	149.25 133.25	3,951
May	135.75	135.75	135.75	134.75	+	.25	175.00 135.75	752
June	....	....		136.25	+	.25	153.75 139.00	5,509
July	....	....		137.50	+	.25	139.50 139.50	303
Sept	....	....		141.25	+	.25	154.25 126.00	1,540
Dec	146.50	146.50	146.50	146.50	+	.50	158.25 136.00	8,443
Est vol 23,000; vol Mn 17,651 ; open int 170,156, +969.								

EXCHANGE ABBREVIATIONS
(for commodity futures and futures options)

CBT-Chicago Board of Trade; CME-Chicago Mercantile Exchange; CSCE-Coffee, Sugar & Cocoa Exchange, New York; CMX-COMEX (Div. of New York Mercantile Exchange); CTN-New York Cotton Exchange; DTB-Deutsche Terminboerse; FINEX-Financial Exchange (Div. of New York Cotton Exchange; IPE-International Petroleum Exchange; KC-Kansas City Board of Trade; LIFFE-London International Financial Futures Exchange; MATIF-Marche a Terme International de France; ME-Montreal Exchange; MCE-MidAmerica Commodity Exchange; MPLS-Minneapolis Grain Exchange; NYFE-New York Futures Exchange (Sub. of New York Cotton Exchange); NYM-New York Mercantile Exchange; SIMEX-Singapore International Monetary Exchange Ltd.; SFE-Sydney Futures Exchange; TFE-Toronto Futures Exchange; WPG-Winnipeg CommodityExchange.

The settlement price is important because it is used for calculating daily gains and losses and margin requirements. In the case of the December 1998 corn futures contract, a trader with a long position in one contract would find that the margin account balance increased by $37.50 (5,000 × 0.75 cent) between August 3 and August 4, 1995. Similarly, a trader with a short position in one contract would find that the margin balance decreased by $37.50 between August 3, 1998, and August 4, 1998.

Lifetime Highs and Lows

The sixth and seventh numbers show the highest futures price and the lowest futures price achieved in the trading of the particular contract. The highest and lowest prices for the December 1998 corn futures contract were $299\frac{1}{2}$ cents and 220 cents. (The contract had traded for over a year on August 4, 1998.)

Open Interest and Volume of Trading

The final column in Table 2.2 shows the *open interest* for each contract. This is the total number of the contracts outstanding. It is the sum of all the long positions, or equivalently, it is the sum of all the short positions. Because of problems in compiling the data, the open interest information is one trading day older than the price information. Thus, in *The Wall Street Journal* of August 5, 1998, the open interest is for the close of trading on August 3, 1998. In the case of the December 1998 corn futures contract, the open interest was 157,619 contracts.

At the end of each commodity's section, Table 2.2 shows the estimated volume of trading in contracts of all maturities on August 4, 1998 and the actual volume of trading in these contracts on August 3, 1998. It also shows the total open interest for all contracts on August 3, 1998 and the change in this open interest from the previous trading day. For all corn futures contracts, the estimated trading volume was 50,000 contracts on August 4, 1998 and the actual trading volume was 64,988 contracts on August 3, 1998. The open interest for all contracts was 317,935 on August 3, 1998—up 4,674 from the previous trading day.

It sometimes happens that the volume of trading in a day is greater than the open interest at the end of the day. This is indicative of a large number of day trades.

Patterns of Futures Prices

A number of different patterns of futures prices can be picked out from Table 2.2. The futures price of gold on the New York Mercantile Exchange increases as the time to maturity increases. This is known as a *normal market*. The opposite situation, where the futures price is a decreasing function of the time to maturity, is known as an *inverted market*. For many assets, the pattern is mixed. The futures price is sometimes an increasing and sometimes a decreasing function of maturity. The factors determining the pattern observed for a commodity are discussed in chapter 3.

2.5   CONVERGENCE OF FUTURES PRICE TO SPOT PRICE

As the delivery month of a futures contract is approached, the futures price converges to the spot price of the underlying asset. When the delivery period is reached, the futures price equals—or is very close to—the spot price.

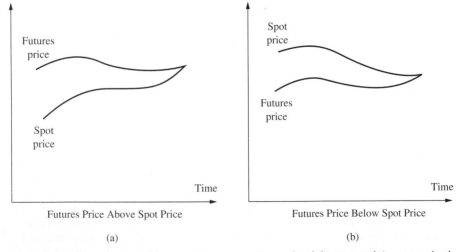

Figure 2.1   Convergence of futures price to spot price as the delivery month is approached.

To show why this is so, suppose first that the futures price is above the spot price during the delivery period. This gives rise to a clear arbitrage opportunity for traders:

1. Short a futures contract.
2. Buy the asset.
3. Make delivery.

This is certain to lead to a profit equal to the amount by which the futures price exceeds the spot price. As traders exploit this arbitrage opportunity, the futures price will fall. Suppose next that the futures price is below the spot price during the delivery period. Companies interested in acquiring the asset will find it attractive to enter into a long futures contract and then wait for delivery to be made. As they do this, the futures price will tend to rise.

Figure 2.1 illustrates the convergence of the futures price to the spot price. In Figure 2.1a the futures price is above the spot price prior to the delivery month. In Figure 2.1b it is below the spot price prior to the delivery month.

2.6 SETTLEMENT

When the exchange has provided alternatives as to when, where, and what will be delivered, it is the party with the short position that makes the choice. When it is ready to deliver, the party with the short position sends a *notice of intention to deliver* to the exchange. The price paid is normally the most recent settlement price (with a possible adjustment for the quality of asset that is chosen and the delivery location). The exchange then selects a party with an outstanding long position to accept delivery.

Cash Settlement

Some financial futures, such as those on stock indices, are settled in cash. This is because it is inconvenient or impossible to deliver the underlying asset. In the case of the futures contract on the S&P 500, for example, delivering the underlying asset would involve delivering a portfolio of 500 stocks. When a contract is settled in cash, it is marked to market at the end of the last trading day and all positions are declared closed. The settlement price on the last trading day is set equal to the closing spot price of the underlying asset. This ensures that the futures price converges to the spot price.

One exception to the rule that the settlement price on the last trading day equals the closing spot price is the S&P 500 futures contract. This bases the final settlement price on the opening price of the index the morning after the last trading day. This procedure is designed to avoid some of the problems connected with the fact that stock index futures, stock index options, and options on stock index futures all expire on the same day. Arbitrageurs often take large offsetting positions in these three contracts, and there may be chaotic trading and significant price movements toward the end of an expiration day as they attempt to close out their positions. The media have coined the term *triple witching hour* to describe trading during the last hour of an expiration day.

2.7   REGULATION

Futures markets in the United States are currently regulated federally by the Commodity Futures Trading Commission (CFTC), which was established in 1974. This body is responsible for licensing futures exchanges and approving contracts. All new contracts and changes to existing contracts must be approved by the CFTC. To be approved, the contract must have some useful economic purpose. Usually, this means that it must serve the needs of hedgers as well as speculators.

The CFTC looks after the public interest. It is responsible for ensuring that prices are communicated to the public and that futures traders report their outstanding positions if they are above certain levels. The CFTC also licenses all individuals who offer their services to the public in the futures area. The backgrounds of these people are investigated and there are minimum capital requirements. The CFTC deals with complaints brought by the public and ensures that disciplinary action is taken against individuals when this is appropriate. It has the authority to force exchanges to take disciplinary action against members who are in violation of exchange rules.

In 1982, the National Futures Association (NFA) was formed. This led to some of the responsibilities of the CFTC being shifted to the futures industry itself. The NFA is an organization of people who participate in the futures industry. Its objective is to prevent fraud and ensure that the market operates in the best interests of the general public. The NFA requires its members to pass an exam. It is authorized to monitor trading and take disciplinary action where appropriate. It has set up an efficient system for arbitrating disputes between individuals and its members.

From time to time, other bodies, such as the Securities and Exchange Commission (SEC), the Federal Reserve Board, and the U.S. Treasury Department, have claimed jurisdictional rights over some aspects of futures trading. These bodies are concerned about the effects of futures trading on the spot markets for securities such as stocks, Treasury bills, and Treasury bonds. The SEC currently has an effective veto over the approval of new stock or bond index futures contracts. However, the basic responsibility for all futures and options on futures rests with the CFTC.

Trading Irregularities

Most of the time, futures markets operate efficiently and in the public interest. However, from time to time, trading irregularities do come to light. One type of trading irregularity occurs when an investor group tries to "corner the market."[1] The investor

---

[1] Possibly the best known example of this is the activities of the Hunt brothers in the silver market in 1979–1980. Between the middle of 1979 and the beginning of 1980, their activities led to a price rise from $9 per ounce to $50 per ounce. The price dropped sharply when the exchange forced them to close out their futures positions.

group takes a huge long futures position and tries to exercise some control over the supply of the underlying commodity. As the maturity of the futures contracts is approached, the investor group does not close out its position, and the number of outstanding futures contracts may exceed the amount of the commodity available for delivery. The holders of short positions realize that they will find it difficult to deliver and become desperate to close out their positions. The result is a large rise in both futures and spot prices. Regulators usually deal with this type of abuse of the market by increasing margin requirements, imposing stricter position limits, prohibiting trades that increase a speculator's open position, and forcing market participants to close out their positions.

Other types of trading irregularities can involve the traders on the floor of the exchange. These received some publicity early in 1989 when it was announced that the FBI had carried out a two-year investigation, using undercover agents, of trading on the Chicago Board of Trade and the Chicago Mercantile Exchange. The investigation was initiated because complaints were filed by a large agricultural concern. The alleged offenses included overcharging customers, not paying customers the full proceeds of sales, and traders using their knowledge of customer orders to trade first for themselves.

2.8 HEDGING USING FUTURES

A company that knows it is due to sell an asset at a particular time in the future can hedge by taking a short futures position. This is known as a *short hedge*. If the price of the asset goes down, the company does not fare well on the sale of the asset but makes a gain on the short futures position. If the price of the asset goes up, the company gains from the sale of the asset but takes a loss on the futures position. Similarly, a company that knows that it is due to buy an asset in the future can hedge by taking a long futures position. This is known as a *long hedge*. It is important to recognize that futures hedging does not necessarily improve the overall financial outcome. In fact, we can expect a futures hedge to make the outcome worse roughly 50% of the time. What the futures hedge does do is reduce risk by making the outcome more certain.

There are a number of reasons why hedging using futures contracts works less than perfectly in practice.

1. The asset whose price is to be hedged may not be exactly the same as the asset underlying the futures contract.
2. The hedger may be uncertain as to the exact date when the asset will be bought or sold.
3. The hedge may require the futures contract to be closed out well before its expiration date.

These problems give rise to what is termed *basis risk*.

Basis Risk

The *basis* in a hedging situation is defined as follows:[2]

basis = spot price of asset to be hedged − futures price of contract used

If the asset to be hedged and the asset underlying the futures contract are the same, the basis should be zero at the expiration of the futures contract. Prior to expiration, as illustrated in Figure 2.1, the basis may be positive or negative.

When the spot price increases by more than the futures price, the basis increases. This is referred to as a *strengthening of the basis*. When the futures price increases by more than the spot price, the basis declines. This is referred to as a *weakening of the basis*.

To examine the nature of basis risk we use the following notation:

S_1: spot price at time t_1
S_2: spot price at time t_2
F_1: futures price at time t_1
F_2: futures price at time t_2
b_1: basis at time t_1
b_2: basis at time t_2

We will assume that a hedge is put in place at time t_1 and closed out at time t_2. We ignore the time value of money. As an example we consider the case where the spot and futures price at the time the hedge is initiated are $2.50 and $2.20, respectively, and that at the time the hedge is closed out they are $2.00 and $1.90, respectively. This means that $S_1 = 2.50$, $F_1 = 2.20$, $S_2 = 2.00$, and $F_2 = 1.90$.

From the definition of the basis,

$$b_1 = S_1 - F_1$$
$$b_2 = S_2 - F_2$$

In our example, $b_1 = 0.30$ and $b_2 = 0.10$.

Consider first the situation of a hedger who knows that the asset will be sold at time t_2 and takes a short futures position at time t_1. The price realized for the asset is S_2 and the profit on the futures position is $F_1 - F_2$. The effective price that is obtained for the asset with hedging is, therefore,

$$S_2 + F_1 - F_2 = F_1 + b_2$$

In our example, this is $2.30. The value of F_1 is known at time t_1. If b_2 were also known at this time, a perfect hedge (i.e., a hedge eliminating all uncertainty about the price obtained) would result. The hedging risk is the uncertainty associated with b_2. This is known as *basis risk*. Consider next a situation where a company knows that it will buy the asset at time t_2 and initiates a long hedge at time t_1. The price paid for

---

[2]This is the usual definition. However, the alternative definition

basis = futures price − spot price

is sometimes used, particularly when the futures contract is on a financial asset.

the asset is S_2 and the loss on the futures position is $F_1 - F_2$. The effective price that is paid with hedging is, therefore,

$$S_2 + F_1 - F_2 = F_1 + b_2$$

This is the same expression as before; it is $2.30 in the example. The value of F_1 is known at time t_1 and the term b_2 represents basis risk.

For investment assets such as currencies, stock indices, gold, and silver, the basis risk tends to be fairly small. This is because, as we will see in chapter 3, arbitrage arguments lead to a well-defined relationship between the futures price and the spot price of an investment asset. The basis risk for an investment asset arises mainly from uncertainty as to the level of the risk-free interest rate and the asset's yield in the future. In the case of a commodity such as oil, corn, or copper, imbalances between supply and demand and the difficulties sometimes associated with storing the commodity can lead to large variations in the basis and, therefore, a much higher basis risk.

The asset that gives rise to the hedger's exposure is sometimes different from the asset underlying the hedge.[3] The basis risk is then usually greater. Define S_2^* as the price of the asset underlying the futures contract at time t_2. As before, S_2 is the price of the asset being hedged at time t_2. By hedging, a company ensures that the price that will be paid (or received) for the asset is

$$S_2 + F_1 - F_2$$

This can be written

$$F_1 + (S_2^* - F_2) + (S_2 - S_2^*)$$

The terms $S_2^* - F_2$ and $S_2 - S_2^*$ represent the two components of the basis. The $S_2^* - F_2$ term is the basis that would exist if the asset being hedged were the same as the asset underlying the futures contract. The $S_2 - S_2^*$ term is the basis arising from the difference between the two assets.

Note that basis risk can lead to an improvement or a worsening of a hedger's position. Consider a short hedge. If the basis strengthens unexpectedly, the hedger's position improves, whereas if the basis weakens unexpectedly, the hedger's position worsens. For a long hedge, the reverse holds.

Choice of Contract

One key factor affecting basis risk is the choice of the futures contract to be used for hedging. This choice has two components:

1. The choice of the asset underlying the futures contract.
2. The choice of the delivery month.

If the asset being hedged exactly matches an asset underlying a futures contract, the first choice is generally fairly easy. In other circumstances, it is necessary to carry out a careful analysis to determine which of the available futures contracts has futures prices that are most closely correlated with the price of the asset being hedged.

---

[3] For example, airlines sometimes use the NYMEX heating oil futures contract to hedge their exposure to the price of jet fuel. See the article by Nikkhah referenced at the end of this chapter for a description of this.

The choice of the delivery month is likely to be influenced by several factors. It might be assumed that when the expiration of the hedge corresponds to a delivery month, the contract with that delivery month is chosen. In fact, a contract with a later delivery month is usually chosen in these circumstances. This is because futures prices are in some instances quite erratic during the delivery month. Also, a long hedger runs the risk of having to take delivery of the physical asset if the contract is held during the delivery month. This can be expensive and inconvenient.

In general, basis risk increases as the time difference between the hedge expiration and the delivery month increases. A good rule of thumb is, therefore, to choose a delivery month that is as close as possible to, but later than, the expiration of the hedge. Suppose that the delivery months are March, June, September, and December for a particular contract. For hedge expirations in December, January, and February, the March contract will be chosen; for hedge expirations in March, April, and May, the June contract will be chosen; and so on. This rule of thumb assumes that there is sufficient liquidity in all contracts to meet the hedger's requirements. In practice, liquidity tends to be greatest in short-maturity futures contracts. Therefore, in some situations the hedger may be inclined to use short-maturity contracts and roll them forward. This strategy is explained in section 2.10.

Example 2.1   It is March 1. A U.S. company expects to receive 50 million Japanese yen at the end of July. Yen futures contracts on the Chicago Mercantile Exchange have delivery months of March, June, September, and December. One contract is for the delivery of 12.5 million yen. The company therefore shorts four September yen futures contracts on March 1. When the yen are received at the end of July, the company closes out its position. We suppose that the futures price on March 1 in cents per yen is 0.7800 and that the spot and futures prices when the contract is closed out are 0.7200 and 0.7250, respectively.

The gain on the futures contract is $0.7800 - 0.7250 = 0.0550$ cents per yen. The basis is $0.7200 - 0.7250 = -0.0050$ cents per yen when the contract is closed out. The effective price obtained in cents per yen is the final spot price plus the gain on the futures:

$$0.7200 + 0.0550 = 0.7750$$

This can also be written as the initial futures price plus the final basis:

$$0.7800 - 0.0050 = 0.7750$$

The total amount received by the company for the 50 million yen is 50×0.00775 million dollars, or $387,500.

Example 2.2   It is June 8 and a company knows that it will need to purchase 20,000 barrels of crude oil at some time in October or November. Oil futures contracts are currently traded for delivery every month on NYMEX, and the contract size is 1,000 barrels. The company therefore decides to use the December contract for hedging and takes a long position in 20 December contracts. The futures price on June 8 is $18.00 per barrel. The company finds that it is ready to purchase the crude oil on November 10. It therefore closes out its futures contract on that date. The spot price and futures price on November 10 are $20.00 per barrel and $19.10 per barrel.

The gain on the futures contract is $19.10 - 18.00 = \$1.10$ per barrel. The basis when the contract is closed out is $20.00 - 19.10 = \$0.90$ per barrel. The effective price paid (in dollars per barrel) is the final spot price less the gain on the futures or

$$20.00 - 1.10 = 18.90$$

This can also be calculated as the initial futures price plus the final basis

$$18.00 + 0.90 = 18.90$$

The total price received is $18.90 \times 20,000 = \$378,000$.

2.9 OPTIMAL HEDGE RATIO

The hedge ratio is the ratio of the size of the position taken in futures contracts to the size of the exposure. Up to now we have always assumed a hedge ratio of 1.0. We now show that if the objective of the hedger is to minimize risk, a hedge ratio of 1.0 is not necessarily optimal.

Define:

ΔS: change in spot price, S, during a period of time equal to the life of the hedge
ΔF: change in futures price, F, during a period of time equal to the life of the hedge
σ_S: standard deviation of ΔS
σ_F: standard deviation of ΔF
ρ: coefficient of correlation between ΔS and ΔF
h: hedge ratio

When the hedger is long the asset and short futures, the change in the value of the hedger's position during the life of the hedge is

$$\Delta S - h\,\Delta F$$

For a long hedge it is

$$h\,\Delta F - \Delta S$$

In either case the variance, v, of the change in value of the hedged position is given by

$$v = \sigma_S^2 + h^2\sigma_F^2 - 2h\rho\sigma_S\sigma_F$$

so that

$$\frac{\partial v}{\partial h} = 2h\sigma_F^2 - 2\rho\sigma_S\sigma_F$$

Setting this equal to zero, and noting that $\partial^2 v/\partial h^2$ is positive, we see that the value of h that minimizes the variance is

$$h = \rho\frac{\sigma_S}{\sigma_F} \qquad (2.1)$$

The optimal hedge ratio is, therefore, the product of the coefficient of correlation between ΔS and ΔF and the ratio of the standard deviation of ΔS to the standard

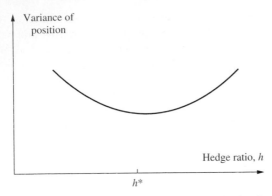

Figure 2.2   Dependence of variance of hedger's position on hedge ratio.

deviation of ΔF. Figure 2.2 shows how the variance of the value of the hedger's position depends on the hedge ratio chosen.

If $\rho = 1$ and $\sigma_F = \sigma_S$, the optimal hedge ratio, h, is 1.0. This is to be expected because in this case the futures price mirrors the spot price perfectly. If $\rho = 1$ and $\sigma_F = 2\sigma_S$, the optimal hedge ratio h is 0.5. This result is also as expected because in this case the futures price always changes by twice as much as the spot price.

> **Example 2.3**   A company knows that it will buy 1 million gallons of jet fuel in three months. The standard deviation of the change in the price per gallon of jet fuel over a three-month period is calculated as 0.032. The company chooses to hedge by buying futures contracts on heating oil. The standard deviation of the change in the futures price over a three-month period is 0.040 and the coefficient of correlation between the three-month change in the price of jet fuel and the three-month change in the futures price is 0.8. The optimal hedge ratio is therefore
>
> $$0.8 \times \frac{0.032}{0.040} = 0.64$$
>
> One heating oil futures contract is on 42,000 gallons. The company should therefore buy
>
> $$0.64 \times \frac{1,000,000}{42,000} = 15.2$$
>
> contracts. Rounding to the nearest whole number, 15 contracts are required.

2.10   ROLLING THE HEDGE FORWARD

Sometimes, the expiration date of the hedge is later than the delivery dates of all the futures contracts that can be used. The hedger must then roll the hedge forward. This involves closing out one futures contract and taking the same position in a futures contract with a later delivery date. Hedges can be rolled forward many times. Consider a company that wishes to use a short hedge to reduce the risk associated with the price to be received for an asset at time T. If there are futures contracts 1, 2, 3, ..., n (not all necessarily in existence at the present time) with progressively later delivery dates, the company can use the following strategy:

Time t_1: Short futures contract 1

Time t_2: Close out futures contract 1
Short futures contract 2

Time t_3: Close out futures contract 2
Short futures contract 3

$\vdots$

Time t_n: Close out futures contract $n - 1$
Short futures contract n

Time T: Close out futures contract n

In this strategy there are n basis risks or sources of uncertainty. At time T there is uncertainty about the difference between the futures price for contract n and the spot price of the asset being hedged. In addition, on each of the $n - 1$ occasions when the hedge is rolled forward, there is uncertainty about the difference between the futures price for the contract being closed out and the futures price for the new contract being entered into. (We will refer to the latter as the *rollover basis*.) In many situations the hedger has some flexibility on the exact time when a switch is made from one contract to the next. This can be used to reduce the rollover basis risk. For example, if the rollover basis is unattractive at the beginning of the period during which the rollover must be made, the hedger can delay the rollover in the hope that the rollover basis will improve.

Example 2.4 In April 1999, a company realizes that it will have 100,000 barrels of oil to sell in June 2000 and decides to hedge its risk with a hedge ratio of 1.0. The current spot price is $19. Although crude oil futures are traded on the New York Mercantile Exchange with maturities up to six years, we suppose that only the first six delivery months have sufficient liquidity to meet the company's needs. The company, therefore, shorts 100 October 1999 contracts. In September 1999 it rolls the hedge forward into the March 2000 contract. In February 2000 it rolls the hedge forward again into the July 2000 contract.

One possible outcome is that the price of oil drops from $19 to $16 per barrel between April 1999 and June 2000. Suppose that the October 1999 futures contract is shorted at $18.20 per barrel and closed out at $17.40 per barrel for a profit of $0.80 per barrel; the March 2000 contract is shorted at $17.00 per barrel and closed out at $16.50 per barrel for a profit of $0.50 per barrel; the July 2000 contract is shorted at $16.30 per barrel and closed out at $15.90 per barrel for a profit of $0.40 per barrel. In this case the futures contracts provide a total of $1.70 per barrel compensation for the $3 per barrel oil price decline.

Metallgesellschaft

Sometimes rolling the hedge forward can lead to cash flow problems. This was illustrated dramatically by the activities of a German company, Metallgesellschaft (MG), in the early 1990s.

MG sold a huge volume of five- to ten-year heating oil and gasoline fixed-price supply contracts to its customers at 6 to 8 cents above market prices. It hedged its exposure with long positions in futures contracts that were rolled over. As it turned out, the price of oil fell and there were margin calls on the futures position. This put considerable short-term cash flow pressures on MG. The members of MG who instigated the hedging strategy argued that these short-term cash outflows were offset by positive cash flows that would ultimately be realized on the long-term fixed-price contracts. However, the company's senior management and their bankers became concerned about the huge cash drain. As a result, the company closed out all the hedge positions and agreed with their customers that the fixed-price contracts would be abandoned. The result was a loss to MG of $1.33 billion.[4]

2.11   ACCOUNTING AND TAX

The full details of the accounting and tax treatment of futures contracts are beyond the scope of this book. A trader who wants detailed information on this should consult experts. In this section we provide some general background information.

Accounting

FASB Statement No. 52, Foreign Currency Translation, established accounting standards in the United States for foreign currency futures. FASB Statement No. 80, Accounting for Futures Contracts, established accounting standards in the United States for all other contracts. The two statements require changes in market value to be recognized when they occur unless the contract qualifies as a hedge. If the contract does qualify as a hedge, gains or losses are generally recognized for accounting purposes in the same period in which the gains or losses from the item being hedged are recognized.

Consider a trader who in September 1998 takes a long position in a March 1999 corn futures contract and closes out the position at the end of February 1999. Suppose that the futures prices are 150 cents per bushel when the contract is entered into, 170 cents per bushel at the end of 1998, and 180 cents per bushel when the contract is closed out. One contract is for the delivery of 5,000 bushels. If the trader is a speculator, the gains for accounting purposes are

$$5,000 \times \$0.20 = \$1,000$$

---

[4]For a discussion of MG, see "MG's Trial by Essay," *RISK*, (October 1994), 228–34; and C. L. Culp and M. H. Miller, "Metallgesellschaft and the Economics of Synthetic Storage," *Journal of Applied Corporate Finance*, 7(4) (Winter 1995), 62–76.

in 1998 and

$$5,000 \times \$0.10 = \$500$$

in 1999. If the trader is hedging the purchase of 5,000 bushels of corn in 1999, the entire gain of $1,500 is realized in 1999 for accounting purposes. We will refer to this treatment as *hedge accounting*.

The treatment of hedging gains and losses is sensible. If the trader in our example is a company that is hedging the purchase of 5,000 bushels of corn at the end of February 1999, the effect of the futures contract is to ensure that the price paid is close to 150 cents per bushel. The accounting treatment reflects that this price is paid in 1999. The 1998 accounts for the trader are unaffected by the futures transaction.

In June, 1998, the Financial Accounting Standards Board issued FASB Statement No. 133, Accounting for Derivative Instruments and Hedging Activities (FAS 133). FAS 133 applies to all types of derivatives (including futures, forwards, swaps, and options) and is effective for fiscal years beginning after June 15, 1999. FAS 133 requires all derivatives to be included on the balance sheet at fair market value.[5] It increases disclosure requirements. It also gives companies far less latitude in using hedge accounting. For hedge accounting to be used, the hedging instrument must be highly effective in offsetting exposures and an assessment of this effectiveness is required every three months.

Tax

Under the U.S. tax rules, two key issues are the nature of a taxable gain or loss and the timing of the recognition of the gain or loss. Gains or losses are either classified as capital gains/losses or as part of ordinary income. For a corporate taxpayer, capital gains are taxed at the same rate as ordinary income while the ability to deduct losses is restricted. Capital losses are deductible only to the extent of capital gains. A corporation may carry back a capital loss for three years and carry it forward for up to five years. For a noncorporate taxpayer, The Taxpayer Relief Act of 1997 widened the rate differential between ordinary income and long-term capital gains. (Long-term capital gains are gains from the sale of a capital asset held for more than one year.) For a noncorporate taxpayer, capital losses are deductible to the extent of capital gains plus ordinary income up to $3,000 and can be carried forward indefinitely.

Generally, positions in futures contracts are treated as if they are closed out on the last day of the tax year. Any gains or losses on contracts other than foreign currency contracts are treated as capital gains/losses. Gains or losses on foreign currency contracts are treated as ordinary income/losses.

Hedging transactions are exempt from the foregoing rule. The definition of a hedge transaction for tax purposes is different from that for accounting purposes. The tax regulations define a hedging transaction as a transaction entered into in the normal

---

[5]Previously, the attraction of derivatives in some situations was that they were "off-balance sheet" items.

course of business primarily for one of the following reasons:

1. To reduce the risk of price changes or currency fluctuations with respect to property that is held or to be held by the taxpayer for the purposes of producing ordinary income.
2. To reduce the risk of price or interest rate changes or currency fluctuations with respect to borrowings made by the taxpayer.

Gains or losses from hedging transactions are treated as ordinary income. The timing of the recognition of gains or losses from hedging transactions generally matches the timing of the recognition of income or deduction from the hedged items.

SUMMARY

In this chapter we have looked at how futures markets operate. In futures markets, contracts are traded on an exchange, and it is necessary for the exchange to define carefully the precise nature of what it is that is traded, the procedures that will be followed, and the regulations that will govern the market. By contrast, forward contracts are negotiated directly over the telephone by two relatively sophisticated individuals. As a result, there is no need to standardize the product, and an extensive set of rules and procedures is not required. The main differences between futures and forward contracts are summarized in Table 2.3.

A very high proportion of futures contracts that are initiated do not lead to the delivery of the underlying asset. They are closed out prior to the delivery period being reached. But, it is the possibility of final delivery that drives the determination of the futures price. For each futures contract, there is a range of days during which delivery can be made and a well-defined delivery procedure. Some contracts, such as those on stock indices, are settled in cash rather than by delivery of the underlying asset.

Table 2.3   Comparison of Forward and Futures Contracts

Forwards	*Futures*
Private contract between two parties	Traded on an exchange
Not standardized	Standardized contract
Usually one specified delivery date	Range of delivery dates
Settled at end of contract	Settled daily
Delivery or final cash settlement usually takes place	Contract usually closed out prior to maturity

The specification of contracts is an important activity for a futures exchange. The two sides to any contract must know what can be delivered, where delivery can take place, and when delivery can take place. They also need to know such details as the trading hours, how prices will be quoted, maximum price movements, and so on.

Margins are an important aspect of futures markets. A trader keeps a margin account with a broker. This is adjusted daily to reflect gains or losses, and the broker may require the account to be topped up from time to time if adverse price movements have taken place. The broker must either be a clearinghouse member or maintain a margin account with a clearinghouse member. Each clearinghouse member maintains a margin account with the exchange clearinghouse. The balance in the account is adjusted daily to reflect gains and losses on the business for which the clearinghouse member is responsible. The exchange ensures that information on prices is collected in a systematic way and relayed within a matter of seconds to traders throughout the world. Many newspapers, such as *The Wall Street Journal*, carry each day a summary of the preceding day's trading.

Futures contracts can be used to hedge a company's exposure to a price of a commodity. A position in the futures markets is taken to offset the effect of the price of the commodity on the rest of the company's business. An important concept in futures hedging is basis. This is the difference between the spot price of an asset and its futures price. The risk in a hedge is the uncertainty about the value of the basis at the maturity of the hedge. This is known as basis risk.

The hedge ratio is the ratio of the size of the position taken in futures contracts to the size of the exposure. If hedgers wish to minimize the variance of their total positions, it may be optimal to use a hedge ratio different from 1.0. When there is no liquid futures contract that matures later than the expiration of the hedge, a strategy known as rolling the hedge forward is sometimes used. This involves entering into a sequence of futures contracts. When the first futures contract is near expiration, it is closed out and the hedger enters into a second contract with a later delivery month. When the second contract is close to expiration, it is closed out and the hedger enters into a third contract with a later delivery month, and so on. Rolling the hedge works well if there is a close correlation between changes in the futures prices and changes in the spot prices.

SUGGESTIONS FOR FURTHER READING

On Futures Markets

Chance, D. *An Introduction to Options and Futures*. Orlando, Fla.: Dryden Press, 1989.

Chicago Board of Trade. *Commodity Trading Manual*. Chicago: 1989.

Duffie, D. *Futures Markets*. Englewood Cliffs, N.J.: Prentice Hall, 1989.

Horn, F. F. *Trading in Commodity Futures*. New York: New York Institute of Finance, 1984.

Kolb, R. *Understanding Futures Markets*. Glenview, Ill.: Scott, Foresman, 1985.

Schwarz, E. W., J. M. Hill, and T. Schneeweis. *Financial Futures*. Homewood, Ill.: Richard D. Irwin, 1986.

Teweles, R. J., and F. J. Jones. *The Futures Game*. New York: McGraw-Hill, 1987.

On Hedging

Chicago Board of Trade. *Introduction to Hedging*. Chicago: 1984.

Culp, C. L., and M. H. Miller "Metallgesellschaft and the Economics of Synthetic Storage," *Journal of Applied Corporate Finance*, 7,4 (Winter 1995), 62–76.

Ederington, L. H. "The Hedging Performance of the New Futures Market," *Journal of Finance*, 34 (March 1979), 157–70.

Frankcle, C. T. "The Hedging Performance of the New Futures Market: Comment," *Journal of Finance*, 35 (December 1980), 1273–79.

Johnson, L. L. "The Theory of Hedging and Speculation in Commodity Futures Markets," *Review of Economics Studies*, 27 (October 1960), 139–51.

Nikkhah, S. "How End Users Can Hedge Fuel Costs in Energy Markets," *Futures* (October 1987), 66–67.

Stulz, R. M. "Optimal Hedging Policies," *Journal of Financial and Quantitative Analysis*, 19 (June 1984), 127–40.

QUESTIONS AND PROBLEMS
(ANSWERS IN SOLUTIONS MANUAL)

2.1. Distinguish between the terms *open interest* and *trading volume*.

2.2. What is the difference between a local and a commission broker?

2.3. What is the difference between the operation of the margin accounts administered by the clearinghouse and those administered by a broker?

2.4. What are the most important aspects of the design of a new futures contract?

2.5. Explain how margins protect traders against the possibility of default.

2.6. Under what circumstances are (a) a short hedge and (b) a long hedge appropriate?

2.7. Explain what is meant by basis risk when futures contracts are used for hedging.

2.8. Does a perfect hedge always lead to a better outcome than an imperfect hedge? Explain your answer.

2.9. Under what circumstances does a minimum variance hedge portfolio lead to no hedging at all?

2.10. Suppose that you enter into a short futures contract to sell July silver for $5.20 per ounce on the New York Commodity Exchange. The size of the contract is 5,000 ounces. The initial margin is $4,000 and the maintenance margin is $3,000. What change in the futures price will lead to a margin call? What happens if you do not meet the margin call?

2.11. The party with a short position in a futures contract sometimes has options as to the precise asset that will be delivered, where delivery will take place, when delivery will take place, and so on. Do these options increase or decrease the futures price? Explain your reasoning.

2.12. A trader enters into two long futures contracts on frozen orange juice. Each contract is for the delivery of 15,000 pounds. The current futures price is 160 cents per pound, the initial margin is $6,000 per contract, and the maintenance margin is $4,500 per contract. What price change would lead to a margin call? Under what circumstances could $2,000 be withdrawn from the margin account?

2.13. At the end of one day, a clearinghouse member is long 100 contracts and the settlement price is $50,000 per contract. The original margin is $2,000 per contract. On the following day, the member becomes responsible for clearing an additional 20 long contracts. These were entered into at a price of $51,000 per contract. The settlement price at the end of this day is $50,200. How much does the member have to add to its margin account with the exchange clearinghouse?

2.14. Suppose that the standard deviation of quarterly changes in the price of a commodity is $0.65, the standard deviation of quarterly changes in a futures price on the commodity is $0.81, and the coefficient of correlation between the two changes is 0.8. What is the optimal hedge ratio for a three-month contract? What does it mean?

2.15. "Speculation in futures markets is pure gambling. It is not in the public interest to allow speculators to buy seats on a futures exchange." Discuss this viewpoint.

2.16. Identify the most actively traded contracts in Table 2.2. Consider each of the following sections separately: grains and oilseeds, livestock and meat, food and fiber, and metals and petroleum.

2.17. What do you think would happen if an exchange started trading a contract where the quality of the underlying asset was incompletely specified?

2.18. "When a futures contract is traded on the floor of the exchange, it may be the case that the open interest increases by one, stays the same, or decreases by one." Explain this statement.

2.19. In the Chicago Board of Trade's corn futures contract, the following delivery months are available: March, May, July, September, and December. Which contract should be used for hedging when the expiration of the hedge is in
(a) June?
(b) July?
(c) January?

2.20. Does a perfect hedge always succeed in locking in the current spot price of an asset for a future transaction? Explain your answer.

2.21. Explain why a short hedger's position improves when the basis strengthens unexpectedly and worsens when the basis weakens unexpectedly.

2.22. Imagine that you are the treasurer of a Japanese company exporting electronic equipment to the United States. Discuss how you would design a foreign exchange hedging strategy and the arguments you would use to sell the strategy to your fellow executives.

2.23. "If the minimum variance hedge ratio is calculated as 1.0, the hedge must be perfect." Is this statement true? Explain your answer.

2.24. "If there is no basis risk, the optimal hedge ratio is always 1.0." Is this statement true? Explain your answer.

2.25. The standard deviation of monthly changes in the spot price of live cattle is (in cents per pound) 1.2. The standard deviation of monthly changes in the futures price of live cattle for the closest contract is 1.4. The correlation between the futures price changes and the spot price changes is 0.7. It is now October 15. A beef producer is committed to purchasing 200,000 pounds of live cattle on November 15. The producer wants to use the December live cattle futures contracts to hedge its risk. Each contract is for the delivery of 40,000 pounds of cattle. What strategy should the beef producer follow?

2.26. A pig farmer expects to have 90,000 pounds of live hogs to sell in three months. The live hogs futures contract on the Chicago Mercantile Exchange is for the delivery of 30,000 pounds of hogs. How can the farmer use this for hedging? From the farmer's viewpoint, what are the pros and cons of hedging?

2.27. It is now July 1999. A mining company has just discovered a small deposit of gold. It will take six months to construct the mine. The gold will then be extracted on a more or less continuous basis for one year. Futures contracts on gold are available on the New York Commodity Exchange. The delivery months range from August 1999 to April 2001 and are at two-month intervals. Each contract is for the delivery of 100 ounces. Discuss how the mining company might use futures markets for hedging.

2.28. An airline executive has argued: "There is no point in our using oil futures. There is just as much chance that the price of oil in the future will be less than the futures price as there is that it will be greater than this price." Discuss this viewpoint.

2.29. What is the effect of using a hedge ratio of 1.5 instead of 1.0 in Example 2.4 of section 2.10?

2.30. "Shareholders can hedge the risks faced by a company. There is no need for the company itself to hedge." Discuss this viewpoint.

2.31. "A company that uses a certain commodity in its manufacturing operations should pass price changes on to its customers. Hedging is then unnecessary." Discuss this viewpoint.

2.32. "Company treasurers should not hedge. They will be blamed when a loss is experienced on the position taken in the hedging instrument." Discuss this viewpoint.

ASSIGNMENT QUESTIONS

2.33. A company enters into a short futures contract to sell 5,000 bushels of wheat for 250 cents per bushel. The initial margin is $3,000 and the maintenance margin is

$2,000. What price change would lead to a margin call? Under what circumstances could $1,500 be withdrawn from the margin account?

2.34. The following table gives data on monthly changes in the spot price and the futures price for a certain commodity. Use the data to calculate a minimum variance hedge ratio for a company that knows it will purchase the commodity in one month.

Spot price change	+0.50	+0.61	−0.22	−0.35	+0.79
Futures price change	+0.56	+0.63	−0.12	−0.44	+0.60

Spot price change	+0.04	+0.15	+0.70	−0.51	−0.41
Futures price change	−0.06	+0.01	+0.80	−0.56	−0.46

Evaluate how well a hedging strategy based on the minimum variance hedge ratio would have worked during each month of the ten-month period covered by the data.

2.35. It is now October, 1999. A company anticipates that it will purchase 1 million pounds of copper in each of February 2000, August 2000, February 2001, and August 2001. The company has decided to use the futures contracts traded in the COMEX division of the New York Mercantile Exchange to hedge its risk. One contract is for the delivery of 25,000 pounds of copper. The initial margin is $2,000 per contract and the maintenance margin is $1,500 per contract. The company's policy is to hedge 80% of its exposure. Contracts with maturities up to 13 months into the future are considered to have sufficient liquidity to meet the company's needs. Devise a hedging strategy for the company.

Assume the market prices (in cents per pound) today and at future dates are as follows. What is the impact of the strategy you propose on the price the company pays for copper? What is the initial margin requirement in October 1999? Is the company subject to any margin calls?

Date	*Oct 1999*	*Feb 2000*	*Aug 2000*	*Feb 2001*	*Aug 2001*
Spot Price	72.00	69.00	65.00	77.00	88.00
Mar 2000 Futures Price	72.30	69.10			
Sep 2000 Futures Price	72.80	70.20	64.80		
Mar 2001 Futures Price		70.70	64.30	76.70	
Sep 2001 Futures Price			64.20	76.50	88.20

CHAPTER 3

FORWARD AND FUTURES PRICES

In this chapter we examine how forward prices and futures prices are related to the spot price of the underlying asset. Forward contracts are easier to analyze than futures contracts because there is no daily settlement. Consequently, most of the analysis in the first part of the chapter is directed toward determining forward prices rather than futures prices. Luckily, for many of the contracts that are traded it can be argued that the forward price and futures price of an asset are very close to each other when the maturities of the two contracts are the same. This means that results obtained for forward prices can be assumed to be true for futures prices as well.

It will prove important for us to distinguish between *investment assets* and *consumption assets*. An investment asset is an asset that is held for investment purposes by significant numbers of investors. Stocks and bonds are clearly investment assets. Gold and silver are also examples of investment assets. Note that an investment asset does not have to be held exclusively for investment. Silver, for example, has a number of industrial uses. However, an investment asset does have to satisfy the requirement that it is held by significant numbers of investors solely for investment. A consumption asset is an asset that is held primarily for consumption. It is not usually held for investment. Examples of consumption assets are commodities such as copper, oil, and live hogs.

As we will see, arbitrage arguments enable the forward and futures prices of investment assets to be determined from spot prices and other observable variables. The same determination is not possible for forward and futures prices of consumption assets.

In the first part of the chapter, key results are provided for forward contracts on

1. Investment assets providing no income.

2. Investment assets providing a known cash income.

3. Investment assets providing a known dividend yield.

In the second part of the chapter, we use these results to calculate forward and futures prices for contracts on stock indices, foreign exchange, gold, and silver, and discuss how the contracts are used for hedging.

50

3.1 SOME PRELIMINARIES

We start by presenting some preliminary material.

Continuous Compounding

In this book the interest rates used will be compounded continuously except where stated otherwise. Readers used to working with interest rates that are compounded annually, semiannually, or in some other way may find this frustrating. However, continuously compounded interest rates are used to such a great extent when options and other complex derivatives are being priced that it makes sense to get used to working with them now.

Consider an amount A invested for n years at an interest rate of R per annum. If the rate is compounded once per annum, the terminal value of the investment is

$$A(1 + R)^n$$

If it is compounded m times per annum, the terminal value of the investment is

$$A\left(1 + \frac{R}{m}\right)^{mn} \tag{3.1}$$

Suppose that $A = \$100$, $R = 10\%$ per annum, and $n = 1$, so that we are considering one year. When we compound once per annum ($m = 1$), this formula shows that the $100 grows to

$$\$100 \times 1.1 = \$110$$

When we compound twice a year ($m = 2$), we earn 5% interest per six months, with the interest being reinvested, and the $100 grows to

$$\$100 \times 1.05 \times 1.05 = \$110.25$$

When we compound four times a year ($m = 4$), we earn 2.5% per six months, with the interest being reinvested, and the $100 grows to

$$\$100 \times 1.025^4 = \$110.38$$

Table 3.1 shows the effect of increasing the compounding frequency further (i.e., of increasing m). The limit as m tends to infinity is known as *continuous compounding*. With continuous compounding, it can be shown that an amount A invested for n years at rate R grows to

$$Ae^{Rn} \tag{3.2}$$

where e is the mathematical constant, 2.71828. In the example in Table 3.1, $A = 100$, $n = 1$, and $R = 0.1$, so that the value to which A grows with continuous compounding is

$$100e^{0.1} = 110.52$$

Table 3.1   Compounding Frequency

The effect of increasing the compounding frequency on the value of $100 at the end of one year when the interest rate is 10% per annum.

Compounding Frequency	Value of $100 at End of One Year (dollars)
Annually ($m = 1$)	110.00
Semiannually ($m = 2$)	110.25
Quarterly ($m = 4$)	110.38
Monthly ($m = 12$)	110.47
Weekly ($m = 52$)	110.51
Daily ($m = 365$)	110.52

This is (to two decimal places) the same as the value using daily compounding. For most practical purposes, continuous compounding can be thought of as being equivalent to daily compounding. Compounding a sum of money at a continuously compounded rate R for n years involves multiplying it by e^{Rn}. Discounting it at a continuously compounded rate R for n years involves multiplying by e^{-Rn}.

The compounding frequency, in effect, defines the units in which an interest rate is measured. A rate expressed with one compounding frequency can be converted into an equivalent rate with a different compounding frequency. For example, from Table 3.1 we see that 10.25% with annual compounding is equivalent to 10% with semiannual compounding.

Suppose that R_c is a rate of interest with continuous compounding and R_m is the equivalent rate with compounding m times per annum. From the results in equations (3.1) and (3.2), we must have

$$Ae^{R_c n} = A\left(1 + \frac{R_m}{m}\right)^{mn}$$

or

$$e^{R_c} = \left(1 + \frac{R_m}{m}\right)^{m}$$

This means that

$$R_c = m \ln\left(1 + \frac{R_m}{m}\right) \tag{3.3}$$

and

$$R_m = m(e^{R_c/m} - 1) \tag{3.4}$$

These equations can be used to convert a rate where the compounding frequency is *m* times per annum to a continuously compounded rate, and vice versa. The function ln is the natural logarithm function. It is defined so that if $y = \ln x$, then $x = e^y$.

Example 3.1   Consider an interest rate that is quoted as 10% per annum with semiannual compounding. From equation (3.3) with $m = 2$ and $R_m = 0.1$, the equivalent rate with continuous compounding is

$$2 \ln (1 + 0.05) = 0.09758$$

or 9.758% per annum.

Example 3.2   Suppose that a lender quotes the interest rate on loans as 8% per annum with continuous compounding and that interest is actually paid quarterly. From equation (3.4), with $m = 4$ and $R_c = 0.08$, the equivalent rate with quarterly compounding is

$$4(e^{0.02} - 1) = 0.0808$$

or 8.08% per annum. This means that on a $10,000 loan, interest payments of $202 would be required each quarter.

Finally, we note that a rate expressed with a compounding frequency of m_1 can be converted to a rate with a compounding frequency of m_2. From equation (3.1)

$$A\left(1 + \frac{R_{m_1}}{m_1}\right)^{m_1 n} = A\left(1 + \frac{R_{m_2}}{m_2}\right)^{m_2 n}$$

so that

$$R_{m_2} = \left[\left(1 + \frac{R_{m_1}}{m_1}\right)^{m_1/m_2} - 1\right] m_2$$

Short Selling

Some of the arbitrage strategies presented in this chapter involve *short selling*. This trade, usually simply referred to as "shorting," involves selling an asset that is not owned with the intention of buying it back later. Short selling is possible for some— but not all—investment assets. It yields a profit when the price of the asset goes down and a loss when it goes up.

To explain the mechanics of short selling, we suppose that an investor contacts a broker to short 500 IBM shares. The broker immediately borrows 500 IBM shares from another client and sells them in the open market in the usual way, depositing the sale proceeds to the investor's account. Provided there are shares that can be borrowed, the investor can continue to maintain the short position for as long as desired. At some stage, however, the investor will choose to instruct the broker to close out the position. The broker then uses funds in the investor's account to purchase 500 IBM shares and replaces them in the account of the client from which the shares were borrowed. The investor makes a profit if the stock price has declined and a loss if it has risen. If at any time while the contract is open, the broker runs out of shares to borrow, the investor is what is known as *short-squeezed* and must close out the position immediately even if not ready to do so.

Regulators often allow securities to be sold short only on an *uptick*, that is, when the most recent movement in the price of the security was an increase. A broker requires significant initial margins from clients with short positions, and as with futures contracts, if there are adverse movements (i.e., increases) in the price of the security, additional margin may be required. The proceeds of the initial sales of the security normally form part of the initial margin requirement. Some brokers pay interest on margin accounts, and marketable securities such as Treasury bills can be deposited with a broker to meet initial margin requirements. As in the case of futures contracts, the margin does not, therefore, represent a real cost.

An investor with a short position must pay to the broker any income, such as dividends or interest, that would normally be received on the securities that have been shorted. The broker will transfer this to the account of the client from whom the securities have been borrowed. Consider the position of an investor who shorts 500 IBM shares in April when the price per share is $120 and closes out the position by buying them back in July when the price per share is $100. Suppose that a dividend of $4 per share is paid in May. The investor receives $500 \times \$120 = \$60,000$ in April when the short position is initiated. The dividend leads to a payment by the investor of $500 \times \$4 = \$2,000$ in May. The investor also pays $500 \times \$100 = \$50,000$ when the position is closed out in July. The net gain is, therefore,

$$\$60,000 - \$2,000 - \$50,000 = \$8,000$$

Assumptions and Notation

In this chapter and subsequent chapters we assume that there are some market participants for which the following are true:

1. The market participants are subject to no transactions costs when they trade.
2. The market participants are subject to the same tax rate on all net trading profits.
3. The market participants can borrow money at the same risk-free rate of interest as they can lend money.
4. The market participants take advantage of arbitrage opportunities as they occur.

Note that we do not require these assumptions to be true for all market participants. All that we require is that they be true for a subset of all market participants, for example, large investment banks. This is not unreasonable. As discussed in chapter 1, the fact that these market participants are prepared to take advantage of arbitrage opportunities as they occur means that in practice arbitrage opportunities disappear almost as soon as they arise. An implication of the assumptions is, therefore, that market prices are such that there are no arbitrage opportunities.

The following notation will be used throughout this chapter:

T: time when the forward contract matures (years)
S_0: price of asset underlying the forward contract today
F_0: forward price today
r: risk-free rate of interest per annum, with continuous compounding, for an investment maturing at time T

3.2 THE FORWARD PRICE FOR AN INVESTMENT ASSET

We now consider the relationship between the forward price and spot price of an investment asset that pays no income. As an example, we consider a stock that is currently selling for $30 and is expected to pay no dividends over the next two years. We assume the two-year risk-free interest rate is 5% per annum with continuous compounding.

Suppose first that the two-year forward price of the stock is $35. This means that the stock can be bought or sold for $35 with delivery in two years. Arbitrageurs can adopt the following strategy:

1. Borrow $3,000 dollars at an interest rate of 5% per annum for 2 years.
2. Buy 100 shares of the stock.
3. Enter into a forward contract to sell 100 shares for $3,500 in two years.

In two years $3,000e^{0.05 \times 2} = \$3,316$ is required to repay the loan. However, under the terms of the forward contract the arbitrageur can sell the shares for $3,500. The result is a riskless profit of $184. It is easy to see that any forward price above $33.16 gives rise to this type of riskless arbitrage profit.

Riskless arbitrage opportunities, if they are observed at all, rarely last for long. In this case, as arbitrageurs enter into short forward contracts, they will then quickly drive the forward price down to $33.16 and eliminate the arbitrage opportunity. We can deduce that a forward price above $33.16 will not be observed in a well-functioning market.

Suppose next that the forward price is relatively low at $31. An arbitrageur can then adopt the following strategy:

1. Short 100 shares of the stock.
2. Invest the $3,000 proceeds at the risk-free rate of 5% for two years.
3. Enter into a long forward contract to buy 100 shares for $3,100 in two years.

In two years the $3,000 investment grows to $3,000e^{0.05 \times 2} = \$3,316$. Under the terms of the forward contract, 100 shares are purchased for $3,100 and the short position is closed out. The result is a riskless profit of $216. This riskless arbitrage opportunity is available whenever the forward price is below $33.16. As traders take advantage of it, the forward price will be driven up and the arbitrage opportunity will disappear.

These arguments show that we should expect the forward price to be $33.16. Any forward price above $33.16 allows arbitrageurs to make money by buying the stock and entering into short forward contracts on the stock. Any forward price below $33.16 allows arbitrageurs to make money by shorting the stock and entering into long forward contracts.

Generalization

We can generalize from this example using the notation introduced earlier. For an investment asset providing no income:

$$F_0 = S_0 e^{rT} \tag{3.5}$$

In our example $S_0 = 30$, $r = 0.05$, and $T = 2$, so that

$$F_0 = 30e^{0.05 \times 2} = 33.16$$

If $F_0 > S_0e^{rT}$, arbitrageurs can buy the asset and short forward contracts on the asset. If $F_0 < S_0e^{rT}$, they can short the asset and buy forward contracts on it.[1]

> **Example 3.3**   Consider a four-month forward contract to buy a zero-coupon bond that will mature one year from today. The current price of the bond is \$930. (Because the bond will have eight months to go when the forward contract matures, we can regard the contract as on an eight-month zero-coupon bond.) We assume that the four-month risk-free rate of interest (continuously compounded) is 6% per annum. We can use equation (3.5) with $T = 4/12$, $r = 0.06$, and $S_0 = 930$ to obtain the forward price
>
> $$F_0 = 930e^{0.06 \times 4/12} = \$948.79$$
>
> This would be the delivery price in a contract negotiated today.

What If Short Sales Are Not Possible?

Short sales are not possible for all investment assets. As it happens, this does not matter. To derive equation (3.5) we do not need to be able to short the asset. All that we require is that there be a significant number of people who hold the asset purely for investment. If the forward price is too low, they will find it attractive to sell the asset and take a long position in a forward contract.

Consider the example of gold. (This is also discussed in section 1.1.) Assume no storage costs. If $F_0 > S_0e^{rT}$, an investor can adopt the following strategy:

1. Borrow S_0 dollars at an interest rate r for T years.
2. Buy one ounce of gold.
3. Short a forward contract on one ounce of gold.

After T years, one ounce of gold is sold for F_0. An amount S_0e^{rT} is required to repay the loan at this time, and the investor makes a profit of $F_0 - S_0e^{rT}$.

Suppose next that $F_0 < S_0e^{rT}$. In this case an investor who owns one ounce of gold can

1. Sell the gold for S_0.
2. Invest the proceeds at interest rate r for T years.
3. Take a long position in a forward contract on one ounce of gold.

After T years the cash invested has grown to S_0e^{rT}. The gold is repurchased for F_0, and the investor makes a profit of $S_0e^{rT} - F_0$ relative to the position the investor would have been in if the gold had been kept.

---

[1]For another way of seeing that equation (3.5) is correct, consider the following strategy: Buy one unit of the asset and enter into a short forward contract to sell it for F_0 at time T. This costs S_0 and is certain to lead to a cash inflow of F_0 at time T. S_0 must, therefore, equal the present value of F_0; that is, $S_0 = F_0e^{-rT}$, or equivalently $F_0 = S_0e^{rT}$.

As in the non-dividend-paying stock example considered earlier, we can expect the forward price to adjust so that neither of the two arbitrage opportunities we have considered exists. This means that the relationship in equation (3.5) must hold.

3.3 THE EFFECT OF KNOWN INCOME

We now move on to consider forward contracts on assets that provide a known cash income. As an example, we consider a long forward contract to purchase a coupon-bearing bond whose current price is $900. We suppose that the forward contract matures in one year and the bond lasts for five years, so that the forward contract is a contract to purchase a four-year bond in one year. We also suppose that coupon payments of $40 are expected after 6 months and 12 months, with the second coupon payment being immediately prior to the delivery date in the forward contract. We assume the six-month and one-year risk-free interest rates (continuously compounded) are 9% per annum and 10% per annum, respectively.

Suppose first that the forward price is relatively high at $930. An arbitrageur can borrow $900 to buy the bond and short a forward contract. The first coupon payment has a present value of $40e^{-0.09 \times 0.5} = \$38.24$. Of the $900, $38.24 is therefore borrowed at 9% per annum for six months so that it can be repaid with the first coupon payment. The remaining $861.76 is borrowed at 10% per annum for one year. The amount owing at the end of the year is $861.76e^{0.1 \times 1} = \$952.39$. The second coupon provides $40 toward this amount, and $930 is received for the bond under the terms of the forward contract. The arbitrageur, therefore, makes a net profit of

$$\$40 + \$930 - \$952.39 = \$17.61$$

Suppose next that the forward price is relatively low at $905. An investor can short the bond and enter into a long forward contract. An investor who shorts a bond must pay the coupons on the bond. (This is similar to an investor who shorts a stock having to pay the dividends declared on the stock.) Of the $900 realized from the short sale, $38.24 is invested for six months at 9% per annum so that it grows into an amount sufficient to pay the first coupon. The remaining $861.76 is invested for 12 months at 10% per annum and grows to $952.39. Of this sum, $40 is used to pay the second coupon on the bond, and $905 is paid under the terms of the forward contract to purchase the bond and close out the short position. The investor, therefore, gains

$$\$952.39 - \$40 - \$905 = \$7.39$$

If the bond cannot be shorted, we will find that investors who own the bond will sell the bond and buy the forward contract in the second situation. They will find that they are $7.39 better off than they would be if they held the bond for the year.

The first strategy produces a profit when the forward price is greater than 912.39, whereas the second strategy produces a profit when it is less than 912.39. It follows that if there are no arbitrage opportunities, the forward price must be $912.39.

A Generalization

We can generalize from this example to argue that, when an investment asset will provide income with a present value of I during the life of a forward contract

$$F_0 = (S_0 - I)e^{rT} \tag{3.6}$$

In the earlier example, $S_0 = 900.00$, $I = 40e^{-0.09 \times 0.5} + 40e^{-0.10 \times 1} = 74.433$, $r = 0.1$, and $T = 1$, so that

$$F_0 = (900.00 - 74.433)e^{0.1 \times 1} = \$912.39$$

This is in agreement with our earlier calculation. Equation (3.6) applies to any investment asset that provides a known cash income.

If $F_0 > (S_0 - I)e^{rT}$, an arbitrageur can lock in a profit by buying the asset and shorting a forward contract on the asset. If $F_0 < (S_0 - I)e^{rT}$, an arbitrageur can lock in a profit by shorting the asset and taking a long position in a forward contract. If short sales are not possible, investors who own the asset will find it profitable to sell the asset and go long forward contracts.[2]

> **Example 3.4**   Consider a 10-month forward contract on a stock with a price of $50. We assume that the risk-free rate of interest (continuously compounded) is 8% per annum for all maturities. We also assume that dividends of $0.75 per share are expected after three months, six months, and nine months. The present value of the dividends, I, is given by
>
> $$I = 0.75e^{-0.08 \times 3/12} + 0.75e^{-0.08 \times 6/12} + 0.75e^{-0.08 \times 9/12} = 2.162$$
>
> The variable T is 10 months or $10/12$ years so that the forward price, F_0, from equation (3.6), is given by
>
> $$F_0 = (50 - 2.162)e^{0.08 \times 10/12} = \$51.14$$
>
> If the forward price were less than this, an arbitrageur would short the stock spot and buy forward contracts. If the forward price were greater than this, an arbitrageur would short forward contracts and buy the stock spot.

3.4   THE EFFECT OF A KNOWN DIVIDEND YIELD

We now move on to consider the situation where the asset underlying a forward contract provides a known dividend yield. This means that the income, when expressed as a percentage of the asset price, is known. We assume first that the dividend yield is paid continuously at a constant annual rate of q. To illustrate what this means, suppose that $q = 0.05$ so that the dividend yield is 5% per annum. When the asset price

---

[2]For another way of seeing that equation (3.6) is correct, consider the following strategy: Buy one unit of the asset and enter into a short forward contract to sell it for F_0 at time T. This costs S_0 and is certain to lead to a cash inflow of F_0 at time T and income with a present value of I. The initial outflow is S_0. The present value of the inflows is $I + F_0e^{-rT}$. Hence $S_0 = I + F_0e^{-rT}$, or equivalently $F_0 = (S_0 - I)e^{rT}$.

is $10, dividends in the next small interval of time are paid at the rate of 5% of $10 (or 50 cents) per annum; when the asset price is $100, dividends in the next small interval of time are paid at the rate of $5 per annum; and so on. In practice, dividends are not paid continuously, but in some situations the continuous dividend yield assumption is a good approximation of reality.

The forward price for an investment asset providing a continuous dividend yield at rate q is

$$F_0 = S_0 e^{(r-q)T} \tag{3.7}$$

This equation is proved in Appendix 3A.

Example 3.5 Consider a six-month forward contract on an investment asset that is expected to provide a continuous dividend yield of 4% per annum. The risk-free rate of interest (with continuous compounding) is 10% per annum. The asset's price is $25. In this case $S_0 = 25$, $r = 0.10$, $T = 0.5$, $q = 0.04$. From equation (3.7), the forward price F_0 is given by

$$F_0 = 25 e^{(0.10-0.04)\times 0.5} = \$25.76$$

When the dividend yield is continuous, but varies throughout the life of the forward contract, q should be set equal to the average dividend yield during the life of the contract. Equation (3.7) can also be used in situations where there is a known dividend yield, but it is paid at discrete points in time. It is necessary to find the continuous dividend yield that is equivalent to the discrete dividend yield. The way this is done is described in Appendix 3A.

3.5 VALUE OF A FORWARD CONTRACT

The value of a forward contract at the time it is first entered into is zero. At a later stage it may prove to have a positive or negative value. Suppose that f is the value today of a long forward contract that has a delivery price of K and that F_0 is the current forward price for the contract. A general result, applicable to a forward contract on either an investment or consumption asset, is

$$f = (F_0 - K)e^{-rT} \tag{3.8}$$

where, as usual, T is the time to maturity of the contract and r is the risk-free rate for a maturity T. To see why equation (3.8) is correct, we compare a long forward contract that has a delivery price of F_0 with an otherwise identical long forward contract that has a delivery price of K. The difference between the two is only in the amount that will be paid for the underlying asset at time T. Under the first contract this amount is F_0; under the second contract it is K. A cash outflow difference of $F_0 - K$ at time T translates to a difference of $(F_0 - K)e^{-rT}$ today. The contract with a delivery price F_0 is, therefore, less valuable than the contract with delivery price K by an amount $(F_0 - K)e^{-rT}$. The value of the contract that has a delivery price of F_0 is by definition zero. It follows that the value of the contract with a delivery price of K is $(F_0 - K)e^{-rT}$. This proves equation (3.8). Similarly, the value of a short forward contract with delivery price K is

$$(K - F_0)e^{-rT}$$

Equation (3.8) shows that we can value a long forward contract on an asset by assuming that the price of the asset at the maturity of the forward contract is the forward price, F_0. This is because, when we make this assumption, a long forward contract will provide a payoff at time T of $F_0 - K$. This is worth $(F_0 - K)e^{-rT}$, the value of the forward contract, today. Similarly, we can value a short forward contract on the asset by assuming that the current forward price of the asset is realized.

Using equation (3.8) in conjunction with equation (3.5) gives the following expression for the value of a long forward contract on an investment asset that provides no income

$$f = S_0 - Ke^{-rT} \qquad (3.9)$$

Similarly, using equation (3.8) in conjunction with equation (3.6) gives the following expression for the value of a long forward contract on an investment asset that provides a known income with present value I

$$f = S_0 - I - Ke^{-rT} \qquad (3.10)$$

Finally, using equation (3.8) in conjunction with equation (3.7) gives the following expression for the value of a long forward contract on an investment asset that provides a known dividend yield at rate q:

$$f = S_0 e^{-qT} - Ke^{-rT} \qquad (3.11)$$

Example 3.6   Consider a six-month long forward contract on a non-dividend-paying stock. The risk-free rate of interest (with continuous compounding) is 10% per annum, the stock price is $25, and the delivery price is $24. In this case $S_0 = 25$, $r = 0.10$, $T = 0.5$, and $K = 24$. From equation (3.5), the forward price, F_0, is given by

$$F_0 = 25e^{0.1 \times 0.5} = \$26.28$$

From equation (3.8), the value of the forward contract is

$$f = (26.28 - 24)e^{-0.1 \times 0.5} = \$2.17$$

Alternatively, equation (3.9) yields

$$f = 25 - 24e^{-0.1 \times 0.5} = \$2.17$$

3.6   FORWARD PRICES VERSUS FUTURES PRICES

Appendix 3B provides an arbitrage argument to show that when the risk-free interest rate is constant and the same for all maturities, the forward price for a contract with a certain delivery date is the same as the futures price for a contract with that delivery date. The argument in Appendix 3B can be extended to cover situations where the interest rate is a known function of time.

When interest rates vary unpredictably (as they do in the real world), forward and futures prices are in theory no longer the same. We can get a sense of the nature of the relationship by considering the situation where the price of the underlying asset, S, is strongly positively correlated with interest rates. When S increases, an investor who holds a long futures position makes an immediate gain because of the daily settlement procedure. Because increases in S tend to occur at the same time as increases in interest rates, this gain will tend to be invested at a higher-than-average rate of interest. Similarly, when S decreases, the investor will take an immediate loss. This loss will tend to be financed at a lower-than-average rate of interest. An investor holding a forward contract rather than a futures contract is not affected in this way by interest rate movements. It follows that, *ceteris paribus*, a long futures contract will be more attractive than a similar long forward contract. Hence, when S is strongly positively correlated with interest rates, futures prices will tend to be higher than forward prices. When S is strongly negatively correlated with interest rates, a similar argument shows that forward prices will tend to be higher than futures prices.

The theoretical differences between forward and futures prices for contracts that last only a few months are in most circumstances sufficiently small to be ignored.[3] In most of this book we therefore assume that forward and futures contracts are the same. The symbol F_0 will be used to represent both the futures price and the forward price of an asset at time zero.

As the life of a futures contract increases, the differences between forward and futures contracts are liable to become significant, and it is then dangerous to assume that forward and futures prices are perfect substitutes for each other. This point is discussed further in connection with Eurodollar futures in chapters 4 and 21.

Empirical Research

Some of the empirical research that has been carried out comparing forward and futures contracts is listed at the end of the chapter. Cornell and Reinganum studied forward and futures prices on the British pound, Canadian dollar, German mark, Japanese yen, and Swiss franc between 1974 and 1979. They found very few statistically significant differences between the two prices. Their results were confirmed by Park and Chen, who as part of their study looked at the British pound, German mark, Japanese yen, and Swiss franc between 1977 and 1981.

French studied copper and silver during the period 1968–1980. The results for silver show that the futures price and the forward price are significantly different (at the 95% confidence level), with the futures price generally above the forward price. The results for copper are less clear-cut. Park and Chen looked at gold, silver, silver coin, platinum, copper, and plywood between 1977 and 1981. Their results are similar to those of French for silver. The forward and futures prices are significantly different,

---

[3]In practice, there are a number of factors, not reflected in theoretical models, that may cause forward and futures prices to be different. These factors include taxes, transactions costs, and the treatment of margins. Also, in some instances, futures contracts are more liquid and easier to trade than are forward contracts.

with the futures price above the forward price. Rendleman and Carabini studied the Treasury bill market between 1976 and 1978. They also found statistically significant differences between futures and forward prices.

3.7   STOCK INDEX FUTURES

A *stock index* tracks changes in the value of a hypothetical portfolio of stocks. The weight of a stock in the portfolio equals the proportion of the portfolio invested in the stock. The percentage increase in the stock index over a small interval of time is set equal to the percentage increase in the value of the hypothetical portfolio. Dividends are usually not included in the calculation so that the index tracks the capital gain/loss from investing in the portfolio.[4]

If the hypothetical portfolio of stocks remains fixed, the weights assigned to individual stocks in the portfolio do not remain fixed. When the price of one particular stock in the portfolio rises more sharply than others, more weight is automatically given to that stock. Some indices are constructed from a hypothetical portfolio consisting of one of each of a number of stocks. The weights assigned to the stocks are then proportional to their market prices, with adjustments being made when there are stock splits. Other indices are constructed so that weights are proportional to market capitalization (stock price $\times$ number of shares outstanding). The underlying portfolio is then automatically adjusted to reflect stock splits, stock dividends, and new equity issues.

Stock Indices

Table 3.2 shows futures prices for contracts on a number of different stock indices as they were reported in *The Wall Street Journal* of August 5, 1998. The prices refer to the close of trading on August 4, 1998.

The *Dow Jones Industrial Average* is based on a portfolio consisting of 30 blue chip stocks in the United States. The weights given to the stocks are proportional to their prices. One futures contract, traded on the CBOT, is on 10 times the index.

The *Standard & Poor's 500 (S&P 500) Index* is based on a portfolio of 500 different stocks: 400 industrials, 40 utilities, 20 transportation companies, and 40 financial institutions. The weights of the stocks in the portfolio at any given time are proportional to their market capitalizations. This index accounts for 80% of the market capitalization of all the stocks listed on the New York Stock Exchange. One futures contract, traded on the Chicago Mercantile Exchange, is on 250 times the index. The *Standard & Poor's MidCap 400 Index* is similar to the S&P 500 but based on a portfolio of 400 stocks that have somewhat lower market capitalizations.

The *Nikkei 225 Stock Average* is based on a portfolio of 225 of the largest stocks trading on the Tokyo Stock Exchange. Stocks are weighted according to their prices.

---

[4]An exception to this is a *total return index*. This is calculated by assuming that dividends on the hypothetical portfolio are reinvested in the portfolio.

Table 3.2   Stock Index Futures Quotes from *The Wall Street Journal,* **August 5, 1998**

DJ INDUSTRIAL AVERAGE (CBOT)-$10 times average

	Open	High	Low	Settle	Chg	High	Low	Open Interest
Sept	8810	8889	8480	8505	− 306	9418	7150	13,882
Dec	8898	8970	8590	8590	− 310	9515	7677	1,453
Mr99	9060	9060	8675	8683	− 305	9586	8675	677

Est vol 25,000; vol Mon 13,496; open int 16,125, +561.
Idx prl: High 8857.03; Low 8487.31; Close 8487.31 −299.43

S&P 500 INDEX (CME)-$250 times index

Sept	111850	112550	107300	107400	− 43.60	119940	879.20	358,508
Dec	113550	113700	108600	108550	− 44.30	121210	890.85	15,835
Mr99	115200	115250	109520	109650	− 45.70	122500	902.85	3,855
June	....	....		110780	− 46.60	123810	914.85	1,666
Dec	116400	118500	113300	113300	− 45.00	126390	981.40	644

Est vol 172,659; vol Mon 113,335; open int 380,587, +3,836.
Idx prl: High 1119.73; Low 1071.82; Close 1072.12 −40.32

MINI S&P 500 INDEX (CME)-$50 times index

Sept	111825	112675	107350	1074.00	− 43.50	119975	107350	9,150

Vol Mon 29,153; open int 9,258, +80.

S&P MIDCAP 400 (CME)-$500 times index

Sept	346.50	347.00	332.90	333.10	− 11.20	388.00	312.40	13,094

Est vol 1,024; vol Mon 805; open int 13,094, −94.
Idx prl: High 345.21; Low 332.24; Close 332.26 −11.03

NIKKEI 225 STOCK AVERAGE (CME)-$5 times index

Sept	16035.	16080.	15790.	15820.	− 135	18680.	14520.	26,298

Est vol 1,958; vol Mon 1,290; open int 26,353, −146.
Idx prl: High 16180.92; Low 16004.25; Close 16023.58 −141.50

NASDAQ 100 (CME)-$100 times index

Sept	137400	139600	131600	131800	− 57.25	150000	980.50	10,286
Dec	136200	141375	133650	133650	− 57.25	151300	119085	36

Est vol 9,157; vol Mon 4,426; open int 10,362, +58.
Idx prl: High 1386.09; Low 1316.37; Close 1317.24 −51.20

GSCI (CME)-$250 times nearby index

Aug	141.90	142.10	141.50	142.00	+ 1.10	177.00	140.70	24,952
Sept	144.60	144.80	144.50	144.80	+ 1.10	177.10	143.60	1,035

Est vol 6,646; vol Mon 1,687; open int 26,079, +465.
Idx prl: High 142.21; Low 141.59; Close 142.07 +.85

RUSSELL 2000 (CME)-$500 times index

Sept	417.75	417.75	399.50	399.75	− 13.75	502.90	399.50	9,552

Est vol 947; vol Mon 525; open int 9,579, +80.
Idx prl: High 415.54; Low 401.32; Close 401.63 −11.73

U.S. DOLLAR INDEX (FINEX)-$1,000 times USDX

Sept	101.60	101.60	100.71	100.92	− .60	102.46	98.23	4,352
Dec	101.07	101.07	100.40	100.65	− .61	102.04	98.11	2,521

Est vol na; vol Mon 1,341; open int 6,873, −72.
Idx prl: High 101.72; Low 100.96; Close 101.13 −.52

ALL ORDINARIES SHARE PRICE INDEX (SFE)
A$25 times index

	Open	High	Low	Settle	Chg	High	Low	Open Interest
Sept	2653.0	2702.0	2652.0	2692.0	+ 7.0	2930.0	905.0	168,562
Dec	....	....		2706.0	+ 9.0	2920.0	2610.0	3,900
Mr99	....	....		2722.0	+ 7.0	2940.0	2590.0	1,609
June	....	....		2735.0	+ 7.0	2850.0	2570.0	1,055

Est vol 11,315; vol Mn 4,152; open int 175,146, +10,118.
The index: High 2687.9; Low 2663.3; Close 2682.3 +8.5

CAC-40 STOCK INDEX (MATIF)-FFr 200 per index pt.

Aug	4095.0	4146.0	4060.0	4060.0	− 45.0	4424.0	4060.0	156,397
Sept	4110.0	4200.0	4088.0	4072.0	− 45.0	4437.0	2936.0	105,226
Dec	....	....		4107.0	− 45.0	4448.5	2807.5	15,610
Mr99	....	....		4145.0	− 45.0	4499.0	2890.0	27,053
Sept	4203.5	4203.5	4203.5	4156.0	− 48.0	4519.5	4130.5	14,905
Mr00	....	....		4253.0	− 45.0	4569.5	4204.0	6,180

Est vol 40,344; vol Mn 53,252; open int 325,371, +442.

DAX-30 GERMAN STOCK INDEX (DTB)
DM 100 times index

Sept	5828.0	5919.0	5828.0	5747.5	− .85	6244.0	4309.0	91,702
Dec	5885.0	5965.0	5885.0	5805.5	− .68	6285.0	5237.0	2,583

Est vol 32,051; vol Mn 27,460; open int 94,561, +2,394.
The index: High 5816.89; Low 5718.70; Close 5718.70 −.96

FT-SE 100 INDEX (LIFFE)-£10 per index point

Sept	5815.0	5851.0	5703.0	5750.0	− 70.0	6280.5	5715.0	180,559
Dec	5909.0	5909.0	5909.0	5839.0	− 70.0	6285.0	5866.0	7,226
Mr99	....	....		5910.0	− 70.0	6234.0	6234.0	970

Est vol 25,350; vol Mn 22,679; open int 188,755, +3,844.

One futures contract (traded on the Chicago Mercantile Exchange) is on five times the index. The *NASDAQ 100* is based on 100 stocks using the National Association of Securities Dealers Automatic Quotations Service. The *CAC-40 Index* is based on 40 large stocks trading in France. The *FT-SE 100 Index* is based on a portfolio of 100 major U.K. shares listed on the London Stock Exchange. The *All Ordinaries Share Price Index* is a broadly based index reflecting the value of a portfolio of Australian stocks.

In the GSCI index futures contract shown in Table 3.2, the underlying asset is the *Goldman Sachs Commodity Index.* This is not a stock index. It is a broadly based index of commodity prices. All the major commodity groups, such as energy, livestock, grains and oilseeds, food and fiber, and metals, are represented in the GSCI. Studies by Goldman Sachs have shown that the GSCI is negatively related to the S&P 500 index, with the correlation being in the range −0.30 to −0.40.

As mentioned in section 2.6, futures contracts on stock indices are settled in cash, not by delivery of the underlying asset. All contracts are marked to market on the last trading day, and the positions are then deemed to be closed. For most contracts, the settlement price on the last trading day is set at the closing value of the index on that day. But as discussed in section 2.6, for the S&P 500 it is set as the value of the index calculated from opening prices the next day. For the futures on the S&P 500, the last trading day is the Thursday before the third Friday of the delivery month.

Futures Prices of Stock Indices

An index can be thought of as an investment asset that pays dividends. The asset is the portfolio of stocks underlying the index, and the dividends are the dividends that would be received by the holder of this portfolio. Often there are many stocks underlying the index providing dividends at different times. To a reasonable approximation, the index can then be considered as an asset providing a continuous dividend yield. If q is the dividend yield rate, equation (3.7) gives the futures price, F_0, as[5]

$$F_0 = S_0 e^{(r-q)T} \tag{3.12}$$

Example 3.7   Consider a three-month futures contract on the S&P 500. Suppose that the stocks underlying the index provide a dividend yield of 3% per annum, that the current value of the index is 900, and that the continuously compounded risk-free interest rate is 8% per annum. In this case, $r = 0.08$, $S_0 = 900$, $T = 0.25$, and $q = 0.03$, and the futures price, F_0, is given by

$$F_0 = 900e^{(0.08-0.03)\times0.25} = 911.32$$

In practice, the dividend yield on the portfolio underlying an index varies week by week throughout the year. For example, a large proportion of the dividends on NYSE stocks are paid in the first week of February, May, August, and November of each year. The value of q that is used should represent the average annualized dividend yield during the life of the contract. The dividends used for estimating q should be those for which the ex-dividend date is during the life of the futures contract. Looking at Table 3.2, we see that the futures prices for the S&P 500 appear to be increasing with maturity at about 1% per three months, or 4% per year, from September 1998 to June 1999. This corresponds to the situation where the risk-free interest rate exceeds the dividend yield by about 4% per annum.

In some countries all companies tend to pay dividends on the same dates. In this case, discrete dividend yields can be estimated for those dates and the result in Appendix 3A can be used to calculate the equivalent continuous dividend yield. Alternatively, the cash amount of the dividends can be estimated and the index can then be considered to be an investment asset providing known income. The result in equation (3.6) is then used to calculate the futures price.

Index Arbitrage

If $F_0 > S_0 e^{(r-q)T}$, profits can be made by buying the stocks underlying the index and shorting futures contracts. If $F_0 < S_0 e^{(r-q)T}$, profits can be made by doing the reverse, that is, shorting or selling the stocks underlying the index and taking a long position in futures contracts. These strategies are known as *index arbitrage*. When $F_0 < S_0 e^{(r-q)T}$, index arbitrage is often done by a pension fund that owns an indexed portfolio of stocks. When $F_0 > S_0 e^{(r-q)T}$, it is often done by a corporation holding

---

[5]For a total return index, dividends are assumed to be reinvested in the portfolio underlying the index so that $q = 0$ and $F_0 = S_0 e^{rT}$.

short-term money market investments. For indices involving many stocks, index arbitrage is sometimes accomplished by trading a relatively small representative sample of stocks whose movements closely mirror those of the index. Often, index arbitrage is implemented using *program trading*. This means that a computer system is used to generate the trades.

October 19, 1987

In normal market conditions, F_0 is very close to $S_0 e^{(r-q)T}$. However, it is interesting to note what happened on October 19, 1987, when the market fell by over 20% and the volume of shares traded on the New York Stock Exchange (604 million) easily exceeded all previous records. For most of the day, futures prices were at a significant discount to the underlying index. For example, at the close of trading, the S&P 500 index was at 225.06 (down 57.88 on the day) while the futures price for December delivery on the S&P 500 was 201.50 (down 80.75 on the day). This was largely because the delays in processing orders to sell equity made index arbitrage too risky. On the next day, October 20, 1987, the New York Stock Exchange placed temporary restrictions on the way in which program trading could be done. The result was that the breakdown of the traditional linkage between stock indices and stock index futures continued. At one point, the futures price for the December contract was 18% less than the S&P 500 index.

Hedging Using Index Futures

Stock index futures can be used to hedge the risk in a well-diversified portfolio of stocks. Readers familiar with the capital asset pricing model will know that the relationship between the expected return on a portfolio of stocks and the return on the market (i.e., the stock market as a whole) is described by a parameter β (beta). This is the slope of the best-fit line obtained when the excess return on the portfolio over the risk-free rate is regressed against the excess return on the market over the risk-free rate. When $\beta = 1.0$, the return on the portfolio tends to mirror the return on the market; when $\beta = 2.0$, the excess return on the portfolio tends to be twice as great as the excess return on the market; when $\beta = 0.5$, it tends to be half as great; and so on.

When the β of the portfolio equals 1, the position in futures contracts should be chosen so that the value of the stocks underlying the futures contracts equals the total value of the portfolio being hedged. When $\beta = 2$, the portfolio is twice as volatile as the stocks underlying the futures contract and the position in futures contracts should be twice as great. When $\beta = 0.5$, the portfolio is half as volatile as the stocks underlying the futures contract and the position should be half as great. In general, if we define

P: value of a portfolio
A: value of assets underlying one futures contract

the correct number of contracts to short in order to hedge the risk in the portfolio is

$$\beta \frac{P}{A}$$

This formula assumes that the maturity of the futures contract is close to the maturity of the hedge and ignores the daily settlement of the futures contract.[6]

> **Example 3.8**   A company wishes to hedge a portfolio worth $2,100,000 over the next three months using an S&P 500 index futures contract with four months to maturity. The current level of the S&P 500 is 900 and the β of the portfolio is 1.5. The value of the assets underlying one futures contract is $900 \times 250 = \$225,000$. The correct number of futures contracts to short is, therefore,
>
> $$1.5 \times \frac{2,100,000}{225,000} = 14$$
>
> To show that the hedge works, we suppose the risk-free rate is 4% per year and the market provides a total return of −7% in the course of the next three months. This is bad news for the portfolio. The risk-free rate is 1% per three months so that the return on the market is 8% below the risk-free rate. We therefore expect the return (including dividends) on the portfolio during the three months to be $1.5 \times 8 = 12\%$ below the risk-free rate, or −11%.[7] Assume that the dividend yield on the index is 2% per annum, or 0.5% per three months. This means that the index declines by 7.5% during the three months, from 900 to 832.5. Equation (3.12) gives the initial futures price as $900e^{(0.04-0.02)\times 1/3} = 906.02$ and the final futures price as $832.5e^{(0.04-0.02)\times 1/12} = 833.89$. The gain on the futures position is
>
> $$(906.02 - 833.89) \times 250 \times 14 = 252,455$$
>
> The total loss on the portfolio is $0.11 \times 2,100,000 = \$231,000$. The net gain from the hedged position is $252,455 - 231,000 = \$21,455$ or about 1% of the value of the portfolio. This is as expected. The return on the hedged position during the three months is the risk-free rate. It is easy to verify that roughly the same return is realized regardless of the performance of the market.

Why Hedge?

As Example 3.8 illustrates, an index futures hedge leads to the value of the hedged position growing at close to the risk-free interest rate. The excess return on the portfolio (whether positive or negative) is offset by the gain or loss on the futures. It is natural to ask why the hedger should go to the trouble of using futures contracts. If the hedger's objective is to earn the risk-free interest rate, then the portfolio can be sold and the proceeds invested in Treasury bills.

---

[6]A small adjustment known as *tailing the hedge* can be used to take account of the daily settlement when a futures contract is used for hedging. For a discussion of this, see D. Duffie, *Futures Markets*, Prentice Hall, 1989; and R. Rendleman, "A Reconciliation of Potentially Conflicting Approaches to Hedging with Futures," *Advances in Futures and Options Research*, 6 (1993). Problem 3.27 deals with this issue.

[7]For ease of exposition, we ignore the distinction between continuously compounded and quarterly compounded rates.

One possible reason for hedging is that the hedger feels that the stocks in the portfolio have been chosen well. There might be some uncertainty about the performance of the market as a whole, but confidence that the stocks in the portfolio will outperform the market (after appropriate adjustments have been made for the β of the portfolio). A hedge using index futures removes the risk arising from market moves and leaves the hedger exposed only to the performance of the portfolio relative to the market. Another possible reason is that the hedger is planning to hold a portfolio for a long period of time and requires short-term protection in an uncertain market situation. The alternative strategy of selling the portfolio and buying it back later might involve unacceptably high transaction costs.

Changing Beta

Stock index futures can be used to change the beta of a portfolio. Consider the situation in Example 3.8. To reduce the beta of the portfolio from 1.5 to 0, a total of 14 contracts are required. To reduce the beta to 0.75, it is necessary to short only one-half of 14, or 7, contracts; to increase the beta from 1.5 to 3.0, a long position in 14 contracts is required; and so on. In general, to change the beta of the portfolio from β to β^* where $\beta > \beta^*$, a short position in

$$(\beta - \beta^*)\frac{P}{A}$$

contracts is required. When $\beta < \beta^*$, a long position in

$$(\beta^* - \beta)\frac{P}{A}$$

contracts is required.

The Nikkei Index

Equation (3.12) does not apply to the futures contract on the Nikkei 225. The reason for this is quite subtle. When S is the value of the Nikkei 225 index, it is the value of a portfolio measured in yen. The variable underlying the CME futures contract on the Nikkei 225 is a variable with a *dollar value* of $5S$. In other words, the futures contract takes a variable that is measured in yen and treats it as though it were dollars. We cannot invest in a portfolio whose value will always be $5S$ dollars. The best we can do is to invest in one that is always worth $5S$ yen or in one that is always worth $5QS$ dollars, where Q is the dollar value of 1 yen. The variable underlying the Nikkei 225 is therefore a dollar amount that does not equal the price of something that is traded. Consequently, we cannot derive a theoretical futures price using arbitrage arguments. The CME Nikkei 225 futures contract is an example of a *quanto*. This is a type of derivative where the payoff is defined by variables in one currency and paid in another. In chapter 19, we explain how quantos can be analyzed.

3.8   FOREIGN CURRENCIES

We now move on to consider forward foreign exchange contracts. The underlying asset in such contracts is a certain number of units of the foreign currency. We will define the variable S_0 as the current spot price, measured in dollars, of one unit of the foreign currency and F_0 as the forward price, measured in dollars, of one unit of the foreign currency. This is consistent with the way we have defined S_0 and F_0 for other assets underlying forward contracts. However, it does not always correspond to the way spot and forward exchange rates are quoted. For all major exchange rates, except the British pound, a spot or forward exchange rate is normally quoted as the number of units of the currency that are equivalent to one dollar. For the British pound, it is quoted as the number of dollars per unit of the foreign currency.

A foreign currency has the property that the holder of the currency can earn interest at the risk-free interest rate prevailing in the foreign country. (For example, the holder can invest the currency in a foreign-denominated bond.) We define r_f as the value of this foreign risk-free interest rate for a maturity T with continuous compounding. As before, r is the domestic risk-free rate for this maturity.

The relationship between F_0 and S_0 is

$$F_0 = S_0 e^{(r-r_f)T} \tag{3.13}$$

This is the well-known interest rate parity relationship from international finance. To understand the relationship, suppose first that $F_0 > S_0 e^{(r-r_f)T}$. An investor can

1. Borrow $S_0 e^{-r_f T}$ in the domestic currency at rate r for time T.
2. Use the cash to buy spot $e^{-r_f T}$ of the foreign currency and invest this at the foreign risk-free rate.
3. Short a forward contract on one unit of the foreign currency.

The holding in the foreign currency grows to one unit at time T because of the interest earned. Under the terms of the forward contract, the holding is exchanged for F_0 at time T. An amount $S_0 e^{(r-r_f)T}$ is required to repay the borrowing. A net profit of $F_0 - S_0 e^{(r-r_f)T}$ is, therefore, made at time T.

Suppose next that $F_0 < S_0 e^{(r-r_f)T}$. An investor can

1. Borrow $e^{-r_f T}$ in the foreign currency at rate r_f for time T.
2. Use the cash to buy $S_0 e^{-r_f T}$ of the domestic currency and invest this at the domestic risk-free rate.
3. Take a long position in a forward contract on one unit of the foreign currency.

In this case, the holding in the domestic currency grows to $S_0 e^{(r-r_f)T}$ at time T because of the interest earned. At time T the investor pays F_0 and receives one unit of the foreign currency. The latter is used to repay the borrowings. A net profit of $S_0 e^{(r-r_f)T} - F_0$ is, therefore, made at time T.

Note that equation (3.13) is identical to equation (3.7) with q replaced by r_f. This is not a coincidence. A foreign currency can be regarded as an investment asset paying a known dividend yield. The "dividend yield" is the risk-free rate of interest in the foreign currency. To see why this is so, note that interest earned on a foreign currency holding is denominated in the foreign currency. Its value when measured in the domestic currency is therefore proportional to the value of the foreign currency.

The value of a forward foreign exchange contract is given by equation (3.11) with q replaced by r_f. It is

$$f = S_0 e^{-r_f T} - K e^{-rT} \tag{3.14}$$

Example 3.9   Suppose that the six-month interest rates in the United States and Japan are 5% and 1% per annum, respectively. The current yen/dollar exchange rate is quoted as 100. This means that there are 100 yen per dollar or 0.01 dollars per yen. For a six-month forward contract on the yen $S_0 = 0.01$, $r = 0.05$, and $r_f = 0.01$. Equation (3.13) gives the forward foreign exchange rate as

$$0.01 e^{(0.05-0.01) \times 0.5} = 0.010202$$

This would be quoted as $1/0.010202$, or 98.02.

Futures Contracts

Table 3.3 shows quotes at the close of trading on August 4, 1998, for Chicago Mercantile Exchange futures contracts on the Japanese yen, deutschemark, Canadian dollar, British pound, Swiss franc, Australian dollar, and Mexican peso. Note that

Table 3.3   Foreign Exchange Futures Quotes from *The Wall Street Journal*, August 5, 1998

	Open	High	Low	Settle	Change	Lifetime High	Lifetime Low	Open Interest
JAPAN YEN (CME)-12.5 million yen; $ per yen (.00)								
Sept	.6909	.6975	.6887	.6941	+ .0033	.8695	.6887	134,116
Dec	.7035	.7050	.7015	.7032	+ .0033	.8445	.6987	2,332
Mr99	.7095	.7135	.7095	.7123	+ .0033	.8315	.7077	1,920
June	....	....	....	.7215	+ .0033	.7800	.7181	649
Est vol 19,047; vol Mon 20,301; open int 139,017, +3,058.								
DEUTSCHEMARK (CME)-125,000 marks; $ per mark								
Sept	.5617	.5664	.5610	.5649	+ .0034	.5944	.5425	106,486
Dec	.5654	.5690	.5645	.5678	+ .0034	.5840	.5496	749
Est vol 18,949; vol Mon 17,605; open int 107,425, +1,970.								
CANADIAN DOLLAR (CME)-100,000 dlrs.; $ per Can $								
Sept	.6604	.6622	.6590	.6590	+ .0001	.7463	.6590	65,939
Dec	.6610	.6628	.6597	.6609	....	.7400	.6597	4,812
Mr99	.6620	.6630	.6608	.6615	− .0001	.7247	.6608	1,218
June	.6615	.6615	.6615	.6621	− .0002	.7170	.6615	309
Est vol 7,528; vol Mon 7,958; open int 72,330, +354.								
BRITISH POUND (CME)-62,500 pds.; $ per pound								
Sept	1.6234	1.6356	1.6220	1.6318	+ .0086	1.6870	1.5690	41,121
Dec	1.6180	1.6280	1.6180	1.6242	+ .0088	1.6760	1.5630	843
Ju99	....	....	1.6096	+ .0088	1.6460	1.5960		140
Est vol 7,159; vol Mon 16,364; open int 42,107, +3,383.								
SWISS FRANC (CME)-125,000 francs; $ per franc								
Sept	.6692	.6743	.6682	.6729	+ .0042	.7420	.6503	70,530
Dec	.6760	.6802	.6753	.6790	+ .0042	.7290	.6569	504
Est vol 13,437; vol Mon 10,077; open int 71,050, +1,501								
AUSTRALIAN DOLLAR (CME)-100,000 dlrs.; $ per A.$								
Sept	.6023	.6075	.6020	.6052	+ .0027	.7010	.5804	24,750
Dec	....	....	....	.6058	+ .0027	.6690	.5890	135
Est vol 817; vol Mon 1,947; open int 24,885, +414.								
MEXICAN PESO (CME)-500,000 new Mex. peso, $ per MP								
Sept	.10972	.10990	.10920	.10935	− .00015	.11680	.08000	27,679
Dec	.10500	.10510	.10450	.10460	− .00020	.11440	.08000	11,535
Mr99	....	....	....	.10015	− .00015	.10565	.09675	2,630
June	....	....	....	.09600	....	.10220	.09350	745
Sept	....	....	....	.09200	....	.09510	.09140	597
Est vol 5,548; vol Mon 6,055; open int 43,186, −171.								

futures exchange rates are always quoted as the value, in U.S. dollars, of the foreign currency. (In the case of the yen, the value of the foreign currency is given in U.S. cents.) As explained above, forward rates are usually quoted the other way around, that is, as the number of units of the foreign currency per U.S. dollar. A forward quote on the Canadian dollar of 1.4000 would become a futures quote of 0.7143. The Chicago Mercantile Exchange also trades futures contracts on the euro (the currency adopted by a number of European countries on January 1, 1999) and the Brazilian real.

Futures prices can be calculated using equation (3.13). When the foreign interest rate is greater than the domestic interest rate ($r_f > r$), the equation shows that F_0 is always less than S_0 and that F_0 decreases as the maturity of the contract, T, increases. Similarly, when the domestic interest rate is greater than the foreign interest rate ($r > r_f$), the equation shows that F_0 is always greater than S_0 and that F_0 increases as T increases. On August 4, 1998, interest rates in Japan, Germany, Canada, Switzerland, and Australia were all lower than in the United States. This corresponds to the $r_f < r$ situation and explains why futures prices for these currencies increase with maturity. Interest rates in Britain and Mexico were higher than in the United States. This corresponds to the $r_f > r$ situation and explains why futures prices for these currencies decrease with maturity.

> **Example 3.10**   The futures price of the Japanese yen in Table 3.3 appears to be increasing at a rate of about 5.2% per annum with the maturity. For example, the March 1999 settlement price is about 2.6% higher than the September 1998 settlement price. This suggests that the short-term risk-free interest rate was about 5.2% per annum higher in the United States than in Japan on August 4, 1998.

3.9   FUTURES ON COMMODITIES

Futures on commodities and the way they can be used for hedging were discussed in chapter 2. We now consider how commodity futures contracts are priced. Some commodities (for example, gold and silver) are investment assets; others (for example, oil) are consumption assets.[8] Arbitrage arguments can be used to obtain exact futures prices in the case of investment commodities, but can only give an upper bound to futures prices in the case of consumption commodities. Before explaining this we consider the impact of storage costs on futures prices.

Storage Costs

Equation (3.5) shows that if an investment asset has no storage costs and produces no income, the relationship between its futures price and its spot price is

$$F_0 = S_0 e^{rT}$$

---

[8] It will be recalled that for an asset to be an investment asset, it need not be held solely for investment purposes. What is required is that some individuals hold it for investment purposes and that these individuals be prepared to sell their holdings and go long futures or forward contracts, if they look more attractive. This explains why silver, although it has significant industrial uses, is an investment asset.

Storage costs can be regarded as negative income. If U is the present value of all the storage costs that will be incurred during the life of a futures contract, it follows from equation (3.6) that

$$F_0 = (S_0 + U)e^{rT} \tag{3.15}$$

If the storage costs incurred at any time are proportional to the price of the commodity, they can be regarded as providing a negative dividend yield. In this case, from equation (3.7),

$$F_0 = S_0 e^{(r+u)T} \tag{3.16}$$

where u is the storage costs per annum as a proportion of the spot price.

Example 3.11   Consider a one-year futures contract on gold. Suppose that it costs $2 per ounce per year to store gold, with the payment being made at the end of the year. Assume that the spot price is $450 and the risk-free rate is 7% per annum for all maturities. This corresponds to $r = 0.07$, $S_0 = 450$, $T = 1$, and

$$U = 2e^{-0.07 \times 1} = 1.865$$

The forward price, F_0, is given by

$$F_0 = (450 + 1.865)e^{0.07 \times 1} = \$484.63$$

If $F_0 > 484.63$, an arbitrageur can buy gold and short one-year gold futures contracts to lock in a profit. If $F_0 < 484.63$, an investor who already owns gold can improve the return by selling the gold and buying gold futures contracts.

Consumption Commodities

For commodities that are not held primarily for investment purposes, the arbitrage arguments used to determine futures prices need to be reviewed carefully.

Suppose that instead of equation (3.15), we have

$$F_0 > (S_0 + U)e^{rT} \tag{3.17}$$

To take advantage of this opportunity, an arbitrageur can implement the following strategy:

1. Borrow an amount $S_0 + U$ at the risk-free rate and use it to purchase one unit of the commodity and to pay storage costs.
2. Short a futures contract on one unit of the commodity.

This strategy is certain to lead to a profit of $F_0 - (S_0 + U)e^{rT}$ at time T. There is no problem in implementing the strategy for any commodity. However, as arbitrageurs do so, there will be a tendency for S_0 to increase and F_0 to decrease until equation (3.17) is no longer true. We conclude that equation (3.17) cannot hold for any significant length of time.

Suppose next that

$$F_0 < (S_0 + U)e^{rT} \tag{3.18}$$

In the case of gold and silver, we can argue that many investors hold the commodity solely for investment. When they observe the inequality in equation (3.18), they will find it profitable to

1. Sell the commodity, save the storage costs, and invest the proceeds at the risk-free interest rate.
2. Take a long position in a futures contract.

If we regard the futures contract as a forward contract, the result is a riskless profit at maturity of $(S_0 + U)e^{rT} - F_0$ relative to the position the investors would have been in if they had held the gold or silver. It follows that equation (3.18) cannot hold for long. Because neither equation (3.17) nor (3.18) can hold for long, we must have $F_0 = (S_0 + U)e^{rT}$.

For commodities that are not, to any significant extent, held for investment, this argument cannot be used. Individuals and companies who keep such a commodity in inventory do so because of its consumption value—not because of its value as an investment. They are reluctant to sell the commodity and buy futures contracts because futures contracts cannot be consumed. There is, therefore, nothing to stop equation (3.18) from holding. This means that all we can assert for a consumption commodity is

$$F_0 \le (S_0 + U)e^{rT} \tag{3.19}$$

If storage costs are expressed as a proportion u of the spot price, the equivalent result is

$$F_0 \le S_0 e^{(r+u)T} \tag{3.20}$$

Convenience Yields

When we do not have equality in equations (3.19) or (3.20), users of the commodity must feel that there are benefits from ownership of the physical commodity that are not obtained by the holder of a futures contract. These benefits may include the ability to profit from temporary local shortages or the ability to keep a production process running. The benefits are sometimes referred to as the *convenience yield* provided by the product. If the dollar amount of storage costs is known and has a present value, U, the convenience yield, y, is defined so that

$$F_0 e^{yT} = (S_0 + U)e^{rT} \tag{3.21}$$

If the storage costs per unit are a constant proportion, u, of the spot price, y is defined so that

$$F_0 e^{yT} = S_0 e^{(r+u)T}$$

or

$$F_0 = S_0 e^{(r+u-y)T} \tag{3.22}$$

The convenience yield simply measures the extent to which the left-hand side is less than the right-hand side in equation (3.19) or (3.20). For investment assets such as gold, the convenience yield must be zero; otherwise, there are arbitrage opportunities. A consumption asset behaves like an investment asset that provides a return equal to the convenience yield. If the futures price decreases as the maturity of the contract increases, equation (3.22) shows that the convenience yield, y, is greater than $r + u$. If the futures price increases with the maturity of the contract, the reverse is true.

The convenience yield reflects the market's expectations concerning the future availability of the commodity. The greater the possibility that shortages will occur during the life of the futures contract, the higher the convenience yield. If users of the commodity have high inventories, there is very little chance of shortages in the near future and the convenience yield tends to be low. On the other hand, low inventories tend to lead to high convenience yields.

3.10 THE COST OF CARRY

The relationship between futures prices and spot prices can be summarized in terms of what is known as the *cost of carry*. This measures the storage cost plus the interest that is paid to finance the asset less the income earned on the asset. For a non-dividend-paying stock, the cost of carry is r since there are no storage costs and no income is earned; for a stock index, it is $r - q$ since income is earned at rate q on the asset; for a currency, it is $r - r_f$; for a commodity with storage costs that are a proportion u of the price, it is $r + u$; and so on.

Define the cost of carry as c. For an investment asset, the futures price is

$$F_0 = S_0 e^{cT} \tag{3.23}$$

For a consumption asset, it is

$$F_0 = S_0 e^{(c-y)T} \tag{3.24}$$

where y is the convenience yield.

3.11 DELIVERY OPTIONS

Whereas a forward contract normally specifies that delivery is to take place on a particular day, a futures contract often allows the party with the short position to choose to deliver at any time during a certain period. (Typically, the party has to give a few days notice of its intention to deliver.) This introduces a complication into the determination of futures prices. Should the maturity of the futures contract be assumed to be the beginning, middle, or end of the delivery period? Even though most futures contracts are closed out prior to maturity, it is important to know when delivery would have taken place, in order to calculate the theoretical futures price.

If the futures price is an increasing function of the time to maturity, it can be seen from equation (3.24) that the benefits from holding the asset (including convenience yield and net of storage costs) are less than the risk-free rate. It is then usually optimal for the party with the short position to deliver as early as possible. This is because the interest earned on the cash received outweighs the benefits of holding the asset. As a general rule, futures prices in these circumstances should, therefore, be calculated on the basis that delivery will take place at the beginning of the delivery period. If futures prices are decreasing as maturity increases, the reverse is true: It is usually optimal for the party with the short position to deliver as late as possible and futures prices should, as a general rule, be calculated on the assumption that this will happen.

3.12 FUTURES PRICES AND THE EXPECTED FUTURE SPOT PRICE

One question that is often raised is whether the futures price of an asset is equal to its expected future spot price. If you had to guess what the price of an asset will be in three months, is the three-month futures price an unbiased estimate? John Maynard Keynes and John Hicks, in the 1930s, argued that if hedgers tend to hold short positions and speculators tend to hold long positions, the futures price will be below the expected future spot price. This is because speculators require compensation for the risks they are bearing. They will trade only if there is an expectation that the futures price will rise over time. Hedgers, on the other hand, because they are reducing their risks, are prepared to enter into contracts where the expected payoff is slightly negative. If hedgers tend to hold long positions while speculators hold short positions, Keynes and Hicks argue that the futures price must be above the expected future spot price. The reason is similar. To compensate speculators for the risks they are bearing, there must be an expectation that the futures prices will decline over time.

The situation where the futures price is below the expected future spot price is known as *normal backwardation;* the situation where the futures price is above the expected future spot price is known as *contango*. We now consider the factors determining normal backwardation and contango from the point of view of the trade-offs that have to be made between risk and return in capital markets.

Risk and Return

In general, the higher the risk of an investment, the higher the expected return demanded by an investor. The capital asset pricing model, outlined in section 3.7, leads to the conclusion that there are two types of risk in the economy: systematic and nonsystematic. Nonsystematic risk should not be important to an investor. This is because it can be almost completely eliminated by holding a well-diversified portfolio. An investor should not, therefore, require a higher expected return for bearing nonsystematic risk. Systematic risk, by contrast, cannot be diversified away. It arises from a correlation between returns from the investment and returns from the stock market as a whole. An investor, in general, requires a higher expected return than the risk-free interest rate for bearing positive amounts of systematic risk. Also, an investor is prepared to accept a lower expected return than the risk-free interest rate when the systematic risk in an investment is negative.

The Risk in a Futures Position

Consider a speculator who takes a long futures position in the hope that the price of the asset will be above the futures price at maturity. We suppose that the speculator puts the present value of the futures price into a risk-free investment at time t while simultaneously taking a long futures position. We assume that the futures contract can be treated as a forward contract and that the delivery date is T. The proceeds of the risk-free investment are used to buy the asset on the delivery date. The asset is then immediately sold for its market price. This means that the cash flows to the speculator are

Time 0: $-F_0 e^{-rT}$
Time T: $+S_T$

where S_T is the price of the asset at time T.

The present value of this investment is

$$-F_0 e^{-rT} + E(S_T) e^{-kT}$$

where k is the discount rate appropriate for the investment (i.e., it is the expected return required by investors on the investment) and E denotes expected value. Assuming that all investment opportunities in securities markets have zero net present value,

$$-F_0 e^{-rT} + E(S_T) e^{-kT} = 0$$

or

$$F_0 = E(S_T) e^{(r-k)T} \tag{3.25}$$

The value of k depends on the systematic risk of the investment. If S_T is uncorrelated with the level of the stock market, the investment has zero systematic risk. In this case, $k = r$ and equation (3.25) shows that $F_0 = E(S_T)$. If S_T is positively correlated with the level of the stock market, the investment has positive systematic risk. In this case, $k > r$ and equation (3.25) shows that $F_0 < E(S_T)$. Finally, if S_T is negatively correlated with the stock market, the investment has negative systematic risk. This means that $k < r$ and equation (3.25) shows that $F_0 > E(S_T)$.

Empirical Evidence

If $F_0 = E(S_T)$, the futures price will drift up or down only if the market changes its views about the expected future spot price. Over a long period of time, we can reasonably assume that the market revises its expectations about future spot prices upward as often as it does so downward. It follows that when $F_0 = E(S_T)$, the average profit from holding futures contracts over a long period of time should be zero. The $F_0 < E(S_T)$ situation corresponds to the positive systematic risk situation. Because the futures price and the spot price must be equal at maturity of the futures contract, this implies that a futures price should, on average, drift up and a trader should over a long period of time make positive profits from consistently holding long futures positions. Similarly, the $F_0 > E(S_T)$ situation implies that a trader should over a long period of time make positive profits from consistently holding short futures positions.

How do futures prices behave in practice? Some of the empirical work that has been carried out is listed at the end of this chapter. The results are mixed. Houthakker's study looked at futures prices for wheat, cotton, and corn during the period 1937–1957. It showed that it was possible to earn significant profits from taking long futures positions. This suggests that an investment in corn has positive systematic risk and $F_0 < E(S_T)$. Telser's study contradicted the findings of Houthakker. His data covered the period 1926–1950 for cotton and 1927–1954 for wheat and gave rise to no significant profits for traders taking either long or short positions. To quote from Telser, "The futures data offer no evidence to contradict the simple ... hypothesis that the futures price is an unbiased estimate of the expected future spot price." Gray's study looked at corn futures prices during the 1921–1959 period and resulted in findings similar to those of Telser. Dusak's study used data on corn, wheat, and soybeans during 1952–1967 and took a different approach. It attempted to estimate the systematic risk of an investment in these commodities by calculating the correlation of movements in the commodity prices with movements in the S&P 500. The results suggest that there is no systematic risk and lend support to the $F_0 = E(S_T)$ hypothesis. However, more recent work by Chang using the same commodities and more advanced statistical techniques supports the $F_0 < E(S_T)$ hypothesis.

SUMMARY

In many situations the futures price of a contract with a certain delivery date can be considered to be the same as the forward price for a contract with the same delivery date. It can be shown that, in theory, the two should be exactly the same when interest rates are perfectly predictable and should be close to each other for short-life contracts when interest rates vary unpredictably.

For the purposes of understanding futures (or forward) prices, it is convenient to divide futures contracts into two categories: those where the underlying asset is held for investment by a significant number of investors and those where the underlying asset is held primarily for consumption purposes. In the case of investment assets, we have considered three different situations:

1. The asset provides no income.
2. The asset provides a known dollar income.
3. The asset provides a known dividend yield.

The results are summarized in Table 3.4. They enable futures prices to be obtained for contracts on stock indices, currencies, gold, and silver.

In the case of consumption assets, it is not possible to obtain the futures price as a function of the spot price and other observable variables. A parameter known as the

Table 3.4   Forward/Futures Contracts on Investment Assets

Summary of results for a contract with maturity T on an asset with price S_0 when the risk-free interest rate for a T-year period is r

Asset	Value of Long Forward Contract with Delivery Price K	Forward/Futures Price
Provides no income	$S_0 - Ke^{-rT}$	$S_0 e^{rT}$
Provides known income with present value, I	$S_0 - I - Ke^{-rT}$	$(S_0 - I)e^{rT}$
Provides known dividend yield, q	$S_0 e^{-qT} - Ke^{-rT}$	$S_0 e^{(r-q)T}$

asset's convenience yield becomes important. This measures the extent to which users of the commodity feel that there are benefits from ownership of the physical asset that are not obtained by the holders of the futures contract. These benefits may include the ability to profit from temporary local shortages or the ability to keep a production process running. It is possible to obtain only an upper bound for the futures price of consumption assets using arbitrage arguments.

The concept of a cost of carry is sometimes useful. The cost of carry is the storage cost of the underlying asset plus the cost of financing it minus the income received from it. In the case of investment assets, the futures price is greater than the spot price by an amount reflecting the cost of carry. In the case of consumption assets, the futures price is greater than the spot price by an amount reflecting the cost of carry net of the convenience yield.

If we assume that the capital asset pricing model is true, the relationship between the futures price and the expected future spot price depends on whether the spot price is positively or negatively correlated with the level of the stock market. Positive correlation will tend to lead to a futures price lower than the expected future spot price. Negative correlation will tend to lead to a futures price higher than the expected future spot price. Only when the correlation is zero will the theoretical futures price be equal to the expected future spot price.

SUGGESTIONS FOR FURTHER READING

On Empirical Research Concerning Forward and Futures Prices

Cornell, B., and M. Reinganum. "Forward and Futures Prices: Evidence from Foreign Exchange Markets," *Journal of Finance*, 36 (December 1981), 1035–45.

French, K. "A Comparison of Futures and Forward Prices," *Journal of Financial Economics*, 12 (November 1983), 311–42.

Park, H. Y., and A. H. Chen. "Differences between Futures and Forward Prices: A Further Investigation of Marking to Market Effects," *Journal of Futures Markets*, 5 (February 1985), 77–88.

Rendleman, R., and C. Carabini. "The Efficiency of the Treasury Bill Futures Markets," *Journal of Finance*, 34 (September 1979), 895–914.

Viswanath, P. V. "Taxes and the Futures-Forward Price Difference in the 91-Day T-Bill Market," *Journal of Money Credit and Banking*, 21, 2 (May 1989), 190–205.

Empirical Research Concerning the Relationship between Futures Prices and Expected Future Spot Prices

Chang, E. C. "Returns to Speculators and the Theory of Normal Backwardation," *Journal of Finance*, 40 (March 1985), 193–208.

Dusak, K. "Futures Trading and Investor Returns: An Investigation of Commodity Risk Premiums," *Journal of Political Economy*, 81 (December 1973), 1387–1406.

Gray, R. W. "The Search for a Risk Premium," *Journal of Political Economy*, 69 (June 1961), 250–60.

Houthakker, H. S. "Can Speculators Forecast Prices?" *Review of Economics and Statistics*, 39 (1957), 143–51.

Telser, L. G. "Futures Trading and the Storage of Cotton and Wheat," *Journal of Political Economy*, 66 (June 1958), 233–55.

On the Theoretical Relationship between Forward and Futures Prices

Cox, J. C., J. E. Ingersoll, and S. A. Ross. "The Relation between Forward Prices and Futures Prices," *Journal of Financial Economics*, 9 (December 1981), 321–46.

Jarrow, R. A., and G. S. Oldfield. "Forward Contracts and Futures Contracts," *Journal of Financial Economics*, 9 (December 1981), 373–82.

Kane, E. J. "Market Incompleteness and Divergences between Forward and Futures Interest Rates," *Journal of Finance*, 35 (May 1980), 221–34.

Margrabe, W. "A Theory of Forward and Futures Prices," Working Paper, Wharton School, University of Pennsylvania, 1976.

Richard, S., and M. Sundaresan. "A Continuous Time Model of Forward and Futures Prices in a Multigood Economy," *Journal of Financial Economics*, 9 (December 1981), 347–72.

Other

Hicks, J. R. *Value and Capital.* Oxford: Oxford University Press, 1939.

Keynes, J. M. *A Treatise on Money.* London: Macmillan, 1930.

QUESTIONS AND PROBLEMS
(ANSWERS IN SOLUTIONS MANUAL)

3.1. A bank quotes you a rate of interest of 14% per annum with quarterly compounding. What is the equivalent rate with (a) continuous compounding, and (b) annual compounding?

3.2. Explain what happens when an investor shorts a certain share.

3.3. Suppose that you enter into a six-month forward contract on a non-dividend-paying stock when the stock price is $30 and the risk-free interest rate (with continuous compounding) is 12% per annum. What is the forward price?

3.4. A stock index currently stands at 350. The risk-free interest rate is 8% per annum (with continuous compounding) and the dividend yield on the index is 4% per annum. What should the futures price for a four-month contract be?

3.5. Explain carefully why the futures price of gold can be calculated from its spot price and other observable variables, whereas the futures price of copper cannot.

3.6. Explain carefully the meaning of the terms *convenience yield* and *cost of carry*. What is the relationship between the futures price, the spot price, the convenience yield, and the cost of carry?

3.7. Is the futures price of a stock index greater than or less than the expected future value of the index? Explain your answer.

3.8. A person receives $1,100 in one year in return for an investment of $1,000 now. What is the percentage return per annum with:
  (a) Annual compounding?
  (b) Semiannual compounding?
  (c) Monthly compounding?
  (d) Continuous compounding?

3.9. What rate of interest with continuous compounding is equivalent to 15% per annum with monthly compounding?

3.10. A deposit account pays 12% per annum with continuous compounding, but interest is actually paid quarterly. How much interest will be paid each quarter on a $10,000 deposit?

3.11. A one-year-long forward contract on a non-dividend-paying stock is entered into when the stock price is $40 and the risk-free rate of interest is 10% per annum with continuous compounding.
  (a) What are the forward price and the initial value of the forward contract?
  (b) Six months later, the price of the stock is $45 and the risk-free interest rate is still 10%. What are the forward price and the value of the forward contract?

3.12. The risk-free rate of interest is 7% per annum with continuous compounding and the dividend yield on a stock index is 3.2% per annum. The current value of an index is 150. What is the six-month futures price?

3.13. Assume that the risk-free interest rate is 9% per annum with continuous compounding and that the dividend yield on a stock index varies throughout the year. In February, May, August, and November, the dividend yield is 5% per annum. In other months, it is 2% per annum. Suppose that the value of the index on July 31, 2000, is 300. What is the futures price for a contract deliverable on December 31, 2000?

3.14. Suppose that the risk-free interest rate is 10% per annum with continuous compounding and the dividend yield on a stock index is 4% per annum. The index is standing at 400 and the futures price for a contract deliverable in four months is 405. What arbitrage opportunities does this create?

3.15. Estimate the difference between risk-free rates of interest in Britain and the United States from the information in Table 3.3.

3.16. The two-month interest rates in Switzerland and the United States with continuous compounding are 3% and 8% per annum, respectively. The spot price of the Swiss franc is $0.6500. The futures price for a contract deliverable in two months is $0.6600. What arbitrage opportunities does this create?

3.17. The current price of silver is $9 per ounce. The storage costs are $0.24 per ounce per year payable quarterly in advance. Assuming that interest rates of all maturities equal 10% per annum with continuous compounding, calculate the futures price of silver for delivery in nine months.

3.18. Suppose that F_1 and F_2 are futures prices for contracts on the same commodity with maturity dates of t_1 and t_2 and $t_2 > t_1$. Prove that

$$F_2 \le (F_1 + U)e^{r(t_2 - t_1)}$$

where r is the risk-free interest rate (assumed to be constant) and U is the cost of storing the commodity between times t_1 and t_2 discounted to time t_1 at the risk-free rate. For the purposes of this problem, assume that a futures contract is the same as a forward contract.

3.19. When a known cash outflow in a foreign currency is hedged by a company using a forward contract, there is no foreign exchange risk. When it is hedged using futures contracts, the marking to market process does leave the company exposed to some risk. Explain the nature of this risk. In particular, consider whether the company is better off using a futures contract or a forward contract when
   (a) The value of the foreign currency falls rapidly during the life of the contract.
   (b) The value of the foreign currency rises rapidly during the life of the contract.
   (c) The value of the foreign currency first rises and then falls back to its initial level.
   (d) The value of the foreign currency first falls and then rises back to its initial level.
   Assume that the forward price equals the futures price.

3.20. It is sometimes argued that a forward exchange rate is an unbiased predictor of future exchange rates. Under what circumstances is this so?

3.21. What is the difference between the way in which prices are quoted in the foreign exchange futures market, the foreign exchange spot market, and the foreign exchange forward market?

3.22. The forward price of the Swiss franc for delivery in 45 days is quoted as 1.8204. The futures price for a contract that will be delivered in 45 days is 0.5479. Explain these two quotes. Which is more favorable for an investor wanting to sell Swiss francs?

3.23. The Value Line Index is designed to reflect changes in the value of a portfolio of over 1,600 equally weighted stocks. Prior to March 9, 1988, the change in the index from one day to the next was calculated as the *geometric* average of the changes in the prices of the stocks underlying the index. In these circumstances, does equation (3.12) correctly relate the futures price of the index to its cash price? If not, does the equation overstate or understate the futures price?

3.24. A company has a $10 million portfolio with a beta of 1.2. The S&P is currently 900 and one futures contract is on 250 times the index. How can the company use futures contracts on the S&P 500 to completely hedge its risk over the next six months? What position should it take to reduce the beta of the portfolio to 0.3?

3.25. On July 1, an investor holds 50,000 shares of a certain stock. The market price is $30 per share. The investor is interested in hedging against movements in the market over the next two months and decides to use a December stock index futures contract. The index level is currently 750 and one contract is for delivery of $500 times the index. The beta of the stock is 1.25. What strategy should the investor follow?

3.26. "When the convenience yield is high, long hedges are likely to be particularly attractive to a company that knows it will require a certain quantity of a commodity on a certain future date." Discuss.

3.27. A U.S. company is interested in using a futures contract maturing at time T to hedge a foreign currency exposure at time t_1. Define r as the interest rate (all maturities) on the U.S. dollar and r_f as the interest rate (all maturities) on the foreign currency. Assume that r and r_f are constant.
(a) Show that the optimal hedge ratio is

$$e^{(r_f - r)(T - t_1)}$$

(b) Show that, when the company wishes to hedge against exchange rate movements over the next day, the optimal hedge ratio is S_0/F_0 where S_0 is the current spot price of the currency and F_0 is the current futures price of the currency for the contract maturing at time T.
(c) Show that the company can take account of the daily settlement of futures contracts for a hedge that lasts longer than one day by adjusting the hedge ratio so that it always equals the spot price of the currency divided by the futures price of the currency. (This is known as tailing the hedge.)

3.28. Show that the growth rate in an index futures price equals the excess return of the index over the risk-free rate. Assume that the risk-free interest rate and dividend yield are constant.

ASSIGNMENT QUESTIONS

3.29. A stock is expected to pay a dividend of $1 per share in two months and again in five months. The stock price is $50 and the risk-free rate of interest is 8% per annum with continuous compounding for all maturities. An investor has just taken a short position in a six-month forward contract on the stock.
(a) What are the forward price and the initial value of the forward contract?
(b) Three months later, the price of the stock is $48 and the risk-free rate of interest is still 8% per annum. What are the forward price and the value of the short position in the forward contract?

3.30. A bank offers a corporate client a choice between borrowing cash at 11% per annum and borrowing gold at 2% per annum. (If gold is borrowed, interest and principal must be repaid in gold. Thus 100 ounces borrowed today would require 102 ounces to be repaid in one year.) The risk-free interest rate is 9.25% per annum and storage costs are 0.5% per annum. Discuss whether the rate of interest on the gold loan is too high or too low in relation to the rate of interest on the cash loan. The interest rates on the two loans are expressed with annual compounding. The risk-free interest rate and storage cost are expressed with continuous compounding.

3.31. A company that is uncertain about the exact date when it will pay a foreign currency sometimes wishes to negotiate with its bank a forward contract where there is a period during which delivery can be made. The company wants to reserve the right to choose the exact delivery date to fit in with its own cash flows. Put yourself in the position of the bank. How would you price the product that the client wants?

3.32. A fund manager has a portfolio worth $50 million with a beta of 0.87. The manager is concerned about the performance of the market over the next two months and plans to use three-month futures contracts on the S&P 500 to hedge the risk. The current level of the index is 1250, one contract is on 250 times the index, the risk-free rate is 6% per annum, and the dividend yield on the index is 3% per annum.

(a) What is the theoretical futures price for the three-month futures contract?

(b) What position should the fund manager take to eliminate all exposure to the market over the next two months?

(c) Calculate the effect of your strategy on the fund manager's returns if the level of the market in two months is 1,000, 1,100, 1,200, 1,300, and 1,400.

3.33. A foreign exchange trader working for a bank enters into a long forward contract to buy one million pounds sterling at an exchange rate of 1.6000 in three months. At the same time, another trader on the next desk takes a long position in 16 three-month futures contracts on sterling. The futures price is 1.6000 and each contract is on 62,500 pounds. Within minutes of the trades being executed the forward and the futures prices both increase to 1.6040. Both traders immediately claim a profit of $4,000. The bank's systems show that the futures trader has made a $4,000 profit, but the forward trader has made a profit of only $3,900. The forward trader immediately picks up the phone to complain to the systems department. Explain what is going on here. Why are the profits different?

APPENDIX 3A

Assets Providing Dividend Yields

In this appendix we explain the relationship

$$F_0 = S_0 e^{(r-q)T} \tag{3A.1}$$

for an asset providing a continuous dividend yield at rate q and explain how it can be used in situations where dividends are paid discretely.

In the continuous dividend yield case, consider an investor adopting the following strategy:

1. Buy spot e^{-qT} of the asset and reinvest income from the asset in the asset.
2. Short a forward contract on one unit of the asset.

The holding of the asset grows at rate q so that $e^{-qT} \times e^{qT}$, or exactly one unit of the asset, is held at time T.[9] Under the terms of the forward contract, the asset is sold for F_0 at time T. The strategy, therefore, leads to an initial outflow of $S_0 e^{-qT}$ and a final inflow of F_0. The present value of the inflow must equal the outflow. Hence

$$S_0 e^{-qT} = F_0 e^{-rT}$$

or

$$F_0 = S_0 e^{(r-q)T}$$

If $F_0 < S_0 e^{(r-q)T}$, an arbitrageur should enter into a long forward contract and short the asset to lock in a riskless profit. If $F_0 > S_0 e^{(r-q)T}$, an arbitrageur should buy the asset and enter into a short forward contract to lock in a riskless profit. If the dividend yield is a known continuous dividend yield but is not constant, we should set q equal to the average dividend yield during the life of the forward contract in equation (3A.1).

Equation (3A.1) can be used in any situation where a known dividend yield is expected—whether or not the dividend is continuous. If discrete dividends of q_1, $q_2, \ldots, q_n$ are expected between time zero and time T, we define

$$Q = (1 + q_1)(1 + q_2) \cdots (1 + q_n) - 1$$

This is the proportional increase in our stock holdings that would result from the dividends being reinvested. The equivalent continuous dividend, q, must satisfy

$$e^{qT} = 1 + Q$$

---

[9]These arguments make the unrealistic assumption that one share is divisible. However, we can magnify the holdings in the two portfolios by 100, 10,000, or 1,000,000 and the basic argument is still the same. To illustrate the fact that the holding grows at rate q when dividends are reinvested, suppose that the stock price is $100, the dividend yield, q, is 5% per annum, and a short time interval of 0.02 years is considered. If we hold 10,000 shares, the dividend received in the short time interval is $10,000 \times \$100 \times 0.05 \times 0.02 = \$1,000$. As a result, 10 new shares can be purchased, so that the holding grows by 0.1% during the time period. This corresponds to the assumed growth rate of 5% per annum.

or,

$$q = \frac{1}{T} \ln (1 + Q)$$

and equation (3A.1) can be used with this value of q.

Example 3.12   Consider a six-month forward contract on a stock that is expected to provide a dividend equal to 4% of the stock price during the first month and during the fourth month. (The precise timing of the dividends does not matter when they are assumed to be a known percentage of the stock price at the time the dividend is paid.) The continuously compounded risk-free interest rate is 6% and the current stock price is $80. In this case, $S_0 = 80$, $r = 0.06$, $T = 0.5$, and $Q = 1.04 \times 1.04 - 1 = 0.0816$. The equivalent continuous dividend yield is

$$\frac{1}{0.5} \ln (1.0816) = 0.1569$$

or, 15.69%. From equation (3.7) the forward price, F_0, is, therefore, given by

$$F_0 = 80e^{(0.06 - 0.1569) \times 0.5} = \$76.22$$

Note that this is an example of a situation where the dividend yield is greater than the risk-free rate so that the forward price is less than the spot price.

Proof That Forward and Futures Prices Are Equal When Interest Rates Are Constant

In this appendix we show that forward and futures prices are equal when interest rates are constant. Suppose that a futures contract lasts for n days and that F_i is the futures price at the end of day i $(0 < i < n)$. Define δ as the risk-free rate per day (assumed constant). Consider the following strategy:[10]

1. Take a long futures position of e^{δ} at the end of day 0 (i.e., at the beginning of the contract).
2. Increase the long position to $e^{2\delta}$ at the end of day 1.
3. Increase the long position to $e^{3\delta}$ at the end of day 2.

And so on.

This strategy is summarized in Table 3.5. By the beginning of day i, the investor has a long position of $e^{\delta i}$. The profit (possibly negative) from the position on day i is

$$(F_i - F_{i-1})e^{\delta i}$$

Assume that this is compounded at the risk-free rate until the end of day n. Its value at the end of day n is

$$(F_i - F_{i-1})e^{\delta i}e^{(n-i)\delta} = (F_i - F_{i-1})e^{n\delta}$$

The value at the end of day n of the entire investment strategy is, therefore,

$$\sum_{i=1}^{n}(F_i - F_{i-1})e^{n\delta}$$

This is

$$[(F_n - F_{n-1}) + (F_{n-1} - F_{n-2}) + \cdots + (F_1 - F_0)]e^{n\delta} = (F_n - F_0)e^{n\delta}$$

Because F_n is the same as the terminal asset price, S_T, the terminal value of the investment strategy can be written

$$(S_T - F_0)e^{n\delta}$$

---

[10]This strategy was proposed by J. C. Cox, J. E. Ingersoll, and S. A. Ross, "The Relationship between Forward Prices and Futures Prices," *Journal of Financial Economics*, 9 (December 1981), 321–46.

Table 3.5 **Investment Strategy to Show that Futures and Forward Prices are Equal**

Day	0	1	2	...	$n-1$	n
Futures price	F_0	F_1	F_2	...	F_{n-1}	F_n
Futures position	e^{δ}	$e^{2\delta}$	$e^{3\delta}$	...	$e^{n\delta}$	0
Gain/loss	0	$(F_1 - F_0)e^{\delta}$	$(F_2 - F_1)e^{2\delta}$	...	...	$(F_n - F_{n-1})e^{n\delta}$
Gain/loss compounded to day n	0	$(F_1 - F_0)e^{n\delta}$	$(F_2 - F_1)e^{n\delta}$	...	...	$(F_n - F_{n-1})e^{n\delta}$

An investment of F_0 in a risk-free bond combined with the strategy just given yields

$$F_0 e^{n\delta} + (S_T - F_0)e^{n\delta} = S_T e^{n\delta}$$

at time T. No investment is required for all the long futures positions described. It follows that an amount F_0 can be invested to give an amount $S_T e^{n\delta}$ at time T.

Suppose next that the forward price at the end of day 0 is G_0. By investing G_0 in a riskless bond and taking a long forward position of $e^{n\delta}$ forward contracts, an amount $S_T e^{n\delta}$ is also guaranteed at time T. Thus, there are two investment strategies, one requiring an initial outlay of F_0, the other requiring an initial outlay of G_0, both of which yield $S_T e^{n\delta}$ at time T. It follows that in the absence of arbitrage opportunities

$$F_0 = G_0$$

In other words, the futures price and the forward price are identical. Note that in this proof there is nothing special about the time period of one day. The futures price based on a contract with weekly settlements is also the same as the forward price when corresponding assumptions are made.

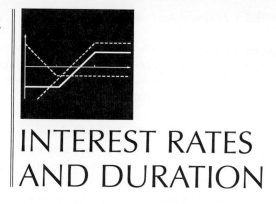

4
INTEREST RATES AND DURATION

In this chapter we take a first look at interest rate markets. We explain zero rates, par yields, forward rates, and the relationships between them. We cover day count conventions, and the way in which the prices of bonds and Treasury bills are quoted in the United States. We discuss the duration measure and explain how it can be used to quantify a company's exposure to interest rates. We also consider interest rate futures markets. Treasury bond futures and Eurodollar futures contracts are described in some detail, and we examine how they can be used for duration-based hedging.

4.1 TYPES OF RATES

For any given currency, many different types of interest rates are regularly quoted. These include mortgage rates, deposit rates, prime borrowing rates, and so on. As will be discussed in chapter 23, the applicable interest rate in a given situation depends on the credit risk. The higher the credit risk, the higher the interest rate. In this section, we introduce three interest rates that are particularly relevant to the analysis of derivatives.

Treasury Rates

The Treasury rate is the rate of interest applicable to borrowing by a government in its own currency. For example the U.S. dollar Treasury rate is the rate at which the U.S. government can borrow in U.S. dollars; the Japanese Treasury rate is the rate at which the Japanese government can borrow in yen; and so on. It is usually assumed that there is no chance that a government will default on an obligation denominated in its own currency.[1] For this reason, Treasury rates are regarded as risk-free rates.

LIBOR Rates

LIBOR is short for the *London Interbank Offer Rate*. It is the rate at which large international banks fund much of their activities. Specifically, it is the rate at which one large international bank is willing to lend money to another large international

---

[1] The reason for this is the government can always meet its obligation by printing more money.

87

bank. LIBOR rates are determined in trading between banks and change as economic conditions change. LIBOR zero rates are generally higher than Treasury zero rates because they are not risk-free. There is always some chance (albeit small) that the bank borrowing the money will default.

Repo Rate

Sometimes an investment dealer will fund trading activities with a *repo* or *repurchase agreement*. This is a contract where the owner of securities agrees to sell them to a counterparty now and buy them back later at a slightly higher price. The counterparty is providing a loan. The difference between the price at which the securities are sold and the price at which they are repurchased is the interest earned by the counterparty. The interest rate is referred to as the *repo rate*. If structured carefully, the loan involves very little credit risk. If the borrowing company does not keep to its side of the agreement, the lender simply keeps the securities. If the lending company does not keep to its side of the agreement, the borrowing company keeps the cash.

The repo rate is only slightly higher than the corresponding Treasury rate. The most common type of repo is an *overnight repo*, in which the agreement is renegotiated each day. However, longer-term arrangements, known as *term repos*, are sometimes used.

4.2   ZERO RATES

The *n*-year *zero rate* (sometimes simply referred to as the *n*-year zero) is the rate of interest earned on an investment that starts today and lasts for *n* years. All the interest and principal is realized at the end of *n* years. There are no intermediate payments. The *n*-year zero rate is sometimes also referred to as the *n*-year *spot rate*. Suppose the five-year Treasury zero rate with annual compounding is quoted as 5% per annum. This means that $100, if invested at the risk-free rate for five years, would grow to

$$100 \times 1.05^5 = 127.63$$

Many of the interest rates we observe directly in the market are not pure zero rates. Consider a five-year government bond that provides a 6% coupon. This does not provide precise information on the five-year Treasury zero rate because some of the return on the bond is realized in the form of coupons prior to the end of year five. Later in this chapter we will discuss how Treasury zero rates can be estimated from data on government bonds. In Appendix 5A we will discuss how LIBOR zero rates are calculated from data on swaps and Eurodollar futures.

4.3   BOND PRICING

Most bonds provide periodic coupons. The theoretical price of a bond can be calculated as the present value of the cash flows received by the owner of the bond using the appropriate zero-coupon interest rates as discount rates. Consider the situation where

Table 4.1	Treasury Zero Rates
Maturity	**Zero Rate (%)**
(years)	**(cont comp)**
0.5	5.0
1.0	5.8
1.5	6.4
2.0	6.8

Treasury zero-coupon interest rates with continuous compounding are as shown in Table 4.1. Suppose that a two-year Treasury bond with a principal of \$100 provides a coupon at the rate of 6% per annum with the coupons being paid semiannually. To calculate the present value of the first coupon of \$3 we discount it at 5.0% for six months; to calculate the present value of the second coupon of \$3 we discount it at 5.8% for one year; and so on. The theoretical price of the bond is, therefore:

$$3e^{-0.05 \times 0.5} + 3e^{-0.058 \times 1.0} + 3e^{-0.064 \times 1.5} + 103e^{-0.068 \times 2.0} = 98.39$$

or \$98.39.

Bond Yield

The yield on a coupon-bearing bond is the discount rate that equates the cash flows on the bond to its market value. Suppose that the theoretical price of the bond we have been considering, \$98.39, is also its market value (that is, the market price of the bond is in exact agreement with the data in Table 4.1). If y is the yield on the bond expressed with continuous compounding, we must have:

$$3e^{-y \times 0.5} + 3e^{-y \times 1.0} + 3e^{-y \times 1.5} + 103e^{-y \times 2.0} = 98.39$$

This equation can be solved using an iterative ("trial and error") procedure to give $y = 6.76\%$.[2]

Par Yield

The *par yield* for a certain maturity is the coupon rate that causes the bond price to equal its face value (i.e., principal). Usually the bond is assumed to provide semiannual coupons. Suppose that the coupon on a two-year bond in our example is c per annum (or $c/2$ every six months). Using the zero-coupon interest rates in Table 4.1, the value

---

[2]One way of solving nonlinear equations of the form $f(y) = 0$, such as this one, is to use the Newton–Raphson method. We start with an estimate y_0 of the solution and produce successively better estimates $y_1, y_2, y_3, \ldots$ using the formula $y_{i+1} = y_i - f(y_i)/f'(y_i)$ where $f'(y)$ denotes the partial derivative of f with respect to y.

of the bond is equal to its face value of 100 when

$$\frac{c}{2}e^{-0.05\times0.5} + \frac{c}{2}e^{-0.058\times1.0} + \frac{c}{2}e^{-0.064\times1.5} + \left(100 + \frac{c}{2}\right)e^{-0.068\times2.0} = 100$$

This equation can be solved in a straightforward way to give $c = 6.87$. The two-year par yield is, therefore, 6.87% per annum with semiannual compounding (or 6.75% with continuous compounding.)

More generally, if P is the present value of $1 received at the maturity of the bond, A is the value of an annuity that pays one dollar on each coupon payment date, and m is the number of coupon payments per year, the par yield c (compounded m times per year) must satisfy

$$100 = A\frac{c}{m} + 100P$$

so that

$$c = \frac{(100 - 100P)m}{A}$$

In our example, $m = 2$, $P = e^{-0.068\times2} = 0.87284$ and $A = e^{-0.05\times0.5} + e^{-0.058\times1.0} + e^{-0.064\times1.5} + e^{-0.068\times2.0} = 3.70027$. The formula confirms that the par yield is 6.87% per annum.

4.4   DETERMINING ZERO RATES

We now discuss how zero-coupon interest rates can be calculated from the prices of coupon-bearing instruments. One approach is known as the *bootstrap method*. To illustrate the nature of the method, consider the data in Table 4.2 on the prices of five bonds. Because the first three bonds pay no coupons, the zero rates corresponding to the maturities of these bonds can easily be calculated. The three-month bond provides a return of 2.5 on an initial investment of 97.5 in three months. With quarterly compounding, the rate is $(4 \times 2.5)/97.5 = 10.256\%$ per annum. When the rate is expressed with continuous compounding, equation (3.3) shows that it becomes

$$4\ln\left(1 + \frac{0.10256}{4}\right) = 0.10127$$

or 10.127% per annum. The six-month bond provides a return of 5.1 on an initial investment of 94.9 in six months. With semiannual compounding, the rate is $(2 \times 5.1)/94.9 = 10.748\%$ per annum. When the rate is expressed with continuous compounding, equation (3.3) shows that it becomes

$$2\ln\left(1 + \frac{0.10748}{2}\right) = 0.10469$$

Table 4.2	Data for Bootstrap Method		
Bond Principal ($)	*Time to Maturity (years)*	*Annual Coupon ($)**	*Bond Price ($)*
100	0.25	0	97.5
100	0.50	0	94.9
100	1.00	0	90.0
100	1.50	8	96.0
100	2.00	12	101.6

*Half the stated coupon is assumed to be paid every six months.

or 10.469% per annum. Similarly, the one-year rate with continuous compounding is

$$\ln \left(1 + \frac{10}{90.0}\right) = 0.10536$$

or 10.536% per annum.

The fourth bond lasts 1.5 years. The payments on the bond are as follows:

6 months: $4
1 year: $4
1.5 years: $104

From our earlier calculations, we know that the discount rate for the payment at the end of six months is 10.469% and the discount rate for the payment at the end of one year is 10.536%. We also know that the bond's price, $96, must equal the present value of all the payments received by the bondholder. Suppose the 1.5-year zero rate is denoted by R. It follows that

$$4e^{-0.10469 \times 0.5} + 4e^{-0.10536 \times 1.0} + 104e^{-R \times 1.5} = 96.0$$

This reduces to

$$e^{-1.5R} = 0.85196$$

or

$$R = -\frac{\ln(0.85196)}{1.5} = 0.10681$$

The 1.5-year zero rate is, therefore, 10.681%. This is the only zero rate that is consistent with the six-month rate, one-year rate, and the data in Table 4.2.

The two-year zero rate can be calculated similarly from the six-month, one-year, and 1.5-year zero rates and the information on the fifth bond in Table 4.2. If R is the two-year zero rate,

$$6e^{-0.10469 \times 0.5} + 6e^{-0.10536 \times 1.0} + 6e^{-0.10681 \times 1.5} + 106e^{-R \times 2.0} = 101.6$$

This gives $R = 0.10808$ or 10.808%.

Table 4.3	Continuously Compounded Zero Rates Determined from Data in Table 4.2
Maturity (years)	**Zero Rate (%) (cont comp)**
0.25	10.127
0.50	10.469
1.00	10.536
1.50	10.681
2.00	10.808

The rates we have calculated are summarized in Table 4.3. A chart showing the zero rate as a function of maturity is known as the *zero curve*. A common assumption is that the zero curve is linear between the points determined using the bootstrap method. (This means that the 1.25-year zero rate is $0.5 \times 10.536 + 0.5 \times 10.681 = 10.608\%$ in our example.) It is usually assumed that the zero curve is horizontal prior to the first point and horizontal beyond the last point. Figure 4.1 shows the zero curve for our data. By using longer maturity bonds, the zero curve would be more accurately determined beyond two years.

In practice, we do not usually have bonds with maturities equal to exactly 1.5 years, 2 years, 2.5 years, and so on. The approach often used by financial engineers is to interpolate between the bond price data before they are used to calculate the zero curve. For example, if we know that a 2.3-year bond with a coupon of 6% sells for 98 and a 2.7-year bond with a coupon of 6.5% sells for 99, we might assume that a 2.5-year bond with a coupon of 6.25% would sell for 98.5.

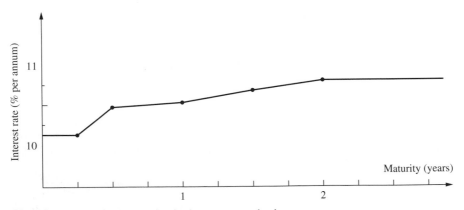

Figure 4.1   Zero rates given by the bootstrap method.

4.5 FORWARD RATES

A forward interest rate is the interest rate implied by current zero rates for a specified future time period. To illustrate how it is calculated, we suppose that the zero rates are as shown in the second column of Table 4.4. The rates are assumed to be continuously compounded. Thus, the 10% per annum rate for one year means that, in return for an investment of $100 today, the investor receives $100e^{0.1} = 110.52 in one year; the 10.5% per annum rate for two years means that, in return for an investment of $100 today, the investor receives $100e^{0.105 \times 2} = 123.37 in two years; and so on.

The forward interest rate in Table 4.4 for year two is 11% per annum. This is the interest rate that is implied by the zero rates for the time period between the end of the first year and the end of the second year. It can be calculated from the one-year zero interest rate of 10% per annum and the two-year zero interest rate of 10.5% per annum. It is the rate of interest for year two that, when combined with 10% per annum for year one, gives 10.5% overall for the two years. To show that the correct answer is 11% per annum, suppose that $100 is invested. A rate of 10% for the first year and 11% for the second year yields

$$100e^{0.1}e^{0.11} = $123.37$$

at the end of the second year. A rate of 10.5% per annum for two years yields

$$100e^{0.105 \times 2}$$

hich is also $123.37. This example illustrates that when interest rates are continuously compounded and rates in successive time periods of equal length are combined, the overall equivalent rate is simply the arithmetic average of the rates (10.5% is the average of 10% and 11%). The result is only approximately true when the rates are not continuously compounded.

The forward rate for year three is the rate of interest that is implied by a 10.5% per annum two-year zero rate and a 10.8% per annum three-year zero rate. It is 11.4% per annum. The reason is that a two-year investment at 10.5% per annum combined with a one-year investment at 11.4% per annum gives an overall return of 10.8% per annum for three years. The other forward rates can be similarly calculated and are

Table 4.4 Calculation of Forward Rates

Year (n)	Zero Rate for an n-Year Investment (% per annum)	Forward Rate for nth Year (% per annum)
1	10.0	
2	10.5	11.0
3	10.8	11.4
4	11.0	11.6
5	11.1	11.5

shown in the third column of the table. In general, if R_1 and R_2 are the zero rates for maturities T_1 and T_2, respectively, and R_F is the forward interest rate for the period of time between T_1 and T_2:

$$R_F = \frac{R_2 T_2 - R_1 T_1}{T_2 - T_1} \qquad (4.1)$$

To illustrate this formula, consider the calculation of the year four forward rate from the data in Table 4.4: $T_1 = 3$, $T_2 = 4$, $R_1 = 0.108$, and $R_2 = 0.11$, and the formula gives $R_F = 0.116$.

Assuming that an investor can borrow or invest at the zero rate, the investor can lock in the forward rate for borrowing or investing during a future time period. Suppose, for example, that the interest rates are as in Table 4.4. If an investor borrows $100 at 10% for one year and then invests the money at 10.5% for two years, the result is a cash outflow of $100e^{0.1} = \$110.52$ at the end of year one and an inflow of $100e^{0.105 \times 2} = \$123.37$ at the end of year two. Because $123.37 = 110.52e^{0.11}$, a return equal to the forward rate (11%) is earned on $110.52 during the second year.

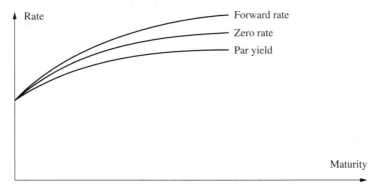

Figure 4.2   Par yields, zero rate, and forward rates when yield curve is upward sloping.

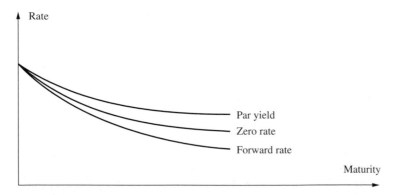

Figure 4.3   Par yields, zero rate, and forward rates when yield curve is downward sloping.

Suppose next that the investor borrows $100 for four years at 11% and invests it for three years at 10.8%. The result is a cash inflow of $100e^{0.108 \times 3} = \$138.26$ at the end of the third year and a cash outflow of $100e^{0.11 \times 4} = \$155.27$ at the end of the fourth year. Because $155.27 = 138.26e^{0.116}$, money is being borrowed for the fourth year at the forward rate of 11.6%.

Equation (4.1) can be written

$$R_F = R_2 + (R_2 - R_1)\frac{T_1}{T_2 - T_1} \tag{4.2}$$

This shows that if the zero curve is upward sloping with $R_2 > R_1$, then $R_F > R_2$. Similarly, if the zero curve is downward sloping with $R_2 < R_1$, then $R_F < R_2$. Figures 4.2 and 4.3 show the par yield, zero rate, and forward rate for cases where the zero curve is upward sloping and downward sloping, respectively. As indicated by these figures, when the yield curve is upward sloping, the par yield for a certain maturity is less than the zero rate for that maturity (when both are expressed with the same compounding frequency). Similarly, when the yield curve is downward sloping, the par yield for a certain maturity is greater than the zero rate for that maturity.

Taking limits as T_2 approaches T_1 in equation (4.2) and letting the common value of the two be T, we obtain

$$R_F = R + T\frac{\partial R}{\partial T}$$

where R is the zero rate for a maturity of T. The value of R_F obtained in this way is known as the *instantaneous forward rate* for a maturity of T. This is the forward rate that is applicable to a very short future time period that begins at time T.

4.6 FORWARD-RATE AGREEMENTS

A *forward-rate agreement* (FRA) is a forward contract where the parties agree that a certain interest rate will apply to a certain principal during a specified future time period. In this section we examine how forward-rate agreements can be valued in terms of forward rates.

Consider a forward-rate agreement where it is specified that an interest rate R_K will be earned for the period of time between T_1 and T_2 on a principal of L. Define:

R_F: The forward interest rate for the period between times T_1 and T_2.

R: The actual interest rate observed at time T_1 for a maturity T_2.

We will depart from our usual assumption of continuous compounding and assume that R_K, R_F, and R are all measured with a compounding frequency corresponding to $T_2 - T_1$. (This means that if $T_2 - T_1 = 0.5$, the rates are expressed with semiannual compounding; if $T_2 - T_1 = 0.25$, the rates are expressed with quarterly compounding; and so on.) The forward-rate agreement is an agreement to the following cash flows:[3]

   Time T_1: $-L$.
   Time T_2: $+L[1 + R_K(T_2 - T_1)]$.

To value the FRA, we first note that it is always worth zero when $R_K = R_F$.[4] This is because, as shown in section 4.5, we can, at no cost, lock in the forward rate for a future time period. For example, we can ensure that we earn the forward rate for the time period between the end of year two and the end of year three by borrowing funds for two years and investing them for three years. Similarly, we can ensure that we pay the forward rate for this time period by borrowing funds for three years and investing them for two years.

We can now use an argument, analogous to that in section 3.5, to calculate the value of the FRA for values of R_K other than R_F. Compare two FRAs. The first promises that the forward rate R_F will be earned on a principal of L between times T_1 and T_2; the second promises that R_K will be earned on the same principal between the same two dates. The two contracts are the same except for the interest payments received at time T_2. The excess value of the FRA promising R_K over the FRA promising R_F is, therefore, the present value of the difference between the interest payments or

$$L(R_K - R_F)(T_2 - T_1)e^{-R_2 T_2}$$

where R_2 is the continously compounded zero-coupon interest rate for a maturity T_2.[5] Because the value of the FRA promising R_F is zero, the value of the FRA promising R_K is

$$V = L(R_K - R_F)(T_2 - T_1)e^{-R_2 T_2} \tag{4.3}$$

When an FRA specifies that the interest rate R_K will be paid rather than received, its value is similarly given by

$$V = L(R_F - R_K)(T_2 - T_1)e^{-R_2 T_2} \tag{4.4}$$

Example 4.1   Assume that the zero-coupon yield curve is the same as in Table 4.4, so that the one-year zero rate is 10% and the two-year zero rate is 10.5%. Suppose we have entered into an FRA where we will receive a rate of 12% with annual compounding on a principal of $1 million between the end of year one and the end of year two. In this case, the forward rate is 11% with continuous compounding or 11.6278% with annual compounding. Because the two-year zero rate is 10.5% with continuous compounding, the value of the FRA is calculated using equation (4.3) as

$$1{,}000{,}000 \times (0.120000 - 0.116278) \times 1 \times e^{-0.105 \times 2} = \$3{,}017$$

---

[3]In practice, an FRA such as the one considered is usually settled in cash at time T_1. The cash settlement is the present value of the agreement or

$$L \frac{1 + R_K(T_2 - T_1)}{1 + R(T_2 - T_1)} - L$$

[4]It is usually the case that R_K is set equal to R_F when the FRA is initiated.

[5]Note that R_K, R, and R_F are expressed with a compounding frequency corresponding to $T_2 - T_1$ while R_2 is expressed with continuous compounding.

Alternative Characterization of FRAs

Consider again an FRA that guarantees that a rate, R_K, will be earned between times T_1 and T_2. The principal, L, can be borrowed at rate R at time T_1 and repaid at time T_2. When this transaction is combined with the FRA, we see that the FRA is equivalent to the following cash flows

Time T_1: 0.
Time T_2: $LR_K(T_2 - T_1)$.
Time T_2: $-LR(T_2 - T_1)$.

In other words, the FRA is equivalent to an agreement where interest at the predetermined rate, R_K, is received and interest at the market rate, R, is paid.

Combining the two cash flows at time T_2, we see that the FRA is equivalent to a single cash flow of

$$L(R_K - R)(T_2 - T_1)$$

at time T_2. From equation (4.3), it follows that the FRA can be valued by assuming that $R = R_F$ and discounting the resultant cash flows at the risk-free rate.

Similar results are obtained for an FRA that guarantees that funds can be borrowed at rate R_K between times T_1 and T_2. We have, therefore, shown:

1. An FRA is equivalent to an agreement where interest at a predetermined rate, R_K, is exchanged for interest at the market rate, R.
2. An FRA can be valued by assuming that the forward interest rate is certain to be realized.

These two results will be useful when we consider interest rate swaps in the next chapter.

4.7 THEORIES OF THE TERM STRUCTURE

It is natural to ask what determines the shape of the zero curve. Why is it sometimes downward sloping and sometimes upward sloping? A number of different theories have been proposed. The simplest of these is *expectations theory*. This conjectures that long-term interest rates should reflect expected future short-term interest rates. More precisely, it argues that a forward interest rate corresponding to a certain period is equal to the expected future zero rate for that period. Another approach, *market segmentation theory*, conjectures that there need be no relationship between short-, medium-, and long-term interest rates. Under this theory, different institutions invest in bonds of different maturities and do not switch maturities. The short-term interest rate is determined by supply and demand in the short-term bond market; the medium-term interest rate is determined by supply and demand in the medium-term bond market; and so on.

The theory that is in some ways most appealing is *liquidity preference theory.* This argues that forward rates should always be higher than expected future zero rates. The basic assumption underlying the theory is that investors prefer to preserve their liquidity and invest funds for short periods of time. Borrowers, on the other hand, usually prefer to borrow at fixed rates for long periods of time. If the interest rates offered by banks and other financial intermediaries were such that the forward rate equaled the expected future zero rate, long-term interest rates would equal the average of expected future short-term interest rates. In the absence of any incentive to do otherwise, investors would tend to deposit their funds for short time periods and borrowers would tend to choose to borrow for long time periods. Financial intermediaries would then find themselves financing substantial amounts of long-term fixed-rate loans with short-term deposits. Excessive interest rate risk would result. In practice, to match depositors with borrowers and avoid interest rate risk, financial intermediaries raise long-term interest rates relative to expected future short-term interest rates. This strategy reduces the demand for long-term fixed-rate borrowing and encourages investors to deposit their funds for long terms.

Liquidity preference theory leads to a situation in which forward rates are greater than expected future zero rates. It is also consistent with the empirical result that yield curves tend to be upward sloping more often than they are downward sloping.

4.8   DAY COUNT CONVENTIONS

We now examine the day count conventions that are used when interest rates are quoted. This is a quite separate issue from the compounding frequency used. The day count defines the way that interest accrues over time. Generally, we know the interest earned over some reference period (e.g., the time between coupon payments) and we are interested in calculating the interest earned over some other period.

The day count convention is usually expressed as X/Y. When we are calculating the interest earned between two dates, X defines the way that the number of days between the two dates is calculated, and Y defines the way that the total number of days in the reference period is calculated. The interest earned between the two dates is

$$\frac{\text{number of days between dates}}{\text{number of days in reference period}} \times \text{interest earned in reference period}$$

Three day count conventions that are commonly used in the United States are:

1. Actual/actual (in period).
2. 30/360.
3. Actual/360.

Actual/actual (in period) is used for U.S. Treasury bonds; 30/360 is used for U.S. corporate and municipal bonds; and actual/360 is used for U.S. Treasury bills and other money market instruments.

The use of actual/actual (in period) for Treasury bonds indicates that the interest earned between two dates is based on the ratio of the actual days elapsed to the actual number of days in the period between coupon payments. Suppose that the bond principal is $100, coupon payment dates are March 1 and September 1, and the coupon rate is 8%. We wish to calculate the interest earned between March 1 and July 3. The reference period is from March 1 to September 1. There are 184 (actual) days in this period, and interest of $4 is earned during the period. There are 124 (actual) days between March 1 and July 3. The interest earned between March 1 and July 3 is, therefore,

$$\frac{124}{184} \times 4 = 2.6957$$

The use of 30/360 for corporate and municipal bonds indicates that we assume 30 days per month and 360 days per year when carrying out calculations. Using 30/360, the total number of days between March 1 and September 1 is 180. The total number of days between March 1 and July 3 is $(4 \times 30) + 2 = 122$. In a corporate bond with the same terms as the Treasury bond just considered, the interest earned between March 1 and July 3 would, therefore, be

$$\frac{122}{180} \times 4 = 2.7111$$

The use of actual/360 for a money market instrument indicates that the reference period is 360 days. The interest earned during part of a year is calculated by dividing the actual number of elapsed days by 360 and then multiplying by the rate. The interest earned in 90 days is, therefore, exactly one-fourth of the quoted rate. Note that the interest earned in a whole year of 365 days is 365/360 times the quoted rate.

4.9 QUOTATIONS

The price quoted for an interest-bearing instrument is often not the same as the cash price you would pay if you purchased it. We illustrate this by considering the way that prices are quoted for Treasury bonds and Treasury bills in the United States.

Bonds

Treasury bond prices in the United States are quoted in dollars and thirty-seconds of a dollar. The quoted price is for a bond with a face value of $100. Thus, a quote of 90-05 means that the indicated price for a bond with a face value of $100,000 is $90,156.25.

The quoted price is not the same as the cash price that is paid by the purchaser. In general,

Cash price = Quoted price + Accrued interest since last coupon date

To illustrate this formula, suppose that it is March 5, 1999, and the bond under consideration is an 11% coupon bond maturing on July 10, 2001, with a quoted price of 95-16, or $95.50. Because coupons are paid semiannually on government bonds, the most recent coupon date is January 10, 1999, and the next coupon date is July 10, 1999. The number of days between January 10, 1999, and March 5, 1999, is 54, whereas the number of days between January 10, 1999, and July 10, 1999, is 181. On a bond with $100 face value, the coupon payment is $5.50 on January 10 and July 10. The accrued interest on March 5, 1999, is the share of the July 10 coupon accruing to the bondholder on March 5, 1999. Because actual/actual in period is used for Treasury bonds, this is

$$\frac{54}{181} \times \$5.5 = \$1.64$$

The cash price per $100 face value for the July 10, 2001, bond is, therefore,

$$\$95.50 + \$1.64 = \$97.14$$

Thus, the cash price of a $100,000 bond is $97,140.

Treasury Bills

As mentioned, the actual/360 day count convention is used for Treasury bills in the United States. Price quotes are for a Treasury bill with a face value of $100. There is a difference between the cash price and quoted price for a Treasury bill. If Y is the cash price of a Treasury bill that has a face value of $100 and n days to maturity, the quoted price is

$$\frac{360}{n}(100 - Y)$$

This is referred to as the *discount rate*. It is the annualized dollar return provided by the Treasury bill expressed as a percentage of the face value. If, for a 90-day Treasury bill, the cash price, Y, were 98, the quoted price would be 8.00.

The discount rate or quoted price is not the same as the rate of return earned on the Treasury bill. The latter is calculated as the dollar return divided by the cost. In the preceding example, where the quoted price is 8.00, the rate of return would be 2/98, or 2.04% per 90 days. This amounts to

$$\frac{2}{98} \times \frac{365}{90} = 0.0828$$

or 8.28% per annum with compounding every 90 days.[6] When converted to semiannual compounding, this rate of return is sometimes referred to as the *bond equivalent yield*.

---

[6]It is interesting to note in passing that, in the United States, the compounding frequency convention for a money market instrument, such as a Treasury bill, is to set the compounding period equal to the life of the instrument. This means that the quoted yields on money market instruments of different maturities are not directly comparable.

4.10 INTEREST RATE FUTURES

We now move on to consider interest rate futures contracts. Table 4.5 shows interest rate futures quotes as they appeared in *The Wall Street Journal* on August 5, 1998. There are two main types of contracts: those where the underlying is a government bond and those where the underlying is a short-term Eurodollar or LIBOR interest rate. Examples of the first type of contract are Treasury bonds futures (CBOT),

Table 4.5 Interest Rate Futures Quotes from *The Wall Street Journal*, August 5, 1998

INTEREST RATE

```
TREASURY BONDS (CBT)-$100,000; pts. 32nds of 100%
                                         Lifetime      Open
      Open   High   Low  Settle Change High   Low  Interest
Sept 123-11 123-20 123-03 123-18 +  7 124-14 103-22 817,311
Dec  123-00 123-20 122-28 123-10 +  7 124-00 103-13 198,733
Mr99 123-07 123-07 123-02 123-02 +  7 123-20 103-04  38,190
Sept  ....   ....   ....  122-14 +  7 121-26 115-11   3,732
Est vol 425,000; vol Mon 403,192; open int 1,058,001, +8,548.
TREASURY BONDS (MCE)-$50,000; pts. 32nds of 100%
Sept 123-05 123-28 123-04 123-27 + 16 124-07 118-07  16,093
Est vol 5,500; vol Mon 5,059; open int 16,148, +314.
TREASURY NOTES (CBT)-$100,000; pts. 32nds of 100%
Sept 113-29 114-08 113-26 114-02 +  5 114-22 110-25 473,591
Dec  113-27 114-07 113-27 114-03 +  6 114-21 111-11  68,414
Mr99  ....   ....   ....  114-06 +  6 113-29 112-04     476
Est vol 90,210; vol Mon 88,300; open int 542,481, +1,919.
5 YR TREAS NOTES (CBT)-$100,000; pts. 32nds of 100%
Sept 109-23 09-305 109-21 09-265 + 3.5 110-05 108-09 267,962
Dec  109-25 110-00 109-24 109-28 + 3.0 110-00 108-30  25,750
Est vol 43,000; vol Mon 57,144; open int 293,712, +11,457.
2 YR TREAS NOTES (CBT)-$200,000; pts. 32nds of 100%
Sept 104-08 104-11 104-06 04-097 + 1.50 4-175 03-225  43,352
Est vol 4,000; vol Mon 2,232; open int 44,454, +221.
30-DAY FEDERAL FUNDS (CBT)-$5 million; pts. of 100%
Aug 94.490 94.495 94.485 94.485 .... 94.830 94.220  5,913
Sept 94.47 94.47 94.47 94.47 + .01 94.64 94.30  4,242
Oct  94.50 94.50 94.49 94.50 + .01 94.60 94.32  3,039
Nov  94.49 94.50 94.49 94.49 + .01 94.60 94.27  3,730
Dec  94.46 94.48 94.46 94.47 + .01 94.59 94.25    968
Ja99 94.42 94.45 94.42 94.44 + .01 94.55 94.25    905
Feb  94.51 94.54 94.51 94.52 + .01 94.55 94.31    276
Est vol 999; vol Mon 2,216; open int 19,156, −4,634.
MUNI BOND INDEX (CBT)-$1,000; times Bond Buyer MBI
Sept 124-09 124-25 124-09 124-16 .... 125-07 119-01 25,263
Dec  124-02 124-07 123-31 124-02 .... 124-10 123-07    538
Est vol 2,500; vol Mon 1,565; open int 25,801, +415.
The index: Close 123-22; Yield 5.38.
TREASURY BILLS (CME)-$1 mil.; pts. of 100%
                                Discount      Open
      Open  High  Low  Settle Chg Settle Chg Interest
Sept 95.02 95.05 95.01 95.01 + .01 4.99 − .01 4,596
Dec  95.07 95.07 95.05 95.06 + .02 4.94 − .02   234
Est vol 408; vol Mon 202; open int 4,841, +162.
LIBOR-1 MO. (CME)-$3,000,000; points of 100%
Aug  94.35 94.36 94.35 94.35 .... 5.65 ....  19,174
Sept 94.35 94.36 94.35 94.36 .... 5.64 ....   8,778
Oct   ....  ....  ....  94.36 .... 5.64 ....   2,759
Nov  94.38 94.38 94.38 94.38 + .01 5.62 − .01  2,159
Dec  94.20 94.21 94.19 94.21 + .01 5.79 − .01  3,542
Ja99  ....  ....  ....  94.41 + .01 5.59 − .01    277
Mar   ....  ....  ....  94.41 + .02 5.59 − .02    128
Est vol 3,658; vol Mon 3,522; open int 36,880, +2,250.
EURODOLLAR (CME)-$1 million; pts of 100%
                                  Yield      Open
      Open  High  Low  Settle Chg Settle Chg Interest
Aug  94.31 94.32 94.31 94.32 .... 5.68 ....  15,402
Sept 94.32 94.34 94.31 94.32 .... 5.68 .... 473,350
Oct  94.28 94.30 94.28 94.29 + .01 5.71 − .01  6,787
Nov  94.28 94.30 94.28 94.29 + .01 5.71 − .01  1,308
Dec  94.29 94.32 94.28 94.30 + .01 5.70 − .01 403,791
Ja99 94.33 94.37 94.33 94.36 + .02 5.64 − .02  1,514
```

```
     Open  High  Low  Settle Change Yield  Chg  Interest
Mar  94.35 94.40 94.33 94.37 + .02 5.63 − .02 354,208
June 94.32 94.37 94.31 94.35 + .03 5.65 − .03 295,205
Sept 94.30 94.35 94.28 94.32 + .02 5.68 − .02 227,003
Dec  94.17 94.22 94.16 94.19 + .02 5.81 − .02 200,016
Mr00 94.22 94.27 94.21 94.24 + .02 5.76 − .02 159,594
June 94.19 94.25 94.19 94.22 + .02 5.78 − .02 143,615
Sept 94.19 94.23 94.18 94.20 + .01 5.80 − .01  97,841
Dec  94.11 94.16 94.11 94.13 + .01 5.87 − .01  81,352
Mr01 94.15 94.19 94.14 94.17 + .01 5.83 − .01  71,664
June 94.13 94.17 94.12 94.15 + .01 5.85 − .01  58,667
Sept 94.12 94.17 94.10 94.14 + .01 5.86 − .01  47,995
Dec  94.05 94.09 94.04 94.07 + .01 5.93 − .01  43,784
Mr02 94.08 94.13 94.07 94.11 + .02 5.89 − .02  47,696
June 94.06 94.12 94.05 94.09 + .02 5.91 − .02  46,157
Sept 94.06 94.11 94.05 94.08 + .02 5.92 − .02  46,601
Dec  93.98 94.04 93.98 94.01 + .02 5.99 − .02  36,566
Mr03 94.02 94.07 94.01 94.05 + .02 5.95 − .02  32,577
June 94.00 94.05 93.99 94.03 + .02 5.97 − .02  25,630
Sept 93.98 94.04 93.96 94.01 + .02 5.99 − .02  16,676
Dec  93.91 93.96 93.90 93.93 + .01 6.07 − .01   9,779
Mr04 93.94 93.99 93.93 93.96 + .01 6.04 − .01   8,264
June 93.91 93.96 93.90 93.93 + .01 6.07 − .01   8,677
Sept 93.89 93.93 93.88 93.91 + .01 6.09 − .01   6,957
Dec  93.82 93.86 93.81 93.84 + .01 6.16 − .01   7,928
Mr05 93.85 93.89 93.84 93.87 + .01 6.13 − .01   5,917
June 93.82 93.86 93.81 93.84 + .01 6.16 − .01   5,587
Sept 93.80 93.84 93.79 93.82 + .01 6.18 − .01   4,220
Dec  93.73 93.77 93.72 93.75 + .01 6.25 − .01   3,339
Mr06 93.76 93.80 93.75 93.78 + .01 6.22 − .01   5,586
June 93.73 93.77 93.72 93.75 + .01 6.25 − .01   3,840
Sept 93.70 93.75 93.70 93.73 + .01 6.27 − .01   4,597
Dec  93.63 93.68 93.63 93.66 + .01 6.34 − .01   5,043
Mr07 93.66 93.71 93.66 93.69 + .01 6.31 − .01   4,230
June 93.66 93.68 93.63 93.66 + .01 6.34 − .01   4,396
Sept 93.61 93.66 93.61 93.64 + .01 6.36 − .01   5,089
Dec  93.54 93.59 93.54 93.57 + .01 6.43 − .01   4,082
Mr08 93.60 93.62 93.59 93.60 + .01 6.40 − .01   3,826
June 93.57 93.59 93.56 93.57 + .01 6.43 − .01   1,163
Est vol 418,701; vol Mon 313,714; open int 3,037,519, −4,986.
EUROYEN (CME) -Yen 100,000,000; pts. of 100%
                                     Lifetime      Open
     Open  High  Low  Settle Change High   Low  Interest
Sept 99.24 99.25 99.24 99.24 ....  99.47 96.62 21,289
Dec  99.26 99.26 99.25 99.26 ....  99.46 96.39 14,492
Mr99 99.26 99.27 99.26 99.27 ....  99.42 96.67 12,613
June 99.27 99.28 99.27 99.28 ....  99.38 97.45 13,730
Sept 99.22 99.23 99.22 99.23 + .01 99.23 97.32  5,934
Dec  99.06 99.08 99.06 99.08 + .01 99.16 97.09  6,534
Mr00 98.97 98.98 98.97 98.98 + .02 98.94 96.92  6,070
June 98.89 98.89 98.89 98.89 + .02 98.94 98.09  1,495
Sept  ....  ....  ....  98.77 + .02 98.82 98.00    743
Dec   ....  ....  ....  98.65 + .02 98.70 97.92    570
Mr01  ....  ....  ....  98.54 + .02 98.59 98.07    573
Est vol 2,004; vol Mon 2,504; open int 83,474, −202.
SHORT STERLING (LIFFE)-£500,000; pts of 100%
                                     Lifetime      Open
     Open  High  Low  Settle Change High   Low  Interest
Sept 92.24 92.25 92.23 92.24 + 0   93.08 91.30 177,158
Dec  92.35 92.36 92.32 92.35 + 0   93.25 91.27 178,459
Mr99 92.54 92.56 92.52 92.55 + .01 93.45 91.45 142,425
June 92.76 92.80 92.75 92.78 + .01 93.61 91.53 162,211
Sept 92.97 93.00 92.95 92.98 + .01 93.70 91.92  99,249
Dec  93.08 93.12 93.08 93.11 + .01 93.76 91.94 119,733
```

Table 4.5 Interest Rate Futures Quotes from *The Wall Street Journal*, August 5, 1998 (Continued)

Mr00	93.26	93.30	93.26	93.29	+	.02	93.83	91.96	98,931
June	93.35	93.40	93.34	93.40	+	.03	93.91	92.47	66,746
Sept	93.45	93.48	93.44	93.47	+	.03	93.96	93.01	44,354
Dec	93.50	93.55	93.50	93.53	+	.03	94.01	93.22	28,214
Mr01	93.58	93.61	93.57	93.61	+	.03	94.06	93.29	20,288
June	93.63	93.64	93.62	93.65	+	.03	93.69	93.37	7,912
Mr02	....	....	....	93.81	+	.02	93.75	93.58	401

Est vol 91,655; vol Mon 129,076; open int 1,146,156, −2,457.

LONG GILT (LIFFE) (Decimal)-£50,000; pts of 100%

Sept	109.54	109.64	109.38	109.59	+	.10	110.86	107.59	160,314
Dec	109.60	109.62	109.60	109.75	+	.10	109.68	107.90	1,111

Est vol 50,032; vol Mon 61,271; open int 161,425, +4,843.

5 YR. GILT (LIFFE)-£50,000; pts of 100%

Sept	103.60	103.60	103.49	103.50	+	0	104.70	102.35	2,316

Est vol 187; vol Mon 22; open int 2,316, −2.

3-MONTH EUROMARK (LIFFE) DM 1,000,000; pts of 100%

Aug	96.46	96.46	96.46	96.46	+	0	96.46	96.28	16,921
Sept	96.42	96.43	96.41	96.42	+	0	96.43	93.38	482,497
Oct	96.31	96.31	96.31	96.31	+	.01	96.31	96.28	8,250
Dec	96.17	96.18	96.17	96.18	+	.01	96.19	93.40	504,115
Mr99	96.09	96.11	96.08	96.10	+	.01	96.11	93.24	464,759
June	95.98	96.00	95.97	95.98	+	.01	96.00	93.29	215,246
Sept	95.88	95.89	95.88	95.89	+	.01	95.89	93.80	193,389
Dec	95.74	95.74	95.73	95.74	+	0	95.75	94.19	197,221
Mr00	95.72	95.72	95.71	95.72	+	.01	95.72	94.24	161,169
June	95.64	95.64	95.63	95.64	+	.01	95.64	93.97	85,671
Sept	95.56	95.57	95.56	95.57	+	.01	95.57	93.84	83,640
Dec	95.48	95.48	95.47	95.48	+	.01	95.49	93.68	21,199
Mr01	95.44	95.44	95.43	95.44	+	.01	95.44	93.50	27,969
June	95.39	95.39	95.38	95.38	+	.01	95.39	93.85	11,893
Sept	95.32	95.32	95.32	95.32	+	.01	95.32	94.01	5,101
Dec	95.22	95.22	95.22	95.22	+	.01	95.22	94.50	3,956
Mr02	95.19	95.19	95.18	95.19	+	.01	95.19	94.75	1,606
June	....	....	....	95.14	+	.01	95.10	94.93	348

Est vol 144,701; vol Mon 119,040; open int 2,484,950, +7,591.

3-MONTH EUROSWISS (LIFFE) SFr 1,000,000; pts of 100%

Sept	98.00	98.01	97.96	98.00	−	.01	98.77	97.10	87,944
Dec	97.78	97.79	97.74	97.78	−	.01	98.60	96.99	46,244
Mr99	97.68	97.69	97.65	97.68	−	.01	98.48	96.90	28,111
June	97.55	97.57	97.54	97.56	−	.02	98.34	97.34	20,049
Sept	97.46	97.47	97.46	97.47	−	.02	97.94	97.34	11,819
Dec	97.33	97.33	97.31	97.33	−	.01	97.51	97.19	2,964
Mr00	97.22	97.22	97.22	97.24	−	.01	97.40	97.10	2,169
June	....	....	....	97.14	−	.01	97.35	96.99	1,063

Est vol 24,924; vol Mon 20,935; open int 200,363, +3,645.

3-MONTH EURO LIRA (LIFFE) ITL 1,000,000; pts of 100%

Sept	95.45	95.47	95.43	95.44	+	0	95.92	92.86	194,777
Dec	96.08	96.09	96.08	96.09	+	.01	96.12	92.84	160,012
Mr99	96.08	96.09	96.07	96.08	+	.01	96.09	92.78	226,933
June	95.99	96.01	95.96	95.97	+	.01	96.01	94.03	57,816
Sept	95.87	95.88	95.86	95.88	+	.01	95.89	94.41	31,735
Dec	95.73	95.74	95.72	95.73	+	0	95.74	94.91	38,922
Mr00	95.70	95.71	95.70	95.71	+	.01	95.71	95.23	21,185
June	....	....	....	95.63	+	.01	95.62	95.40	4,956

Est vol 28,608; vol Mon 26,166; open int 736,336, −536.

GERMAN GOVT. BOND (LIFFE) 250,000 marks; pts of 100%

Sept	109.55	109.84	109.55	109.75	+	.21	109.84	105.70	72,405
Dec	....	....	....	109.02	+	.22	108.62	107.21	453

Est vol 6,676; vol Mon 8,175; open int 72,858, +1,006.

ITALIAN GOVT. BOND (LIFFE) ITL 200,000,000; pts of 100%

Sept	121.41	121.60	121.40	121.48	+	.15	121.60	118.15	100,554
Dec	107.72	107.82	107.72	107.79	+	.16	107.82	106.35	8,035

Est vol 10,256; vol Mon 11,026; open int 108,589, +725.

CANADIAN BANKERS ACCEPTANCE (ME)-C$1,000,000

Aug	....	....	....	94.72	+	.04	94.96	94.72	701
Sept	94.62	94.65	94.61	94.64	+	.03	95.14	94.55	95,460
Oct	....	....	....	94.59	+	.04	94.76	94.69	260
Dec	94.46	94.51	94.46	94.51	+	.04	95.04	94.46	74,362
Mr99	94.43	94.48	94.43	94.47	+	.04	94.96	94.42	37,490
June	94.41	94.45	94.41	94.45	+	.04	94.90	94.40	20,473
Sept	94.40	94.41	94.40	94.42	+	.04	94.83	94.38	17,301
Dec	94.31	94.31	94.31	94.31	+	.03	94.74	94.30	8,718
Mr00	94.33	94.33	94.33	94.33	+	.03	94.71	94.31	4,051
June	....	....	....	94.30	+	.03	94.49	94.28	1,183

Est vol 30,833; vol Fr 0; open int 260,074, −2,371.

10 YR. CANADIAN GOVT. BONDS (ME)-C$100,000

Sept	124.26	124.43	124.17	124.32	+	.27	126.18	123.65	45,829

Est vol 6,190; vol Fr 0; open int 45,830, −85.

5 YR. FRENCH GOVT. BONDS (MATIF) FFr 500,000; 100ths of 100%

Sept	100.42	100.46	100.41	100.45	+	.07	104.63	99.00	36,103

Est vol 6,014; vol Mn 5,807; open int 36,103, −366.

10 YR. FRENCH GOVT. BONDS (MATIF) FFr 500,000; 100ths of 100%

Sept	....	....	....	105.47	+	.19	105.49	102.35	135,741
Dec	105.08	105.15	105.07	105.21	+	.18	105.15	103.80	221

Est vol 74,564; vol Mn 49,123; open int 135,962, +970.

PIBOR-3 MONTH (MATIF) FF5,000,000

Sept	....	....	....	96.40	....		96.41	92.90	52,692
Dec	96.18	96.19	96.18	96.19	+	.01	96.20	93.77	71,005
Mr99	96.09	96.10	96.08	96.09	....		96.13	93.52	50,734
June	95.98	96.00	95.97	95.98	+	.01	96.00	93.37	20,270
Sept	95.87	95.88	95.87	95.88	+	.01	95.89	94.23	18,817
Dec	95.74	95.74	95.72	95.74	....		95.75	94.45	12,666
Mr00	95.71	95.72	95.71	95.71	....		95.96	94.42	7,638
June	95.63	95.63	95.63	95.63	+	.01	95.66	94.48	3,585
Sept	....	....	....	95.55	+	.01	95.52	94.36	2,315
Dec	95.48	95.48	95.48	95.48	+	.02	95.48	95.00	870
Mr01	....	....	....	95.42	+	.01	95.28	95.28	322

Est vol 15,366; vol Mn 16,230; open int 240.994, +2,995.

3 YR. COMMONWEALTH T-BONDS (SFE)-A$100,000

Sept	94.82	94.82	94.77	94.81	+	.02	95.21	94.24	291,331

Est vol 19,987; vol Mn 1,194; open int 291,331, +12,860.

EUROYEN (SIMEX)-Yen 100,000,000 pts. of 100%

Sept	99.25	99.25	99.23	99.24	−	.15	99.49	96.50	130,816
Dec	99.26	99.26	99.23	99.25	−	.10	99.48	96.37	104,680
Mr99	99.27	99.28	99.25	99.26	−	.20	99.44	96.24	109,985
June	99.27	99.27	99.25	99.26	−	.15	99.38	96.65	75,609
Sept	99.23	99.23	99.20	99.21	−	.02	99.31	96.99	38,217
Dec	99.06	99.07	99.06	99.07	−	.01	99.16	97.23	46,125
Mr00	98.97	98.98	98.96	98.98	−	.01	99.07	97.10	36,644
June	....	....	....	98.87	−	.01	98.92	97.39	5,165
Sept	....	....	....	98.78	+	.01	98.81	97.94	2,173
Dec	....	....	....	98.66	+	.01	98.69	97.90	2,174
Mr01	....	....	....	98.54	+	.01	98.59	98.08	1,783
June	....	....	....	98.45	+	.01	99.40	98.26	441

Est vol 22,311; vol Mn 25,634; open int 553,812, −6,313.

BOBL-MED.TERM BOND (DTB)-DM 250,000; DM per $

Sept	106.03	106.03	105.94	106.20	+	.05	106.23	104.54	318,465

Est vol 91,808; vol Mn 135,234; open int 334,622, −13,817.

LONG TERM GOVT. BOND-BUND (DTB) DM 250,000; pts of 100%

Sept	109.70	109.34	109.19	109.85	+	.14	109.42	85.01	793,484
Dec	108.90	108.57	108.45	109.02	+	.23	108.66	107.93	48,329

Est vol 342,071; vol Mn 410,930; open int 841,853, −39,344.

Treasury notes futures (CBOT), and long gilt futures (LIFFE). Examples of the second type of contract are Eurodollar futures (CME), Euroyen futures (CME and SIMEX), and EuroSwiss futures(LIFFE). With the advent of the euro on January 1, 1999, several exchanges have started trading contracts on three-month Euribor, and contracts on eurobonds have been initiated. We explain how a typical bond futures contract works in section 4.11 by examining the Treasury bond futures contract traded on the CBOT. In section 4.12, we then explain how a typical short-term interest rate futures contract works by considering the Eurodollar futures contract traded on the CME.

4.11 TREASURY BOND FUTURES

In the Treasury bond futures contract, any government bond with more than 15 years to maturity on the first day of the delivery month and not callable within 15 years from that day can be delivered. As will be explained later, the exchange has developed a procedure for adjusting the price received by the party with the short position according to the particular bond delivered.[7] Treasury bond futures prices are quoted in a similar way to the prices of Treasury bonds. Thus the quote of 123-18 for the September contract in Table 4.5 indicates that the price is $123\frac{18}{32}$ per $100 face value of bonds. Each contract is for $100,000 face value of bonds.

Conversion Factors

As mentioned, there is a provision in the Treasury bond futures contract for the party with the short position to choose to deliver any bond with a maturity over 15 years and not callable within 15 years. When a particular bond is delivered, a parameter known as its *conversion factor* defines the price received by the party with the short position. The quoted price applicable to the delivery is the product of the conversion factor and the quoted futures price. Taking accrued interest into account, we have the following relationship for each $100 face value of the bond delivered:

$$
\begin{array}{c}
\text{cash received by party} \\
\text{with short position}
\end{array}
=
\begin{array}{c}
\text{quoted futures} \\
\text{price}
\end{array}
\times
\begin{array}{c}
\text{conversion factor} \\
\text{for bond delivered}
\end{array}
$$

$$
+
\begin{array}{c}
\text{accrued interest since last} \\
\text{coupon date on bond delivered}
\end{array}
$$

Suppose that the quoted futures price is 90-00, the conversion factor for the bond delivered is 1.3800, and the accrued interest on this bond at the time of delivery is $3.00 per $100 face value. The cash received by the party with the short position when it delivers the bond (and the cash paid by the party with the long position when it takes delivery) is

$$(1.38 \times 90.00) + 3.00 = \$127.20$$

per $100 face value. The party with the short position in one contract would, therefore, deliver bonds with face value of $100,000 and receive $127,200.

The conversion factor for a bond is equal to the value of the bond on the first day of the delivery month on the assumption that the interest rate for all maturities equals 8% per annum (with semiannual compounding). The bond maturity and the times to the coupon payment dates are rounded down to the nearest three months for the purposes of the calculation. This enables the CBOT to produce comprehensive tables. If, after rounding, the bond lasts for an exact number of half years, the first coupon is assumed to be paid in six months. If, after rounding, the bond does not last

---

[7]The Treasury note futures contract shown in Table 4.5 works similarly to the Treasury bond futures contract, except that the maturity of the bond delivered must be between $6\frac{1}{2}$ and 10 years.

for an exact number of six months (i.e., there is an extra three months), the first coupon is assumed to be paid after three months and accrued interest is subtracted.

> **Example 4.2**   Consider a 14% coupon bond with 20 years and two months to maturity. For the purposes of calculating the conversion factor, the bond is assumed to have exactly 20 years to maturity. The first coupon payment is assumed to be made after six months. Coupon payments are then assumed to be made at six-month intervals until the end of the 20 years, when the principal payment is made. We will work in terms of a $100 face value bond. On the assumption that the discount rate is 8% per annum with semiannual compounding (or 4% per six months), the value of the bond is
>
> $$\sum_{i=1}^{40} \frac{7}{1.04^i} + \frac{100}{1.04^{40}} = 159.38$$
>
> Dividing by the face value, the credit conversion factor is 1.5938.

> **Example 4.3**   Consider a 14% coupon bond with 18 years and four months to maturity. For the purposes of calculating the conversion factor, the bond is assumed to have exactly 18 years and three months to maturity. Discounting all the payments back to a point in time three months from today gives a value of
>
> $$7 + \sum_{i=1}^{36} \frac{7}{1.04^i} + \frac{100}{1.04^{36}} = 163.72$$
>
> The interest rate for a three-month period is $\sqrt{1.04} - 1$ or 1.9804%. Hence, discounting back to the present gives the bond's value as $163.72/1.019804 = 160.55$. Subtracting the accrued interest of 3.5, this becomes 157.05. The conversion factor is, therefore, 1.5705.

Cheapest-to-Deliver Bond

At any given time, there are many bonds that can be delivered in the CBOT Treasury bond futures contract. These vary widely as far as coupon and maturity are concerned. The party with the short position can choose which of the available bonds is "cheapest" to deliver. Because the party with the short position receives

$$(\text{quoted futures price} \times \text{conversion factor}) + \text{accrued interest}$$

and the cost of purchasing a bond is

$$\text{quoted price} + \text{accrued interest}$$

the cheapest-to-deliver bond is the one for which

$$\genfrac{}{}{0pt}{}{\text{quoted}}{\text{price}} - \left(\genfrac{}{}{0pt}{}{\text{quoted futures}}{\text{price}} \times \genfrac{}{}{0pt}{}{\text{conversion}}{\text{factor}} \right)$$

is least. This can be found by examining each of the bonds in turn.

> **Example 4.4**   The party with the short position has decided to deliver and is trying to choose between the three bonds in Table 4.6. Assume that the current quoted futures price is 93-08, or 93.25. The cost of delivering each of the bonds is as follows:

Bond 1:   99.50 − (93.25 × 1.0382) = 2.69
Bond 2: 143.50 − (93.25 × 1.5188) = 1.87
Bond 3: 119.75 − (93.25 × 1.2615) = 2.12

The cheapest-to-deliver bond is bond 2.

Table 4.6   Deliverable Bonds in Example 4.4

Bond	Quoted Price	Conversion Factor
1	99.50	1.0382
2	143.50	1.5188
3	119.75	1.2615

A number of factors determine the cheapest-to-deliver bond. When yields are in excess of 8%, there is a tendency for the conversion factor system to favor the delivery of low-coupon, long-maturity bonds. When yields are less than 8%, there is a tendency for it to favor the delivery of high-coupon, short-maturity bonds. Also, when the yield curve is upward sloping, there is a tendency for bonds with a long time to maturity to be favored; whereas when it is downward sloping, there is a tendency for bonds with a short time to maturity to be delivered. Finally, some bonds tend to sell for more than their theoretical value. Examples are low-coupon bonds and bonds where the coupons can be stripped from the bond. These bonds are unlikely to prove to be cheapest to deliver in any circumstances.

The Wild Card Play

Trading in the CBOT Treasury bond futures contracts ceases at 2 p.m. (Chicago time). However, Treasury bonds themselves continue trading until 4 p.m. Furthermore, the party with the short position has until 8 p.m. to issue to the clearinghouse a notice of intention to deliver. If the notice is issued, the invoice price is calculated on the basis of the settlement price that day. This is the price at which trading was being done just before the bell at 2 p.m.

This gives the party with the short position an option known as a *wild card play*. If bond prices decline after 2 p.m., the party can issue a notice of intention to deliver and proceed to buy cheapest-to-deliver bonds in preparation for delivery. If the bond price does not decline, the party with the short position keeps the position open and waits until the next day when the same strategy can be used.

Like the other options open to the party with the short position, the wild card option is not free. Its value is reflected in the futures price, which is lower than it would be without the option.

Determining the Quoted Futures Price

An exact theoretical futures price for the Treasury bond contract is difficult to determine because the short party's options concerned with the timing of delivery and choice of the bond that is delivered cannot easily be valued. However, if we assume that both the cheapest-to-deliver bond and the delivery date are known, the Treasury bond futures contract is a futures contract on a security providing the holder with known income. Equation (3.6) then shows that today's futures price, F_0, is related to today's spot bond price, B, by

$$F_0 = (B - I)e^{rT} \tag{4.5}$$

where I is the present value of the coupons during the life of the futures contract, T is the time when the futures contract matures, and r is the risk-free interest rate applicable to an investment maturing at time T.

In equation (4.5), F_0 is the cash futures price and B is the cash bond price. The correct procedure, therefore, is as follows:

1. Calculate the cash price of the cheapest-to-deliver bond from the quoted price.
2. Calculate the cash futures price from the cash bond price using equation (4.5).
3. Calculate the quoted futures price from the cash futures price.
4. Divide the quoted futures price by the conversion factor to allow for the difference between the cheapest-to-deliver bond and the standard 15-year 8% bond.

The procedure is best illustrated with an example.

Example 4.5   Suppose that in a T-bond futures contract, it is known that the cheapest-to-deliver bond will be a 12% coupon bond with a conversion factor of 1.4000. Suppose also that it is known that delivery will take place in 270 days' time. Coupons are payable semiannually on the bond. As illustrated in Figure 4.4, the last coupon date was 60 days ago, the next coupon date is in 122 days' time, and the next-but-one coupon date is in 305 days' time. The term structure is flat and the rate of interest (with continuous compounding) is 10% per annum. We assume that the current quoted bond price is $120. (This is for a bond with a face value of $100.) The cash price of the bond is obtained by adding to this quoted price the proportion of the next coupon payment that accrues to the holder. The cash price is, therefore,

$$120 + \frac{60}{60 + 122} \times 6 = 121.978$$

A coupon payment of $6 will be received after 122 days ($= 0.3342$ year). The present value of this is

$$6e^{-0.3342 \times 0.1} = 5.803$$

The futures contract lasts for 270 days ($= 0.7397$ year). The cash futures price if the contract were written on the 12% bond, therefore, would be

$$(121.978 - 5.803)e^{0.7397 \times 0.1} = 125.094$$

Figure 4.4   Time chart for Example 4.5.

At delivery, there are 148 days of accrued interest. The quoted futures price if the contract were written on the 12% bond would, therefore, be

$$125.094 - 6 \times \frac{148}{148 + 35} = 120.242$$

The contract is in fact written on a standard 8% bond, and 1.4000 standard bonds are considered equivalent to each 12% bond. The quoted futures price should, therefore, be

$$\frac{120.242}{1.4000} = 85.887$$

4.12 EURODOLLAR FUTURES

The most popular of the futures contracts on short-term interest rates is the three-month Eurodollar futures contract traded on the CME. A Eurodollar is a dollar deposited in a U.S. or foreign bank outside the United States. The three-month Eurodollar interest rate is the rate of interest earned on Eurodollars deposited for three months by one bank with another bank. It is the same as the three-month London Interbank Offer Rate (LIBOR) mentioned earlier in this chapter.

Three-month Eurodollar futures contracts trade with delivery months of March, June, September, and December up to ten years into the future. In addition, as can be seen from Table 4.5, the CME trades short-maturity contracts with other delivery months. The variable underlying the contract is the Eurodollar interest rate applicable to a 90-day period beginning on the third Wednesday of the delivery month.

If Z is the quoted price for a Eurodollar futures contract, the contract price is

$$10,000[100 - 0.25(100 - Z)] \tag{4.6}$$

Thus, the quote of 94.32 for the September 1998 contract in Table 4.5 corresponds to a contract price of

$$10,000[100 - 0.25(100 - 94.32)] = \$985,800$$

It can be seen from equation (4.6) that a change of one basis point, or 0.01, in a Eurodollar futures quote corresponds to a contract price change of $25.

When the third Wednesday of the delivery month is reached and the actual interest rate for the 90-day period is known, the contract is settled in cash. The final marking to market sets the futures price equal to $100 - R$, where R is the 90-day Eurodollar interest rate expressed with quarterly compounding and an actual/360 day count convention. Thus, if the 90-day Eurodollar interest rate underlying the contract proves to be 8%, the final marking to market is 92 and the final contract price is

$$10,000[100 - 0.25(100 - 92)] = \$980,000$$

Forward Interest Rates

If a futures contract were settled at the end of its life, rather than being marked to market daily, a Eurodollar futures quote of Z would mean that the forward interest rate is $100 - Z$ for the three month period following the third Wednesday of the delivery month. Thus, the quote of 94.32 for the September 1998 contract in Table 4.5 would imply a forward rate of 5.68%, for a 90-day period starting on the third Wednesday in September. (The day count convention is actual/360 and the compounding frequency is every 90 days.)

As pointed out in section 3.6, futures prices and forward prices are not exactly equal and the difference between the two is greatest for long-dated contracts. It is, therefore, dangerous to assume that relatively long-dated Eurodollar futures prices can be translated into forward rates in the way that has just been described.

The forward rate is less than the futures rate.[8] Analysts make what is termed a *convexity adjustment* to convert Eurodollar futures rates to forward interest rates. One way this is done is by using the formula

$$\text{Forward Rate} = \text{Futures Rate} - \frac{1}{2}\sigma^2 t_1 t_2$$

where t_1 is the time to maturity of the futures contract, t_2 is the time to the maturity of the rate underlying the futures contract, and σ is the standard deviation of the change in the short-term interest rate in one year. Both rates are expressed with continuous compounding.[9] A typical value for σ is 1.2%, or 0.012.

> **Example 4.6** Consider the situation where $\sigma = 0.012$ and we wish to calculate a forward rate when the eight-year Eurodollar futures price is 94. In this case $t_1 = 8$, $t_2 = 8.25$, and the convexity adjustment is
>
> $$\frac{1}{2} \times 0.012^2 \times 8 \times 8.25 = 0.00475$$
>
> or 0.475%. The futures rate is 6% per annum with quarterly compounding, or 5.96% with continuous compounding. The forward rate is, therefore, $5.96 - 0.475 = 5.485\%$ per annum with continuous compounding. Note that the convexity adjustment is roughly proportional to the square of the time to maturity of the futures contract. Thus the convexity adjustment for the eight-year contract is approximately four times that used for the four-year contract.

4.13   DURATION

Duration is an important concept in the use of interest rate futures for hedging. The duration of a bond is a measure of how long, on average, the holder of the bond has to wait before receiving cash payments. A zero-coupon bond that matures in n years

---

[8] Arguments similar to those in section 3.6 can be used to show this is true. See Problem 4.26.

[9] This formula comes from the Ho–Lee interest rate model. which is covered in chapter 21.

has a duration of n years. However, a coupon-bearing bond maturing in n years has a duration of less than n years. This is because some of the cash payments are received by the holder prior to year n.

Suppose that a bond provides the holder with payments c_i at time t_i ($1 \leq i \leq n$). The bond's price, B, and its continuously compounded yield, y, are related by

$$B = \sum_{i=1}^{n} c_i e^{-yt_i} \tag{4.7}$$

The duration, D, of the bond is defined as

$$D = \frac{\sum_{i=1}^{n} t_i c_i e^{-yt_i}}{B} \tag{4.8}$$

This can be written

$$D = \sum_{i=1}^{n} t_i \left[\frac{c_i e^{-yt_i}}{B} \right]$$

The term in square brackets is the ratio of the present value of the payment at time t_i to the bond price. The bond price is the present value of all payments. The duration is, therefore, a weighted average of the times when payments are made, with the weight applied to time t_i being equal to the proportion of the bond's total present value provided by the payment at time t_i. The sum of the weights is 1.0. We now show why duration is an important concept in hedging.

From equation (4.7),

$$\frac{\partial B}{\partial y} = -\sum_{i=1}^{n} c_i t_i e^{-yt_i} \tag{4.9}$$

and from equation (4.8) this can be written

$$\frac{\partial B}{\partial y} = -BD \tag{4.10}$$

If we make a small parallel shift to the yield curve, increasing all interest rates by a small amount, Δy, the yields on all bonds also increase by Δy. Equation (4.10) shows that the bond's price increases by ΔB, where

$$\frac{\Delta B}{\Delta y} = -BD$$

or

$$\frac{\Delta B}{B} = -D\Delta y \tag{4.11}$$

This shows that the percentage change in a bond price is equal to its duration multiplied by the size of the parallel shift in the yield curve.

Table 4.7   Calculation of Duration

Time (yrs.)	Payment ($)	Present Value	Weight	Time × Weight
0.5	5	4.709	0.050	0.025
1.0	5	4.435	0.047	0.047
1.5	5	4.176	0.044	0.066
2.0	5	3.933	0.042	0.084
2.5	5	3.704	0.039	0.098
3.0	105	73.256	0.778	2.334
Total	130	94.213	1.000	2.654

Example 4.7   Consider a three-year 10% coupon bond with a face value of $100. Suppose that the yield on the bond is 12% per annum with continuous compounding. This means that $y = 0.12$. Coupon payments of $5 are made every six months. Table 4.7 shows the calculations necessary to determine the bond's duration. The present values of the payments using the yield as the discount rate are shown in column three. (For example, the present value of the first payment is $5e^{-0.12 \times 0.5} = 4.709$.) The sum of the numbers in column three is the bond's price of $94.213. The weights are calculated by dividing the numbers in column three by 94.213. The sum of the numbers in column five gives the duration as 2.654 years. From equation (4.11),

$$\Delta B = -94.213 \times 2.654 \Delta y$$

that is,

$$\Delta B = -250.04 \Delta y$$

If $\Delta y = +0.001$ so that y increases to 0.121, this formula indicates that we expect ΔB to be -0.25. In other words, we expect the bond price to go down to $94.213 - 0.250 = 93.963$. By recomputing the bond price for a yield of 12.1%, the reader can verify that this is indeed what happens.

The duration of a bond portfolio can be defined as a weighted average of the durations of the individual bonds in the portfolio with the weights being proportional to the bond prices. Equation (4.11) then shows that the proportional effect on a portfolio of a parallel shift of Δy in the yield curve is the duration of the portfolio multiplied by Δy.

The preceding analysis is based on the assumption that y is expressed with continuous compounding. If y is expressed with annual compounding, a similar analysis to that given above shows that equation (4.11) becomes

$$\Delta B = -\frac{BD \Delta y}{1 + y}$$

More generally, if y is expressed with a compounding frequency of m times per year,

$$\Delta B = -\frac{BD\Delta y}{1 + y/m}$$

The variable D^* defined by

$$D^* = \frac{D}{1 + y/m}$$

is sometimes referred to as *modified duration*. It has the property that

$$\Delta B = -BD^*\Delta y \tag{4.12}$$

when y is expressed with a compounding frequency of m times per year.

It is worth noting that the duration concept can be used for assets other than bonds. Suppose that B is the price of an instrument that depends, in some way, on the level of interest rates. Define Δy as a small parallel shift in the zero curve and ΔB to be the impact of this shift on B. We can define the duration of the instrument as

$$-\frac{1}{B}\frac{\Delta B}{\Delta y}$$

The relation in equation (4.11) then holds.

4.14 DURATION-BASED HEDGING STRATEGIES

Consider the situation where a position in an interest-rate-dependent asset such as a bond portfolio or a money market security is being hedged using an interest rate futures contract. Define

F_C: Contract price for the interest rate futures contract.

D_F: Duration of the asset underlying the futures contract at the maturity of the futures contract.

P: Forward value of the portfolio being hedged at the maturity of the hedge.[10]

D_P: Duration of the portfolio at the maturity of the hedge.

We assume that the change in the yield, Δy, is the same for all maturities, which means that only parallel shifts in the yield curve can occur. It is approximately true that

$$\Delta P = -PD_P\Delta y$$

To a reasonable approximation, it is also true that

$$\Delta F_C = -F_C D_F \Delta y$$

---

[10]It is usually a reasonable approximation to assume that the forward value of the portfolio equals its value today.

The number of contracts required to hedge against an uncertain Δy is, therefore,

$$N^* = \frac{PD_P}{F_C D_F} \tag{4.13}$$

This is the *duration-based hedge ratio*. It is sometimes also called the *price sensitivity hedge ratio.*[11] Using it has the effect of making the duration of the entire position zero.

When the hedging instrument is a Treasury bond futures contract, the hedger must base D_F on an assumption that one particular bond will be delivered. This means that the hedger must estimate which of the available bonds is likely to be cheapest to deliver at the time the hedge is put in place. If, subsequently, the interest rate environment changes so that it looks as though a different bond will be cheapest to deliver, the hedge has to be adjusted and its performance may be worse than anticipated.

> **Example 4.8**   It is August 2 and a fund manager with $10 million invested in government bonds is concerned that interest rates are expected to be highly volatile over the next three months. The fund manager decides to use the December T-bond futures contract to hedge the value of the portfolio. The current futures price is 93-02, or 93.0625. Because each contract is for the delivery of $100,000 face value of bonds, the futures contract price is $93,062.50.
>
> We suppose that the duration of the bond portfolio in three months will be 6.80 years. The cheapest-to-deliver bond in the T-bond contract is expected to be a 20-year 12% per annum coupon bond. The yield on this bond is currently 8.80% per annum, and the duration will be 9.20 years at maturity of the futures contract.
>
> The fund manager requires a short position in T-bond futures to hedge the bond portfolio. If interest rates go up, a gain will be made on the short futures position and a loss will be made on the bond portfolio. If interest rates decrease, a loss will be made on the short position, but there will be a gain on the bond portfolio. The number of bond futures contracts that should be shorted can be calculated from equation (4.13) as
>
> $$\frac{10,000,000}{93,062.50} \times \frac{6.80}{9.20} = 79.42$$
>
> Rounding to the nearest whole number, the portfolio manager should short 79 contracts.

4.15   LIMITATIONS OF DURATION

The duration concept provides a simple approach to interest rate risk management. However, the hedge to which it gives rise is far from perfect. There are two main reasons for this. The first concerns a concept known as *convexity*. The second concerns the underlying assumption of parallel shifts in the yield curve.

---

[11] For a more detailed discussion of equation (4.13) together with the tailing and other adjustments that can be made, see R. Rendleman, "Duration-Based Hedging with Treasury Bond Futures," Working paper, Kenan-Flagler Business School, University of North Carolina.

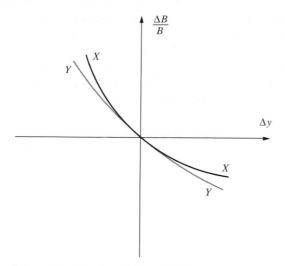

Figure 4.5   Bond portfolios with different convexities.

Convexity

For very small parallel shifts in the yield curve, the change in value of a portfolio depends solely on its duration. When moderate or large changes in interest rates are considered, a factor known as *convexity* is important. Figure 4.5 shows the relationship between the percentage change in value and change in yield, Δy, for two portfolios having the same duration. The gradients of the two curves are the same when $\Delta y = 0$ (and equal to minus the duration of the portfolio). This means that both portfolios change in value by the same percentage for small yield changes, which is consistent with equation (4.11). For large interest rate changes, the portfolios behave differently. Portfolio X has more convexity (or curvature) than portfolio Y. Its value increases by a greater percentage amount than that of portfolio Y when yields decline, and its value decreases by less than that of portfolio Y when yields increase.

A measure of convexity is

$$C = \frac{1}{B}\frac{\partial^2 B}{\partial y^2} = \frac{\sum_{i=1}^{n} c_i t_i^2 e^{-yt_i}}{B}$$

The convexity of a bond portfolio tends to be greatest when the portfolio provides payments evenly over a long period of time. It is least when the payments are concentrated around one particular point in time.

When convexity is taken into account, it can be shown that equation (4.11) becomes

$$\frac{\Delta B}{B} = -D\Delta y + \frac{1}{2}C\Delta y^2$$

Nonparallel Shifts

One serious problem with the duration concept is that it assumes all interest rates change by the same amount. In practice, short-term rates are usually more volatile than, and are not highly correlated with, long-term rates. Sometimes it even happens that short- and long-term rates move in opposite directions to each other. For this reason, financial institutions often hedge their interest rate exposure by dividing the zero-coupon yield curve into segments and ensuring that they are hedged against a movement in each segment. Suppose that the ith segment is the part of the zero-coupon yield curve between time t_i and t_{i+1}. A financial institution would examine the effect of a small increase, Δy, in all the zero-coupon yields for maturities between t_i and t_{i+1} while keeping the rest of the zero-coupon yield curve unchanged. If the exposure were unacceptable, trades would be undertaken in carefully selected instruments to reduce it. In the context of a bank managing a portfolio of assets and liabilities, this approach is sometimes referred to as *GAP management*.

SUMMARY

Many different types of interest rates are important in financial markets. The n-year zero rate or n-year spot rate is the rate applicable to an investment lasting for n years when all of the return is realized at the end. Forward rates are the rates applicable to future periods of time as implied by today's zero rates. The par yield on a bond of a certain maturity is the coupon rate that causes the bond to sell for its par value.

Interest rate markets are riddled with conventions. These conventions include the compounding frequency with which rates are quoted, the day count conventions used for bonds and money market instruments, and the ways in which prices are quoted for bonds and money market instruments. The conventions vary from country to country. It is important to have a full understanding of the relevant conventions before carrying out or recommending trades in a particular market.

The two most popular interest rate futures contracts in the United States are the Treasury bond and Eurodollar contracts. In the Treasury bond futures contract, any bond with a maturity of more than 15 years and not callable within 15 years can be delivered. The Eurodollar futures contract is settled in cash. The underlying variable is the three-month Eurodollar interest rate. This is also known as the three-month LIBOR rate. It is the rate paid on deposits in the interbank market.

In the Treasury bond futures contract, the party with the short position has a number of interesting delivery options:

1. Delivery can be made on any day during the delivery month.
2. There are a number of alternative bonds that can be delivered.
3. On any day during the delivery month, the notice of intention to deliver at the 2 p.m. settlement price can be made any time up to 8 p.m.

These options all tend to reduce the futures price.

The concept of duration is important in hedging interest rate risk. Duration measures how long, on average, an investor has to wait before receiving payments. A key result is

$$\Delta B = -BD\Delta y$$

where B is a bond price, D is its duration, Δy is a small change in its yield (continuously compounded), and ΔB is the resultant small change in B. The equation enables a hedger to assess the sensitivity of a bond to small changes in its yield. It also enables the hedger to assess the sensitivity of an interest rate futures price to small changes in the yield of the underlying bond. If the hedger is prepared to assume that Δy is the same for all bonds, the result enables the hedger to calculate the number of futures contracts necessary to protect a bond or bond portfolio against small changes in interest rates.

The key assumption underlying duration-based hedging is that all interest rates change by the same amount. This means that only parallel shifts in the term structure are allowed for. In practice, short-term interest rates are generally more volatile than long-term interest rates, and hedge performance is liable to be poor if the duration of the bond underlying the futures contract and the duration of the asset being hedged are markedly different.

SUGGESTIONS FOR FURTHER READING

Allen, S. L., and A. D. Kleinstein. *Valuing Fixed Income Investments and Derivative Securities.* New York: New York Institute of Finance, 1991.

Chicago Board of Trade. *Interest Rate Futures for Institutional Investors.* Chicago: 1987.

Fabozzi, F. J. *Fixed Income Mathematics: Analytical and Statistical Techniques.* Chicago: Probus, 1993.

Fabozzi, F. J. *Handbook of Fixed Income Securities,* 5th ed. McGraw-Hill, 1997.

Fabozzi, F. J. *Valuation of Fixed Income Securities and Derivatives,* 3rd ed., Frank J. Fabozzi Associates, 1998.

Figlewski, S. *Hedging with Financial Futures for Institutional Investors.* Cambridge, Mass.: Ballinger, 1986.

Gay, G. D., R. W. Kolb, and R. Chiang. "Interest Rate Hedging: An Empirical Test of Alternative Strategies," *Journal of Financial Research,* 6 (Fall 1983), 187–97.

Klemkosky, R. C., and D. J. Lasser. "An Efficiency Analysis of the T-Bond Futures Market," *Journal of Futures Markets,* 5 (1985), 607–20.

Kolb, R. W. *Interest Rate Futures: A Comprehensive Introduction.* Richmond, Va.: R. F. Dame, 1982.

Kolb, R. W., and R. Chiang. "Improving Hedging Performance Using Interest Rate Futures," *Financial Management,* 10 (Autumn 1981), 72–79.

Resnick, B. G. "The Relationship between Futures Prices for U.S. Treasury Bonds," *Review of Research in Futures Markets,* 3 (1984), 88–104.

Resnick, B. G., and E. Hennigar. "The Relationship between Futures and Cash Prices for U.S. Treasury Bonds," *Review of Research in Futures Markets*, 2 (1983), 282–99.

Senchak, A. J., and J. C. Easterwood. "Cross Hedging CDs with Treasury Bill Futures," *Journal of Futures Markets*, 3 (1983), 429–38.

Stigum, M. *The Money Market*. Homewood, Ill.: Dow Jones-Irwin, 1983.

Veit, W. T., and W. W. Reiff. "Commercial Banks and Interest Rate Futures: A Hedging Survey," *Journal of Futures Markets*, 3 (1983), 283–93.

QUESTIONS AND PROBLEMS
(ANSWERS IN SOLUTIONS MANUAL)

4.1. Suppose that zero rates with continuous compounding are as follows:

Maturity (years)	Rate (% per annum)
1	8.0
2	7.5
3	7.2
4	7.0
5	6.9

Calculate forward interest rates for the second, third, fourth, and fifth years.

4.2. The term structure is upward sloping. Put the following in order of magnitude:
   (a) The five-year zero rate.
   (b) The yield on a five-year coupon-bearing bond.
   (c) The forward rate corresponding to the period between 5 and $5\frac{1}{4}$ years in the future.

   What is the answer to this question when the term structure is downward sloping?

4.3. The six-month and the one-year zero rates are both 10% per annum. For a bond that lasts 18 months and pays a coupon of 8% per annum (with a coupon payment having just been made), the yield is 10.4% per annum. What is the bond's price? What is the 18-month zero rate? All rates are quoted with semiannual compounding.

4.4. It is January 9, 2001. The price of a Treasury bond with a 12% coupon that matures on October 12, 2007, is quoted as 102-07. What is the cash price? The bond pays coupons on April 12 and October 12 each year.

4.5. The price of a 90-day Treasury bill is quoted as 10.00. What continuously compounded return does an investor earn on the Treasury bill for the 90-day period?

4.6. What assumptions does a duration-based hedging scheme make about the way that the term structure moves?

4.7. It is January 30. You are managing a bond portfolio worth $6 million. The average duration of the portfolio in six months will be 8.2 years. The September Treasury bond futures price is currently 108-15 and the cheapest-to-deliver bond will have a duration of 7.6 years when the futures contract matures. How should you hedge against changes in interest rates over the next seven months?

4.8. Suppose that zero interest rates with continuous compounding are as follows:

Maturity (years)	Rate (% per annum)
1	12.0
2	13.0
3	13.7
4	14.2
5	14.5

Calculate forward interest rates for the second, third, fourth, and fifth years.

4.9. Suppose that zero interest rates with continuous compounding are as follows:

Maturity (months)	Rate (% per annum)
3	8.0
6	8.2
9	8.4
12	8.5
15	8.6
18	8.7

Calculate forward interest rates for the second, third, fourth, fifth, and sixth quarters.

4.10. The cash prices of six-month and one-year Treasury bills are 94.0 and 89.0. A $1\frac{1}{2}$-year bond that will pay coupons of $4 every six months currently sells for $94.84. A two-year bond that will pay coupons of $5 every six months currently sells for $97.12. Calculate the six-month, one-year, $1\frac{1}{2}$-year, and two-year zero rates.

4.11. A 10-year 8% coupon bond currently sells for $90. A 10-year 4% coupon bond currently sells for $80. What is the 10-year zero rate? (*Hint:* Consider taking a long position in two of the 4% coupon bonds and a short position in one of the 8% coupon bonds.)

4.12. Explain carefully why liquidity preference theory is consistent with the observation that the term structure tends to be upward sloping more often than it is downward sloping.

4.13. It is May 5, 2001. The quoted price of a government bond with a 12% coupon that matures on July 27, 2009, is 110-17. What is the cash price? The bond pays coupons on January 27 and July 27 each year.

4.14. Suppose that the T-bond futures price is 101-12. Which of the following four bonds is cheapest to deliver?

Bond	Price	Conversion Factor
1	125-05	1.2131
2	142-15	1.3792
3	115-31	1.1149
4	144-02	1.4026

4.15. It is July 30, 2000. The cheapest-to-deliver bond in a September 2000 Treasury bond futures contract is a 13% coupon bond, and delivery is expected to be made on September 30, 2000. Coupon payments on the bond are made on February 4 and August 4 each year. The term structure is flat and the rate of interest with semiannual compounding is 12% per annum. The conversion factor for the bond is 1.5. The current quoted bond price is $110. Calculate the quoted futures price for the contract.

4.16. An investor is looking for arbitrage opportunities in the Treasury bond futures market. What complications are created by the fact that the party with a short position can choose to deliver any bond with a maturity of over 15 years?

4.17. Assuming that zero rates are as in Problem 4.9, what is the value of an FRA that enables the holder to earn 9.5% for a three-month period starting in one year on a principal of $1,000,000. The interest rate is expressed with quarterly compounding.

4.18. Suppose that the nine-month interest rate is 8% per annum and the six-month interest rate is 7.5% per annum (both with continuous compounding). Estimate the futures price of a 90-day Treasury bill with a face value of $1 million for delivery in six months.

4.19. A five-year bond with a yield of 11% (continuously compounded) pays an 8% coupon at the end of each year.
   (a) What is the bond's price?
   (b) What is the bond's duration?
   (c) Use the duration to calculate the effect on the bond's price of a 0.2% decrease in its yield.
   (d) Recalculate the bond's price on the basis of a 10.8% per annum yield and verify that the result is in agreement with your answer to (c).

4.20. Suppose that a bond portfolio with a duration of 12 years is hedged using a futures contract where the underlying asset has a duration of four years. What is likely to be the impact on the hedge if the 12-year rate is less volatile than the four-year rate?

4.21. Suppose that it is February 20 and a treasurer of a company realizes that on July 17, the company will have to issue $5 million of commercial paper with a maturity of 180 days. If the paper were issued today, it would realize $4,820,000. (In other words, the company would receive $4,820,000 for its paper and have to redeem it at $5,000,000 in 180 days' time.) The September Eurodollar futures price is quoted as 92.00. How should the treasurer hedge the company's exposure?

4.22. On August 1, a portfolio manager has a bond portfolio worth $10 million. The duration of the portfolio in two months will be 7.1 years. The December Treasury bond futures price is currently 91-12, and the cheapest-to-deliver bond will have a duration of 8.8 years in December. How should the portfolio manager immunize the portfolio against changes in interest rates over the next two months?

4.23. How can the portfolio manager change the duration of the portfolio to 3.0 years in Problem 4.22?

4.24. Between February 28, 2001, and March 1, 2001, you have a choice between owning a government bond paying a 10% coupon and a corporate bond paying a 10% coupon. Consider carefully the day count conventions discussed in section 4.8 and decide which of the two bonds you would prefer to own. Ignore the risk of default.

4.25. Prove that when a bond yield, y, is expressed with a compounding frequency of m times per year

$$\Delta B = -\frac{BD\Delta y}{1 + y/m}$$

where B is the price of the bond and D is its duration.

4.26. Explain why the forward interest rate is less than the corresponding futures interest rate calculated from a Eurodollar futures contract. Use the argument in section 3.6.

4.27. The three-month Eurodollar futures price for a contract maturing in six years is quoted as 95.20. The standard deviation of the change in the short-term interest rate in one year is 1.1%. Estimate the forward LIBOR interest rate for the period between 6.00 and 6.25 years in the future.

ASSIGNMENT QUESTIONS

4.28. Assume that a bank can borrow or lend money at the same interest rate in Eurodollar markets. The 90-day rate is 10% per annum and the 180-day rate is 10.2% per annum both expressed with continuous compounding. The Eurodollar futures price for a contract maturing in 90 days is quoted as 89.5. What arbitrage opportunities are open to the bank?

4.29. A Canadian company wishes to create a futures contract on Canadian LIBOR from a U.S. Eurodollar futures contract and forward contracts on foreign exchange. Using an example, explain how this can be done. For the purposes of this problem, assume that a futures contract is the same as a forward contract.

4.30. Portfolio A consists of a one-year zero-coupn bond with a face value of $2,000 and a 10-year zero-coupon bond with a face value of $6,000. Portfolio B consists of a 5.95 year zero-coupon bond with a face value of $5,000. The current yield on all bonds is 10% per annum.
(a) Show that both portfolios have the same duration.
(b) Show that the percentage changes in the values of the two portfolios for a 10-basis-point increase in yields is the same.
(c) What are the percentage changes in the values of the two portfolios for a 5% per annum increase in yields?
(d) Which portfolio has the higher convexity?

4.31. The following table gives the prices of bonds

Bond Principal ($)	Time to Maturity (years)	Annual Coupon ($)*	Bond Price ($)
100	0.50	0.0	98
100	1.00	0.0	95
100	1.50	6.2	101
100	2.00	8.0	104

*Half the stated coupon is assumed to be paid every six months.

(a) Calculate zero rates for maturities of 6 months, 12 months, 18 months, and 24 months.

(b) What are the forward rates for the periods: 6 months to 12 months, 12 months to 18 months, 18 months to 24 months?

(c) What are the 6-month, 12-month, 18-month, and 24-month par yields for bonds that provide semiannual coupon payments?

(d) Estimate the price and yield of a two-year bond providing a semiannual coupon of 7% per annum.

4.32. It is June 25, 1999. The futures price for the June 1999 CBOT bond futures contract is 118-23.

(a) Calculate the conversion factor for a bond maturing on January 1, 2015, paying a coupon of 10%.

(b) Calculate the conversion factor for a bond maturing on October 1, 2020, paying a coupon of 7%.

(c) Suppose that the quoted prices of the bonds in (a) and (b) are 144.00 and 112.00, respectively. Which bond is cheaper to deliver?

(d) Assuming that the cheapest-to-deliver bond is actually delivered, what is the cash price received for the bond?

4.33. A portfolio manager plans to use a Treasury bond futures contract to hedge a bond portfolio over the next three months. The portfolio is worth $100 million and will have a duration of 4.0 years in three months. The futures price is 122 and each futures contract is on $100,000 of bonds. The bond that is expected to be cheapest to deliver will have a duration of 9.0 years at the maturity of the futures contract. What position in futures contracts is required?

(a) What adjustments to the hedge are necessary if after one month the bond that is expected to be cheapest to deliver changes to one with a duration of 7 years?

(b) Suppose that all rates increase over the three months, but long-term rates increase less than short-term and medium-term rates. What is the effect of this on the performance of the hedge?

CHAPTER 5

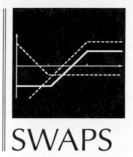

SWAPS

A swap is an agreement between two companies to exchange cash flows in the future. The agreement defines the dates when the cash flows are to be paid and the way that they are to be calculated. Usually the calculation of the cash flows involves the future values of one or more market variables.

A forward contract can be viewed as a simple example of a swap. Suppose it is March 1, 1999, and a company enters into a forward contract to buy 100 ounces of gold for $300 per ounce in one year. The company can sell the gold in one year as soon as it is received. The forward contract is, therefore, equivalent to a swap agreement where the company pays a cash flow of $30,000 on March 1, 2000, and receives a cash flow equal to $100S$ on the same date, where S is the market price of one ounce of gold.

Whereas a forward contract leads to the exchange of cash flows on just one future date, swaps typically lead to cash flow exchanges on several future dates. The first swap contracts were negotiated in the early 1980s. Since then, the market has grown very rapidly. Hundreds of billions of dollars of contracts are currently negotiated each year. In this chapter we examine how swaps are designed, how they are used, and how they can be valued. Most of our discussion will center on the two most popular types of swaps: interest rate swaps and currency swaps.

5.1 MECHANICS OF INTEREST RATE SWAPS

The most common type of swap is a "plain vanilla" interest rate swap. In this, company B agrees to pay company A cash flows equal to interest at a predetermined fixed rate on a notional principal for a number of years. At the same time, company A agrees to pay company B cash flows equal to interest at a floating rate on the same notional principal for the same period of time. The currencies of the two sets of cash flows are the same.

London Interbank Offer Rate

The floating rate in many interest rate swap agreements is the London Interbank Offer Rate (LIBOR), introduced in chapter 4. LIBOR is the rate of interest offered by banks on deposits from other banks in Eurocurrency markets. One-month LIBOR is the rate offered on one-month deposits; three-month LIBOR is the rate offered on

121

three-month deposits; and so on. LIBOR rates are determined by trading between banks and change continuously as economic conditions change. Just as prime is often the reference rate of interest for floating-rate loans in the domestic financial market, LIBOR is frequently a reference rate of interest for loans in international financial markets. To understand how it is used, consider a loan with a rate of interest specified as six-month LIBOR plus 0.5% per annum. The life of the loan is divided into six-month periods. For each period, the rate of interest is set at 0.5% per annum above the six-month LIBOR rate at the beginning of the period. Interest is paid at the end of the period.

An Interest Rate Swap Example

Consider a three-year swap initiated on March 1, 1999, in which company B agrees to pay to company A an interest rate of 5% per annum on a notional principal of $100 million and in return company A agrees to pay to company B the six-month LIBOR rate on the same notional principal. We assume the agreement specifies that payments are to be exchanged every six months and the 5% interest rate is quoted with semiannual compounding. This swap is represented diagrammatically in Figure 5.1.

The first exchange of payments would take place on September 1, 1999, six months after the initiation of the agreement. Company B would pay company A $2.5 million. This is the interest on the $100 million principal for six months at the rate of 5% per annum. Company A would pay company B interest on the $100 million principal at the six-month LIBOR rate prevailing six months prior to September 1, 1999—that is, on March 1, 1999. Suppose that six-month LIBOR rate on March 1, 1999, is 4.2% per annum. Company A pays company B $0.5 \times 0.042 \times \$100 = \$2.1$ million.[1] Note that there is no uncertainty about this first exchange of payments because it is determined by the LIBOR rate at the time the contract is entered into.

The second exchange of payments would take place on March 1, 2000, one year after the initiation of the agreement. Company B would pay $2.5 million to company A. Company A would pay interest on the $100 million principal to company B at the six-month LIBOR rate prevailing six months prior to March 1, 2000—that is, on September 1, 1999. Suppose that the six-month LIBOR rate on September 1, 1999, is 4.8% per annum. Company A pays $0.5 \times 0.048 \times \$100 = \$2.4$ million to company B.

Figure 5.1　Interest rate swap between companies A and B.

---

[1] Note that the calculations here are not perfectly accurate because they ignore day count and business day conventions. This point is discussed in more detail later in the chapter.

Table 5.1 Cash Flows (Millions of Dollars) to Company B in a $100 Million Three-Year Interest Rate Swap When a Fixed Rate of 5% Is Paid and LIBOR Is Received

Date	LIBOR Rate (%)	Floating Cash Flow Received	Fixed Cash Flow Paid	Net Cash Flow
March 1, 1999	4.20			
September 1, 1999	4.80	+2.10	−2.50	−0.40
March 1, 2000	5.30	+2.40	−2.50	−0.10
September 1, 2000	5.50	+2.65	−2.50	+0.15
March 1, 2001	5.60	+2.75	−2.50	+0.25
September 1, 2001	5.90	+2.80	−2.50	+0.30
March 1, 2002	6.40	+2.95	−2.50	+0.45

In total, there are six exchanges of payment on the swap. The fixed payments are always $2.5 million. The floating-rate payments on a payment date are calculated using the six-month LIBOR rate prevailing six months before the payment date. An interest rate swap is generally structured so that one side remits the difference between the two payments to the other side. In the example given, company B would pay company A $0.4 million (= $2.5 million − $2.1 million) on September 1, 1999, and $0.1 million (= $2.5 million − $2.4 million) on March 1, 2000.

Table 5.1 provides a complete example of the payments made under the swap for one particular set of six-month LIBOR rates. The table shows the swap cash flows from the perspective of company B. Note that the $100 million principal is used only for the calculation of interest payments. The principal itself is not exchanged. This is why it is termed the *notional principal*.

If the principal were exchanged at the end of the life of the swap, the nature of the deal would not be changed in any way. The principal is the same for both the fixed and floating payments. Exchanging $100 million for $100 million at the end of the life of the swap is a transaction that would have no financial value to either party. Table 5.2 shows the cash flows in Table 5.1 with a final exchange of principal added in. This provides an interesting way of viewing the swap. The cash flows in the third column of this table are the cash flows from a long position in a floating-rate bond. The cash flows in the fourth column of the table are the cash flows from a short position in a fixed-rate bond. The table shows that the swap can be regarded as the exchange of a fixed-rate bond for a floating-rate bond. Company B, whose position is described by Table 5.2, is long a floating-rate bond and short a fixed-rate bond. Company A is long a fixed-rate bond and short a floating-rate bond.

This characterization of the cash flows in the swap helps to explain why the floating rate in the swap is set six months before it is paid. On a floating-rate instrument, interest is generally set at the beginning of the period to which it will apply and is paid at the end of the period. The timing of the floating-rate payments in a "plain vanilla" interest-rate swap, such as the one in Table 5.2, reflects this.

Table 5.2   Cash Flows (Millions of Dollars) from Table 5.1 When There Is a Final Exchange of Principal

Date	LIBOR Rate (%)	Floating Cash Flow Received	Fixed Cash Flow Paid	Net Cash Flow
March 1, 1999	4.20			
September 1, 1999	4.80	+2.10	−2.50	−0.40
March 1, 2000	5.30	+2.40	−2.50	−0.10
September 1, 2000	5.50	+2.65	−2.50	+0.15
March 1, 2001	5.60	+2.75	−2.50	+0.25
September 1, 2001	5.90	+2.80	−2.50	+0.30
March 1, 2002	6.40	+102.95	−102.50	+0.45

Using the Swap to Transform a Liability

For company B, the swap could be used to transform a floating-rate loan into a fixed-rate loan. Suppose that company B has arranged to borrow $100 million at LIBOR plus 80 basis points. (One basis point is one-hundredth of 1% so the rate is LIBOR plus 0.8%.) After company B has entered into the swap, it has three sets of cash flows:

1. It pays LIBOR plus 0.8% to its outside lenders.
2. It receives LIBOR under the terms of the swap.
3. It pays 5% under the terms of the swap.

These three sets of cash flows net out to an interest rate payment of 5.8%. Thus, for company B the swap could have the effect of transforming borrowings at a floating rate of LIBOR plus 80 basis points into borrowings at a fixed rate of 5.8%.

For company A, the swap could have the effect of transforming a fixed-rate loan into a floating-rate loan. Suppose that company A has a three-year $100 million loan outstanding on which it pays 5.2% per annum. After it has entered into the swap, it has three sets of cash flows:

1. It pays 5.2% per annum to its outside lenders.
2. It pays LIBOR under the terms of the swap.
3. It receives 5% per annum under the terms of the swap.

These three sets of cash flows net out to an interest rate payment of LIBOR plus 0.2% (or LIBOR plus 20 basis points). Thus, for company A, the swap could have the effect of transforming borrowings at a fixed rate of 5.2% into borrowings at a floating rate of LIBOR plus 20 basis points. These potential uses of the swap by companies A and B are illustrated in Figure 5.2.

Using the Swap to Transform an Asset

Swaps can also be used to transform the nature of an asset. Consider company B in our example. The swap could have the effect of transforming an asset earning a fixed rate of interest into an asset earning a floating rate of interest. Suppose that company

5.2% 5%

LIBOR LIBOR + 0.8%

Figure 5.2 Companies A and B use the swap to transform a liability.

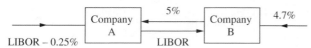

5% 4.7%

LIBOR − 0.25% LIBOR

Figure 5.3 Companies A and B use the swap to transform an asset.

B owns $100 million in bonds that will provide interest at 4.7% per annum over the next three years. After company B has entered into the swap, it has three sets of cash flows:

1. It receives 4.7% per annum on the bonds.
2. It receives LIBOR under the terms of the swap.
3. It pays 5% per annum under the terms of the swap.

These three sets of cash flows net out to an interest rate inflow of LIBOR minus 30 basis points. Thus, one possible use of the swap for company B is to transform an asset earning 4.7% per annum into an asset earning LIBOR minus 30 basis points.

Consider next company A. The swap could have the effect of transforming an asset earning a floating rate of interest into an asset earning a fixed rate of interest. Suppose that company A has an investment of $100 million that yields LIBOR minus 25 basis points. After it has entered into the swap, it has three sets of cash flows:

1. It receives LIBOR minus 25 basis points on its investment.
2. It pays LIBOR under the terms of the swap.
3. It receives 5% under the terms of the swap.

These three sets of cash flows net out to an interest rate inflow of 4.75% per annum. Thus, one possible use of the swap for company A is to transform an asset earning LIBOR minus 25 basis points into an asset earning 4.75% per annum. These potential uses of the swap by companies A and B are illustrated in Figure 5.3.

Role of Financial Intermediary

Usually, two nonfinancial companies do not get in touch directly to arrange a swap in the way indicated in Figures 5.2 and 5.3. They each deal with a financial intermediary such as a bank or other financial institution. "Plain vanilla" fixed-for-floating swaps on U.S. interest rates are usually structured so that the financial institution earns 3 to 4 basis points (0.03 to 0.04% per annum) on a pair of offsetting transactions.

Figure 5.4 shows what the role of the financial institution might be in the situation in Figure 5.2. The financial institution enters into two offsetting swap transactions

Figure 5.4   Interest rate swap from Figure 5.2 when financial institution is used.

Figure 5.5   Interest rate swap from Figure 5.3 when financial institution is used.

with companies A and B. Assuming that neither A nor B defaults, the financial institution is certain to make a profit of 0.03% (3 basis points) per year multiplied by the notional principal of $100 million. (This amounts to $30,000 per year for the three-year period.) Company B ends up borrowing at 5.815% (instead of 5.8%, as in Figure 5.2). Company A ends up borrowing at LIBOR plus 21.5 basis points (instead of at LIBOR plus 20 basis points, as in Figure 5.2).

Figure 5.5 illustrates the role of the financial institution in the situation in Figure 5.3. Again, the financial institution is certain to make a profit of 3 basis points if neither company defaults on the swap. Company B ends up earning LIBOR minus 31.5 basis points (instead of LIBOR minus 30 basis points, as in Figure 5.3). Company A ends up earning 4.735% (instead of 4.75%, as in Figure 5.3).

Note that in each case the financial institution has two separate contracts, one with company A and the other with company B. In most instances, company A will not even know that the financial institution has entered into an offsetting swap with company B, and vice versa. If one of the companies defaults, the financial institution still has to honor its agreement with the other company. The 3-basis-point spread earned by the financial institution is partly to compensate it for the default risk it is bearing.

Pricing Schedules

The fixed rate in a "plain vanilla" swap is sometimes quoted as a certain number of basis points above the Treasury note yield. Table 5.3 shows an example of an *indication pricing schedule* that might be used by swap traders working for financial institutions. It indicates the prices quoted to prospective counterparties. For example, it shows that in a five-year swap where the financial institution will pay fixed and receive six-month LIBOR, the fixed rate should be set 23 basis points above the current five-year Treasury note rate. The latter is 6.24% per annum so that the financial institution should set the fixed rate at 6.47% per annum. When it is negotiating a five-year swap where it will receive fixed and pay six-month LIBOR for five years, the schedule indicates that the institution should set the fixed rate at 27 basis points above the current five-year Treasury note rate, or at 6.51% per annum. The bank's profit, or

Maturity (years)	Bank Pays Fixed Rate	Bank Receives Fixed Rate	Current TN Rate (%)
Table 5.3	Sample Pricing Schedule for Interest Rate Swaps (TN = Treasury Note; bps = basis points)		
2	2-yr TN + 17 bps	2-yr TN + 20 bps	5.86
3	3-yr TN + 19 bps	3-yr TN + 22 bps	6.02
4	4-yr TN + 22 bps	4-yr TN + 26 bps	6.13
5	5-yr TN + 23 bps	5-yr TN + 27 bps	6.24
7	7-yr TN + 30 bps	7-yr TN + 33 bps	6.35
10	10-yr TN + 32 bps	10-yr TN + 36 bps	6.51

its bid-ask spread from negotiating two offsetting five-year swaps, would be 4 basis points (0.04%) per annum.[2]

The average of the bid and ask rates exchanged for floating is referred to as the *swap rate*. Thus, in Table 5.3 the five-year swap rate is 6.49%. The average excess of the fixed rate in a swap agreement over the corresponding Treasury rate is known as the *swap spread*. Thus, in Table 5.3 the five-year swap spread is 25 basis points. At any given time, swap spreads are determined by supply and demand. If more market participants want to receive fixed than receive floating, swap spreads tend to fall. If the reverse is true, swap spreads tend to rise. Table 5.3 would be updated regularly as market conditions changed.

Day Count and Business Day Conventions

The day count conventions discussed in chapter 4 affect payments on a swap, and some of the numbers calculated in the examples we have given so far do not exactly reflect the day count conventions. Consider, for example, the six-month LIBOR payments in Table 5.1. Because it is a money market rate, six-month LIBOR is quoted on an actual/360 basis. The first floating payment in Table 5.1, based on the LIBOR rate of 4.2%, is shown as $2.10 million. Because there are 184 days between March 1 and September 1, it should be

$$100 \times 0.042 \times \frac{184}{360} = 2.1467$$

In general, a LIBOR-based floating-rate cash flow on a swap payment date is calculated as $LRn/360$, where L is the principal, R is the relevant LIBOR rate, and n is the number of days since the last payment date.

The fixed rate that is paid in a swap transaction is similarly quoted with a particular day count basis being specified. As a result the fixed payments may not be exactly

[2]In the early days of swaps, bid-ask spreads as high as 100 basis points were possible. Now the market is much more competitive and, as mentioned earlier, the bid-ask spread on a vanilla deal is 3 to 4 basis points.

equal on each payment date. If the fixed rate is quoted as actual/365 or 30/360, it is not directly comparable with LIBOR since it applies to a full year. To make a six-month LIBOR rate comparable with a Treasury note rate in a 365-day year, either the six-month LIBOR rate must be multiplied by 365/360, or the Treasury note rate must be multiplied by 360/365.

Another complication is the way that holidays and weekends are handled. Cash flows in swap agreements are specified as occurring on particular days. If the day for a cash flow proves to be a weekend or holiday, a convention is needed to determine the actual payment day. This is known as the *business day convention*. The *following* business day convention means that if the day specified for a cash flow turns out to be a non-business day, the cash flow actually occurs on the next business day. In the case of the *modified following* business day convention, the cash flow occurs on the next business day except when that day falls in a different month. In the latter case, it occurs on the immediately preceding business day. *Preceding* and *modified preceding* business day conventions are defined analogously. In the preceding business day convention, a cash flow occurs on the specified day or the immediately preceding business day. In the modified preceding business day convention, the cash flow occurs on the next business day whenever the specified day is a nonbusiness day and the immediately preceding business day is in a different month.

For ease of exposition, we will continue to ignore day count and business day conventions in this book.

Warehousing

In practice, it is unlikely that two companies will contact a financial institution at the same time and want to take opposite positions in exactly the same swap. For this reason, a large financial institution is prepared to enter into a swap without having an offsetting swap with another counterparty. This is known as *warehousing* interest-rate swaps. The financial institution must carefully quantify and hedge the risks it is taking. Bonds, forward rate agreements, and interest rate futures are examples of the instruments that can be used for hedging.

5.2   THE COMPARATIVE ADVANTAGE ARGUMENT

An explanation commonly put forward to explain the popularity of swaps concerns comparative advantages. Consider the use of an interest-rate swap to transform a liability. Some companies, it is argued, have a comparative advantage when borrowing in fixed-rate markets, whereas other companies have a comparative advantage in floating-rate markets. To obtain a new loan, it makes sense for a company to go to the market where it has a comparative advantage. As a result, the company may borrow fixed when it wants floating, or borrow floating when it wants fixed. The swap is used to transform a fixed-rate loan into a floating-rate loan, or vice versa.

Table 5.4	Borrowing Rates That Provide a Basis for the Comparative Advantage Argument	
	Fixed	*Floating*
Company A	10.0%	6-month LIBOR + 0.3%
Company B	11.2%	6-month LIBOR + 1.0%

An Example

Suppose that two companies, A and B, both wish to borrow $10 million for five years and have been offered the rates shown in Table 5.4. We assume that company B wants to borrow at a fixed rate of interest, whereas company A wants to borrow floating funds at a rate linked to six-month LIBOR. Company B clearly has a worse credit rating than company A because it pays a higher rate of interest than company A in both fixed and floating markets.

A key feature of the rates offered to companies A and B is that the difference between the two fixed rates is greater than the difference between the two floating rates. Company B pays 1.2% per annum more than company A in fixed-rate markets and only 0.7% per annum more than company A in floating-rate markets. Company B appears to have a comparative advantage in floating-rate markets, whereas company A appears to have a comparative advantage in fixed-rate markets.[3] It is this apparent anomaly that can lead to a swap being negotiated. Company A borrows fixed-rate funds at 10% per annum. Company B borrows floating-rate funds at LIBOR plus 1% per annum. They then enter into a swap agreement to ensure that A ends up with floating-rate funds and B ends up with fixed-rate funds.

To understand how the swap might work, we first assume that A and B get in touch with each other directly. The sort of swap they might negotiate is shown in Figure 5.6. This is very similar to our example in Figure 5.2. Company A agrees to pay company B interest at six-month LIBOR on $10 million. In return, company B agrees to pay company A interest at a fixed rate of 9.95% per annum on $10 million.

Company A has three sets of interest-rate cash flows:

1. It pays 10% per annum to outside lenders.
2. It receives 9.95% per annum from B.
3. It pays LIBOR to B.

The net effect of the three cash flows is that A pays LIBOR plus 0.05% per annum. This is 0.25% per annum less than it would pay if it went directly to floating-rate

---

[3]Note that B's comparative advantage in floating-rate markets does not imply that B pays less than A in this market. It means that the extra amount that B pays over the amount paid by A is less in this market. One of my students summarized the situation as follows: "A pays more less in fixed-rate markets; B pays less more in floating-rate markets."

Figure 5.6   Swap agreement between A and B when rates in
Table 5.4 apply.

Figure 5.7   Swap agreement between A and B when rates in Table 5.4 apply and
a financial intermediary is involved.

markets. Company B also has three sets of interest rate cash flows:

1. It pays LIBOR + 1% per annum to outside lenders.
2. It receives LIBOR from A.
3. It pays 9.95% per annum to A.

The net effect of the three cash flows is that B pays 10.95% per annum. This is 0.25% per annum less than it would pay if it went directly to fixed-rate markets.

The swap arrangement appears to improve the position of both A and B by 0.25% per annum. The total gain is, therefore, 0.5% per annum. It can be shown that the total apparent gain in this type of interest rate swap agreement is always $a - b$, where a is the difference between the interest rates facing the two companies in fixed-rate markets, and b is the difference between the interest rates facing the two companies in floating-rate markets. In this case, $a = 1.2\%$ and $b = 0.70\%$.

If A and B did not deal directly with each other and used a financial institution, an arrangement, such as that shown in Figure 5.7, might result. (This is similar to the example in Figure 5.4.) In this case, A ends up borrowing at LIBOR + 0.07%, B ends up borrowing at 10.97%, and the financial institution earns a spread of four basis points per year. The gain to company A is 0.23%; the gain to company B is 0.23%; and the gain to the financial institution is 0.04%. The total gain to all three parties is 0.50% as before.

Criticism of the Comparative Advantage Argument

The comparative advantage argument we have just outlined for explaining the attractiveness of interest rate swaps is open to question. Why in Table 5.4 should the spreads between the rates offered to A and B be different in fixed and floating markets? Now that the swap market has been in existence for some time, we might reasonably expect these types of differences to have been arbitraged away.

The reason that spread differentials appear to exist is due to the nature of the contracts available to companies in fixed and floating markets. The 10.0% and 11.2% rates available to A and B in fixed-rate markets are five-year rates (for example, the rates at which the companies can issue five-year fixed-rate bonds.) The LIBOR +

0.3% and LIBOR + 1.0% rates available to A and B in floating-rate markets are six-month rates. In the floating-rate market, the lender usually has the opportunity to review the floating rates every six months. If the creditworthiness of A or B has declined, the lender has the option of increasing the spread over LIBOR that is charged. In extreme circumstances, the lender can refuse to roll over the loan at all. The providers of fixed-rate financing do not have the option to change the terms of the loan in this way.[4]

The spreads between the rates offered to A and B are a reflection of the extent to which B is more likely to default than A. During the next six months, there is very little chance that either A or B will default. As we look further ahead, default statistics show that the probability of a default by a company with a relatively low credit rating (such as B) increases faster than the probability of a default by a company with a relatively high credit rating (such as A). This is why the spread between the five-year rates is greater than the spread between the six-month rates.[5]

After negotiating a floating-rate loan at LIBOR + 1.0% and entering into the swap shown in Figure 5.7, B appears to obtain a fixed-rate loan at 10.97%. The arguments just presented show that this is not really the case. In practice, the rate paid is 10.97% only if B can continue to borrow floating-rate funds at a spread of 1.0% over LIBOR. If, for example, the credit rating of B declines so that the floating-rate loan is rolled over at LIBOR + 2.0%, the rate paid by B increases to 11.97%. If B's spread over six-month LIBOR is more likely to rise than to fall, B's expected average borrowing rate when it enters into the swap is greater than 10.97%.

The swap in Figure 5.7 locks in LIBOR + 0.07% for company A for the whole of the next five years, not just for the next six months. This appears to be a good deal for company A. The downside of the arrangement to A is that it is bearing the risk of a default by the financial institution. If it borrowed floating rate funds in the usual way, it would not be bearing this risk.

5.3 VALUATION OF INTEREST RATE SWAPS

If we assume no possibility of default, an interest-rate swap can be valued either as a long position in one bond combined with a short position in another bond, or as a portfolio of forward-rate agreements.

The Discount Rate

When swaps and other over-the-counter derivatives are valued, the cash flows are usually discounted using LIBOR zero-coupon interest rates. This is because LIBOR is the cost of funds for a financial institution. The implicit assumption is that the risk

---

[4]If the floating rate loans are structured so that the spread over LIBOR is guaranteed in advance regardless of changes in credit rating, there is, in practice, little or no comparative advantage.

[5]Chapter 23 provides statistics on default rates for bonds with different credit ratings.

associated with the cash flows on the derivative is the same as the risk associated with a loan in the interbank market. The way in which the LIBOR zero-coupon yield curve is usually calculated is described in Appendix 5A.

Relationship of Swaps to Bonds

We now return to the interest rate swap in Figure 5.1. We showed, in Table 5.2, that it can be characterized as the difference between two bonds. Although the principal is not exchanged, we can assume without changing the value of the swap that, at the end of the agreement, A pays B the notional principal of $100 million and B pays A the same notional principal. The swap is then the same as an arrangement in which

1. Company B has lent company A $100 million at the six-month LIBOR rate.
2. Company A has lent company B $100 million at a fixed rate of 5% per annum.

To put it another way, company B has purchased a $100 million floating-rate (LIBOR) bond from company A and has sold a $100 million fixed-rate (5% per annum) bond to company A. The value of the swap to company B is, therefore, the difference between the values of the two bonds.

Define

B_{fix}: Value of fixed-rate bond underlying the swap.

B_{fl}: Value of floating-rate bond underlying the swap.

It follows that the value of the swap to company B is

$$V_{swap} = B_{fl} - B_{fix} \tag{5.1}$$

To see how equation (5.1) is used, we define

t_i: Time when ith payments are exchanged ($1 \leq i \leq n$).

L: Notional principal in swap agreement.

r_i: LIBOR zero rate for a maturity t_i.

k: Fixed payment made on each payment date.

The fixed-rate bond, B_{fix}, can be valued as described in section 4.3. The cash flows from the bond are k at time t_i ($1 \leq i \leq n$) and L at time t_n so that

$$B_{fix} = \sum_{i=1}^{n} ke^{-r_i t_i} + Le^{-r_n t_n}$$

Consider next the floating-rate bond. Immediately after a payment date this is identical to a newly issued floating-rate bond. It follows that $B_{fl} = L$ immediately after a payment date. Between payment dates, we can use the fact that B_{fl} will equal L immediately after the next payment date and argue as follows. Immediately before the next payment date $B_{fl} = L + k^*$ where k^* is the floating-rate payment (already known) that will be made on the next payment date. In our notation, the time until the next payment date is t_1. The value of the swap today is its value just before the next payment date discounted at rate r_1 for time t_1:

$$B_{fl} = (L + k^*)e^{-r_1 t_1}$$

Equation (5.1) gives the value of the swap in the situation where a company is paying fixed and receiving floating. When the company is receiving fixed and paying floating, B_{fix} and B_{fl} are calculated in the same way and equation (5.1) becomes

$$V_{swap} = B_{fix} - B_{fl} \tag{5.2}$$

The fixed rate in a swap is usually chosen so that the swap is worth approximately zero when it is first negotiated. During its life it may have a positive or negative value. In these respects a swap is like a forward contract.

Example 5.1 Suppose that, under the terms of a swap, a financial institution has agreed to pay six-month LIBOR and receive 8% per annum (with semiannual compounding) on a notional principal of $100 million. The swap has a remaining life of 1.25 years. LIBOR rates with continuous compounding for 3-month, 9-month, and 15-month maturities are 10%, 10.5%, and 11%, respectively. The 6-month LIBOR rate at the last payment date was 10.2% (with semiannual compounding). In this case, $k = \$4$ million and $k^* = \$5.1$ million, so that

$$B_{fix} = 4e^{-0.1\times0.25} + 4e^{-0.105\times0.75} + 104e^{-0.11\times1.25}$$
$$= \$98.24 \text{ million}$$
$$B_{fl} = (100 + 5.1)e^{-0.1\times0.25}$$
$$= \$102.51 \text{ million}$$

Hence the value of the swap is

$$98.24 - 102.51 = -\$4.27 \text{ million}$$

If the bank had been in the opposite position of paying fixed and receiving floating, the value of the swap would be +$4.27 million. Note that a more precise calculation would take account of the actual/360 day count convention in calculating k^* and the exact timing of cash flows, as discussed earlier.

Relationship of Swaps to Forward Rate Agreements

Forward rate agreements were introduced in chapter 4. They are agreements that a certain predetermined interest rate will apply to a certain principal for a certain period of time in the future. In section 4.6 we showed that an FRA can be characterized as an agreement where interest at the predetermined rate is exchanged for interest at the market interest rate for the period in question. This shows that an interest rate swap is nothing more than a portfolio of forward rate agreements.

Consider again the swap agreement between company A and company B in Figure 5.1. As illustrated in Table 5.1, this commits company B to six exchanges of cash flow. The first exchange is known at the time the swap is negotiated. The other five exchanges can be regarded as FRAs. The exchange on March 1, 2000, is an FRA where interest at 5% is exchanged for interest at the six-month rate observed in the market on September 1, 1999; the exchange on September 1, 2000, is an FRA where interest at 5% is exchanged for interest at the six-month rate observed in the market on March 1, 2000; and so on.

As shown in section 4.6, an FRA can be valued by assuming that forward interest rates are realized. Because it is a portfolio of forward rate agreements, a plain vanilla interest rate swap can also be valued by making the assumption that forward interest rates are realized. The procedure is as follows:

1. Calculate forward rates for each of the LIBOR rates that will determine swap cash flows.
2. Calculate swap cash flows on the assumption that the LIBOR rates will equal the forward rates.
3. Set the swap value equal to the present value of these cash flows.

Example 5.2   Consider again the situation in Example 5.1. The cash flows that will be exchanged in three months are known. Interest for six months at a rate of 8% per annum will be exchanged for interest at a rate of 10.2% per annum for six months. The value of the exchange to the financial institution is

$$0.5 \times 100 \times (0.08 - 0.102)e^{-0.1 \times 0.25} = -1.07$$

To calculate the value of the exchange in nine months, we must first calculate the forward rate corresponding to the period between three and nine months. From equation (4.1), this is

$$\frac{0.105 \times 0.75 - 0.10 \times 0.25}{0.5} = 0.10750$$

or 10.750% per annum with continuous compounding. From equation (3.4), this value becomes 11.044% per annum with semiannual compounding. The value of the FRA corresponding to the exchange in nine months is, therefore

$$0.5 \times 100 \times (0.08 - 0.11044)e^{-0.105 \times 0.75} = -1.41$$

To calculate the value of the exchange in 15 months, we must first calculate the forward rate corresponding to the period between 9 and 15 months. From equation (4.1), this is

$$\frac{0.11 \times 1.25 - 0.105 \times 0.75}{0.5} = 0.1175$$

or 11.75% per annum with continuous compounding. From equation (3.4), this value becomes 12.102% per annum with semiannual compounding. The value of the FRA corresponding to the exchange in 15 months is, therefore

$$0.5 \times 100 \times (0.08 - 0.12102)e^{-0.11 \times 1.25} = -1.79$$

The total value of the swap is

$$-1.07 - 1.41 - 1.79 = -4.27$$

or $-\$4.27$ million. This is in agreement with the calculation based on bond prices.

As already mentioned, the fixed rate in an interest rate swap is chosen so that the swap is initially worth zero. This means that the sum of the values of the FRAs underlying the swap is zero. It does not mean that the value of each individual FRA is zero. In general, some FRAs will have positive values whereas others have negative values.

Consider again the FRAs underlying the swap between the financial institution and company B in Figure 5.4.

Value of FRA to financial institution < 0 when forward interest rate $> 5.015\%$.
Value of FRA to financial institution $= 0$ when forward interest rate $= 5.015\%$.
Value of FRA to financial institution > 0 when forward interest rate $< 5.015\%$.

Suppose that the term structure is upward sloping at the time the swap is negotiated. This means that the forward interest rates increase as the maturity of the FRA increases. Because the sum of the values of the FRAs is zero, the forward interest rate must be less than 5.015% per annum for the early payment dates and greater than 5.015% per annum for the later payment dates. The value to the financial institution of the FRAs corresponding to early payment dates is, therefore, positive whereas the value of the FRAs corresponding to later payment dates is negative. If the term structure is downward sloping at the time the swap is negotiated, the reverse is true. The impact of the shape of the term structure on the values of the forward contracts underlying a swap is summarized in Figure 5.8.

5.4 CURRENCY SWAPS

Another popular type of swap is known as a *currency swap*. In its simplest form, this involves exchanging principal and interest payments in one currency for principal and interest payments in another currency.

A currency swap agreement requires that a principal be specified in each of the two currencies. The principal amounts are usually exchanged at the beginning and at the end of the life of the swap. Usually, the principal amounts are chosen to be approximately equivalent using the exchange rate at the time the swap is initiated.

Currency Swap Example

Consider a five-year currency swap agreement between companies A and B entered into on February 1, 1999. We suppose that company A pays a fixed interest rate of 11% in sterling and receives a fixed interest rate of 8% in dollars.[6] Interest rate payments are made once a year and the principal amounts are $15 million and £10 million. The swap is shown in Figure 5.9. Initially, the principal amounts flow in the opposite direction to the arrows in Figure 5.9. The interest payments during the life of the swap and the final principal payment flow in the same direction as the arrows. Thus, at the outset of the swap, company A pays $15 million and receives £10 million. Each year during the life of the swap contract, company A receives $1.20 million (= 8% of $15 million) and pays £1.10 million (= 11% of £10 million). At the end of the life of the swap, it pays a principal of £10 million and receives a principal of $15 million. These cash flows are shown in Table 5.5.

---

[6]This is termed a "fixed for fixed" currency swap.

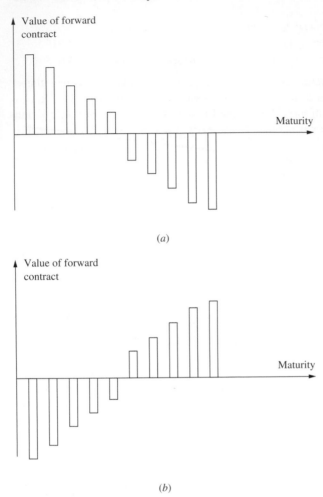

(a)

(b)

Figure 5.8   Value of forward contracts underlying a swap as a function of maturity. In (*a*) the yield curve is upward sloping and we receive fixed or the yield curve is downward sloping and we receive floating; in (*b*) the yield curve is upward sloping and we receive floating or the yield curve is downward sloping and we receive fixed.

Use of Currency Swap to Transform Loans and Assets

A swap, such as the one just considered, can be used to transform borrowings in one currency to borrowings in another currency. Suppose that company A can issue $15 million worth of U.S. dollar denominated bonds at 8% interest. The swap transforms the transaction into one where company A has borrowed £10 million at 11% interest. The initial exchange of principal converts the proceeds of the bond issue from U.S.

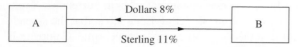

Figure 5.9　A currency swap.

Table 5.5	Cash Flows to Company A in Currency Swap	
Date	*Dollar Cash Flow (millions)*	*Sterling Cash Flow (millions)*
February 1, 1999	−15.00	+10.00
February 1, 2000	+1.20	−1.10
February 1, 2001	+1.20	−1.10
February 1, 2002	+1.20	−1.10
February 1, 2003	+1.20	−1.10
February 1, 2004	+16.20	−11.10

dollars to sterling. The subsequent exchanges have the effect of swapping the interest and principal payments from dollars to sterling.

The swap can also be used to transform the nature of assets. Suppose that company A can invest £10 million in the U.K. to yield 11% per annum for the next five years, but feels that the U.S. dollar will strengthen against sterling and prefers a U.S. denominated investment. The swap can be used to transform the U.K. investment into a $15 million investment in the U.S. yielding 8%.

Comparative Advantage

Suppose the five-year borrowing costs to company A and company B in U.S. dollars (USD) and Australian dollars (AUD) are as shown in Table 5.6. (The rates have been adjusted to reflect the impact on the companies of any differences in the tax regimes in the two countries.) The data in the table suggest that Australian rates are higher than U.S. interest rates. Also, company A is more creditworthy than company

Table 5.6	Borrowing Rates Providing Basis for Currency Swap	
	*USD**	*AUD**
Company A	5.0%	12.6%
Company B	7.0%	13.0%

*Quoted rates have been adjusted to reflect the differential impact of taxes.

B, because it is offered a more favorable rate of interest in both currencies. From the viewpoint of a swap trader, the interesting aspect of Table 5.6 is that the spreads between the rates paid by A and B in the two markets are not the same. Company B pays 2% more than company A in the U.S. dollar market and only 0.4% more than company A in the AUD market.

This situation is analogous to that in Table 5.4. Company A has a comparative advantage in the U.S. dollar market, whereas company B has a comparative advantage in the AUD market. In Table 5.4, where a plain vanilla interest rate swap is considered, we argued that comparative advantages were largely illusory. Here we are comparing the rates offered in two different currencies, and it is more likely that the comparative advantages are genuine. One possible source of comparative advantage is tax. Company A's position might be such that USD borrowings lead to lower taxes on its worldwide income than AUD borrowings. Company B's position might be the reverse. (Note that we have adjusted the interest rates in Table 5.6 to reflect these types of tax advantages.)

We assume that A wants to borrow AUD and B wants to borrow USD. This creates a perfect situation for a currency swap. Company A and company B each borrow in the market where they have a comparative advantage; that is, company A borrows USD whereas company B borrows AUD. They then use a currency swap to transform A's loan into a AUD loan and B's loan into a USD loan.

As already mentioned, the difference between the dollar interest rates is 2% whereas the difference between the AUD interest rates is 0.4%. By analogy with the interest rate swap case, we expect the total gain to all parties to be $2.0 - 0.4 = 1.6\%$ per annum.

There are many ways in which the swap can be organized. Figure 5.10 shows one possible arrangement. Company A borrows USD and company B borrows AUD. The effect of the swap is to transform the USD interest rate of 5% per annum to an AUD interest rate of 11.9% per annum for company A. As a result, company A is 0.7% per annum better off than it would be if it went directly to AUD markets. Similarly, company B exchanges an AUD loan at 13% per annum for a USD loan at 6.3% per annum and ends up 0.7% per annum better off than it would be if it went directly to USD markets. The financial intermediary gains 1.3% per annum on its USD cash flows and loses 1.1% per annum on its AUD flows. If, for the moment, we ignore the difference between the two currencies, the intermediary makes a net gain of 0.2% per annum. As predicted, the total gain to all parties is 1.6% per annum.

It can be seen from Figure 5.10 that the financial institution is exposed to foreign exchange risk. Each year it makes a gain of USD 156,000 (= 1.3% of 12 million)

Figure 5.10   A currency swap motivated by comparative advantage.

Figure 5.11   Alternative arrangement for currency swap: Company B bears some foreign exchange risk.

Figure 5.12   Alternative arrangement for currency swap: Company A bears some foreign exchange risk.

and incurs a loss of AUD 220,000 ($=$ 1.1% of 20 million). The financial institution can avoid this risk by buying AUD 220,000 per annum in the forward market for each year of the life of the swap, thus locking in a net gain in U.S. dollars.

It is possible to redesign the swap so that the financial institution makes a 0.2% spread in USD. Figure 5.11 and Figure 5.12 present two alternatives. These alternatives are unlikely to be used in practice because they do not lead to the companies being free of foreign exchange risk.[7] In Figure 5.11, company B bears some foreign exchange risk because it pays 1.1% per annum in AUD and 5.2% per annum in USD. In Figure 5.12, company A bears some foreign exchange risk because it receives 1.1% per annum in USD and pays 13% per annum in AUD.

5.5   VALUATION OF CURRENCY SWAPS

In the absence of default risk, a currency swap can be decomposed into a position in two bonds, as is the case with an interest rate swap. Consider the position of company A in Table 5.6 some time after the initial exchange of principal. It is short a sterling bond that pays interest at 11% per annum and long a dollar bond that pays interest at 8% per annum.

If we define V_{swap} as the value in U.S. dollars of a swap where dollars are received and a foreign currency is paid

$$V_{swap} = B_D - S_0 B_F$$

where B_F is the value, measured in the foreign currency, of the foreign-denominated bond underlying the swap; B_D is the value in U.S. dollars of the U.S. dollar bond underlying the swap; and S_0 is the current spot exchange rate (expressed as number

---

[7]Usually it makes sense for the financial institution to bear the foreign exchange risk, because it is in the best position to hedge the risk.

of dollars per unit of foreign currency). The value of the swap can, therefore, be determined from LIBOR rates in the two currencies and the spot exchange rate. The value of a swap where the foreign currency is received and dollars are paid is

$$V_{swap} = S_0 B_F - B_D$$

Example 5.3   Suppose that the term structure of LIBOR interest rates is flat in both Japan and the United States. The Japanese rate is 4% per annum and the U.S. rate is 9% per annum (both with continuous compounding). A financial institution has entered into a currency swap where it receives 5% per annum in yen and pays 8% per annum in dollars once a year. The principals in the two currencies are $10 million and 1,200 million yen. The swap will last for another three years and the current exchange rate is 110 yen = $1. In this case

$$B_D = 0.8e^{-0.09\times1} + 0.8e^{-0.09\times2} + 10.8e^{-0.09\times3}$$

$$= 9.644 \text{ million dollars}$$

$$B_F = 60e^{-0.04\times1} + 60e^{-0.04\times2} + 1,260e^{-0.04\times3}$$

$$= 1,230.55 \text{ million yen}$$

The value of the swap is

$$\frac{1,230.55}{110} - 9.644 = \$1.543 \text{ million}$$

If the financial institution had been paying yen and receiving dollars, the value of the swap would have been $-\$1.543$ million.

Decomposition into Forward Contracts

An alternative decomposition of the currency swap is into a series of forward contracts. Consider again the situation in Table 5.5. On each payment date, company A has agreed to exchange an inflow of $1.2 million and an outflow of £1.1 million. In addition, at the final payment date, it has agreed to exchange a $15 million inflow for a £10 million outflow. Each of these exchanges represents a forward contract. In section 3.5 we saw that forward contracts can be valued on the assumption that the forward price of the underlying asset is realized. This provides a convenient way of valuing the forward contracts underlying a currency swap.

Example 5.4   Consider the situation in Example 5.3. The current spot rate is 110 yen per dollar, or 0.009091 dollar per yen. Because the difference between the dollar and yen interest rates is 5% per annum, equation (3.13) can be used to give the one-year, two-year, and three-year forward exchange rates as

$$0.009091e^{0.05\times1} = 0.009557$$

$$0.009091e^{0.05\times2} = 0.010047$$

$$0.009091e^{0.05\times3} = 0.010562$$

respectively. The exchange of interest involves receiving 60 million yen and paying $0.8 million. The risk-free interest rate in dollars is 9% per annum. The forward contracts can be valued on the assumption that the forward rates just calculated are realized. The values of the forward contracts corresponding to the exchanges in one year, two years, and three years are, therefore (in millions of dollars)

$$(60 \times 0.009557 - 0.8)e^{-0.09 \times 1} = -0.2071$$
$$(60 \times 0.010047 - 0.8)e^{-0.09 \times 2} = -0.1647$$
$$(60 \times 0.010562 - 0.8)e^{-0.09 \times 3} = -0.1269$$

The final exchange of principal involves receiving 1,200 million yen and paying $10 million. This can also be valued on the assumption that the three-year forward rate is realized. Its value (in millions of dollars) is

$$(1{,}200 \times 0.010562 - 10)e^{-0.09 \times 3} = 2.0416$$

The total value of the swap is $2.0416 - 0.1269 - 0.1647 - 0.2071 = \$1.543$ million, which is in agreement with the result of the calculations in Example 5.3.

The value of a currency swap is normally zero when it is first negotiated. If the two principals are exactly equal using the exchange rate at the start of the swap, the value of the swap is also zero immediately after the initial exchange of principal. However, as in the case of interest rate swaps, this does not mean that each of the individual forward contracts underlying the swap has zero value. It can be shown that when interest rates in two currencies are significantly different, the payer of the low-interest-rate currency is in the position where the forward contracts corresponding to the early exchanges of cash flows have positive values and the forward contract corresponding to the final exchange of principals has a negative expected value. The payer of the high-interest-rate currency is likely to be in the opposite position; that is, the early exchanges of cash flows have negative values and the final exchange has a positive expected value.

For the payer of the low-interest-rate currency, the swap will tend to have a negative value during most of its life. The forward contracts corresponding to the early exchanges of payments have positive values, and once these exchanges have taken place, there is a tendency for the remaining forward contracts to have, in total, a negative value. For the payer of the high-interest-rate currency, the reverse is true and the value of the swap will tend to be positive during most of its life. These results are important when the credit risk in the swap is being evaluated.

5.6 OTHER SWAPS

A swap in its most general form is a contract that involves the exchange of cash flows according to a formula that depends on the value of one or more market variables. Many different types of swaps have been developed by financial engineers.

In an interest rate swap, a number of different floating reference rates can be used. In the United States, six-month LIBOR is the most common floating reference rate. Among the others used are three-month LIBOR, the one-month commercial paper rate, the Treasury bill rate, and the municipal bond tax-exempt rate. Swaps can be constructed to swap one floating rate (say, LIBOR) for another floating rate (say, the Treasury bill rate). This flexibility allows a company to hedge its exposure when assets subject to one floating rate are financed by liabilities subject to a different floating rate.

The principal in a swap agreement can be varied throughout the term of the swap to meet the needs of a counterparty. In an *amortizing swap*, the principal reduces in a predetermined way. The agreement might be designed to correspond to the amortization schedule on a loan. In a *step-up swap*, the principal increases in a predetermined way that might be designed to correspond to drawdowns on a loan agreement. *Deferred swaps* or *forward swaps* where the parties do not begin to exchange interest payments until some future date can also be arranged.

One popular swap is an agreement to exchange a fixed interest rate in one currency for a floating interest rate in another currency. This is a combination of an interest-rate swap and currency swap. It is known as a *cross-currency swap* or *currency coupon swap*.

Swaps can be extendable or puttable. In an *extendable swap*, one party has the option to extend the life of the swap beyond the specified period. In a *puttable swap*, one party has the option to terminate the swap early. Options on swaps, or *swaptions*, are also available. These provide one party with the right at a future time to enter into a swap where a predetermined fixed rate is exchanged for floating. Swaptions are discussed further in chapter 20.

A *constant maturity swap* (CMS swap) is an agreement to exchange a LIBOR rate for a swap rate. An example would be an agreement to exchange six-month LIBOR applied to a certain principal for the 10-year swap rate applied to the same principal every six months for the next five years. A *constant maturity Treasury swap* (CMT swap) is a similar agreement to exchange a LIBOR rate for a particular Treasury rate (e.g., the 10-year Treasury rate). In an *index amortizing rate swap* (sometimes also called an *indexed principal swap*), the principal reduces in a way dependent on the level of interest rates. (The lower the interest rate, the greater the reduction in the principal.) In a *differential swap*, or *diff swap*, a floating interest rate in the domestic currency is exchanged for a floating interest rate in a foreign currency, with both interest rates being applied to the same domestic principal.

An *equity swap* is an agreement to exchange the dividends and capital gains realized on an equity index for either a fixed or a floating rate of interest. Equity swaps can be used by portfolio managers to convert returns from a fixed or floating investment to the returns from investing in an equity index, or vice versa. *Commodity swaps* are now becoming increasingly popular. A company that consumes 100,000 barrels of oil per year could agree to pay \$2 million each year for the next 10 years and to receive in return $100,000S$, where S is the current market price of oil per barrel. The agreement would, in effect, lock in the company's oil cost at \$20 per barrel. An oil producer might agree to the opposite exchange, thereby locking in the price it realized for its oil at $20 per barrel. *Credit swaps* are a recent innovation in swap markets. These are discussed further in chapter 23.

5.7   CREDIT RISK

Contracts, such as swaps, that are private arrangements between two companies entail credit risks. Consider a financial institution that has entered into offsetting contracts with two companies, A and B (see, for example, Figures 5.4, 5.5, or 5.7). If neither party defaults, the financial institution remains fully hedged. A decline in the value of one contract will always be offset by an increase in the value of the other contract. However, there is a chance that one party will get into financial difficulties and default. The financial institution still has to honor the contract it has with the other party.

Suppose that some time after the initiation of the contracts in Figure 5.4, the contract with company B has a positive value to the financial institution whereas the contract with company A has a negative value. If company B defaults, the financial institution is liable to lose the whole of the positive value it has in this contract. To maintain a hedged position, it would have to find a third party willing to take company B's position. To induce the third party to take the position, the financial institution would have to pay the third party an amount roughly equal to the value of its contract with B prior to the default.

A financial institution has credit risk exposure from a swap only when the value of the swap to the financial institution is positive. What happens when this value is negative and the counterparty gets into financial difficulties? In theory, the financial institution could realize a windfall gain, because a default would lead to it getting rid of a liability. In practice, it is likely that the counterparty would choose to sell the contract to a third party or rearrange its affairs in some way so that its positive value in the contract is not lost. The most realistic assumption for the financial institution is, therefore, as follows. If the counterparty goes bankrupt, there will be a loss if the value of the swap to the financial institution is positive, and there will be no effect on the financial institution's position if the value of the swap to the financial institution is negative. This situation is summarized in Figure 5.13.

Potential losses from defaults on a swap are much less than the potential losses from defaults on a loan with the same principal. This is because the value of the swap is usually only a small fraction of the value of the loan. Potential losses from defaults on a currency swap are greater than on an interest rate swap. The reason is that, because principal amounts in two different currencies are exchanged at the end of the life of a currency swap, a currency swap can have a greater value than an interest rate swap.

Sometimes a financial institution can predict which of two offsetting contracts is more likely to have a positive value. Consider the currency swap in Figure 5.10. AUD interest rates are higher than USD interest rates. This means that, as time passes, the

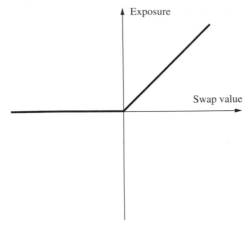

Figure 5.13   The credit exposure in a swap.

financial institution is likely to find that its swap with A has a negative value whereas its swap with B has a positive value. The creditworthiness of B is, therefore, more important than the creditworthiness of A.

It is important to distinguish between the credit risk and market risk to a financial institution in any contract. As discussed earlier, the credit risk arises from the possibility of a default by the counterparty when the value of the contract to the financial institution is positive. The market risk arises from the possibility that market variables such as interest rates and exchange rates will move in such a way that the value of a contract to the financial institution becomes negative. Market risks can be hedged by entering into offsetting contracts; credit risks are less easy to hedge. Credit risk issues are discussed in more detail in chapter 23. Market risk issues are discussed in more detail in chapters 13 and 14.

SUMMARY

The two most common types of swaps are interest rate swaps and currency swaps. In an interest rate swap, one party agrees to pay the other party interest at a fixed rate on a notional principal for a number of years. In return, it receives interest at a floating rate on the same notional principal for the same period of time. In a currency swap, one party agrees to pay interest and principal in one currency. In return, it receives interest and principal in another currency.

Principal amounts are not usually exchanged in an interest rate swap. In a currency swap, principal amounts are usually exchanged at both the beginning and the end of the life of the swap. For a party paying interest in the foreign currency, the foreign principal is received and the domestic principal is paid at the beginning of the life of the swap. At the end of the life of the swap, the foreign principal is paid and the domestic principal is received.

An interest rate swap can be used to transform a floating-rate loan into a fixed-rate loan, or vice versa. It can also be used to transform a floating-rate investment to a fixed-rate investment, or vice versa. A currency swap can be used to transform a loan in one currency into a loan in another currency. It can also be used to transform an investment denominated in one currency into an investment denominated in another currency.

There are two ways of valuing interest rate swaps and currency swaps. In the first, the swap is decomposed into a long position in one bond and a short position in another bond. In the second, the swap is regarded as a portfolio of forward contracts.

When a financial institution enters into a swap, it is exposed to credit risk. If the counterparty defaults when the financial institution has positive value in the swap, the financial institution loses money. If the counterparty defaults when the financial institution has negative value in the swap, it is reasonable to assume that the financial institution makes neither a gain nor a loss.

SUGGESTIONS FOR FURTHER READING

Bicksler, J., and A. H. Chen. "An Economic Analysis of Interest Rate Swaps," *Journal of Finance* 41, 3 (1986), 645–55.

Hull, J. "Assessing Credit Risk in a Financial Institution's Off-Balance Sheet Commitments," *Journal of Financial and Quantitative Analysis*, 24 (December 1989), 489–502.

Hull, J., and A. White. "The Impact of Default Risk on the Prices of Options and Other Derivative Securities," *Journal of Banking and Finance*, 19 (1985), 299-322.

Hull, J., and A. White. "The Price of Default," *RISK* (September 1992), 101–03.

International Swaps and Derivatives Association. *Code of Standard, Working Assumptions and Provisions for Swaps*. New York.

Layard-Liesching, R. "Swap Fever," *Euromoney* supplement (January 1986), 108–13.

Litzenberger, R. H. "Swaps: Plain and Fanciful," *Journal of Finance* 47, 3 (1992), 831–50.

Marshall, J. F., and K. R. Kapner. *Understanding Swap Finance*. Cincinnati, OH: South-Western, 1990.

Smith, C. W., C. W. Smithson, and L. M. Wakeman. "The Evolving Market for Swaps," *Midland Corporate Finance Journal*, 3 (Winter 1986), 20–32.

Turnbull, S. M. "Swaps: A Zero Sum Game," *Financial Management* 16, 1 (Spring 1987), 15–21.

Wall, L. D., and J. J. Pringle. "Alternative Explanations of Interest Rate Swaps: A Theoretical and Empirical Analysis," *Financial Management* 18, 2 (Summer 1989), 59–73.

QUESTIONS AND PROBLEMS
(ANSWERS IN SOLUTIONS MANUAL)

5.1. Companies A and B have been offered the following rates per annum on a $20 million five-year loan:

	Fixed rate	*Floating rate*
Company A	12.0%	LIBOR + 0.1%
Company B	13.4%	LIBOR + 0.6%

Company A requires a floating-rate loan; company B requires a fixed-rate loan. Design a swap that will net a bank, acting as intermediary, 0.1% per annum and that will appear equally attractive to both companies.

5.2. Company X wishes to borrow U.S. dollars at a fixed rate of interest. Company Y wishes to borrow Japanese yen at a fixed rate of interest. The amounts required by the two companies are roughly the same at the current exchange rate. The companies have been quoted the following interest rates, which have been adjusted for the impact of taxes:

	Yen	*Dollars*
Company X	5.0%	9.6%
Company Y	6.5%	10.0%

Design a swap that will net a bank, acting as intermediary, 50 basis points per annum. Make the swap equally attractive to the two companies and ensure that all foreign exchange risk is assumed by the bank.

5.3. A $100 million interest rate swap has a remaining life of 10 months. Under the terms of the swap, six-month LIBOR is exchanged for 12% per annum (compounded semiannually). The average of the bid-ask rate being exchanged for six-month LIBOR in swaps of all maturities is currently 10% per annum with continuous compounding. The six-month LIBOR rate was 9.6% per annum two months ago. What is the current value of the swap to the party paying floating? What is its value to the party paying fixed?

5.4. What is meant by warehousing swaps?

5.5. A currency swap has a remaining life of 15 months. It involves exchanging interest at 14% on £20 million for interest at 10% on $30 million once a year. The term structure of interest rates in both the United Kingdom and the United States is currently flat, and if the swap were negotiated today the interest rates exchanged would be 8% in dollars and 11% in sterling. All interest rates are quoted with annual compounding. The current exchange rate (dollars per pound sterling) is 1.6500. What is the value of the swap to the party paying sterling? What is the value of the swap to the party paying dollars?

5.6. Explain the difference between the credit risk and the market risk in a financial contract.

5.7. Explain why a bank is subject to credit risk when it enters into two offsetting swap contracts.

5.8. Companies X and Y have been offered the following rates per annum on a $5 million 10-year investment:

	Fixed rate	Floating rate
Company X	8.0%	LIBOR
Company Y	8.8%	LIBOR

Company X requires a fixed-rate investment; company Y requires a floating-rate investment. Design a swap that will net a bank, acting as intermediary, 0.2% per annum and will appear equally attractive to X and Y.

5.9. A financial institution has entered into an interest rate swap with company X. Under the terms of the swap, it receives 10% per annum and pays six-month LIBOR on a principal of $10 million for five years. Payments are made every six months. Suppose that company X defaults on the sixth payment date (end of year three) when the interest rate (with semiannual compounding) is 8% per annum for all maturities. What is the loss to the financial institution? Assume that six-month LIBOR was 9% per annum halfway through year three.

5.10. A financial institution has entered into a 10-year currency swap with company Y. Under the terms of the swap, it receives interest at 3% per annum in Swiss francs and pays interest at 8% per annum in U.S. dollars. Interest payments are exchanged once a year. The principal amounts are $7 million and 10 million francs. Suppose that company Y defaults at the end of year six, when the exchange rate is $0.80 per franc. What is the cost to the financial institution? Assume that, at the end of year six, the interest rate is 3% per annum in Swiss francs and 8% per annum in U.S. dollars for all maturities. All interest rates are quoted with annual compounding.

5.11. Companies A and B face the following interest rates:

	A	B
U.S. dollars (floating rate)	LIBOR + 0.5%	LIBOR + 1.0%
Canadian (fixed rate)	5.0%	6.5%

Assume that A wants to borrow U.S. dollars at a floating rate of interest and B wants to borrow Canadian dollars at a fixed rate of interest. A financial institution is planning to arrange a swap and requires a 50 basis point spread. If the swap is equally attractive to A and B, what rates of interest will A and B end up paying?

5.12. After it hedges its foreign exchange risk using forward contracts, is the financial institution's average spread in Figure 5.10 likely to be greater than or less than 40 basis points? Explain your answer.

5.13. How can a deferred swap be created from two other swaps?

5.14. "Companies with high credit risks are the ones that cannot access fixed-rate markets directly. They are the companies that are most likely to be paying fixed and receiving floating in an interest rate swap." Assume that this statement is true. Do you think it increases or decreases the risk of a financial institution's swap portfolio? Assume that companies are most likely to default when interest rates are high.

5.15. Why is the expected loss from a default on an interest rate swap less than the expected loss from the default on a loan with the same principal?

5.16. A bank finds that its assets are not matched with its liabilities. It is taking floating-rate deposits and making fixed-rate loans. How can swaps be used to offset the risk?

5.17. Explain how you would value a swap where a floating rate is received in currency A and a fixed rate is paid in currency B. No principal is exchanged.

ASSIGNMENT QUESTIONS

5.18. Company A, a British manufacturer, wishes to borrow U.S. dollars at a fixed rate of interest. Company B, a U.S. multinational, wishes to borrow sterling at a fixed rate of interest. They have been quoted the following rates per annum (adjusted for tax effects):

	Sterling	*U.S. dollars*
Company A	11.0%	7.0%
Company B	10.6%	6.2%

Design a swap that will net a bank, acting as intermediary, 10 basis points per annum and that will produce a gain of 15 basis points per annum for each of the two companies.

5.19. Under the terms of an interest rate swap, a financial institution has agreed to pay 10% per annum and to receive three-month LIBOR in return on a notional principal of $100 million with payments being exchanged every three months. The swap has a remaining life of 14 months. The average of the bid-ask fixed rate currently being swapped for three-month LIBOR is 12% per annum for all maturities. The three-month LIBOR rate one month ago was 11.8% per annum. All rates are compounded quarterly. What is the value of the swap?

5.20. Suppose that the term structure of interest rates is flat in the United States and Australia. The USD interest rate is 7% per annum and the AUD rate is 9% per annum (both continuously compounded). The current value of the AUD is 0.62 USD. Under the terms of a swap agreement, a financial institution pays 8% per annum in AUD and receives 4% per annum in USD. The principals in the two currencies are $12 million USD and 20 million AUD. Payments are exchanged every year, with one exchange having just taken place. The swap will last two more years. What is the value of the swap to the financial institution?

5.21. Company X is based in the United Kingdom and would like to borrow $50 million at a fixed interest rate for five years in U.S. funds. Because the company is not well known in the United States, this has proved to be impossible. However, the company has been quoted 12% per annum on fixed-rate five-year sterling funds. Company Y is based in the United States and would like to borrow the equivalent of $50 million in sterling funds for five years at a fixed rate of interest. It has been unable to get a quote but has been offered U.S. dollar funds at 10.5% per annum. Five-year government bonds currently yield 9.5% per annum in the United States and 10.5% per annum in the United Kingdom. Suggest an appropriate currency swap that will net the financial intermediary 0.5% per annum.

APPENDIX 5A

Construction of the Zero-Coupon LIBOR Curve

In this appendix, we explain the way the zero-coupon LIBOR curve is usually constructed.

A common practice is to use LIBOR rates to define the zero curve for maturities up to one year, Eurodollar futures for maturities between one year and N years, and swap rates beyond N years. The value of N depends on the country. For U.S. LIBOR it is common to use $N = 5$.

Once a convexity adjustment similar to that described in section 4.12 is made, the Eurodollar futures contracts define forward rates for periods of 90 days. Most of the time we are in the situation where one 90-day period begins the day after the previous 90-day period ends. This means we can use an inductive procedure to define the zero curve. From equation (4.1) the forward rate, R_F, for the period between times T_1 and T_2 can be combined with the zero rate, R_1, for maturity T_1 to give the zero rate, R_2, for maturity T_2 using the following formula:

$$R_2 = \frac{R_F(T_2 - T_1) + R_1 T_1}{T_2}$$

Example 5.5 Suppose that the three-year zero rate is 4.8% and the forward rate for the period between 3 and 3.25 years is 5.3%. The zero rate for a maturity of 3.25 years is

$$\frac{0.053 \times 0.25 + 0.048 \times 3}{3.25} = 0.04838$$

or 4.838%.

We now describe how swap rates are used to determine the zero curve beyond five years. Consider the seven-year swap rate and suppose that it is 7.5%. This is the average of the bid and ask fixed rate that is exchanged for floating in a seven-year swap. Section 5.3 shows that a seven-year swap is the difference between a seven-year fixed-rate bond and a seven-year floating-rate bond. At the start of the life of the swap, the swap is worth zero and the floating-rate bond is worth par. It follows that the fixed-rate bond is also worth par. A seven-year bond paying coupon of 7.5% per annum, therefore, has a value of par. Other swap rates define other bonds that are worth par. These bonds are used in conjunction with the bootstrap techniques described in section 4.4 to calculate zero rates.

CHAPTER

6

OPTIONS MARKETS

Options were introduced in chapter 1. It will be recalled that a call option is the right to buy an asset for a certain price; a put option is the right to sell an asset for a certain price. A European option can be exercised only at the end of its life; an American option can be exercised at any time during its life. In this chapter we explain the way that exchange-traded options markets are organized, the terminology used, how contracts are traded, how margin requirements are set, and so on. Later chapters will discuss trading strategies involving options, the pricing of options, and ways in which portfolios of options can be hedged. Options are fundamentally different from the forward, futures, and swap contracts discussed in the last few chapters. An option gives the holder of the option the right to do something. The holder does not have to exercise this right. By contrast, in a forward, futures, or swap contract, the two parties have committed themselves to some action.

This chapter will focus primarily on exchange-traded stock options. (Exchange-traded options on currencies, indices, and futures are covered in chapter 12.) Options are traded very actively in the over-the-counter market as well as on exchanges. The main advantage of an over-the-counter option is that it can be tailored by a financial institution to meet the needs of a client. The strike price and maturity do not have to correspond to those specified by the exchange. Also, nonstandard features can be incorporated into the design of the option.

6.1 UNDERLYING ASSETS

Options trade on many different exchanges throughout the world. The underlying assets include stocks, foreign currencies, stock indices, and many different futures contracts.

Stock Options

The exchanges trading stock options in the United States are the Chicago Board Options Exchange (CBOE), the Philadelphia Exchange (PHLX), the American Stock Exchange (AMEX), and the Pacific Stock Exchange (PSE). Options trade on over 500 different stocks. They are American-style (that is, they can be exercised early).

One contract gives the holder the right to buy or sell 100 shares at the specified strike price. This is convenient because the shares themselves are normally traded in lots of 100.

Foreign Currency Options

The major exchange for trading foreign currency options is the Philadelphia Exchange. It offers both European and American contracts on currencies such as the Australian dollar, British pound, Canadian dollar, euro, German mark, Japanese yen, and Swiss franc. The size of one contract depends on the currency. For example, in the case of the British pound, one contract gives the holder the right to buy or sell £31,250; in the case of the Japanese yen, one contract gives the holder the right to buy or sell 6.25 million yen.

Index Options

Many different index options trade in the United States. The two most popular are those on the S&P 100 and S&P 500 traded on the CBOE. The S&P 500 option is European, whereas the S&P 100 option is American. One contract is to buy or sell 100 times the index at the specified strike price. Settlement is in cash rather than by delivering the portfolio underlying the index. Consider, for example, one call contract on the S&P 100 with a strike price of 980. If it is exercised when the value of the index is 992, the writer of the contract pays the holder $(992 - 980) \times 100 = \$1,200$. This cash payment is based on the index value at the end of the day on which exercise instructions are issued. Not surprisingly, traders usually wait until the end of a day before issuing these instructions.

Futures Options

In a futures option (or option on futures), the underlying asset is a futures contract. The futures contract normally matures shortly after the expiration of the option. Futures options are now available for most of the assets on which futures contracts are traded. When the holders of a call option exercise, they acquire from the writers a long position in the underlying futures contract plus a cash amount equal to the excess of the futures price over the strike price. When the holders of a put option exercise, they acquire a short position in the underlying futures contract plus a cash amount equal to the excess of the strike price over the futures price. The most actively traded futures options are the Treasury bond futures option traded on CBOT and the Eurodollar futures option traded on CME. The contracts on corn, soybeans, crude oil, and Treasury notes are also popular.

6.2 SPECIFICATION OF STOCK OPTIONS

In the rest of this chapter we focus on the trading of stock options in the United States. The trading of index options, currency options, and futures options are discussed further in chapter 12.

An exchange-traded stock option contract is an American-style option contract to buy or sell 100 shares of the stock. Details of the contract, such as the expiration date, the strike price, what happens when dividends are declared, how large a position traders can hold, and so on, are specified by the exchange.

Expiration Dates

A stock option is referred to by the month that the expiration date occurs. Thus, a January call on IBM is a call option on IBM with an expiration date in January. The precise expiration date is 10:59 p.m. Central Time on the Saturday immediately following the third Friday of the expiration month. The last day on which options trade is the third Friday of the expiration month. A trader with a long position in an option normally has until 4:30 p.m. Central Time on that Friday to instruct a broker to exercise the option. The broker then has until 10:59 p.m. the next day to complete the paperwork notifying the exchange that the exercise is to take place.

Stock options are on a January, February, or March cycle. The January cycle consists of the months of January, April, July, and October. The February cycle consists of the months of February, May, August, and November. The March cycle consists of the months of March, June, September, and December. If the expiration date for the current month has not been reached, options trade with expiration dates in the current month, the following month, and the next two months in the cycle. If the expiration date of the current month has passed, options trade with expiration dates in the next month, the next-but-one month, and the next two months of the expiration cycle. For example, IBM is on a January cycle. At the beginning of January, options are traded with expiration dates in January, February, April, and July; at the end of January, they are traded with expiration dates in February, March, April, and July; at the beginning of May, they are traded with expiration dates in May, June, July, and October; and so on. When one option reaches expiration, trading in another is started.

Longer-dated stock options known as *long-term equity anticipation securities* or LEAPS also trade on exchanges. These have January expiration dates. In August 1998, for example, options on a range of stocks traded with expiration dates of January 2000 and January 2001.

Strike Prices

The exchange chooses the strike prices at which options can be written. When the stock price is relatively low (for example, $20), the spacing between strike prices is $2\frac{1}{2}$; when it is higher (for example, $100), the spacing between strike prices is $5. When it is very high (for example, $300), the spacing between strike prices is $10. An exception occurs when there has been a stock split or a stock dividend, as will be described shortly.

When a new expiration date is introduced, the two strike prices closest to the current stock price are usually selected by the exchange. If one of these is very close to the existing stock price, the third strike price closest to the current stock price may also be selected. If the stock price moves outside the range defined by the highest and lowest strike price, trading is usually introduced in an option with a new strike price. To illustrate these rules, suppose that the stock price is $83 when trading in the October options starts. Call and put options would first be offered with strike prices of 80 and 85. If the stock price rose above $85, a strike price of 90 would be offered; if it fell below $80, a strike price of 75 would be offered; and so on.

Terminology

For any given asset at any given time, there may be many different option contracts trading. Consider a stock where there are four expiration dates and five strike prices. If call and put options trade with every expiration date and every strike price, there are a total of 40 different contracts. All options of the same type (calls or puts) are referred to as an *option class*. For example, IBM calls are one class whereas IBM puts are another class. An *option series* consists of all the options of a given class with the same expiration date and strike price. In other words, an option series refers to a particular contract that is traded. The IBM 110 January calls are an option series.

Options are referred to as *in the money*, *at the money*, or *out of the money*. An in-the-money option is one that would lead to a positive cash flow to the holder if it were exercised immediately. Similarly, an at-the-money option would lead to zero cash flow if it were exercised immediately, and an out-of-the-money option would lead to a negative cash flow if it were exercised immediately. If S is the stock price and X is the strike price, a call option is in the money when $S > X$, at the money when $S = X$, and out of the money when $S < X$. A put option is in the money when $S < X$, at the money when $S = X$, and out of the money when $S > X$. Clearly, an option will be exercised only if it is in the money. In the absence of transactions costs, an in-the-money option will always be exercised on the expiration date if it has not been exercised previously.

The *intrinsic value* of an option is defined as the maximum of zero and the value it would have if it were exercised immediately. For a call option, the intrinsic value is, therefore, $\max(S - X, 0)$. For a put option, it is $\max(X - S, 0)$. An in-the-money American option must be worth at least as much as its intrinsic value because the holder can realize the intrinsic value by exercising immediately. Often it is optimal for the holder of an in-the-money American option to wait rather than exercise immediately. The option is then said to have *time value*. The total value of an option can be thought of as the sum of its intrinsic value and its time value.

Flex Options

Some exchanges now offer *flex options*. These are options where the traders on the floor of the exchange agree to nonstandard terms. These nonstandard terms might involve a strike price or an expiration date that is different from those usually offered by the exchange. Flex options are an attempt by the exchanges to regain business from the over-the-counter markets.

Dividends and Stock Splits

The early over-the-counter options were dividend protected. If a company declared a cash dividend, the strike price for options on the company's stock was reduced on the ex-dividend day by the amount of the dividend. Now, both exchange-traded and over-the-counter options are not generally adjusted for cash dividends. As we will see in chapter 11, this has significant implications for the way that options are valued.

Exchange-traded options are adjusted for stock splits. A stock split occurs when the existing shares are "split" into more shares. For example, in a 3-for-1 stock split, three new shares are issued to replace each existing share. Because a stock split does not change the assets or the earning ability of a company, we should not expect it to have any effect on the wealth of the company's shareholders. All else being equal, the 3-for-1 stock split just referred to should cause the stock price to go down to one-third of its previous value. In general, an n-for-m stock split should cause the stock price to go down to m/n of its previous value. The terms of option contracts are adjusted to reflect expected changes in a stock price arising from a stock split. After an n-for-m stock split, the exercise price is reduced to m/n of its previous value and the number of shares covered by one contract is increased to n/m of its previous value. If the stock price reduces in the way expected, the positions of both the writer and the purchaser of a contract remain unchanged.

> ***Example 6.1*** Consider a call option to buy 100 shares of a company for $30 per share. Suppose that the company makes a 2-for-1 stock split. The terms of the option contract are then changed so that it gives the holder the right to purchase 200 shares for $15 per share.

Stock options are adjusted for stock dividends. A stock dividend involves a company issuing more shares to its existing shareholders. For example, a 20% stock dividend means that investors receive one new share for each five already owned. Like a stock split, a stock dividend has no effect on either the assets or the earning power of a company. The stock price can be expected to go down as a result of a stock dividend. The 20% stock dividend referred to is essentially the same as a 6-for-5 stock split. All else being equal, it should cause the stock price to decline to five-sixths of its previous value. The terms of an option are adjusted to reflect the expected price decline arising from a stock dividend in the same way as they are for that arising from a stock split.

> ***Example 6.2*** Consider a put option to sell 100 shares of a company for $15 per share. Suppose that the company declares a 25% stock dividend. This is equivalent to a 5-for-4 stock split. The terms of the option contract are changed so that it gives the holder the right to sell 125 shares for $12.

Adjustments are also made for rights issues. A rights issue gives existing shareholders the right to buy more shares at a specified price. The basic procedure is to calculate the theoretical price of the rights and then to reduce the strike price by this amount. As pointed out by Brown, this procedure leaves the option holder slightly worse off than prior to the issue.[1]

---

[1] See R. L. Brown, "Adjusting Option Contracts to Reflect Capitalization Changes," *Journal of Business Finance and Accounting*, 16 (1989), 247–54.

Position Limits and Exercise Limits

The exchange specifies a *position limit* for each stock upon which options are traded. This defines the maximum number of option contracts that a trader can hold on one side of the market. For this purpose, long calls and short puts are considered to be on the same side of the market. Also, short calls and long puts are considered to be on the same side of the market. The *exercise limit* equals the position limit. It defines the maximum number of contracts that can be exercised by any individual (or group of individuals acting together) in any period of five consecutive business days. The position/exercise limit is usually 3,000, 5,500, or 8,000 contracts. Options on actively traded stocks with high market capitalizations normally have position/exercise limits of 8,000 contracts. Options on smaller capitalization stocks usually have position/exercise limits of 3,000 or 5,500 contracts. Position limits and exercise limits are designed to prevent the market from being unduly influenced by the activities of an individual trader or group of traders.

6.3   NEWSPAPER QUOTES

Many newspapers carry option quotations. In *The Wall Street Journal*, stock option quotations can currently be found under the heading "Listed Options" in the Money and Investing section. Table 6.1 shows an extract from the quotations as they appeared in *The Wall Street Journal* of Wednesday, August 5, 1998. These refer to trading that took place on the previous day (i.e., Tuesday, August 4, 1998).

The company on whose stock the option is written, together with the closing stock price, are listed in the first column. The strike price and maturity month appear in the second and third columns. If a call option with the specified strike price and the specified maturity month traded during the previous day, the next two columns show the volume of trading and price at last trade for the call option. The final two columns show the same for a put option.

The quoted price is the price of an option to buy or sell one share. As mentioned earlier, one contract is for the purchase or sale of 100 shares. A contract, therefore, costs 100 times the price shown. Because most options are priced at less than $10 and some are priced at less than $1, individuals do not have to be extremely wealthy to trade options.

The Wall Street Journal also shows the total call volume, put volume, call open interest, and put open interest for each exchange. The numbers for Tuesday, August 4, 1998, are shown in Table 6.2. The volume is the total number of contracts traded on the day. The open interest is the number of contracts outstanding.

From Table 6.1, it appears that there were arbitrage opportunities on May 11, 1995. For example, an August put option on Chase with a strike price of 75 is quoted as $5\frac{1}{4}$. Because the stock price is $69\frac{5}{8}$, it appears that this put and the stock could be purchased, and the put exercised immediately, for a profit of $\frac{1}{8}$. In fact, arbitrage opportunities such as this almost certainly did not exist. For both options and

Table 6.1 Stock Option Quotations from *The Wall Street Journal* on August 5, 1998

Option/Strike		Exp.	—Call— Vol.	—Call— Last	—Put— Vol.	—Put— Last
AscendC	40	Aug	768	8 1/4	80	3/8
47 11/16	40	Sep	217	8 7/8	716	1 1/16
47 11/16	45	Aug	1118	3 7/8	1003	1 5/16
47 11/16	45	Sep	823	5 1/8	289	2 1/2
47 11/16	50	Aug	3232	1 1/2	1075	3 3/8
47 11/16	50	Sep	831	2 3/4	120	5
47 11/16	55	Aug	1821	5/16	13	7 7/8
47 11/16	55	Sep	1337	1 1/2	...	...
AsiaPlp	12 1/2	Sep	600	1/4	...	...
AspctT	25	Mar	...	...	500	2
AtlCstAir	22 1/2	Sep	1000	2 1/8	20	13/16
22 3/4	25	Aug	...	...	1000	2 3/16
BMC Sft	45	Aug	...	...	393	1 5/16
Baan	30	Aug	400	8 1/8	20	1/16
38 1/8	35	Aug	300	3 3/4	30	5/8
38 1/8	40	Aug	255	1 1/4	140	2 3/8
BakrHu	22 1/2	Aug	50	1 9/16	2056	1/2
22 5/8	25	Aug	437	3/8	2012	2 1/4
BallyTotF	30	Sep	1000	1 1/8	2	5 1/8
BancOne o	50	Aug	531	1/2	50	2 7/8
BankAm	85	Sep	297	4 1/4	226	3
83 3/4	90	Aug	627	1/2	76	5 1/4
BellAtl	45	Sep	515	1 3/4	75	1 1/2
44 3/16	55	Oct	300	5/16	...	...
BergBrun	40	Aug	3	3 3/8	280	1/2
41 3/4	45	Aug	342	7/8	591	3
41 3/4	50	Aug	730	1/4	103	7
41 3/4	60	Sep	272	1/4	...	...
BestBuy	45	Aug	36	2 3/4	240	1 5/8
BeverlyE	10	Sep	2000	7/8	...	...
Blk Dk	55	Nov	...	...	962	3 1/2
Boeing	35	Aug	1533	2 1/2	75	5/8
36 13/16	40	Aug	197	3/8	359	3 3/8
36 13/16	40	Feb	595	3 1/2	7	5
36 13/16	42 1/2	Aug	815	3/16	10	5
36 13/16	45	Sep	265	5/16	10	7 1/2
36 13/16	45	Nov	351	7/8	10	7 3/4
BostChkn	7 1/2	Jan	...	...	3000	6 1/2
Bowatr	40	Sep	...	...	440	1 3/8
41 7/8	45	Aug	286	9/16	...	...
BrMSq	100	Sep	318	10 3/4	185	1 5/8
107 1/4	110	Aug	506	2 3/8	135	3 1/8
107 1/4	120	Aug	394	3/8	2	11
107 1/4	120	Sep	439	1	3	12 3/8
BwnFer	40	Sep	1524	5/16	...	...
BudgetGp	30	Aug	1000	3/16	...	...
CBS Cp	35	Aug	610	9/16	70	1 5/8
CHS El	17 1/2	Aug	582	1	30	1 15/16
CMG Inf	70	Sep	863	9 1/4	...	...
CNS Inc	5	Oct	250	1/4	100	7/8
4 3/16	5	Jan	250	1/2	...	...
Cadence	25	Aug	5	3 1/8	520	1/2
27 9/16	27 1/2	Aug	53	1 1/16	520	1
CapOne	110	Aug	13	4 3/8	1240	3 1/2
CashAmer	15	Oct	254	1 1/4	...	...
Caterp	45	Sep	26	4	320	15/16
Cellstar	15	Aug	460	1/4	56	3 1/2
Cendant	15	Aug	324	1 1/8	429	13/16
15 3/8	15	Sep	318	1 13/16	25	1 3/8
15 3/8	15	Nov	1266	2 11/16	251	1 11/16
15 3/8	17 1/2	Aug	568	3/8	596	2 1/4
15 3/8	17 1/2	Sep	426	3/4	7	2 3/4
15 3/8	20	Aug	630	1/8	35	4 7/8
15 3/8	20	Nov	265	7/8	40	5 1/8
15 3/8	22 1/2	Nov	320	7/16	4	7 3/8
Centocor	30	Oct	502	6 1/2	...	...
32 15/16	35	Aug	107	3/4	312	2 9/16
32 15/16	35	Sep	27	2 5/8	305	2 3/4
Chase n	65	Aug	354	5 1/8	360	3/4
69 5/8	70	Aug	496	2 1/4	734	2 1/4
69 5/8	70	Sep	243	3 3/4	199	2 3/4
69 5/8	75	Aug	836	3/4	613	5 1/4
Chiqta	10	Sep	10	2 3/8	300	1/2
Chryslr	40	Oct	...	...	2250	3/8
CienaCp	60	Aug	...	...	357	11/16
72 3/16	70	Aug	50	5	275	2 5/8
Cisco	75	Jan	14	23 3/8	1005	2 5/8
93 1/8	80	Aug	3668	13 1/4	134	9/16
93 1/8	80	Oct	214	16	2065	2 1/4
93 1/8	85	Aug	2156	9 7/8	7630	1
93 1/8	85	Oct	253	12 5/8	102	2 3/4
93 1/8	90	Aug	2143	6	7692	2 3/8
93 1/8	95	Aug	6778	3 1/4	1215	4 7/8
93 1/8	95	Sep	3083	5 1/8	1358	6 1/4
93 1/8	95	Oct	314	7	162	8
93 1/8	100	Aug	9690	1 11/16	226	8
93 1/8	100	Sep	862	3	80	9 1/2
93 1/8	100	Oct	467	4 1/2	3	10
93 1/8	100	Jan	694	8 3/8	14	13
93 1/8	105	Aug	5184	11/16	20	12 1/8
93 1/8	105	Sep	367	2	...	3 1/8
93 1/8	105	Oct	559	3	...	...
93 1/8	110	Aug	357	3/8	50	11 3/4
93 1/8	110	Sep	617	1 1/16	...	...
93 1/8	110	Jan	318	4 3/4	...	...
Citicp	150	Aug	35	7	337	2 5/8
154	160	Aug	451	3	112	7 1/8
154	165	Aug	375	1 1/2	244	10 1/8
154	170	Aug	266	1	130	13
Coke	65	Aug	...	...	263	1/16
78 5/8	75	Aug	1727	4 7/8	2060	1 1/16
78 5/8	75	Nov	3	8 1/4	334	2 7/8
78 5/8	80	Aug	1757	1 7/8	4822	2 3/4
78 5/8	80	Sep	988	3	157	3 7/8
78 5/8	85	Aug	576	5/8	450	6 1/2
78 5/8	85	Sep	1102	1 1/4	90	7 1/4
78 5/8	85	Nov	475	2 7/8	35	7
78 5/8	90	Nov	236	1 1/2	20	10 1/4
ColgPl	90	Sep	...	...	517	3 1/4
ComScop	17 1/2	Aug	255	1 1/8	5	1 3/4
16 3/4	17 1/2	Sep	231	2 3/16	5	2 9/16
CANTV	22 1/2	Sep	...	...	300	2 5/8
Compaq	25	Jan	135	8 3/4	259	3/4
32 1/16	27 1/2	Aug	27	5 3/8	484	1/8
32 1/16	30	Aug	7064	2 1/2	1064	1/2
32 1/16	30	Sep	367	3 3/8	110	1 1/16
32 1/16	30	Oct	518	3 7/8	189	1 3/8
32 1/16	30	Jan	311	5 1/8	131	2 9/16
32 1/16	32 1/2	Aug	1967	1 5/16	1275	1 1/2
32 1/16	32 1/2	Sep	196	1 7/8	535	2
32 1/16	32 1/2	Oct	473	2 1/2	71	2 3/8
32 1/16	35	Aug	3633	7/16	467	3 1/4
32 1/16	35	Sep	2177	1	85	3 3/8
32 1/16	35	Oct	894	1 3/4	144	4 1/8
32 1/16	35	Jan	644	3	35	5
32 1/16	40	Jan	992	1 7/16	35	8 1/2
CompAssoc	35	Aug	1841	3/4	163	3 1/2
31 7/8	35	Sep	289	1 9/16	79	4 1/4
31 7/8	40	Aug	801	1/4	35	8 1/4
CptrLrn	25	Aug	112	1 11/16	423	2 3/4
Cmpuwr	50	Sep	22	5 3/4	1030	4
50	55	Sep	196	2 1/2	1000	7
50	65	Feb	2000	2 1/8	...	...
Comvrs	55	Oct	621	1 3/4	...	...
Cnseco	40	Aug	760	1 1/16	39	2 1/2
37 5/16	40	Nov	708	2 3/4	48	3 7/8
37 5/16	45	Sep	555	15/16	55	7 1/2
ConsCap	30	Nov	1000	1/4	...	...
CoopCam	35	Aug	17	9/16	500	4
CresRE	30	Jan	...	...	300	3 3/8
Deere	45	Aug	10	1/2	257	5 1/8
DellCptr	80	Aug	348	26 1/8	55	7/16
105 13/16	90	Aug	136	18	810	1 1/4
105 13/16	95	Aug	277	13 1/8	1075	2 1/4
105 13/16	100	Aug	1062	9 3/4	1340	3 1/2
105 13/16	100	Sep	70	13 1/2	295	7
105 13/16	105	Aug	1084	6 7/8	1692	5 1/2
105 13/16	105	Sep	220	11 1/4	358	9 1/4
105 13/16	110	Aug	3609	4 3/4	510	8 1/2
105 13/16	110	Sep	655	8 5/8	25	12
105 13/16	115	Aug	2995	3	340	12
105 13/16	115	Sep	506	6 3/4	10	13
105 13/16	120	Aug	3727	1 7/8	39	15
105 13/16	120	Sep	353	5	...	...
105 13/16	130	Aug	1749	11/16	105	23 1/2
105 13/16	130	Sep	267	2 7/8	20	26
105 13/16	140	Sep	291	1 1/2	...	...
105 13/16	140	Nov	237	5	...	...
DeltaAr	120	Aug	348	3 1/8	150	6 3/8
DiaOff	30	Sep	20	1 7/8	547	2 1/2
Diebold	30	Sep	...	...	400	5 1/4
Disney	30	Jan	35	5 1/4	502	1 11/16
32 13/16	32 1/2	Aug	512	1 3/8	21	1
32 13/16	32 1/2	Sep	21	2 1/2	343	1 7/16
32 13/16	33 3/8	Aug	112	1 5/8	507	1 1/2
32 13/16	35	Aug	537	9/16	531	2 1/2
32 13/16	35	Sep	300	1 1/4	94	2 1/2
32 13/16	36 5/8	Aug	241	5/16	130	3 3/8
32 13/16	36 5/8	Oct	214	1 5/16	330	3 5/8
32 13/16	40	Aug	186	1/8	573	5 3/4
32 13/16	40	Oct	975	11/16	123	6 3/4
32 13/16	42 1/2	Oct	285	7/16	...	...
32 13/16	43 3/8	Oct	6950	3/8	...	...
DollarGn	40	Nov	500	3 1/4	23	3 3/4
Dressr	45	Oct	...	...	2000	11 7/8
31 1/2	45	Jan	...	...	4000	12 7/8
DuPont	65	Sep	786	1 1/4	5	3 3/8
60 3/4	70	Aug	505	1/8	111	7 3/8
ECI	35	Aug	...	...	2090	2 15/16
32 7/8	35	Nov	...	...	2000	3 3/4
EMC	50	Aug	469	1 7/8	1619	2 5/8
48 3/4	50	Oct	654	4 1/4	...	...
48 3/4	55	Jan	260	4 1/8	...	...
48 3/4	60	Jan	1442	2 1/2	...	...
EVI Inc	45	Nov	400	3/8	...	...
EastCh	55	Mar	515	5 3/4	...	...
EKodak	80	Aug	127	2 5/16	413	1 11/16
81 1/16	85	Aug	244	5/8	72	4 1/8
Egghead	20	Aug	516	1/4	27	6 7/8
ElPNGs	30	Oct	400	5 1/8	...	...
Enron	45	Aug	1325	5 1/4	...	...
50	45	Oct	300	6 1/8	...	...
50	50	Aug	368	1 3/4	150	1
Entrgy	25	Sep	810	2 1/2	...	...
27 3/16	25	Mar	810	3 1/8	...	...
EnvoyCp	35	Aug	...	...	1080	2
35	35	Sep	10	3 3/8	350	3 1/8
EnzoBi	10	Jan	1495	2	910	1 7/16
10 1/8	12 1/2	Jan	1789	1 3/16	10	3 1/2
EricTel	27 1/2	Oct	817	2	797	2 1/2
Excite	30	Nov	6	10 5/8	310	3 1/4
38 1/2	32 1/2	Nov	...	...	400	4 1/8
38 1/2	35	Aug	71	4 7/8	776	1 1/2
38 1/2	35	Sep	1	5 5/8	311	2 9/16
38 1/2	37 1/2	Aug	123	3	460	2 1/4
38 1/2	40	Aug	553	2 7/16	95	3 3/4
38 1/2	45	Aug	396	1 1/16	127	7 1/8
38 1/2	45	Sep	1095	2 11/16	20	9 1/2
Exxon	60	Oct	145	9 1/4	325	5/8
67 1/16	65	Sep	10	3 7/8	329	1 5/8
67 1/16	65	Oct	75	4 3/8	650	1 3/4
67 1/16	70	Aug	359	1/2	43	3 3/8
67 1/16	70	Oct	145	1 7/8	433	4 1/4
FamDolr	17 1/2	Aug	500	3/8	...	...
FamGolf	25	Aug	27	3/8	486	3
F N M	60	Aug	337	2 1/4	193	1 1/2
FedDSt	55	Aug	10	7/16	410	4 1/2
FChNBD	90	Oct	400	3/4	10	12 7/8
FUnion	55	Aug	280	1 3/4	210	1 1/2
Firstplus	40	Oct	317	2 1/2	15	7 1/2
Fleetw	35	Sep	...	...	300	1 1/8
FordMot	60	Sep	514	7/8	...	...
53 7/8	65	Aug	800	1/8	...	...
ForeSys	25	Aug	267	9/16	22	2 1/16
FrnklRes	50	Aug	...	...	800	7 3/4
G T E	55	Sep	310	15/16	14	3 1/8
Gtwy2000	50	Sep	56	5 5/8	1565	3 5/8
51 9/16	55	Aug	228	1 7/16	244	4 5/8

stocks, Table 6.1 gives the prices at which the last trade took place on August 4, 1998. The last trade for the August Chase put with a strike price of 75 probably occurred much earlier in the day than the last trade on the stock. If an option trade had been attempted at the time of the last trade on the stock, the put price would have been higher than $5\frac{1}{4}$.

Table 6.2   Volume and Open Interest, August 4, 1998

Exchange	Call Volume	Call Open Interest	Put Volume	Put Open Interest
Chicago Board	627,875	12,110,413	509,873	8,579,424
American	278,263	8,771,292	138,633	4,790,149
Pacific	166,021	4,859,096	90,411	2,628,679
Philadelphia	103,383	3,719,449	62,537	2,082,897
Total	1,175,542	29,460,250	801,454	18,081,149

6.4   TRADING

Options trading is in many respects similar to futures trading (see chapter 2). An exchange has a number of members (individuals and firms) who are referred to as having seats on the exchange. Membership in an exchange entitles one to go on the floor of the exchange and trade with other members.

Market Makers

Most options exchanges (including the CBOE) use a market maker system to facilitate trading. A *market maker* for a certain option is a person who will quote both a bid and an ask price on the option whenever asked to do so. The bid is the price at which the market maker is prepared to buy and the ask is the price at which the market maker is prepared to sell. At the time the bid and the ask are quoted, the market maker does not know whether the trader who asked for the quotes wants to buy or sell the option. The ask is, of course, higher than the bid, and the amount by which the ask exceeds the bid is referred to as the *bid–ask spread*. The exchange sets upper limits for the bid–ask spread. For example, it might specify that it be no more than $0.25 for options priced at less than $0.50, $0.50 for options priced between $0.50 and $10, $0.75 for options priced between $10 and $20, and $1 for options priced over $20.

The existence of the market maker ensures that buy and sell orders can always be executed at some price without delays. Market makers, therefore, add liquidity to the market. The market makers themselves make their profits from the bid–ask spread. To hedge their risks, they use the procedures discussed in chapter 13.

Floor Broker

Floor brokers execute trades for the general public. When an individual contacts a broker to buy or sell an option, the broker relays the order to the firm's floor broker in the exchange on which the option trades. If the brokerage house does not have its own floor broker, it generally has an arrangement whereby it uses either an independent floor broker or the floor broker of another firm.

The floor broker trades either with another floor broker or with the market maker. Floor brokers may be on commission or may be paid a salary by the brokerage house for whom they execute trades.

Order Book Official

Many orders that are relayed to floor brokers are limit orders. This means that they can be executed only at the specified price or a more favorable price. Often, when a limit order reaches a floor broker, it cannot be executed immediately. (For example, a limit order to buy a call at $5 cannot be executed immediately when the market maker is quoting a bid of $4\frac{3}{4}$ and an ask of $5\frac{1}{4}$.) In most exchanges, the floor broker will then pass the order to a person known as an *order book official* (or board broker). This person enters the order into a computer along with other public limit orders. This ensures that as soon as the limit price is reached, the order is executed. The information on all outstanding limit orders is available to all traders.

The market maker/order book official system can be contrasted with the *specialist system* that is used in a few options exchanges (e.g., AMEX and PHLX) and is the most common system for trading stocks. Under this system, a person known as a specialist is responsible for being a market maker and keeping a record of limit orders. Unlike an order book official, a specialist does not make information on limit orders available to other traders.

Offsetting Orders

A trader who has purchased an option can close the position by issuing an offsetting order to sell the same option. Similarly, a trader who has written an option can close out the position by issuing an offsetting order to buy the same option. If, when an option contract is traded, neither trader is offsetting an existing position, the open interest increases by one contract. If one trader is offsetting an existing position and the other is not, the open interest stays the same. If both traders are offsetting existing positions, the open interest goes down by one contract.

6.5 COMMISSIONS

For the retail investor, commissions vary significantly from broker to broker. Discount brokers generally charge lower commissions than those charged by full-service brokers. The actual amount charged is usually calculated as a fixed cost plus a proportion of the dollar amount of the trade. Table 6.3 shows the sort of schedule that might be offered by a discount broker. Under this schedule, the purchase or sale of one contract always costs $30 (because both the maximum and minimum commission is $30 for the first contract). The purchase of eight contracts when the option price is $3 would cost $20 + (0.02 \times 2{,}400) = \$68$ in commissions.

If an option position is closed out by entering into an offsetting trade, the commission must be paid again. If the option is exercised, a trader pays the same com-

Table 6.3	A Typical Commission Schedule for a Discount Broker		

Dollar amount of Trade	Commission*
< $2,500	$20 + 0.02 of the dollar amount
$2,500 to $10,000	$45 + 0.01 of the dollar amount
> $10,000	$120 + 0.0025 of the dollar amount

*Maximum commission is $30 per contract for the first five contracts plus $20 per contract for each additional contract. Minimum commission is $30 per contract for the first contract plus $2 per contract for each additional contract.

mission as when placing an order to buy or sell the underlying stock. Typically, this is 1 to 2% of the stock's value.

Consider a trader who buys one call contract with a strike price of $50 when the stock price is $49. We suppose the option price is $4.50, so the cost of the contract is $450. Using the schedule in Table 6.3, the commission paid when the option is bought is $30. Suppose that the stock price rises and the option is exercised when it reaches $60. Assuming that the trader pays a 1.5% commission on stock trades, the commission payable when the option is exercised is

$$0.015 \times \$60 \times 100 = \$90$$

The total commission paid is, therefore, $120. Note that if the trader could sell the option for $10 instead of exercising it, there would be a saving of $60 in commissions. (This is because the commission payable when an option is sold is only $30 in our example.) In general, the commission system tends to push traders in the direction of selling options rather than exercising them.

A hidden cost in option trading (and in stock trading) is the market maker's bid–ask spread. Suppose that in the example just considered, the bid price was $4.00 and the ask price was $4.50 at the time the option was purchased. We can reasonably assume that a "fair" price for the option is halfway between the bid and the ask price, or $4.25. The cost to the buyer and to the seller of the market maker system is the difference between the fair price and the price paid. This is $0.25 per option, or $25 per contract.

6.6   MARGINS

When shares are purchased, an investor can either pay cash or use a margin account. The initial margin required is usually 50% of the value of the shares, and the maintenance margin is usually 25% of the value of the shares. The margin account operates in the same way as it does for a trader entering into a futures contract (see section 2.3).

When call and put options are purchased, the option price must be paid in full. Traders are not allowed to buy options on margin. This is because options already contain substantial leverage. Buying on margin would raise this leverage to an unacceptable level. When a trader writes options, there is a requirement that funds be maintained in a margin account. This is because the trader's broker and the exchange want to be satisfied that the trader will not default if the option is exercised. The size of the margin required depends on the circumstances.

Writing Naked Options

Consider first the situation where a stock option is naked. This means that the option position is not combined with an offsetting position in the underlying stock. The initial margin in the United States is the greater of the results of the following two calculations:

1. A total of 100% of the proceeds of the sale plus 20% of the underlying share price less the amount, if any, by which the option is out of the money.
2. A total of 100% of the proceeds of the sale plus 10% of the underlying share price.

For options on a broadly based index, the 20% in the preceding calculations is replaced by 15%. This is because an index is usually less volatile than the price of an individual stock.

> **Example 6.3**   A trader writes four naked call option contracts on a stock. The option price is $5, the strike price is $40, and the stock price is $38. Because the option is $2 out of the money, the first calculation gives
>
> $$400(5 + 0.2 \times 38 - 2) = 4,240$$
>
> The second calculation gives
>
> $$400(5 + 0.1 \times 38) = 3,520$$
>
> The initial margin requirement is, therefore, $4,240. Note that if the option had been a put, it would be $2 in the money and the margin requirement would be
>
> $$400(5 + 0.2 \times 38) = \$5,040$$
>
> In both cases the proceeds of the sale, $2,000, can be used to form part of the margin account.

A calculation similar to the initial margin calculation (but with the current market price replacing the proceeds of sale) is repeated every day. Funds can be withdrawn from the margin account when the calculation indicates that the margin required is less than the current balance in the margin account. When the calculation indicates that a significantly greater margin is required, a margin call will be made.

Writing Covered Calls

Writing covered calls involves writing call options when the shares that might have to be delivered are already owned. Covered calls are far less risky than naked calls because the worst that can happen is that the trader is required to sell shares already owned at below their market value. If covered call options are out of the money, no margin is required. The shares owned can be purchased using a margin account as described previously, and the price received for the option can be used to partially fulfill this margin requirement. If the options are in the money, no margin is required for the options. However, for the purposes of calculating the trader's equity position, the share price is reduced by the extent, if any, to which the option is in the money. This may limit the amount that the trader can withdraw from the margin account if the share price increases.

> **Example 6.4**   A trader decides to buy 200 shares of a certain stock on margin and to write two call option contracts on the stock. The stock price is $63, the strike price is $65, and the price of the option is $7. Because the options are out of the money, the margin account allows the trader to borrow 50% of the price of the stock, or $6,300. The trader is also able to use the price received for the option, $7 × 200 or $1,400, to finance the purchase of the shares. The shares cost $63 × 200 = $12,600. The minimum cash initially required from the trader for his or her trades is, therefore,

$$\$12,600 - \$6,300 - \$1,400 = \$4,900$$

In chapter 8 we discuss more complicated option trading strategies, such as spreads, combinations, straddles, strangles, and so on. There are special rules for determining the margin requirements when these trading strategies are used.

6.7   THE OPTIONS CLEARING CORPORATION

The Options Clearing Corporation (OCC) performs much the same sort of function for options markets as the clearinghouse does for futures markets (see chapter 2). It guarantees that option writers will fulfill their obligations under the terms of the option contract and keeps a record of all long and short positions. The OCC has a number of members, and all option trades must be cleared through a member. If a brokerage house is not itself a member of an exchange's OCC, it must arrange to clear its trades with a member. Members are required to have a certain minimum amount of capital and to contribute to a special fund that can be used if any member defaults on an option obligation.

When purchasing an option, the buyer must pay for it in full by the morning of the next business day. These funds are deposited with the OCC. The writer of the option maintains a margin account with a broker, as described earlier. The broker maintains a margin account with the OCC member that clears its trades. The OCC member, in turn, maintains a margin account with the OCC. The margin requirements described in the preceding section are the margin requirements imposed by the OCC on its members. A brokerage house may require higher margins from its clients. However, it cannot require lower margins.

Exercising an Option

When a trader wishes to exercise an option, the trader notifies the broker handling the trade. The broker in turn notifies the OCC member that clears its trades. This member then places an exercise order with the OCC. The OCC randomly selects a member with an outstanding short position in the same option. The member, using a procedure established in advance, selects a particular client who has written the option. If the option is a call, this client is required to sell stock at the strike price. If it is a put, the client is required to buy stock at the strike price. The client is said to be *assigned*. When an option is exercised, the open interest goes down by one.

At the expiration of the option, all in-the-money options should be exercised unless the transactions costs are so high as to wipe out the payoff from the option. Some brokerage firms will automatically exercise options for their clients at expiration when it is in their clients' interest to do so. Many exchanges also have rules for exercising stock options that are in the money at expiration.

6.8 REGULATION

Options markets in the United States are regulated in a number of ways. Both the exchanges and the Options Clearing Corporations have rules governing the behavior of traders. In addition, there are both federal and state regulatory authorities. In general, options markets have demonstrated a willingness to regulate themselves. There have been no major scandals or defaults by OCC members. Traders can have a high level of confidence in the way the market is run.

The Securities and Exchange Commission is responsible for regulating options markets in stocks, stock indices, currencies, and bonds at the federal level. The Commodity Futures Trading Commission is responsible for regulating markets for options on futures. The major options markets are in the states of Illinois and New York. These states actively enforce their own laws on unacceptable trading practices.

6.9 TAXATION

Determining the tax implications of options strategies can be tricky and an investor who is in doubt about this should consult a tax specialist. In the United States, the general rule is that (unless the taxpayer is a professional trader) gains and losses from the trading of stock options are taxed as capital gains or losses. The way that capital gains and losses are taxed in the United States was discussed in section 2.11. For both the holder and the writer of a stock option, a gain or loss is recognized when (a) the option expires unexercised or (b) the option is sold. If the option is exercised, the gain or loss from the option is rolled into the position taken in the stock and recognized when the stock position is closed out. For example, when a call option is exercised, the party with a long position is deemed to have purchased the stock at the strike price plus the call price. This is then used as a basis for calculating this party's gain or loss when the stock is eventually sold. Similarly, when a put option is exercised, the writer is deemed to have bought stock for the strike price less the original put price and the purchaser is deemed to have sold the stock for this price.

Wash Sale Rule

One tax consideration in option trading in the United States is the wash sale rule. To understand this rule, imagine an investor who buys a stock when the price is $60 and plans to keep it for the long term. If the stock price drops to $40, the investor might be tempted to sell the stock and then immediately repurchase it so that the $20 loss is realized for tax purposes. To prevent this sort of thing, the tax authorities have ruled that when the repurchase is within 30 days of the sale (i.e., between 30 days before the sale and 30 days after the sale), any loss on the sale is not deductible. The disallowance also applies where, within the 61-day period, the taxpayer enters into an option or similar contract to acquire the stock. Thus, selling a stock at a loss and buying a call option within a 30-day period will lead to the loss being disallowed. The wash sale rule does not apply if the taxpayer is a dealer in stocks or securities and the loss is sustained in the ordinary course of business.

Constructive Sales

Prior to 1997, if a United States taxpayer sold short a security while holding a long position in a substantially identical security, no gain or loss was recognized until the short position was closed out. This means that short positions could be used to defer recognition of a gain for tax purposes. The situation was changed by the Tax Relief Act of 1997. An appreciated property is now treated as "constructively sold" when the owner

1. Enters into a short sale of the same or substantially identical property;
2. Enters into a futures or forward contract to deliver the same or substantially identical property; or
3. Enters into one or more positions that eliminate substantially all of the loss and opportunity for gain.

It should be noted that transactions reducing only the risk of loss or only the opportunity for gain should not result in constructive sales. Therefore, an investor holding a long position in a stock can buy in-the-money put options on the stock without triggering a constructive sale because the upside potential is not limited.

Tax Planning Using Derivatives

Tax practitioners sometimes use options and other derivatives to minimize tax costs or maximize tax benefits. One simple transaction is a cross-border arbitrage. A company buys an option in one tax jurisdiction where the cost of the option can be offset against tax immediately while selling an identical option in another jurisdiction where the income arising from the option sale is taxed only when the option is exercised or expires. Other transactions are more complex. For example, it is sometimes advantageous to receive the income from a security in Country A and the capital gain/loss in Country B. This could be the case if Country A has a tax regime that provides for a low effective tax rate on interest and dividends and a relatively high tax rate on capital gains. One can accomplish this by arranging for a company in Country A to have legal ownership of the security and for it to enter into a forward contract to sell the security to a related company in Country B at some future time. If carefully structured, options can also be used to create a hybrid instrument that is treated as equity for rating or financial reporting purposes and as debt for tax purposes. As a debt instrument, the corporation obtains the tax benefit on the interest/dividend it pays. This can significantly reduce its cost of capital.

Tax authorities in many jurisdictions have proposed legislation designed to combat the use of derivatives for tax purposes. Before entering into any tax-motivated transaction, a treasurer should explore in detail how the structure could be unwound in the event of legislative change and how costly this process could be.

6.10 WARRANTS, EXECUTIVE STOCK OPTIONS, AND CONVERTIBLES

Usually, when a call option on a stock is exercised, the party with the short position acquires shares that have already been issued and sells them to the party with the long position for the strike price. The company whose stock underlies the option is not involved in any way. Warrants and executive stock options are call options that work slightly differently. They are written by a company on its own stock. When they are exercised, the company issues more of its own stock and sells them to the option holder for the strike price. The exercise of a warrant or executive stock option, therefore, leads to an increase in the number of shares of the company's stock that are outstanding.[2]

Warrants are call options that often come into existence as a result of a bond issue. They are added to the bond issue to make it more attractive to investors. Typically, a warrant lasts for a number of years. Once they have been created, they sometimes trade separately from the bonds to which they were originally attached.

Executive stock options are call options issued to executives to motivate them to act in the best interests of the company's shareholders. They are usually at-the-money when they are first issued. After a period of time they become vested and can be exercised. Unlike warrants and exchange-traded stock options they cannot be sold. They often last as long 10 or 15 years.

A *convertible bond* is a bond issued by a company that can be converted into equity at certain times using a predetermined exchange ratio. It is, therefore, a bond with an embedded call option on the company's stock. Convertibles are like warrants and executive stock options in that their exercise leads to more shares being issued by the company. Convertibles will be discussed in more detail in chapter 23.

---

[2]This in turn leads to some dilution in the value of the equity. The impact of this on the price of the option will be discussed in chapter 11.

SUMMARY

Options trade on a wide range of different assets on exchanges and in the over-the-counter market. An exchange must specify the terms of the option contracts it trades. In particular, it must specify the size of the contract, the precise expiration time, and the strike price.

The terms of a stock option are not adjusted for cash dividends. However, they are adjusted for stock dividends and stock splits. The aim of the adjustment is to keep the positions of both the writer and the buyer of a contract unchanged.

Most option exchanges use a market-maker system. A market maker is a person who is prepared to quote both a bid (the market maker's buying price) and an ask (the market maker's selling price). Market makers improve the liquidity of the market and ensure that there is never any delay in executing market orders. They themselves make a profit from the difference between their bid and ask prices (known as their bid–ask spread). The exchange has rules specifying upper limits for the bid–ask spread.

Writers of options have potential liabilities and are required to maintain margins with their brokers. The broker, if not a member of the Options Clearing Corporation, will maintain a margin account with a firm that is a member. This firm will in turn maintain a margin account with the Options Clearing Corporation. The Options Clearing Corporation is responsible for keeping a record of all outstanding contracts, handling exercise orders, and so on.

SUGGESTIONS FOR FURTHER READING

Chance, D. M. *An Introduction to Derivatives,* 4th ed. Orlando, Fla.: Dryden Press, 1998.

Cox, J. C., and M. Rubinstein. *Options Markets.* Englewood Cliffs, N.J.: Prentice Hall, 1985.

Kolb, R. W. *Futures, Options, and Swaps*, 2nd ed. New York: Blackwell, 1997.

McMillan, L. G. *Options as a Strategic Investment*, 3rd ed. New York: New York Institute of Finance, 1992.

QUESTIONS AND PROBLEMS
(ANSWERS IN SOLUTIONS MANUAL)

6.1. Explain why brokers require margins from clients when they write options but not when they buy options.

6.2. A stock option is on a February-May-August-November cycle. What options trade on (a) April 1 and (b) May 30?

6.3. A company declares a 3-for-1 stock split. Explain how the terms of a call option contract with a strike price of $60 change.

6.4. Explain the difference between the specialist system and the market maker/order book official system for the organization of trading at an exchange.

6.5. Explain carefully the difference between writing a put option and buying a call option.

6.6. The treasurer of a corporation is trying to choose between the use of options and forward contracts to hedge the corporation's foreign exchange risk. Discuss the advantages and disadvantages of each.

6.7. Consider an exchange-traded call option contract to buy 500 shares with an exercise price of $40 and maturity in four months. Explain how the terms of the option contract change when there is
   (a) A 10% stock dividend.
   (b) A 10% cash dividend.
   (c) A 4-for-1 stock split.

6.8. "If most of the call options on a stock are in the money, it is likely that the stock price has risen rapidly in the last few months." Discuss this statement.

6.9. What is the effect of an unexpected cash dividend on (a) a call option price and (b) a put option price?

6.10. Options on General Motors' stock are on a March-June-September-December cycle. What options trade on (a) March 1; (b) June 30; and (c) August 5?

6.11. Explain why the market maker's bid–ask spread represents a real cost to options traders.

6.12. A trader writes five naked call option contracts. The option price is $3.50, the strike price is $60, and the stock price is $57. What is the initial margin requirement?

ASSIGNMENT QUESTIONS

6.13. An trader buys 500 shares of a stock and sells five call option contracts on the stock. The strike price is $30. The price of the option is $3. What is the trader's minimum cash investment (a) if the stock price is $28 and (b) if the stock price is $32?

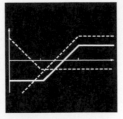

CHAPTER 7

PROPERTIES OF STOCK OPTION PRICES

This chapter looks at the factors affecting stock option prices. It then uses a number of different arbitrage arguments to explore the relationships between European option prices, American option prices, and the underlying stock price. The most important of these relationships is put–call parity. The chapter examines whether American options should be exercised early. It shows that it is never optimal to exercise an American call option on a non-dividend-paying stock prior to the option's expiration, but that under some circumstances the early exercise of an American put option on such a stock is optimal.

7.1 FACTORS AFFECTING OPTION PRICES

There are six factors affecting the price of a stock option:

1. The current stock price.
2. The strike price.
3. The time to expiration.
4. The volatility of the stock price.
5. The risk-free interest rate.
6. The dividends expected during the life of the option.

In this section we consider what happens to option prices when one of these factors changes with all the others remaining fixed. The results are summarized in Table 7.1.

Stock Price and Strike Price

If it is exercised at some time in the future, the payoff from a call option is the amount by which the stock price exceeds the strike price. Call options, therefore, become more valuable as the stock price increases and less valuable as the strike price increases. For a put option, the payoff on exercise is the amount by which the strike price exceeds the stock price. Put options, therefore, behave in the opposite way to call options. They become less valuable as the stock price increases and more valuable as the strike price increases.

Table 7.1	Summary of the Effect on the Price of a Stock Option of Increasing One Variable While Keeping all Others Fixed			
Variable	*European Call*	*European Put*	*American Call*	*American Put*
Stock price	+	−	+	−
Strike price	−	+	−	+
Time to expiration	?	?	+	+
Volatility	+	+	+	+
Risk-free rate	+	−	+	−
Dividends	−	+	−	+

Time to Expiration

Consider next the effect of the expiration date. Both put and call American options become more valuable as the time to expiration increases. To see this, consider two options that differ only with respect to the expiration date. The owner of the long-life option has all the exercise opportunities open to the owner of the short-life option— and more. The long-life option must, therefore, always be worth at least as much as the short-life option.

European put and call options do not necessarily become more valuable as the time to expiration increases. This is because the owner of a long-life European option does not have all the exercise opportunities open to the owner of a short-life European option. The owner of the long-life European option can exercise only at the maturity of that option. Consider two European call options on a stock, one with an expiration date in one month and the other with an expiration date in two months. Suppose that a very large dividend is expected in six weeks. The dividend will cause the stock price to decline. It is possible that this will lead to the short-life option being worth more than the long-life option.

Volatility

The volatility of a stock price, σ, is defined so that $\sigma \sqrt{\Delta t}$ is the standard deviation of the return on the stock in a short length of time, Δt. It is a measure of how uncertain we are about future stock price movements. As volatility increases, the chance that the stock will do very well or very poorly increases. For the owner of a stock, these two outcomes tend to offset each other. However, this is not so for the owner of a call or put. The owner of a call benefits from price increases but has limited downside risk in the event of price decreases because the most that the owner can lose is the price of the option. Similarly, the owner of a put benefits from price decreases but has limited downside risk in the event of price increases. The value of both calls and puts, therefore, increases as volatility increases.

Risk-Free Interest Rate

The risk-free interest rate affects the price of an option in a less clear-cut way. As interest rates in the economy increase, the expected growth rate of the stock price tends to increase. However, the present value of any future cash flows received by the holder of the option decreases. These two effects tend to decrease the value of a put option. Hence, put option prices decline as the risk-free interest rate increases. In the case of calls, the first effect tends to increase the price and the second effect tends to decrease it. It can be shown that the first effect always dominates the second effect; that is, the price of a call always increases as the risk-free interest rate increases.

It should be emphasized that these results assume that all other variables remain fixed. In practice, when interest rates rise (fall), stock prices tend to fall (rise). The net effect of an interest rate change and the accompanying stock price change, therefore, may be different from that just given.

Dividends

Dividends have the effect of reducing the stock price on the ex-dividend date. This is bad news for the value of call options and good news for the value of put options. The value of a call option is, therefore, negatively related to the size of any anticipated dividend, and the value of a put option is positively related to the size of any anticipated dividend.

7.2   ASSUMPTIONS AND NOTATION

We now move on to derive some relationships between option prices that do not require any assumptions about volatility and the probabilistic behavior of stock prices. The assumptions we do make are similar to those we made when deriving forward and futures prices in chapter 3. We assume that there are some market participants, such as large investment banks, for which

1. There are no transactions costs.
2. All trading profits (net of trading losses) are subject to the same tax rate.
3. Borrowing and lending at the risk-free interest rate is possible.

We assume that these market participants are prepared to take advantage of arbitrage opportunities as they arise. As discussed in chapters 1 and 3, this means that any available arbitrage opportunities disappear very quickly. For the purposes of our analyses, it is, therefore, reasonable to assume that there are no arbitrage opportunities.

We will use the following notation:

S_0: current stock price
S_T: stock price at time T
X: strike price of option
T: time of expiration of option
r: risk-free rate of interest for maturity T (continuously compounded)
C: value of American call option to buy one share
P: value of American put option to sell one share
c: value of European call option to buy one share
p: value of European put option to sell one share

It should be noted that r is the nominal rate of interest, not the real rate of interest. We can assume that $r > 0$. Otherwise, a risk-free investment would provide no advantages over cash.

7.3 UPPER AND LOWER BOUNDS FOR OPTION PRICES

In this section we derive upper and lower bounds for option prices. These do not depend on any particular assumptions about the factors mentioned in section 7.1 (except $r > 0$). If the option price is above the upper bound or below the lower bound, there are profitable opportunities for arbitrageurs.

Upper Bounds

An American or European call option gives the holder the right to buy one share of a stock for a certain price. No matter what happens, the option can never be worth more than the stock. Hence, the stock price is an upper bound to the option price:

$$c \le S_0 \text{ and } C \le S_0$$

If these relationships do not hold, an arbitrageur can easily make a riskless profit by buying the stock and selling the call option.

An American or European put option gives the holder the right to sell one share of a stock for X. No matter how low the stock price becomes, the option can never be worth more than X. Hence

$$p \le X \text{ and } P \le X$$

For European put options, we know that at time T the option will not be worth more than X. It follows that its value today cannot be more than the present value of X:

$$p \le Xe^{-rT}$$

If this were not true, an arbitrageur could make a riskless profit by selling the option and investing the proceeds of the sale at the risk-free interest rate.

Lower Bound for European Calls on Non-Dividend-Paying Stocks

A lower bound for the price of a European call option on a non-dividend-paying stock is

$$S_0 - Xe^{-rT}$$

We first illustrate this with a numerical example and then present a more formal argument.

Suppose that $S_0 = \$20$, $X = \$18$, $r = 10\%$ per annum, and $T = 1$ year. In this case,

$$S_0 - Xe^{-rT} = 20 - 18e^{-0.1} = 3.71$$

or $3.71. Consider the situation where the European call price is $3.00, which is less than the theoretical minimum of $3.71. An arbitrageur can buy the call and short the stock. This provides a cash inflow of $20.00 − $3.00 = $17.00. If invested for one year at 10% per annum, the $17.00 grows to $17e^{0.1}$ = $18.79. At the end of the year, the option expires. If the stock price is greater than $18, the arbitrageur exercises the option, closes out the short position, and makes a profit of

$$\$18.79 - \$18.00 = \$0.79$$

If the stock price is less than $18, the stock is bought in the market and the short position is closed out. The arbitrageur then makes an even greater profit. For example, if the stock price is $17, the arbitrageur's profit is

$$\$18.79 - \$17.00 = \$1.79$$

For a more formal argument, we consider the following two portfolios:

> *Portfolio A*: one European call option plus an amount of cash equal to Xe^{-rT}
> *Portfolio B*: one share

In portfolio A, if the cash is invested at the risk-free interest rate, it will grow to X at time T. If $S_T > X$, the call option is exercised at time T and portfolio A is worth S_T. If $S_T < X$, the call option expires worthless and the portfolio is worth X. Hence, at time T portfolio A is worth

$$\max(S_T, X)$$

Portfolio B is worth S_T at time T. Hence, portfolio A is always worth at least as much as, and is sometimes worth more than, portfolio B at time T. It follows that it must be worth at least as much as portfolio B today. Hence

$$c + Xe^{-rT} \geq S_0$$

or

$$c \geq S_0 - Xe^{-rT}$$

Because the worst that can happen to a call option is that it expires worthless, its value must be positive. This means that $c \geq 0$ and, therefore,

$$c \geq \max(S_0 - Xe^{-rT}, 0) \tag{7.1}$$

Example 7.1 Consider a European call option on a non-dividend-paying stock where the stock price is $51, the exercise price is $50, the time to maturity is six months, and the risk-free rate of interest is 12% per annum. In this case, $S_0 = 51, X = 50, T = 0.5$, and $r = 0.12$. From equation (7.1), a lower bound for the option price is $S_0 - Xe^{-rT}$, or

$$51 - 50e^{-0.12 \times 0.5} = \$3.91$$

Lower Bound for European Puts on Non-Dividend-Paying Stocks

For a European put option on a non-dividend-paying stock, a lower bound for the price is

$$Xe^{-rT} - S_0$$

Again, we first illustrate this with a numerical example and then present a more formal argument.

Suppose that $S_0 = \$37$, $X = \$40$, $r = 5\%$ per annum, and $T = 0.5$ year. In this case,

$$Xe^{-rT} - S_0 = 40e^{-0.05 \times 0.5} - 37 = 2.01$$

or $2.01. Consider the situation where the European put price is $1.00, which is less than the theoretical minimum of $2.01. An arbitrageur can borrow $38.00 for six months to buy both the put and the stock. At the end of the six months, the arbitrageur will be required to repay $38e^{0.05 \times 0.5} = \$38.96$. If the stock price is below $40.00, the arbitrageur exercises the option to sell the stock for $40.00, repays the loan, and makes a profit of

$$\$40.00 - \$38.96 = \$1.04$$

If the stock price is greater than $40.00, the arbitrageur discards the option, sells the stock, and repays the loan for an even greater profit. For example, if the stock price is $42.00, the arbitrageur's profit is

$$\$42.00 - \$38.96 = \$3.04$$

For a more formal argument, we consider the following two portfolios:

Portfolio C: one European put option plus one share
Portfolio D: an amount of cash equal to Xe^{-rT}

If $S_T < X$, the option in portfolio C is exercised at time T, and the portfolio becomes worth X. If $S_T > X$, the put option expires worthless, and the portfolio is worth S_T at time T. Hence portfolio C is worth

$$\max(S_T, X)$$

at time T. Assuming that the cash is invested at the risk-free interest rate, portfolio D is worth X at time T. Hence, portfolio C is always worth as much as, and is sometimes worth more than, portfolio D at time T. It follows that in the absence of arbitrage opportunities, portfolio C must be worth at least as much as portfolio D today. Hence

$$p + S_0 \geq Xe^{-rT}$$

or

$$p \geq Xe^{-rT} - S_0$$

Because the worst that can happen to a put option is that it expires worthless, its value must be non-negative. This means that

$$p \geq \max(Xe^{-rT} - S_0, 0) \qquad (7.2)$$

Example 7.2 Consider a European put option on a non-dividend-paying stock where the stock price is $38, the exercise price is $40, the time to maturity is three months, and the risk-free rate of interest is 10% per annum. In this case, $S_0 = 38$,

$X = 40$, $T = 0.25$, and $r = 0.10$. From equation (7.2), a lower bound for the option price is $Xe^{-rT} - S_0$, or

$$40e^{-0.1 \times 0.25} - 38 = \$1.01$$

7.4 PUT–CALL PARITY

We now derive an important relationship between p and c for a non-dividend-paying stock. Consider the following two portfolios:

Portfolio A: one European call option plus an amount of cash equal to Xe^{-rT}
Portfolio C: one European put option plus one share

Both are worth

$$\max(S_T, X)$$

at expiration of the options. Because the options are European, they cannot be exercised prior to the expiration date. The portfolios must, therefore, have identical values today. This means that

$$c + Xe^{-rT} = p + S_0 \tag{7.3}$$

This relationship is known as *put–call parity*. It shows that the value of a European call with a certain exercise price and exercise date can be deduced from the value of a European put with the same exercise price and date, and vice versa.

If equation (7.3) does not hold, there are arbitrage opportunities. Suppose that the stock price is $31, the exercise price is $30, the risk-free interest rate is 10% per annum, the price of a three-month European call option is $3, and the price of a three-month European put option is $2.25. In this case,

$$c + Xe^{-rT} = 3 + 30e^{-0.1 \times 0.25} = 32.26$$
$$p + S_0 = 2.25 + 31 = 33.25$$

Portfolio C is overpriced relative to portfolio A. The correct arbitrage strategy is to buy the securities in portfolio A and short the securities in portfolio C. This involves buying the call and shorting both the put and the stock. The strategy generates a positive cash flow of

$$-3 + 2.25 + 31 = 30.25$$

upfront. When invested at the risk-free interest rate, this grows to $30.25e^{0.1 \times 0.25} = 31.02$ in three months.

If the stock price at expiration of the option is greater than $30, the call will be exercised. If it is less than $30, the put will be exercised. In either case, the investor ends up buying one share for $30. This share can be used to close out the short position. The net profit is therefore

$$\$31.02 - \$30.00 = \$1.02$$

For an alternative situation, suppose that the call price is \$3 and the put price is \$1. In this case,

$$c + Xe^{-rT} = 3 + 30e^{-0.1\times0.25} = 32.26$$
$$p + S_0 = 1 + 31 = 32.00$$

Portfolio A is overpriced relative to portfolio C. An arbitrageur can short the securities in portfolio A and buy the securities in portfolio C to lock in a profit. This involves shorting the call and buying both the put and the stock. The strategy involves an initial investment of

$$\$31 + \$1 - \$3 = \$29$$

at time zero. When financed at the risk-free interest rate, a repayment of $29e^{0.1\times0.25} = 29.73$ is required at the end of the three months. As in the previous case, either the call or the put will be exercised. The short call and long put option position, therefore, leads to the stock being sold for \$30.00. The net profit is, therefore,

$$\$30.00 - \$29.73 = \$0.27$$

7.5 EARLY EXERCISE: CALLS ON A NON-DIVIDEND-PAYING STOCK

This section demonstrates that it is never optimal to exercise an American call option on a non-dividend-paying stock before the expiration date.

To illustrate the general nature of the argument, consider an American call option on a non-dividend-paying stock with one month to expiration when the stock price is \$50 and the strike price is \$40. The option is deep in the money, and the trader who owns the option might well be tempted to exercise it immediately. However, if the trader plans to hold the stock for more than one month, this is not the best strategy. A better course of action is to keep the option and exercise it at the end of the month. The \$40 strike price is then paid out one month later than it would be if the option were exercised immediately, so that interest is earned on the \$40 for one month. Because the stock pays no dividend, no income from the stock is sacrificed. A further advantage of waiting rather than exercising immediately is that there is some small chance that the stock price will fall below \$40 in one month. While holding the option, the trader has insurance against a decline in the stock price below \$40. As soon as the option is exercised, this insurance is given up.

These arguments show that there are no advantages to exercising early if the trader plans to keep the stock for the remaining life of the option (one month, in this case). What if the trader thinks the stock is currently overpriced and is wondering whether to exercise the option and sell the stock? In this case, the trader is better off selling the option than exercising it.[1] The option will be bought by a trader who does want to hold the stock. (Such traders must exist. Otherwise the current stock price

---

[1] As an alternative strategy, the trader can keep the option and short the stock to lock in a better profit than \$10.

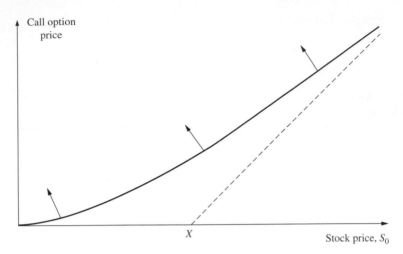

Figure 7.1   Variation of price of an American or European call option on a non-dividend-paying stock with the stock price, S_0.

would be less than \$50.) The price obtained for the option should be greater than its intrinsic value of \$10. In fact, equation (7.1) shows that the market price of the option must always be greater than

$$50 - 40e^{-0.1 \times 0.08333} = 10.33$$

Otherwise there are arbitrage opportunities.

For a more formal proof, we note from equation (7.1) that

$$c \geq S_0 - Xe^{-rT}$$

Because $C \geq c$, it follows that

$$C \geq S_0 - Xe^{-rT}$$

Assuming that $r > 0$, this equation shows that whenever $T > 0$, $C > S_0 - X$. If it were optimal to exercise early, C would equal $S_0 - X$. We deduce that it can never be optimal to exercise early.

Figure 7.1 shows the general way in which the call price varies with S_0 and X. It indicates that the call price is always above its intrinsic value of max $(S_0 - X, 0)$. As r or T or the volatility increases, the call price moves in the direction indicated by the arrows (i.e., farther away from the intrinsic value).

7.6   EARLY EXERCISE: PUTS ON A NON-DIVIDEND-PAYING STOCK

It can be optimal to exercise an American put option on a non-dividend-paying stock early. Indeed, at any given time during its life, a put option should always be exercised early if it is sufficiently deep in the money.

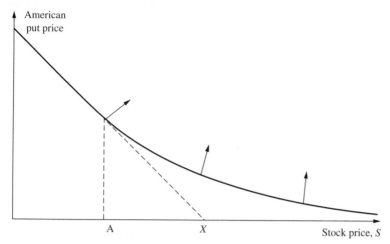

Figure 7.2   Variation of price of an American put option with the stock price, *S*.

To illustrate, we consider an extreme situation. Suppose that the strike price is $10 and the stock price is virtually zero. By exercising immediately, a trader makes an immediate gain of $10. If the trader waits, the gain from exercise might be less than $10 but cannot be more than $10, because negative stock prices are impossible. Furthermore, receiving $10 now is preferable to receiving $10 in the future. It follows that the option should be exercised immediately.

Consider an investor who holds the stock plus an in-the-money put option. The advantage of exercising immediately is that the strike price is received early and can be invested to earn additional interest. The disadvantage is that, in the event the stock price rises above the strike price, the investor will be worse off. The decision to exercise early is in essence a trade-off of these two considerations. In general, the early exercise of a put option becomes more attractive as S_0 decreases, as r increases, and as the volatility decreases.

Recall from equation (7.2) that

$$p \geq Xe^{-rT} - S_0$$

For an American put with price P, the stronger condition

$$P \geq X - S_0$$

must always hold, because immediate exercise is always possible.

Figure 7.2 shows the general way in which the price of an American put varies with S_0. Assuming $r > 0$, it is always optimal to exercise an American put immediately when the stock price is sufficiently low. When early exercise is optimal, the value of the option is $X - S_0$. The curve representing the value of the put, therefore, merges into the put's intrinsic value, $X - S_0$, for a sufficiently small value of S_0. In Figure 7.2 this value of S_0 is shown as point A. The value of the put moves in the direction indicated by the arrows when r decreases, when the volatility increases, and when T increases.

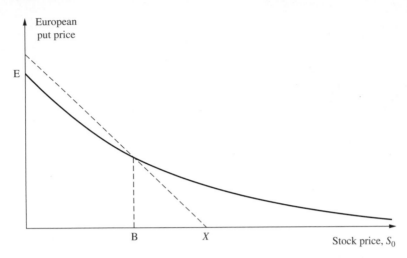

Figure 7.3   Variation of price of a European put option with the stock price, S_0.

Because there are some circumstances when it is desirable to exercise an American put option early, it follows that an American put option is always worth more than the corresponding European put option. Further, because an American put is sometimes worth its intrinsic value (see Figure 7.2), it follows that a European put option must sometimes be worth less than its intrinsic value. Figure 7.3 shows the variation of the European put price with the stock price. Note that point B in Figure 7.3, at which the price of the option is equal to its intrinsic value, must represent a higher value of the stock price than point A in Figure 7.2. Point E in Figure 7.3 is where $S_0 = 0$ and the European put price is Xe^{-rT}.

7.7   RELATIONSHIP BETWEEN AMERICAN PUT AND CALL PRICES

Put–call parity holds only for European options. However, it is possible to derive some relationships for American option prices. It can be shown (see Problem 7.19) that, when the stock pays no dividends,

$$S_0 - X \leq C - P \leq S_0 - Xe^{-rT} \tag{7.4}$$

Example 7.3   An American call option on a non-dividend-paying stock with exercise price $20.00 and maturity in five months is worth $1.50. This must also be the value of a European call option on the same stock with the same exercise price and maturity. Suppose that the current stock price is $19.00 and the risk-free interest rate is 10% per annum. From a rearrangement of equation (7.3), the price of a European put with exercise price $20 and maturity in five months is

$$1.50 + 20e^{-0.1 \times 5/12} - 19 = 1.68$$

From equation (7.4),

$$19 - 20 \leq C - P \leq 19 - 20e^{-0.1 \times 5/12}$$

or

$$1 \geq P - C \geq 0.18$$

which shows that $P - C$ lies between $1.00 and $0.18. With C at $1.50, P must lie between $1.68 and $2.50. In other words, upper and lower bounds for the price of an American put with the same strike price and expiration date as the American call are $2.50 and $1.68.

7.8 THE EFFECT OF DIVIDENDS

The results produced so far in this chapter have assumed that we are dealing with options on a non-dividend-paying stock. In this section we examine the impact of dividends. In the United States, exchange-traded stock options generally have less than a year to maturity. The dividends payable during the life of the option can usually be predicted with reasonable accuracy. We will use D to denote the present value of the dividends during the life of the option. In the calculation of D, a dividend is assumed to occur at the time of its ex-dividend date.

Lower Bound for Calls and Puts

We can redefine portfolios A and B as follows:

> *Portfolio A*: one European call option plus an amount of cash equal to $D + Xe^{-rT}$
> *Portfolio B*: one share

An argument similar to the one used to derive equation (7.1) shows that

$$c \geq S_0 - D - Xe^{-rT} \tag{7.5}$$

We can also redefine portfolios C and D as follows:

> *Portfolio C*: one European put option plus one share
> *Portfolio D*: an amount of cash equal to $D + Xe^{-rT}$

An argument similar to the one used to derive equation (7.2) shows that

$$p \geq D + Xe^{-rT} - S_0 \tag{7.6}$$

Early Exercise

When dividends are expected, we can no longer assert than an American call option will not be exercised early. Sometimes it is optimal to exercise an American call immediately prior to an ex-dividend date. This is because the dividend causes the stock price to jump down, making the option less attractive. It is never optimal to exercise a call at other times. This point is discussed further in chapter 11.

Put–Call Parity

Comparing the value at time T of the redefined portfolios A and C shows that, with dividends, the put–call parity result in equation (7.3) becomes

$$c + D + Xe^{-rT} = p + S_0 \tag{7.7}$$

Dividends cause equation (7.4) to be modified (see Problem 7.20) to

$$S_0 - D - X \le C - P \le S_0 - Xe^{-rT} \tag{7.8}$$

7.9   EMPIRICAL RESEARCH

Empirical research to test the results in this chapter might seem relatively simple to carry out once the appropriate data have been assembled. In fact, there are a number of complications:

1. It is important to be sure that option prices and stock prices are being observed at exactly the same time. For example, it is inappropriate to test for arbitrage opportunities by looking at the price at which the last trade is done each day. This point has already been made in connection with the numbers in Table 6.1.

2. It is important to consider carefully whether a trader could have taken advantage of any observed arbitrage opportunity. If the opportunity exists only momentarily, there might in practice be no way of exploiting it.

3. Transactions costs must be taken into account in determining whether arbitrage opportunities were possible.

4. Put–call parity holds only for European options. Exchange-traded stock options are American.

5. Dividends to be paid during the life of the option must be estimated.

Some of the empirical research that has been carried out is described in the papers by Bhattacharya, Galai, Gould and Galai, Klemkosky and Resnick, and Stoll that are referenced at the end of this chapter. Galai and Bhattacharya test whether option prices are ever less than their lower bounds; Stoll, Gould and Galai, and the two papers by Klemkosky and Resnick test whether put–call parity holds. We will consider the results of Bhattacharya and of Klemkosky and Resnick.

Bhattacharya's study examined whether the theoretical lower bounds for call options applied in practice. He used data consisting of the transaction prices for options on 58 stocks over a 196-day period between August 1976 and June 1977. The first test examined whether the options satisfied the condition that price be greater than intrinsic value, that is, whether $C > \max(S_0 - X, 0)$. Over 86,000 option prices were examined, and about 1.3% were found to violate this condition. In 29% of the cases, the violation disappeared by the next trade, indicating that in practice traders would not have been able to take advantage of it. When transactions costs were taken into account, the profitable opportunities created by the violation disappeared. Bhattacharya's second test examined whether options sold for less than the lower bound

$S_0 - D - Xe^{-rT}$ [see equation (7.5)]. He found that 7.6% of the option prices were less than this lower bound. However, when transactions costs were taken into account, there were no profitable opportunities.

Klemkosky and Resnick's tests of put–call parity used data on option prices taken from trades between July 1977 and June 1978. They subjected their data to several tests to determine the likelihood of options being exercised early and discarded data where early exercise was considered probable. In doing this, they felt they were justified in treating American options as European. They identified 540 situations where the call price was too low relative to the put and 540 situations where the call price was too high relative to the put. After allowing for transactions costs, they found that 38 of the first set of situations gave rise to profitable arbitrage opportunities and 147 of the second set of situations did so. The opportunities persisted when either a 5- or a 15-minute delay between the opportunity being noted and trades being executed was assumed. Klemkosky and Resnick's conclusion is that arbitrage opportunities were available to some traders, particularly market makers, during the period they studied.

SUMMARY

There are six factors affecting the value of a stock option: the current stock price, the strike price, the expiration date, the stock price volatility, the risk-free interest rate, and the dividends expected during the life of the option. The value of a call generally increases as the current stock price, the time to expiration, the volatility, and the risk-free interest rate increase. The value of a call decreases as the strike price and expected dividends increase. The value of a put generally increases as the strike price, the time to expiration, the volatility, and the expected dividends increase. The value of a put decreases as the current stock price and the risk-free interest rate increase.

It is possible to reach some conclusions about the values of stock options without making any assumptions about the probabilistic behavior of stock prices. For example, the price of a call option on a stock cannot be worth more than the price of the stock itself. Similarly, the price of a put option on a stock cannot be worth more than the option's strike price.

A call option on a non-dividend-paying stock cannot be worth less than

$$\max (S_0 - Xe^{-rT}, 0)$$

where S_0 is the stock price, X is the exercise price, r is the risk-free interest rate, and T is the time to expiration. A put option on a non-dividend-paying stock cannot be worth less than

$$\max (Xe^{-rT} - S_0, 0)$$

When dividends with present value D will be paid, the lower bound for a call option becomes

$$\max (S_0 - D - Xe^{-rT}, 0)$$

and the lower bound for a put option becomes

$$\max\left(Xe^{-rT} + D - S_0,\ 0\right)$$

Put–call parity is a relationship between the price, c, of a European call option on a stock and the price, p, of a European put option on a stock. For a non-dividend-paying stock, it is

$$c + Xe^{-rT} = p + S_0$$

For a dividend-paying stock, the put–call parity relationship is

$$c + D + Xe^{-rT} = p + S_0$$

Put–call parity does not hold for American options. However, it is possible to obtain upper and lower bounds for the difference between the price of an American call and the price of an American put.

In later chapters we carry the analyses in this chapter further by making some specific assumptions about the probabilistic behavior of stock prices. This will enable us to derive exact pricing formulas for European stock options. It will also enable us to develop numerical procedures for pricing American options.

SUGGESTIONS FOR FURTHER READING

Bhattacharya, M. "Transaction Data Tests of Efficiency of the Chicago Board Options Exchange," *Journal of Financial Economics*, 12 (1983), 161–85.

Galai, D. "Empirical Tests of Boundary Conditions for CBOE Options," *Journal of Financial Economics*, 6 (1978), 187–211.

Gould, J. P., and D. Galai. "Transactions Costs and the Relationship Between Put and Call Prices," *Journal of Financial Economics*, 1 (1974), 105–29.

Klemkosky, R. C., and B. G. Resnick. "An Ex-Ante Analysis of Put–Call Parity," *Journal of Financial Economics*, 8 (1980), 363–78.

Klemkosky, R. C., and B. G. Resnick. "Put–Call Parity and Market Efficiency," *Journal of Finance*, 34 (December 1979), 1141–55.

Merton, R. C. "The Relationship between Put and Call Prices: Comment," *Journal of Finance*, 28 (March 1973), 183–84.

Merton, R. C. "Theory of Rational Option Pricing," *Bell Journal of Economics and Management Science*, 4 (Spring 1973), 141–83.

Stoll, H. R. "The Relationship Between Put and Call Option Prices," *Journal of Finance*, 24 (December 1969), 801–24.

QUESTIONS AND PROBLEMS
(ANSWERS IN SOLUTIONS MANUAL)

7.1. An investor buys a call with strike price X and writes a put with the same strike price. Describe the investor's position.

7.2. Explain why an American option is always worth at least as much as a European option on the same asset with the same strike price and exercise date.

7.3. Explain why an American option is always worth at least as much as its intrinsic value.

7.4. List the six factors affecting stock option prices.

7.5. What is a lower bound for the price of a four-month call option on a non-dividend-paying stock when the stock price is $28, the strike price is $25, and the risk-free interest rate is 8% per annum?

7.6. What is a lower bound for the price of a one-month European put option on a non-dividend-paying stock when the stock price is $12, the strike price is $15, and the risk-free interest rate is 6% per annum?

7.7. Give two reasons why the early exercise of an American call option on a non-dividend-paying stock is not optimal. The first reason should involve the time value of money. The second reason should apply even if interest rates are zero.

7.8. "The early exercise of an American put is a trade-off between the time value of money and the insurance value of a put." Explain this statement.

7.9. Explain why the arguments leading to put–call parity for European options cannot be used to give a similar result for American options.

7.10. What is a lower bound for the price of a six-month call option on a non-dividend-paying stock when the stock price is $80, the strike price is $75, and the risk-free interest rate is 10% per annum?

7.11. What is a lower bound for the price of a two-month European put option on a non-dividend-paying stock when the stock price is $58, the strike price is $65, and the risk-free interest rate is 5% per annum?

7.12. A four-month European call option on a dividend-paying stock is currently selling for $5. The stock price is $64, the strike price is $60, and a dividend of $0.80 is expected in one month. The risk-free interest rate is 12% per annum for all maturities. What opportunities are there for an arbitrageur?

7.13. A one-month European put option on a non-dividend-paying stock is currently selling for $2\frac{1}{2}$. The stock price is $47, the strike price is $50, and the risk-free interest rate is 6% per annum. What opportunities are there for an arbitrageur?

7.14. Give an intuitive explanation of why the early exercise of an American put becomes more attractive as the risk-free interest rate increases and volatility decreases.

7.15. The price of a European call that expires in six months and has a strike price of $30 is $2. The underlying stock price is $29, and a dividend of $0.50 is expected in two months and in five months. The term structure is flat, with all risk-free interest rates being 10%. What is the price of a European put option that expires in six months and has a strike price of $30?

7.16. Explain carefully the arbitrage opportunities in Problem 7.15 if the European put price is $3.

7.17. The price of an American call on a non-dividend-paying stock is $4. The stock price is $31, the strike price is $30, and the expiration date is in three months. The risk-free interest rate is 8%. Derive upper and lower bounds for the price of an American put on the same stock with the same strike price and expiration date.

7.18. Explain carefully the arbitrage opportunities in Problem 7.17 if the American put price is greater than the calculated upper bound.

7.19. Prove the result in equation (7.4). [*Hint:* For the first part of the relationship consider (a) a portfolio consisting of a European call plus an amount of cash equal to X and (b) a portfolio consisting of an American put option plus one share.]

7.20. Prove the result in equation (7.8). [*Hint:* For the first part of the relationship consider (a) a portfolio consisting of a European call plus an amount of cash equal to $D + X$ and (b) a portfolio consisting of an American put option plus one share.]

7.21. Even when the company pays no dividends, there is a tendency for executive stock options to be exercised early. (See section 6.10 for a discussion of executive stock options.) Give a possible reason for this.

ASSIGNMENT QUESTIONS

7.22. European call and put options on a stock each have a strike price of $20 and an expiration date in three months. Each sells for $3. The risk-free interest rate is 10% per annum, the current stock price is $19, and a $1 dividend is expected in one month. Identify the arbitrage opportunity open to a trader.

7.23. Suppose that c_1, c_2, and c_3 are the prices of European call options with strike prices X_1, X_2, and X_3, respectively, where $X_3 > X_2 > X_1$ and $X_3 - X_2 = X_2 - X_1$. All options have the same maturity. Show that

$$c_2 \leq 0.5(c_1 + c_3)$$

(*Hint:* Consider a portfolio that is long one option with strike price X_1, long one option with strike price X_3, and short two options with strike price X_2.)

7.24. What is the result corresponding to that in Problem 7.23 for European put options?

7.25. Suppose that you are the manager and sole owner of a highly leveraged company. All the debt will mature in one year. If at that time the value of the company is greater than the face value of the debt, you will pay off the debt. If the value of the company is less than the face value of the debt, you will declare bankruptcy and the debtholders will own the company.
(a) Express your position as an option on the value of the company.
(b) Express the position of the debtholders in terms of options on the value of the company.
(c) What can you do to increase the value of your position?

CHAPTER 8

TRADING STRATEGIES INVOLVING OPTIONS

The profit from an investment in a single call or put option was discussed in chapter 1. In this chapter we cover more fully the range of profit patterns obtainable using options. These are presented with the assumption that the underlying asset is a stock, but similar patterns can be obtained for other underlying assets such as foreign currencies, stock indices, and futures contracts.

In the first section we consider what happens when a position in a stock option is combined with a position in the stock itself. We then move on to examine the profit patterns obtained when an investment is made in two or more different options on the same stock. One of the attractions of options is that they can be used to create a very wide range of payoff patterns. If European options were available with every single possible strike price, any payoff pattern could, in theory, be created.

8.1 STRATEGIES INVOLVING A SINGLE OPTION AND A STOCK

There are a number of different trading strategies involving a single option on a stock and the stock itself. The profits from these are illustrated in Figure 8.1. In this figure and in other figures throughout this chapter, the dashed line shows the relationship between profit and stock price for the individual securities constituting a portfolio, and the solid line shows the relationship between profit and stock price for the whole portfolio.

In Figure 8.1(a) the portfolio consists of a long position in a stock plus a short position in a call option. This is known as *writing a covered call*. The long stock position "covers" or protects a trader from the payoff on the short call that becomes necessary if there is a sharp rise in the stock price. In Figure 8.1(b) a short position in a stock is combined with a long position in a call option. This is the reverse of writing a covered call. In Figure 8.1(c) the investment strategy involves buying a put option on a stock and the stock itself. This is sometimes referred to as a *protective put* strategy. In Figure 8.1(d) a short position in a put option is combined with a short position in the stock. This is the reverse of a protective put.

The profit patterns for the portfolios in Figures 8.1 (a–d) have the same general shape as the profit patterns discussed in chapter 1 for short put, long put, long call,

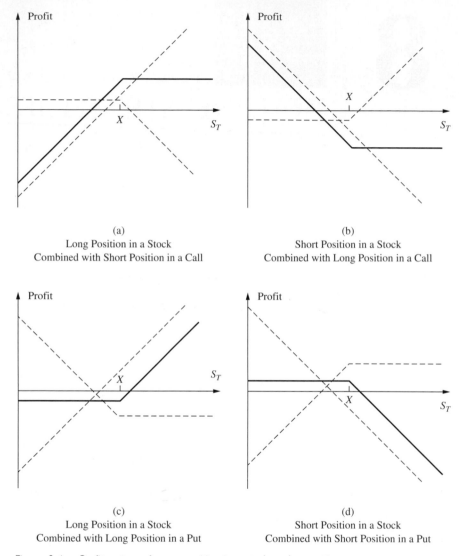

(a)
Long Position in a Stock
Combined with Short Position in a Call

(b)
Short Position in a Stock
Combined with Long Position in a Call

(c)
Long Position in a Stock
Combined with Long Position in a Put

(d)
Short Position in a Stock
Combined with Short Position in a Put

Figure 8.1   Profit patterns from a position in a stock and an option.

and short call, respectively. Put–call parity provides a way of understanding why this is so. From equation (7.7) the put–call parity relationship is

$$p + S_0 = c + Xe^{-rT} + D \tag{8.1}$$

where p is the price of a European put, S_0 is the current stock price, c is the price of a European call, X is the strike price of both call and put, r is the risk-free interest rate, T is the time to maturity of both call and put, and D is the present value of the dividends anticipated during the life of the option.

Equation (8.1) shows that a long position in a put combined with a long position in the stock is equivalent to a long call position plus a certain amount $(Xe^{-rT} + D)$ of cash. This explains why the profit pattern in Figure 8.1(c) is similar to the profit pattern from a long call position. The position in Figure 8.1(d) is the reverse of that in Figure 8.1(c) and, therefore, leads to a profit pattern similar to that from a short call position.

Equation (8.1) can be rearranged to become

$$S_0 - c = Xe^{-rT} + D - p$$

In other words, a long position in a stock combined with a short position in a call is equivalent to a short put position plus a certain amount $(Xe^{-rT} + D)$ of cash. This equality explains why the profit pattern in Figure 8.1(a) is similar to the profit pattern from a short put position. The position in Figure 8.1(b) is the reverse of that in Figure 8.1(a) and, therefore, leads to a profit pattern similar to that from a long put position.

8.2 SPREADS

A spread trading strategy involves taking a position in two or more options of the same type (i.e., two or more calls or two or more puts).

Bull Spreads

One of the most popular types of spreads is a *bull spread*. It can be created by buying a call option on a stock with a certain strike price and selling a call option on the same stock with a higher strike price. Both options have the same expiration date. The strategy is illustrated in Figure 8.2. The profits from the two option positions taken separately are shown by the dashed lines. The profit from the whole strategy is the sum of the profits given by the dashed lines and is indicated by the solid line. Since a call price always decreases as the strike price increases, the value of the option sold is always less than the value of the option bought. A bull spread, when created from calls, therefore, requires an initial investment.

Suppose that X_1 is the strike price of the call option bought, X_2 is the strike price of the call option sold, and S_T is the stock price on the expiration date of the options.

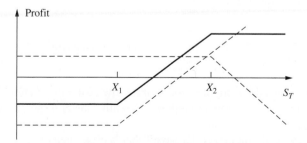

Figure 8.2   Bull spread created using call options.

Table 8.1	Payoff from a Bull Spread		
Stock Price Range	*Payoff From Long Call Option*	*Payoff From Short Call Option*	*Total Payoff*
$S_T \geq X_2$	$S_T - X_1$	$X_2 - S_T$	$X_2 - X_1$
$X_1 < S_T < X_2$	$S_T - X_1$	0	$S_T - X_1$
$S_T \leq X_1$	0	0	0

Table 8.1 shows the total payoff that will be realized from a bull spread in different circumstances. If the stock price does well and is greater than X_2, the payoff is the difference between the two strike prices, $X_2 - X_1$. If the stock price on the expiration date lies between the two strike prices, the payoff is $S_T - X_1$. If the stock price on the expiration date is below X_1, the payoff is zero. The profit in Figure 8.2 is calculated by subtracting the initial investment from the payoff.

A bull spread strategy limits the trader's upside as well as downside risk. The strategy can be described by saying that the trader has a call option with a strike price equal to X_1 and has chosen to give up some upside potential by selling a call option with strike price X_2 ($X_2 > X_1$). In return for giving up the upside potential, the trader gets the price of the option with strike price X_2. Three types of bull spreads can be distinguished:

1. Both calls are initially out of the money.
2. One call is initially in the money; the other call is initially out of the money.
3. Both calls are initially in the money.

The most aggressive bull spreads are those of type 1. They cost very little to set up and have a small probability of giving a relatively high payoff ($X_2 - X_1$). As we move from type 1 to type 2 and from type 2 to type 3, the spreads become more conservative.

Example 8.1 A trader buys for $3 a call with a strike price of $30 and sells for $1 a call with a strike price of $35. The payoff from this bull spread strategy is $5 if the stock price is above $35 and zero if it is below $30. If the stock price is between $30 and $35, the payoff is the amount by which the stock price exceeds $30. The cost of the strategy is $3 − $1 = $2. The profit is therefore as follows:

Stock Price Range	*Profit*
$S_T \leq 30$	−2
$30 < S_T < 35$	$S_T - 32$
$S_T \geq 35$	3

Bull spreads can also be created by buying a put with a low strike price and selling a put with a high strike price, as illustrated in Figure 8.3. Unlike the bull spread created from calls, bull spreads created from puts involve a positive cash flow to the trader up front (ignoring margin requirements) and a payoff that is either negative or zero.

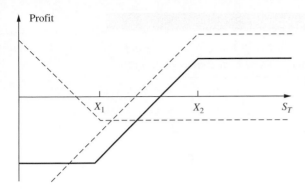

Figure 8.3   Bull spread created using put options.

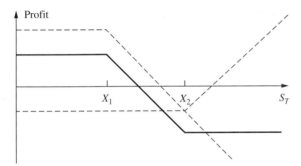

Figure 8.4   Bear spread created using call options.

Bear Spreads

A trader who enters into a bull spread is hoping that the stock price will increase. By contrast, a trader who enters into a *bear spread* is hoping that the stock price will decline. Like a bull spread, a bear spread can be created by buying a call with one strike price and selling a call with another strike price. However, in the case of a bear spread, the strike price of the option purchased is greater than the strike price of the option sold. In Figure 8.4 the profit from the spread is shown by the solid line. A bear spread created from calls involves an initial cash inflow (when margin requirements are ignored), because the price of the call sold is greater than the price of the call purchased.

Assume that the strike prices are X_1 and X_2, with $X_1 < X_2$. Table 8.2 shows the payoff that will be realized from a bear spread in different circumstances. If the stock price is greater than X_2, the payoff is negative at $-(X_2 - X_1)$. If the stock price is less than X_1, the payoff is zero. If the stock price is between X_1 and X_2, the payoff is $-(S_T - X_1)$. The profit is calculated by adding the initial cash inflow to the payoff.

> **Example 8.2**   A trader buys for $1 a call with a strike price of $35 and sells for $3 a call with a strike price of $30. The payoff from this bear spread strategy is –$5 if the stock price is above $35 and zero if it is below $30. If the stock price is between $30 and $35, the payoff is $-(S_T - 30)$. The investment generates $3 - $1 = $2 up front. The

Table 8.2   Payoff from a Bear Spread

Stock Price Range	Payoff From Long Call Option	Payoff From Short Call Option	Total Payoff
$S_T \geq X_2$	$S_T - X_2$	$X_1 - S_T$	$-(X_2 - X_1)$
$X_1 < S_T < X_2$	0	$X_1 - S_T$	$-(S_T - X_1)$
$S_T \leq X_1$	0	0	0

profit is therefore as follows:

Stock price range	Profit
$S_T \leq 30$	$+2$
$30 < S_T < 35$	$32 - S_T$
$S_T \geq 35$	-3

Like bull spreads, bear spreads limit both the upside profit potential and the downside risk. Bear spreads can be created using puts instead of calls. The trader buys a put with a high strike price and sells a put with a low strike price, as illustrated in Figure 8.5. Bear spreads created with puts require an initial investment. In essence, the trader has bought a put with a certain strike price and chosen to give up some of the profit potential by selling a put with a lower strike price. In return for the profit given up, the trader gets the price of the option sold.

Butterfly Spreads

A *butterfly spread* involves positions in options with three different strike prices. It can be created by buying a call option with a relatively low strike price, X_1; buying a call option with a relatively high strike price, X_3; and selling two call options with a strike price, X_2, halfway between X_1 and X_3. Generally, X_2 is close to the current stock price. The pattern of profits from the strategy is shown in Figure 8.6. A butterfly spread leads to a profit if the stock price stays close to X_2 but gives rise to a small loss if there is a significant stock price move in either direction. It is, therefore, an

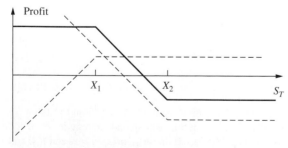

Figure 8.5   Bear spread created using put options.

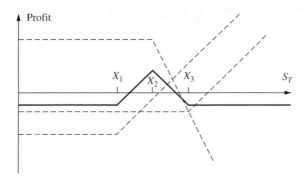

Figure 8.6   Butterfly spread created using call options.

Table 8.3   Payoff from a Butterfly Spread

Stock Price Range	Payoff From First Long Call	Payoff From Second Long Call	Payoff From Short Calls	Total Payoff*
$S_T < X_1$	0	0	0	0
$X_1 < S_T < X_2$	$S_T - X_1$	0	0	$S_T - X_1$
$X_2 < S_T < X_3$	$S_T - X_1$	0	$-2(S_T - X_2)$	$X_3 - S_T$
$S_T > X_3$	$S_T - X_1$	$S_T - X_3$	$-2(S_T - X_2)$	0

*These Payoffs are calculated using the relationship $X_2 = 0.5(X_1 + X_3)$.

appropriate strategy for a trader who feels that large stock price moves are unlikely. The strategy requires a small investment initially. The payoff from a butterfly spread is shown in Table 8.3.

Example 8.3   Suppose that a certain stock is currently worth $61. Consider a trader who feels that a significant price move in the next six months is unlikely. Suppose that the market prices of six-month calls are as follows:

Strike Price ($)	Call Price ($)
55	10
60	7
65	5

The trader could create a butterfly spread by buying one call with a $55 strike price, buying one call with a $65 strike price, and selling two calls with a $60 strike price. It costs $10 + $5 − (2 × $7) = $1 to create the spread. If the stock price in six months is greater than $65 or less than $55, there is no payoff, and the trader takes a net loss of $1. If the stock price is between $56 and $64, a profit is made. The maximum profit, $4, occurs when the stock price in six months is $60.

Butterfly spreads can be created using put options. The trader buys a put with a low strike price, buys a put with a high strike price, and sells two puts with an

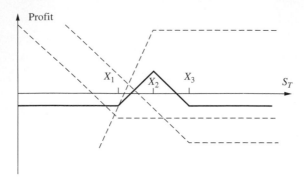

Figure 8.7   Butterfly spread created using put options.

intermediate strike price, as illustrated in Figure 8.7. The butterfly spread in Example 8.3 would be created by buying a put with a strike price of $55, buying a put with a strike price of $65, and selling two puts with a strike price of $60. If all options are European, the use of put options results in exactly the same spread as the use of call options. Put–call parity can be used to show that the initial investment is the same in both cases.

A butterfly spread can be sold or shorted by following the reverse strategy. Options are sold with strike prices of X_1 and X_3, and two options with the middle strike price, X_2, are purchased. This strategy produces a modest profit if there is a significant movement in the stock price.

Calendar Spreads

Up to now we have assumed that the options used to create a spread all expire at the same time. We now move on to *calendar spreads*, in which the options have the same strike price and different expiration dates.

A calendar spread can be created by selling a call option with a certain strike price and buying a longer-maturity call option with the same strike price. The longer the maturity of an option, the more expensive it is. A calendar spread, therefore, requires an initial investment. Figure 8.8 shows the profit from a calendar spread at the time when the short-maturity option expires. (It is assumed that the long-maturity option is sold at this time.) The pattern is similar to the profit from the butterfly spread in Figure 8.6. The trader makes a profit if the stock price at the expiration of the short-maturity option is close to the strike price of the short-maturity option. However, a loss is incurred if the stock price is significantly above or significantly below this strike price.

To understand the profit pattern from a calendar spread, first consider what happens if the stock price is very low when the short-maturity option expires. The short-maturity option is worthless, and the value of the long-maturity option is close to zero. The trader, therefore, incurs a loss that is only a little less than the cost of setting up the spread initially. Consider next what happens if the stock price, S_T, is very high when the short-maturity option expires. The short-maturity option costs the trader $S_T - X$, and the long-maturity option is worth a little more than $S_T - X$, where X is the strike

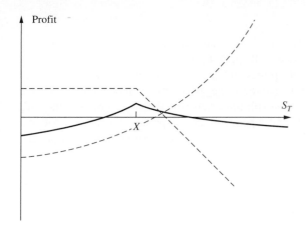

Figure 8.8   Calendar spread created using two calls.

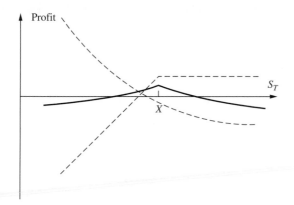

Figure 8.9   Calendar spread created using two puts.

price of the options. Again, the trader has a net loss that is a little less than the cost of setting up the spread initially. If S_T is close to X, the short-maturity option costs the trader either a small amount or nothing at all. However, the long-maturity option is still quite valuable. In this case, a significant net profit is made.

In a *neutral calendar spread* a strike price close to the current stock price is chosen. A *bullish calendar spread* involves a higher strike price, whereas a *bearish calendar spread* involves a lower strike price.

Calendar spreads can be created with put options as well as call options. The trader buys a long-maturity put option and sells a short-maturity put option. As shown in Figure 8.9, the profit pattern is similar to that obtained from using calls.

A *reverse calendar spread* is the opposite trading strategy to that in Figures 8.8 and 8.9. The trader buys a short-maturity option and sells a long-maturity option. A small profit arises if the stock price at the expiration of the short-maturity option is well above or well below the strike price of the short-maturity option. However, a significant loss results if it is close to the strike price.

Diagonal Spreads

Bull, bear, and calendar spreads can all be created from a long position in one call (put) and a short position in another call (put). In the case of bull and bear spreads, the calls (puts) have different strike prices and the same expiration date. In the case of calendar spreads, the calls (puts) have the same strike price and different expiration dates. In a *diagonal spread* both the expiration dates and the strike prices of the calls (puts) are different. There are several types of diagonal spreads. Their profit patterns are generally variations on the profit patterns from the corresponding bull or bear spreads.

8.3 COMBINATIONS

A *combination* is an option trading strategy that involves taking a position in both calls and puts on the same stock. We will consider straddles, strips, straps, and strangles.

Straddle

One popular combination is a *straddle*, which involves buying a call and a put with the same strike price and expiration date. The profit pattern is shown in Figure 8.10. The strike price is denoted by X. If the stock price is close to this strike price at expiration of the options, the straddle leads to a loss. However, if there is a sufficiently large move in either direction, a significant profit will result. The payoff from a straddle is calculated in Table 8.4.

A straddle is appropriate when a trader is expecting a large move in a stock price but does not know in which direction the move will be. Consider a trader who feels that the price of a certain stock, currently valued at $69 by the market, will move significantly in the next three months. The trader could create a straddle by buying both a put and a call with a strike price of $70 and an expiration date in three months. Suppose that the call costs $4 and the put costs $3. If the stock price stays at $69, it is easy to see that the strategy costs the trader $6. (An up-front investment of $7 is required, the call expires worthless, and the put expires worth $1.) If the stock price moves to $70, a loss of $7 is experienced. (This is the worst that can happen.)

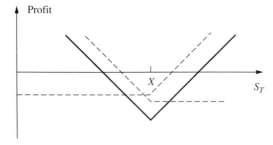

Figure 8.10   A straddle.

Table 8.4   Payoff from a Straddle

Range of Stock Price	Payoff From Call	Payoff From Put	Total Payoff
$S_T \leq X$	0	$X - S_T$	$X - S_T$
$S_T > X$	$S_T - X$	0	$S_T - X$

However, if the stock price jumps to $90, a profit of $13 is made; if the stock moves down to $55, a profit of $8 is made; and so on.

A straddle seems like a natural trading strategy when a big jump in the price of a company's stock is expected—for example, when there is a takeover bid for the company or when the outcome of a major lawsuit is expected to be announced soon. However, this is not necessarily the case. If the general view of the market is that there will be a big jump in the stock price soon, that view will be reflected in the prices of options. A trader will find options on the stock to be significantly more expensive than options on a similar stock for which no jump is expected. For a straddle to be an effective strategy, the trader must believe that there are likely to be big movements in the stock price, and this belief must be different from those of most other market participants.

The straddle in Figure 8.10 is sometimes referred to as a *bottom straddle* or *straddle purchase*. A *top straddle* or *straddle write* is the reverse position. It is created by selling a call and a put with the same exercise price and expiration date. It is a highly risky strategy. If the stock price on the expiration date is close to the strike price, a significant profit results. However, the loss arising from a large move in either direction is unlimited.

Strips and Straps

A *strip* consists of a long position in one call and two puts with the same strike price and expiration date. A *strap* consists of a long position in two calls and one put with the same strike price and expiration date. The profit patterns from strips and straps are shown in Figure 8.11. In a strip the trader is betting that there will be a big stock price move and considers a decrease in the stock price to be more likely than an increase. In a strap the trader is also betting that there will be a big stock price move. However, in this case, an increase in the stock price is considered to be more likely than a decrease.

Strangles

In a *strangle*, sometimes called a *bottom vertical combination*, a trader buys a put and a call with the same expiration date and different strike prices. The profit pattern that is obtained is shown in Figure 8.12. The call strike price, X_2, is higher than the put strike price, X_1. The payoff function for a strangle is calculated in Table 8.5.

A strangle is a similar strategy to a straddle. The trader is betting that there will be a large price move but is uncertain whether it will be an increase or a decrease.

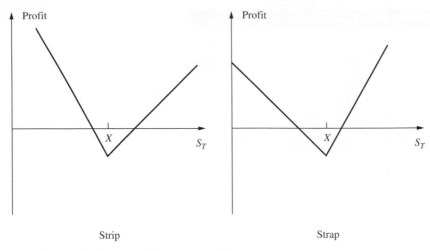

Strip   Strap

Figure 8.11   Profit patterns from a strip and a strap.

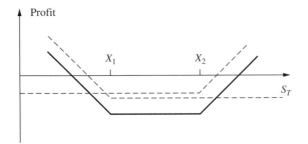

Figure 8.12   A strangle.

Comparing Figures 8.12 and 8.10, we see that the stock price has to move farther in a strangle than in a straddle for the trader to make a profit. However, the downside risk if the stock price ends up at a central value is less with a strangle.

The profit pattern obtained with a strangle depends on how close together the strike prices are. The farther apart they are, the less the downside risk and the farther the stock price has to move for a profit to be realized.

Table 8.5   Payoff from a Strangle

Range of Stock Price	Payoff From Call	Payoff From Put	Total Payoff
$S_T \leq X_1$	0	$X_1 - S_T$	$X_1 - S_T$
$X_1 < S_T < X_2$	0	0	0
$S_T \geq X_2$	$S_T - X_2$	0	$S_T - X_2$

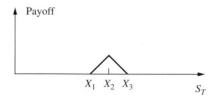

Figure 8.13 Payoff from a butterfly spread.

The sale of a strangle is sometimes referred to as a *top vertical combination*. It can be appropriate for a trader who feels that large stock price moves are unlikely. However, like the sale of a straddle, it is a risky strategy involving unlimited potential loss to the trader.

8.4 OTHER PAYOFFS

The preceding sections have demonstrated just a few of the ways in which options can be used to produce an interesting relationship between profit and stock price. If European options expiring at time T were available with every single possible strike price, any payoff function at time T could, in theory, be obtained. The simplest illustration of this involves the use of butterfly spreads. Recall that a butterfly spread is created by buying options with strike prices X_1 and X_3 and selling two options with strike price X_2, where $X_1 < X_2 < X_3$ and $X_3 - X_2 = X_2 - X_1$. Figure 8.13 shows the payoff from a butterfly spread. The pattern can be described as a spike. As X_1 and X_3 move closer together, the spike becomes smaller. Through the judicious combination of a large number of very small spikes, any payoff function can be approximated.

SUMMARY

A number of common trading strategies involve a single option and the underlying stock. For example, a covered call involves buying the stock and selling a call option on the stock, and a protective put involves buying a put option and buying the stock. The former is similar to selling a put option; the latter is similar to buying a call option.

Spreads involve either taking a position in two or more calls or taking a position in two or more puts. A bull spread can be created by buying a call (put) with a low strike price and selling a call (put) with a high strike price. A bear spread can be created by buying a call (put) with a high strike price and selling a call (put) with a low strike price. A butterfly spread involves buying calls (puts) with a low and a high strike price and selling two calls (puts) with some intermediate strike price. A calendar spread involves selling a call (put) with a short time to expiration and buying a call (put) with a longer time to expiration. A diagonal spread involves a long position in one option and a short position in another option for which both the strike prices and the expiration dates are different.

Combinations involve taking a position in both calls and puts on the same stock. A straddle combination involves taking a long position in a call and a long position in a put with the same strike price and expiration date. A strip consists of a long position in one call and two puts with the same strike price and expiration date. A strap consists of a long position in two calls and one put with the same strike price and expiration date. A strangle consists of a long position in a call and a put with different strike prices and the same expiration date. There are many other ways in which options can be used to produce interesting payoffs. It is not surprising that option trading has steadily increased in popularity and continues to fascinate investors.

SUGGESTIONS FOR FURTHER READING

Bookstaber, R. M. *Option Pricing and Strategies in Investing.* Reading, Mass.: Addison-Wesley, 1981.

Chance, D. M. *An Introduction to Derivatives,* 4th ed. Orlando, Fla.: Dryden Press, 1989.

Degler, W. H., and H. P. Becker. "19 Option Strategies and When to Use Them," *Futures* (June 1984).

McMillan, L. G. *Options as a Strategic Investment.* 3rd ed. New York: New York Institute of Finance, 1992.

Slivka, R. "Call Option Spreading," *Journal of Portfolio Management,* 7 (Spring 1981), 71–76.

Welch, W. W. *Strategies for Put and Call Option Trading.* Cambridge, Mass.: Winthrop, 1982.

Yates, J. W., and R. W. Kopprasch. "Writing Covered Call Options: Profits and Risks," *Journal of Portfolio Management,* 6 (Fall 1980), 74–80.

QUESTIONS AND PROBLEMS
(ANSWERS IN SOLUTIONS MANUAL)

8.1. What is meant by a protective put? What position in call options is equivalent to a protective put?

8.2. Explain two ways in which a bear spread can be created.

8.3. When is it appropriate for a trader to purchase a butterfly spread?

8.4. Call options on a stock are available with strike prices of $15, $17\frac{1}{2}$, and $20 and expiration dates in three months. Their prices are $4, $2, and $\frac{1}{2}$, respectively.

Explain how the options can be used to create a butterfly spread. Construct a table showing how profit varies with stock price for the butterfly spread.

8.5. What trading strategy creates a reverse calendar spread?

8.6. What is the difference between a strangle and a straddle?

8.7. A call option with a strike price of $50 costs $2. A put option with a strike price of $45 costs $3. Explain how a strangle can be created from these two options. What is the pattern of profits from the strangle?

8.8. Use put–call parity to relate the initial investment for a bull spread created from calls to the initial investment for a bull spread created from puts.

8.9. Explain how an aggressive bear spread can be created from put options.

8.10. Suppose that put options on a stock with strike prices $30 and $35 cost $4 and $7, respectively. How can the options be used to create (a) a bull spread and (b) a bear spread? Construct a table that shows the profit and payoff for both spreads.

8.11. Use put–call parity to show that the cost of a butterfly spread created from European puts is identical to the cost of a butterfly spread created from European calls.

8.12. A call with a strike price of $60 costs $6. A put with the same strike price and expiration date costs $4. Construct a table that shows the profit from a straddle. For what range of stock prices would the straddle lead to a loss?

8.13. Construct a table showing the payoff from a bull spread when puts with strike prices X_1 and X_2 are used ($X_2 > X_1$).

8.14. A trader believes that there will be a big jump in a stock price but is uncertain as to the direction. Identify six different strategies the trader can follow, and explain the differences among them.

8.15. How can a forward contract on a stock with a certain delivery price and delivery date be created from options?

8.16. A box spread is a combination of a bull call spread with strike prices X_1 and X_2 and a bear put spread with the same strike prices. The expiration date is the same for all options. What are the characteristics of a box spread?

8.17. What is the result if the strike price of the put is higher than the strike price of the call in a strangle?

8.18. One Australian dollar is currently worth $0.64. A one-year butterfly spread is set up using European call options with strike prices of $0.60, $0.65, and $0.70. The risk-free interest rates in the United States and Australia are 5% and 4%, respectively, and the volatility of the exchange rate is 15%. Use the DerivaGem software to calculate the cost of setting up the butterfly spread position. Show that the cost is the same if European put options are used instead of European call options.

ASSIGNMENT QUESTIONS

8.19. Draw a diagram showing the variation of a trader's profit or loss with the terminal stock price for a portfolio consisting of
(a) One share and a short position in one call option.
(b) Two shares and a short position in one call option.

(c) One share and a short position in two call options.

(d) One share and a short position in four call options.

In each case, assume that the call option has a strike price equal to the current stock price.

8.20. Three put options on a stock have the same expiration date and strike prices of $55, $60, and $65. The market prices are $3, $5, and $8, respectively. Explain how a butterfly spread can be created. Construct a table showing the profit from the strategy. For what range of stock prices would the butterfly spread lead to a loss?

8.21. A diagonal spread is created by buying a call with strike price X_2 and exercise date T_2 and selling a call with strike price X_1 and exercise date T_1 ($T_2 > T_1$). Draw a diagram showing the profit when (a) $X_2 > X_1$ and (b) $X_2 < X_1$.

CHAPTER 9

INTRODUCTION TO BINOMIAL TREES

A useful and very popular technique for pricing a stock option involves constructing a *binomial tree*. This is a diagram representing different possible paths that might be followed by the stock price over the life of the option. In this chapter we will take a first look at binomial trees and their relationship to an important principle known as risk-neutral valuation. The general approach adopted here is similar to that in an important paper published by Cox, Ross, and Rubinstein in 1979.[1]

The material in this chapter is intended to be introductory. More details on the use of numerical procedures involving binomial trees are in chapter 16. Risk-neutral valuation is explained more fully in chapters 11 and 19.

9.1 A ONE-STEP BINOMIAL MODEL

We start by considering a very simple situation: A stock price is currently $20, and it is known that at the end of three months the stock price will be either $22 or $18. We are interested in valuing a European call option to buy the stock for $21 in three months. This option will have one of two values at the end of the three months. If the stock price turns out to be $22, the value of the option will be $1; if the stock price turns out to be $18, the value of the option will be zero. The situation is illustrated in Figure 9.1.

It turns out that a relatively simple argument can be used to price the option in this example. The only assumption needed is that no arbitrage opportunities exist. We set up a portfolio of the stock and the option in such a way that there is no uncertainty about the value of the portfolio at the end of the three months. We then argue that, because the portfolio has no risk, the return earned on it must equal the risk-free interest rate. This enables us to work out the cost of setting up the portfolio and, therefore, the option's price. Because there are two securities (the stock and the stock option) and only two possible outcomes, it is always possible to set up the riskless portfolio.

Consider a portfolio consisting of a long position in Δ shares of the stock and a short position in one call option. We calculate the value of Δ that makes the portfolio

---

[1] See J. Cox, S. Ross, and M. Rubinstein, "Option Pricing: A Simplified Approach," *Journal of Financial Economics*, 7 (October 1979), 229-64.

Stock price = $22
Option price = $1

Stock price = $20

Stock price = $18
Option price = $0

Figure 9.1   Stock price movements in numerical example.

riskless. If the stock price moves up from $20 to $22, the value of the shares is 22Δ and the value of the option is 1, so that the total value of the portfolio is $22\Delta - 1$. If the stock price moves down from $20 to $18, the value of the shares is 18Δ and the value of the option is zero, so that the total value of the portfolio is 18Δ. The portfolio is riskless if the value of Δ is chosen so that the final value of the portfolio is the same for both alternatives. This means

$$22\Delta - 1 = 18\Delta$$

or

$$\Delta = 0.25$$

A riskless portfolio is, therefore,

Long: 0.25 shares.

Short: 1 option.

If the stock price moves up to $22, the value of the portfolio is

$$22 \times 0.25 - 1 = 4.5$$

If the stock price moves down to $18, the value of the portfolio is

$$18 \times 0.25 = 4.5$$

Regardless of whether the stock price moves up or down, the value of the portfolio is always 4.5 at the end of the life of the option.

Riskless portfolios must, in the absence of arbitrage opportunities, earn the risk-free rate of interest. Suppose that in this case the risk-free rate is 12% per annum. It follows that the value of the portfolio today must be the present value of 4.5, or

$$4.5e^{-0.12 \times 0.25} = 4.367$$

The value of the stock price today is known to be $20. Suppose the option price is denoted by f. The value of the portfolio today is

$$20 \times 0.25 - f = 5 - f$$

It follows that

$$5 - f = 4.367$$

or

$$f = 0.633$$

This shows that, in the absence of arbitrage opportunities, the current value of the option must be 0.633. If the value of the option were more than 0.633, the portfolio would cost less than 4.367 to set up and would earn more than the risk-free rate. If the value of the option were less than 0.633, shorting the portfolio would provide a way of borrowing money at less than the risk-free rate.

A Generalization

We can generalize the argument just presented by considering a stock whose price is initially S_0 and an option on the stock (or any other derivative dependent on the stock) whose current price is f. We suppose that the option lasts for time T and that during the life of the option the stock price can either move up from S_0 to a new level, S_0u, or down from S_0 to a new level, S_0d ($u > 1$; $d < 1$). The proportional increase in the stock price when there is an up movement is $u - 1$; the proportional decrease when there is a down movement is $1 - d$. If the stock price moves up to S_0u, we suppose that the payoff from the option is f_u; if the stock price moves down to S_0d, we suppose the payoff from the option is f_d. The situation is illustrated in Figure 9.2.

As before, we imagine a portfolio consisting of a long position in Δ shares and a short position in one option. We calculate the value of Δ that makes the portfolio riskless. If there is an up movement in the stock price, the value of the portfolio at the end of the life of the option is

$$S_0u\Delta - f_u$$

If there is a down movement in the stock price, the value becomes

$$S_0d\Delta - f_d$$

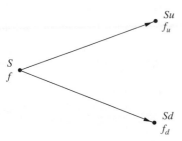

Figure 9.2 Stock and option prices in a general one-step tree.

The two are equal when

$$S_0 u \Delta - f_u = S_0 d \Delta - f_d$$

or

$$\Delta = \frac{f_u - f_d}{S_0 u - S_0 d} \tag{9.1}$$

In this case, the portfolio is riskless and must earn the risk-free interest rate. Equation (9.1) shows that Δ is the ratio of the change in the option price to the change in the stock price as we move between the nodes.

If we denote the risk-free interest rate by r, the present value of the portfolio is

$$(S_0 u \Delta - f_u)e^{-rT}$$

The cost of setting up the portfolio is

$$S_0 \Delta - f$$

It follows that

$$S_0 \Delta - f = (S_0 u \Delta - f_u)e^{-rT}$$

or

$$f = S_0 \Delta - (S_0 u \Delta - f_u)e^{-rT}$$

Substituting from equation (9.1) for Δ and simplifying, this equation reduces to

$$f = e^{-rT}[pf_u + (1 - p)f_d] \tag{9.2}$$

where

$$p = \frac{e^{rT} - d}{u - d} \tag{9.3}$$

Equations (9.2) and (9.3) enable an option to be priced using a one-step binomial model.

In the numerical example considered previously (see Figure 9.1), $u = 1.1, d = 0.9, r = 0.12, T = 0.25, f_u = 1$, and $f_d = 0$. From equation (9.3)

$$p = \frac{e^{0.12 \times 0.25} - 0.9}{1.1 - 0.9} = 0.6523$$

and from equation (9.2)

$$f = e^{-0.12 \times 0.25}[0.6523 \times 1 + 0.3477 \times 0] = 0.633$$

The result agrees with the answer obtained earlier in this section.

Irrelevance of the Stock's Expected Return

The option pricing formula in equation (9.2) does not involve the probabilities of the stock price moving up or down. For example, we get the same option price when the probability of an upward movement is 0.5 as we do when it is 0.9. This is surprising and seems counterintuitive. It is natural to assume that, as the probability of an upward movement in the stock price increases, the value of a call option on the stock increases and the value of a put option on the stock decreases. This is not the case.

The key reason is that we are not valuing the option in absolute terms. We are calculating its value in terms of the price of the underlying stock. The probabilities of future up or down movements are already incorporated into the price of the stock. It turns out that we do not need to take them into account again when valuing the option in terms of the stock price.

9.2 RISK-NEUTRAL VALUATION

Although we do not need to make any assumptions about the probabilities of up and down movements in order to derive equation (9.2), it is natural to interpret the variable p in equation (9.2) as the probability of an up movement in the stock price. The variable $1 - p$ is then the probability of a down movement, and the expression

$$p f_u + (1 - p) f_d$$

is the expected payoff from the option. With this interpretation of p, equation (9.2) then states that the value of the option today is its expected future value discounted at the risk-free rate.

We now investigate the expected return from the stock when the probability of an up movement is assumed to be p. The expected stock price at time T, $E(S_T)$, is given by

$$E(S_T) = p S_0 u + (1 - p) S_0 d$$

or

$$E(S_T) = p S_0 (u - d) + S_0 d$$

Substituting from equation (9.3) for p, this reduces to

$$E(S_T) = S_0 e^{rT} \tag{9.4}$$

showing that the stock price grows, on average, at the risk-free rate. Setting the probability of the up movement equal to p is, therefore, equivalent to assuming that the return on the stock equals the risk-free rate.

In a *risk-neutral world* all individuals are indifferent to risk. They require no compensation for risk, and the expected return on all securities is the risk-free interest rate. Equation (9.4) shows that we are assuming a risk-neutral world when we set the probability of an up movement to p. Equation (9.2) shows that the value of the option is its expected payoff in a risk-neutral world discounted at the risk-free rate.

This result is an example of an important general principle in option pricing known as *risk-neutral valuation*. The principle states that it is valid to assume the world is risk neutral when pricing options. The resulting option prices are correct not just in a risk-neutral world, but in the real world as well.

The One-Step Binomial Example Revisited

We now return to the numerical example in Figure 9.1 to illustrate that risk-neutral valuation gives the same answer as no-arbitrage arguments. In Figure 9.1, the stock price is currently $20 and will move either up to $22 or down to $18 at the end of three months. The option considered is a European call option with a strike price of $21 and an expiration date in three months. The risk-free interest rate is 12% per annum.

We define p as the probability of an upward movement in the stock price in a risk-neutral world. (We know from the analysis given earlier in this section that p is given by equation (9.3). However, for the purpose of this illustration we suppose that we do not know this.) In a risk-neutral world the expected return on the stock must be the risk-free rate of 12%. This means that p must satisfy

$$22p + 18(1 - p) = 20e^{0.12 \times 0.25}$$

or

$$4p = 20e^{0.12 \times 0.25} - 18$$

That is, p must be 0.6523.

At the end of the three months, the call option has a 0.6523 probability of being worth 1 and a 0.3477 probability of being worth zero. Its expected value is, therefore,

$$0.6523 \times 1 + 0.3477 \times 0 = 0.6523$$

In a risk-neutral world, this should be discounted at the risk-free rate. The value of the option today is, therefore,

$$0.6523e^{-0.12 \times 0.25}$$

or $0.633. This is the same as the value obtained earlier, illustrating that no-arbitrage arguments and risk-neutral valuation give the same answer.

9.3 TWO-STEP BINOMIAL TREES

We can extend the analysis to a two-step binomial tree, such as that shown in Figure 9.3. Here the stock price starts at $20 and in each of two time steps may go up by 10% or down by 10%. We suppose that each time step is three months long and the risk-free interest rate is 12% per annum. As before, we consider an option with a strike price of $21.

The objective of the analysis is to calculate the option price at the initial node of the tree. This can be done by repeatedly applying the principles established earlier in the chapter. Figure 9.4 shows the same tree as Figure 9.3, but with both the stock price and the option price at each node. (The stock price is the upper number and the option price is the lower number.) The option prices at the final nodes of the tree are

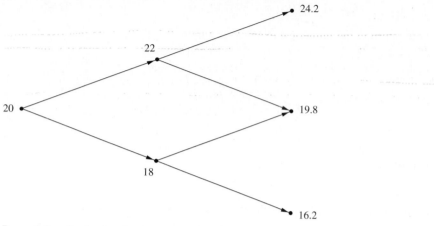

Figure 9.3   Stock prices in a two-step tree.

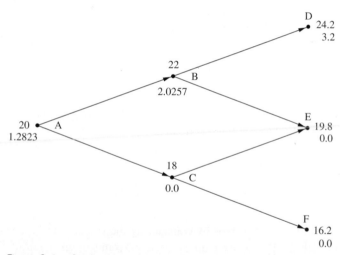

Figure 9.4   Stock option prices in a two step tree. The upper number at each node is the stock price; the lower number is the option price.

easily calculated. They are the payoffs from the option. At node D, the stock price is 24.2 and the option price is $24.2 - 21 = 3.2$; at nodes E and F, the option is out of the money and its value is zero.

At node C, the option price is zero, because node C leads to either node E or node F and at both nodes the option price is zero. We calculate the option price at node B by focusing our attention on the part of the tree shown in Figure 9.5. Using the notation introduced earlier in the chapter, $u = 1.1$, $d = 0.9$, $r = 0.12$, and $T = 0.25$ so that

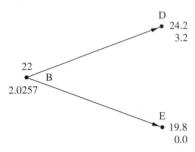

Figure 9.5   Evaluation of option price at node B.

$p = 0.6523$. Equation (9.2) gives the value of the option at node B as

$$e^{-0.12 \times 0.25}[0.6523 \times 3.2 + 0.3477 \times 0] = 2.0257$$

It remains for us to calculate the option price at the initial node, A. We do so by focusing on the first step of the tree. We know that the value of the option at node B is 2.0257 and that at node C it is zero. Equation (9.2), therefore, gives the value at node A as

$$e^{-0.12 \times 0.25}[0.6523 \times 2.0257 + 0.3477 \times 0] = 1.2823$$

The value of the option is $1.2823.

Note that this example was constructed so that u and d (the proportional up and down movements) were the same at each node of the tree and so that the time steps were of equal length. As a result, the risk-neutral probability, p, as calculated by equation (9.3) is the same at each node.

A Generalization

We can generalize the case of two time steps by considering the situation in Figure 9.6. The stock price is initially S_0. During each time step, it either moves up to u times its initial value or moves down to d times its initial value. The notation for the value of the option is shown on the tree. (For example, after two up movements, the value of the option is f_{uu}.) We suppose that the risk-free interest rate is r and the length of the time step is Δt years.

Repeated application of equation (9.2) gives

$$f_u = e^{-r\Delta t}[pf_{uu} + (1 - p)f_{ud}] \tag{9.5}$$

$$f_d = e^{-r\Delta t}[pf_{ud} + (1 - p)f_{dd}] \tag{9.6}$$

$$f = e^{-r\Delta t}[pf_u + (1 - p)f_d] \tag{9.7}$$

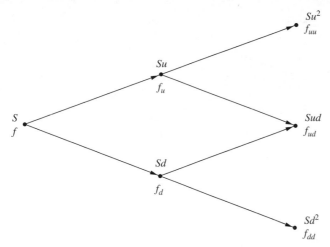

Figure 9.6   Stock and option prices in a general two-step tree.

Substituting from equations (9.5) and (9.6) in (9.7), we get

$$f = e^{-2r\Delta t}[p^2 f_{uu} + 2p(1-p)f_{ud} + (1-p)^2 f_{dd}] \qquad (9.8)$$

This is consistent with the principle of risk-neutral valuation mentioned earlier. The variables p^2, $2p(1-p)$, and $(1-p)^2$ are the probabilities that the upper, middle, and lower final nodes will be reached. The option price is equal to its expected payoff in a risk-neutral world discounted at the risk-free interest rate.

As we add more steps to a binomial tree, the risk-neutral valuation principle continues to hold. The option price is always equal to its expected payoff in a risk-neutral world, discounted at the risk-free interest rate.

9.4   A PUT OPTION EXAMPLE

The procedures described in this chapter can be used to price any derivative dependent on a stock whose price changes are binomial. Problem 9.13, for example, considers a derivative whose payoff is the square of the final stock price. Here we consider a two-year European put option with a strike price of $52 on a stock whose current price is $50. We suppose that there are two time steps of one year, and in each time step the stock price either moves up by a proportional amount of 20% or moves down by a proportional amount of 20%. We also suppose that the risk-free interest rate is 5%.

The tree is shown in Figure 9.7. The value of the risk-neutral probability, p, is given by

$$p = \frac{e^{0.05\times1} - 0.8}{1.2 - 0.8} = 0.6282$$

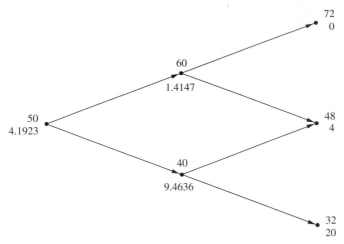

Figure 9.7   Use of two-step tree to value a European put option. At each node the upper number is the stock price; the lower number is the option price.

The possible final stock prices are: $72, $48, and $32. In this case $f_{uu} = 0$, $f_{ud} = 4$, and $f_{dd} = 20$. From equation (9.8)

$$f = e^{-2 \times 0.05 \times 1}[0.6282^2 \times 0 + 2 \times 0.6282 \times 0.3718 \times 4 + 0.3718^2 \times 20]$$
$$= 4.1923$$

The value of the put is $4.1923. This result can also be obtained using equation (9.2) and working back through the tree one step at a time. Figure 9.7 shows the intermediate option prices that are calculated.

9.5   AMERICAN OPTIONS

Up to now, all the options we have considered have been European. We now move on to consider how American options can be valued using a binomial tree such as that in Figures 9.4 or 9.7. The procedure is to work back through the tree from the end to the beginning, testing at each node to see whether early exercise is optimal. The value of the option at the final nodes is the same as for the European option. At earlier nodes the value of the option is the greater of

1. The value given by equation (9.2).
2. The payoff from early exercise.

Figure 9.8 shows how Figure 9.7 is affected if the option under considera-tion is American rather than European. The stock prices and their probabilities are

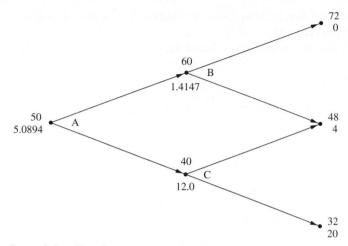

Figure 9.8   Use of two-step tree to value an American put option. At each node the upper number is the stock price; the lower number is the option price.

unchanged. The values for the option at the final nodes are also unchanged. At node B, equation (9.2) gives the value of the option as 1.4147, and the payoff from early exercise is negative (= −8). Clearly early exercise is not optimal at node B and the value of the option at this node is 1.4147. At node C, equation (9.2) gives the value of the option as 9.4636, whereas the payoff from early exercise is 12. In this case, early exercise is optimal and the value of the option at the node is 12. At the initial node A, the value given by equation (9.2) is

$$e^{-0.05 \times 1}[0.6282 \times 1.4147 + 0.3718 \times 12.0] = 5.0894$$

and the payoff from early exercise is 2.0. In this case early exercise is not optimal. The value of the option is, therefore, $5.0894.

More details on the use of binomial trees to value American options are given in chapter 16.

9.6 DELTA

At this stage it is appropriate to discuss *delta*, an important parameter in the pricing and hedging of options.

The delta of a stock option is the ratio of the change in the price of the stock option to the change in the price of the underlying stock. It is the number of units of the stock we should hold for each option shorted in order to create a riskless hedge. It is the same as the Δ introduced earlier in this chapter. The construction of a riskless hedge is sometimes referred to as *delta hedging*. The delta of a call option is positive, whereas the delta of a put option is negative.

From Figure 9.1 we can calculate the value of the delta of the call option being considered as

$$\frac{1 - 0}{22 - 18} = 0.25$$

This is because when the stock price changes from \$18 to \$22, the option price changes from \$0 to \$1.

In Figure 9.4 the delta corresponding to stock price movements over the first time step is

$$\frac{2.0257 - 0}{22 - 18} = 0.5064$$

The delta for stock price movements over the second time step is

$$\frac{3.2 - 0}{24.2 - 19.8} = 0.7273$$

if there is an upward movement over the first time step and

$$\frac{0 - 0}{19.8 - 16} = 0$$

if there is a downward movement over the first time step.

From Figure 9.7 delta is

$$\frac{1.4147 - 9.4636}{60 - 40} = -0.4024$$

at the end of the first time step and either

$$\frac{0 - 4}{72 - 48} = -0.1667$$

or

$$\frac{4 - 20}{48 - 32} = -1.0000$$

at the end of the second time step.

The two-step examples show that delta changes over time. (In Figure 9.4 delta changes from 0.5064 to either 0.7273 or 0; in Figure 9.7 it changes from -0.4024 to either -0.1667, or -1.0000.) Thus, in order to maintain a riskless hedge using an option and the underlying stock, the holdings in the stock must be adjusted at the end of each step. We will discuss this point further in chapters 11 and 13.

9.7 MATCHING VOLATILITY WITH u AND d

In practice, when constructing a binomial tree to represent the movements in a stock price, we choose the parameters u and d to match the volatility of the stock price. To see how this is done, we suppose that the expected return on a stock (in the real world) is μ and its volatility is σ. Figure 9.9a shows stock price movements over the first step of a binomial tree. The step is of length Δt. The stock price either moves up by a proportional amount u or moves down by a proportional amount d. The probability of an up movement (in the real world) is assumed to be q.

The expected stock price at the end of the first time step is $S_0 e^{\mu \Delta t}$. On the tree the expected stock price at this time is

$$qS_0 u + (1 - q)S_0 d$$

In order to match the expected return on the stock with the tree's parameters, we must, therefore, have

$$qS_0 u + (1 - q)S_0 d = S_0 e^{\mu \Delta t}$$

or

$$q = \frac{e^{\mu \Delta t} - d}{u - d} \tag{9.9}$$

As mentioned in section 7.1, the volatility of a stock price, σ, is defined so that $\sigma \sqrt{\Delta t}$ is the standard deviation of the return on the stock price in a short period of time of length Δt. Equivalently, the variance of the return is $\sigma^2 \Delta t$. On the tree in Figure 9.9a the variance of the stock price return is[2]

$$qu^2 + (1 - q)d^2 - [qu + (1 - q)d]^2$$

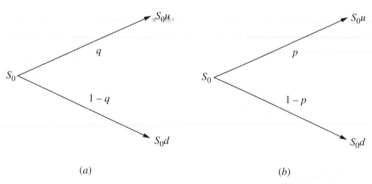

(a)   (b)

Figure 9.9   Change in stock price in time Δt in (a) the real world and (b) the risk-neutral world.

---

[2]This uses the result that the variance of a variable Q equals $E(Q^2) - [E(Q)]^2$ where E denotes expected value.

In order to match the stock price volatility with the tree's parameters we must, therefore, have

$$qu^2 + (1-q)d^2 - [qu + (1-q)d]^2 = \sigma^2 \Delta t \qquad (9.10)$$

Substituting from equation (9.9) into equation (9.10) we get

$$e^{\mu \Delta t}(u + d) - ud - e^{2\mu \Delta t} = \sigma^2 \Delta t$$

When terms in Δt^2 and higher powers of Δt are ignored, one solution to this equation is

$$u = e^{\sigma \sqrt{\Delta t}} \qquad (9.11)$$

$$d = e^{-\sigma \sqrt{\Delta t}} \qquad (9.12)$$

These are the values of u and d proposed by Cox, Ross, and Rubinstein (1979) for matching u and d.

The analysis in this chapter shows that we can replace the tree in Figure 9.9a with the tree in Figure 9.9b, where the probability of an up movement is p, and then behave as though the world is risk neutral. The variable p is given by equation (9.3) as

$$p = \frac{e^{r \Delta t} - d}{u - d}$$

It is the risk-neutral probability of an up movement. In Figure 9.9b, the expected stock price at the end of the time step is $S_0 e^{r \Delta t}$, as shown in equation (9.4). The variance of the stock price return is

$$pu^2 + (1-p)d^2 - [pu + (1-p)d]^2 = [e^{r \Delta t}(u + d) - ud - e^{2r \Delta t}]$$

Substituting for u and d from equations (9.11) and (9.12), we can find this equals $\sigma^2 \Delta t$ when terms in Δt^2 and higher powers of Δt are ignored.

 This analysis shows that when we move from the real world to the risk-neutral world the expected return on the stock changes, but its volatility remains the same (at least in the limit as Δt tends to zero). This is an illustration of an important general result known as *Girsanov's theorem*. When we move from a world with one set of risk preferences to a world with another set of risk preferences, the expected growth rates in variables change, but their volatilities remain the same. We will examine the impact of risk preferences on the behavior of market variables in more detail in chapter 19. Moving from one set of risk preferences to another is sometimes referred to as *changing the measure*.

9.8   BINOMIAL TREES IN PRACTICE

The binomial models presented so far have been unrealistically simple. Clearly an analyst can expect to obtain only a very rough approximation to an option price by assuming that stock price movements during the life of the option consist of one or two binomial steps.

When binomial trees are used in practice, the life of the option is typically divided into 30 or more time steps of length Δt. In each time step there is a binomial stock price movement. With 30 time steps this means that 31 terminal stock prices and 2^{30}, or about 1 billion, possible stock price paths are considered.

The parameters u and d are chosen to match the stock price volatility. A popular way of doing this is by setting

$$u = e^{\sigma \sqrt{\Delta t}} \qquad d = e^{-\sigma \sqrt{\Delta t}}$$

as indicated in the previous section. Chapter 16 provides a much more detailed discussion of the practical issues involved in the construction and use of binomial trees.

SUMMARY

This chapter has provided a first look at the valuation of stock options. If stock price movements during the life of an option are governed by a one-step binomial tree, it is possible to set up a portfolio consisting of a stock option and the stock that is riskless. In a world with no arbitrage opportunities, riskless portfolios must earn the risk-free interest. This enables the stock option to be priced in terms of the stock. It is interesting to note that no assumptions are required about the probabilities of up and down movements in the stock price at each node of the tree.

When stock price movements are governed by a multistep binomial tree, we can treat each binomial step separately and work back from the end of the life of the option to the beginning to obtain the current value of the option. Again, only no-arbitrage arguments are used, and no assumptions are required about the probabilities of up and down movements in the stock price at each node.

Another approach to valuing stock options involves risk-neutral valuation. This very important principle states that it is permissible to assume the world is risk neutral when valuing an option in terms of the underlying stock. This chapter has shown, through both numerical examples and algebra, that no-arbitrage arguments and risk-neutral valuation lead to the same option prices.

The delta of a stock option, Δ, considers the effect of a small change in the underlying stock price on the change in the option price. It is the ratio of the change in the option price to the change in the stock price. For a riskless position, a trader should buy Δ shares for each option sold. An inspection of a typical binomial tree shows that delta changes during the life of an option. This means that, to maintain a riskless portfolio, the position in the underlying stock must also change.

In chapter 11 we examine the Black–Scholes analytic approach to pricing stock options. We review other types of options in chapter 12. Chapter 13 considers the properties of delta in more detail. In chapter 16 we return to binomial trees and give a more complete discussion of how they are implemented.

SUGGESTIONS FOR FURTHER READING

Cox, J., S. Ross, and M. Rubinstein. "Option Pricing: A Simplified Approach," *Journal of Financial Economics*, 7 (October 1979), 229–64.

Rendleman, R., and B. Bartter. "Two State Option Pricing," *Journal of Finance*, 34 (1979), 1092–1110.

QUESTIONS AND PROBLEMS
(ANSWERS IN SOLUTIONS MANUAL)

9.1. A stock price is currently $40. It is known that at the end of one month it will be either $42 or $38. The risk-free interest rate is 8% per annum with continuous compounding. What is the value of a one-month European call option with a strike price of $39?

9.2. Explain the no-arbitrage and risk-neutral valuation approaches to valuing a European option using a one-step binomial tree.

9.3. What is meant by the delta of a stock option?

9.4. A stock price is currently $50. It is known that at the end of six months it will be either $45 or $55. The risk-free interest rate is 10% per annum with continuous compounding. What is the the value of a six-month European put option with a strike price of $50?

9.5. A stock price is currently $100. Over each of the next two six-month periods it is expected to go up by 10% or down by 10%. The risk-free interest rate is 8% per annum with continuous compounding. What is the value of a one-year European call option with a strike price of $100?

9.6. For the situation considered in Problem 9.5, what is the value of a one-year European put option with a strike price of $100? Verify that the European call and European put prices satisfy put–call parity.

9.7. Consider the situation in which stock price movements during the life of a European option are governed by a two-step binomial tree. Explain why it is not possible to set up a position in the stock and the option that remains riskless for the whole of the life of the option.

9.8. A stock price is currently $50. It is known that at the end of two months it will be either $53 or $48. The risk-free interest rate is 10% per annum with continuous compounding. What is the value of a two-month European call option with a strike price of $49? Use no-arbitrage arguments.

9.9. A stock price is currently $80. It is known that at the end of four months it will be either $75 or $85. The risk-free interest rate is 5% per annum with continuous compounding. What is the value of a four-month European put option with a strike price of $80? Use no-arbitrage arguments.

9.10. A stock price is currently $40. It is known that at the end of three months it will be either $45 or $35. The risk-free rate of interest with quarterly compounding is 8% per annum. Calculate the value of a three-month European put option on the stock with an exercise price of $40. Verify that no-arbitrage arguments and risk-neutral valuation arguments give the same answers.

9.11. A stock price is currently $50. Over each of the next two three-month periods it is expected to go up by 6% or down by 5%. The risk-free interest rate is 5% per annum with continuous compounding. What is the value of a six-month European call option with a strike price of $51?

9.12. For the situation considered in Problem 9.11, what is the value of a six-month European put option with a strike price of $51? Verify that the European call and European put prices satisfy put–call parity. If the put option were American, would it ever be optimal to exercise it early at any of the nodes on the tree?

9.13. A stock price is currently $25. It is known that at the end of two months it will be either $23 or $27. The risk-free interest rate is 10% per annum with continuous compounding. Suppose S_T is the stock price at the end of two months. What is the value of a derivative that pays off S_T^2 at this time?

ASSIGNMENT QUESTIONS

9.14. A stock price is currently $50. It is known that at the end of six months it will be either $60 or $42. The risk-free rate of interest with continuous compounding is 12% per annum. Calculate the value of a six-month European call option on the stock with an exercise price of $48. Verify that no-arbitrage arguments and risk-neutral valuation arguments give the same answers.

9.15. A stock price is currently $40. Over each of the next two three-month periods it is expected to go up by 10% or down by 10%. The risk-free interest rate is 12% per annum with continuous compounding.
   (a) What is the value of a six-month European put option with a strike price of $42?
   (b) What is the value of a six-month American put option with a strike price of $42?

9.16. Estimate how high the strike price has to be in Problem 9.15 for it to be optimal to exercise the option immediately.

10

MODEL OF THE BEHAVIOR OF STOCK PRICES

Any variable whose value changes over time in an uncertain way is said to follow a *stochastic process*. Stochastic processes can be classified as *discrete time* or *continuous time*. A discrete-time stochastic process is one where the value of the variable can change only at certain fixed points in time, whereas a continuous-time stochastic process is one where changes can take place at any time. Stochastic processes can also be classified as *continuous variable* or *discrete variable*. In a continuous-variable process, the underlying variable can take any value within a certain range, whereas in a discrete-variable process, only certain discrete values are possible.

This chapter develops a continuous-variable, continuous-time stochastic process for stock prices. An understanding of this process is the first step to understanding the pricing of options and other more complicated derivatives. It should be noted that, in practice, we do not observe stock prices following continuous-variable, continuous-time processes. Stock prices are restricted to discrete values (often multiples of $\$\frac{1}{8}$ in the United States) and changes can be observed only when the exchange is open. Nevertheless, the continuous-variable, continuous-time process proves to be a useful model for many purposes.

Many people feel that continuous-time stochastic processes are so complicated that they should be left entirely to "rocket scientists." This is not so. The biggest hurdle to understanding these processes is the notation. Here we present a step-by-step approach aimed at getting the reader over this hurdle. We also explain an important result known as *Ito's lemma* that is central to a full understanding of the theory underlying the pricing of derivatives.

10.1 THE MARKOV PROPERTY

A *Markov process* is a particular type of stochastic process where only the present value of a variable is relevant for predicting the future. The past history of the variable and the way that the present has emerged from the past are irrelevant.

Stock prices are usually assumed to follow a Markov process. Suppose that the price of IBM stock is $100 now. If the stock price follows a Markov process, our predictions for the future should be unaffected by the price one week ago, one month ago, or one year ago. The only relevant piece of information is that the price is now $100.[1] Predictions for the future are uncertain and must be expressed in terms of probability distributions. The Markov property implies that the probability distribution of the price at any particular future time is not dependent on the particular path followed by the price in the past.

The Markov property of stock prices is consistent with the weak form of market efficiency. This states that the present price of a stock impounds all the information contained in a record of past prices. If the weak form of market efficiency were not true, technical analysts could make above-average returns by interpreting charts of the past history of stock prices. There is very little evidence that they are, in fact, able to do this.

It is competition in the marketplace that tends to ensure that weak-form market efficiency holds. There are many, many investors watching the stock market closely. Trying to make a profit from it leads to a situation where a stock price, at any given time, reflects the information in past prices. Suppose that it was discovered that a particular pattern in stock prices always gave a 65% chance of subsequent steep price rises. Investors would attempt to buy a stock as soon as the pattern was observed, and demand for the stock would immediately rise. This would lead to an immediate rise in its price and the observed effect would be eliminated, as would any profitable trading opportunities.

10.2   CONTINUOUS TIME STOCHASTIC PROCESSES

Consider a variable that follows a Markov stochastic process. Suppose that its current value is 10 and that the change in its value during one year is $\phi(0, 1)$, where $\phi(\mu, \sigma)$ denotes a probability distribution that is normally distributed with mean μ and standard deviation σ. What is the probability distribution of the change in the value of the variable during two years?

The change in two years is the sum of two normal distributions, each of which has a mean of zero and standard deviation of 1.0. Because the variable is Markov, the two probability distributions are independent. When we add two independent normal distributions, the result is a normal distribution where the mean is the sum of the means and the variance is the sum of the variances.[2] The mean of the change during two years in the variable we are considering is, therefore, zero and the variance of this change is 2.0. The change in the variable over two years is, therefore, $\phi(0, \sqrt{2})$.

Consider next the change in the variable during six months. The variance of the change in the value of the variable during one year equals the variance of the

---

[1] Statistical properties of the stock price history of IBM may be useful in determining the characteristics of the stochastic process followed by the stock price (e.g., its volatility). The point being made here is that the particular path followed by the stock in the past is irrelevant.

[2] The variance of a probability distribution is the square of its standard deviation. The variance of a one-year change in the value of the variable we are considering is, therefore, 1.0.

change during the first six months plus the variance of the change during the second six months. We assume these are the same. It follows that the variance of the change during a six month period must be 0.5. Equivalently, the standard deviation of the change is $\sqrt{0.5}$ so that the probability distribution for the change in the value of the variable during six months is $\phi(0, \sqrt{0.5})$.

A similar argument shows that the change in the value of the variable during three months is $\phi(0, \sqrt{0.25})$. More generally, the change during any time period of length T is $\phi(0, \sqrt{T})$. In particular, the change during a very short time period of length Δt is $\phi(0, \sqrt{\Delta t})$.

The square root signs in these results may seem strange. They arise because, when Markov processes are considered, the variance of the changes in successive time periods are additive. The standard deviations of the changes in successive time periods are not additive. The variance of the change in the variable in our example is 1.0 per year, so that the variance of the change in two years is 2.0 and the variance of the change in three years is 3.0. The standard deviation of the change in two and three years is $\sqrt{2}$ and $\sqrt{3}$, respectively. Strictly speaking, we should not refer to the standard deviation of the variable as 1.0 per year. It should be "1.0 per square root of years". The results explain why uncertainty is often referred to as being proportional to the square root of time.

Wiener Processes

The process followed by the variable we have been considering is known as a *Wiener process*. It is a particular type of Markov stochastic process with a mean change of zero and a variance rate of 1.0 per year. It has been used in physics to describe the motion of a particle that is subject to a large number of small molecular shocks and is sometimes referred to as *Brownian motion*.

Expressed formally, a variable z follows a Wiener process if it has the following two properties:

> *Property 1.*
> The change Δz during a small period of time Δt is

$$\Delta z = \epsilon \sqrt{\Delta t} \qquad (10.1)$$

> where ϵ is a random drawing from a standardized normal distribution, $\phi(0, 1)$.

> *Property 2.*
> The values of Δz for any two different short intervals of time Δt are independent.

It follows from the first property that Δz itself has a normal distribution with

$$\text{mean of } \Delta z = 0$$
$$\text{standard deviation of } \Delta z = \sqrt{\Delta t}$$
$$\text{variance of } \Delta z = \Delta t$$

The second property implies that z follows a Markov process.

Consider the increase in the value of z during a relatively long period of time, T. This can be denoted by $z(T) - z(0)$. It can be regarded as the sum of the increases in z in N small time intervals of length Δt, where

$$N = \frac{T}{\Delta t}$$

Thus,

$$z(T) - z(0) = \sum_{i=1}^{N} \epsilon_i \sqrt{\Delta t} \tag{10.2}$$

where the ϵ_i ($i = 1, 2, \ldots, N$) are random drawings from $\phi(0, 1)$. From the second property of Wiener processes, the ϵ_i's are independent of each other. It follows from equation (10.2) that $z(T) - z(0)$ is normally distributed with

$$\text{mean of } [z(T) - z(0)] = 0$$
$$\text{variance of } [z(T) - z(0)] = N\Delta t = T$$
$$\text{standard deviation of } [z(T) - z(0)] = \sqrt{T}$$

This is consistent with the discussion earlier in this section.

> **Example 10.1** Suppose that the value, z, of a variable that follows a Wiener process is initially 25 and that time is measured in years. At the end of one year, the value of the variable is normally distributed with a mean of 25 and a standard deviation of 1.0. At the end of five years, it is normally distributed with a mean of 25 and a standard deviation of $\sqrt{5}$, or 2.236. Note that our uncertainty about the value of the variable at a certain time in the future, as measured by its standard deviation, increases as the square root of how far we are looking ahead.

In ordinary calculus it is usual to proceed from small changes to the limit as the small changes become closer to zero. Thus $\Delta y / \Delta x$ becomes dy / dx in the limit, and so on. We can proceed similarly when dealing with stochastic processes. A Wiener process is the limit as $\Delta t \longrightarrow 0$ of the process described above for z.

Figure 10.1 illustrates what happens to the path followed by z as the limit $\Delta t \longrightarrow 0$ is approached. Note that the path is quite "jagged". This is because the size of a movement in z in time Δt is proportional to $\sqrt{\Delta t}$ and, when Δt is small, $\sqrt{\Delta t}$ is much bigger than Δt. Two intriguing properties of Wiener processes, related to this $\sqrt{\Delta t}$ property, are

1. The expected length of the path followed by z in any time interval is infinite.
2. The expected number of times z equals any particular value in any time interval is infinite.

Generalized Wiener Process

The basic Wiener process, dz, that has been developed so far has a drift rate of zero and a variance rate of 1.0. The drift rate of zero means that the expected value of z at any future time is equal to its current value. The variance rate of 1.0 means that

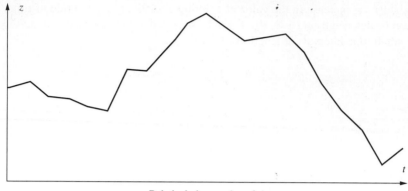

Relatively large value of Δt

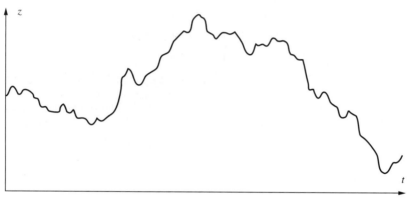

Smaller value of Δt

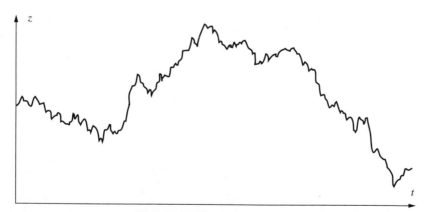

The true process obtained as $\Delta t \longrightarrow 0$

Figure 10.1   How a Wiener process is obtained when $\Delta t \longrightarrow 0$ in equation (10.1).

the variance of the change in z in a time interval of length T equals T. A *generalized Wiener process* for a variable x can be defined in terms of dz as follows:

$$dx = a\,dt + b\,dz \qquad (10.3)$$

where a and b are constants.

To understand equation (10.3), it is useful to consider the two components on the right-hand side separately. The $a\,dt$ term implies that x has an expected drift rate of a per unit of time. Without the $b\,dz$ term, the equation is

$$dx = a\,dt$$

which implies that

$$\frac{dx}{dt} = a$$

or

$$x = x_0 + at$$

where x_0 is the value of x at time zero. In a period of time of length T, x increases by an amount aT. The $b\,dz$ term on the right-hand side of equation (10.3) can be regarded as adding noise or variability to the path followed by x. The amount of this noise or variability is b times a Wiener process. A Wiener process has a standard deviation of 1.0. It follows that b times a Wiener process has a standard deviation of b. In a small time interval Δt, the change in the value of x, Δx, is from equations (10.1) and (10.3) given by

$$\Delta x = a\,\Delta t + b\epsilon\,\sqrt{\Delta t}$$

where, as before, ϵ is a random drawing from a standardized normal distribution. Thus, Δx has a normal distribution with

$$\text{mean of } \Delta x = a\,\Delta t$$

$$\text{standard deviation of } \Delta x = b\,\sqrt{\Delta t}$$

$$\text{variance of } \Delta x = b^2\,\Delta t$$

Similar arguments to those given for a Wiener process show that the change in the value of x in any time interval T is normally distributed with

$$\text{mean of change in } x = aT$$

$$\text{standard deviation of change in } x = b\,\sqrt{T}$$

$$\text{variance of change in } x = b^2 T$$

Thus, the generalized Wiener process given in equation (10.3) has an expected drift rate (i.e., average drift per unit of time) of a and a variance rate (i.e., variance per unit of time) of b^2. It is illustrated in Figure 10.2.

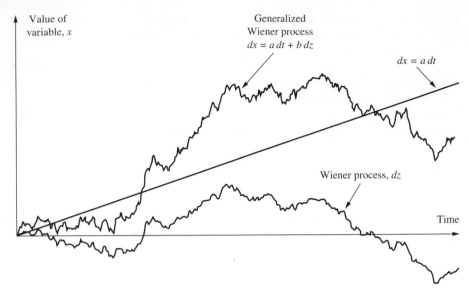

Figure 10.2 Generalized Wiener process; $a = 0.3$, $b = 1.5$.

Example 10.2

Consider the situation where the cash position of a company, measured in thousands of dollars, follows a generalized Wiener process with a drift of 20 per year and a variance rate of 900 per year. Initially, the cash position is 50. At the end of one year the cash position will have a normal distribution with a mean of 70 and a standard deviation of $\sqrt{900}$, or 30. At the end of six months it will have a normal distribution with a mean of 60 and a standard deviation of $30\sqrt{0.5} = 21.21$. Note that our uncertainty about the cash position at some time in the future, as measured by its standard deviation, increases as the square root of how far ahead we are looking. Also, note that the cash position can become negative (we can interpret this as a situation where the company is borrowing funds).

Ito Process

A further type of stochastic process can be defined. This is known as an *Ito process*. It is a generalized Wiener process where the parameters a and b are functions of the value of the underlying variable, x, and time, t. Algebraically, an Ito process can be written

$$dx = a(x, t)dt + b(x, t)z \tag{10.4}$$

Both the expected drift rate and variance rate of an Ito process are liable to change over time. In a small time interval between t and $t + \Delta t$, the variable changes from x to $x + \Delta x$ where:

$$\Delta x = a(x, t)\Delta t + b(x, t)\epsilon\sqrt{\Delta t}$$

This relationship involves a small approximation. It assumes that the drift and variance rate of x remain constant, equal to $a(x, t)$ and $b(x, t)^2$ respectively, during the time interval between t and $t + \Delta t$.

10.3 THE PROCESS FOR STOCK PRICES

In this section we discuss the stochastic process usually assumed for the price of a non-dividend-paying stock.

It is tempting to suggest that a stock price follows a generalized Wiener process; that is, that it has a constant expected drift rate and a constant variance rate. However, this model fails to capture a key aspect of stock prices. This is that the expected percentage return required by investors from a stock is independent of the stock's price. If investors require a 14% per annum expected return when the stock price is $10, then, *ceteris paribus*, they will also require a 14% per annum expected return when it is $50.

Clearly, the constant expected drift-rate assumption is inappropriate and needs to be replaced by the assumption that the expected return (that is, expected drift divided by the stock price) is constant. If S is the stock price at time t, the expected drift rate in S should be assumed to be μS for some constant parameter, μ. This means that in a short interval of time, Δt, the expected increase in S is $\mu S \Delta t$. The parameter, μ, is the expected rate of return on the stock, expressed in decimal form. If the volatility of the stock price is always zero, this model implies that

$$\Delta S = \mu S \Delta t$$

In the limit as $\Delta t \longrightarrow 0$

$$dS = \mu S \, dt$$

or

$$\frac{dS}{S} = \mu \, dt$$

so that

$$S_T = S_0 e^{\mu T} \tag{10.5}$$

where S_0 and S_T are the stock price at time zero and time T. Equation (10.5) shows that when the variance rate is zero, the stock price grows at a continuously compounded rate of μ per unit of time.

In practice, of course, a stock price does exhibit volatility. A reasonable assumption is that the variability of the percentage return in a short period of time, Δt, is the same regardless of the stock price. In other words, an investor is just as uncertain of the percentage return when the stock price is $50 as when it is $10. This suggests that the standard deviation of the change in a short period of time Δt should be proportional to the stock price and leads to the model

$$dS = \mu S \, dt + \sigma S \, dz$$

or

$$\frac{dS}{S} = \mu \, dt + \sigma \, dz \qquad (10.6)$$

Equation (10.6) is the most widely used model of stock price behavior. The variable σ is the volatility of the stock price. The variable μ is its expected rate of return.

Example 10.3   Consider a stock that pays no dividends, has a volatility of 30% per annum, and provides an expected return of 15% per annum with continuous compounding. In this case $\mu = 0.15$ and $\sigma = 0.30$. The process for the stock price is

$$\frac{dS}{S} = 0.15 \, dt + 0.30 \, dz$$

If S is the stock price at a particular time and ΔS is the increase in the stock price in the next small interval of time,

$$\frac{\Delta S}{S} = 0.15 \, \Delta t + 0.30 \epsilon \sqrt{\Delta t}$$

where ϵ is a random drawing from a standardized normal distribution. Consider a time interval of one week or 0.0192 year and suppose that the initial stock price is $100. Then $\Delta t = 0.0192$, $S = 100$, and

$$\Delta S = 100(0.00288 + 0.0416 \epsilon)$$

or

$$\Delta S = 0.288 + 4.16 \epsilon$$

showing that the price increase is a random drawing from a normal distribution with mean $0.288 and standard deviation $4.16.

10.4   REVIEW OF THE MODEL

The model of stock price behavior developed in the previous section is sometimes known as *geometric Brownian motion*. The discrete-time version of the model is

$$\frac{\Delta S}{S} = \mu \, \Delta t + \sigma \epsilon \sqrt{\Delta t} \qquad (10.7)$$

or

$$\Delta S = \mu S \, \Delta t + \sigma S \epsilon \sqrt{\Delta t} \qquad (10.8)$$

The variable ΔS is the change in the stock price, S, in a small interval of time, Δt; and ϵ is a random drawing from a standardized normal distribution (i.e., a normal distribution with a mean of zero and standard deviation of 1.0). The parameter, μ, is the expected rate of return per unit of time from the stock and the parameter, σ, is the volatility of the stock price. Both of these parameters are assumed constant.

The left-hand side of equation (10.7) is the return provided by the stock in a short period of time, Δt. The term $\mu \, \Delta t$ is the expected value of this return, and the term $\sigma \epsilon \sqrt{\Delta t}$ is the stochastic component of the return. The variance of the stochastic component (and, therefore, of the whole return) is $\sigma^2 \Delta t$. This is consistent with the definition of the volatility, σ, given in sections 7.1 and 9.7; that is, σ is such that $\sigma \sqrt{\Delta t}$ is the standard deviation of the return in a short time period, Δt.

Equation (10.7) shows that $\Delta S / S$ is normally distributed with mean $\mu \, \Delta t$ and standard deviation $\sigma \sqrt{\Delta t}$. In other words,

$$\frac{\Delta S}{S} \sim \phi(\mu \, \Delta t, \, \sigma \sqrt{\Delta t}) \tag{10.9}$$

Monte Carlo Simulation

A Monte Carlo simulation of a stochastic process is a procedure for sampling random outcomes for the process. We will use it as a way of developing some understanding of the nature of the stock price process in equation (10.6).

Suppose that the expected return from a stock is 14% per annum and that the standard deviation of the return (i.e., the volatility) is 20% per annum. This means that $\mu = 0.14$ and $\sigma = 0.20$. Suppose that $\Delta t = 0.01$ so that we are considering changes in the stock price in time intervals of length 0.01 year (or 3.65 days). From equation (10.8)

$$\Delta S = 0.14 \times 0.01 S + 0.2 \sqrt{0.01} S \epsilon$$

or

$$\Delta S = 0.0014 S + 0.02 S \epsilon \tag{10.10}$$

A path for the stock price can be simulated by sampling repeatedly for ϵ from $\phi(0, 1)$ and substituting into equation (10.10). Table 10.1 shows one particular set of results from doing this. The initial stock price is assumed to be $20. For the first period, ϵ is sampled as 0.52. From equation (10.10), the change during the first time period is

$$\Delta S = 0.0014 \times 20 + 0.02 \times 20 \times 0.52 = 0.236$$

At the beginning of the second time period the stock price is, therefore, $20.236. The value of ϵ sampled for the next period is 1.44. From equation (10.10), the change during the second time period is

$$\Delta S = 0.0014 \times 20.236 + 0.02 \times 20.236 \times 1.44 = 0.611$$

At the beginning of the next period the stock price is, therefore, $20.847; and so on. Note that, because the process we are simulating is Markov, the samples for ϵ should be independent of each other.

Table 10.1   Simulation of Stock Price When $\mu = 0.14$ and $\sigma = 0.20$ during Periods of Length 0.01 Year.

Stock Price at Start of Period	Random Sample, for ϵ	Change in Stock Price During Period
20.000	0.52	0.236
20.236	1.44	0.611
20.847	−0.86	−0.329
20.518	1.46	0.628
21.146	−0.69	−0.262
20.883	−0.74	−0.280
20.603	0.21	0.115
20.719	−1.10	−0.427
20.292	0.73	0.325
20.617	1.16	0.507
21.124	2.56	1.111

Table 10.1 assumes that stock prices are measured to the nearest 0.001. It is important to realize that the table shows only one possible pattern of stock price movements. Different random samples would lead to different price movements. Any small time interval Δt can be used in the simulation. In the limit as $\Delta t \longrightarrow 0$ is a perfect description of the stochastic process obtained. The final stock price of 21.124 in Table 10.1 can be regarded as a random sample from the distribution of stock prices at the end of 10 time intervals; that is, at the end of one-tenth of a year. By repeatedly simulating movements in the stock price, as in Table 10.1, a complete probability distribution of the stock price at the end of this time is obtained.

10.5   THE PARAMETERS

The process for stock prices developed in this chapter involves two parameters, μ and σ. The parameter, μ, is the expected continuously compounded return earned by an investor per year. Most investors require higher expected returns to induce them to take higher risks. It follows that the value of μ should depend on the risk of the return from the stock.[3] It should also depend on the level of interest rates in the economy. The higher the level of interest rates, the higher the expected return required on any given stock.

Fortunately, we do not have to concern ourselves with the determinants of μ in any detail because the value of a derivative dependent on a stock is, in general, independent of μ. The parameter σ, the stock price volatility, is, by contrast,

---

[3] More precisely, μ depends on that part of the risk that cannot be diversified away by the investor.

critically important to the determination of the value of most derivatives. Procedures for estimating σ are discussed in chapter 11. Typical values of σ for a stock are in the range 0.20 to 0.40 (i.e., 20 to 40%).

The standard deviation of the proportional change in the stock price in a small interval of time Δt is $\sigma \sqrt{\Delta t}$. As a rough approximation, the standard deviation of the proportional change in the stock price over a relatively long period of time, T, is $\sigma \sqrt{T}$. This means that as an approximation, volatility can be interpreted as the standard deviation of the change in the stock price in one year. In chapter 11 we will show that the volatility of a stock price is exactly equal to the standard deviation of the continuously compounded return provided by the stock in one year.

10.6 ITO'S LEMMA

The price of a stock option is a function of the underlying stock's price and time. More generally, we can say that the price of any derivative is a function of the stochastic variables underlying the derivative and time. A serious student of derivatives must, therefore, acquire some understanding of the behavior of functions of stochastic variables. An important result in this area was discovered by a mathematician, K. Ito, in 1951.[4] It is known as *Ito's lemma*.

Suppose that the value of a variable x follows an Ito process:

$$dx = a(x, t)\, dt + b(x, t)\, dz \tag{10.11}$$

where dz is a Wiener process and a and b are functions of x and t. The variable x has a drift rate of a and a variance rate of b^2. Ito's lemma shows that a function, G, of x and t follows the process

$$dG = \left(\frac{\partial G}{\partial x} a + \frac{\partial G}{\partial t} + \frac{1}{2} \frac{\partial^2 G}{\partial x^2} b^2 \right) dt + \frac{\partial G}{\partial x} b\, dz \tag{10.12}$$

where the dz is the same Wiener process as in equation (10.11). Thus, G also follows an Ito process. It has a drift rate of

$$\frac{\partial G}{\partial x} a + \frac{\partial G}{\partial t} + \frac{1}{2} \frac{\partial^2 G}{\partial x^2} b^2$$

and a variance rate of

$$\left(\frac{\partial G}{\partial x} \right)^2 b^2$$

A completely rigorous proof of Ito's lemma is beyond the scope of this book. In Appendix 10A, we show that the lemma can be viewed as an extension of well-known results in differential calculus.

---

[4]See K. Ito, "On Stochastic Differential Equations," *Memoirs, American Mathematical Society*, 4 (1951), 1–51.

Earlier we argued that

$$dS = \mu S\, dt + \sigma S\, dz \tag{10.13}$$

with μ and σ constant, is a reasonable model of stock price movements. From Ito's lemma, it follows that the process followed by a function, G, of S and t is

$$dG = \left(\frac{\partial G}{\partial S} \mu S + \frac{\partial G}{\partial t} + \frac{1}{2} \frac{\partial^2 G}{\partial S^2} \sigma^2 S^2 \right) dt + \frac{\partial G}{\partial S} \sigma S\, dz \tag{10.14}$$

Note that both S and G are affected by the same underlying source of uncertainty, dz. This proves to be very important in the derivation of the Black–Scholes results.

Application to Forward Contracts

To illustrate Ito's lemma, consider a forward contract on a non-dividend-paying stock. Assume that the risk-free rate of interest is constant and equal to r for all maturities. From equation (3.5),

$$F_0 = S_0 e^{rT}$$

where F_0 is the forward price at time zero, S is the spot price at time zero, and T is the time to maturity of the forward contract.

We are interested in what happens to the forward price as time passes. We define F as the forward price at a general time t and S as the stock price at time t with $(t < T)$. The relationship between F and S is

$$F = S e^{r(T-t)} \tag{10.15}$$

Assuming that the process for S is given by equation (10.13), we can use Ito's lemma to determine the process for F.

From equation (10.15)

$$\frac{\partial F}{\partial S} = e^{r(T-t)} \qquad \frac{\partial^2 F}{\partial S^2} = 0 \qquad \frac{\partial F}{\partial t} = -rS e^{r(T-t)}$$

From equation (10.14) the process for F is given by

$$dF = \left[e^{r(T-t)} \mu S - rS e^{r(T-t)} \right] dt + e^{r(T-t)} \sigma S\, dz$$

Substituting $F = S e^{r(T-t)}$, this becomes

$$dF = (\mu - r) F\, dt + \sigma F\, dz \tag{10.16}$$

Like S, F follows geometric Brownian motion. It has an expected growth rate of $\mu - r$ rather than μ. The growth rate in F is the excess return of S over the risk-free rate.

Application to the Logarithm of the Stock Price

We now use Ito's lemma to derive the process followed by $\ln S$. Define

$$G = \ln S$$

Because

$$\frac{\partial G}{\partial S} = \frac{1}{S} \qquad \frac{\partial^2 G}{\partial S^2} = -\frac{1}{S^2} \qquad \frac{\partial G}{\partial t} = 0$$

it follows from equation (10.14) that the process followed by G is

$$dG = \left(\mu - \frac{\sigma^2}{2}\right)dt + \sigma\,dz \qquad\qquad (10.17)$$

Because μ and σ are constant, this equation indicates that G follows a generalized Wiener process. It has constant drift rate $\mu - \sigma^2/2$ and constant variance rate σ^2. The change in G between time zero and some future time, T, is, therefore, normally distributed with mean

$$\left(\mu - \frac{\sigma^2}{2}\right)T$$

and variance

$$\sigma^2 T$$

We will make use of this result in chapter 11.

SUMMARY

Stochastic processes describe the probabilistic evolution of the value of a variable through time. A Markov process is one where only the present value of the variable is relevant for predicting the future. The past history of the variable and the way in which the present has emerged from the past is irrelevant.

A Wiener process, dz, is a process describing the evolution of a normally distributed variable. The drift of the process is zero and the variance rate is 1.0 per unit time. This means that, if the value of the variable is x_0 at time zero, at time T it is normally distributed with mean x_0 and standard deviation $\sqrt{T}$.

A generalized Wiener process describes the evolution of a normally distributed variable with a drift of a per unit time and a variance rate of b^2 per unit time, where a and b are constants. This means that if, as before, the value of the variable is x_0 at time zero, it is normally distributed with a mean of $x_0 + aT$ and a standard deviation of $b\sqrt{T}$ at time T.

An Ito process is a process where the drift and variance rate of x can be a function of both x itself and time. The change in x in a very short period of time is, to a good approximation, normally distributed, but its change over longer periods of time is liable to be non-normal.

In this chapter, we have developed a plausible Markov stochastic process for the behavior of a stock price over time. The process is widely used in the valuation of derivatives. It is known as geometric Brownian motion. Under this process, the proportional rate of return to the holder of the stock in any small interval of time is normally distributed and the returns in any two different small intervals of time are independent.

One way of gaining an intuitive understanding of a stochastic process for a variable is to simulate the behavior of the variable. This involves dividing a time interval into many small time steps and randomly sampling possible paths for the variable. The future probability distribution for the variable can then be calculated. Monte Carlo simulation is discussed further in chapter 16.

Ito's lemma is a way of calculating the stochastic process followed by a function of a variable from the stochastic process followed by the variable itself. As we will see in chapter 11, Ito's lemma is very important in the pricing of derivatives. A key point is that the Wiener process, dz, underlying the stochastic process for the variable is exactly the same as the Wiener process underlying the stochastic process for the function of the variable. Both are subject to the same underlying source of uncertainty.

SUGGESTIONS FOR FURTHER READING

On Efficient Markets and the Markov Property of Stock Prices

Brealey, R. A. *An Introduction to Risk and Return from Common Stock*, 2nd ed. Cambridge, Mass.: MIT Press, 1983.

Cootner, P. H. (ed.) *The Random Character of Stock Market Prices*. Cambridge, Mass.: MIT Press, 1964.

On Stochastic Processes

Cox, D. R., and H. D. Miller. *The Theory of Stochastic Processes*. London: Chapman and Hall, 1965.

Feller, W. *Probability Theory and Its Applications*, vols. 1 and 2. New York: John Wiley and Sons, 1950.

Karlin, S., and H. M. Taylor. *A First Course in Stochastic Processes*, 2nd ed. New York: Academic Press, 1975.

Neftci, S. *Introduction to Mathematics of Financial Derivatives*, New York: Academic Press, 1996.

QUESTIONS AND PROBLEMS
(ANSWERS IN SOLUTIONS MANUAL)

10.1. What would it mean to assert that the temperature at a certain place follows a Markov process? Do you think that temperatures do, in fact, follow a Markov process?

10.2. Can a trading rule based on the past history of a stock's price ever produce returns that are consistently above average? Discuss.

10.3. A company's cash position, measured in millions of dollars, follows a generalized Wiener process with a drift rate of 0.5 per quarter and a variance rate of 4.0 per quarter. How high does the company's initial cash position have to be for the company to have a less than 5% chance of a negative cash position by the end of one year?

10.4. Variables X_1 and X_2 follow generalized Wiener processes with drift rates μ_1 and μ_2 and variances σ_1^2 and σ_2^2. What process does $X_1 + X_2$ follow if:
   (a) The changes in X_1 and X_2 in any short interval of time are uncorrelated?
   (b) There is a correlation ρ between the changes in X_1 and X_2 in any short interval of time?

10.5. Consider a variable, S, that follows the process

$$dS = \mu\, dt + \sigma\, dz$$

For the first three years, $\mu = 2$ and $\sigma = 3$; for the next three years, $\mu = 3$ and $\sigma = 4$. If the initial value of the variable is 5, what is the probability distribution of the value of the variable at the end of year six?

10.6. Suppose that G is a function of a stock price, S, and time. Suppose that σ_S and σ_G are the volatilities of S and G. Show that, when the expected return of S increases by $\lambda\sigma_S$, the growth rate of G increases by $\lambda\sigma_G$, where λ is a constant.

10.7. Stock A and stock B both follow geometric Brownian motion. Changes in any short interval of time are uncorrelated with each other. Does the value of a portfolio consisting of one of stock A and one of stock B follow geometric Brownian motion? Explain your answer.

10.8. The process for the stock price in equation (10.8) is

$$\Delta S = \mu S\, \Delta t + \sigma S \epsilon \sqrt{\Delta t}$$

where μ and σ are constant. Explain carefully the difference between this model and each of the following:

$$\Delta S = \mu\, \Delta t + \sigma \epsilon \sqrt{\Delta t}$$

$$\Delta S = \mu S\, \Delta t + \sigma \epsilon \sqrt{\Delta t}$$

$$\Delta S = \mu\, \Delta t + \sigma S \epsilon \sqrt{\Delta t}$$

Why is the model in equation (10.8) a more appropriate model of stock price behavior than any of these three alternatives?

10.9. It has been suggested that the short-term interest rate, r, follows the stochastic process

$$dr = a(b - r)\, dt + rc\, dz$$

where a, b, and c are positive constants and dz is a Wiener process. Describe the nature of this process.

10.10. Suppose that a stock price, S, follows geometric Brownian motion with expected return μ and volatility σ:

$$dS = \mu S\, dt + \sigma S\, dz$$

What is the process followed by the variable S^n? Show that S^n also follows geometric Brownian motion.

10.11. Suppose that x is the yield to maturity with continuous compounding on a zero-coupon bond that pays off $1 at time T. Assume that x follows the process

$$dx = a(x_0 - x)\,dt + sx\,dz$$

where a, x_0, and s are positive constants and dz is a Wiener process. What is the process followed by the bond price?

ASSIGNMENT QUESTIONS

10.12. Suppose that a stock price has an expected return of 16% per annum and a volatility of 30% per annum. When the stock price at the end of a certain day is $50, calculate the following:
(a) The expected stock price at the end of the next day.
(b) The standard deviation of the stock price at the end of the next day.
(c) The 95% confidence limits for the stock price at the end of the next day.

10.13. A company's cash position, measured in millions of dollars, follows a generalized Wiener process with a drift rate of 0.1 per month and a variance rate of 0.16 per month. The initial cash position is 2.0.
(a) What are the probability distributions of the cash position after one month, six months, and one year?
(b) What are the probabilities of a negative cash position at the end of six months and one year?
(c) At what time in the future is the probability of a negative cash position greatest?

10.14. Suppose that x is the yield on a perpetual government bond that pays interest at the rate of $1 per annum. Assume that x is expressed with continuous compounding, that interest is paid continuously on the bond, and that x follows the process

$$dx = a(x_0 - x)\,dt + sx\,dz$$

where a, x_0, and s are positive constants and dz is a Wiener process. What is the process followed by the bond price? What is the expected instantaneous return (including interest and capital gains) to the holder of the bond?

APPENDIX 10A

Derivation of Ito's Lemma

In this appendix, we show how Ito's lemma can be regarded as a natural extension of other, simpler results. Consider a continuous and differentiable function, G, of a variable x. If Δx is a small change in x and ΔG is the resulting small change in G, a well known result from ordinary calculus is

$$\Delta G \approx \frac{dG}{dx} \Delta x \qquad (10A.1)$$

In other words, ΔG is approximately equal to the rate of change of G with respect to x multiplied by Δx. The error involves terms of order Δx^2. If more precision is required, a Taylor series expansion of ΔG can be used:

$$\Delta G = \frac{dG}{dx} \Delta x + \frac{1}{2} \frac{d^2 G}{dx^2} \Delta x^2 + \frac{1}{6} \frac{d^3 G}{dx^3} \Delta x^3 + \cdots$$

For a continuous and differentiable function, G, of two variables, x and y, the result analogous to equation (10A.1) is

$$\Delta G \approx \frac{\partial G}{\partial x} \Delta x + \frac{\partial G}{\partial y} \Delta y \qquad (10A.2)$$

and the Taylor series expansion of ΔG is

$$\Delta G = \frac{\partial G}{\partial x} \Delta x + \frac{\partial G}{\partial y} \Delta y + \frac{1}{2} \frac{\partial^2 G}{\partial x^2} \Delta x^2 + \frac{\partial^2 G}{\partial x \partial y} \Delta x \Delta y + \frac{1}{2} \frac{\partial^2 G}{\partial y^2} \Delta y^2 + \cdots \qquad (10A.3)$$

In the limit as Δx and Δy tend to zero, equation (10A.3) becomes

$$dG = \frac{\partial G}{\partial x} dx + \frac{\partial G}{\partial y} dy \qquad (10A.4)$$

We now extend equation (10A.4) to cover functions of variables following Ito processes. Suppose that a variable, x, follows the Ito process in equation (10.4)

$$dx = a(x, t) dt + b(x, t) dz \qquad (10A.5)$$

and that G is some function of x and of time, t. By analogy with equation (10A.3), we can write

$$\Delta G = \frac{\partial G}{\partial x} \Delta x + \frac{\partial G}{\partial t} \Delta t + \frac{1}{2} \frac{\partial^2 G}{\partial x^2} \Delta x^2 + \frac{\partial^2 G}{\partial x \partial t} \Delta x \Delta t + \frac{1}{2} \frac{\partial^2 G}{\partial t^2} \Delta t^2 + \cdots \qquad (10A.6)$$

Equation (10A.5) can be discretized to

$$\Delta x = a(x, t) \Delta t + b(x, t) \epsilon \sqrt{\Delta t}$$

235

or if arguments are dropped,

$$\Delta x = a\,\Delta t + b\epsilon\,\sqrt{\Delta t} \qquad (10\text{A}.7)$$

This equation reveals an important difference between the situation in equation (10A.6) and the situation in equation (10A.3). When limiting arguments were used to move from equation (10A.3) to equation (10A.4), terms in Δx^2 were ignored because they were second-order terms. From equation (10A.7),

$$\Delta x^2 = b^2\epsilon^2\,\Delta t + \text{terms of higher order in } \Delta t \qquad (10\text{A}.8)$$

This shows that the term involving Δx^2 in equation (10A.6) has a component that is of order Δt and cannot be ignored.

The variance of a standardized normal distribution is 1.0. This means that

$$E(\epsilon^2) - [E(\epsilon)]^2 = 1$$

where E denotes expected value. Because $E(\epsilon) = 0$, it follows that $E(\epsilon^2) = 1$. The expected value of $\epsilon^2\,\Delta t$ is, therefore, Δt. It can be shown that the variance of $\epsilon^2\,\Delta t$ is of order Δt^2 and that as a result of this, we can treat $\epsilon^2\,\Delta t$ as nonstochastic and equal to its expected value of Δt as Δt tends to zero. It follows from equation (10A.8) that Δx^2 becomes nonstochastic and equal to $b^2\,dt$ as Δt tends to zero. Taking limits as Δx and Δt tend to zero in equation (10A.6), and using this last result, we obtain

$$dG = \frac{\partial G}{\partial x}dx + \frac{\partial G}{\partial t}dt + \frac{1}{2}\frac{\partial^2 G}{\partial x^2}b^2\,dt \qquad (10\text{A}.9)$$

This is Ito's lemma. Substituting for dx from equation (10A.5), equation (10A.9) becomes

$$dG = \left(\frac{\partial G}{\partial x}a + \frac{\partial G}{\partial t} + \frac{1}{2}\frac{\partial^2 G}{\partial x^2}b^2\right)dt + \frac{\partial G}{\partial x}b\,dz$$

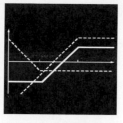

THE BLACK–SCHOLES MODEL

In the early 1970s, Fischer Black, Myron Scholes, and Robert Merton made a major breakthrough in the pricing of stock options by developing what has become known as the Black–Scholes model.[1] The model has had a huge influence on the way that traders price and hedge options. It has also been pivotal to the growth and success of financial engineering in the 1980s and 1990s. In 1997, the importance of the model was recognized when Myron Scholes and Robert Merton were awarded the Nobel prize for economics. Sadly, Fischer Black died in 1995, otherwise he also would undoubtedly have been one of the recipients of this prize.

This chapter shows how the Black–Scholes model for valuing European call and put options on a non-dividend-paying stock is derived. We explain how volatility can be either estimated from historical data or implied from option prices using the model. We discuss the risk-neutral valuation argument introduced in chapter 9. Later in the chapter we show how the Black–Scholes model can be extended to deal with European call and put options on dividend-paying stocks. We also present some results on the pricing of American call options on dividend-paying stocks.

11.1 LOGNORMAL PROPERTY OF STOCK PRICES

A variable has a lognormal distribution if the natural logarithm of the variable is normally distributed. In equation (10.17) we showed that if a stock price, S, follows geometric Brownian motion,

$$dS = \mu S \, dt + \sigma S \, dz$$

then

$$d \ln S = \left(\mu - \frac{\sigma^2}{2} \right) dt + \sigma \, dz$$

---

[1] See F. Black and M. Scholes, "The Pricing of Options and Corporate Liabilities," *Journal of Political Economy,* 81 (May–June 1973), 637–659; and R. C. Merton, "Theory of Rational Option Pricing," *Bell Journal of Economics and Management Science,* 4 (Spring 1973), 141–183.

From this equation we see that the variable $\ln S$ follows a generalized Wiener process. The change in $\ln S$ between time 0 and T is normally distributed so that

$$\ln S_T - \ln S_0 \sim \phi\left[\left(\mu - \frac{\sigma^2}{2}\right)T, \ \sigma\sqrt{T}\right]$$

From this it follows that

$$\ln \frac{S_T}{S_0} \sim \phi\left[\left(\mu - \frac{\sigma^2}{2}\right)T, \ \sigma\sqrt{T}\right] \tag{11.1}$$

and

$$\ln S_T \sim \phi\left[\ln S_0 + \left(\mu - \frac{\sigma^2}{2}\right)T, \ \sigma\sqrt{T}\right] \tag{11.2}$$

where S_T is the stock price at a future time T, S_0 is the stock price at time 0, and $\phi(m, s)$ denotes a normal distribution with mean m and standard deviation s. Equation (11.2) shows that $\ln S_T$ is normally distributed so that S_T has a lognormal distribution.

The model we developed in chapter 10, therefore, implies that a stock's price at time T, given its price today, is lognormally distributed. The standard deviation of the logarithm of the stock price is $\sigma\sqrt{T}$. It is proportional to the square root of how far ahead we are looking.

Example 11.1   Consider a stock with an initial price of \$40, an expected return of 16% per annum, and a volatility of 20% per annum. From equation (11.2), the probability distribution of the stock price, S_T, in six months' time is given by

$$\ln S_T \sim \phi[\ln 40 + (0.16 - 0.2^2/2) \times 0.5, \ 0.2\sqrt{0.5}]$$
$$\ln S_T \sim \phi(3.759, \ 0.141)$$

There is a 95% probability that a normally distributed variable has a value within 1.96 standard deviations of its mean. Hence, with 95% confidence,

$$3.759 - 1.96 \times 0.141 < \ln S_T < 3.759 + 1.96 \times 0.141$$

This can be written

$$e^{3.759-1.96\times0.141} < S_T < e^{3.759+1.96\times0.141}$$

or

$$32.55 < S_T < 56.56$$

Thus, there is a 95% probability that the stock price in six months will lie between 32.55 and 56.56.

A variable that has a lognormal distribution can take any value between zero and infinity. Figure 11.1 illustrates the shape of a lognormal distribution. Unlike the normal distribution, it is skewed so that the mean, median, and mode are all different. From equation (11.2) and the properties of the lognormal distribution, it can be shown that the expected value of S_T, $E(S_T)$, is given by[2]

$$E(S_T) = S_0 e^{\mu T} \tag{11.3}$$

This fits in with the definition of μ as the expected rate of return. The variance of S_T, var (S_T), can be shown to be given by

$$\text{var}(S_T) = S_0^2 e^{2\mu T}[e^{\sigma^2 T} - 1] \tag{11.4}$$

Example 11.2   Consider a stock where the current price is \$20, the expected return is 20% per annum, and the volatility is 40% per annum. The expected stock price in one year, $E(S_T)$, and the variance of the stock price in one year, var (S_T), are given by

$$E(S_T) = 20e^{0.2 \times 1} = 24.43$$

$$\text{var}(S_T) = 400e^{2 \times 0.2 \times 1}(e^{0.4^2 \times 1} - 1) = 103.54$$

The standard deviation of the stock price in one year is $\sqrt{103.54}$, or 10.18.

11.2   THE DISTRIBUTION OF THE RATE OF RETURN

The lognormal property of stock prices can be used to provide information on the probability distribution of the continuously compounded rate of return earned on a stock between times 0 and T. Define the continuously compounded rate of return per annum realized between times 0 and T as η.[3] It follows that

$$S_T = S_0 e^{\eta T} \tag{11.5}$$

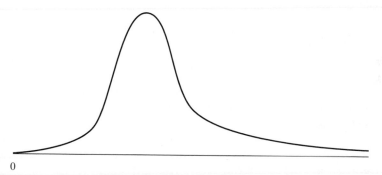

Figure 11.1   Lognormal distribution.

[2]For a discussion of the properties of the lognormal distribution, see J. Aitchison and J. A. C. Brown, *The Lognormal Distribution* (Cambridge: Cambridge University Press, 1966).

[3]It is important to distinguish between the continuously compounded rate of return, η, and the annualized return with no compounding (see section 3.1). The latter is

$$\frac{1}{T}\left(\frac{S_T - S_0}{S_0}\right)$$

and is always greater than η.

and

$$\eta = \frac{1}{T} \ln \frac{S_T}{S_0} \tag{11.6}$$

It follows from equation (11.1) that

$$\eta \sim \phi \left(\mu - \frac{\sigma^2}{2}, \frac{\sigma}{\sqrt{T}} \right) \tag{11.7}$$

Thus, the continuously compounded rate of return per annum is normally distributed with mean $\mu - \sigma^2/2$ and standard deviation $\sigma/\sqrt{T}$.

> **Example 11.3**   Consider a stock with an expected return of 17% per annum and a volatility of 20% per annum. The probability distribution for the actual rate of return (continuously compounded) realized over three years is normal with mean
>
> $$0.17 - \frac{0.2^2}{2} = 0.15$$
>
> or 15% per annum and standard deviation
>
> $$\frac{0.2}{\sqrt{3}} = 0.1155$$
>
> or 11.55% per annum. Because there is a 95% chance that a normally distributed variable will lie within 1.96 standard deviations of its mean, we can be 95% confident that the actual return realized over three years will be between -7.6% and $+37.6\%$ per annum.

What Is the Expected Rate of Return?

Equation (10.7) shows that $\mu \Delta t$ is the expected return provided by S in a very short period of time, Δt. It is natural to assume that μ is also the expected return on the stock over a relatively long period of time when this return is expressed with continuous compounding. However, this is not the case. Equation (11.7) shows that the expected continuously compounded return is $\mu - \sigma^2/2$ per year.[4]

To understand this further, define

   U: The expected return on an asset per annum in a period Δt.

   V: The expected return on the asset per annum realized over a longer period of time, expressed with a compounding frequency of Δt.

An important general result is that, whenever there is some uncertainty about the return, $U > V$. As Δt tends to zero, U becomes μ and V becomes the expected continuously compounded return. Our assumptions about the behavior of stock prices imply that this expected continuously compounded return is $\mu - \sigma^2/2$.

---

[4]It is tempting to argue that we can take logarithms in equation (11.3) to get $\ln [E(S_T)] = \ln (S_0) + \mu T$. Setting $\ln [E(S_T)] = E[\ln (S_T)]$ leads to $E(S_T/S_0) = \mu T$. However, this argument is flawed. Because $\ln$ is a nonlinear function, it is not true that $\ln [E(S_T)] = E[\ln (S_T)]$.

We illustrate the general result with a simple example where Δt is one year. Suppose that the following is a sequence of returns per annum on a stock, measured using annual compounding:

$$15\%, \quad 20\%, \quad 30\%, \quad -20\%, \quad 25\%$$

Our best estimate of the expected return in one year is calculated by taking the sum of the returns and dividing by five. It is 14%. To estimate the expected return realized over five years with annual compounding, we imagine investing $100 in the stock. Its value at the end of the five year period would be

$$100 \times 1.15 \times 1.20 \times 1.30 \times 0.80 \times 1.25 = \$179.40$$

This corresponds to a return of

$$(1.7940)^{1/5} - 1 = 0.124$$

or 12.4% per annum with annual compounding. The expected return per annum over five years with annual compounding is, therefore, less than the expected return in one year.

The arguments in this section show that the term *expected return* is ambiguous. It can refer either to μ or to $\mu - \sigma^2/2$. Unless otherwise stated, it will be used to refer to μ throughout this book.

11.3 VOLATILITY

As discussed in section 10.5, the volatility of a stock, σ, is a measure of our uncertainty about the returns provided by the stock. Typical values of the volatility of a stock are in the range of 20% to 40% per annum.

From equation (11.7), the volatility of a stock price can be defined as the standard deviation of the return provided by the stock in one year when the return is expressed using continuous compounding. Equation (11.2) shows that volatility is also the standard deviation of the natural logarithm of the stock price at the end of one year.

When Δt is small, equation (10.7) shows that $\sigma \sqrt{\Delta t}$ is approximately equal to the standard deviation of the proportional change in the stock price in time Δt. Suppose $\sigma = 0.3$, or 30% per annum and the current stock price is $50. The standard deviation of the proportional change in the stock price in one week is approximately

$$0.3 \times \sqrt{\frac{1}{52}} = 0.0416$$

A one standard deviation move in the stock price in one week is, therefore, 50×0.0416 or $2.08. Our uncertainty about a future stock price, as measured by its standard deviation, increases—at least approximately—with the square root of how far ahead we are looking. For example, the standard deviation of the stock price in four weeks is approximately twice the standard deviation in one week.

Estimating Volatility from Historical Data

To estimate the volatility of a stock price empirically, the stock price is usually observed at fixed intervals of time (e.g., every day, week, or month).

Define:

$n + 1$: Number of observations

S_i: Stock price at end of ith interval ($i = 0, 1, \ldots, n$)

τ: Length of time interval in years

and let

$$u_i = \ln\left(\frac{S_i}{S_{i-1}}\right)$$

for $i = 1, 2, \ldots, n$.

Because $S_i = S_{i-1}e^{u_i}$, u_i is the continuously compounded return (not annualized) in the ith interval. The usual estimate, s, of the standard deviation of the u_i's is given by

$$s = \sqrt{\frac{1}{n-1}\sum_{i=1}^{n}(u_i - \bar{u})^2}$$

or

$$s = \sqrt{\frac{1}{n-1}\sum_{i=1}^{n}u_i^2 - \frac{1}{n(n-1)}\left(\sum_{i=1}^{n}u_i\right)^2}$$

where $\bar{u}$ is the mean of the u_i's.

From equation (11.1), the standard deviation of the u_i, s is $\sigma\sqrt{\tau}$. The variable, s, is, therefore, an estimate of $\sigma\sqrt{\tau}$. It follows that σ itself can be estimated as σ^*, where

$$\sigma^* = \frac{s}{\sqrt{\tau}}$$

The standard error of this estimate can be shown to be approximately $\sigma^*/\sqrt{2n}$.

Choosing an appropriate value for n is not easy. *Ceteris paribus,* more data generally lead to more accuracy. However, σ does change over time and data that are too old may not be relevant for predicting the future. A compromise that seems to work reasonably well is to use closing prices from daily data over the most recent 90 to 180 days. An often used rule of thumb is to set the time period over which the volatility is measured equal to the time period over which it is to be applied. Thus, if the volatility is to be used to value a two-year option, two years of historical data are used. More sophisticated approaches involving GARCH models are discussed in chapter 15.

An important issue is whether time should be measured in calendar days or trading days when volatility parameters are being estimated and used. Later in this chapter, we show that empirical research indicates that trading days should be used. In other words, days when the exchange is closed should be ignored for the purposes of the volatility calculation.

Example 11.4 Table 11.1 shows a possible sequence of stock prices over a 20-day period. Because

$$\sum u_i = 0.09531 \quad \text{and} \quad \sum u_i^2 = 0.00333$$

an estimate of the standard deviation of the daily return is

$$\sqrt{\frac{0.00333}{19} - \frac{0.09531^2}{380}} = 0.0123$$

Assuming that time is measured in trading days and that there are 252 trading days per year, $\tau = 1/252$ and the data give an estimate for the volatility per annum of $0.0123 \times \sqrt{252} = 0.195$. The estimated volatility is 19.5% per annum. The standard error of this estimate is

$$\frac{0.195}{\sqrt{2 \times 20}} = 0.031$$

or 3.1% per annum.

Table 11.1 Computation of Volatility

Day	Closing Stock Price (dollars)	Price Relative, S_i/S_{i-1}	Daily Return, $u_i = \ln(S_i/S_{i-1})$
0	20		
1	$20\frac{1}{8}$	1.00625	0.00623
2	$19\frac{7}{8}$	0.98758	−0.01250
3	20	1.00629	0.00627
4	$20\frac{1}{2}$	1.02500	0.02469
5	$20\frac{1}{4}$	0.98781	−0.01227
6	$20\frac{7}{8}$	1.03086	0.03040
7	$20\frac{7}{8}$	1.00000	0.00000
8	$20\frac{7}{8}$	1.00000	0.00000
9	$20\frac{3}{4}$	0.99401	−0.00601
10	$20\frac{3}{4}$	1.00000	0.00000
11	21	1.01205	0.01198
12	$21\frac{1}{8}$	1.00595	0.00593
13	$20\frac{7}{8}$	0.98817	−0.01190
14	$20\frac{7}{8}$	1.00000	0.00000
15	$21\frac{1}{4}$	1.01796	0.01780
16	$21\frac{3}{8}$	1.00588	0.00587
17	$21\frac{3}{8}$	1.00000	0.00000
18	$21\frac{1}{4}$	0.99415	−0.00587
19	$21\frac{3}{4}$	1.02353	0.02326
20	22	1.01149	0.01143

This analysis assumes that the stock pays no dividends, but it can be adapted to accommodate dividend-paying stocks. The return, u_i, during a time interval that includes an ex-dividend day is given by

$$u_i = \ln \frac{S_i + D}{S_{i-1}}$$

where D is the amount of the dividend. The return in other time intervals is still

$$u_i = \ln \frac{S_i}{S_{i-1}}$$

However, as tax factors play a part in determining returns around an ex-dividend date, it is probably best to discard altogether data for intervals that include an ex-dividend date.

11.4   CONCEPTS UNDERLYING THE BLACK–SCHOLES– MERTON DIFFERENTIAL EQUATION

The Black–Scholes–Merton differential equation is an equation that must be satisfied by the price, f, of any derivative dependent on a non-dividend-paying stock. The equation is derived in the next section. Here we consider the nature of the arguments used.

The Black–Scholes–Merton analysis is analogous to the no-arbitrage analysis used in chapter 9 to value options when stock price changes are binomial. A riskless portfolio consisting of a position in the option and a position in the underlying stock is created. In the absence of arbitrage opportunities, the return from the portfolio must be the risk-free interest rate, r.

The reason why a riskless portfolio can be created is that the stock price and the option price are both affected by the same underlying source of uncertainty: stock price movements. In any short period of time, the price of a call option is perfectly positively correlated with the price of the underlying stock; the price of a put option is perfectly negatively correlated with the price of the underlying stock. In both cases, when an appropriate portfolio of the stock and the option is established, the gain or loss from the stock position always offsets the gain or loss from the option position so that the overall value of the portfolio at the end of the short period of time is known with certainty.

Suppose, for example, that at a particular point in time the relationship between a small change in the stock price, ΔS, and the resultant small change in the price of a European call option, Δc, is given by

$$\Delta c = 0.4 \, \Delta S$$

This means that the slope of the line representing the relationship between c and S is 0.4, as indicated in Figure 11.2. The riskless portfolio would consist of

1. A long position in 0.4 share.
2. A short position in one call option.

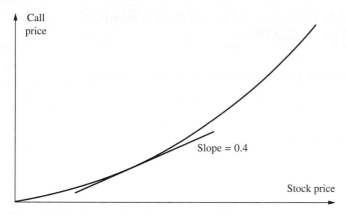

Figure 11.2   Relationship between *c* and *S*.

There is one important difference between the Black–Scholes–Merton analysis and our analysis using a binomial model in chapter 9. In Black–Scholes–Merton, the position in the stock and the option is riskless for only a very short period of time. (Theoretically, it remains riskless only for an instantaneously short period of time.) To remain riskless it must be adjusted or *rebalanced* frequently.[5] For example, the relationship between Δc and ΔS might change from $\Delta c = 0.4\,\Delta S$ today to $\Delta c = 0.5\,\Delta S$ in two weeks. This would mean that 0.5 rather than 0.4 shares must then be owned for each call option sold. It is nevertheless true that the return from the riskless portfolio in any very short period of time must be the risk-free interest rate. This is the key element in the Black–Scholes arguments and leads to their pricing formulas.

Assumptions

The assumptions we use to derive the Black–Scholes–Merton differential equation are as follows:

1. The stock price follows the process developed in chapter 10 with μ and σ constant.
2. The short selling of securities with full use of proceeds is permitted.
3. There are no transactions costs or taxes. All securities are perfectly divisible.
4. There are no dividends during the life of the derivative.
5. There are no riskless arbitrage opportunities.
6. Security trading is continuous.
7. The risk-free rate of interest, r, is constant and the same for all maturities.
   8. Frequent Rebalancing

As we discuss in chapters 17 and 19, some of these assumptions can be relaxed. For example σ can be a known function of t and interest rates can be stochastic.

---

[5] We discuss the rebalancing of portfolios in more detail in chapter 13.

11.5   DERIVATION OF THE BLACK–SCHOLES–MERTON DIFFERENTIAL EQUATION

The stock price process we are assuming is the one developed in section 10.3:

$$dS = \mu S \, dt + \sigma S \, dz \tag{11.8}$$

Suppose that f is the price of a call option or other derivative contingent on S. The variable f must be some function of S and t. Hence from equation (10.14),

$$df = \left(\frac{\partial f}{\partial S} \mu S + \frac{\partial f}{\partial t} + \frac{1}{2} \frac{\partial^2 f}{\partial S^2} \sigma^2 S^2\right) dt + \frac{\partial f}{\partial S} \sigma S \, dz \tag{11.9}$$

The discrete versions of equations (11.8) and (11.9) are

$$\Delta S = \mu S \, \Delta t + \sigma S \, \Delta z \tag{11.10}$$

and

$$\Delta f = \left(\frac{\partial f}{\partial S} \mu S + \frac{\partial f}{\partial t} + \frac{1}{2} \frac{\partial^2 f}{\partial S^2} \sigma^2 S^2\right) \Delta t + \frac{\partial f}{\partial S} \sigma S \, \Delta z \tag{11.11}$$

where ΔS and Δf are the changes in f and S in a small time interval Δt. Recall from the discussion of Ito's lemma in section 10.6 that the Wiener processes underlying f and S are the same. In other words, the $\Delta z \, (= \epsilon \sqrt{\Delta t})$ in equations (11.10) and (11.11) are the same. It follows that by choosing a portfolio of the stock and the derivative, the Wiener process can be eliminated.

The appropriate portfolio is

$$-1: \quad \text{derivative}$$

$$+\frac{\partial f}{\partial S}: \quad \text{shares}$$

The holder of this portfolio is short one derivative and long an amount $\partial f / \partial S$ of shares. Define Π as the value of the portfolio. By definition

$$\Pi = -f + \frac{\partial f}{\partial S} S \tag{11.12}$$

The change $\Delta \Pi$ in the value of the portfolio in the time interval Δt is given by

$$\Delta \Pi = -\Delta f + \frac{\partial f}{\partial S} \Delta S \tag{11.13}$$

Substituting equations (11.10) and (11.11) into equation (11.13) yields

$$\Delta \Pi = \left(-\frac{\partial f}{\partial t} - \frac{1}{2} \frac{\partial^2 f}{\partial S^2} \sigma^2 S^2\right) \Delta t \tag{11.14}$$

Because this equation does not involve Δz, the portfolio must be riskless during time Δt. The assumptions listed in the preceding section imply that the portfolio must instantaneously earn the same rate of return as other short-term risk-free securities. If it earned more than this return, arbitrageurs could make a riskless profit by shorting the risk-free securities and using the proceeds to buy the portfolio; if it earned less, they could make a riskless profit by shorting the portfolio and buying risk-free securities. It follows that

$$\Delta \Pi = r \Pi \, \Delta t$$

where r is the risk-free interest rate. Substituting from equations (11.12) and (11.14), this becomes

$$\left(\frac{\partial f}{\partial t} + \frac{1}{2} \frac{\partial^2 f}{\partial S^2} \sigma^2 S^2 \right) \Delta t = r \left(f - \frac{\partial f}{\partial S} S \right) \Delta t$$

so that

$$\frac{\partial f}{\partial t} + r S \frac{\partial f}{\partial S} + \frac{1}{2} \sigma^2 S^2 \frac{\partial^2 f}{\partial S^2} = r f \qquad (11.15)$$

Equation (11.15) is the Black–Scholes–Merton differential equation. It has many solutions, corresponding to all the derivatives that can be defined with S as the underlying variable. The particular derivative that is obtained when the equation is solved depends on the *boundary conditions* that are used. These specify the values of the derivative at the boundaries of possible values of S and t. In the case of a European call option, the key boundary condition is

$$f = \max (S - X, \, 0) \qquad \text{when } t = T$$

In the case of a European put option, it is

$$f = \max (X - S, \, 0) \qquad \text{when } t = T$$

One point that should be emphasized about the portfolio used in the derivation of equation (11.15) is that it is not permanently riskless. It is riskless only for an infinitesimally short period of time. As S and t change, $\partial f / \partial S$ also changes. To keep the portfolio riskless, it is, therefore, necessary to frequently change the relative proportions of the derivative and the stock in the portfolio.

Example 11.5 A forward contract on a non-dividend-paying stock is a derivative dependent on the stock. As such, it should satisfy equation (11.15). From equation (3.9), the value of the forward contract, f, at a general time t is given in terms of the stock price S at this time by

$$f = S - K e^{-r(T-t)}$$

where K is the delivery price. This means that

$$\frac{\partial f}{\partial t} = -r K e^{-r(T-t)} \qquad \frac{\partial f}{\partial S} = 1 \qquad \frac{\partial^2 f}{\partial S^2} = 0$$

When these are substituted into the left-hand side of equation (11.15), we obtain

$$-rKe^{-r(T-t)} + rS$$

This equals rf, showing that equation (11.15) is indeed satisfied.

The Prices of Tradeable Derivatives

Any function $f(S, t)$ that is a solution of the differential equation (11.15) is the theoretical price of a derivative that could be traded. If a derivative with that price existed, it would not create any arbitrage opportunities. Conversely, if a function $f(S, t)$ does not satisfy the differential equation (11.15), it cannot be the price of a derivative without creating arbitrage opportunities for traders.

To illustrate this point, consider first the function $\exp(S)$. This does not satisfy the differential equation (11.15). It is, therefore, not a candidate for being the price of a derivative dependent on the stock price. If an instrument whose price was always $\exp(S)$ existed, there would be an arbitrage opportunity. As another example, consider the function

$$\frac{e^{(\sigma^2 - 2r)(T-t)}}{S}$$

This does satisfy the differential equation and so is, in theory, the price of a tradeable security. (It is the price of a derivative that pays off $1/S_T$ at time T.) For other examples of tradeable derivatives see Problems 11.11, 11.12, and 11.27.

11.6   RISK-NEUTRAL VALUATION

Risk-neutral valuation was introduced in connection with the binomial model in chapter 9. It is without doubt the single most important tool for the analysis of derivatives. It arises from one key property of the Black–Scholes–Merton differential equation (11.15). This property is that the equation does not involve any variables that are affected by the risk preferences of investors. The variables that do appear in the equation are the current stock price, time, stock price volatility, and the risk-free rate of interest. All are independent of risk preferences.

The Black–Scholes–Merton differential equation would not be independent of risk preferences if it involved the expected return on the stock, μ. This is because the value of μ does depend on risk preferences. The higher the level of risk aversion by investors, the higher μ will be for any given stock. It is fortunate that μ happens to drop out in the derivation of the differential equation.

Because the Black–Scholes–Merton differential equation is independent of risk preferences, an ingenious argument can be used. If risk preferences do not enter the equation, they cannot affect its solution. Any set of risk preferences can, therefore, be used when evaluating f. In particular, the very simple assumption that all investors are risk neutral can be made.

In a world where investors are risk neutral, the expected return on all securities is the risk-free rate of interest, r. The reason is that risk-neutral investors do not require a premium to induce them to take risks. It is also true that the present value of any cash flow in a risk-neutral world can be obtained by discounting its expected value at the risk-free rate. The assumption that the world is risk neutral does, therefore, considerably simplify the analysis of derivatives.

Consider a derivative that provides a payoff at one particular time. It can be valued using risk-neutral valuation by using the following procedure:

1. Assume that the expected return from the underlying asset is the risk-free interest rate, r (i.e., assume $\mu = r$).
2. Calculate the expected payoff from the option at its maturity.
3. Discount the expected payoff at the risk-free interest rate.

It is important to appreciate that risk-neutral valuation (or the assumption that all investors are risk neutral) is merely an artificial device for obtaining solutions to the Black–Scholes differential equation. The solutions that are obtained are valid in all worlds, not just those where investors are risk neutral. When we move from a risk-neutral world to a risk-averse world, two things happen. The expected growth rate in the stock price changes and the discount rate that must be used for any payoffs from the derivative changes. It happens that these two changes always offset each other exactly.

Application to Forward Contracts on a Stock

Forward contracts on a non-dividend-paying stock have already been valued in section 3.5. They will be valued again in this section to provide a simple illustration of risk-neutral valuation. We make the assumption that interest rates are constant and equal to r. This is somewhat more restrictive than the assumption in chapter 3. Consider a long forward contract that matures at time T with delivery price, K. As described in chapter 1, the value of the contract at maturity is

$$S_T - K$$

where S_T is the stock price at time T. From the risk-neutral valuation argument, the value of the forward contract at time $t\,(< T)$ is its expected value at time T in a risk-neutral world, discounted to time t at the risk-free rate of interest. Denoting the value of the forward contract at time t by f, this means that

$$f = e^{-r(T-t)}\hat{E}(S_T - K) \tag{11.16}$$

where $\hat{E}$ denotes expected value in a risk-neutral world. Because K is a constant, equation (11.16) becomes

$$f = e^{-r(T-t)}\hat{E}(S_T) - Ke^{-r(T-t)} \tag{11.17}$$

The expected growth rate of the stock price, μ, becomes r in a risk-neutral world. Hence, from equation (11.3),

$$\hat{E}(S_T) = Se^{r(T-t)} \tag{11.18}$$

Substituting equation (11.18) into equation (11.17) gives

$$f = S - Ke^{-r(T-t)} \qquad (11.19)$$

This is in agreement with equation (3.9). Example 11.5 shows that this expression for f satisfies the Black–Scholes differential equation.

11.7 BLACK–SCHOLES PRICING FORMULAS

The Black–Scholes formulas for the prices at time zero of a European call option on a non-dividend-paying stock and a European put option on a non-dividend-paying stock are

$$c = S_0 N(d_1) - Xe^{-rT} N(d_2) \qquad (11.20)$$

and

$$p = Xe^{-rT} N(-d_2) - S_0 N(-d_1) \qquad (11.21)$$

where

$$d_1 = \frac{\ln(S_0/X) + (r + \sigma^2/2)T}{\sigma \sqrt{T}}$$

$$d_2 = \frac{\ln(S_0/X) + (r - \sigma^2/2)T}{\sigma \sqrt{T}} = d_1 - \sigma \sqrt{T}$$

and $N(x)$ is the cumulative probability distribution function for a variable that is normally distributed with a mean of zero and a standard deviation of 1.0 (i.e., it is the probability that such a variable will be less than x). As usual, S_0 is the stock price at time zero, X is the strike price, r is the continuously compounded risk-free rate, σ is the stock price volatility, and T is the time to maturity of the option.

One way of deriving the Black–Scholes formulas is by solving the differential equation (11.15) subject to the boundary conditions mentioned in section 11.5.[6] To see that equations (11.20) and (11.21) have properties consistent with the boundary conditions, look at what happens to d_1 and d_2 as $T \longrightarrow 0$. If $S_0 > X$, they both tend to $+\infty$ so that $N(d_1) = N(d_2) = 1$ and $N(-d_1) = N(-d_2) = 0$. This means that equations (11.20) and (11.21) give

$$c = S_0 - X \qquad\qquad p = 0$$

---

[6]The differential equation gives the call and put prices at a general time t. For example, the call price that satisfies the differential equation is $c = SN(d_1) - Xe^{-r(T-t)}N(d_2)$ where

$$d_1 = \frac{[\ln(S/X) + (r + \sigma^2/2)(T - t)]}{\sigma \sqrt{T - t}}$$

and $d_2 = d_1 - \sigma \sqrt{T - t}$. See Problem 11.17 to prove that the differential equation is satisfied.

If $S_0 < X$, both d_1 and d_2 tend to $-\infty$ as $T \longrightarrow 0$ so that $N(d_1) = N(d_2) = 0$ and $N(-d_1) = N(-d_2) = 1$. This means that equations (11.20) and (11.21) give

$$c = 0 \qquad\qquad p = X - S_0$$

The Black–Scholes formulas in equations (11.20) and (11.21) can also be derived using risk-neutral valuation. Consider a European call option. The expected value of the option at maturity in a risk-neutral world is

$$\hat{E}[\max (S_T - X, 0)]$$

where, as before, $\hat{E}$ denotes expected value in a risk-neutral world. From the risk-neutral valuation argument, the European call option price, c, is this expected value discounted at the risk-free rate of interest, that is,

$$c = e^{-rT}\hat{E}[\max (S_T - X, 0)] \tag{11.22}$$

Appendix 11A shows that this equation leads to the result in equation (11.20).

To provide an interpretation of the terms in equation (11.20), we note that it can be written

$$c = e^{-rT}[S_0 N(d_1)e^{rT} - XN(d_2)] \tag{11.23}$$

The expression $N(d_2)$ is the probability that the option will be exercised in a risk-neutral world, so that $XN(d_2)$ is the strike price times the probability that the strike price will be paid. The expression $S_0 N(d_1)e^{rT}$ is the expected value of a variable that equals S_T if $S_T > X$ and is zero otherwise in a risk-neutral world.

Because $c = C$ when there are no dividends, equation (11.20) also gives the value of an American call option on a non-dividend-paying stock. Unfortunately, no exact analytic formula for the value of an American put option on a non-dividend-paying stock has been produced. Numerical procedures and analytic approximations for calculating American put values are discussed in chapter 16.

Up to now we have been assuming r is constant. When interest rates are stochastic, the usual practice is to set r equal to the zero-coupon risk-free interest rate for a maturity T in the Black–Scholes formulas. This is theoretically correct, as we will show in chapter 19.

Properties of the Black–Scholes Formulas

We now show that the Black–Scholes formulas have the right general properties by considering what happens when some of the parameters take extreme values.

When the stock price, S_0, becomes very large, a call option is almost certain to be exercised. It then becomes very similar to a forward contract with delivery price X. From equation (3.9), we expect the call price to be

$$S_0 - Xe^{-rT}$$

This is, in fact, the call price given by equation (11.20) because when S_0 becomes very large, both d_1 and d_2 become very large, and $N(d_1)$ and $N(d_2)$ are both close to 1.0. When the stock price becomes very large, the price of a European put option, p, approaches zero. This is consistent with equation (11.21) because $N(-d_1)$ and $N(-d_2)$ are both close to zero.

Consider next what happens when the volatility σ approaches zero. Because the stock is virtually riskless, its price will grow at rate r to $S_0 e^{rT}$ at time T and the payoff from a call option is

$$\max [S_0 e^{rT} - X, \, 0]$$

Discounting at rate r, the value of the call today is

$$e^{-rT} \max [S_0 e^{rT} - X, \, 0] = \max [S_0 - X e^{-rT}, \, 0]$$

To show that this is consistent with equation (11.20), consider first the case where $S_0 > X e^{-rT}$. This implies that $\ln (S_0/X) + rT > 0$. As σ tends to zero, d_1 and d_2 tend to $+\infty$ so that $N(d_1)$ and $N(d_2)$ tend to 1.0 and equation (11.20) becomes

$$c = S_0 - X e^{-rT}$$

When $S_0 < X e^{-rT}$, it follows that $\ln(S_0/X) + rT < 0$. As σ tends to zero, d_1 and d_2 tend to $-\infty$ so that $N(d_1)$ and $N(d_2)$ tend to zero and equation (11.20) gives a call price of zero. The call price is, therefore, always $\max [S_0 - X e^{-rT}, \, 0]$ as σ tends to zero. Similarly, it can be shown that the put price is always $\max [X e^{-rT} - S_0, \, 0]$ as σ tends to zero.

11.8 CUMULATIVE NORMAL DISTRIBUTION FUNCTION

The only problem in applying equations (11.22) and (11.23) is in calculating the cumulative normal distribution function, N. Tables for $N(x)$ are provided at the end of this book. A polynomial approximation can be used that gives six-decimal-place accuracy is[7]

$$N(x) = \begin{cases} 1 - N'(x)(a_1 k + a_2 k^2 + a_3 k^3 + a_4 k^4 + a_5 k^5) & \text{when } x \geq 0 \\ 1 - N(-x) & \text{when } x < 0 \end{cases}$$

where

$$k = \frac{1}{1 + \gamma x}$$

$$\gamma = 0.2316419$$

$$a_1 = 0.319381530$$

$$a_2 = -0.356563782$$

$$a_3 = 1.781477937$$

$$a_4 = -1.821255978$$

$$a_5 = 1.330274429$$

---

[7] See M. Abramowitz and I. Stegun, *Handbook of Mathematical Functions*. New York: Dover Publications, 1972.

and

$$N'(x) = \frac{1}{\sqrt{2\pi}} e^{-x^2/2}$$

Example 11.6 Consider the situation where the stock price six months from the expiration of an option is $42, the exercise price of the option is $40, the risk-free interest rate is 10% per annum, and the volatility is 20% per annum. This means that $S_0 = 42$, $X = 40, r = 0.1, \sigma = 0.2, T = 0.5$,

$$d_1 = \frac{\ln(42/40) + (0.1 + 0.2^2/2) \times 0.5}{0.2 \sqrt{0.5}} = 0.7693$$

$$d_2 = \frac{\ln(42/40) + (0.1 - 0.2^2/2) \times 0.5}{0.2 \sqrt{0.5}} = 0.6278$$

and

$$Xe^{-rT} = 40e^{-0.05} = 38.049$$

Hence, if the option is a European call, its value, c, is given by

$$c = 42N(0.7693) - 38.049N(0.6278)$$

If the option is a European put, its value, p, is given by

$$p = 38.049N(-0.6278) - 42N(-0.7693)$$

Using the polynomial approximation,

$$N(0.7693) = 0.7791 \qquad N(-0.7693) = 0.2209$$
$$N(0.6278) = 0.7349 \qquad N(-0.6278) = 0.2651$$

so that

$$c = 4.76 \qquad p = 0.81$$

The stock price has to rise by $2.76 for the purchaser of the call to break even. Similarly, the stock price has to fall by $2.81 for the purchaser of the put to break even.

11.9 WARRANTS ISSUED BY A COMPANY ON ITS OWN STOCK

The Black–Scholes formula, with some adjustments for the impact of dilution, can be used to value European warrants issued by a company on its own stock.[8] Consider a company with N outstanding shares and M outstanding European warrants. Suppose

---

[8]See F. Black and M. Scholes, "The Pricing of Options and Corporate Liabilities," *Journal of Political Economy,* 81 (May–June 1973), 637–59; D. Galai and M. Schneller, "Pricing Warrants and the Value of the Firm," *Journal of Finance,* 33 (1978), 1339–42; B. Lauterbach and P. Schultz, "Pricing Warrants: An Empirical Study of the Black–Scholes Model and Its Alternatives," *Journal of Finance,* 45 (1990), 1181–1209.

that each warrant entitles the holder to purchase γ shares from the company at time T at a price of X per share.

If V_T is the value of the company's equity (including the warrants) at time T and the warrant holders exercise, the company receives a cash inflow from the payment of the exercise price of $M\gamma X$ and the value of the company's equity increases to $V_T + M\gamma X$. This value is distributed among $N + M\gamma$ shares so that the share price immediately after exercise becomes

$$\frac{V_T + M\gamma X}{N + M\gamma}$$

The payoff to the warrant holder if the warrant is exercised is, therefore,

$$\gamma\left(\frac{V_T + M\gamma X}{N + M\gamma} - X\right)$$

or

$$\frac{N\gamma}{N + M\gamma}\left(\frac{V_T}{N} - X\right)$$

The warrants should be exercised only if this payoff is positive. The payoff to the warrant holder is, therefore,

$$\frac{N\gamma}{N + M\gamma} \max\left(\frac{V_T}{N} - X, 0\right)$$

This shows that the value of the warrant is the value of

$$\frac{N\gamma}{N + M\gamma}$$

regular call options on V/N, where V is the value of the company's equity.

The value of V at time zero is given by

$$V_0 = NS_0 + MW$$

where S_0 is the stock price at time zero and W is the warrant price at that time, so that

$$\frac{V_0}{N} = S_0 + \frac{M}{N}W$$

The Black–Scholes formula in equation (11.20), therefore, gives the warrant price W if

1. The stock price S_0 is replaced by $S_0 + (M/N)W$.
2. The volatility σ is the volatility of the equity of the company (i.e., it is the volatility of the value of the shares plus the warrants, not just the shares).
3. The formula is multiplied by $(N\gamma)/(N + M\gamma)$.

When these adjustments are made we end up with a formula for W as a function of W. This can be solved numerically.

11.10   IMPLIED VOLATILITIES

The one parameter in the Black–Scholes pricing formulas that cannot be directly observed is the volatility of the stock price. In section 11.3, we discussed how this can be estimated from a history of the stock price. At this stage, it is appropriate to mention an alternative approach that involves what is termed an *implied volatility*. This is the volatility implied by an option price observed in the market.

To illustrate the basic idea, suppose that the value of a call on a non-dividend-paying stock is 1.875 when $S_0 = 21$, $X = 20$, $r = 0.1$, and $T = 0.25$. The implied volatility is the value of σ, that when substituted into equation (11.20) gives $c = 1.875$. Unfortunately, it is not possible to invert equation (11.20) so that σ is expressed as a function of S_0, X, r, T, and c. However, an iterative search procedure can be used to find the implied σ. For example, we start by trying $\sigma = 0.20$. This gives a value of c equal to 1.76, which is too low. Because c is an increasing function of σ, a higher value of σ is required. We can next try a value of 0.30 for σ. This gives a value of c equal to 2.10, which is too high and means that σ must lie between 0.20 and 0.30. Next, a value of 0.25 can be tried for σ. This also proves to be too high, showing that σ lies between 0.20 and 0.25. Proceeding in this way the range for σ can be halved at each iteration and the correct value of σ can be calculated to any required accuracy.[9] In this example, the implied volatility is 0.235, or 23.5% per annum.

Implied volatilities can be used to monitor the market's opinion about the volatility of a particular stock. Analysts often calculate implied volatilities from actively traded options on a certain stock and use them to calculate the price of a less actively traded option on the same stock. This procedure is discussed in chapter 17. It is important to note that the prices of deep-in-the-money and deep-out-of-the-money options are relatively insensitive to volatility. Implied volatilities calculated from these options, therefore, tend to be unreliable.

11.11   THE CAUSES OF VOLATILITY

Some analysts have claimed that the volatility of a stock price is caused solely by the random arrival of new information about the future returns from the stock. Others have claimed that volatility is caused largely by trading. An interesting question, therefore, is whether the volatility of an exchange-traded instrument is the same when the exchange is open as when it is closed.

---

[9]This method is presented for illustration. Other more powerful methods, such as the Newton–Raphson method, are often used in practice. (See footnote 2 in chapter 4 for further information on the Newton–Raphson method.)

Fama and K. French have tested this question empirically.[10] They collected data on the stock price at the close of each trading day over a long period of time, and then calculated:

1. The variance of stock price returns between the close of trading on one day and the close of trading on the next trading day when there are no intervening nontrading days.
2. The variance of the stock price returns between the close of trading on Fridays and the close of trading on Mondays.

If trading and nontrading days are equivalent, the variance in the second case should be three times as great as the variance in the first case. Fama found that it was only 22% higher. French's results were similar. He found that it was 19% higher.

These results suggest that volatility is far larger when the exchange is open than when it is closed. Proponents of the view that volatility is caused only by new information might be tempted to argue that most new information on stocks arrives during trading days.[11] However, studies of futures prices on agricultural commodities, which depend largely on the weather, have shown that they exhibit much the same behavior as stock prices; that is, they are much more volatile during trading hours. Presumably, news about the weather is equally likely to arise on any day. The only reasonable conclusion seems to be that volatility is largely caused by trading itself.[12]

What are the implications of all of this for the measurement of volatility and the Black–Scholes model? If daily data are used to measure volatility, the results suggest that days when the exchange is closed should be ignored. The volatility per annum can then be calculated from the volatility per trading day using the formula

$$\text{volatility per annum} = \frac{\text{volatility per}}{\text{trading day}} \times \sqrt{\frac{\text{number of trading}}{\text{days per annum}}}$$

This approach was used in Example 11.4 and is the one generally used by practitioners. The normal assumption in equity markets is that there are 252 trading days per year.

Although volatility appears to be a phenomenon that is related largely to trading days, interest is paid by the calendar day. This has led D. French to suggest that, when

---

[10]See E. E. Fama, "The Behavior of Stock Market Prices," *Journal of Business,* 38 (January 1965), 34–105; K. R. French, "Stock Returns and the Weekend Effect," *Journal of Financial Economics,* 8 (March 1980), 55–69.

[11]In fact, this is questionable. Frequently, important announcements (e.g., those concerned with sales and earnings) are made when exchanges are closed.

[12]For a discussion of this, see K. French and R. Roll, "Stock Return Variances: The Arrival of Information and the Reaction of Traders," *Journal of Financial Economics,* 17 (September 1986), 5–26. We consider one way in which trading can generate volatility when we discuss portfolio insurance schemes in chapter 13.

options are being valued, two time measures should be calculated:[13]

$$\tau_1: \frac{\text{trading days until maturity}}{\text{trading days per year}}$$

$$\tau_2: \frac{\text{calendar days until maturity}}{\text{calendar days per year}}$$

and that the Black–Scholes formulas should be adjusted to

$$c = S_0 N(d_1) - X e^{-r\tau_2} N(d_2)$$

and

$$p = X e^{-r\tau_2} N(-d_2) - S_0 N(-d_1)$$

where

$$d_1 = \frac{\ln(S_0/X) + r\tau_2 + \sigma^2 \tau_1/2}{\sigma \sqrt{\tau_1}}$$

$$d_2 = \frac{\ln(S_0/X) + r\tau_2 - \sigma^2 \tau_1/2}{\sigma \sqrt{\tau_1}} = d_1 - \sigma \sqrt{\tau_1}$$

In practice, this adjustment makes little difference except for very short life options.

11.12 DIVIDENDS

Up to now, we have assumed that the stock upon which the option is written pays no dividends. In practice, this is not usually true. In this section, we modify the Black–Scholes model to take account of dividends. We assume that the amount and timing of the dividends during the life of an option can be predicted with certainty. As most exchange-traded stock options last for less than a year, this is not an unreasonable assumption.

A dividend-paying stock can reasonably be expected to follow the stochastic process developed in chapter 10 except when the stock goes ex-dividend. At this point, the stock's price goes down by an amount reflecting the dividend paid per share. For tax reasons, the stock price may go down by somewhat less than the cash amount of the dividend. To take account of this, the word *dividend* in this section should be interpreted as the reduction in the stock price on the ex-dividend date caused by the dividend. Thus, if a dividend of $1 per share is anticipated and the share price normally goes down by 80% of the dividend on the ex-dividend date, the dividend should be assumed to be $0.80 for the purposes of the analysis.

---

[13] See D. W. French, "The Weekend Effect on the Distribution of Stock Prices: Implications for Option Pricing," *Journal of Financial Economics*, 13 (September 1984), 547–59.

European Options

European options can be analyzed by assuming that the stock price is the sum of two components: a riskless component that corresponds to the known dividends during the life of the option and a risky component. The riskless component, at any given time, is the present value of all the dividends during the life of the option discounted from the ex-dividend dates to the present at the risk-free rate. By the time the option matures, the dividends will have been paid and the riskless component will no longer exist. The Black–Scholes formula is, therefore, correct if S_0 is equal to the risky component of the stock price and σ is the volatility of the process followed by the risky component.[14] Operationally, this means that the Black–Scholes formula can be used provided that the stock price is reduced by the present value of all the dividends during the life of the option, the discounting being done from the ex-dividend dates at the risk-free rate. A dividend is counted as being during the life of the option only if its ex-dividend date occurs during the life of the option.

> **Example 11.7**   Consider a European call option on a stock when there are ex-dividend dates in two months and five months. The dividend on each ex-dividend date is expected to be $0.50. The current share price is $40, the exercise price is $40, the stock price volatility is 30% per annum, the risk-free rate of interest is 9% per annum, and the time to maturity is six months. The present value of the dividends is
>
> $$0.5e^{-0.1667 \times 0.09} + 0.5e^{-0.4167 \times 0.09} = 0.9741$$
>
> The option price can, therefore, be calculated from the Black–Scholes formula with $S_0 = 39.0259$, $X = 40$, $r = 0.09$, $\sigma = 0.3$, and $T = 0.5$.
>
> $$d_1 = \frac{\ln(39.0259/40) + (0.09 + 0.3^2/2) \times 0.5}{0.3\sqrt{0.5}} = 0.2017$$
>
> $$d_2 = \frac{\ln(39.0259/40) + (0.09 - 0.3^2/2) \times 0.5}{0.3\sqrt{0.5}} = -0.0104$$
>
> Using the polynomial approximation in section 11.8 gives us
>
> $$N(d_1) = 0.5800 \qquad N(d_2) = 0.4959$$
>
> and from equation (11.20), the call price is
>
> $$39.0259 \times 0.5800 - 40e^{-0.09 \times 0.5} \times 0.4959 = 3.67$$
>
> or $3.67.

---

[14] In theory this is not quite the same as the volatility of the stochastic process followed by the whole stock price. The volatility of the risky component is approximately equal to the volatility of the whole stock price multiplied by $S_0/(S_0 - D)$, where D is the present value of the dividends. In practice, the two are often assumed to be the same.

American Options

Consider next American call options. In section 7.5, we presented an argument to show that these should never be exercised early in the absence of dividends. An extension to the argument shows that when there are dividends, it is optimal to exercise only at a time immediately before the stock goes ex-dividend. We assume that n ex-dividend dates are anticipated and that $t_1, t_2, \ldots, t_n$ are moments in time immediately prior to the stock going ex-dividend with $t_1 < t_2 < t_3 < \cdots < t_n$. The dividends corresponding to these times will be denoted by $D_1, D_2, \ldots, D_n$, respectively.

We start by considering the possibility of early exercise just prior to the final ex-dividend date (i.e., at time t_n). If the option is exercised at time t_n, the investor receives

$$S(t_n) - X$$

If the option is not exercised, the stock price drops to $S(t_n) - D_n$. As shown by equation (7.5), the value of the option is then greater than

$$S(t_n) - D_n - Xe^{-r(T-t_n)}$$

It follows that if

$$S(t_n) - D_n - Xe^{-r(T-t_n)} \geq S(t_n) - X$$

that is,

$$D_n \leq X\left[1 - e^{-r(T-t_n)}\right] \tag{11.24}$$

it cannot be optimal to exercise at time t_n. On the other hand, if

$$D_n > X\left[1 - e^{-r(T-t_n)}\right] \tag{11.25}$$

for any reasonable assumption about the stochastic process followed by the stock price, it can be shown that it is always optimal to exercise at time t_n for a sufficiently high value of $S(t_n)$. The inequality in (11.25) will tend to be satisfied when the final ex-dividend date is fairly close to the maturity of the option (i.e., $T - t_n$ is small) and the dividend is large.

Consider next time t_{n-1}, the penultimate ex-dividend date. If the option is exercised at time t_{n-1}, the investor receives

$$S(t_{n-1}) - X$$

If the option is not exercised at time t_{n-1}, the stock price drops to $S(t_{n-1}) - D_{n-1}$ and the earliest subsequent time at which exercise could take place is t_n. Hence, from equation (7.5) a lower bound to the option price if it is not exercised at time t_{n-1} is

$$S(t_{n-1}) - D_{n-1} - Xe^{-r(t_n - t_{n-1})}$$

It follows that if

$$S(t_{n-1}) - D_{n-1} - Xe^{-r(t_n - t_{n-1})} \geq S(t_{n-1}) - X$$

or

$$D_{n-1} \leq X\left[1 - e^{-r(t_n - t_{n-1})}\right]$$

it is not optimal to exercise at time t_{n-1}. Similarly, for any $i < n$, if

$$D_i \leq X\left[1 - e^{-r(t_{i+1} - t_i)}\right] \tag{11.26}$$

it is not optimal to exercise at time t_i.

The inequality in (11.26) is approximately equivalent to

$$D_i \leq Xr(t_{i+1} - t_i)$$

Assuming that X is fairly close to the current stock price, the dividend yield on the stock would have to be either close to or above the risk-free rate of interest for this inequality not to be satisfied. This is not often the case.

We can conclude from this analysis that in most circumstances, the only time that needs to be considered for the early exercise of an American call is the final ex-dividend date, t_n. Furthermore, if inequality (11.26) holds for $i = 1, 2, \ldots, n - 1$ and inequality (11.24) holds, we can be certain that early exercise is never optimal.

Black's Approximation

Black suggests an approximate procedure for taking account of early exercise.[15] This involves calculating, as described earlier in this section, the prices of European options that mature at times T and t_n, and then setting the American price equal to the greater of the two. This approximation seems to work well in most cases. A more exact procedure suggested by Roll, Geske, and Whaley is given in Appendix 11B.[16]

> **Example 11.8** Consider the situation in Example 11.7, but suppose that the option is American rather than European. In this case $D_1 = D_2 = 0.5$, $S_0 = 40$, $X = 40$, $r = 0.09$, t_1 occurs after two months, and t_2 occurs after five months. Because
>
> $$X\left[1 - e^{-r(t_2 - t_1)}\right] = 40(1 - e^{-0.09 \times 0.25}) = 0.89$$
>
> is greater than 0.5, it follows [see inequality (11.26)] that the option should never be exercised on the first ex-dividend date. In addition, because
>
> $$X\left[1 - e^{-r(T - t_2)}\right] = 40(1 - e^{-0.09 \times 0.0833}) = 0.30$$
>
> is less than 0.5, it follows [see inequality (11.24)] that when it is sufficiently deeply in-the-money, the option should be exercised on its second ex-dividend date.

---

[15] See F. Black, "Fact and Fantasy in the Use of Options," *Financial Analysts Journal*, 31 (July–August 1975), 36–41, 61–72.

[16] See R. Roll, "An Analytic Formula for Unprotected American Call Options on Stocks with Known Dividends," *Journal of Financial Economics*, 5 (1977), 251–58; R. Geske, "A Note on an Analytic Valuation Formula for Unprotected American Call Options on Stocks with Known Dividends," *Journal of Financial Economics*, 7 (1979), 375–80; R. Whaley, "On the Valuation of American Call Options on Stocks with Known Dividends," *Journal of Financial Economics*, 9 (June 1981), 207–11; R. Geske, "Comments on Whaley's Note," *Journal of Financial Economics*, 9 (June 1981), 213–215.

We now use Black's approximation to value the option. The present value of the first dividend is

$$0.5e^{-0.1667 \times 0.09} = 0.4926$$

so that the value of the option, on the assumption that it expires just before the final ex-dividend date, can be calculated using the Black–Scholes formula with $S_0 = 39.5074$, $X = 40$, $r = 0.09$, $\sigma = 0.30$, and $T = 0.4167$. It is \$3.52. Black's approximation involves taking the greater of this and the value of the option when it can only be exercised at the end of six months. From Example 11.7, we know that the latter is \$3.67. Black's approximation, therefore, gives the value of the American call as \$3.67.

The value of the option given by the Roll, Geske, and Whaley (RGW) formula is \$3.72. There are two reasons for differences between RGR and Black's approximation (BA). The first concerns the timing of the early exercise decision and tends to make RGW greater than BA. In BA, the assumption is that holder has to decide today whether the option will be exercised after five months or after six months; RGW allows the decision on early exercise at the five-month point to depend on the stock price. The second concerns the way in which volatility is applied and tends to make BA greater than RGW. In BA, when we assume exercise takes place after five months, the volatility is applied to the stock price less the present value of the first dividend; when we assume exercise takes place after six months, the volatility is applied to the stock price less the present value of both dividends. In RGW, it is always applied to the stock price less the present value of both dividends.

Whaley[17] has empirically tested three models for the pricing of American calls on dividend-paying stocks: (1) the formula in Appendix 10B; (2) Black's model; and (3) the European option pricing model described at the beginning of this section. He used 15,582 Chicago Board options. The models produced pricing errors with means of 1.08%, 1.48%, and 2.15%, respectively. The typical bid–ask spread on a call option is greater than 2.15% of the price. On average, therefore, all three models work well and within the tolerance imposed on the options market by trading imperfections.

Up to now, our discussion has centered on American call options. The results for American put options are less clear cut. Dividends make it less likely that an American put option will be exercised early. It can be shown that it is never worth exercising an American put for a period immediately prior to an ex-dividend date.[18] Indeed, if

$$D_i \geq X \left[1 - e^{-r(t_{i+1} - t_i)} \right]$$

for all $i < n$ and

$$D_n \geq X \left[1 - e^{-r(T - t_n)} \right]$$

an argument analogous to that just given shows that the put option should never be exercised early. In other cases, numerical procedures must be used to value a put.

---

[17] See R. E. Whaley, "Valuation of American Call Options on Dividend Paying Stocks: Empirical Tests," *Journal of Financial Economics,* 10 (March 1982), 29–58.

[18] See H. E. Johnson, "Three Topics in Option Pricing," Ph.D. thesis, University of California, Los Angeles, 1981, p. 42.

SUMMARY

We started this chapter by examining the properties of the process for stock prices introduced in chapter 10. The process implies that the price of a stock at some future time, given its price today, is lognormal. It also implies that the continuously compounded return from the stock in a period of time is normally distributed. Our uncertainty about future stock prices increases as we look further ahead. The standard deviation of the logarithm of the stock price is proportional to the square root of how far ahead we are looking.

To estimate the volatility, σ, of a stock price empirically, the stock price is observed at fixed intervals of time (e.g., every day, every week, or every month). For each time period, the natural logarithm of the ratio of the stock price at the end of the time period to the stock price at the beginning of the time period is calculated. The volatility is estimated as the standard deviation of these numbers divided by the square root of the length of the time period in years. Usually, days when the exchanges are closed are ignored in measuring time for the purposes of volatility calculations.

The differential equation for the price of any derivative dependent on a stock can be obtained by creating a riskless position in the option and the stock. Because the derivative and the option price both depend on the same underlying source of uncertainty, this can always be done. The position that is created remains riskless for only a very short period of time. However, the return on a riskless position must always be the risk-free interest rate if there are to be no arbitrage opportunities.

The expected return on the stock does not enter into the Black–Scholes differential equation. This leads to a useful result known as risk-neutral valuation. This result states that when valuing a derivative dependent on a stock price, we can assume that the world is risk neutral. This means that we can assume that the expected return from the stock is the risk-free interest rate, and then discount expected payoffs at the risk-free interest rate. The Black–Scholes equations for European call and put options can be derived by either solving their differential equation or by using risk-neutral valuation.

An implied volatility is the volatility that, when used in conjunction with the Black–Scholes option pricing formula, gives the market price of the option. Traders monitor implied volatilities and sometimes use the implied volatility from one stock option price to calculate the price of another option on the same stock. Empirical results show that the volatility of a stock is much higher when the exchange is open than when it is closed. This suggests that, to some extent, trading itself causes stock price volatility.

The Black–Scholes results can easily be extended to cover European call and put options on dividend-paying stocks. The procedure is to use the Black–Scholes formula with the stock price reduced by the present value of the dividends anticipated during the life of the option, and the volatility equal to the volatility of the stock price net of the present value of these dividends.

In theory, American call options are liable to be exercised early, immediately before any ex-dividend date. In practice, only the final ex-dividend date usually needs to be considered. Fischer Black has suggested an approximation. This involves setting the American call option price equal to the greater of two European call option prices. The first European call option expires at the same time as the American call option; the second expires immediately prior to the final ex-dividend date. A more exact approach involving bivariate normal distributions is explained in Appendix 11B.

SUGGESTIONS FOR FURTHER READING

On the Distribution of Stock Price Changes

Blattberg, R., and N. Gonedes. "A Comparison of the Stable and Student Distributions as Statistical Models for Stock Prices," *Journal of Business,* 47 (April 1974), 244–80.

Fama, E. F. "The Behavior of Stock Prices," *Journal of Business,* 38 (January 1965), 34–105.

Kon, S. J. "Models of Stock Returns—A Comparison," *Journal of Finance,* 39 (March 1984), 147–65.

Richardson, M., and T. Smith. "A Test for Multivariate Normality in Stock Returns," *Journal of Business,* 66 (1993), 295–321.

On the Black–Scholes Analysis

Black, F. "Fact and Fantasy in the Use of Options and Corporate Liabilities," *Financial Analysts Journal,* 31 (July–August 1975), 36–41, 61–72.

Black, F., and M. Scholes. "The Pricing of Options and Corporate Liabilities," *Journal of Political Economy,* 81 (May–June 1973), 637–59.

Merton, R. C. "Theory of Rational Option Pricing," *Bell Journal of Economics and Management Science,* 4 (Spring 1973), 141–183.

On Risk-Neutral Valuation

Cox, J. C., and S. A. Ross. "The Valuation of Options for Alternative Stochastic Processes," *Journal of Financial Economics,* 3 (1976), 145–66.

Smith, C. W. "Option Pricing: A Review," *Journal of Financial Economics,* 3 (1976), 3–54.

On Analytic Solutions to the Pricing of American Calls

Geske, R. "Comments on Whaley's Note," *Journal of Financial Economics,* 9 (June 1981), 213–15.

Geske, R. "A Note on an Analytic Valuation Formula for Unprotected American Call Options on Stocks with Known Dividends," *Journal of Financial Economics,* 7 (1979), 375–80.

Roll, R. "An Analytical Formula for Unprotected American Call Options on Stocks with Known Dividends," *Journal of Financial Economics,* 5 (1977), 251–58.

Whaley, R. "On the Valuation of American Call Options on Stocks with Known Dividends," *Journal of Financial Economics,* 9 (1981), 207–11.

QUESTIONS AND PROBLEMS
(ANSWERS IN SOLUTIONS MANUAL)

11.1. What does the Black–Scholes stock option pricing model assume about the probability distribution of the stock price in one year?

11.2. The volatility of a stock price is 30% per annum. What is the standard deviation of the proportional price change in one trading day?

11.3. Explain the principle of risk-neutral valuation.

11.4. Calculate the price of a three-month European put option on a non-dividend-paying stock with a strike price of $50 when the current stock price is $50, the risk-free interest rate is 10% per annum, and the volatility is 30% per annum.

11.5. What difference does it make to your calculations in Problem 11.4 if a dividend of $1.50 is expected in two months?

11.6. What is *implied volatility*? How can it be calculated?

11.7. A stock price is currently $40. Assume that the expected return from the stock is 15% and that its volatility is 25%. What is the probability distribution for the rate of return (with continuous compounding) earned over a two-year period?

11.8. A stock price follows geometric Brownian motion with an expected return of 16% and a volatility of 35%. The current price is $38.
   (a) What is the probability that a European call option on the stock with an exercise price of $40 and a maturity date in six months will be exercised?
   (b) What is the probability that a European put option on the stock with the same exercise price and maturity will be exercised?

11.9. Prove that with the notation in the chapter, a 95% confidence interval for S_T is between

$$S_0 e^{(\mu-\sigma^2/2)T - 1.96\sigma\sqrt{T}} \quad \text{and} \quad S_0 e^{(\mu-\sigma^2/2)T + 1.96\sigma\sqrt{T}}$$

11.10. A portfolio manager announces that the average of the returns realized in each year of the last 10 years is 20% per annum. In what respect is this statement misleading?

11.11. Assume that a non-dividend-paying stock has an expected return of μ and a volatility of σ. An innovative financial institution has just announced that it will trade a security that pays off a dollar amount equal to $\ln S_T$ at time T where S_T denotes the value of the stock price at time T.
   (a) Use risk-neutral valuation to calculate the price of the security at time t in terms of the stock price, S, at time t.
   (b) Confirm that your price satisfies the differential equation (11.15).

11.12. Consider a derivative that pays off S_T^n at time T where S_T is the stock price at that time. When the stock price follows geometric Brownian motion, it can be shown that its price at time t ($t \le T$) has the form

$$h(t, T)S^n$$

where S is the stock price at time t and h is a function only of t and T.
  (a) By substituting into the Black–Scholes partial differential equation derive an ordinary differential equation satisfied by $h(t, T)$.
  (b) What is the boundary condition for the differential equation for $h(t, T)$?
  (c) Show that

$$h(t, T) = e^{[0.5\sigma^2 n(n-1)+r(n-1)](T-t)}$$

  where r is the risk-free interest rate and σ is the stock price volatility.

11.13. What is the price of a European call option on a non-dividend-paying stock when the stock price is \$52, the strike price is \$50, the risk-free interest rate is 12% per annum, the volatility is 30% per annum, and the time to maturity is three months?

11.14. What is the price of a European put option on a non-dividend-paying stock when the stock price is \$69, the strike price is \$70, the risk-free interest rate is 5% per annum, the volatility is 35% per annum, and the time to maturity is six months?

11.15. Consider an American call option on a stock. The stock price is \$70, the time to maturity is eight months, the risk-free rate of interest is 10% per annum, the exercise price is \$65, and the volatility is 32%. A dividend of \$1 is expected after three months and again after six months. Show that it can never be optimal to exercise the option on either of the two dividend dates. Use DerivaGem to calculate the price of the option.

11.16. A call option on a non-dividend-paying stock has a market price of $\$2\frac{1}{2}$. The stock price is \$15, the exercise price is \$13, the time to maturity is three months, and the risk-free interest rate is 5% per annum. What is the implied volatility?

11.17. With the notation used in this chapter
  (a) What is $N'(x)$?
  (b) Show that $SN'(d_1) = Xe^{-r(T-t)}N'(d_2)$, where S is the stock price at time t and

$$d_1 = \frac{\ln(S/X) + (r + \sigma^2/2)(T - t)}{\sigma\sqrt{T - t}}$$

$$d_2 = \frac{\ln(S/X) + (r - \sigma^2/2)(T - t)}{\sigma\sqrt{T - t}}$$

  (c) Calculate $\partial d_1/\partial S$ and $\partial d_2/\partial S$.
  (d) Show that when

$$c = SN(d_1) - Xe^{r(T-t)}N(d_2)$$

$$\frac{\partial c}{\partial t} = -rXe^{-r(T-t)}N(d_2) - SN'(d_1)\frac{\sigma}{2\sqrt{T - t}}$$

  where c is the price of a call option on a non-dividend-paying stock.
  (e) Show that $\partial c/\partial S = N(d_1)$.
  (f) Show that c satisfies the Black–Scholes differential equation.

11.18. Show that the Black–Scholes formulas for call and put options satisfy put–call parity.

11.19. A stock price is currently $50 and the risk-free interest rate is 5%. Use the DerivaGem software to translate the following table of European call options on the stock into a table of implied volatilities, assuming no dividends. Are the option prices consistent with Black–Scholes?

Strike Price ($)	Maturity (months)		
	3	6	12
45	7.0	8.3	10.5
50	3.7	5.2	7.5
55	1.6	2.9	5.1

11.20. Explain carefully why Black's approach to evaluating an American call option on a dividend-paying stock may give an approximate answer even when only one dividend is anticipated. Does the answer given by Black's approach understate or overstate the true option value? Explain your answer.

11.21. Consider an American call option on a stock. The stock price is $70, the time to maturity is eight months, the risk-free rate of interest is 10% per annum, the exercise price is $65, and the volatility is 32%. Dividends of $1 are expected after three months and six months. Show that it can never be optimal to exercise the option on either of the two dividend dates. Calculate the price of the option.

11.22. Show that the probability that a European call option will be exercised in a risk-neutral world is, with the notation introduced in this chapter, $N(d_2)$. What is an expression for the value of a derivative that pays off $100 if the price of a stock at time T is greater than X?

11.23. Show that S^{-2r/σ^2} could be the price of a traded security.

ASSIGNMENT QUESTIONS

11.24. A stock price is currently $50. Assume that the expected return from the stock is 18% and its volatility is 30%. What is the probability distribution for the stock price in two years? Calculate the mean and standard deviation of the distribution. Determine 95% confidence intervals.

11.25. Suppose that observations on a stock price (in dollars) at the end of each of 15 consecutive weeks are as follows: $30\frac{1}{4}$, 32, $31\frac{1}{8}$, $30\frac{1}{8}$, $30\frac{1}{4}$, $30\frac{3}{8}$, $30\frac{5}{8}$, 33, $32\frac{7}{8}$, 33, $33\frac{1}{2}$, $33\frac{1}{2}$, $33\frac{3}{4}$, $33\frac{1}{2}$, $33\frac{1}{4}$. Estimate the stock price volatility. What is the standard error of your estimate?

11.26. A financial institution plans to offer a security that pays off a dollar amount equal to S_T^2 at time T.
  (a) Use risk-neutral valuation to calculate the price of the security at time t in terms of the stock price, S, at time t. (*Hint:* The expected value of S_T^2 can be calculated from the mean and variance of S_T given in section 11.1.)
  (b) Confirm that your price satisfies the differential equation (11.15).

11.27. Consider an option on a non-dividend-paying stock when the stock price is $30, the exercise price is $29, the risk-free interest rate is 5%, the volatility is 25% per annum, and the time to maturity is 4 months.
(a) What is the price of the option if it is a European call?
(b) What is the price of the option if it is an American call?
(c) What is the price of the option if it is a European put?
(d) Verify that put–call parity holds.

11.28. Assume that the stock in Problem 11.28 is due to go ex-dividend in $1\frac{1}{2}$ months. The expected dividend is 50 cents.
(a) What is the price of the option if it is a European call?
(b) What is the price of the option if it is a European put?
(c) If the option is an American call, are there any circumstances under which it will be exercised early?

11.29. Consider an American call option when the stock price is $18, the exercise price is $20, the time to maturity is six months, the volatility is 30% per annum, and the risk-free interest rate is 10% per annum. Two equal dividends are expected during the life of the option with ex-dividend dates at the end of two months and five months. Assume the dividends are 40 cents. Use Black's approximation and the DerivaGem software to value the option. How high can the dividends be without the American option being worth more than the corresponding European option?

APPENDIX 11A

Proof of Black–Scholes–Merton Formula

We will prove the Black–Scholes result by first proving another key result that will also be useful in future chapters.

Key Result

If V is lognormally distributed and the standard deviation of $\ln V$ is s then

$$E[\max(V - X, 0)] = E(V)N(d_1) - XN(d_2) \qquad (11A.1)$$

where

$$d_1 = \frac{\ln[E(V)/X] + s^2/2}{s}$$

$$d_2 = \frac{\ln[E(V)/X] - s^2/2}{s}$$

and E denotes expected value.

Proof of Key Result

Define $g(V)$ as the probability density function of V. It follows that

$$E[\max(V - X), 0] = \int_X^\infty (V - X)g(V)dV \qquad (11A.2)$$

The variable $\ln V$ is normally distributed with standard deviation s. From the properties of the lognormal distribution the mean of $\ln V$ is m where

$$m = \ln[E(V)] - s^2/2 \qquad (11A.3)$$

Define a new variable

$$Q = \frac{\ln V - m}{s} \qquad (11A.4)$$

This variable is normally distributed with a mean of zero and a standard deviation of 1.0. Denote the density function for Q by $h(Q)$ so that

$$h(Q) = \frac{1}{\sqrt{2\pi}}e^{-Q^2/2}$$

Using equation (11A.4) to convert the expression on the right-hand side of equation (11A.2) from an integral over V to an integral over Q we get

$$\hat{E}[\max(V - X, 0)] = \int_{(\ln X - m)/s}^\infty (e^{Qs+m} - X)h(Q)dQ$$

or

$$\hat{E}[\max (V - X, 0)] = \int_{(\ln X - m)/s}^{\infty} e^{Qs+m} h(Q)dQ - X \int_{(\ln X-m)/s}^{\infty} h(Q)dQ \quad (11A.5)$$

Now

$$e^{Qs+m} h(Q) = \frac{1}{\sqrt{2\pi}} e^{(-Q^2+2Qs+2m)/2}$$

$$= \frac{1}{\sqrt{2\pi}} e^{[-(Q-s)^2+2m+s^2]/2}$$

$$= \frac{e^{m+s^2/2}}{\sqrt{2\pi}} e^{[-(Q-s)^2]/2}$$

$$= e^{m+s^2/2} h(Q - s)$$

This means that equation (11A.5) becomes

$$\hat{E}[\max(V - X, 0)] = e^{m+s^2/2} \int_{(\ln X-m)/s}^{\infty} h(Q - s)dQ - X \int_{(\ln X-m)/s}^{\infty} h(Q)dQ$$

$$(11A.6)$$

If we define $N(x)$ as the probability that a variable with a mean of zero and a standard deviation of 1.0 is less than x, the first integral in equation (11A.6) is

$$1 - N\left[(\ln X - m)/s - s\right]$$

or

$$N\left[(- \ln X + m)/s + s\right]$$

Substituting for m from equation (11A.3) this becomes

$$N\left[\frac{\ln[E(V)/X] + s^2/2}{s}\right] = N(d_1)$$

Similarly the second integral in equation (11A.6) is $N(d_2)$. Equation (11A.6), therefore, becomes

$$\hat{E}[\max (V - X, 0)] = e^{m+s^2/2} N(d_1) - XN(d_2)$$

Substituting for m from equation (11A.3) the key result follows.

The Black–Scholes Result

We now consider a call option on a non-dividend-paying stock maturing at time T. The strike price is X, the risk-free rate is r, the current stock price is S_0, and the volatility is σ. As shown in equation (11.22), the call price, c, is given by

$$c = e^{-rT} \hat{E}\left[\max(S_T - X, 0)\right] \quad (11A.7)$$

where S_T is the stock price at time T and $\hat{E}$ denotes expectations in a risk-neutral world. Under the stochastic process assumed by Black–Scholes, S_T is lognormal. Also from equations (11.2) and (11.3), $\hat{E}(S_T) = S_0 e^{rT}$ and the standard deviation of $\ln S_T$ is $\sigma\sqrt{T}$.

From the key result just proved, equation (11A.7) implies

$$c = e^{-rT}[S_0 e^{rT} N(d_1) - X N(d_2)]$$

or

$$c = S_0 N(d_1) - X e^{-rT} N(d_2)$$

where

$$d_1 = \frac{\ln(S_0/X) + (r + \sigma^2/2)T}{\sigma\sqrt{T}}$$

$$d_2 = \frac{\ln(S_0/X) + (r - \sigma^2/2)T}{\sigma\sqrt{T}}$$

Exact Procedure for Calculating Values of American Calls on Dividend-Paying Stocks

The Roll, Geske, and Whaley formula for the value of an American call option on a stock paying a single dividend D_1 at time t_1 is

$$C = (S_0 - D_1 e^{-rt_1})N(b_1) + (S_0 - D_1 e^{-rt_1})M\left(a_1, -b_1; -\sqrt{\frac{t_1}{T}}\right)$$

$$- Xe^{-rT}M\left(a_2, -b_2; -\sqrt{\frac{t_1}{T}}\right) - (X - D_1)e^{-rt_1}N(b_2) \qquad (11B.1)$$

where

$$a_1 = \frac{\ln[(S_0 - D_1 e^{-rt_1})/X] + (r + \sigma^2/2)T}{\sigma\sqrt{T}}$$

$$a_2 = a_1 - \sigma\sqrt{T}$$

$$b_1 = \frac{\ln[(S_0 - D_1 e^{-rt_1})/S^*] + (r + \sigma^2/2)t_1}{\sigma\sqrt{t_1}}$$

$$b_2 = b_1 - \sigma\sqrt{t_1}$$

The variable σ is the volatility of the stock price less the present value of the dividend. The function, $M(a, b; \rho)$, is the cumulative probability, in a standardized bivariate normal distribution, that the first variable is less than a and the second variable is less than b, when the coefficient of correlation between the variables is ρ. We give a procedure for calculating the M function in Appendix 11C. The variable S^* is the solution to

$$c(S^*) = S^* + D_1 - X$$

where $c(S^*)$ is the Black–Scholes option price given by equation (11.20) when the stock price is S^* and the time to maturity is $T - t_1$. When early exercise is never optimal, $S^* = \infty$. In this case $b_1 = b_2 = -\infty$ and equation (11B.1) reduces to the Black–Scholes equation with S_0 replaced by $S_0 - D_1 e^{-rt_1}$. In other situations, $S^* < \infty$ and the option should be exercised at time t_1 when $S(t_1) > S^* + D_1$.

When several dividends are anticipated, early exercise is normally optimal only on the final ex-dividend date (see section 11.12). It follows that the Roll, Geske, and Whaley formula can be used with S_0 reduced by the present value of all dividends except the final one. The variable, D_1, should be set equal to the final dividend and t_1 should be set equal to the final ex-dividend date.

Calculation of Cumulative Probability in Bivariate Normal Distribution

As in Appendix 11B, we define $M(a, b; \rho)$ as the cumulative probability in a standardized bivariate normal distribution that the first variable is less than a and the second variable is less than b, when the coefficient of correlation between the variables is ρ. Drezner provides a way of calculating $M(a, b; \rho)$ to four-decimal-place accuracy.[19] If $a \leq 0$, $b \leq 0$, and $\rho \leq 0$,

$$M(a, b; \rho) = \frac{\sqrt{1-\rho^2}}{\pi} \sum_{i,j=1}^{4} A_i A_j f(B_i, B_j)$$

where

$$f(x, y) = \exp[a'(2x - a') + b'(2y - b') + 2\rho(x - a')(y - b')]$$

$$a' = \frac{a}{\sqrt{2(1-\rho^2)}} \qquad b' = \frac{b}{\sqrt{2(1-\rho^2)}}$$

$A_1 = 0.3253030$	$A_2 = 0.4211071$	$A_3 = 0.1334425$	$A_4 = 0.006374323$
$B_1 = 0.1337764$	$B_2 = 0.6243247$	$B_3 = 1.3425378$	$B_4 = 2.2626645$

In other circumstances where the product of a, b, and ρ is negative or zero, one of the following identities can be used:

$$M(a, b; \rho) = N(a) - M(a, -b; -\rho)$$
$$M(a, b; \rho) = N(b) - M(-a, b; -\rho)$$
$$M(a, b; \rho) = N(a) + N(b) - 1 + M(-a, -b; \rho)$$

In circumstances where the product of a, b, and ρ is positive, the identity

$$M(a, b; \rho) = M(a, 0; \rho_1) + M(b, 0; \rho_2) - \delta$$

can be used in conjunction with the previous results, where

$$\rho_1 = \frac{(\rho a - b)\,\mathrm{sgn}(a)}{\sqrt{a^2 - 2\rho ab + b^2}} \qquad \rho_2 = \frac{(\rho b - a)\,\mathrm{sgn}(b)}{\sqrt{a^2 - 2\rho ab + b^2}}$$

$$\delta = \frac{1 - \mathrm{sgn}(a)\,\mathrm{sgn}(b)}{4} \qquad \mathrm{sgn}(x) = \begin{cases} +1 & \text{when } x \geq 0 \\ -1 & \text{when } x < 0 \end{cases}$$

---

[19] Z. Drezner, "Computation of the Bivariate Normal Integral," *Mathematics of Computation*, 32 (January 1978), 277–79. Note that the presentation here corrects a typo in Drezner's paper.

CHAPTER

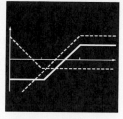

12

OPTIONS
ON STOCK INDICES,
CURRENCIES, AND
FUTURES

In this chapter we tackle the problem of valuing options on stock indices, currencies, and futures contracts. As a first step, the analysis in chapter 11 is extended to cover European options on a stock paying a continuous dividend. The argument is then made that stock indices, currencies, and futures prices are analogous to stocks paying continuous dividends. The basic results for options on a stock paying a continuous dividend can, therefore, be extended to value options on these other assets.

12.1 RESULTS FOR A STOCK PAYING A CONTINUOUS DIVIDEND YIELD

Consider the difference between a stock that pays a continuous dividend yield at a rate q per annum and an otherwise identical stock that pays no dividends. Both stocks should provide the same overall return (dividends plus capital gain). The payment of a continuous dividend yield causes the growth rate in the stock price to be less than it would otherwise be by an amount q. If, with a continuous dividend yield of q, the stock price grows from S_0 at time zero to S_T at time T, then in the absence of dividends it would grow from S_0 at time zero to $S_T e^{qT}$ at time T. Alternatively, in the absence of dividends it would grow from $S_0 e^{-qT}$ at time zero to S_T at time T.

This argument shows that we get the same probability distribution for the stock price at time T in each of the following two cases:

1. The stock starts at price S_0 and pays a continuous dividend yield at rate q.
2. The stock starts at price $S_0 e^{-qT}$ and pays no dividend yield.

This leads to a simple rule. When valuing a European option lasting for time T on a stock paying a known dividend yield at rate q, we reduce the current stock price from S_0 to $S_0 e^{-qT}$ and then value the option as though the stock pays no dividends.

Lower Bounds for Option Prices

As a first application of this rule, consider the problem of determining bounds for the price of a European option on a stock providing a dividend yield equal to q. From equation (7.1) the lower bound for the price at time zero of a European call option on a non-dividend-paying stock maturing at time T is

$$c \geq \max(S_0 - Xe^{-rT}, 0)$$

Substituting $S_0 e^{-qT}$ for S_0 in this equation, we see that a lower bound for the price of a European call option on a stock paying a dividend yield of q is given by

$$c \geq \max(S_0 e^{-qT} - Xe^{-rT}, 0) \tag{12.1}$$

We can also prove this directly by considering the following two portfolios:

Portfolio A: one European call option plus an amount of cash equal to Xe^{-rT}

Portfolio B: e^{-qT} shares, with dividends being reinvested in additional shares

In portfolio A, the cash, if it is invested at the risk-free interest rate, will grow to X at time T. If $S_T > X$, the call option is exercised at time T and portfolio A is worth S_T. If $S_T < X$, the call option expires worthless and the portfolio is worth X. Hence, at time T, portfolio A is worth

$$\max(S_T, X)$$

Because of the reinvestment of dividends, portfolio B becomes one share at time T. It is, therefore, worth S_T at this time. It follows that portfolio A is always worth as much as, and is sometimes worth more than, portfolio B at time T. In the absence of arbitrage opportunities, this must also be true today. Hence,

$$c + Xe^{-rT} \geq S_0 e^{-qT}$$

or

$$c \geq S_0 e^{-qT} - Xe^{-rT}$$

To obtain a lower bound for a European put option, we note from equation (7.2) that a lower bound for the price at time zero of a European put option on a non-dividend-paying stock maturing at time T is given by

$$p \geq \max(Xe^{-rT} - S_0, 0)$$

As in the case of call options, we can replace S_0 by $S_0 e^{-qT}$ in this equation to get a lower bound for the price of a put option on a stock paying a dividend yield at rate q:

$$p \geq \max(Xe^{-rT} - S_0 e^{-qT}, 0) \tag{12.2}$$

This result can also be proved directly by considering the following portfolios:

> *Portfolio C:* one European put option plus e^{-qT} shares, with dividends on the shares being reinvested in additional shares
>
> *Portfolio D:* an amount of cash equal to Xe^{-rT}

Put–Call Parity

From equation (7.3), put–call parity for a non-dividend-paying stock is

$$c + Xe^{-rT} = p + S_0$$

Replacing S_0 by S_0e^{-qT} in this equation, we obtain put–call parity for an option on a stock providing a continuous dividend yield equal to q:

$$c + Xe^{-rT} = p + S_0e^{-qT} \tag{12.3}$$

This result can also be proved directly by considering the following two portfolios:

> *Portfolio A:* one European call option plus an amount of cash equal to Xe^{-rT}
>
> *Portfolio C:* one European put option plus e^{-qT} shares, with dividends on the shares being reinvested in additional shares

Both portfolios are worth $\max(S_T, X)$ at time T. They must, therefore, be worth the same today, and the put–call parity result in equation (12.3) follows.

For American options the put–call parity result is (see Problem 12.19)

$$S_0e^{-qT} - X \le C - P \le S_0 - Xe^{-rT}$$

12.2 OPTION PRICING FORMULAS

By replacing S_0 by S_0e^{-qT} in the Black–Scholes formulas, equations (11.20) and (11.21), we obtain the price, c, of a European call and the price, p, of a European put on a stock providing a continuous dividend yield at rate q as

$$c = S_0e^{-qT}N(d_1) - Xe^{-rT}N(d_2) \tag{12.4}$$
$$p = Xe^{-rT}N(-d_2) - S_0e^{-qT}N(-d_1) \tag{12.5}$$

Because

$$\ln\left(\frac{S_0e^{-qT}}{X}\right) = \ln\frac{S_0}{X} - qT$$

d_1 and d_2 are given by

$$d_1 = \frac{\ln(S_0/X) + (r - q + \sigma^2/2)T}{\sigma\sqrt{T}}$$

and

$$d_2 = \frac{\ln(S_0/X) + (r - q - \sigma^2/2)T}{\sigma\sqrt{T}} = d_1 - \sigma\sqrt{T}$$

These results were first derived by Merton.[1] If the dividend yield is not constant during the life of the option, equations (12.4) and (12.5) are still true, with q equal to the average annualized dividend yield during the life of the option.

Risk-Neutral Valuation

Appendix 12A derives, in a similar way to section 11.5, the differential equation that must be satisfied by any derivative whose price, f, depends on a stock providing a continuous dividend yield q. Like the Black–Scholes differential equation (11.15), it does not involve any variable affected by risk preferences. Therefore, the risk-neutral valuation procedure, described in section 11.6, can be used. In a risk-neutral world, the total return from the stock must be r. The dividends provide a return of q. The expected growth rate in the stock price, therefore, must be $r - q$. The risk-neutral process for the stock price is

$$dS = (r - q)S\,dt + \sigma S\,dz \qquad (12.6)$$

To value a derivative dependent on a stock that provides a continuous dividend yield equal to q, we set the expected growth rate of the stock equal to $r - q$ and discount the expected payoff at rate r. This approach can be used to derive equations (12.4) and (12.5). The math is similar to that in Appendix 11A.

Binomial Trees

We now examine the effect of a dividend yield equal to q on the binomial model in chapter 9. Consider the situation in Figure 12.1, in which a stock price starts at S_0 and, during time T, moves either up to S_0u or down to S_0d. As in chapter 9, we define p as the probability of an up movement in a risk-neutral world. The total return provided by the stock in a risk-neutral world must be the risk-free interest rate, r. The dividends provide a return equal to q. The return in the form of capital gains must be $r - q$. This means that p must satisfy

$$pS_0u + (1 - p)S_0d = S_0e^{(r-q)T}$$

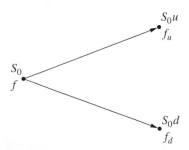

Figure 12.1   Stock price and option price in one-step binomial tree when stock pays a dividend at rate q.

[1] See R. Merton, "Theory of Rational Option Pricing," *Bell Journal of Economics and Management Science*, 4 (Spring 1973), 141–83.

or

$$p = \frac{e^{(r-q)T} - d}{u - d} \tag{12.7}$$

Because the value of the derivative is the expected payoff in a risk-neutral world discounted at the risk-free rate,

$$f = e^{-rT}[pf_u + (1 - p)f_d] \tag{12.8}$$

Example 12.1 Suppose that the initial stock price is $30 and the stock price will move either up to $36 or down to $24 during a six-month period. The six-month risk-free interest rate is 5%, and the stock is expected to provide a dividend yield of 3% during the six-month period. In this case $u = 1.2, d = 0.8$, and

$$p = \frac{e^{(0.05-0.03)\times0.5} - 0.8}{1.2 - 0.8} = 0.5251$$

Consider a six-month put option on the stock with a strike price of $28. If the stock price moves up, the payoff is zero; if it moves down, the payoff is $4. The value of the option is, therefore,

$$e^{-0.05\times0.5}[0.5251 \times 0 + 0.4749 \times 4] = 1.85$$

12.3 OPTIONS ON STOCK INDICES

Options on stock indices trade in both the over-the-counter and exchange-traded markets. Some of the indices used track the movement of the stock market as a whole; some are based on the performance of a particular sector (e.g., mining, computer technology, or utilities).

Two popular exchange-traded index options in the United States are those on the S&P 100 and S&P 500 trading on the Chicago Board Options Exchange. The options on the S&P 500 are European, whereas those on the S&P 100 are American. Both options have maturity dates on the Saturday following the third Friday of the expiration month.

Index options are settled in cash rather than by delivering the securities underlying the index. This means that, upon exercise of the option, the holder of a call option receives $S - X$ in cash and the writer of the option pays this amount in cash, where S is the value of the index at the time of exercise and X is the strike price. Similarly, the holder of a put option receives $X - S$ in cash and the writer of the option pays this amount in cash. The cash payment is based on the index value at the end of the day on which the exercise instructions are issued. Each contract is for $100 times the value of the index.

Quotes

Table 12.1 shows some of the quotes on index options as they appeared in the *Wall Street Journal* of August 5, 1998. These quotes refer to the price at which the last trade was done on the preceding day.

Table 12.1 Quotes for Stock Index Options from *The Wall Street Journal*, August 5, 1998

DJ INDUS AVG(DJX)

Dec	64p	20	9/16	+ 3/16	858
Dec	66p	25	7 1/4	+ 2	1,010
Dec	68p	2	15/16	+ 3/8	1,353
Dec	72p	70	1 1/4	+ 1/8	36,937
Sep	76p	4	1/2	+ 1/8	2,516
Dec	76p	55	2 1/16	+ 1/2	47,457
Mar	76c	5	14 7/8	...	...
Mar	76p	50	3 1/8	+ 3/8	1,260
Aug	80c	116	6	− 3 3/8	297
Aug	80p	1,648	11/16	+ 1/2	1,201
Sep	80c	2	7 7/8	− 4 1/4	10,395
Sep	80p	200	1 3/16	+ 7/16	14,612
Dec	80c	36	10 3/8	− 2 3/8	3,809
Dec	80p	156	3	+ 1	13,100
Mar	80p	2	3 3/4	+ 3/4	1,485
Aug	82c	73	4 3/8	− 2 3/8	50
Aug	82p	482	1 1/8	+ 11/16	1,044
Sep	82p	6	1 11/16	+ 9/16	664
Aug	84c	23	2 5/8	− 3 3/4	85
Aug	84p	1,056	1 3/4	+ 1 1/16	1,213
Sep	84c	96	4	− 3 1/2	11,839
Sep	84p	433	2 5/8	+ 1 1/4	18,441
Dec	84p	40	4 1/8	+ 1 1/4	617
Mar	84c	1	9	...	...
Mar	84p	5	5 1/8	+ 1 1/4	387
Aug	85c	278	2 3/16	− 2 7/16	150
Aug	85p	303	2 1/8	+ 1 3/16	527
Sep	85c	89	3 1/2	− 1 7/8	41
Sep	85p	162	3 1/8	+ 1 3/8	9,166
Dec	85c	16	6	− 3 1/2	15
Dec	85p	68	4 5/8	+ 1 5/8	270
Aug	86c	1,080	1 5/8	− 2 1/2	131
Aug	86p	1,134	2 5/8	+ 1 9/16	3,447
Sep	86c	78	3	− 1 7/8	1,590
Sep	86p	459	3 1/4	+ 1 3/8	2,377
Dec	86p	32	4 1/2	+ 1	536
Aug	87c	539	1 3/16	− 1 5/16	216
Aug	87p	710	3	+ 1 9/16	6,485
Sep	87c	63	2 3/8	− 1 5/8	210
Sep	87p	463	3 3/8	+ 1 1/16	2,262
Aug	88c	925	7/8	− 13/16	737
Aug	88p	1,748	3 7/8	+ 2	3,089
Sep	88c	728	1 15/16	− 1 3/16	15,645
Sep	88p	709	4 1/2	+ 1 11/16	6,803
Dec	88c	51	4 1/4	− 1 1/2	5,556
Dec	88p	64	6	+ 1 7/8	2,807
Mar	88c	4	6 3/4	− 1 1/4	225
Mar	88p	76	7 1/8	+ 1 5/8	4,431
Aug	89c	392	1/2	− 11/16	1,189
Aug	89p	725	4 1/2	+ 2 1/4	2,351
Sep	89c	80	1 15/16	− 1/2	270
Sep	89p	470	5	+ 2	831
Aug	90c	879	5/16	− 1/2	2,593
Aug	90p	1,368	5 3/8	+ 2 9/16	4,076
Sep	90c	1,122	1 3/16	− 13/16	5,125
Sep	90p	198	5 7/8	+ 2 3/8	4,795
Dec	90c	58	3 1/4	− 1 1/4	719
Dec	90p	177	7	+ 1 3/4	1,988
Mar	90p	20	7 1/4	...	...
Aug	91c	398	5/16	− 3/16	3,495
Aug	91p	5,104	6	+ 2 5/8	2,303
Sep	91c	89	1	− 7/8	213
Sep	91p	46	5	+ 1 1/8	2,046
Aug	92c	615	1/8	− 3/16	2,995
Aug	92p	175	7	+ 3 1/2	1,330
Sep	92c	225	3/4	− 7/16	6,090
Sep	92p	230	7	+ 2 5/8	4,368
Mar	92p	25	8 1/8	+ 1 3/4	1,338
Aug	93c	25	3/16	...	1,374
Aug	93p	252	7 5/8	+ 2 3/4	2,225
Sep	93c	15	5/8	− 7/16	698
Aug	94c	228	1/16	− 1/16	2,120
Sep	94p	170	8 1/8	+ 2	935
Dec	94c	113	2 5/16	− 9/16	361
Dec	94p	20	9	+ 1 1/2	404
Aug	96p	1	10 5/8	+ 4 3/4	395
Sep	96c	20	1/4	− 3/16	1,074
Sep	96p	63	10 1/2	+ 4 1/8	385
Dec	96c	5	1 3/8	− 1 5/16	1,063
Mar	96c	3	3	− 1 1/4	799
Sep	98p	10	10	+ 1 3/8	46
Sep	100p	8	11 1/4	− 1/8	156
Mar	100c	4	1 3/4	− 7/8	171
Mar	100p	3	13 1/2	+ 3 1/8	2,388

S & P 100 INDEX(OEX)

Aug	470c	17	67	− 12	77
Aug	470p	5,738	2 3/8	+ 1 9/16	6,333
Sep	470c	7	71 3/8	− 41 1/8	27
Sep	470p	203	5 3/4	+ 3	1,506
Aug	480c	10	69	− 30 1/2	52
Aug	480p	938	3 1/4	+ 2 1/8	3,638
Sep	480c	21	67 5/8	− 23 3/8	1
Sep	480p	329	6 1/2	+ 2 7/8	1,722
Oct	480c	6	66	− 30	27
Oct	480p	79	10 3/8	+ 4 3/8	1,238
Aug	490c	1	50	− 23 1/2	78
Aug	490p	1,953	4 3/8	+ 3	9,012
Sep	490p	101	9	+ 4 3/8	2,470
Oct	490p	31	13	+ 6 1/2	448
Aug	500c	2	40 3/4	− 21 1/4	46
Aug	500p	5,363	5 5/8	+ 3 1/2	8,248
Sep	500p	822	10 3/4	+ 4 7/8	3,946
Oct	500p	382	13 7/8	+ 5 1/8	786
Nov	500p	2	12 3/8	...	...
Aug	510c	5	26	− 45 3/4	46
Aug	510p	3,327	8	+ 5 1/8	6,742
Sep	510p	633	13 5/8	+ 6 5/8	1,008
Oct	510c	30	44 7/8	− 9 5/8	53
Oct	510p	23	18	+ 7 1/4	1,519
Aug	515p	2,129	9 1/2	+ 6	6,434
Sep	515p	51	15 1/4	+ 7 3/8	455
Aug	520c	214	18 7/8	− 13 3/8	1,481
Aug	520p	7,443	11 1/4	+ 7 1/8	13,667
Sep	520c	12	28 5/8	− 21 3/8	149
Sep	520p	2,867	17 1/2	+ 8 1/8	7,438
Oct	520c	1,317	33	− 12 1/4	2,178
Oct	520p	216	21 1/2	+ 9 1/4	424
Nov	520c	1	42 5/8	− 8	4
Nov	520p	12	20 1/2	+ 4 7/8	178
Aug	525c	410	15	− 13	794
Aug	525p	8,275	13 3/4	+ 8 3/4	5,931
Sep	525c	20	22 1/2	− 40 1/4	4
Sep	525p	279	19	+ 8 7/8	1,041
Aug	530c	1,926	12	− 11 7/8	2,974
Aug	530p	9,500	15 7/8	+ 9 7/8	8,801
Sep	530c	81	20	− 12 3/4	2,066
Sep	530p	1,018	21 1/2	+ 9 5/8	3,340
Oct	530c	146	25	− 12 3/4	108
Oct	530p	287	25	+ 9 7/8	1,880
Nov	530c	2	35 1/4	...	...
Nov	530p	2	24 1/2	+ 5 1/4	184
Aug	535c	2,240	9 1/2	− 10 3/4	883
Aug	535p	7,280	17 5/8	+ 10 1/2	11,457
Sep	535c	35	17 1/2	− 33 1/8	1,116
Sep	535p	132	23	+ 11	1,757
Aug	540c	12,296	7 1/4	− 9 1/4	4,689
Aug	540p	14,322	21	+ 12 3/8	14,764
Sep	540c	1,241	14	− 12 1/4	1,013
Sep	540p	949	24 3/4	+ 9 7/8	2,929
Oct	540c	15	20	− 11 3/4	32
Oct	540p	274	29 1/8	+ 10 5/8	1,293
Nov	540c	8	25 3/4	− 11 1/4	4
Nov	540p	10	30	+ 7	585
Aug	545c	6,450	5 1/8	− 7 7/8	1,820
Aug	545p	6,900	23 7/8	+ 13 3/8	15,375
Sep	545c	62	12 3/8	− 9 5/8	19
Sep	545p	215	28	+ 12 3/8	1,542
Oct	545c	150	25 5/8	...	...
Oct	545p	18	28 1/2	...	...
Aug	550c	10,202	3 7/8	− 6	6,754
Aug	550p	10,364	28	+ 15 1/2	16,118
Sep	550c	787	10 3/8	− 7 1/8	4,667
Sep	550p	950	31	+ 12 3/4	1,741
Oct	550c	31	20	− 4 3/8	4,644
Oct	550p	77	33 1/2	+ 12 3/4	4,724
Nov	550c	60	21 1/4	...	...
Nov	550p	15	34 1/2	+ 8 1/4	477
Aug	555c	11,604	2 3/4	− 4 3/4	10,282
Aug	555p	1,929	32	+ 16 5/8	9,129
Sep	555c	82	8 1/2	− 8	4,930
Sep	555p	73	34	+ 13 5/8	2,921
Aug	560c	16,088	1 7/8	− 3 1/2	16,202
Aug	560p	4,754	36 3/8	+ 17 7/8	11,124
Sep	560c	736	7 1/2	− 4 3/4	2,671
Sep	560p	254	39	+ 16 1/4	1,972
Oct	560c	649	14 1/4	− 5 3/4	3,026
Oct	560p	72	33	+ 6 1/4	3,578
Nov	560c	5	20 1/4	− 11 1/4	264
Nov	560p	15	42	+ 11 1/2	1,238
Aug	565c	13,347	1 1/4	− 2 1/4	14,661
Aug	565p	1,865	42	+ 20	8,013
Sep	565c	994	5 1/2	− 4 3/4	2,793
Sep	565p	92	42	+ 18 1/4	1,335
Oct	565c	1,500	13	...	...
Aug	570c	10,608	15/16	− 1 3/8	14,732
Aug	570p	1,342	45 3/8	+ 19 3/8	8,912
Sep	570c	556	5 1/4	− 3	1,919

S & P 500 INDEX-AM(SPX)

Aug	20c	1,191	1/4	...	3,676
Aug	400c	1,500	709	...	3,540
Sep	600c	75	490	− 52	2,171
Sep	600p	100	3/16	+ 1/8	13,303
Sep	700p	22	1 1/8	+ 3/4	8,485
Aug	800p	1,235	5/16	+ 1/8	14,840
Sep	800p	1,039	2	+ 1	7,888
Aug	850p	127	1 1/8	+ 7/8	4,744
Sep	850p	31	4	+ 2 1/8	4,944
Sep	875p	152	4 1/4	+ 1 7/8	14,402
Aug	900p	278	2 1/4	+ 1 5/8	13,894
Sep	900c	630	203	− 35	22,524
Sep	900p	615	3 3/8	+ 1/4	18,698
Sep	920p	15	5 1/8	+ 1 3/4	532
Sep	925p	13	6	+ 2 3/8	13,461
Aug	950p	395	3	+ 1 5/8	10,182
Sep	950c	20	138	− 36 1/2	3,481
Sep	950p	756	9	+ 4	22,746
Oct	950p	370	16	+ 7 1/2	740
Aug	975p	146	5	+ 3 7/8	856
Sep	975p	204	12	+ 5 1/2	12,428
Aug	990p	392	5	+ 2 3/4	1,275
Aug	995c	4	105	− 23 1/2	63
Aug	995p	153	5 3/8	+ 3 1/8	4,392
Sep	995p	261	15 3/4	+ 7 3/8	21,112
Aug	1005c	237	88	− 46	308
Aug	1005p	1,415	8 3/8	+ 5 5/8	5,025
Aug	1010p	130	9 1/2	+ 6 1/2	300
Sep	1010p	262	13 7/8	+ 3 7/8	642
Aug	1025c	3	75	− 18	248
Aug	1025p	1,427	11 1/2	+ 7 1/2	10,961
Sep	1025c	12	109	+ 5 1/2	2,840
Sep	1025p	1,192	22	+ 10 3/4	13,779
Aug	1040p	211	13 1/2	+ 7 3/4	3,650
Sep	1040p	2,090	21	+ 7	1,415
Aug	1050c	222	42	− 43	1,027
Aug	1050p	7,625	18	+ 11 1/2	8,850
Sep	1050c	1,422	58	− 29	19,831
Sep	1050p	983	30	+ 14 1/2	32,354
Oct	1050c	100	90 1/4	...	...
Oct	1050p	524	36	+ 14	4,778
Aug	1060c	8	46 1/2	...	...
Aug	1060p	160	21	...	...
Sep	1060c	1	67	− 12	10,246
Sep	1060p	311	25	+ 8 3/4	1,363
Aug	1065p	30	16 1/2	...	...
Aug	1070p	5	22	...	...
Aug	1075c	1,864	25 1/2	− 29	1,594
Aug	1075p	9,791	27	+ 16 3/4	12,259
Sep	1075c	160	39	− 28 1/4	13,908
Sep	1075p	289	38	+ 17	25,658
Oct	1075p	1,042	45	+ 17 3/4	12,151
Aug	1080c	665	23	− 22 1/2	663
Aug	1080p	1,490	27 3/4	+ 16 5/8	5,271
Sep	1080c	23	47	− 33	32
Sep	1080p	61	39	+ 18 1/2	786
Aug	1090c	5,683	18	− 26 1/2	69
Aug	1090p	2,276	33	+ 18 1/2	4,186
Sep	1090c	310	39	− 71	769
Sep	1090p	2,770	44 1/4	+ 19 3/4	5,143
Sep	1095c	292	37	− 13 5/8	1,939
Sep	1095p	316	47	+ 20 1/2	2,719
Aug	1100c	6,029	13	− 17 1/2	5,554
Aug	1100p	12,019	39	+ 22 1/4	19,411
Sep	1100c	544	29	− 18 1/2	27,092
Sep	1100p	1,601	52	+ 22 7/8	36,669
Oct	1100c	150	40	− 24 1/2	8
Oct	1100p	1,430	57	+ 20	3,419
Sep	1105c	261	37	...	...
Sep	1105p	106	45	+ 14 1/4	19
Aug	1110c	1,048	9 1/2	− 15	2,422
Aug	1110p	10,811	45	+ 24	7,453
Sep	1110c	172	27	− 13	3,834
Sep	1110p	3,010	54 1/2	+ 21 1/2	3,668
Aug	1115c	2,790	8	− 15	1,002
Aug	1115p	539	48	+ 26	1,865
Sep	1115c	158	20	− 16	1,736
Sep	1115p	470	52	+ 19	3,785
Aug	1120c	1,078	6 1/2	− 13	2,476
Aug	1120p	2,901	52	+ 27 1/8	7,519
Sep	1120c	745	26 1/2	− 7 1/2	4,306
Sep	1120p	1,225	62	+ 26	4,951
Aug	1125c	1,779	5	− 15 1/2	3,687
Aug	1125p	1,421	54	+ 27 1/2	5,441
Sep	1125c	1,011	17	− 13 1/2	19,679
Sep	1125p	1,343	64	+ 28	16,250
Oct	1125c	2	33 1/2	− 19	2,001
Oct	1125p	7	53	+ 8 1/8	2,653

Example 12.2 In Table 12.1, one October call option on the S&P 100 with a strike price of 520 costs $33. One contract is on 100 times the index and costs $3,300. The value of the index at the close of trading on August 4, 1998, was 525.64, so that the option was in the money. If the option contract were exercised on August 4, 1998, the holder would receive ($525.64 − $520) × 100 = $564 in cash. (Because this is less than $3,300, it is clearly not optimal to exercise.) From DerivaGem, the implied volatility for this option is 28.84%. This is based on a risk-free rate of 5% per annum, a dividend yield of 2%, and 52 trading days to maturity (or a time to maturity of $52/252 = 0.206$ years).

In addition to relatively short-dated options, the exchanges trade longer-maturity contracts known as LEAPS. The acronym LEAPS stands for "Long-term Equity AnticiPation Securities" and was originated by the CBOE. LEAPS last up to three years. The index is divided by 10 for the purposes of quoting the strike price and the option price. One contract is an option on 100 times one-tenth of the index (or 10 times the index). LEAPS on indices have expiration dates in December. (As mentioned in chapter 6, LEAPS also trade on many individual stocks. These have expirations in January.)

Another innovation of the CBOE is a product known as a CAP. This trades with the S&P 100 and S&P 500 as the underlying market variables. CAPs are options in which the payout is capped so that it cannot exceed $30. The options are European except for the following: A call CAP is automatically exercised on a day when the index closes at more than $30 above the strike price; a put CAP is automatically exercised on a day when the index closes at more than $30 below the cap level.

As mentioned in chapter 6, the CBOE also trades what are known as *flex options*. These are options in which traders can choose the expiration date, the strike price, whether the option is American or European, and the settlement basis.

Portfolio Insurance

Portfolio managers can use index options to limit their downside risk. Suppose that the value of an index is S_0. Consider a manager in charge of a well-diversified portfolio whose beta is 1.0. A beta of 1.0 implies that the returns from the portfolio mirror those from the index. If the dividend yield from the portfolio is the same as the dividend yield from the index, the percentage changes in the value of the portfolio can be expected to be approximately the same as the percentage changes in the value of the index. Each contract on the S&P 500 is on 100 times the index. It follows that the value of the portfolio is protected against the possibility of the index falling below X if, for each $100S_0$ dollars in the portfolio, the manager buys one put option contract with strike price X. Suppose that the manager's portfolio is worth $500,000 and the value of the index is 1,000. The portfolio is worth 500 times the index. The manager can obtain insurance against the value of the portfolio dropping below $480,000 in the next three months by buying five put option contracts with a strike price of 960. To illustrate how this works, consider the situation where the index drops to 900 in three months. The portfolio will be worth about $450,000. The payoff from the options will be 5 × ($960 − $900) × 100 = $30,000, bringing the total value of the portfolio up to the insured value of $480,000.

When the Portfolio's Beta Is Not 1.0

When the portfolio's beta is not equal to 1.0, the capital asset pricing model can be used. This model asserts that the expected excess return of a portfolio over the risk-free interest rate equals β times the excess return of a market index over the risk-free interest rate. Consider a portfolio with $\beta = 2.0$. Suppose that it is currently worth $1 million. Suppose further that the current risk-free interest rate is 12% per annum, the dividend yield on both the portfolio and the index is expected to be 4% per annum, and the current value of the index is 1,000. Table 12.2 shows the expected relationship between the level of the index and the value of the portfolio in three months. To illustrate the sequence of calculations necessary to derive Table 12.2, consider what happens when the value of the index in three months proves to be 1,040:

Value of index in three months	1,040
Return from change in index	40/1,000, or 4% per three months
Dividends from index	$0.25 \times 4 = 1\%$ per three months
Total return from index	$4 + 1 = 5\%$ per three months
Risk-free interest rate	$0.25 \times 12 = 3\%$ per three months
Excess return from index over risk-free interest rate	$5 - 3 = 2\%$ per three months
Expected return from portfolio above risk-free interest rate	$2 \times 2 = 4\%$ per three months
Expected return from portfolio	$3 + 4 = 7\%$ per three months
Dividends from portfolio	$0.25 \times 4 = 1\%$ per three months
Increase in value of portfolio	$7 - 1 = 6\%$ per three months
Value of portfolio	$1 \times 1.06 = \$1.06$ million

Suppose that S_0 is the value of the index. It can be shown that for each $100S_0$ dollars in the portfolio, a total of β put contracts should be purchased. The strike price should be the value that the index is expected to have when the value of the

Table 12.2 Relation between Value of Index and Value of Portfolio for $\beta = 2.0$

Value of Index in Three Months	Expected Value of Portfolio in Three Months ($ millions)
1,080	1.14
1,040	1.06
1,000	0.98
960	0.90
920	0.82

portfolio reaches the insured value. Suppose that the insured value is $0.90 million in our example. Table 12.2 shows that the appropriate strike price for the put options purchased is 960. In this case, $100S_0 = \$100,000$ and $\beta = 2.0$ so that 2 put contracts are required for each $100,000 in the portfolio. Because the portfolio is worth $1 million, a total of 20 contracts should be purchased.

To illustrate that the required result is obtained, consider what happens if the value of the index falls to 920. As shown in Table 12.2, the expected value of the portfolio is $0.82 million. The put options pay off ($960 − $920) × 20 × 100 = $80,000, and this is exactly what is necessary to move the total value of the portfolio manager's position up from $0.82 million to the required level of $0.90 million.

Valuation

When options on stock indices are valued, it is usual to assume that the stock index follows geometric Brownian motion.[2] Equation (12.6) gives the process for the stock index in a risk-neutral world. This means that equations (12.4) and (12.5) can be used to value European call and put options on an index with S_0 equal to the value of the index, σ equal to the volatility of the index, and q equal to the dividend yield on the index.

The variable q in equations (12.1) to (12.5) should be set equal to the average dividend yield (continuously compounded and annualized) during the life of the option. For the purposes of calculating this average dividend yield, a dividend is counted as occurring during the life of the option if the ex-dividend date is during its life. In the United States there is some seasonality in the way dividends are paid. For example, it is popular to pay dividends during the first week of February, May, August, and November. At any given time the correct value of q is therefore likely to depend on the life of the option.

In some countries a small number of ex-dividend dates tend to be used by all companies. It is appropriate to assume that stock indices in these countries provide dividend yields at discrete points in time. These dividend yields can be converted to an equivalent continuous dividend yield as described in Appendix 3A in order to use equations (12.1) to (12.5).

> **Example 12.3**   Consider a European call option on the S&P 500 that is two months from maturity. The current value of the index is 930, the exercise price is 900, the risk-free interest rate is 8% per annum, and the volatility of the index is 20% per annum. Continuous dividend yields of 0.2% and 0.3% per month are expected in the first month and the second month, respectively. In this case, $S_0 = 930$, $X = 900$, $r = 0.08$, $\sigma = 0.2$, and $T = 2/12$. The average dividend yield is 0.25% per two months or 3% per annum. Hence $q = 0.03$ and
>
> $$d_1 = \frac{\ln(930/900) + (0.08 - 0.03 + 0.2^2) \times 2/12}{0.2 \times \sqrt{2/12}} = 0.5444$$

---

[2]This presents a small theoretical problem because it is inconsistent to assume that both stock prices and a weighted average of stock prices follow geometric Brownian motion. For practical purposes, however, this inconsistency is not really important. Neither individual stocks nor stock indices follow geometric Brownian motion exactly, but for both it is a reasonable approximation.

$$d_2 = \frac{\ln(930/900) + (0.08 - 0.03 - 0.2^2) \times 2/12}{0.2 \times \sqrt{2/12}} = 0.4628$$

$$N(d_1) = 0.7069 \qquad N(d_2) = 0.6782$$

so that the call price, c, is given by equation (12.4) as

$$c = 930 \times 0.7069e^{-0.03 \times 2/12} - 900 \times 0.6782e^{-0.08 \times 2/12} = 51.83$$

One contract would cost $5,183.

In some circumstances it is optimal to exercise American put options on an index prior to the exercise date. To a lesser extent this is also true of American call options on an index. American stock index option prices are, therefore, always worth slightly more than the corresponding European stock index option prices. Numerical procedures and analytic approximations for valuing American index options are discussed in chapter 16.

12.4 CURRENCY OPTIONS

European and American options on foreign currencies are actively traded in both the over-the-counter and exchange-traded markets. The Philadelphia Stock Exchange has been trading currency options since 1982. The currencies traded include the Australian dollar, British pound, Canadian dollar, German mark, Japanese yen, French franc, and Swiss franc.

For a corporation wishing to hedge a foreign exchange exposure, foreign currency options are an interesting alternative to forward contracts. A company due to receive sterling at a known time in the future can hedge its risk by buying put options on sterling that mature at that time. The strategy guarantees that the value of the sterling will not be less than the exercise price while allowing the company to benefit from any favorable exchange-rate movements. Similarly, a company due to pay sterling at a known time in the future can hedge by buying calls on sterling that mature at that time. The approach guarantees that the cost of the sterling will not exceed a certain amount while allowing the company to benefit from favorable exchange-rate movements. Whereas a forward contract locks in the exchange rate for a future transaction, an option provides a type of insurance. This insurance is, of course, not free. It costs nothing to enter into a forward transaction, whereas options require a premium to be paid up front.

Quotes

Table 12.3 shows the closing prices of some of the currency options traded on the Philadelphia Exchange on August 4, 1998. Options are traded with expiration dates in the three nearest months; in March, June, September, and December for the first year; and in June and December for the following two years. The expiration date

Table 12.3 Currency Option Prices on the Philadelphia Exchange, August 4, 1998

OPTIONS
PHILADELPHIA EXCHANGE

	Calls Vol.	Calls Last	Puts Vol.	Puts Last
ADollr				60.48
50,000 Australian Dollars-European				
63½ Sep	20	0.36	...	...
CDollr				66.00
50,000 Canadian Dollars-cents per unit.				
72 Sep	...	...	20	5.95
British Pound				163.62
31,250 Brit. Pound EOM-European				
164 Aug	16	0.67	...	...
165 Sep	32	0.78	...	...
31,250 Brit. Pounds-European Style.				
163 Aug	10	0.72	...	...
164 Aug	16	0.38	...	...
164 Aug	20	0.91	...	...
165 Aug	100	0.18	...	...
31,250 Brit. Pounds-cents per unit.				
160 Sep	...	...	13	0.38
165 Sep	10	0.78	...	...
Canadian Dollar				66.00
50,000 Canadian Dollars-European Style.				
69 Sep	...	...	20	2.93
50,000 Canadian Dollars-cents per unit.				
69½ Sep	...	...	15	3.32

	Calls Vol.	Calls Last	Puts Vol.	Puts Last
50,000 Canadian Dollars-cents per unit.				
70 Sep	...	...	6	3.83
66 Dec	...	...	23	0.92
66½ Aug	...	...	300	0.80
67½ Aug	...	...	300	1.38
68 Aug	...	...	9	1.81
68½ Aug	...	...	11	2.34
69 Sep	...	...	20	2.84
French Franc				168.07
250,000 French Francs-European Style				
15½ Aug	3	0.16	...	...
GMark-JYen				81.66
62,500 German Mark-Japanese Yen cross.				
76 Dec	1	5.30	...	...
German Mark				56.35
62,500 German Marks-European Style.				
55 Dec	...	...	62	0.50

	Calls Vol.	Calls Last	Puts Vol.	Puts Last
Japanese Yen				68.65
6,250,000 J.Yen-100ths of a cent per unit.				
68 Aug	...	...	1	0.35
69 Sep	...	...	4	1.26
70 Sep	...	...	25	1.77
70½ Aug	1	0.30	...	...
71 Dec	6	2.36	...	...
72 Dec	...	...	1	3.70
74 Dec	2	1.32	...	...
75 Sep	20	0.18	...	...
6,250,000 J.Yen-EuropeanStyle.				
68 Sep	...	...	20	0.88
72 Sep	54	0.52	...	...
73 Sep	32	0.36	...	...
Swiss Franc				66.98
62,500 Swiss Francs-European Style.				
67½ Aug	100	0.13	...	...
69 Dec	...	...	16	2.23
70 Sep	...	...	16	3.20
62,500 Swiss Francs-cents per unit.				
67½ Sep	10	0.47	...	...

Call Vol 561   Open Int ... 77,046
Put Vol 1,010   Open Int ... 98,863

for regular PHLX currency options is the Friday before the third Wednesday of the expiration month. For the "EOM" options the expiration date is the last Friday of the month. Table 12.3 shows only the three contracts in each category with the shortest times to maturity.

The sizes of contracts are indicated at the beginning of each section in Table 12.3. The option prices are for the purchase or sale of one unit of a foreign currency with U.S. dollars. For the Japanese yen, the prices are in hundredths of a cent. For the other currencies they are in cents. Thus one call option contract on the Australian dollar with strike price $63\frac{1}{2}$ cents and exercise month September would give the holder the right to purchase 50,000 Australian dollars for U.S. $31,750. The indicated price of the contract is $50,000 \times 0.36$ cents, or $180. The spot exchange rate for the Australian dollar is shown as 60.48 cents per Australian dollar.

Valuation

To value currency options, we define S as the spot exchange rate (the value of one unit of the foreign currency measured in the domestic currency). We assume that S follows a geometric Brownian motion process similar to that assumed for stocks in chapter 11. In a risk-neutral world the process is

$$dS = (r - r_f)S\,dt + \sigma S\,dz$$

where r is the domestic risk-free interest rate, r_f is the foreign risk-free interest rate, and σ is the exchange rate's volatility.

This process is the same as that in equation (12.6) with $q = r_f$. This is because, as noted in section 3.8, a foreign currency is analogous to a stock providing a known dividend yield. The owner of foreign currency receives a "dividend yield" equal to the risk-free interest rate, r_f, in the foreign currency. Because the stochastic process for a foreign currency is the same as that for a stock paying a dividend yield equal to the foreign risk-free rate, the formulas derived in section 12.2 are correct with q replaced by r_f. The European call price, c, and put price, p, are therefore given by

$$c = S_0 e^{-r_f T} N(d_1) - X e^{-rT} N(d_2) \tag{12.9}$$
$$p = X e^{-rT} N(-d_2) - S_0 e^{-r_f T} N(-d_1) \tag{12.10}$$

where S_0 is the value of the exchange rate at time zero,

$$d_1 = \frac{\ln(S_0/X) + (r - r_f + \sigma^2/2)T}{\sigma\sqrt{T}}$$

and

$$d_2 = \frac{\ln(S_0/X) + (r - r_f - \sigma^2/2)T}{\sigma\sqrt{T}} = d_1 - \sigma\sqrt{T}$$

Both the domestic interest rate, r, and the foreign interest rate, r_f, are the rates for a maturity T. Put and call options on a currency are symmetrical in that a put option to sell X_A units of currency A for X_B units of currency B is the same as a call option to buy X_B units of currency B for X_A units of currency A.

From equation (3.13), the forward rate, F_0, for a maturity T is given by

$$F_0 = S_0 e^{(r - r_f)T}$$

This enables equations (12.9) and (12.10) to be simplified to

$$c = e^{-rT}\left[F_0 N(d_1) - X N(d_2)\right] \tag{12.11}$$
$$p = e^{-rT}\left[X N(-d_2) - F_0 N(-d_1)\right] \tag{12.12}$$

where

$$d_1 = \frac{\ln(F_0/X) + \sigma^2 T/2}{\sigma\sqrt{T}}$$

$$d_2 = \frac{\ln(F_0/X) - \sigma^2 T/2}{\sigma\sqrt{T}} = d_1 - \sigma\sqrt{T}$$

Note that the maturities of the forward contract and the option must be the same for equations (12.11) and (12.12) to apply.

> **Example 12.4** Consider a four-month European call option on the British pound. Suppose that the current exchange rate is 1.6000, the strike price is 1.6000, the risk-free interest rate in the United States is 8% per annum, the risk-free interest rate in Britain is 11% per annum, and the option price is 4.3 cents. In this case $S_0 = 1.6$, $X = 1.6$, $r = 0.08$, $r_f = 0.11$, $T = 4/12$, and $c = 0.043$. The implied volatility can be calculated iteratively. A volatility of 20% gives an option price of 0.0639, a volatility of 10% gives an option price of 0.0285, and so on. The implied volatility is 14.1%.

In some circumstances it is optimal to exercise American currency options prior to maturity. Thus American currency options are worth more than their European counterparts. In general, call options on high-interest currencies and put options on low-interest currencies are the most likely to be exercised prior to maturity. This is because a high-interest-rate currency is expected to depreciate relative to the U.S. dollar (making it potentially attractive to buy the currency now at the strike price and sell at the market price), and a low-interest-rate currency is expected to appreciate relative to the U.S. dollar (making it potentially attractive to buy now at the market price and sell at the strike price). Unfortunately, analytic formulas do not exist for the evaluation of American currency options. Numerical procedures and analytic approximations are discussed in chapter 16.

12.5 FUTURES OPTIONS

Options on futures contracts, or futures options, are now traded on many different exchanges. They require the delivery of an underlying futures contract when exercised. If a call futures option is exercised, the holder acquires a long position in the underlying futures contract plus a cash amount equal to the most recent settlement futures price minus the strike price. If a put futures option is exercised, the holder acquires a short position in the underlying futures contract plus a cash amount equal to the strike price minus the most recent settlement futures price. As the following examples show, the effective payoff from a call futures option is the excess of the futures price at the time of exercise less the strike price; the effective payoff from a put futures option is the strike price less the futures price at the time of exercise.

> **Example 12.5** Suppose it is August 15 and an investor has one September futures call option contract on copper with a strike price of 70 cents per pound. One futures contract is on 25,000 pounds of copper. Suppose that the futures price of copper for delivery in September is currently 81 cents, and at the close of trading on August 14 (the last settlement) it was 80 cents. If the option is exercised, the investor receives a cash amount of
>
> $$25,000 \times (80 - 70) \text{ cents} = \$2,500$$
>
> plus a long position in a futures contract to buy 25,000 pounds of copper in September. If desired, the position in the futures contract can be closed out immediately. This would leave the investor with the $2,500 cash payoff plus an amount
>
> $$25,000 \times (81 - 80) \text{ cents} = \$250$$
>
> reflecting the change in the futures price since the last settlement. The total payoff from exercising the option on August 15 is $2,750, which equals $25,000(F - X)$, where F is the futures price at the time of exercise and X is the strike price.

> **Example 12.6** An investor has one December futures put option on corn with a strike price of 200 cents per bushel. One futures contract is on 5,000 bushels of corn. Suppose that the current futures price of corn for delivery in December is 180, and the most recent settlement price is 179 cents. If the option is exercised, the investor receives a cash amount of
>
> $$5,000 \times (200 - 179) \text{ cents} = \$1,050$$

plus a short position in a futures contract to sell 5,000 bushels of corn in December. If desired, the position in the futures contract can be closed out. This would leave the investor with the $1,050 cash payoff minus an amount

$$5,000 \times (180 - 179) \text{ cents} = \$50$$

reflecting the change in the futures price since the last settlement. The net payoff from exercise is $1,000, which equals $5,000(X - F)$, where F is the futures price at the time of exercise and X is the strike price.

Futures options are written on both financial futures and commodity futures. Table 12.4 shows the closing prices of a variety of futures options on August 4, 1998. The month shown is the expiration month of the underlying futures contract. The maturity date of the options contract is generally on, or a few days before, the earliest delivery date of the underlying futures contract. For example, the NYSE index futures option and the S&P index futures options both expire on the same day as the underlying futures contract, whereas the IMM currency futures options expire two business days prior to the expiration of the futures contract.

Options on Interest Rate Futures

The most actively traded futures options in the United States are those on Treasury bond futures, Treasury note futures, and Eurodollar futures. A Treasury bond futures option is an option to enter a Treasury bond futures contract. As mentioned in chapter 4, one Treasury bond futures contract is for the delivery of Treasury bonds with a face value of $100,000. The price of a Treasury bond futures option is quoted as a percentage of the face value of the underlying Treasury bonds to the nearest $\frac{1}{64}$ of 1%. Table 12.4 gives the price of the September call futures option on Treasury bonds as 1-50 or $1\frac{50}{64}\%$ of the debt principal when the strike price is 122 (implying that one contract costs $1,781.25). The quotes for options on Treasury notes are similar.

An option on Eurodollar futures is an option to enter into a Eurodollar futures contract. As explained in chapter 4, the asset underlying a Eurodollar futures contract is a $1 million three-month deposit. When the Eurodollar quote changes by one basis point, or 0.01, there is a gain or loss on the contract of $25. Similarly, in the pricing of options on Eurodollar futures, one basis point represents $25. Table 12.4 gives the price of the CME September call futures option on Eurodollars as 0.57 when the strike price is 93.75. This implies that one contract costs $57 \times \$25 = \$1,425$.

Interest rate futures contracts work in the same way as other futures contracts. For example, the payoff from a call is $\max(F - X, 0)$, where F is the futures price at the time of exercise and X is the strike price. In addition to the cash payoff, the option holder obtains a long position in the futures contract at exercise and the option writer obtains a corresponding short position.

Interest rate futures prices increase when bond prices increase (i.e., when interest rates fall). They decrease when bond prices decrease (i.e., when interest rates rise). An investor who thinks that short-term interest rates will rise can speculate by buying put options on Eurodollar futures, and an investor who thinks that they will fall

Table 12.4   Closing Prices of Futures Options, August 4, 1998

FUTURES OPTIONS PRICES

Tuesday, August 4, 1998

AGRICULTURAL

CORN (CBT)
5,000 bu.; cents per bu.

Strike	Calls—Settle			Puts—Settle		
Price	Sep	Dec	Mar	Sep	Dec	Mar
190	23½	31¾	....	⅛	⅞	....
200	14⅛	23	32¾	⅞	2	1⅜
210	6⅛	15½	....	2¾	4¼	2⅞
220	2¼	9¼	17¼	8½	8¼	5¾
230	¾	5½	12	17	14¼	10
240	½	3⅜	8	26¾	22	15⅞

Est vol 20,000 Mn   11,144 calls 10, 817 puts
Op int Mon 259,524 calls 143,561 puts

SOYBEANS (CBT)
5,000 bu.; cents per bu.

Strike	Calls—Settle			Puts—Settle		
Price	Sep	Nov	Jan	Sep	Nov	Jan
500	51½	49½	....	¼	2¼	2¾
525	....	30	39½	1½	7½	7½
550	9½	16	....	8¼	18	16
575	2½	8¼	14½	25½	35¼	31
600	1	4⅝	8¾	49	56¼	50
625	½	2⅜	5½	73½	79	....

Est vol 15,000 Mn 14,991 calls 7,746 puts
Op int Mon 160,851 calls 72,197 puts

SOYBEAN MEAL (CBT)
100 tons; $ per ton

Strike	Calls—Settle			Puts—Settle		
Price	Sep	Oct	Dec	Sep	Oct	Dec
130	....	....	....	....	....	1.45
135	....	....	1.00	2.75	2.25	
140	3.25	4.30	7.00	2.50	4.75	4.45
145	1.75	2.80	4.75	6.00	8.15	7.20
150	.85	1.60	3.25	10.00	11.60	10.50
155	.65	1.30	2.25	14.75	16.30	14.45

Est vol 2,000 Mn 1,479 calls 2,672 puts
Op int Mon 43,757 calls 30,794 puts

SOYBEAN OIL (CBT)
60,000 lbs.; cents per lb.

Strike	Calls—Settle			Puts—Settle		
Price	Sep	Dec	Mar	Sep	Dec	Mar
2300	....	....	....	....	....	.370
2350	....	....	....	.180	.300	.540
2400	.300	.520	.840	.430	.540	.750
2450	.150	.360	.650	.770	.880	1.060
2500	.100	.250	.520	1.220	1.270	1.430
2550	.060	.170	.420	1.690	1.690	1.830

Est vol 1,000 Mn 876 calls 1,172 puts
Op int Mon 40,108 calls 27,202 puts

WHEAT (CBT)
5,000 bu.; cents per bu.

Strike	Calls—Settle			Puts—Settle		
Price	Sep	Dec	Mar	Sep	Dec	Mar
230	17¼	....	....	....	1	....
240	9	25¼	40½	2	2	2½
250	3¾	17¾	32¼	6¼	4⅝	....
260	1½	11¾	25½	14	8½	
270	¾	7¾	19¼	23	14	1
280	¼	5	15	32¾	–21¼	16½

Est vol 5,000 Mn 3,174 calls 1,270 puts
Op int Mon 90,677 calls 37,622 puts

COTTON (CTN)
50,000 lbs.; cents per lb.

Strike	Calls—Settle			Puts—Settle		
Price	Oct	Dec	Mar	Oct	Dec	Mar
68	3.03	3.57	....	.60	1.45	1.97
69	2.49	2.99	....	1.05	1.84	2.37
70	1.95	2.47	3.59	1.40	2.24	2.82
71	1.43	2.02	3.11	1.90	2.84	3.31
72	1.05	1.63	2.69	2.58	3.42	3.84
73	.75	1.30	2.30	3.28	4.08	4.42

Est vol 3,006 Mn 7,831 calls 5,798 puts
Op int Mon 79,514 calls 54,357 puts

ORANGE JUICE (CTN)
15,000 lbs.; cents per lb.

Strike	Calls—Settle			Puts—Settle		
Price	Sep	Nov	Jan	Sep	Nov	Jan
100	9.35	14.20	....	1.20	2.60	2.40
105	6.00	10.45	13.00	2.65	3.85	4.30
110	3.50	7.45	....	5.05	5.70	5.80
115	1.70	5.10	7.35	8.15	8.25	8.00
120	.65	3.20	5.20	12.10	11.25	10.90
125	.40	2.20	3.55	16.85	....	...

Est vol 1,600 Mn 906 calls 836 puts
Op int Mon 24,292 calls 28,276 puts

COFFEE (CSCE)
37,500 lbs.; cents per lb.

Strike	Calls—Settle			Puts—Settle		
Price	Sep	Oct	Nov	Sep	Oct	Nov
120	9.77	7.85	9.90	.77	5.20	7.25
125	5.75	5.75	8.00	1.75	8.10	10.35
130	3.12	4.00	6.25	4.12	11.35	13.60
135	1.40	3.00	5.00	7.40	15.35	17.35
140	.65	2.35	4.00	11.65	19.70	21.35
145	.35	1.80	3.25	16.35	24.15	25.60

Est vol 4,861 Mn 4,631 calls 2,985 puts
Op int Mon 35,528 calls 27,446 puts

SUGAR-WORLD (CSCE)
112,000 lbs.; cents per lb.

Strike	Calls—Settle			Puts—Settle		
Price						
750	1.22	1.26	1.62	.01	.05	.05
800	.72	.80	1.16	.01	.09	.09
850	.28	.45	.73	.07	.24	.16
900	.08	.19	.37	.37	.48	.30
950	.01	.08	.17	.80	.87	.60
1000	.01	.03	.09	1.30	1.32	1.02

Est vol 3,604 Mn 3,552 calls 2,706 puts
Op int Mon 117,909 calls 64,620 puts

COCOA (CSCE)
10 metric tons; $ per ton

Strike	Calls—Settle			Puts—Settle		
Price						
1450	105	145	149	1	3	7
1500	56	100	107	2	8	15
1550	17	62	71	13	20	29
1600	3	34	50	49	42	58
1650	2	19	33	98	77	91
1700	1	9	21	147	117	129

Est vol 800 Mn 443 calls 285 puts
Op int Mon 25,580 calls 14,729 puts

OIL

CRUDE OIL (NYM)
1,000 bbls.; $ per bbl.

Strike	Calls—Settle			Puts—Settle		
Price	Sep	Oct	Nov	Sep	Oct	Nov
1300	.90	....	....	.15	.30	.30
1350	.56	1.06	....	.31	.46	.45
1400	.30	.77	1.06	.55	.67	.64
1450	.17	.56	.80	.92	.96	.88
1500	.10	.39	.60	1.35	1.29	1.18
1550	.05	.27	.45	1.80	1.66	1.52

Est vol 15,811 Mn 10,974 calls 7,374 puts
Op int Mon 294,030 calls 208,548 puts

HEATING OIL No.2 (NYM)
42,000 gal.; $ per gal.

Strike	Calls—Settle			Puts—Settle		
34	....	....	....	.0045	.0060	....
35	....	....	....	.0075	.0085	.0110
36	.0144	....	....	.0120	.0125	.0145
37	.0095	....	....	.0171	.0165	.0185
38	.0065	.0195	....	.0241	.0201	.0235
39	.0045	.0155	.0279	.0320	.0270	.0296

Est vol 2,131 Mn 1,737 calls 218 puts
Op int Mon 45,215 calls 23,722 puts

GASOLINE-Unlead (NYM)
42,000 gal.; $ per gal.

Strike	Calls—Settle			Puts—Settle		
40	....	....	....	.0060	.0106	.0119
41	.0221	....	....	.0092	.0145	....
42	.0164	.0231	....	.0135	.0190	.0200
43	.0118	.0185	....	.0189	.0244	.0250
44	.0083	.0146	.0210	.0254	.0304	.0304
45	.0057	.0116	.0172	.0327	.0374	....

Est vol 1,067 Mn 821 calls 411 puts
Op int Mon 29,384 calls 18,023 puts

NATURAL GAS (NYM)
10,000 MMBtu.; $ per MMBtu.

Strike	Calls—Settle			Puts—Settle		
Price	Sep	Oct	Nov	Sep	Oct	Nov
180	....	....	....	.069	.089	.048
185	.133	....	....	.088	.109	.060
190	.106	.180	....	.112	.133	.072
195	.087	.158	....	.142	.159	.088
200	.070	.138	....	.175	.191	.106
205	.055	.120	....	.210	.223	.127

Est vol 5,140 Mn 3,359 calls 4,151 puts
Op int Mon 178,787 calls 128,273 puts

BRENT CRUDE (IPE)
1,000 net bbls.; $ per bbl.

Strike	Calls—Settle			Puts—Settle		
Price	Sep	Oct	Nov	Sep	Oct	Nov
1100	1.70	1.99	2.33	....	.06	.08
1150	1.21	1.56	1.90	.01	.13	.15
1200	.77	1.17	1.51	.07	.24	.26
1250	.39	.84	1.17	.19	.41	.42
1300	.14	.58	.88	.44	.65	.63
1350	.05	.38	.64	.85	.95	.89

Est vol 1,550 Mn 35 calls 255 puts
Op int Mon 16,759 calls 10,305 puts

can speculate by buying call options on Eurodollar futures. An investor who thinks that long-term interest rates will rise can speculate by buying put options on Treasury note futures or Treasury bond futures, and an investor who thinks they will fall can speculate by buying call options on these instruments.

Example 12.7   Suppose it is February and the futures price for the June Eurodollar contract is 93.82. (This corresponds to a three-month Eurodollar interest rate of 6.18%

Table 12.4 Closing Prices of Futures Options, August 4, 1998 (Continued)

FUTURES OPTIONS PRICES

GAS OIL (IPE)
100 metric tons; $ per ton

Strike	Calls-Settle			Puts-Settle		
Price	Aug	Sep	Oct	Aug	Sep	Oct
950	14.00	17.80	22.10	....	0.05	0.10
100	9.00	13.00	17.40	....	0.25	0.40
105	4.25	8.70	13.00	0.25	0.95	1.00
110	1.05	5.15	9.20	2.05	2.40	2.20
115	0.10	2.60	6.10	6.10	4.85	4.10
120	....	1.10	3.60	11.00	8.35	6.60

Est vol Mn 250 calls 350 puts
Op int Mon 10,705 calls 5,225 puts

LIVESTOCK

CATTLE-FEEDER (CME)
50,000 lbs.; cents per lb.

Strike	Calls-Settle			Puts-Settle		
Price	Aug	Sep	Oct	Aug	Sep	Oct
66	....	....	....	0.40	1.00	1.30
67	1.60	....	....	0.55	....	....
68	1.10	1.40	1.90	0.90	1.85	2.20
69	0.65	1.00	....	1.70	2.45	....
70	0.40	0.62	1.15	2.47	3.07	3.42
71	0.20	0.42	....	3.27	3.85	....

Est vol 964 Mn 328 calls 1,102 puts
Op int Mon 11,195 calls 12,693 puts

CATTLE-LIVE (CME)
40,000 lbs.; cents per lb.

Strike	Calls-Settle			Puts-Settle		
Price	Aug	Oct	Dec	Aug	Oct	Dec
58	2.12	....	....	0.02	0.62	0.90
59	1.15	1.90	....	0.05	0.92	....
60	0.40	1.35	3.22	0.30	1.30	1.40
61	0.10	0.97	....	1.00	1.75	....
62	0.02	0.65	2.15	1.92	2.35	2.30
63	....	0.45	....	2.90	3.02	....

Est vol 4009 Mn 1,962 calls 2,676 puts
Op int Mon 41,474 calls 35,541 puts

HOGS-LEAN (CME)
40,000 lbs.; cents per lb.

Strike	Calls-Settle			Puts-Settle		
Price	Aug	Oct	Dec	Aug	Oct	Dec
48	2.75	0.62	1.20	0.35	5.67	6.17
49	2.05	0.50	....	0.65	6.55	....
50	1.40	0.35	0.85	1.00	7.37	7.80
51	0.90	....	....	1.50	....	....
52	0.60	....	....	2.20	....	....
53	0.35	....	....	2.95	....	....

Est vol 684 Mn 732 calls 223 puts
Op int Mon 5,572 calls 3,284 puts

METALS

COPPER (CMX)
25,000 lbs.; cents per lb.

Strike	Calls-Settle			Puts-Settle		
Price	Sep	Oct	Nov	Sep	Oct	Nov
70	4.50	5.50	6.25	.60	1.40	2.00
72	3.10	4.20	5.05	1.20	2.15	2.80
74	2.00	3.15	4.00	2.10	3.05	3.70
76	1.20	2.30	3.15	3.30	4.15	4.80
78	.65	1.60	2.40	4.75	5.50	6.05
80	.40	1.15	1.85	6.50	7.00	7.50

Est vol 300 Mn 187 calls 504 puts
Op int Mon 15,753 calls 4,713 puts

GOLD (CMX)
100 troy ounces; $ per troy ounce

Strike	Calls-Settle			Puts-Settle		
Price	Sep	Oct	Dec	Sep	Oct	Dec
280	10.50	12.30	17.10	.60	2.00	4.70
285	5.50	8.30	13.10	1.20	3.10	5.60
290	3.00	5.60	10.00	2.80	5.20	7.50
295	1.30	3.10	7.30	5.90	7.70	9.80
300	.50	1.50	4.90	9.00	11.20	12.20
305	....	.80	3.40	14.80	14.90	15.90

Est vol 8,500 Mn 3,273 calls 2,786 puts
Op int Mon 246,625 calls 131,231 puts

SILVER (CMX)
5,800 troy ounces; cts per troy ounce

Strike	Calls-Settle			Puts-Settle		
500	45.5	50.5	56.5	.4	2.0	8.0
525	22.3	29.7	37.5	2.0	6.0	14.8
550	6.0	16.0	25.7	10.7	17.0	27.0
575	1.9	8.0	17.3	31.5	33.8	43.0
600	1.0	4.5	12.0	55.5	55.0	62.0
625	.7	3.0	8.8	80.2	78.0	83.0

Est vol 2,000 Mn 1,527 calls 1,624 puts
Op int Mon 68,488 calls 21,828 puts

INTEREST RATE

T-BONDS (CBT)
$100,000; points and 64ths of 100%

Strike	Calls-Settle			Puts-Settle		
Price	Sep	Dec	Mar	Sep	Dec	Mar
122	1-50	2-42	3-11	0-14	1-22	2-09
123	1-03	....	....	0-31	....	....
124	0-34	1-38	2-14	0-62	2-19	3-08
125	0-14	....	....	1-42	....	....
126	0-05	0-57	1-29	2-33	3-36	4-20
127	0-02	....	....	3-29	....	....

Est. vol. 150,000;
Mn vol. 69,541 calls; 67,677 puts
Op. int. Mon 646,956 calls; 511,432 puts

T-NOTES (CBT)
$100,000; points and 64ths of 100%

Strike	Calls-Settle			Puts-Settle		
112	2-04	2-23	....	0-01	0-19	....
113	1-07	1-40	....	0-03	0-35	0-56
114	0-25	1-02	1-30	0-20	0-60	1-18
115	0-05	0-39	1-01	....	1-32	....
116	0-01	0-22	....	....	2-14	....
117	0-01	0-11	....	....	....	....

Est vol 36,000 Mn 10,861 calls 5,271 puts
Op int Mon 301,320 calls 251,901 puts

5 YR TREAS NOTES (CBT)
$100,000; points and 64ths of 100%

10800	1-53	....	....	0-01	0-08	....
10850	1-22	....	....	0-01	0-13	....
10900	0-56	1-12	....	0-02	0-20	....
10950	0-28	0-55	....	0-07	0-31	....
11000	0-10	0-38	....	0-21	0-46	....
11050	0-02	0-25	....	....	....	....

Est vol 7,000 Mn 3,185 calls 3,049 puts
Op int Mon 121,099 calls 78,563 puts

MUNI BOND INDEX (CBT)
$1,000; times Bond Buyer MBI

Strike	Calls-Settle			Puts-Settle		
Price	Sep	Dec	....	Sep	Dec	....
122	....	....	....	0-19	....	....
123	....	....	....	0-39	....	....
124	1-21	....	....	0-58	....	....
125	0-52	....	....	....	....	....
126	0-30	....	....	....	....	....
127	....	....	....	....	....	....

Est vol 55 Mn 100 calls 100 puts
Op int Mon 1,702 calls 11,180 puts

EURODOLLAR (CME)
$ million; pts. of 100%

Strike	Calls-Settle			Puts-Settle		
Price	Aug	Sep	Oct	Aug	Sep	Oct
9375	....	0.57	....	....	0.00	0.00
9400	0.32	0.32	0.31	0.00	0.00	0.01
9425	0.08	0.08	0.09	0.00	0.01	0.04
9450	0.00	0.00	0.02	....	0.18	....
9475	....	0.00	....	....	0.42	....
9500	0.00	0.00	....	....	0.67	....

Est. vol. 62,556;
Mon vol. 33,612 calls; 10,325 puts
Op. int. Mon 1,446,720 calls; 959,989 puts

1 YR. MID-CURVE EURODLR (CME)
$1,000,000 contract units; pts. of 100%

Strike	Calls-Settle			Puts-Settle		
9375	....	0.57	....	0.00	0.00	0.01
9400	....	0.32	....	0.00	0.00	0.04
9425	0.09	0.12	0.08	0.02	0.05	0.14
9450	0.00	0.02	0.02	0.18	0.20	....
9475	....	0.00	0.00	....	....	....
9500	....	0.00	....	....	....	....

Est vol 53,740 Mn   29,059 calls 20,-568 puts
Op int Mon 334,588 calls 286,000 puts

2 YR. MID-CURVE EURODLR (CME)
$1,000,000 contract units; pts. of 100%

Strike	Calls-Settle			Puts-Settle		
Price	Sep	Dec	....	Sep	Dec	....
9375	....	....	....	0.00	0.04	....
9400	0.21	0.23	....	0.01	0.10	....
9425	0.05	0.10	....	0.10	0.22	....
9450	0.01	0.04	....	0.40	0.40	....
9475	0.01	0.00	....	....	....	....
9500	....	....	....	....	....	....

Est vol Mn 0 calls 0 puts
Op int Mon 22,444 calls 22,230 puts

EUROMARK (LIFFE)
$1 million; pts. of 100%

Strike	Calls-Settle			Puts-Settle		
Price	Aug	Sep	Oct	Aug	Sep	Oct
9600	0.41	0.42	0.19	....	....	0.02
9625	0.16	0.17	0.04	....	0.01	0.11
9650	....	....	0.01	0.09	0.09	0.33
9675	....	....	....	0.33	0.33	0.58
9700	....	....	....	0.58	0.58	0.82
9725	....	....	....	0.83	0.83	1.07

Vol Tu 3,806 calls 4,492 puts
Op int Mon 305,603 calls 408,581 puts

---

per annum.) The price of a call option on this contract with a strike price of 94.00 is quoted as 0.20. This option could be attractive to an investor who feels that interest rates are likely to come down. Suppose that short-term interest rates do decline by about 100 basis points over the next three months, and the investor exercises the call when the Eurodollar futures price is 94.78. (This corresponds to a three-month Eurodollar interest rate of 5.22% per annum.) The payoff is $25 \times 78 = \$1,950$. The cost of the contract is $20 \times 25 = \$500$. The investor's profit, therefore, is $1,450.

Example 12.8   Suppose it is August and the futures price for the December Treasury bond contract traded on the CBOT is 96-09 (or $96\frac{9}{32} = 96.28125$). The yield on long-term government bonds is about 8.4% per annum. An investor who feels that this yield

Table 12.4   Closing Prices of Futures Options, August 4, 1998 (Continued)

FUTURES OPTIONS PRICES

LONG GILT (LIFFE) (decimal)
£50,000; pts. of 100%

Strike	Calls-Settle			Puts-Settle		
Price	Sep	Oct	Nov	Sep	Oct	Nov
10850	1.21	1.53	1.72	0.12	0.28	0.47
10900	0.83	1.18	1.39	0.24	0.43	0.64
10950	0.52	0.88	1.10	0.43	0.63	0.85
11000	0.29	0.64	0.85	0.70	0.89	1.10
11050	0.15	0.44	0.64	1.06	1.19	1.39
11100	0.07	0.29	0.48	1.48	1.54	1.73

Vol Tu 6,437 calls 4,183 puts
Op int Mon 82,399 calls 26,850 puts

GERMAN GOVT BOND (LIFFE)
$250,000 marks; pts. of 100%

Strike	Calls			Puts		
10900	0.81	0.48	0.62	0.06	0.46	0.60
10950	0.41	0.26	0.38	0.16	0.74	0.86
11000	0.15	0.13	0.22	0.40	1.11	1.20
11050	0.05	0.06	0.12	0.80	1.54	1.60
11100	0.01	0.03	0.06	1.26	2.01	2.04
11150	....	0.01	0.03	1.75	2.50	2.51

Vol Tu 8,074 calls 2,077 puts
Op int Mon 124,189 calls 101,005 puts

CURRENCY

JAPANESE YEN (CME)
12,500,000 yen; cents per 100 yen

Strike	Calls-Settle			Puts-Settle		
Price	Aug	Sep	Oct	Aug	Sep	Oct
6850	1.07	....	....	0.16	0.85	....
6900	0.70	1.47	....	0.28	1.06	1.35
6950	0.42	1.21	....	0.51	1.30	1.54
7000	0.26	0.99	....	0.85	1.58	1.75
7050	0.15	0.81	....	1.24	1.89	1.98
7100	0.09	0.65	1.57	1.68	2.23	2.24

Est vol 10,950 Mon 3,591 calls 7,315 puts
Op int Mon 60,138 calls 113,165 puts

DEUTSCHEMARK (CME)
125,000 marks; cents per mark

Strike	Calls-Settle			Puts-Settle		
Price	Aug	Sep	Oct	Aug	Sep	Oct
5550	1.01	1.18	....	0.02	0.19	....
5600	0.54	0.82	....	0.05	0.33	....
5650	0.17	0.51	0.92	0.18	0.52	....
5700	0.04	0.32	0.67	0.55	0.83	....
5750	0.02	0.19	....	1.03	....	1.17
5800	....	0.11	....	1.51	1.61	....

Est vol 1,862 Mon 387 calls 436 puts
Op int Mon 45,836 calls 31,061 puts

CANADIAN DOLLAR (CME)
100,000 Can.$, cents per Can.$

Strike	Calls-Settle			Puts-Settle		
Price	Aug	Sep	Oct	Aug	Sep	Oct
6500	....	....	....	....	0.18	....
6550	....	0.83	....	0.09	0.30	....
6600	0.24	0.51	....	0.21	0.48	....
6650	0.08	0.28	....	0.55	0.76	....
6700	0.04	0.18	....	1.01	1.14	....
6750	0.02	0.11	....	1.49	1.57	....

Est vol 1,201 Mon 584 calls 202 puts
Op int Mon 32,857 calls 7,845 puts

BRITISH POUND (CME)
62,500 pounds; cents per pound

Strike	Calls-Settle			Puts-Settle		
Price	Aug	Sep	Oct	Aug	Sep	Oct
16100	....	....	....	0.08	0.46	....
16200	1.30	1.94	....	0.12	0.76	1.72
16300	0.52	1.34	....	0.34	1.15	0.00
16400	0.16	0.90	....	0.98	1.72	2.78
16500	0.06	0.57	....	1.88	2.40	....
16600	0.02	0.36	0.64	2.84	3.18	....

Est vol 555 Mon 1,806 calls 325 puts
Op int Mon 15,553 calls 11,073 puts

SWISS FRANC (CME)
125,000 francs; cents per franc

Strike	Calls-Settle			Puts-Settle		
Price	Aug	Sep	Oct	Aug	Sep	Oct
6650	0.85	1.12	....	0.06	0.34	....
6700	0.42	0.81	1.46	0.13	0.52	0.56
6750	0.17	0.56	....	0.38	0.77	....
6800	0.07	0.38	....	0.78	1.09	....
6850	0.04	0.25	....	1.25	1.45	....
6900	0.03	0.16	....	1.74	1.86	....

Est vol 1,103 Mon 262 calls 586 puts
Op int Mon 9,129 calls 10,435 puts

BRAZILIAN REAL (CME)
100,000 Braz. reais; $ per reais

Est vol 0 Mon 0 calls 0 puts
0 Op int Mon 0 calls 500 puts

MEXICAN PESO (CME)
500,000 new Mex. pesos; $ per MP

Strike	Calls-Settle			Puts-Settle		
Price	Aug	Sep	Oct	Aug	Sep	Oct
1062	....	1062	....	....	0.60	....
1075	....	....	....	....	0.95	....
1087	....	....	....	....	....	....
1100	....	1.05	....	....	1.70	....
1112	....	....	....	....	....	....
1125	....	0.25	....	....	3.37	....

Est vol 2 Mon 10 calls 30 puts
Op int Mon 2,078 calls 3,259 puts

INDEX

DJ INDUSTRIAL AVG (CBOT)
$100 times premium

Strike	Calls-Settle			Puts-Settle		
Price	Aug	Sep	Oct	Aug	Sep	Oct
83	....	44.85	....	14.00	24.45	....
84	....	38.50	....	17.20	28.05	....
85	21.55	....	....	21.05	31.95	....
86	16.25	26.90	....	25.75	36.35	....
87	11.75	21.80	33.35	31.20	41.25	....
88	....	17.45	28.05	37.45	46.80	48.60

Est vol 1,750 Mon 523 calls 244 puts
Op int Mon 17,625 calls 17,393 puts

S&P 500 STOCK INDEX (CME)
$250 times premium

Strike	Calls-Settle			Puts-Settle		
Price	Aug	Sep	Oct	Aug	Sep	Oct
1065	....	....	....	23.10	36.60	. . .
1070	....	....	....	25.00	38.50	....
1075	23.20	39.50	....	24.20	40.50	46.00
1080	23.20	36.60	....	29.20	42.60	48.00
1085	20.60	33.90	....	31.60	44.80	....
1090	18.10	31.30	....	34.10	47.20	....

Est vol 39,286 Mn 9,040 calls 14,448 puts
Op int Mon 90,989 calls 216,685 puts

will fall by December might choose to buy December calls with a strike price of 98. Assume that the price of these calls is 1-04 (or $1\frac{4}{64} = 1.0625\%$ of the principal). If long-term rates fall to 8% per annum and the Treasury bond futures price rises to 100-00, the investor will make a net profit per $100 of bond futures of

$$100.00 - 98.00 - 1.0625 = 0.9375$$

Because one option contract is for the purchase or sale of instruments with a face value of $100,000, the investor would make a profit of $937.50 per option contract bought.

Reasons for the Popularity of Futures Options

Futures options are more attractive to investors than options on the underlying asset when it is cheaper or more convenient to deliver futures contracts on the asset rather than the asset itself. This is true of many commodities. For example, it is much easier and more convenient to make or take delivery of a live hogs futures contract than it is to make or take delivery of the hogs themselves.

An important point about a futures option is that the exercise of the option does not usually lead to delivery of the underlying asset, because in most circumstances the underlying futures contract is closed out prior to delivery. Futures options are, therefore, normally settled in cash. This is appealing to many investors, particularly those with limited capital, who may find it difficult to come up with the funds to buy the underlying asset when an option is exercised.

Another advantage sometimes cited for futures options is that the trading of futures and futures options are arranged in pits side by side in the same exchange. This facilitates hedging, arbitrage, and speculation. It also tends to make the markets more efficient.

A final point is that futures options tend to entail lower transactions costs than spot options in many situations.

Put–Call Parity

In chapter 7 we derived a put–call parity relationship for European stock options. We now present a similar argument to derive a put–call parity relationship for European futures options on the assumption that there is no difference between the payoffs from futures and forward contracts.

Consider European call and put futures options, both with strike price X and time to expiration T. We can form two portfolios:

> *Portfolio A:* a European call futures option plus an amount of cash equal to Xe^{-rT}
>
> *Portfolio B:* a European put futures option plus a long futures contract plus an amount of cash equal to $F_0 e^{-rT}$

In portfolio A the cash can be invested at the risk-free rate, r, and will grow to X at time T. Let F_T be the futures price at maturity of the option. If $F_T > X$, the call option in portfolio A is exercised and portfolio A is worth F_T. If $F_T \leq X$, the call is not exercised and portfolio A is worth X. The value of portfolio A at time T is, therefore,

$$\max (F_T, X)$$

In portfolio B the cash can be invested at the risk-free rate to grow to F_0 at time T. The put option provides a payoff of $\max (X - F_T, 0)$. The futures contract provides a payoff of $F_T - F_0$. The value of portfolio B at time T is, therefore,

$$F_0 + (F_T - F_0) + \max (X - F_T, 0) = \max (F_T, X)$$

Because the two portfolios have the same value at time T and there are no early exercise opportunities, it follows that they are worth the same today. The value of portfolio A today is

$$c + Xe^{-rT}$$

where c is the price of the call futures option. The marking-to-market process ensures that the futures contract in portfolio B is worth zero today. Therefore, portfolio B is worth

$$p + F_0 e^{-rT}$$

where p is the price of the put futures option. Hence

$$c + Xe^{-rT} = p + F_0e^{-rT} \tag{12.13}$$

For American futures the put–call parity relationship is (see Problem 12.20)

$$F_0e^{-rT} - X \le C - P \le F_0 - Xe^{-rT}$$

Example 12.9   Suppose that the price of a European call option on silver futures for delivery in six months is \$0.56 per ounce when the exercise price is \$8.50. Assume that the silver futures price for delivery in six months is currently \$8.00 and the risk-free interest rate for an investment that matures in six months is 10% per annum. From a rearrangement of equation (12.13), the price of a European put option on silver futures with the same maturity and exercise date as the call option is

$$0.56 + 8.50e^{-0.1\times0.5} - 8.00e^{-0.1\times0.5} = 1.04$$

12.6   VALUATION OF FUTURES OPTIONS USING BINOMIAL TREES

This section uses a binomial tree approach similar to that in chapter 9 to price futures options. The key difference between futures options and stock options is that there are no up-front costs when a futures contract is entered into.

Suppose that the current futures price is 30 and it is expected to move either up to 33 or down to 28 over the next month. Consider a one-month call option on the futures with a strike price of 29. The situation is shown in Figure 12.2. If the futures price proves to be 33, the payoff from the option is 4 and the value of the futures contract is 3. If the futures price proves to be 28, the payoff from the option is zero and the value of the futures contract is -2.

To set up a riskless hedge, we consider a portfolio consisting of a short position in one options contract and a long position in Δ futures contracts. If the futures price moves up to 33, the value of the portfolio is $3\Delta - 4$; if it moves down to 28, the value of the portfolio is -2Δ. The portfolio is riskless when these are the same—that is, when

$$3\Delta - 4 = -2\Delta$$

or $\Delta = 0.8$.

Figure 12.2   Futures price movements in numerical example.

For this value of Δ, we know the portfolio will be worth $3 \times 0.8 - 4 = -1.6$ in one month. Assume a risk-free interest rate of 6%. The value of the portfolio today must be

$$-1.6e^{-0.06 \times 0.08333} = -1.592$$

The portfolio consists of one short option and Δ futures contracts. Because the value of the futures contract today is zero, the value of the option today must be 1.592.

A Generalization

We can generalize this analysis by considering a futures price that starts at F_0 and is anticipated to rise to F_0u or move down to F_0d over the time period T. We consider a derivative maturing at the end of the time period, and we suppose that its payoff is f_u if the futures price moves up and f_d if it moves down. The situation is summarized in Figure 12.3.

The riskless portfolio in this case consists of a short position in one option combined with a long position in Δ futures contracts, where

$$\Delta = \frac{f_u - f_d}{F_0u - F_0d}$$

The value of the portfolio at the end of the time period, then, is always

$$(F_0u - F_0)\Delta - f_u$$

Denoting the risk-free interest rate by r, we obtain the value of the portfolio today:

$$[(F_0u - F_0)\Delta - f_u]e^{-rT}$$

Another expression for the present value of the portfolio is $-f$, where f is the value of the option today. It follows that

$$-f = [(F_0u - F_0)\Delta - f_u]e^{-rT}$$

Substituting for Δ and simplifying reduces this equation to

$$f = e^{-rT}[pf_u + (1-p)f_d] \qquad (12.14)$$

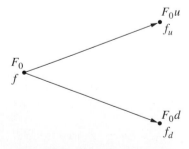

Figure 12.3   Futures price and option price in general situation.

where

$$p = \frac{1 - d}{u - d} \tag{12.15}$$

In the numerical example considered previously (see Figure 12.2), $u = 1.1$, $d = 0.9333$, $r = 0.06$, $T = 0.08333$, $f_u = 4$, and $f_d = 0$. From equation (12.15),

$$p = \frac{1 - 0.9333}{1.1 - 0.9333} = 0.4$$

and from equation (12.14),

$$f = e^{-0.06 \times 0.08333}[0.4 \times 4 + 0.6 \times 0] = 1.592$$

This result agrees with the answer obtained for this example earlier.

12.7 A FUTURES PRICE AS A STOCK PAYING A CONTINUOUS DIVIDEND YIELD

There is a general result that makes the analysis of futures options analogous to the analysis of options on a stock paying a continuous dividend yield. This result is that futures prices behave in the same way as a stock paying a continuous dividend yield at the domestic risk-free interest rate r.

One clue that this might be so is given by comparing equations (12.14) and (12.15) with equations (12.7) and (12.8). The two sets of equations are identical when we set $q = r$. Another clue is that the put–call parity relationship for futures options prices are the same as those for options on a stock paying a continuous dividend yield at rate q when the stock price is replaced by the futures price and $q = r$.

Appendix 12B derives the differential equation for a derivative dependent on a futures price. Comparing this with the differential equation in Appendix 12A for a derivative dependent on a stock providing a known dividend yield confirms that a futures price can be regarded as a stock paying a dividend yield at rate r.

The Expected Growth Rate of a Futures Price

The expected growth rate in the price of a stock that pays dividends at rate q is $r - q$ in a risk-neutral world. (This is because, with this growth rate, the total expected return in the form of dividends and capital gains is r.) Because a futures price behaves like a stock where the dividend yield, q, equals r, it follows that the expected growth rate in a futures price in a risk-neutral world is zero. This is as might be expected. It costs nothing to enter into a futures contract. The expected gain to the holder of a futures contract in a risk-neutral world should, therefore, be zero.

This result, that the expected growth rate in a futures price in a risk-neutral world is zero, is a very general one. It is true for all futures prices. It applies in the world where interest rates are stochastic as well as the world where they are constant.

Because the expected growth rate of the futures price is zero,

$$F_0 = \hat{E}(F_T)$$

where F_T is the futures price at the maturity of the contract, F_0 is the futures price at time zero, and $\hat{E}$ denotes expected value in a risk-neutral world. Because $F_T = S_T$, where S_T is the spot price at time T, it follows that

$$F_0 = \hat{E}(S_T) \qquad (12.16)$$

This means that for all assets the futures price equals the expected future spot price in a risk-neutral world.

12.8   BLACK'S MODEL FOR VALUING FUTURES OPTIONS

European futures options can be valued by extending the results we have produced. Fischer Black was the first to show this in a paper published in 1976.[3] The underlying assumption is that futures prices have the same lognormal property that we assumed for stock prices in chapter 10. The European call price, c, and the European put price, p, for a futures option are given by equations (12.4) and (12.5) with S_0 replaced by F_0 and $q = r$:

$$c = e^{-rT}[F_0 N(d_1) - X N(d_2)] \qquad (12.17)$$
$$p = e^{-rT}[X N(-d_2) - F_0 N(-d_1)] \qquad (12.18)$$

where

$$d_1 = \frac{\ln(F_0/X) + \sigma^2 T/2}{\sigma\sqrt{T}}$$

$$d_2 = \frac{\ln(F_0/X) - \sigma^2 T/2}{\sigma\sqrt{T}} = d_1 - \sigma\sqrt{T}$$

and σ is the volatility of the futures price. When the cost of carry and the convenience yield are functions only of time, it can be shown that the volatility of the futures price is the same as the volatility of the underlying asset. Note that Black's model does not require the options contract and the futures contract to mature at the same time.

> ***Example 12.10***   Consider a European put futures option on crude oil. The time to maturity is four months, the current futures price is $20, the exercise price is $20, the risk-free interest rate is 9% per annum, and the volatility of the futures price is

---

[3] See F. Black, "The Pricing of Commodity Contracts," *Journal of Financial Economics,* 3 (March 1976), 167–79.

25% per annum. In this case $F_0 = 20$, $X = 20$, $r = 0.09$, $T = 4/12$, $\sigma = 0.25$, and $\ln(F_0/X) = 0$, so that

$$d_1 = \frac{\sigma\sqrt{T}}{2} = 0.07216$$

$$d_2 = -\frac{\sigma\sqrt{T}}{2} = -0.07216$$

$$N(-d_1) = 0.4712, \qquad N(-d_2) = 0.5288$$

and the put price p is given by

$$p = e^{-0.09 \times 4/12}(20 \times 0.5288 - 20 \times 0.4712) = 1.12$$

or $1.12.

12.9 COMPARISON OF FUTURES OPTION AND SPOT OPTION PRICES

In this section we compare options on futures and options on spot when they have the same strike price and time to maturity.

The payoff from a European spot call option with strike price X is

$$\max(S_T - X, 0)$$

where S_T is the spot price at the option's maturity. The payoff from a European futures call option with the same strike price is

$$\max(F_T - X, 0)$$

where F_T is the futures price at the option's maturity. If the European futures option matures at the same time as the futures contract, $F_T = S_T$ and the two options are in theory equivalent. If the European call futures option matures before the futures contract, it is worth more than the corresponding spot option in a normal market (where futures prices are higher than spot prices) and less than the corresponding spot option in an inverted market (where futures prices are lower than spot prices).

Similarly, a European futures put option is worth the same as its spot option counterpart when the futures option matures at the same time as the futures contract. If the European put futures option matures before the futures contract, it is worth less than the corresponding spot option in a normal market and more than the corresponding spot option in an inverted market.

Results for American Options

Traded futures options are, in practice, usually American. Assuming that the risk-free rate of interest, r, is positive, there is always some chance that it will be optimal to exercise an American futures option early. American futures options are, therefore, worth more than their European counterparts. We will look at numerical procedures for valuing futures options in chapter 16.

It is not generally true that an American futures option is worth the same as the corresponding American option on the underlying asset when the futures and options contracts have the same maturity. Suppose, for example, that there is a normal market with futures prices consistently higher than spot prices prior to maturity. This is the case with most stock indices, gold, silver, low-interest currencies, and some commodities. An American call futures option must be worth more than the corresponding American call option on the underlying asset. The reason is that in some situations the futures option will be exercised early, in which case it will provide a greater profit to the holder. Similarly, an American put futures option must be worth less than the corresponding American put option on the underlying asset. If there is an inverted market with futures prices consistently lower than spot prices, as is the case with high-interest currencies and some commodities, the reverse must be true. American call futures options are worth less than the corresponding American call option on the underlying asset, whereas American put futures options are worth more than the corresponding American put option on the underlying asset.

The differences just described between American futures options and American asset options hold true when the futures contract expires later than the options contract as well as when the two expire at the same time. In fact, the differences tend to be greater the later the futures contract expires.

SUMMARY

The Black–Scholes formula for valuing European options on a non-dividend-paying stock can be extended to cover European options on a stock providing a continuous known dividend yield. In practice, stocks do not provide continuous dividend yields. However, a number of other assets on which options are written can be considered to be analogous to a stock providing a continuous dividend yield. In particular,

1. An index is analogous to a stock providing a continuous dividend yield. The dividend yield is the average dividend yield on the stocks composing the index.
2. A foreign currency is analogous to a stock providing a continuous dividend yield where the dividend yield is the foreign risk-free interest rate.
3. A futures price is analogous to a stock providing a continuous dividend yield where the dividend yield is equal to the domestic risk-free interest rate.

The extension to Black–Scholes can, therefore, be used to value European options on indices, foreign currencies, and futures contracts. As we will see in Chapter 16, these analogies are also useful in numerically valuing American options on indices, currencies, and futures contracts.

Index options are settled in cash. Upon exercise of an index call option, the holder receives the amount by which the index exceeds the strike price at close of trading. Similarly, upon exercise of an index put option, the holder receives the amount by which the strike price exceeds the index at close of trading. Index options can be used for portfolio insurance. If the portfolio has a β of 1.0, it is appropriate to buy one put option for each $100S_0$ dollars in the portfolio, where S_0 is the value of the index; otherwise, β put options should be purchased for each $100S_0$ dollars in the portfolio, where β is the beta of the portfolio calculated using the capital asset pricing model. The strike price of the put options purchased should reflect the level of insurance required.

Currency options are traded both on organized exchanges and over the counter. They can be used by corporate treasurers to hedge foreign exchange exposure. For example, a U.S. corporate treasurer who knows that sterling will be received at a certain time in the future can hedge by buying put options that mature at that time. Similarly, a U.S. corporate treasurer who knows that sterling will be paid at a certain time in the future can hedge by buying call options that mature at that time.

Futures options require the delivery of the underlying futures contract upon exercise. When a call is exercised, the holder acquires a long futures posit ion plus a cash amount equal to the excess of the futures price over the strike price. Similarly, when a put is exercised, the holder acquires a short position plus a cash amount equal to the excess of the strike price over the futures price. The futures contract that is delivered typically expires slightly later than the option. If we assume that the two expiration dates are the same, a European futures op tion is worth exactly the same as the corresponding European option on the under lying asset. However, this is not true of American options. If the futures market is normal, an American call futures is worth more than the American call on the underlying asset, while an American put futures is worth less than the American put on the underlying asset. If the futures market is inverted, the reverse is true.

SUGGESTIONS FOR FURTHER READING

General

Merton, R. C. "Theory of Rational Option Pricing," *Bell Journal of Economics and Management Science,* 4 (Spring 1973), 141–83.

Stoll, H. R., and R. E. Whaley. "New Option Instruments: Arbitrageable Linkages and Valuation," *Advances in Futures and Options Research,* 1, pt. A (1986), 25–62.

On Options on Stock Indices

Chance, D. M. "Empirical Tests of the Pricing of Index Call Options," *Advances in Futures and Options Research,* 1, pt. A (1986), 141–66.

On Options on Currencies

Amin, K., and R. A. Jarrow. "Pricing Foreign Currency Options under Stochastic Interest Rates," *Journal of International Money and Finance,* 10 (1991), 310–29.

Biger, N., and J. Hull. "The Valuation of Currency Options," *Financial Management,* 12 (Spring 1983), 24–28.

Bodurtha, J. N., and G. R. Courtadon. "Tests of an American Option Pricing Model on the Foreign Currency Options Market," *Journal of Financial and Quantitative Analysis,* 22 (June 1987), 153–67.

Garman, M. B., and S. W. Kohlhagen. "Foreign Currency Option Values," *Journal of International Money and Finance,* 2 (December 1983), 231–37.

Grabbe, J. O. "The Pricing of Call and Put Options on Foreign Exchange," *Journal of International Money and Finance,* 2 (December 1983), 239–53.

On Options on Futures

Black, F. "The Pricing of Commodity Contracts," *Journal of Financial Economics,* 3 (March 1976), 167–79.

Brenner, M., G. Courtadon, and M. Subrahmanyam. "Options on the Spot and Options on Futures," *Journal of Finance,* 40 (December 1985), 1303–17.

Hilliard, J. E., and J. Reis. "Valuation of Commodity Futures and Options under Stochastic Convenience Yields, Interest Rates, and Jump Diffusions in the Spot," *Journal of Financial and Quantitative Analysis,* 33, 1 (March 1998), 61–86.

Miltersen, K. R., and E. S. Schwartz. "Pricing of Options on Commodity Futures with Stochastic Term Structures of Convenience Yields and Interest Rates," *Journal of Financial and Quantitative Analysis,* 33, 1 (March 1998), 33–59.

Ramaswamy, K., and S. M. Sundaresan. "The Valuation of Options on Futures Contracts," *Journal of Finance,* 40 (December 1985), 1319–40.

Wolf, A. "Fundamentals of Commodity Options on Futures," *Journal of Futures Markets,* 2 (1982), 391–408.

QUESTIONS AND PROBLEMS

12.1. A portfolio is currently worth $10 million and has a beta of 1.0. The S&P 100 is currently standing at 500. Explain how a put option on the S&P 100 with a strike of 480 can be used to provide portfolio insurance.

12.2. "Once we know how to value options on a stock paying a continuous dividend yield, we know how to value options on stock indices, currencies, and futures." Explain this statement.

12.3. A stock index is currently 300, the dividend yield on the index is 3% per annum, and the risk-free interest rate is 8% per annum. What is a lower bound for the price of a six-month European call option on the index when the strike price is 290?

12.4. A currency is currently worth $0.80. Over each of the next two months it is expected to increase or decrease in value by 2%. The domestic and foreign risk-free interest rates are 6% and 8%, respectively. What is the value of a two-month European call option with a strike price of $0.80?

12.5. Explain the difference between a call option on yen and a call option on yen futures.

12.6. Explain how currency options can be used for hedging.

12.7. Calculate the value of a three-month at-the-money European call option on a stock index when the index is at 250, the risk-free interest rate is 10% per annum, the volatility of the index is 18% per annum, and the dividend yield on the index is 3% per annum.

12.8. Consider an American call futures option where the futures contract and the option contract expire at the same time. Under what circumstances is the futures option worth more than the corresponding American option on the underlying asset?

12.9. Calculate the value of an eight-month European put option on a currency with a strike price of 0.50. The current exchange rate is 0.52, the volatility of the exchange rate is 12%, the domestic risk-free interest rate is 4% per annum, and the foreign risk-free interest rate is 8% per annum.

12.10. Why are options on bond futures more actively traded than options on bonds?

12.11. "A futures price is like a stock paying a continuous dividend yield." What is the continuous dividend yield?

12.12. A futures price is currently 50. At the end of six months it will be either 56 or 46. The risk-free interest rate is 6% per annum. What is the value of a six-month European call option with a strike price of 50?

12.13. Calculate the value of a five-month European put futures option when the futures price is $19, the strike price is $20, the risk-free interest rate is 12% per annum, and the volatility of the futures price is 20% per annum.

12.14. A total return index tracks the return, including dividends, on a certain portfolio. Explain how you would value (a) forward contracts and (b) European options on the index.

12.15. The S&P100 index currently stands at 696 and has a volatility of 30% per annum. The risk-free rate of interest is 7% per annum, and the index provides a dividend yield of 4% per annum. Calculate the value of a three-month European put with strike price 700.

12.16. What is the put–call parity relationship for European currency options?

12.17. A foreign currency is currently worth $1.50. The domestic and foreign risk-free interest rates are 5% and 9%, respectively. Calculate a lower bound for the value of a six-month call option on the currency with a strike price of $1.40 if it is (a) European and (b) American.

12.18. Consider a stock index currently standing at 250. The dividend yield on the index is 4% per annum, and the risk-free rate is 6% per annum. A three-month European call option on the index with a strike price of 245 is currently worth $10. What is the value of a three-month European put option on the index with a strike price of 245?

12.19. Show that if C is the price of an American call with strike price X and maturity T on a stock providing a dividend yield of q, and P is the price of an American put on the same stock with the same strike price and exercise date,

$$S_0 e^{-qT} - X \le C - P \le S_0 - X e^{-rT}$$

where S_0 is the stock price, r is the risk-free interest rate, and $r > 0$. (*Hint*: To obtain the first half of the inequality, consider possible values of

Portfolio A: a European call option plus an amount X invested at the risk-free rate

Portfolio B: an American put option plus e^{-qT} of stock, with dividends being reinvested in the stock

To obtain the second half of the inequality, consider possible values of

Portfolio C: an American call option plus an amount $Xe^{-r(T-t)}$ invested at the risk-free rate

Portfolio D: a European put option plus one stock, with dividends being reinvested in the stock)

12.20. Show that if C is the price of an American call option on a futures contract when the strike price is X and the maturity is T, and P is the price of an American put on the same futures contract with the same strike price and exercise date,

$$F_0 e^{-rT} - X \le C - P \le F_0 - Xe^{-rT}$$

where F_0 is the futures price and r is the risk-free rate. Assume that $r > 0$ and that there is no difference between forward and futures contracts. (*Hint:* Use an analogous approach to that indicated for Problem 12.19.)

12.21. If the price of currency A expressed in terms of the price of currency B follows the process

$$dS = (r_B - r_A)dt + \sigma \, dz$$

where r_A is the risk-free interest rate in currency A and r_B is the risk-free interest rate in currency B. What is the process followed by the price of currency B expressed in terms of currency A?

12.22. Would you expect the volatility of a stock index to be greater or less than the volatility of a typical stock? Explain your answer.

12.23. Does the cost of portfolio insurance increase or decrease as the beta of the portfolio increases? Explain your answer.

12.24. Suppose that a portfolio is worth $60 million and the S&P 500 is at 1200. If the value of the portfolio mirrors the value of the index, what options should be purchased to provide protection against the value of the portfolio falling below $54 million in one year's time?

12.25. Consider again the situation in Problem 12.24. Suppose that the portfolio has a beta of 2.0, that the risk-free interest rate is 5% per annum, and that the dividend yield on both the portfolio and the index is 3% per annum. What options should be purchased to provide protection against the value of the portfolio falling below $54 million in one year's time?

12.26. Show that the put–call parity relationship for European index options is

$$c + Xe^{-rT} = p + S_0 e^{-qT}$$

where q is the dividend yield on the index, c is the price of a European call option, p is the price of a European put option, and both options have strike price X and maturity T.

12.27. Suppose you buy a put option contract on October gold futures with a strike price of $400 per ounce. Each contract is for the delivery of 100 ounces. What happens if you exercise when the October futures price is $377 and the most recent settlement price is $380?

12.28. Suppose you sell a call option contract on April live-cattle futures with a strike price of 70 cents per pound. Each contract is for the delivery of 40,000 pounds. What happens if the contract is exercised when the futures price is 76 cents and the most recent settlement price is 75 cents?

12.29. Consider a two-month call futures option with a strike price of 40 when the risk-free interest rate is 10% per annum. The current futures price is 47. What is a lower bound for the value of the futures option if it is (a) European and (b) American?

12.30. Consider a four-month put futures option with a strike price of 50 when the risk-free interest rate is 10% per annum. The current futures price is 47. What is a lower bound for the value of the futures option if it is (a) European and (b) American?

12.31. A futures price is currently 60. It is known that over each of the next two three-month periods it will either rise by 10% or fall by 10%. The risk-free interest rate is 8% per annum. What is the value of a six-month European call option on the futures with a strike price of 60? If the call were American, would it ever be worth exercising it early?

12.32. In Problem 12.31, what is the value of a six-month European put option on futures with a strike price of 60? If the put were American, would it ever be worth exercising it early? Verify that the call prices calculated in Problem 12.31 and the put prices calculated here satisfy put–call parity relationships.

12.33. A futures price is currently 25, its volatility is 30% per annum, and the risk-free interest rate is 10% per annum. What is the value of a nine-month European call on the futures with a strike price of 26?

12.34. A futures price is currently 70, its volatility is 20% per annum, and the risk-free interest rate is 6% per annum. What is the value of a five-month European put on the futures with a strike price of 65?

12.35. Suppose that a futures price is currently 35. A European call option and a European put option on the futures with a strike price of 34 are both priced at 2 in the market. The risk-free interest rate is 10% per annum. Identify an arbitrage opportunity. Both options have one year to maturity.

12.36. "The price of an at-the-money European call futures option always equals the price of a similar at-the-money European put futures option." Explain why this statement is true.

12.37. Suppose that a futures price is currently 30. The risk-free interest rate is 5% per annum. A three-month American call futures option with a strike price of 28 is worth 4. Calculate bounds for the price of a three-month American put futures option with a strike price of 28.

12.38. Consider
   (a) A call CAP on the S&P 500 (traded on the CBOT) with a strike price of 300 (see section 12.3 for a discussion of this instrument).
   (b) A bull spread created from European calls on the S&P 500 with strike prices of 300 and 330 and the same maturity as the CAP.

   What is the difference between the two? Which is worth more?

12.39. Can an option on the yen–euro exchange rate be created from two options, one on the dollar–euro exchange rate and the other on the dollar–yen exchange rate? Explain your answer.

ASSIGNMENT QUESTIONS

12.40. A futures price is currently 40. It is known that at the end of three months the price will be either 35 or 45. What is the value of a three-month European call option on the futures with a strike price of 42 if the risk-free interest rate is 7% per annum?

12.41. A stock index currently stands at 300. It is expected to increase or decrease by 10% over each of the next two time periods of three months. The risk-free interest rate is 8% and the dividend yield on the index is 3%. What is the value of a six-month put option on the index with a strike price of 300 if it is (a) European and (b) American?

12.42. Suppose that the spot price of the Canadian dollar is U.S. $0.75 and that the Canadian dollar–U.S. dollar exchange rate has a volatility of 4% per annum. The risk-free rates of interest in Canada and the United States are 9% and 7% per annum, respectively. Calculate the value of a European call option to buy one Canadian dollar for U.S. $0.75 in nine months. Use put-call parity to calculate the price of a European put option to sell one Canadian dollar for U.S. $0.75 in nine months. What is the price of an option to buy U.S. $0.75 with one Canadian dollar in nine months?

12.43. Calculate the implied volatility of soybean futures prices from the following information concerning a European put on soybean futures:

Current futures price	525
Exercise price	525
Risk-free rate	6% per annum
Time to maturity	5 months
Put price	20

12.44. A mutual fund announces that the salaries of its fund managers will depend on the performance of the fund. If the fund loses money, the salaries will be zero. If the fund makes a profit, the salaries will be proportional to the profit. Describe the salary of a fund manager as an option. How is a fund manager motivated to behave with this type of remuneration package?

Derivation of Differential Equation Satisfied by a Derivative Dependent on a Stock Providing a Continuous Dividend Yield

Define f as the price of a derivative dependent on a stock that provides a continuous dividend yield at rate q. We suppose that the stock price, S, follows the process

$$dS = \mu S\,dt + \sigma S\,dz$$

where dz is a Wiener process. The variables μ and σ are the expected proportional growth rate in the stock price and the volatility of the stock price, respectively. Because the stock price provides a continuous dividend yield, μ is only part of the expected return on the stock.[4]

Because f is a function of S and t, it follows from Ito's lemma that

$$df = \left(\frac{\partial f}{\partial S}\mu S + \frac{\partial f}{\partial t} + \frac{1}{2}\frac{\partial^2 f}{\partial S^2}\sigma^2 S^2\right)dt + \frac{\partial f}{\partial S}\sigma S\,dz$$

Similarly to the procedure of section 11.5, we can set up a portfolio consisting of

$$-1: \quad \text{derivative}$$
$$+\frac{\partial f}{\partial S}: \quad \text{stock}$$

If Π is the value of the portfolio,

$$\Pi = -f + \frac{\partial f}{\partial S}S \tag{12A.1}$$

and the change, $\Delta\Pi$, in the value of the portfolio in a time period Δt is as given by equation (11.14):

$$\Delta\Pi = \left(-\frac{\partial f}{\partial t} - \frac{1}{2}\frac{\partial^2 f}{\partial S^2}\sigma^2 S^2\right)\Delta t$$

---

[4]From equation (12.6), $\mu = r - q$ in a risk-neutral world.

303

In time Δt the holder of the portfolio earns capital gains equal to $\Delta\Pi$ and dividends on the stock position equal to

$$qS\frac{\partial f}{\partial S}\Delta t$$

Define ΔW as the change in the wealth of the portfolio holder in time Δt. It follows that

$$\Delta W = \left(-\frac{\partial f}{\partial t} - \frac{1}{2}\frac{\partial^2 f}{\partial S^2}\sigma^2 S^2 + qS\frac{\partial f}{\partial S}\right)\Delta t \qquad (12A.2)$$

Because this expression is independent of the Wiener process, the portfolio is instantaneously riskless. Hence

$$\Delta W = r\Pi\,\Delta t \qquad (12A.3)$$

Substituting from equations (12A.1) and (12A.2) into equation (12A.3) gives

$$\left(-\frac{\partial f}{\partial t} - \frac{1}{2}\frac{\partial^2 f}{\partial S^2}\sigma^2 S^2 + qS\frac{\partial f}{\partial S}\right)\Delta t = r\left(-f + \frac{\partial f}{\partial S}S\right)\Delta t$$

so that

$$\frac{\partial f}{\partial t} + (r - q)S\frac{\partial f}{\partial S} + \frac{1}{2}\sigma^2 S^2\frac{\partial^2 f}{\partial S^2} = rf \qquad (12A.4)$$

This is the differential equation that must be satisfied by f.

Derivation of Differential Equation Satisfied by a Derivative Dependent on a Futures Price

Suppose that the futures price F follows the process

$$dF = \mu F\, dt + \sigma F\, dz \qquad (12B.1)$$

where dz is a Wiener process and σ is constant.[5] Because f is a function of F and t, it follows from Ito's lemma that

$$df = \left(\frac{\partial f}{\partial F}\mu F + \frac{\partial f}{\partial t} + \frac{1}{2}\frac{\partial^2 f}{\partial F^2}\sigma^2 F^2\right)dt + \frac{\partial f}{\partial F}\sigma F\, dz \qquad (12B.2)$$

Consider a portfolio consisting of

$$-1: \quad \text{derivative}$$
$$+\frac{\partial f}{\partial F}: \quad \text{futures contracts}$$

Define Π as the value of the portfolio and let $\Delta\Pi$, Δf, and ΔF be the change in Π, f, and F in time Δt, respectively. Because it costs nothing to enter into a futures contract,

$$\Pi = -f \qquad (12B.3)$$

In a time period Δt, the holder of the portfolio earns capital gains equal to $-\Delta f$ from the derivative and income of

$$\frac{\partial f}{\partial F}\Delta F$$

from the futures contract. Define ΔW as the total change in wealth of the portfolio holder in time Δt. It follows that

$$\Delta W = \frac{\partial f}{\partial F}\Delta F - \Delta f$$

The discrete versions of equations (12B.1) and (12B.2) are

$$\Delta F = \mu F\,\Delta t + \sigma F\,\Delta z$$

---

[5]From the arguments in section 12.7, $\mu = 0$ in a risk-neutral world.

and

$$\Delta f = \left(\frac{\partial f}{\partial F}\mu F + \frac{\partial f}{\partial t} + \frac{1}{2}\frac{\partial^2 f}{\partial F^2}\sigma^2 F^2\right)\Delta t + \frac{\partial f}{\partial F}\sigma F\,\Delta z$$

where $\Delta z = \epsilon\sqrt{\Delta t}$ and ϵ is a random sample from a standardized normal distribution. It follows that

$$\Delta W = \left(-\frac{\partial f}{\partial t} - \frac{1}{2}\frac{\partial^2 f}{\partial F^2}\sigma^2 F^2\right)\Delta t \qquad (12\text{B}.4)$$

This is riskless. Hence it must also be true that

$$\Delta W = r\Pi\,\Delta t \qquad (12\text{B}.5)$$

If we substitute for Π from equation (12B.3), equations (12B.4) and (12B.5) give

$$\left(-\frac{\partial f}{\partial t} - \frac{1}{2}\frac{\partial^2 f}{\partial F^2}\sigma^2 F^2\right)\Delta t = -rf\,\Delta t$$

Hence

$$\frac{\partial f}{\partial t} + \frac{1}{2}\frac{\partial^2 f}{\partial F^2}\sigma^2 F^2 = rf$$

This has the same form as equation (12A.4) with q set equal to r. We deduce that a futures price can be treated in the same way as a stock providing a dividend yield at rate r for the purpose of valuing derivatives.

CHAPTER 13

THE GREEK LETTERS

A financial institution that sells an option or other derivative to a client in the over-the-counter markets is faced with the problem of managing its risk. If the option happens to be the same as one that is traded on an exchange, the financial institution can neutralize its exposure by buying on the exchange the same option as it has sold. But, when the option has been tailored to the needs of a client and does not correspond to the standardized products traded by exchanges, hedging the exposure is far more difficult.

In this chapter we discuss some of the alternative approaches to this problem. We cover what are commonly referred to as the "Greek letters" or simply the "Greeks." Each Greek letter measures a different dimension of the risk in an option position and the aim of a trader is to manage the Greeks so that all risks are acceptable. The analysis presented here is applicable to market makers in options on an exchange as well as to traders working for financial institutions.

Toward the end of the chapter, we consider the creation of options synthetically. This turns out to be very closely related to the hedging of options. This is because creating an option position synthetically is essentially the same task as hedging the opposite option position. For example, creating a long call option synthetically is the same as hedging a short position in the call option.

13.1 EXAMPLE

The next few sections use as an example the position of a financial institution that has sold for $300,000 a European call option on 100,000 shares of a non-dividend-paying stock. We assume that the stock price is $49, the strike price is $50, the risk-free interest rate is 5% per annum, the stock price volatility is 20% per annum, the time to maturity is 20 weeks (0.3846 years), and the expected return from the stock is 13% per annum.[1] With our usual notation, this means that

$$S_0 = 49, \; X = 50, \; r = 0.05, \; \sigma = 0.20, \; T = 0.3846, \; \mu = 0.13$$

---

[1] As shown in chapter 11, the expected return is irrelevant to the pricing of an option. It is given here because it can have some bearing on the effectiveness of a hedging scheme.

The Black–Scholes price of the option is about $240,000. The financial institution has, therefore, sold the option for $60,000 more than its theoretical value. It is faced with the problem of hedging its exposure.[2]

13.2 NAKED AND COVERED POSITIONS

One strategy open to the financial institution is to do nothing. This is sometimes referred to as adopting a *naked position*. It is a strategy that works well if the stock price is below $50 at the end of the 20 weeks. The option then costs the financial institution nothing and it makes a profit of $300,000. A naked position does not work as well if the call is exercised because the financial institution must then buy 100,000 shares at the prevailing market price in 20 weeks to cover the call. The cost to the financial institution is 100,000 times the amount by which the stock price exceeds the strike price. For example, if after 20 weeks the stock price is $60, the option costs the financial institution $1,000,000. This is considerably greater than the $300,000 premium received.

As an alternative to a naked position, the financial institution can adopt a *covered position*. This involves buying 100,000 shares as soon as the option has been sold. If the option is exercised, this strategy works well, but in other circumstances it could lead to a significant loss. For example, if the stock price drops to $40, the financial institution loses $900,000 on its stock position. This is considerably greater than the $300,000 charged for the option.[3]

Neither a naked position nor a covered position provides a satisfactory hedge. If the assumptions underlying the Black–Scholes formula hold, the cost to the financial institution should always be $240,000 on average for both approaches.[4] But on any one occasion, the cost is liable to range from zero to over $1,000,000. A perfect hedge would ensure that the cost is always $240,000. For a perfect hedge, the standard deviation of the cost of writing the option and hedging it is zero.

13.3 A STOP-LOSS STRATEGY

One hedging idea that is sometimes proposed involves what is known as a *stop-loss strategy*. To illustrate the basic idea, consider an institution that has written a European call option with strike price, X, to buy one unit of a stock. The hedging scheme

---

[2]Financial institutions do not normally write call options on individual stocks. However, a call option on a stock is a convenient example with which to develop our ideas. The points that will be made apply to other types of options and to other derivatives.

[3]Put–call parity shows that the exposure from writing a covered call is the same as the exposure from writing a naked put.

[4]More precisely, the present value of the expected cost is $240,000 for both approaches assuming that appropriate risk-adjusted discount rates are used.

involves buying the stock as soon as its price rises above X, and selling as soon as it falls below X. The objective is to hold a naked position whenever the stock price is less than X and a covered position whenever the stock price is greater than X. The scheme is designed to ensure that the institution owns the stock at time T if the option closes in the money and that it does not own the stock if the option closes out of the money. It appears to produce payoffs that are the same as the payoffs on the option. In the situation illustrated in Figure 13.1, the stop-loss strategy involves buying the stock at time t_1, selling it at time t_2, buying it at time t_3, selling it at time t_4, buying it at time t_5, and delivering it at time T.

The cost of setting up the hedge at time zero is the stock price, S_0, if $S_0 > X$ and zero otherwise. At first blush, the total cost, Q, of writing and hedging the option would appear to be given by

$$Q = \max[S_0 - X, 0] \tag{13.1}$$

because all purchases and sales subsequent to time zero are made at price X. If this were correct, the hedging scheme would work perfectly in the absence of transactions costs. Furthermore, the cost of hedging the option would always equal the intrinsic value of the option, which is less than its Black–Scholes price. Thus, one could earn riskless profits by writing options and hedging them.

There are two basic reasons why equation (13.1) is incorrect. The first is that the cash flows to the hedger occur at different times and must be discounted. The second is that purchases and sales cannot be made at exactly the same price, X. This second point is critical. If we assume a risk-neutral world with zero interest rates, we can justify ignoring the time value of money. But, we cannot legitimately assume that both purchases and sales are made at the same price. If markets are efficient, the

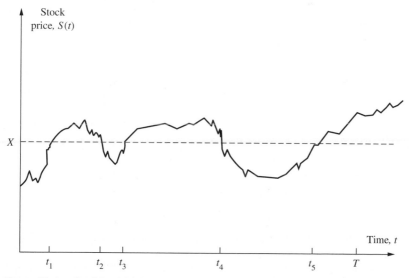

Figure 13.1   Stop-loss strategy.

Table 13.1   Performance of Stop-Loss Strategy

The performance measure is the ratio of standard deviation of cost of writing the option and hedging it to theoretical price of option.

Δt (weeks)	5	4	2	1	0.5	0.25
Performance Measure	1.02	0.93	0.82	0.77	0.76	0.76

hedger cannot know when the stock price equals X, whether it will continue to be above or below X.

As a practical matter, purchases must be made at $X + \delta$ and sales must be made at $X - \delta$, for some positive δ. Thus, every purchase and subsequent sale includes a cost (apart from transactions costs) of 2δ. A natural response to this on the part of the hedger is to reduce δ. Assuming that stock prices change continuously, δ can be made arbitrarily small by monitoring the prices closely. However, as δ is made smaller, the expected number of trades increases. The cost per trade is reduced, but this is offset by an increase in the expected frequency of trading. As $\delta \longrightarrow 0$, the expected number of trades tends to infinity.[5]

The stop-loss strategy, although superficially attractive, does not work particularly well as a hedging scheme. Consider, for example, its use for an out-of-the-money option. If the stock price never reaches the strike price, X, the hedging scheme costs nothing. If the path of the stock price crosses the strike price level many times, the scheme is quite expensive. Monte Carlo simulation can be used to assess the overall performance of the scheme. Table 13.1 shows the results for the option considered in section 13.1. It assumes that the stock price is observed at the end of time intervals of length Δt.[6] The hedge performance measure is the ratio of the standard deviation of the cost of writing the option and hedging it to the Black–Scholes price of the option. Each result is based on 1,000 sample paths for the stock price and has a standard error of about 2%. It appears to be impossible to produce a performance measure for the scheme that is below 0.70 regardless of how small Δt is made.

13.4   DELTA HEDGING

Most traders use more sophisticated hedging schemes than those mentioned so far. These involve calculating measures such as delta, gamma, and vega. In this section, we consider the role played by delta.

The *delta* of an option, Δ, was introduced in chapter 9. It is defined as the rate of change of the option price with respect to the price of the underlying asset. It is the

---

[5]Note the connection between this and the point made in section 10.2 that the expected number of times a Wiener process equals any particular value in any time interval is infinite.

[6]The precise hedging rule used was as follows. If the stock price moves from below X to above X in a time interval of length Δt, it is bought at the end of the interval. If it moves from above X to below X in the time interval, it is sold at the end of the interval. Otherwise, no action is taken.

slope of the curve that relates the option price to the underlying asset price. Suppose that the delta of a call option on a stock is 0.6. This means that when the stock price changes by a small amount, the option price changes by about 60% of that amount. Figure 13.2 shows the relationship between a call price and the underlying stock price. When the stock price corresponds to point A, the option price corresponds to point B, and Δ is the gradient indicated. Expressed mathematically, delta is the partial derivative of the call price with respect to underlying asset price

$$\Delta = \frac{\partial c}{\partial S} \qquad (13.2)$$

Suppose that in Figure 13.2, the stock price is $100 and the option price is $10. Imagine an investor who has sold 20 option contracts—that is, options to buy 2,000 shares. The investor's position could be hedged by buying $0.6 \times 2,000 = 1,200$ shares. The gain (loss) on the option position would then tend to be offset by the loss (gain) on the stock position. For example, if the stock price goes up by $1 (producing a gain of $1,200 on the shares purchased), the option price will tend to go up by $0.6 \times \$1 = \$0.60$ (producing a loss of $1,200 on the options written); if the stock price goes down by $1 (producing a loss of $1,200 on the shares purchased), the option price will tend to go down by $0.60 (producing a gain of $1,200 on the options written).

In this example, the delta of the investor's option position is $0.6 \times (-2,000) = -1,200$. In other words, the investor loses $1,200\Delta S$ on the short option position when the stock price increases by ΔS. The delta of the stock is 1.0 and the long position in 1,200 shares has a delta of +1,200. The delta of the investor's overall position is, therefore, zero. The delta of the stock position offsets the delta of the option position. A position with a delta of zero is referred to as being *delta neutral*.

It is important to realize that, because delta changes, the investor's position remains delta hedged (or delta neutral) for only a relatively short period of time. The hedge has to be adjusted periodically. This is known as *rebalancing*. In our example, by the end of three days the stock price might have increased to $110. From Figure 13.2, it can be seen that an increase in the stock price leads to an increase in delta.

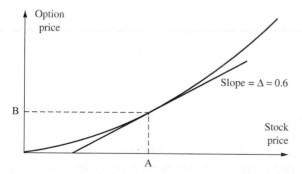

Figure 13.2　Calculation of delta.

Suppose that delta increased from 0.60 to 0.65. An extra $0.05 \times 2,000 = 100$ shares would then have to be purchased to maintain the hedge.

The delta-hedging scheme just described is an example of a *dynamic hedging scheme*. This scheme requires the hedge position to be adjusted periodically. Dynamic hedging can be contrasted with *static hedging,* where the hedge, once set up, is never adjusted. Static hedging schemes are sometimes also referred to as *hedge-and-forget schemes.*

Delta is closely related to the Black–Scholes analysis. Black and Scholes showed that it is possible to set up a riskless portfolio consisting of a position in a derivative on a stock and a position in the stock. Expressed in terms of Δ, their portfolio is

$$-1 : \quad \text{derivative}$$
$$+\Delta : \quad \text{shares of the stock}$$

Using our new terminology, we can say that Black and Scholes valued options by setting up a delta-neutral position and arguing that the return on the position in a short period of time equals the risk-free interest rate.

Delta of Forward Contracts

The concept of delta can be applied to other derivatives besides options. For any derivative whose price, f, depends on S

$$\Delta = \frac{\partial f}{\partial S}$$

Consider a forward contract on a non-dividend-paying stock. Equation (3.9) shows that when the price of the stock changes by ΔS, and all else remains the same, the value of a forward contract on the stock also changes by ΔS. The delta of a forward contract on one share of a non-dividend-paying stock is, therefore, always 1.0. Thus, a short forward contract on one share can be hedged by purchasing one share, whereas a long forward contract on one share can be hedged by shorting one share. These are hedge-and-forget schemes. Because delta is always 1.0, no changes need to be made to the position in the stock during the life of the contract.

Deltas of European Calls and Puts

For a European call option on a non-dividend-paying stock, it can be shown from the Black–Scholes formulas that

$$\Delta = N(d_1)$$

where d_1 is defined as in equation (11.20). Using delta hedging for a short position in a European call option, therefore, involves keeping a long position of $N(d_1)$ shares at any given time. Similarly, using delta hedging for a long position in a European call option involves maintaining a short position of $N(d_1)$ shares at any given time.

For a European put option on a non-dividend-paying stock, it can be shown from the Black–Scholes formulas that delta is given by

$$\Delta = N(d_1) - 1$$

This is negative, which means that a long position in a put option should be hedged with a long position in the underlying stock, and a short position in a put option should be hedged with a short position in the underlying stock. The variation of the delta of a call option and a put option with the stock price is shown in Figure 13.3. Figure 13.4 shows typical patterns for the variation of delta with time to maturity for at-the-money, in-the-money, and out-of-the-money options.

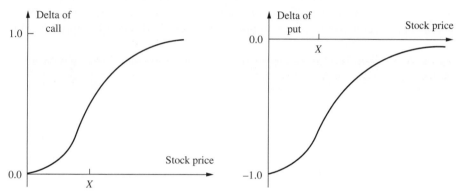

Figure 13.3   Variation of delta with the stock price for a call option and a put option on a non-dividend-paying stock.

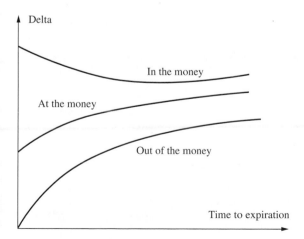

Figure 13.4   Typical patterns for variation of delta with the time to maturity for a call option.

Simulations

Tables 13.2 and 13.3 provide two simulations of the operation of delta hedging for the example in section 13.1. The hedge is assumed to be adjusted or rebalanced weekly. The initial value of delta is calculated from $S_0 = 49$, $X = 50$, $r = 5\%$, $\sigma = 20\%$, and $T = 20$ weeks and is equal to 0.522. This means that as soon as the option is written, \$2,557,800 must be borrowed to buy 52,200 shares at a price of \$49. Because the interest rate is 5%, interest costs totaling \$2,500 are incurred in the first week.

In Table 13.2, the stock price falls to $48\frac{1}{8}$ by the end of the first week. Delta is recomputed at the end of the first week using $S_0 = 48\frac{1}{8}$, $X = 50$, $r = 5\%$, $\sigma = 20\%$, and $T = 19$ weeks and is equal to 0.458. A total of 6,400 shares must be sold to maintain the hedge. This realizes \$308,000 in cash and the cumulative borrowings at the end of week one are reduced to \$2,252,300. During the second week the stock price reduces to $47\frac{3}{8}$ and delta declines again; and so on. Toward the end of the life of the option it becomes apparent that the option will be exercised and delta approaches 1.0.

Table 13.2 Simulation of Delta Hedging; Option Closes in the Money; Cost of Option to Writer = $263,400

Week	Stock Price	Delta	Shares Purchased	Cost of Shares Purchased (Thousands of Dollars)	Cumulative Cost (Incl. Interest, in Thousands of Dollars	Interest Cost (Thousands of Dollars)
0	49	0.522	52,200	2,557.8	2,557.8	2.5
1	$48\frac{1}{8}$	0.458	(6,400)	(308.0)	2,252.3	2.2
2	$47\frac{3}{8}$	0.400	(5,800)	(274.8)	1,979.7	1.9
3	$50\frac{1}{4}$	0.596	19,600	984.9	2,966.5	2.9
4	$51\frac{3}{4}$	0.693	9,700	502.0	3,471.3	3.3
5	$53\frac{1}{8}$	0.774	8,100	430.3	3,904.9	3.8
6	53	0.771	(300)	(15.9)	3,892.8	3.7
7	$51\frac{7}{8}$	0.706	(6,500)	(337.2)	3,559.3	3.4
8	$51\frac{3}{8}$	0.674	(3,200)	(164.4)	3,398.4	3.3
9	53	0.787	11,300	598.9	4,000.5	3.8
10	$49\frac{7}{8}$	0.550	(23,700)	(1,182.0)	2,822.3	2.7
11	$48\frac{1}{2}$	0.413	(13,700)	(664.4)	2,160.6	2.1
12	$49\frac{7}{8}$	0.542	12,900	643.4	2,806.1	2.7
13	$50\frac{3}{8}$	0.591	4,900	246.8	3,055.6	2.9
14	$52\frac{1}{8}$	0.768	17,700	922.6	3,981.2	3.8
15	$51\frac{7}{8}$	0.759	(900)	(46.7)	3,938.3	3.8
16	$52\frac{7}{8}$	0.865	10,600	560.5	4,502.6	4.3
17	$54\frac{7}{8}$	0.978	11,300	620.1	5,127.0	4.9
18	$54\frac{5}{8}$	0.990	1,200	65.6	5,197.5	5.0
19	$55\frac{7}{8}$	1.000	1,000	55.9	5,258.3	5.1
20	$57\frac{1}{4}$	1.000	0	0.0	5,263.4	

By week 20, therefore, the hedger has a fully covered position. The hedger receives $5,000,000 for the stock held, so that the total cost of writing the option and hedging it is $263,400.

Table 13.3 illustrates an alternative sequence of events such that the option closes out of the money. As it becomes progressively clearer that the option will not be exercised, delta approaches zero. By week 20 the hedger has a naked position and has incurred costs totaling $256,600.

In Tables 13.2 and 13.3, the costs of hedging the option, when discounted to the beginning of the period, are close to but not exactly the same as the Black–Scholes price of $240,000. If the hedging scheme worked perfectly, the cost of hedging would, after discounting, be exactly equal to the theoretical price of the option on every simulation. The reason that there is a variation in the cost of delta hedging is that the hedge is rebalanced only once a week. As rebalancing takes place more frequently, the uncertainty in the cost of hedging is reduced. Of course, the simulations in Tables

Table 13.3 Simulation of Delta Hedging; Option Closes out of the Money; Cost of Option to Writer = $256,600

Week	Stock Price	Delta	Shares Purchased	Cost of Shares Purchased (Thousands of Dollars)	Cumulative Cost (Incl. Interest, in Thousands of Dollars	Interest Cost (Thousands of Dollars)
0	49	0.522	52,200	2,557.8	2,557.8	2.5
1	$49\frac{3}{4}$	0.568	4,600	228.9	2,789.1	2.7
2	52	0.705	13,700	712.4	3,504.2	3.4
3	50	0.579	(12,600)	(630.0)	2,877.6	2.8
4	$48\frac{3}{8}$	0.459	(12,000)	(580.5)	2,299.8	2.2
5	$48\frac{1}{4}$	0.443	(1,600)	(77.2)	2,224.8	2.1
6	$48\frac{3}{4}$	0.475	3,200	156.0	2,383.0	2.3
7	$49\frac{5}{8}$	0.540	6,500	322.6	2,707.8	2.6
8	$48\frac{1}{4}$	0.420	(12,000)	(579.0)	2,131.4	2.0
9	$48\frac{1}{4}$	0.410	(1,000)	(48.2)	2,085.2	2.0
10	$51\frac{1}{8}$	0.658	24,800	1,267.9	3,355.1	3.2
11	$51\frac{1}{2}$	0.692	3,400	175.1	3,533.5	3.4
12	$49\frac{7}{8}$	0.542	(15,000)	(748.1)	2,788.7	2.7
13	$49\frac{7}{8}$	0.538	(400)	(20.0)	2,771.5	2.7
14	$48\frac{3}{4}$	0.400	(13,800)	(672.7)	2,101.4	2.0
15	$47\frac{1}{2}$	0.236	(16,400)	(779.0)	1,324.4	1.3
16	48	0.261	2,500	120.0	1,445.7	1.4
17	$46\frac{1}{4}$	0.062	(19,900)	(920.4)	526.7	0.5
18	$48\frac{1}{8}$	0.183	12,100	582.3	1,109.5	1.1
19	$46\frac{5}{8}$	0.007	(17,600)	(820.6)	290.0	0.3
20	$48\frac{1}{8}$	0.000	(700)	(33.7)	256.6	

13.2 and 13.3 are idealized in that they assume that the volatility is constant and that there are no transactions costs.

Table 13.4 shows statistics on the performance of delta hedging from 1,000 simulations of stock price movements for our example. As in Table 13.1, the performance measure is the ratio of the standard deviation of the cost of writing the option and hedging it to the Black–Scholes price of the option. It is clear that delta hedging is a great improvement over the stop-loss strategy. Unlike the stop-loss strategy, the performance of delta hedging gets steadily better as the hedge is monitored more frequently.

Delta hedging aims to keep the total wealth of the financial institution as unchanged as possible. Initially, the value of the written option is $240,000. In the situation depicted in Table 13.2, the value of the option can be calculated as $414,500 on week nine. Thus, the financial institution has lost $174,500 on its option position between week 0 and week 9. Its cash position, as measured by the cumulative cost, is $1,442,700 worse in week 9 than in week 0. The value of the shares held has increased from $2,557,800 to $4,171,100 between week 0 and week 9. The net effect of all this is that the overall wealth of the financial institution has changed by only $3,900 during the nine-week period.

Where the Cost Comes From

The delta-hedging scheme in Tables 13.2 and 13.3, in effect, creates a long position in the option synthetically. This neutralizes the short position arising from the written option. The scheme generally involves selling stock just after the price goes down and buying stock just after the price goes up. It might be termed a buy high, sell low scheme! The cost of $240,000 comes from the average difference between the price paid for the stock and the price realized for it.

Delta of Other European Options

For European call options on a stock index paying a dividend yield q,

$$\Delta = e^{-qT} N(d_1)$$

where d_1 is defined in equation (12.4). For European put options on the stock index,

$$\Delta = e^{-qT} [N(d_1) - 1]$$

Table 13.4   Performance of Delta Hedging

The performance measure is the ratio of standard deviation of cost of writing the option and hedging it to theoretical price of option

Time Between Hedge Rebalancing (Weeks)	5	4	2	1	0.5	0.25
Performance measure	0.43	0.39	0.26	0.19	0.14	0.09

For European call options on a currency,

$$\Delta = e^{-r_f T} N(d_1)$$

where r_f is the foreign risk-free interest rate and d_1 is defined as in equation (12.9), and for European put options on a currency,

$$\Delta = e^{-r_f T}[N(d_1) - 1]$$

For European futures call options,

$$\Delta = e^{-rT} N(d_1)$$

where d_1 is defined as in equation (12.17), and for European futures put options,

$$\Delta = e^{-rT}[N(d_1) - 1]$$

Example 13.1   A bank has written a six-month European option to sell £1,000,000 at an exchange rate of 1.6000. Suppose that the current exchange rate is 1.6200, the risk-free interest rate in the United Kingdom is 13% per annum, the risk-free interest rate in the United States is 10% per annum, and the volatility of sterling is 15%. In this case, $S_0 = 1.6200$, $X = 1.6000$, $r = 0.10$, $r_f = 0.13$, $\sigma = 0.15$, and $T = 0.5$. The delta of a put option on a currency is

$$[N(d_1) - 1]e^{-r_f T}$$

where d_1 is given by equation (12.9).

$$d_1 = 0.0287$$
$$N(d_1) = 0.5115$$

The delta of the put option is, therefore, $(0.5115 - 1)e^{-0.13 \times 0.5} = -0.458$. This is the delta of a long position in one put option. (It means that for small exchange rate changes the price of the put goes down by 45.8% of the increase in the value of the currency.) The delta of the bank's total short position is $-1,000,000 \times 0.458$ or $+458,000$. Delta hedging, therefore, requires that a short sterling position of £458,000 be set up initially. This short sterling position has a delta of $-458,000$ and neutralizes the delta of the option position. As time passes, the short position must be changed.

Using Futures

In practice, delta hedging is often carried out using a position in futures rather than one in the underlying asset. The contract used does not have to mature at the same time as the derivative. Define:

T^*: Maturity of futures contract.
H_A: Position in asset at time zero for delta hedging.
H_F: Required position in futures contracts at time zero for delta hedging.

If the underlying asset is a non-dividend-paying stock, the futures price, F_0, at time zero is from equation (3.5) given by

$$F_0 = S_0 e^{rT^*}$$

When the stock price increases by ΔS, the futures price increases by $\Delta S e^{rT^*}$. The delta of the futures contract is, therefore, e^{rT^*}. Thus, e^{-rT^*} futures contracts have the same sensitivity to stock price movements as one share of the stock. Hence,

$$H_F = e^{-rT^*} H_A$$

When the underlying asset is a stock or stock index paying a dividend yield q, a similar argument shows that

$$H_F = e^{-(r-q)T^*} H_A \tag{13.3}$$

When it is a currency

$$H_F = e^{-(r-r_f)T^*} H_A \tag{13.4}$$

Example 13.2   Consider again the option in Example 13.1. Suppose that the bank decides to hedge using nine-month currency futures contracts. In this case $T^* = 0.75$ and

$$e^{-(r-r_f)T^*} = 1.0228$$

so that the short position in currency futures required for delta hedging is $1.0228 \times 458,000 = £468,442$. Because each futures contract is for the purchase or sale of £62,500, this means that (to the nearest whole number) seven contracts should be shorted.

Futures versus Forwards

It is interesting to note that the delta of a futures contract is different from the delta of the corresponding forward. This is true even when interest rates are constant and the forward price equals the futures price. Consider the situation where the underlying asset is a non-dividend-paying stock. The delta of a futures contract on one unit of the asset is e^{rT^*}, whereas the delta of a forward contract on one unit of the asset is, as previously discussed, 1.0.

Delta of a Portfolio

The delta of an options portfolio dependent on a single asset whose price is S is

$$\frac{\partial \Pi}{\partial S}$$

where Π is the value of the portfolio.

The delta of the portfolio can be calculated from the deltas of the individual options in the portfolio. If a portfolio consists of an amount, w_i, of option i ($1 \le i \le n$), the delta of the portfolio is given by

$$\Delta = \sum_{i=1}^{n} w_i \Delta_i$$

where Δ_i is the delta of ith option. The formula can be used to calculate the position in the underlying asset, or in a futures contract on the underlying asset, necessary to carry out delta hedging. When this position is taken, the delta of the portfolio, including the new position in the underlying asset, is zero so that the portfolio is delta neutral.

Suppose a financial institution in the United States has the following three positions in options on the Australian dollar:

1. A long position in 100,000 call options with a strike price 0.55 and an expiration date in three months. The delta of each option is 0.533.
2. A short position in 200,000 call options with a strike price 0.56 and an expiration date in five months. The delta of each option is 0.468.
3. A short position in 50,000 put options with a strike price 0.56 and an expiration date in two months. The delta of each option is -0.508.

The delta of the whole portfolio is

$$0.533 \times 100,000 - 200,000 \times 0.468 - 50,000 \times (-0.508) = -14,900$$

This means that the portfolio can be made delta neutral with a long position of 14,900 Australian dollars.

A six-month forward contract could also be used to achieve delta neutrality in this example. Suppose that the risk-free rate of interest is 8% per annum in Australia and 5% in the United States ($r = 0.05$ and $r_f = 0.08$.) From equation (3.11) with $q = r_f$, the delta of the forward contract maturing at time T on one Australian dollar is $e^{-r_f T}$, or $e^{-0.08 \times 0.5} = 0.9608$. The long position in Australian dollar forward contracts for delta neutrality is, therefore, $14,900/0.9608 = 15,508$.

Another alternative is to use a six-month futures contract. From equation (13.4), the long position in Australian dollar futures contracts for delta neutrality is

$$14,900 e^{-(0.05-0.08) \times 0.5} = 15,125$$

Transactions Costs

Maintaining a delta-neutral position in a single option and the underlying asset, in the way just described, is liable to be prohibitively expensive because of the transactions costs incurred on trades. For a large portfolio of options, delta neutrality is more feasible. Only one trade in the underlying asset is necessary to zero out delta for the whole portfolio. The hedging transactions costs are absorbed by the profits on many different trades.

13.5 THETA

The *theta* of a portfolio of derivatives, Θ, is the rate of change of the portfolio value with respect to the passage of time when all else remains the same. Equivalently, it is the rate of change of the portfolio value with respect to a decrease in the times to maturity of the derivatives in the portfolio.

Theta is also sometimes referred to as the *time decay* of the portfolio. For a European call option on a non-dividend-paying stock, it can be shown from the Black–Scholes formulas that

$$\Theta = -\frac{S_0 N'(d_1)\sigma}{2\sqrt{T}} - rXe^{-rT}N(d_2)$$

where d_1 and d_2 are defined as in equation (11.20) and

$$N'(x) = \frac{1}{\sqrt{2\pi}}e^{-x^2/2} \qquad (13.5)$$

For a European put option on the stock,

$$\Theta = -\frac{S_0 N'(d_1)\sigma}{2\sqrt{T}} + rXe^{-rT}N(-d_2)$$

For a European call option on a stock index paying a dividend at rate q,

$$\Theta = -\frac{S_0 N'(d_1)\sigma e^{-qT}}{2\sqrt{T}} + qS_0 N(d_1)e^{-qT} - rXe^{-rT}N(d_2)$$

where d_1 and d_2 are defined as in equation (12.4). For a European put option on the stock index

$$\Theta = -\frac{S_0 N'(d_1)\sigma e^{-qT}}{2\sqrt{T}} - qS_0 N(-d_1)e^{-qT} + rXe^{-rT}N(-d_2)$$

With q equal to r_f, these last two equations give thetas for European call and put options on currencies. With q equal to r and S_0 equal to F_0, they give thetas for European futures options.

In these formulas, time is measured in years. Usually when theta is quoted, time is measured in days so that theta is the change in the portfolio value in one day, when all else remains the same. To obtain the theta with time measured in days, the results of using the formulas must be divided by 252, the number of trading days in one year.

> **Example 13.3** Consider a four-month European put option on a stock index. The current value of the index is 305, the strike price is 300, the dividend yield is 3% per annum, the risk-free interest rate is 8% per annum, and the volatility of the index is 25% per annum. In this case, $S_0 = 305$, $X = 300$, $q = 0.03$, $r = 0.08$, $\sigma = 0.25$, and $T = 1/3$. From the formula just given, the option's theta is
>
> $$-\frac{S_0 N'(d_1)\sigma e^{-qT}}{2\sqrt{T}} - qS_0 N(-d_1)e^{-qT} + rXe^{-rT}N(-d_2) = -18.15$$
>
> This means that, when time is measured in days, theta is $18.15/252 = 0.072$.

Theta is usually negative for an option.[7] This is because as time passes, the option tends to become less valuable. The variation of Θ with stock price for a call

---

[7] An exception to this could be an in-the-money European put option on a non-dividend-paying stock or an in-the-money European call option on a currency with a very high interest rate.

option on a stock is shown in Figure 13.5. When the stock price is very low, theta is close to zero. For an at-the-money call option, theta is large and negative. As the stock price increases, theta tends to $-rXe^{-rT}$. Figure 13.6 shows typical patterns for the variation of Θ with the time to maturity for in-the-money, at-the-money, and out-of-the-money call options.

Theta is not the same type of hedge parameter as delta. There is uncertainty about the future stock price, but there is no uncertainty about the passage of time. It makes sense to hedge against changes in the price of the underlying asset, but it does not make any sense to hedge against the effect of the passage of time on an

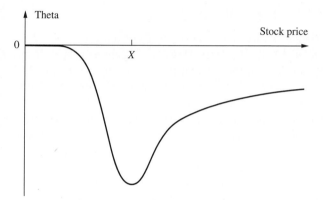

Figure 13.5　Variation of theta of a European call option with stock price.

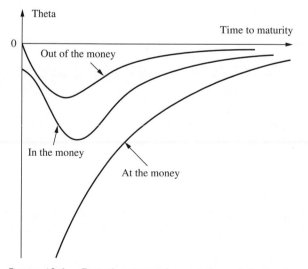

Figure 13.6　Typical patterns for variation of theta of a European call option with time to maturity.

option portfolio. In spite of this, many traders regard theta as a useful descriptive statistic for a portfolio. This is because, as we will see, in a delta-neutral portfolio theta is a proxy for another Greek letter, gamma.

13.6 GAMMA

The *gamma*, Γ, of a portfolio of derivatives on an underlying asset is the rate of change of the portfolio's delta with respect to the price of the underlying asset. It is the second partial derivative of the portfolio value with respect to the asset price:

$$\Gamma = \partial^2 \Pi / \partial S^2$$

If gamma is small, delta changes slowly and adjustments to keep a portfolio delta neutral need only be made relatively infrequently. However, if gamma is large in absolute terms, delta is highly sensitive to the price of the underlying asset. It is then quite risky to leave a delta-neutral portfolio unchanged for any length of time. Figure 13.7 illustrates this point. When the stock price moves from S to S', delta hedging assumes that the option price moves from C to C' when in actual fact it moves from C to C''. The difference between C' and C'' leads to a hedging error. The error depends on the curvature of the relationship between the option price and the stock price. Gamma measures this curvature.[8]

Suppose that ΔS is the price change of an underlying asset during a small interval of time, Δt, and $\Delta \Pi$ is the corresponding price change of the portfolio. If terms of higher order than Δt are ignored, Appendix 13A shows that for a delta-neutral portfolio,

$$\Delta \Pi = \Theta \Delta t + \frac{1}{2} \Gamma \Delta S^2 \tag{13.6}$$

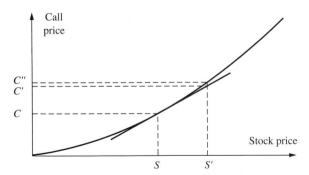

Figure 13.7   Error in delta hedging.

---

[8] Indeed, the gamma of an option is sometimes referred to by traders as its curvature.

where Θ is the theta of the portfolio. Figure 13.8 shows the nature of this relationship between $\Delta\Pi$ and ΔS. When gamma is positive, theta tends to be negative. The portfolio declines in value if there is no change in the S, but increases in value if there is a large positive or negative change in S. When gamma is negative, theta tends to be positive and the reverse is true; the portfolio increases in value if there is no change in S but decreases in value if there is a large positive or negative change in S. As the absolute value of gamma increases, the sensitivity of the value of the portfolio to S increases.

> ***Example 13.4*** Suppose that the gamma of a delta-neutral portfolio of options on an asset is $-10,000$. Equation (13.6) shows that if a change of $+2$ or -2 in the price of the asset occurs over a short period of time, there is an unexpected decrease in the value of the portfolio of approximately $0.5 \times 10,000 \times 2^2 = \$20,000$.

Making a Portfolio Gamma Neutral

A position in either the underlying asset itself or a forward contract on the underlying asset has zero gamma and cannot be used to change the gamma of a portfolio. To adjust the gamma of a portfolio, we must take a position in an instrument such as an option that is not linearly dependent on the underlying asset.

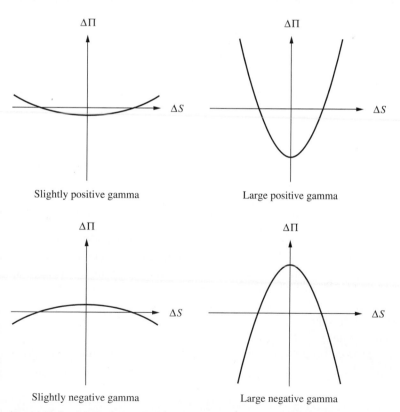

Slightly positive gamma

Large positive gamma

Slightly negative gamma

Large negative gamma

Figure 13.8   Alternative relationships between $\Delta\Pi$ and ΔS for a delta-neutral portfolio.

Suppose that a delta-neutral portfolio has a gamma equal to Γ and a traded option has a gamma equal to Γ_T. If the number of traded options added to the portfolio is w_T, the gamma of the portfolio becomes

$$w_T \Gamma_T + \Gamma$$

Hence, the position in the traded option necessary to make the portfolio gamma neutral is $-\Gamma/\Gamma_T$. Including the traded option is likely to change the delta of the portfolio, so the position in the underlying asset then has to be changed to maintain delta neutrality. Note that the portfolio is gamma neutral only for a short period of time. As time passes, gamma neutrality can be maintained only if the position in the traded option is adjusted so that it is always equal to $-\Gamma/\Gamma_T$.

Making a delta-neutral portfolio gamma neutral can be regarded as a first correction for the fact that the position in the underlying asset cannot be changed continuously when delta hedging is used. Delta neutrality provides protection against relatively small stock price moves between rebalancing. Gamma neutrality provides protection against larger movements in this stock price between hedge rebalancing. Suppose that a portfolio is delta neutral and has a gamma of –3,000. The delta and gamma of a particular traded call option are 0.62 and 1.50, respectively. The portfolio can be made gamma neutral by including in the portfolio a long position of

$$\frac{3,000}{1.5} = 2,000$$

in the traded option. However, the delta of the portfolio will then change from zero to $2,000 \times 0.62 = 1,240$. A quantity, 1,240, of the underlying asset must, therefore, be sold from the portfolio to keep it delta neutral.

Calculation of Gamma

The gamma of a European call or put option on a non-dividend-paying stock is

$$\Gamma = \frac{N'(d_1)}{S_0 \sigma \sqrt{T}}$$

where d_1 is defined as in equation (11.20) and $N'(x)$ is given in equation (13.5). This is always positive and varies with S_0 in the way indicated in Figure 13.9. Typical patterns for the variation of gamma with time to maturity for out-of-the-money, at-the-money, and in-the-money options are shown in Figure 13.10. For an at-the-money option, gamma increases as the time to maturity decreases. Short-life at-the-money options have very high gammas, meaning that the value of the option holder's position is highly sensitive to jumps in the stock price.

For a European call or put option on a stock index paying a continuous dividend at rate q,

$$\Gamma = \frac{N'(d_1)e^{-qT}}{S_0 \sigma \sqrt{T}}$$

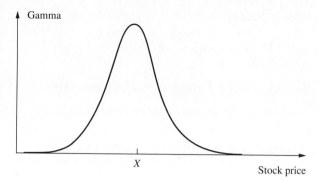

Figure 13.9   Variation of gamma with stock price for an option.

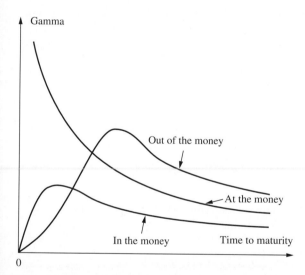

Figure 13.10   Variation of gamma with time to maturity for a stock option.

where d_1 is defined as in equation (12.4). This formula gives the gamma for a European option on a currency when q is put equal to the foreign risk-free rate and gives the gamma for a European futures option with $q = r$ and $S_0 = F_0$.

> **Example 13.5**   Consider a four-month put option on a stock index. Suppose that the current value of the index is 305, the strike price is 300, the dividend yield is 3% per annum, the risk-free interest rate is 8% per annum, and volatility of the index is 25% per annum. In this case, $S_0 = 305, X = 300, q = 0.03, r = 0.08, \sigma = 0.25$, and $T = 4/12$.

The gamma of the index option is given by

$$\frac{N'(d_1)e^{-qT}}{S_0 \sigma \sqrt{T}} = 0.00857$$

Thus an increase of 1.0 (from 305 to 306) in the index increases the delta of the option by approximately 0.00857.

13.7 RELATIONSHIP AMONG DELTA, THETA, AND GAMMA

The price of a single derivative dependent on a non-dividend-paying stock must satisfy the differential equation (11.15). It follows that the value of a portfolio of such derivatives, Π, also satisfies the differential equation:

$$\frac{\partial \Pi}{\partial t} + rS\frac{\partial \Pi}{\partial S} + \frac{1}{2}\sigma^2 S^2 \frac{\partial^2 \Pi}{\partial S^2} = r\Pi$$

Because

$$\Theta = \frac{\partial \Pi}{\partial t} \qquad \Delta = \frac{\partial \Pi}{\partial S} \qquad \Gamma = \frac{\partial^2 \Pi}{\partial S^2}$$

it follows that

$$\Theta + rS\Delta + \frac{1}{2}\sigma^2 S^2 \Gamma = r\Pi \tag{13.7}$$

Similar results can be produced for other underlying assets. (See Problem 13.19). For a delta-neutral portfolio, $\Delta = 0$ and

$$\Theta + \frac{1}{2}\sigma^2 S^2 \Gamma = r\Pi$$

This shows that when Θ is large and positive, gamma tends to be large and negative, and vice versa. This is consistent with the way in which Figure 13.8 has been drawn and explains why theta can be regarded as a proxy for gamma.

13.8 VEGA

Up to now, we have implicitly assumed that the volatility of the asset underlying a derivative is constant. In practice, volatilities change over time. This means that the value of a derivative is liable to change because of movements in volatility as well as because of changes in the asset price and the passage of time.

The *vega* of a portfolio of derivatives, $\mathcal{V}$, is the rate of change of the value of the portfolio with respect to the volatility of the underlying asset:[9]

$$\mathcal{V} = \frac{\partial \Pi}{\partial \sigma}$$

If vega is high in absolute terms, the portfolio's value is very sensitive to small changes in volatility. If vega is low in absolute terms, volatility changes have relatively little impact on the value of the portfolio.

A position in the underlying asset or in a forward contract has zero vega. However, the vega of a portfolio can be changed by adding a position in a traded option. If $\mathcal{V}$ is the vega of the portfolio and $\mathcal{V}_T$ is the vega of a traded option, a position of $-\mathcal{V}/\mathcal{V}_T$ in the traded option makes the portfolio instantaneously vega neutral. Unfortunately, a portfolio that is gamma neutral will not, in general, be vega neutral, and vice versa. (See Problem 13.15 for an elaboration of this.) If a hedger requires a portfolio to be both gamma and vega neutral, at least two traded derivatives dependent on the underlying asset must usually be used.

Example 13.6 Consider a portfolio that is delta neutral, with a gamma of $-5,000$ and a vega of $-8,000$. Suppose that a traded option has a gamma of 0.5, a vega of 2.0, and a delta of 0.6. The portfolio can be made vega neutral by including a long position in 4,000 traded options. This would increase delta to 2,400 and require that 2,400 units of the asset be sold to maintain delta neutrality. The gamma of the portfolio would change from $-5,000$ to $-3,000$.

To make the portfolio gamma and vega neutral, we suppose that there is a second traded option with a gamma of 0.8, a vega of 1.2, and a delta of 0.5. If w_1 and w_2 are the amounts of the two traded options included in the portfolio, we require that

$$-5,000 + 0.5w_1 + 0.8w_2 = 0$$
$$-8,000 + 2.0w_1 + 1.2w_2 = 0$$

The solution to these equations is $w_1 = 400$, $w_2 = 6,000$. The portfolio can, therefore, be made gamma and vega neutral by including 400 of the first traded option and 6,000 of the second traded option. The delta of the portfolio after the addition of the positions in the two traded options is $400 \times 0.6 + 6,000 \times 0.5 = 3,240$. Hence 3,240 units of the asset would have to be sold to maintain delta neutrality.

For a European call or put option on a non-dividend-paying stock, it can be shown from the Black–Scholes formulas that vega is given by

$$\mathcal{V} = S_0 \sqrt{T} N'(d_1)$$

where d_1 is defined as in equation (11.20). The formula for $N'(x)$ is given in equation (13.5). For a European call or put option on a stock or stock index paying a continuous

---

[9] Vega is usually considered to be one of the Greeks even though it is not one of the letters in the Greek alphabet.

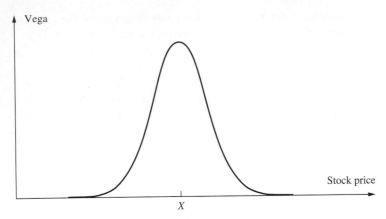

Figure 13.11   Variation of vega with stock price for an option.

dividend yield at rate q,

$$\mathcal{V} = S_0 \sqrt{T} N'(d_1)e^{-qT}$$

where d_1 is defined as in equation (12.4). This equation gives the vega for a European currency option with q replaced by r_f. It also gives the vega for a European futures option with q replaced by r, and S_0 replaced by F_0. The vega of a long position in a call or put option is always positive. The general way that it varies with S_0 is shown in Figure 13.11. Whereas the gamma of an at-the-money option increases as the maturity date approaches (see Figure 13.10), the reverse is true of vega.

Calculating vega from the Black–Scholes model and its extensions may seem strange because one of the assumptions underlying Black–Scholes is that volatility is constant. It would be theoretically more correct to calculate vega from a model where volatility is assumed to be stochastic. However, it turns out that the vega calculated from a stochastic volatility model is very similar to the Black–Scholes vega so the practice of calculating vega from a model where volatility is constant works reasonably well.[10] Stochastic volatility models are discussed in chapter 17.

Gamma neutrality protects against large changes in the price of the underlying asset between hedge rebalancing. Vega neutrality protects against variations in σ. As might be expected, whether it is best to use an available traded option for vega or gamma hedging depends on the time between hedge rebalancing and the volatility of the volatility.[11]

Example 13.7   Consider again the put option in Example 13.5. Its vega is given by

$$S_0 \sqrt{T} N'(d_1)e^{-qT} = 66.44$$

[10]See J. Hull and A. White, "The Pricing of Options on Assets with Stochastic Volatilities," *Journal of Finance*, 42 (June 1987), 281–300; J. Hull and A. White, "An Analysis of the Bias in Option Pricing Caused by a Stochastic Volatility," *Advances in Futures and Options Research*, 3 (1988), 27–61.

[11]For a discussion of this issue, see J. Hull and A. White, "Hedging the Risks from Writing Foreign Currency Options," *Journal of International Money and Finance*, 6 (June 1987), 131–52.

Thus a 1% or 0.01 increase in volatility (from 25% to 26%) increases the value of the option by approximately 0.6644 (= 0.01 × 66.44). Usually vega is quoted as the change in value per 1% change in volatility. In this example, vega would, therefore, be quoted as 0.6644 rather than 66.44.

13.9 RHO

The *rho* of a portfolio of derivatives is the rate of change of the portfolio value with respect to the interest rate:

$$rho = \partial \Pi / \partial r$$

It measures the sensitivity of the portfolio value to interest rates. For a European call option on a non-dividend-paying stock,

$$rho = XTe^{-rT}N(d_2)$$

and for a European put option on the stock,

$$rho = -XTe^{-rT}N(-d_2)$$

where d_2 is defined as in equation (11.20). These same formulas apply to European call and put options on stocks and stock indices paying a dividend yield at rate q.

Example 13.8   Consider again the four-month put option on a stock index in Example 13.5. The current value of the index is 305, the strike price is 300, the dividend yield is 3% per annum, the risk-free interest rate is 8% per annum, and the volatility of the index is 25% per annum. In this case, $S_0 = 305$, $X = 300$, $q = 0.03$, $r = 0.08$, $\sigma = 0.25$, $T = 1/3$. The option's rho is

$$-XTe^{-rT}N(-d_2) = -42.57$$

This means that for a one-percentage-point or 0.01 increase in the risk-free interest rate (from 8% to 9%), the value of the option decreases by 0.4257 (= 0.01 × 42.57).

In the case of currency options, there are two rhos corresponding to the two interest rates. The rho corresponding to the domestic interest rate is given by previous formulas. The rho corresponding to the foreign interest rate for a European call on a currency is given by

$$rho = -Te^{-r_fT}S_0N(d_1)$$

and, for a European put it is

$$rho = Te^{-r_fT}S_0N(-d_1)$$

13.10 HEDGING IN PRACTICE

In an ideal world, traders working for financial institutions would be able to rebalance their portfolios very frequently in order to maintain a zero delta, a zero gamma, a zero vega, and so on. In practice, this is not possible. When managing a large portfolio dependent on a single underlying asset, traders can usually zero out delta at least once a day by trading the underlying asset. Unfortunately, zero gamma and zero vega are less easy to achieve because it is difficult to find options or other nonlinear derivatives that can be traded in the volume required at competitive prices. In most cases, gamma and vega are monitored. When they get too large in either a positive or negative direction, either corrective action is taken or trading is curtailed.

It is worth noting that there are big economies of scale in being an options trader. As noted earlier, maintaining delta neutrality for an individual option on, say, the S&P 500 by trading daily would be prohibitively expensive. But it is realistic to do this for a portfolio of several hundred options on the S&P 500. This is because the cost of daily rebalancing (either by trading the stocks underlying the index or by trading index futures) is covered by the profit on many different trades.

In many markets, financial institutions find that the majority of their trades are sales of call and put options to their clients. Short calls and short puts have negative gammas and negative vegas. It follows that, as time goes by, both the gamma and vega of a financial institution's portfolio tend to become progressively more negative. Traders working for the financial institution are then always looking for ways to buy options (i.e., acquire positive gamma and vega) at competitive prices. There is one aspect of an options book that mitigates the traders' problems somewhat in this situation. Options are usually close to the money when they are first sold so that they have relatively high gammas and vegas. After some time has elapsed, they often become deep-out-of-the-money or deep-in-the-money. In this case, their gammas and vegas become very small and of little consequence. The worst situation for an options trader occurs when written options remain very close to the money right until maturity.

13.11 SCENARIO ANALYSIS

In addition to monitoring risks such as delta, gamma, and vega, option traders often also carry out a scenario analysis. The analysis involves calculating the gain or loss on their portfolio over a specified period under a variety of different scenarios. The time period chosen is likely to depend on the liquidity of the instruments. The scenarios can be either chosen by management or generated by a model.

Consider a bank with a portfolio of options on a foreign currency. There are two main variables upon which the value of the portfolio depends. These are the exchange rate and the exchange rate volatility. Suppose that the exchange rate is currently 1.0000 and its volatility is 10% per annum. The bank could calculate a table, such as Table 13.5, showing the profit or loss experienced during a two-week period under different scenarios. This table considers seven different exchange rates and three different volatilities. Because a one-standard-deviation move in the exchange rate during a two-week period is about 0.02, the exchange rate moves considered are approximately one, two, and three standard deviations.

In Table 13.5, the greatest loss is in the lower right corner of the table. The loss corresponds to the volatility increasing to 12% and the exchange rate moving up to 1.06. Usually the greatest loss in a table such as 13.5 corresponds to one of the

Table 13.5	Profit or Loss Realized in Two Weeks under Different Scenarios (Millions of Dollars)						
	Exchange Rate						
Volatility	*0.94*	*0.96*	*0.98*	*1.00*	*1.02*	*1.04*	*1.06*
8%	+102	+55	+25	+6	−10	−34	−80
10%	+80	+40	+17	+2	−14	−38	−85
12%	+60	+25	+9	−2	−18	−42	−90

corners, but this is not always so. Consider, for example, the situation where a bank's portfolio consists of a reverse butterfly spread (see section 8.2). The greatest loss will be experienced if the exchange rate stays where it is.

13.12 PORTFOLIO INSURANCE

Portfolio managers holding a well-diversified stock portfolio are sometimes interested in insuring themselves against the value of the portfolio dropping below a certain level. One way of doing this is by holding, in conjunction with the stock portfolio, put options on a stock index. This strategy was discussed in section 12.3.

Consider a fund manager holding a $90 million portfolio whose value mirrors the value of the S&P 500. Suppose that the S&P 500 is standing at 900 and the manager wishes to insure against the value of the portfolio dropping below $87 million in the next six months. The manager can buy 1,000 six-month put option contracts on the S&P 500 with an exercise price of 870 and a maturity in six months. If the index drops below 870, the put options will be in the money and provide the manager with compensation for the decline in the value of the portfolio. Consider the case where the index drops to 810 at the end of six months. The value of the manager's stock portfolio is likely to be about $81 million. Because each option contract is on 100 times the index, the total value of the put options is $6 million. This brings the value of the entire holding back up to $87 million.

Creating Options Synthetically

An alternative to buying an option is creating it synthetically. This strategy involves taking a varying position in the underlying asset (or futures on the underlying asset) so that the delta of the position is maintained equal to the delta of the required option.[12] The position necessary to create an option synthetically is the reverse of that necessary to hedge it. This reflects the fact that a procedure for hedging an option involves the creation of an equal and opposite option synthetically.

---

[12] In theory, this strategy could be carried one stage further by using traded options to match the gamma and vega of the required option. In practice this is not usually done.

There are two reasons why it may be more attractive for the portfolio manager to create the required put option synthetically rather than to buy it in the market. The first is that options markets do not always have the liquidity to absorb the trades that managers of large funds would like to carry out. The second is that fund managers often require strike prices and exercise dates that are different from those available in exchange-traded options markets.

The synthetic option can be created from trading the portfolio or from trading in index futures contracts. We first examine the creation of a put option by trading the portfolio. Recall that the delta of a European put on the portfolio is

$$\Delta = e^{-qT}[N(d_1) - 1] \tag{13.8}$$

where, with the usual notation,

$$d_1 = \frac{\ln(S_0/X) + (r - q + \sigma^2/2)T}{\sigma\sqrt{T}}$$

S_0 is the value of the portfolio, X is the strike price, r is the risk-free rate, q is the dividend yield on the portfolio, σ is the volatility of the portfolio, and T is the life of the option. The volatility of the portfolio can be assumed to be its beta times the volatility of an appropriate well diversified index.

To create the put option synthetically, the fund manager should ensure that at any given time a proportion

$$e^{-qT}[1 - N(d_1)]$$

of the stocks in the original $30 million portfolio have been sold and the proceeds invested in riskless assets. As the value of the original portfolio declines, the delta of the put becomes more negative and the proportion of the portfolio sold must be increased. As the value of the original portfolio increases, the delta of the put becomes less negative and the proportion of the portfolio sold must be decreased (i.e., some of the original portfolio must be repurchased).

Using this strategy to create portfolio insurance means that, at any given time, funds are divided between the stock portfolio on which insurance is required and riskless assets. As the value of the stock portfolio increases, riskless assets are sold and the position in the stock portfolio is increased. As the value of the stock portfolio declines, the position in the stock portfolio is decreased and riskless assets are purchased. The cost of the insurance arises because the portfolio manager is always selling after a decline in the market and buying after a rise in the market.

> **Example 13.9**   Consider a portfolio worth $100 million. Suppose that a one-year European put option on the portfolio with a strike price of $85 million is required. Assume that the risk-free rate is 6% per annum, the dividend yield is 2% per annum, and the volatility is 20% per annum. This means that $S_0 = 100$, $X = 85$, $r = 0.06$, $q = 0.02$, $\sigma = 0.2$, and $T = 1$ so that the delta of the portfolio is
>
> $$e^{-qT}[1 - N(d_1)] = -0.130$$

This shows that 13% of the portfolio should be sold initially. If the value of the portfolio reduces to $98 million soon after this has been done, the delta of the portfolio changes to -0.153 and a further 2.3% should be sold.

Use of Index Futures

Using index futures to create portfolio insurance can be preferable to using the underlying stocks, provided that the index futures market is sufficiently liquid to handle the required trades. This is because the transactions costs associated with trades in index futures are generally less than those associated with the corresponding trades in the underlying stocks. The portfolio manager keeps the stock portfolio intact and shorts index futures contracts. From equations (13.3) and (13.8), the dollar amount of futures contracts shorted as a proportion of the value of the portfolio should be

$$e^{-qT}e^{-(r-q)T^*}[1 - N(d_1)] = e^{q(T^*-T)}e^{-rT^*}[1 - N(d_1)]$$

where T^* is the maturity date of the futures contract. If the portfolio is worth K_1 times the index and each index futures contract is on K_2 times the index, this means that the number of futures contracts shorted at any given time should be

$$e^{q(T^*-T)}e^{-rT^*}[1 - N(d_1)]\frac{K_1}{K_2}$$

Example 13.10   In the example given at the beginning of this section, the manager of a \$90 million portfolio mirroring the index wishes to create a six-month put option with strike price of \$87 million. Suppose that the volatility of the market is 25% per annum, the risk-free interest rate is 9% per annum, and the dividend yield on the market is 3% per annum. In this case, $S_0 = 900$, $X = 870$, $r = 0.09$, $q = 0.03$, $\sigma = 0.25$, and $T = 0.5$. The delta of the option that is required is

$$e^{-qT}[N(d_1) - 1] = -0.322$$

Hence, if trades in the portfolio are used to create the option, 32.2% of the portfolio should be sold initially. If nine-month futures contracts on the S&P 500 are used, $T^*-T = 0.25$, $T^* = 0.75$, $K_1 = 100,000$, $K_2 = 250$, so that the number of futures contracts shorted should be

$$e^{q(T^*-T)}e^{-rT^*}[1 - N(d_1)]\frac{K_1}{K_2} = 123.2$$

or 123, rounding to the nearest whole number.

When the portfolio does not mirror the index, the hedging scheme can be adjusted as explained in section 12.3. The strike price for the options created should be the expected level of the market index when the portfolio's value reaches its insured value. The number of options created is β times the number of options that would be required if the portfolio had a beta of 1.0.

Frequency of Rebalancing and October 19, 1987

An important issue when put options are created synthetically is the frequency with which the portfolio manager's position should be adjusted or rebalanced. With no transactions costs, continuous rebalancing is optimal. However, as transaction costs increase, the optimal frequency of rebalancing declines. This issue is discussed by Leland.[13]

Creating put options on the index synthetically does not work well if the volatility of the index changes rapidly or if the index exhibits large jumps. On Monday, October 19, 1987, the Dow Jones Industrial Average dropped by over 500 points. Portfolio managers who had insured themselves by buying put options in the exchange-traded or over-the-counter market survived this crash well. Those who had chosen to create put options synthetically found that they were unable to sell either stocks or index futures fast enough to protect their position.

13.13   STOCK MARKET VOLATILITY

We have already considered the issue of whether volatility is caused solely by the arrival of new information or whether trading itself generates volatility. Portfolio insurance schemes such as those just described have the potential to increase volatility. When the market declines, they cause portfolio managers either to sell stock or to sell index futures contracts. Either action may accentuate the decline. The sale of stock is liable to drive down the market index further in a direct way. The sale of index futures contracts is liable to drive down futures prices. This creates selling pressure on stocks via the mechanism of index arbitrage (see chapter 3), so that the market index is liable to be driven down in this case as well. Similarly, when the market rises, the portfolio insurance schemes cause portfolio managers either to buy stock or to buy futures contracts. This may accentuate the rise.

In addition to formal portfolio insurance schemes, we can speculate that many investors consciously or subconsciously follow portfolio insurance schemes of their own. For example, an investor may be inclined to enter the market when it has just risen, but will sell after a fall to limit the downside risk.

Whether portfolio insurance schemes (formal or informal) affect volatility depends on how easily the market can absorb the trades that are generated by portfolio insurance. If portfolio insurance trades are a very small fraction of all trades, there is likely to be no effect. As portfolio insurance becomes more popular, it is liable to have a destabilizing effect on the market.

Brady Commission Report

The report of the Brady Commission on the October 19, 1987, crash provides interesting insights into the effect of portfolio insurance on the market at that time.[14] The Brady Commission estimated that $60 billion to $90 billion of equity assets were under portfolio insurance administration in October 1987. During the period Wednes-

---

[13] See H. E. Leland, "Option Pricing and Replication with Transactions Costs," *Journal of Finance,* 40 (December 1985), 1283–1301.

[14] See "Report of the Presidential Task Force on Market Mechanisms," January 1988.

day, October 14, 1987, to Friday, October 16, 1987, the market declined by about 10% with much of this decline taking place on Friday afternoon. The decline should have generated at least $12 billion of equity or index futures sales as a result of portfolio insurance schemes.[15] In fact, less than $4 billion were sold, so that portfolio insurers approached the following week with huge amounts of selling already dictated by their models. The Brady Commission estimated that on Monday, October 19, sell programs by three portfolio insurers accounted for almost 10% of the sales on the New York Stock Exchange, and that portfolio insurance sales amounted to 21.3% of all sales in index futures markets. It seems likely that portfolio insurance caused some downward pressure on the market. It is significant that, in aggregate, portfolio insurers executed only a relatively small proportion of the total trades generated by their models. Needless to say, the popularity of portfolio insurance schemes based on dynamic trading in stocks and futures has declined considerably since October 1987.

SUMMARY

Financial institutions offer a variety of option products to their clients. Often the options do not correspond to the standardized products traded by exchanges. The financial institutions are then faced with the problem of hedging their exposure. Naked and covered positions leave them subject to an unacceptable level of risk. One course of action that is sometimes proposed is a stop-loss strategy. This involves holding a naked position when an option is out of the money and converting it to a covered position as soon as the option moves in the money. Although superficially attractive, the strategy does not work at all well.

The delta, Δ, of an option is the rate of change of its price with respect to the price of the underlying asset. Delta hedging involves creating a position with zero delta (sometimes referred to as a delta-neutral position). Because the delta of the underlying asset is 1.0, one way of doing this is to take a position in the underlying asset equal to minus the delta of the portfolio being hedged. The delta of a portfolio changes over time. This means that the position in the underlying asset has to be frequently adjusted.

Once an option position has been made delta neutral, the next stage is often to look at its gamma. The gamma of an option is the rate of change of its delta with respect to the price of the underlying asset. It is a measure of the curvature of the relationship between the option price and the asset price. The impact of this curvature on the performance of delta hedging can be reduced by making an option position gamma neutral. If Γ is the gamma of the position being hedged, this is usually achieved by taking a position in a traded option that has a gamma of $-\Gamma$.

Delta and gamma hedging are both based on the assumption that the volatility of the underlying asset is constant. In practice, volatilities do change over time.

---

[15]To put this in perspective, on Monday, October 19, all previous records were broken when 604 million shares worth $21 billion were traded on the New York Stock Exchange. Approximately $20 billion of S&P 500 futures contracts were traded on that day.

The vega of an option or an option portfolio measures the rate of change of its value with respect to volatility. A trader who wishes to hedge an option position against volatility changes can make the position vega neutral. As with the procedure for creating gamma neutrality, this usually involves taking an offsetting position in a traded option. If the trader wishes to achieve both gamma and vega neutrality, two traded options are usually required.

Two other measures of the risk of an option position are theta and rho. Theta measures the rate of change of the position's value with respect to the passage of time, with all else remaining constant. Rho measures the rate of change of the position's value with respect to the short-term interest rate, with all else remaining constant.

In practice, option traders usually rebalance their portfolios at least once a day to maintain delta neutrality. It is usually not feasible to maintain gamma and vega neutrality on a regular basis. Typically, a trader monitors these measures. If they get too large, either corrective action is taken or trading is curtailed.

Portfolio managers are sometimes interested in creating put options synthetically for the purposes of insuring an equity portfolio. They can do so either by trading the portfolio or by trading index futures on the portfolio. Trading the portfolio involves splitting the portfolio between equities and risk-free securities. As the market declines, more is invested in risk-free securities. As the market increases, more is invested in equities. Trading index futures involves keeping the equity portfolio intact and selling index futures. As the market declines, more index futures are sold; as it rises, fewer are sold. The strategy works reasonably well in normal market conditions. On Monday, October 19, 1987, when the Dow Jones Industrial Average dropped by over 500 points, it worked badly. Portfolio insurers were unable to sell either stocks or index futures fast enough to protect their positions. As a result, the popularity of such schemes has declined.

SUGGESTIONS FOR FURTHER READING

On Hedging Option Positions

Boyle, P. P., and D. Emanuel. "Discretely Adjusted Option Hedges," *Journal of Financial Economics,* 8 (1980), 259–82.

Dillman, S., and J. Harding. "Life after Delta: the Gamma Factor," *Euromoney,* Supplement (February 1985), 14–17.

Figlewski, S. "Options Arbitrage in Imperfect Markets," *Journal of Finance,* 44 (December 1989), 1289–1311.

Galai, D. "The Components of the Return from Hedging Options Against Stocks," *Journal of Business,* 56 (January 1983), 45–54.

Hull, J., and A. White. "Hedging the Risks from Writing Foreign Currency Options," *Journal of International Money and Finance,* 6 (June 1987), 131–52.

On Portfolio Insurance

Asay, M., and C. Edelberg. "Can a Dynamic Strategy Replicate the Returns on an Option?" *Journal of Futures Markets,* 6 (Spring 1986), 63–70.

Bookstaber, R., and J. A. Langsam. "Portfolio Insurance Trading Rules," *Journal of Futures Markets,* 8 (February 1988), 15–31.

Etzioni, E. S. "Rebalance Disciplines for Portfolio Insurance," *Journal of Portfolio Insurance,* 13 (Fall 1986), 59–62.

Leland, H. E. "Option Pricing and Replication with Transactions Costs," *Journal of Finance,* 40 (December 1985), 1283–1301.

Leland, H. E. "Who Should Buy Portfolio Insurance," *Journal of Finance,* 35 (May 1980), 581–94.

Rubinstein, M. "Alternative Paths for Portfolio Insurance," *Financial Analysts Journal,* 41 (July–August 1985), 42–52.

Rubinstein, M., and H. E. Leland. "Replicating Options with Positions in Stock and Cash," *Financial Analysts Journal,* 37 (July–August 1981), 63–72.

Schwartz, E. S. "Options and Portfolio Insurance," *Finanzmarkt und Portfolio Management,* 1 (1986), 9–17.

Tilley, J. A., and G. O. Latainer. "A Synthetic Option Framework for Asset Allocation," *Financial Analysts Journal,* 41 (May–June 1985), 32–41.

QUESTIONS AND PROBLEMS

13.1. What does it mean to assert that the delta of a call option is 0.7? How can a short position in 1,000 call options be made delta neutral when the delta of each option is 0.7?

13.2. Calculate the delta of an at-the-money six-month European call option on a non-dividend-paying stock when the risk-free interest rate is 10% per annum and the stock price volatility is 25% per annum.

13.3. What does it mean to assert that the theta of an option position is -0.1 when time is measured in years? If a trader feels that neither a stock price nor its implied volatility will change, what value of theta is appropriate?

13.4. What is meant by the gamma of an option position? Consider the situation of an option writer whose gamma is large and negative and the delta is zero. What are the risks?

13.5. "The procedure for creating an option position synthetically is the reverse of the procedure for hedging the option position." Explain this statement.

13.6. Why did portfolio insurance not work well on October 19, 1987?

13.7. The Black–Scholes price of an out-of-the-money call option with a strike price of $40 is $4.00. A trader who has written the option plans to use the stop-loss strategy in section 13.3. The trader's plan is to buy at $40\frac{1}{8}$ and to sell at $39\frac{7}{8}$. Estimate the expected number of times the stock will be bought or sold.

13.8. Use the put–call parity relationship to derive, for a non-dividend-paying stock, the relationship between:
(a) The delta of a European call and the delta of a European put.
(b) The gamma of a European call and the gamma of a European put.
(c) The vega of a European call and the vega of a European put.
(d) The theta of a European call and the theta of a European put.

13.9. Suppose that a stock price is currently $20 and that a call option with strike price $25 is created synthetically using a position in the stock that is changed frequently. Consider the following two scenarios:
(a) Stock price increases steadily from $20 to $35 during the life of the option.
(b) Stock price oscillates wildly, ending up at $35.
Which scenario would make the synthetically created option more expensive? Explain your answer.

13.10. What is the delta of a short position in European call options on futures contracts on 1,000 ounces of silver? The options mature in eight months and the futures contract underlying the option matures in nine months. The current nine-month futures price is $8.00 per ounce, the strike price of the options is $8.00, the risk-free interest rate is 12% per annum, and the volatility of silver futures is 18% per annum.

13.11. In Problem 13.10, what initial position in nine-month silver futures is necessary for delta hedging? If silver itself is used, what is the initial position? If one-year silver futures are used, what is the initial position? Assume no storage costs for silver.

13.12. A company uses delta hedging to hedge a portfolio of long positions in put and call options on a currency. Which of the following would give the most favorable result?
(a) A virtually constant spot rate.
(b) Wild movements in the spot rate.
Explain your answer.

13.13. Repeat Problem 13.12 for a financial institution with a portfolio of short positions in put and call options on a currency.

13.14. A financial institution has just sold some seven-month European call options on the Japanese yen. Suppose that the spot exchange rate is 0.80 cent per yen, the strike price is 0.81 cent per yen, the risk-free interest rate in the United States is 8% per annum, the risk-free interest rate in Japan is 5% per annum, and the volatility of the yen is 15% per annum. Calculate the delta, gamma, vega, theta, and rho of the option. Interpret each number.

13.15. Under what circumstances is it possible to make a position in an over-the-counter European option on a stock index both gamma neutral and vega neutral by introducing a single traded European option into the portfolio?

13.16. A fund manager has a well-diversified portfolio that mirrors the performance of the S&P 500 and is worth $360 million. The value of the S&P 500 is 1200 and the portfolio manager would like to buy insurance against a reduction of more than 5% in the value of the portfolio over the next six months. The risk-free interest rate is 6% per annum. The dividend yield on both the portfolio and the S&P 500 is 3%, and the volatility of the index is 30% per annum.

(a) If the fund manager buys traded European put options, how much would the insurance cost?

(b) Can the fund manager obtain the insurance by buying traded call options?

(c) If the fund manager decides to provide insurance by keeping part of the portfolio in risk-free securities, what should the initial position be?

(d) If the fund manager decides to provide insurance by using nine-month index futures, what should the initial position be?

13.17. Repeat Problem 13.16 on the assumption that the portfolio has a beta of 1.5. Assume that the dividend yield on the portfolio is 4% per annum.

13.18. Show by substituting for Θ, Δ, Γ, and Π that the relationship in equation (13.7) is true for:

(a) A single European call option on a non-dividend-paying stock.

(b) A single European put option on a non-dividend-paying stock.

(c) Any portfolio of European put and call options on a non-dividend-paying stock.

13.19. What is the equation corresponding to equation (13.7) for (a) a portfolio of derivatives on a currency and (b) a portfolio of derivatives on a futures contract?

13.20. Suppose that $70 billion of equity assets are the subject of portfolio insurance schemes. Assume that the schemes are designed to provide insurance against the value of the assets declining by more than 5% within one year. Making whatever estimates you find necessary, calculate the value of the stock or futures contracts that the administrators of the portfolio insurance schemes will attempt to sell if the market falls by 23% in a single day.

13.21. Does a forward contract on an asset providing a dividend yield at rate q have the same delta as the corresponding futures contract? Explain your answer.

13.22. A bank's position in options on the dollar-euro exchange rate has a delta of 30,000 and a gamma of $-80,000$. Explain how these numbers can be interpreted. The exchange rate is 0.90. What position would you take to make the position delta neutral? After a short period of time, the exchange rate moves to 0.93. Estimate the new delta. What additional trade is necessary to keep the position delta neutral? Assuming the bank did set up a delta-neutral position originally, has it gained or lost money from the exchange-rate movement?

ASSIGNMENT QUESTIONS

13.23. Consider a one-year European call option on a non-dividend-paying stock when the stock price is $30, the strike price is $30, the risk-free interest rate is 5%, and the volatility is 25% per annum. Use the DerivaGem software to calculate the price, delta, gamma, vega, theta, and rho of the option. Verify that delta is correct by changing the stock price to $30.1 and recomputing delta. Verify that gamma is correct by recomputing the delta for the situation where the stock price is $30.1. Carry out similar calculations to verify that vega, theta, and rho are correct. Use the DerivaGem software to plot the option price, delta, gamma, vega, theta, and rho against the stock price for the stock option.

13.24. A financial institution has the following portfolio of over-the-counter options on sterling:

Type	Postition	Delta of option	Gamma of option	Vega of option
Call	−1,000	0.50	2.2	1.8
Call	−500	0.80	0.6	0.2
Put	−2,000	−0.40	1.3	0.7
Call	−500	0.70	1.8	1.4

A traded option is available with a delta of 0.6, a gamma of 1.5, and a vega of 0.8.

(a) What position in the traded option and in sterling would make the portfolio both gamma neutral and delta neutral?

(b) What position in the traded option and in sterling would make the portfolio both vega neutral and delta neutral?

13.25. Consider again the situation in Problem 13.24. Suppose that a second traded option with a delta of 0.1, a gamma of 0.5, and a vega of 0.6 is available. How could the portfolio be made delta, gamma, and vega neutral?

13.26. A deposit instrument offered by a bank guarantees that investors will receive a return during a six-month period that is the greater of (a) zero and (b) 40% of the return provided by a market index. An investor is planning to put $100,000 in the instrument. Describe the payoff as an option on the index. Assuming that the risk-free rate of interest is 8% per annum, the dividend yield on the index is 3% per annum, and the volatility of the index is 25% per annum, is the product a good deal for the investor?

APPENDIX 13A

Taylor Series Expansions and Hedge Parameters

A Taylor series expansion of the change in the portfolio value in a short period of time shows the role played by different Greek letters. If the volatility of the underlying asset is assumed to be constant, the value of the portfolio, Π, is a function of the asset price, S, and time t. The Taylor series expansion gives

$$\Delta\Pi = \frac{\partial\Pi}{\partial S}\Delta S + \frac{\partial\Pi}{\partial t}\Delta t + \frac{1}{2}\frac{\partial^2\Pi}{\partial S^2}\Delta S^2 + \frac{1}{2}\frac{\partial^2\Pi}{\partial t^2}\Delta t^2 + \frac{\partial^2\Pi}{\partial S\partial t}\Delta S\Delta t + \cdots \quad (13A.1)$$

where $\Delta\Pi$ and ΔS are the change in Π and S in a small time interval Δt. Delta hedging eliminates the first term on the right-hand side. The second term is nonstochastic. The third term (which is of order Δt) can be made zero by ensuring that the portfolio is gamma neutral as well as delta neutral. Other terms are of higher order than Δt.

For a delta-neutral portfolio, the first term on the right-hand side of equation (13A.1) is zero, so that

$$\Delta\Pi = \Theta\,\Delta t + \frac{1}{2}\Gamma\,\Delta S^2$$

when terms of higher order than Δt are ignored. This is equation (13.6).

When the volatility of the underlying asset is uncertain, Π is a function of σ, S, and t. Equation (13A.1) then becomes

$$\Delta\Pi = \frac{\partial\Pi}{\partial S}\Delta S + \frac{\partial\Pi}{\partial\sigma}\Delta\sigma + \frac{\partial\Pi}{\partial t}\Delta t + \frac{1}{2}\frac{\partial^2\Pi}{\partial S^2}\Delta S^2 + \frac{1}{2}\frac{\partial^2\Pi}{\partial\sigma^2}\Delta\sigma^2 + \cdots$$

where $\Delta\sigma$ is the change in σ in time Δt. In this case, delta hedging eliminates the first term on the right-hand side. The second term is eliminated by making the portfolio vega neutral. The third term is nonstochastic. The fourth term is eliminated by making the portfolio gamma neutral. Other Greek letters can be (and in practice are) defined to correspond to higher order terms.

CHAPTER 14

VALUE AT RISK

Chapter 13 looked at measures such as delta, gamma, and vega for describing different aspects of the risk in a portfolio consisting of options and other financial assets. A financial institution usually calculates each of these measures each day for every market variable to which it is exposed. Often there are hundreds, or even thousands, of these market variables. A delta-gamma-vega analysis, therefore, leads to a huge number of different risk measures being produced each day. These risk measures provide valuable information for the traders who are responsible for managing the various components of the financial institution's portfolio, but they are of limited use to senior management.

Value at risk (VaR) is an attempt to provide a single number for senior management summarizing the total risk in a portfolio of financial assets. It has become widely used by corporate treasurers and fund managers as well as by financial institutions. Central bank regulators also use VaR in determining the capital a bank is required to keep to reflect the market risks it is bearing.[1]

The VaR calculation is aimed at making a statement of the following form: "We are X percent certain that we will not lose more than V dollars in the next N days." The variable V is the VaR of the portfolio. It is a function of two parameters: N, the time horizon, and X, the confidence level. One attractive feature of VaR is that it is easy to understand. In essence, it asks the simple question "How bad can things get?" In calculating a bank's capital, regulators use $N = 10$ and $X = 99$. They are, therefore, considering losses over a 10-day period that are expected to happen only one percent of the time. The required capital for market risk is, at the time of writing, three times the 10-day 99% VaR.

14.1 DAILY VOLATILITIES

Before getting into the details of how VaR is calculated, it is appropriate to mention one issue concerned with the units for measuring volatility. In option pricing we usually measure time in years. The volatility of an asset is, therefore, usually quoted as a "volatility per year". In VaR calculations we usually measure time in days and the volatility of an asset is usually quoted as a "volatility per day".

---

[1] See P. Jackson, D. J. Maude, and W. Perraudin. "Bank Capital and Value at Risk," *Journal of Derivatives*, 4, 3, (Spring 1997), 73–90 for a discussion of this.

What is the relationship between the volatility per year used in option pricing and the volatility per day used in VaR calculations? Let us define σ_{yr} as the volatility per year of a certain asset and σ_{day} as the equivalent volatility per day of the asset. Assuming 252 trading days in a year, we can use equation (11.1) to write the standard deviation of the continuously compounded return on the asset in one year as either σ_{yr} or $\sigma_{day}\sqrt{252}$. It follows that

$$\sigma_{yr} = \sigma_{day}\sqrt{252}$$

or

$$\sigma_{day} = \frac{\sigma_{yr}}{\sqrt{252}}$$

so that daily volatility is about 6% of annual volatility.

As pointed out in sections 10.5 and 11.3, σ_{day} is approximately equal to the standard deviation of the return on the asset in one day. For the purposes of calculating VaR we assume exact equality. We define the daily volatility of an asset price as equal to the standard deviation of the asset's daily return.

In this chapter, we will assume that estimates of daily volatilities of assets, as well as estimates of the correlations between asset returns, are available. In chapter 15 we discuss how these estimates are produced.

14.2 CALCULATION OF VaR IN SIMPLE SITUATIONS

We first consider how VaR can be calculated in simple situations. Consider a portfolio consisting of a position worth $10 million in shares of IBM. We suppose that $N = 10$ and $X = 99$, so that we are interested in a 99% confidence level for losses over 10 days.

We assume that the volatility of IBM is 2% per day (corresponding to about 32% per year). Because the size of the position is $10 million, the standard deviation of daily changes in the value of the position is 2% of $10 million, or $200,000. Assuming that the changes on successive days are independent, we expect the standard deviation of the change over a 10-day period to be $\sqrt{10}$ times the change over a one-day period. The standard deviation of the change in the value of the IBM portfolio over a 10-day period is, therefore, $200,000\sqrt{10}$, or $632,456.

It is customary in VaR calculations to assume that the expected change in the price of a market variable over the time period considered is zero. This is not exactly true but it is a reasonable assumption. The expected change in the price of a market variable over a short time period is generally small when compared with the standard deviation of the change. Suppose, for example, that IBM has an expected return of 13% per annum. Over a one-day period, the expected return is $0.13/252$, or about 0.05%, whereas the standard deviation of the return is 2%. Over a 10-day period, the expected return is $13/25.2$, or about 0.5%, whereas the standard deviation of the return is $2\sqrt{10}$, or about 6.3%.

So far, we have established that the change in the value of the portfolio of IBM shares over a 10-day period has a standard deviation of $632,456 and (at least approximately) a mean of zero. We assume that the change is normally distributed.[2] From the tables at the end of this book, $N(-2.33) = 0.01$. This means that there is a 1% probability that a normally distributed variable will decrease in value by more than 2.33 standard deviations. Equivalently, it means that we are 99% certain that a normally distributed variable will not decrease in value by more than 2.33 standard deviations. The 10-day 99% VaR for our portfolio consisting of a $10 million position in IBM is, therefore,

$$2.33 \times 632,456 = \$1,473,621$$

Consider next a portfolio consisting of a $5 million position in AT&T, and suppose the daily volatility of AT&T is 1% (approximately 16% per year). A similar calculation to that for IBM shows that the standard deviation of the change in the value of the portfolio per 10 days is

$$5,000,000 \times 0.01 \times \sqrt{10} = 158,114$$

Assuming the change is normally distributed, the 10-day 99% VaR is

$$158,114 \times 2.33 = \$368,405$$

A Two-Asset Portfolio

Now consider a portfolio consisting of both $10 million of IBM shares and $5 million of AT&T shares. We suppose that the returns on the two shares have a bivariate normal distribution with a correlation of 0.7. A standard result in statistics tells us that, if two variables X and Y have standard deviations equal to σ_X and σ_Y with the coefficient of correlation between them being equal to ρ, the standard deviation of $X + Y$ is given by

$$\sigma_{X+Y} = \sqrt{\sigma_X^2 + \sigma_Y^2 + 2\rho\sigma_X\sigma_Y}$$

To apply this result, we set X equal to the change in the value of the position in IBM over a 10-day period and Y equal to the change in the value of the position in AT&T over a 10-day period, so that

$$\sigma_X = 632,456 \qquad \sigma_Y = 158,114$$

The standard deviation of the change in the value of the portfolio consisting of both stocks over a 10-day period is, therefore,

$$\sqrt{632,456^2 + 158,114^2 + 2 \times 0.7 \times 632,456 \times 158,114} = 751,665$$

The change in the portfolio value is normally distributed. This means that the 10-day 99% VaR for the portfolio is

$$751,665 \times 2.33 = \$1,751,379$$

---

[2]The usual geometric Brownian motion assumption for asset prices, discussed in chapter 10, is consistent with price changes over a short time period being normal.

The Benefits of Diversification

In the example we have just considered:

1. The VaR for the portfolio of IBM shares is $1,473,621.
2. The VaR for the portfolio of AT&T shares is $368,405.
3. The VaR for the portfolio of both IBM and AT&T shares is $1,751,379.

The amount

$$(1,473,621 + 368,405) - 1,751,379 = \$90,647$$

represents the benefits of diversification. If IBM and AT&T were perfectly correlated, the VaR for the portfolio of both IBM and AT&T would equal the VaR for the IBM portfolio plus the VaR for the AT&T portfolio. Less than perfect correlation leads to some of the risk being "diversified away".[3]

14.3   A LINEAR MODEL

The example we have just considered illustrates that VaR calculations are straightforward when

1. We are considering a portfolio of assets; and
2. The changes in the values of the asset prices have a multivariate normal distribution.

To generalize the example, we suppose that we have a portfolio worth P consisting of n assets with an amount α_i being invested in asset i ($1 \leq i \leq n$). We define Δx_i as the return on asset i in one day. It follows that the dollar change in the value of our investment in asset i in one day is $\alpha_i \Delta x_i$ and

$$\Delta P = \sum_{i=1}^{n} \alpha_i \Delta x_i \qquad (14.4)$$

where ΔP is the dollar change in the portfolio value in one day.

In the example considered in the previous section, $10 million was invested in the first asset (IBM) and $5 million was invested in the second asset (AT&T) so that (in millions of dollars) $\alpha_1 = 10$, $\alpha_2 = 5$ and

$$\Delta P = 10\Delta x_1 + 5\Delta x_2$$

Because the Δx_i in equation (14.4) are multivariate normal, ΔP is normally distributed. To calculate VaR we, therefore, need to calculate only the mean and standard deviation of ΔP. We assume, as discussed in the previous section, that the expected value of each Δx_i is zero. This implies that the mean of ΔP is zero.

---

[3] Harry Markowitz was one of the first researchers to study the benefits of diversification to a portfolio manager. He was awarded a Nobel prize for this research in 1990. See H. Markowitz, "Portfolio Selection," *Journal of Finance*, 7, 1, (March 1952), 77–91.

To calculate the standard deviation of ΔP, we define σ_i as the daily volatility of the ith asset and ρ_{ij} as the coefficient of correlation between returns on asset i and asset j. This means that σ_i is the standard deviation of Δx_i and ρ_{ij} is the coefficient of correlation between Δx_i and Δx_j. The standard deviation of ΔP, σ_P, is given by

$$\sigma_P^2 = \sum_{i=1}^{n}\sum_{j=1}^{n} \rho_{ij}\alpha_i\alpha_j\sigma_i\sigma_j$$

This equation can also be written

$$\sigma_P^2 = \sum_{i=1}^{n} \alpha_i^2\sigma_i^2 + 2\sum_{i=1}^{n}\sum_{j<i} \rho_{ij}\alpha_i\alpha_j\sigma_i\sigma_j \tag{14.5}$$

The standard deviation of the change over N days is $\sigma_P\sqrt{N}$ and the 99% VaR for an N-day time horizon is $2.33\sigma_P\sqrt{N}$.

In the example considered in the previous section, $\sigma_1 = 0.02$, $\sigma_2 = 0.01$, and $\rho_{12} = 0.7$. As already noted $\alpha_1 = 10$ and $\alpha_2 = 5$ so that

$$\sigma_P^2 = 10^2 \times 0.02^2 + 5^2 \times 0.01^2 + 2 \times 10 \times 5 \times 0.7 \times 0.02 \times 0.01 = 0.0565$$

and $\sigma_P = 0.238$. This is the standard deviation of the change in the portfolio value per day (in millions of dollars). The 10-day 99% VaR is $2.33 \times 0.238 \times \sqrt{10} = \$1.751$ million. This agrees with the calculation in the previous section.

Extension

Up to now, we have considered a portfolio consisting of positions in a number of different assets and the Δx_i's have been the returns on the assets. The linear model can be used in a much wider range of situations than this. It is appropriate for any portfolio whose value is to a reasonable approximation linearly dependent on a number of market variables. These market variables may be asset prices, as in the cases just considered, but they do not have to be. For example, some of the market variables could be implied volatilities or interest rates. The market variables are assumed to have a multivariate normal distribution.

Define Δx_i as the proportional change in market variable i in one day. (If the ith market variable is the price of an asset, this is the return on the asset in one day.) From the linearity assumption, equation (14.4) holds with α_i equal to the sensitivity of the portfolio value to proportional changes in the ith market variable. Equation (14.5) can, therefore, be used to calculate σ_P.

14.4   HOW INTEREST RATES ARE HANDLED

We now discuss how interest rate dependent instruments are handled in VaR calculations. It is clearly out of the question to define a separate market variable for every single bond price or interest rate to which a company is exposed. Some simplifications are necessary. We describe two approaches in this section. A third approach involving principal components analysis will be covered in section 14.10.

Duration

If we are prepared to assume that all shifts in a zero-coupon yield curve are small parallel shifts, we can use the approximate duration relationship:

$$\Delta P = -DP\Delta y \tag{14.6}$$

introduced in section 4.13. The variable P is the value of a portfolio dependent on interest rates, D is the modified duration of the portfolio, Δy is the size of the parallel shift in the yield curve in one day, and ΔP is the resultant change in the portfolio value.

We will denote the yield volatility per day by σ_y. There are two alternative ways of defining σ_y. The first is as the standard deviation of Δy. From equation (14.6) it then follows that

$$\sigma_P = DP\sigma_y$$

The alternative definition for σ_y, which is consistent with the definition of volatility for asset prices, is as the standard deviation of $\Delta y / y$ where y is the zero-coupon yield for maturity D. From equation (14.6)

$$\Delta P = -DPy\frac{\Delta y}{y}$$

and the relationship between σ_P and σ_y is then

$$\sigma_P = DPy\sigma_y$$

Example 14.1 Consider a bond portfolio worth $10 million with a duration of 5.0 years. Suppose that the volatility of the daily change in the 5-year yield (defined as the standard deviation of the actual changes in the yield) is 0.12%. The standard deviation of the daily change in the portfolio value is

$$5 \times 10,000,000 \times 0.0012 = \$60,000$$

The 10-day 99% VaR is

$$60,000 \times 2.33 \times \sqrt{10} = \$442,086$$

The duration approach can be extended to include a convexity term as explained in section 4.15. It then takes account of the impact of parallel shifts in the yield curve on ΔP more precisely. However, the approach still has the disadvantage that it does not allow for the possibility of nonparallel shifts in the yield curve.

Cash Flow Mapping

An alternative approach for handling interest rates is to use as market variables the prices of zero-coupon bonds with standard maturities. The maturities usually chosen are one month, three months, one year, two years, five years, seven years, ten years, and thirty years. Consider a portfolio of Treasury bonds. The first stage is to regard each Treasury bond as a portfolio of its constituent zero-coupon bonds. The position in each of the zero-coupon bonds is then mapped into an equivalent position in the adjacent standard-maturity zero-coupon bonds.

We will illustrate the procedure by considering a simple example where the portfolio consists of a long position in single bond with a principal of $1 million maturing in 0.8 years. We suppose that the bond provides a coupon of 10% per annum payable semiannually. This means that the bond provides coupon payments of $50,000 in 0.3 years and 0.8 years. It also provides a principal payment of $1 million in 0.8 years. The Treasury bond can, therefore, be regarded as a position in a 0.3-year zero-coupon bond with a principal of $50,000 and a position in a 0.8-year zero-coupon bond with a principal of $1,050,000.

The position in the 0.3-year zero-coupon bond is mapped into an equivalent position in three-month and six-month zero-coupon bonds. The position in the 0.8-year zero-coupon bond is mapped into an equivalent position in six-month and one-year zero-coupon bonds. The result is that the position in the 0.8-year coupon-bearing bond is, for VaR purposes, regarded as a position in zero-coupon bonds having maturities of three months, six months, and one year.

The Mapping Procedure

To explain the mapping procedure, we consider the $1,050,000 that will be received in 0.8 years.[4] We suppose that zero rates, daily bond price volatilities, and correlations between bond returns are as shown in Table 14.1.

The first stage is to interpolate between the six-month rate of 6.0% and the one-year rate of 7.0% to obtain a 0.8-year rate of 6.6%. (Annual compounding is assumed for all rates.) The present value of the $1,050,000 cash flow to be received in 0.8

Table 14.1 Data for the Example

Maturity	3-month	6-month	1-year
Zero rate (% with ann. comp.)	5.50	6.00	7.00
Bond price vol (% per day)	0.06	0.10	0.20

Correlation between daily returns	3-month bond	6-month bond	1-year bond
3-month bond	1.0	0.9	0.6
6-month bond	0.9	1.0	0.7
1-year bond	0.6	0.7	1.0

---

[4]This approach is described in J. P. Morgan, *RiskMetrics Monitor*, (Fourth Quarter 1995). Note that it is more robust than interpolating between yield volatilities, as suggested in an early *RiskMetrics Monitor*.

years is

$$\frac{1,050,000}{1.066^{0.8}} = 997,662$$

We also interpolate between the 0.1% volatility for the six-month bond and the 0.2% volatility for the one-year bond to get a 0.16% volatility for the 0.8-year bond.

Suppose we allocate α of the present value to the six-month bond and $1 - \alpha$ of the present value to the one-year bond. Using equation (14.5) and matching variances we obtain

$$0.0016^2 = 0.001^2\alpha^2 + 0.002^2(1 - \alpha)^2 + 2 \times 0.7 \times 0.001 \times 0.002\alpha(1 - \alpha)$$

This is a quadratic equation that can be solved in the usual way to give $\alpha = 0.3203$. This means that 32.03% of the value should be allocated to a six-month zero-coupon bond and 67.97% of the value should be allocated to a one-year zero-coupon bond. The 0.8-year bond worth \$997,662 is, therefore, replaced by a six-month bond worth

$$997,662 \times 0.3203 = \$319,589$$

and a one-year bond worth

$$997,662 \times 0.6797 = \$678,073$$

The cash flow mapping scheme has the advantage that it preserves both the value and the variance of the cash flow. Also, it can be shown that the weights assigned to two adjacent zero-coupon bonds are always positive.

For the \$50,000 cash flow received at time 0.3 years we can carry out similar calculations. (See Problem 14.9.) It turns out that the present value of the cash flow is \$49,189. It can be mapped into a position worth \$37,397 in a three-month bond and a position worth \$11,793 in a six-month bond.

The results of the calculations are summarized in Table 14.2. The 0.8-year coupon-bearing bond is mapped into a position worth \$37,397 in a three-month bond, a position worth \$331,382 in a six-month bond, and a position worth \$678,074 in a one-year bond. Using the volatilities and correlations in Table 14.1, equation (14.5) gives the variance of the change in the price of the 0.8-year bond with $n = 3$, $\alpha_1 = 37,397$, $\alpha_2 = 331,382$, $\alpha_3 = 678,074$, $\sigma_1 = 0.0006$, $\sigma_2 = 0.001$, $\sigma_3 = 0.002$, $\rho_{12} = 0.9$, $\rho_{13} = 0.6$, and $\rho_{23} = 0.7$. This variance is 2,628,518. The standard deviation of the

Table 14.2 **Example to Illustrate Mapping Scheme**

	\$50,000 received in 0.3 years	*\$1,050,000 received in 0.8 years*	*Total*
Position in 3-month bond (\$)	37,397		37,397
Position in 6-month bond (\$)	11,793	319,589	331,382
Position in 1-year bond (\$)		678,074	678,074

change in the price of the bond is, therefore, $\sqrt{2,628,519} = 1,621$. Because we are assuming that the bond is the only instrument in the portfolio, the 10-day 99% VaR is

$$1621 \times \sqrt{10} \times 2.33 = 11,946$$

or about $11,950.

14.5   WHEN THE LINEAR MODEL CAN BE USED

The simplest application of the linear model is to a portfolio with no derivatives consisting of positions in stocks, bonds, foreign exchange, and commodities. In this case, the change in the value of the portfolio is linearly dependent on the change in the value of the underlying market variables (stock prices, zero-coupon bond prices, exchange rates, and commodity prices), and the use of equation (14.5) is an extension of the examples in section 14.2.

For the purposes of VaR calculations, all asset prices are measured in the domestic currency. The market variables considered by a large bank in the United States are, therefore, likely to include the FTSE index measured in dollars, the price of a three-month U.K. Treasury bill measured in dollars, the price of a six-month U.K. Treasury bill measured in dollars, and so on. This means that the linear model can accommodate positions in assets such as foreign equities and foreign bonds.

An example of a derivative that can be handled by the linear model is a forward contract to buy a foreign currency. Suppose the contract matures at time T. It can be regarded as the exchange of a foreign zero-coupon bond maturing at time T for a domestic zero-coupon bond maturing at time T. For the purposes of calculating VaR, the forward contract is, therefore, treated as a long position in the foreign bond combined with a short position in the domestic bond. Each bond can be handled in the way described in the previous section.

Consider next an interest rate swap. As explained in chapter 5, this can be regarded as the exchange of a floating-rate bond for a fixed-rate bond. The fixed-rate bond is a regular coupon-bearing bond. The floating-rate bond is worth par just after the next payment date. It can be regarded as a zero-coupon bond with a maturity date equal to the next reset date. The interest rate swap, therefore, reduces to a bond portfolio and can be handled in the way described in the previous section.

The Linear Model and Options

The linear model is only an approximation when the portfolio contains options. Consider, for example, a portfolio consisting of options on a single stock whose current price is S. Suppose that the delta of the position (calculated in the way described in chapter 13) is δ. Because δ is the rate of change of the value of the portfolio with S, it is approximately true that

$$\delta = \frac{\Delta P}{\Delta S}$$

or

$$\Delta P = \delta \Delta S \qquad (14.7)$$

where ΔS is the dollar change in the stock price in one day and ΔP is, as usual, the dollar change in the portfolio in one day. We define Δx as the proportional change in the stock price in one day so that:

$$\Delta x = \frac{\Delta S}{S}$$

It follows that an approximate relationship between ΔP and Δx is

$$\Delta P = S\delta \Delta x$$

When we have a position in several underlying market variables that includes options, we can derive an approximately linear relationship between ΔP and the Δx_i's similarly. This relationship is

$$\Delta P = \sum_{i=1}^{n} S_i \delta_i \Delta x_i \qquad (14.8)$$

where S_i is the value of the ith market variable and δ_i is the delta of the portfolio with respect to the ith market variable. This corresponds to equation (14.4)

$$\Delta P = \sum_{i=1}^{n} \alpha_i \Delta x_i$$

with $\alpha_i = S_i \delta_i$. Equation (14.5) can, therefore, be used to calculate the standard deviation of ΔP.

Example 14.2 Consider a portfolio consisting of options on IBM and AT&T. The options on IBM have a delta of 1,000 and the options on AT&T have a delta of 20,000. The IBM share price is $120 and the AT&T share price is $30. From equation (14.8) it is approximately true that

$$\Delta P = 120 \times 1,000 \times \Delta x_1 + 30 \times 20,000 \times \Delta x_2$$

or

$$\Delta P = 120,000\Delta x_1 + 600,000\Delta x_2$$

where Δx_1 and Δx_2 are the proportional changes in the prices of IBM and AT&T in one day and ΔP is the resultant change in the value of the portfolio. Assuming that the daily volatility of IBM is 2% and the daily volatility of AT&T is 1% and the correlation between the daily changes is 0.7, the standard deviation of ΔP (in thousands of dollars) is

$$\sqrt{(120 \times 0.02)^2 + (600 \times 0.01)^2 + 2 \times 120 \times 0.02 \times 600 \times 0.01 \times 0.7} = 7.869$$

Because $N(-1.65) = 0.05$, the 5-day 95% value at risk is

$$1.65 \times \sqrt{5} \times 7,869 = \$29,033$$

14.6   A QUADRATIC MODEL

When a portfolio includes options, the linear model is an approximation. It does not take account of the gamma of the portfolio. As discussed in chapter 13, delta is defined as the rate of change of the portfolio value with respect to an underlying market variable and gamma is defined as the rate of change of the delta with respect to the market variable. Gamma measures the curvature of the relationship between the portfolio value and an underlying market variable.

Figure 14.1 shows the impact of a non-zero gamma on the probability distribution of ΔP. When gamma is positive, the probability distribution of ΔP tends to be positively skewed; when gamma is negative, it tends to be negatively skewed. Figures 14.2 and 14.3 illustrate the reason for this result. Figure 14.2 shows the relationship between the value of a long call option and the price of the underlying asset. A long call is an example of an option position with positive gamma. The figure shows that, when the probability distribution for the price of the underlying asset is normal, the probability distribution for the option price is positively skewed. Figure 14.3 shows the relationship between the value of a short call position and the price of the underlying asset. A short call position has negative gamma. In this case, we see that a normal distribution for the price of the underlying asset gets mapped into a negatively skewed distribution for the value of the option position.

The VaR for a portfolio is critically dependent on the left tail of the probability distribution of ΔP. For example, when the confidence level used is 99%, the VaR is the value in the left tail below which there is only 1% of the distribution. As indicated in Figures 14.1(a) and 14.2, a positive gamma portfolio tends to have a thinner left tail than the normal distribution. If we assume the distribution is normal, we will tend to calculate a VaR that is too high. Similarly, as indicated in Figures 14.1(b) and 14.3, a negative gamma portfolio tends to have a fatter left tail than the normal distribution. If we assume the distribution is normal, we will tend to calculate a VaR that is too low.

For a more accurate estimate of VaR than that given by the linear model, we can use both delta and gamma measures to relate ΔP to the Δx_i's. Consider a portfolio

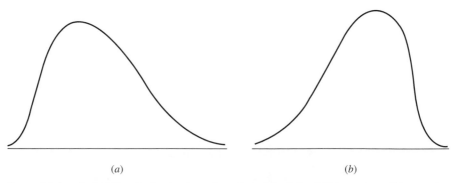

(a)   (b)

Figure 14.1   Probability distribution for value of portfolio (a) positive gamma, (b) negative gamma.

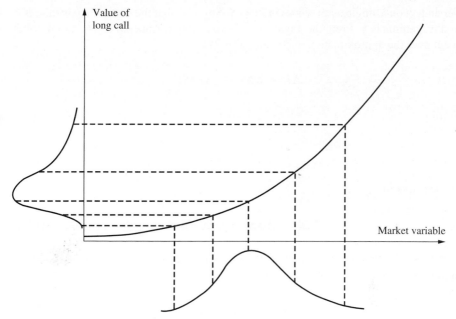

Figure 14.2 Translation of normal probability distribution for asset price into probability distribution for value of a long call on asset.

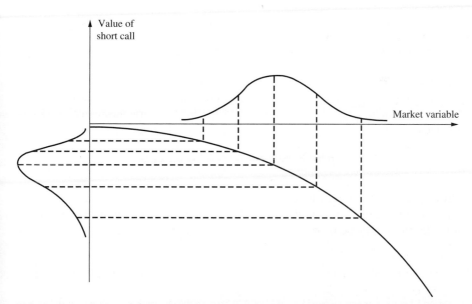

Figure 14.3 Translation of normal probability distribution for asset price into probability distribution for value of a short call on asset.

dependent on a single asset whose price is S. Suppose that the delta of a portfolio is δ and its gamma is γ. From the Taylor series expansion in Appendix 13A, an improvement over the approximation in equation (14.7) is[5]

$$\Delta P = \delta \Delta S + \frac{1}{2}\gamma(\Delta S)^2$$

Setting

$$\Delta x = \frac{\Delta S}{S}$$

reduces this to

$$\Delta P = S\delta \Delta x + \frac{1}{2}S^2\gamma(\Delta x)^2 \qquad (14.9)$$

The variable ΔP is not normal. Assuming that Δx is normal with mean zero and standard deviation σ, the first three moments of ΔP are

$$E(\Delta P) = \frac{1}{2}S^2\gamma\sigma^2$$

$$E[(\Delta P)^2] = S^2\delta^2\sigma^2 + \frac{3}{4}S^4\gamma^2\sigma^4$$

$$E[(\Delta P)^3] = \frac{9}{2}S^4\delta^2\gamma\sigma^4 + \frac{15}{8}S^6\gamma^3\sigma^6$$

The first two moments can be fitted to a normal distribution. This is better than ignoring gamma altogether, but as already pointed out, the assumption that ΔP is normal is less than ideal. An alternative approach is to use the three moments in conjunction with the Cornish–Fisher expansion as described in Appendix 14A.[6]

For a portfolio with n underlying market variables, with each instrument in the portfolio being dependent on only one of the market variables, equation (14.9) becomes

$$\Delta P = \sum_{i=1}^{n} S_i\delta_i\Delta x_i + \sum_{i=1}^{n} \frac{1}{2}S_i^2\gamma_i(\Delta x_i)^2$$

where S_i is the value of the ith market variable, and δ_i and γ_i are the delta and gamma of the portfolio with respect to the ith market variable. When individual instruments in the portfolio may be dependent on more than one market variable, this equation

---

[5] The theta term in the Taylor series expansion measures the expected change in ΔP due to the passage of time. As in the case of the linear model, we assume this is zero.

[6] The Cornish–Fisher expansion provides a relationship between the moments of a distribution and its percentiles. For a description, see N. L. Johnson and S. Kotz, *Distributions in Statistics: Continuous Univariate Distributions 1* (New York: John Wiley and Sons, 1972).

takes the more general form

$$\Delta P = \sum_{i=1}^{n} S_i \delta_i \Delta x_i + \sum_{i=1}^{n} \sum_{j=1}^{n} \frac{1}{2} S_i S_j \gamma_{ij} \Delta x_i \Delta x_j \qquad (14.10)$$

where γ_{ij} is a "cross gamma" defined as

$$\gamma_{ij} = \frac{\partial^2 P}{\partial S_i S_j}$$

Equation 14.10 can be written as

$$\Delta P = \sum_{i=1}^{n} \alpha_i \Delta x_i + \sum_{i=1}^{n} \sum_{j=1}^{n} \beta_{ij} \Delta x_i \Delta x_j \qquad (14.11)$$

where $\alpha_i = S_i \delta_i$ and $\beta_i = S_i S_j \gamma_{ij}/2$.

Equation 14.11 is not as easy to work with as equation (14.4), but it can be used to calculate moments for ΔP. Appendix 14A gives the first three moments and describes how they can be used in conjunction with the Cornish–Fisher expansion to estimate the percentiles of the probability distribution of ΔP that correspond to the required VaR.

14.7   MONTE CARLO SIMULATION

As an alternative to the approaches described so far, we can use Monte Carlo simulation to generate the probability distribution for ΔP. Suppose we wish to calculate a one-day VaR for a portfolio. The procedure is as follows:

1. Value the portfolio today in the usual way using the current values of market variables.

2. Sample once from the multivariate normal probability distribution of the Δx_i's.[7]

3. Use the values of the Δx_i's that are sampled to determine the value of each market variable at the end of one day.

4. Revalue the portfolio at the end of the day in the usual way.

5. Subtract the value calculated in step one from the value in step four to determine a sample ΔP.

6. Repeat steps two to five many times to build up a probability distribution for ΔP.

The VaR is calculated as the appropriate percentile of the probability distribution of ΔP. Suppose, for example, that we calculate 5,000 different sample values of ΔP in the way just described. The 1-day 99% VaR is the value of ΔP for the 50th worst outcome; the 1-day 95% VaR is the value of ΔP for the 250th worst outcome;

---

[7]One way of doing so is given in chapter 16.

and so on.[8] The N-day VaR is usually assumed to be the 1-day VaR multiplied by $\sqrt{N}$.[9]

The drawback of Monte Carlo simulation is that it tends to be slow because a company's complete portfolio (which might consist of hundreds of thousands of different instruments) has to be revalued many times.[10] One way of speeding things up is to assume that equation (14.11) describes the relationship between ΔP and the Δx_i's. We can then jump straight from step two to step five in the Monte Carlo simulation and avoid the need for a complete revaluation of the portfolio. This is sometimes referred to as the *partial simulation* approach.

14.8 HISTORICAL SIMULATION

One disadvantage of the approaches suggested so far is that the market variables are assumed to be normally distributed. In practice, the distributions of daily changes in many market variables have fatter tails than the normal distribution.[11] This has led some companies to base VaR calculations on historical simulation. The first step is to create a database consisting of the daily movements in all market variables over a few years. The first simulation trial assumes that the percentage changes in each market variable are the same as those on the first day covered by the database; the second simulation trial assumes that the percentage changes are the same as those on the second day; and so on. The change in the portfolio value, ΔP, is calculated for each simulation trial and the VaR is set equal to the appropriate percentile of the probability distribution of ΔP. The change in the portfolio value can be obtained either by revaluing the portfolio or by using equation (14.11).[12]

The historical simulation approach has the advantage that it accurately reflects the historical probability distribution of the market variables, but this must be weighed against a number of disadvantages. The number of simulation trials in a historical simulation is limited to the number of days of data that are available. Sensitivity analyses are difficult. The volatility updating schemes described in the next chapter cannot be used.[13] Also, it is difficult to deal with variables where no market data or limited market data are available.

---

[8] Extreme value theory provides a way of "smoothing the tails" so that better estimates of extreme percentiles are obtained. See for example P. Embrechts, C. Kluppelberg, and T. Mikosch. *Modeling Extremal Events for Insurance and Finance*, Springer, 1997.

[9] This is only approximately true when the portfolio includes options, but it is the assumption that is made in practice for all VaR calculation methods.

[10] An approach for limiting the number of portfolio revaluations is proposed in F. Jamshidian and Y. Zhu, "Scenario simulation model: theory and methodology," *Finance and Stochastics*, 1 (1997), 43–67.

[11] For a discussion of this problem and a way of overcoming it without resorting to historical simulation, see J. Hull and A. White, "Value at risk when daily changes in market variables are not normally distributed," *Journal of Derivatives*, 5, 3 (Spring 1998), 9–19.

[12] As in the case of Monte Carlo simulation, extreme value theory can be used. See footnote 8.

[13] For a way of incorporating volatility updating into a historical simulation see J. Hull and A. White, "Incorporating Volatility Updating into the Historical Simulation Method for Value-at-Risk," *Journal of Risk*, 1, 1 (1998), 5–19.

14.9 STRESS TESTING AND BACK-TESTING

In addition to calculating a VaR, many companies carry out what is known as a *stress test* of their portfolio. Stress testing involves estimating how the portfolio would have performed under some of the most extreme market moves seen in the last 10 to 20 years.

For example, to test the impact of an extreme movement in U.S. equity prices, a company might set the proportional changes in all market variables equal to those on October 19, 1987 (when the S&P 500 moved by 22.3 standard deviations). If this is considered to be too extreme, the company might choose January 8, 1988 (when the S&P 500 moved by 6.8 standard deviations). To test the effect of extreme movements in U.K. interest rates, the company might set the proportional changes in all market variables equal to those on April 10, 1992 (when 10-year bond yields moved by 7.7 standard deviations).

Stress testing can be considered as a way of taking into account extreme events that do occur from time to time but that are virtually impossible according to the probability distributions assumed for market variables. A five-standard-deviation daily move in a market variable is one such extreme event. Under the assumption of a normal distribution, it happens about once every 7,000 years but, in practice, it is not uncommon to see a five-standard-deviation daily move once or twice every 10 years.

Whatever the method used for calculating VaR, an important reality check is *back-testing*. It involves testing how well the VaR estimates would have performed in the past. Suppose that we are calculating a 1-day 99% VaR. Back-testing would involve looking at how often the loss in a day exceeded the 1-day 99% VaR. If this happened on about one percent of the days, we can feel reasonably comfortable with the methodology for calculating VaR. If it happened on, say, 10% of days the methodology is suspect.

14.10 PRINCIPAL COMPONENTS ANALYSIS

One approach to handling the risk arising from groups of highly correlated market variables is principal components analysis. This takes historical data on movements in the market variables and attempts to define a set of components or factors that explain the movements.

The approach is best illustrated with an example. The market variables we will consider are ten U.S. Treasury rates with maturities between three months and 30 years. Tables 14.3 and 14.4 show results produced by Frye for these market variables using 1,543 daily observations between 1989 and 1995.[14] The first column in Table 14.3 shows the maturities of the rates that were considered. The remaining ten columns in the table show the ten factors (or principal components) describing the rate

---

[14]See J. Frye, "Principals of Risk: Finding VAR through Factor-Based Interest Rate Scenarios." In *VAR: Understanding and Applying Value at Risk.* (Risk Publications, London, 1997), 275–288.

Table 14.3   Factor Loadings for U.S. Treasury Data

	PC1	PC2	PC3	PC4	PC5	PC6	PC7	PC8	PC9	PC10
3 mo.	0.21	−0.57	0.50	0.47	−0.39	−0.02	0.01	0.00	0.01	0.00
6 mo.	0.26	−0.49	0.23	−0.37	0.70	0.01	−0.04	−0.02	−0.01	0.00
12 mo.	0.32	−0.32	−0.37	−0.58	−0.52	−0.23	−0.04	−0.05	0.00	0.01
2 yr.	0.35	−0.10	−0.38	0.17	0.04	0.59	0.56	0.12	−0.12	−0.05
3 yr.	0.36	0.02	−0.30	0.27	0.07	0.24	−0.79	0.00	−0.09	−0.00
4 yr.	0.36	0.14	−0.12	0.25	0.16	−0.63	0.15	0.55	−0.14	−0.08
5 yr.	0.36	0.17	−0.04	0.14	0.08	−0.10	0.09	−0.26	0.71	0.48
7 yr.	0.34	0.27	0.15	0.01	0.00	−0.12	0.13	−0.54	0.00	−0.68
10 yr.	0.31	0.30	0.28	−0.10	−0.06	0.01	0.03	−0.23	−0.63	0.52
30 yr.	0.25	0.33	0.46	−0.34	−0.18	0.33	−0.09	0.52	0.26	−0.13

Table 14.4   Standard Deviation of Factor Scores (Basis Points)

PC1	PC2	PC3	PC4	PC5	PC6	PC7	PC8	PC9	PC10
17.49	6.05	3.10	2.17	1.97	1.69	1.27	1.24	0.80	0.79

moves. The first factor, shown in the column labeled PC1, corresponds to a roughly parallel shift in the yield curve. When we have one unit of that factor, the three-month rate increases by 0.21 basis points, the six-month rate increases by 0.26 basis points, and so on. The second factor is shown in the column labeled PC2. It corresponds to a "twist" or "steepening" of the yield curve. Rates between 3 months and 2 years move in one direction; rates between 3 years and 30 years move in the other direction. The third factor corresponds to a "bowing" of the yield curve. Rates at the short end and long end of the yield curve move in one direction; rates in the middle move in the other direction. The interest rate move for a particular factor is known as *factor loading*. In our example, the first factor's loading for the three-month rate is 0.21.[15]

Because there are ten rates and ten factors, the interest rate changes observed on any given day can always be expressed as a linear sum of the factors by solving a set of ten simultaneous equations. The amounts of the factors in the rate moves on a particular day are known as the *factor scores*.

The importance of a factor is measured by the standard deviation of its factor score. The standard deviation of the factor scores in our example are shown in Table 14.4 and the factors are listed in order of their importance. The numbers in Table 14.4 are measured in basis points (bps). A one standard deviation move in the first factor, therefore, corresponds to the three-month rate moving by $0.21 \times 17.49 = 3.67$ bps, the six-month rate moving by $0.26 \times 17.49 = 4.55$ bps, and so on.

The technical details of how the factors are determined are not covered here. It is sufficient for us to note that the factors are chosen so that the factor scores are

---

[15]The factor loadings have the property that the sum of their squares for each factor is 1.0.

uncorrelated. For instance, in our example, the first factor score (amount of parallel shift) is uncorrelated with the second factor score (amount of twist) across the 1,543 days.

The variances of the factor scores (i.e., the squares of the standard deviations) have the property that they add up to the total variance of the data. From Table 14.3, the total variance of the original data (that is, sum of the variance of the observations on the three-month rate, the variance of the observations on the six-month rate, and so on) is

$$17.49^2 + 6.05^2 + 3.10^2 + \cdots + 0.79^2 = 367.9$$

From this it can be seen that the first factor accounts for $17.49^2/367.9 = 83.1\%$ of the variation in the original data; the first two factors account for $(17.49^2 + 6.05^2)/367.9 = 93.1\%$ of the variation in the data; the third factor accounts for a further 2.8% of the variation. This shows most of the risk in interest rate moves is accounted for by the first two or three factors. It suggests that we can relate the risks in a portfolio of interest rate dependent instruments to movements in these factors instead of considering all ten interest rates. The three most important factors from Table 14.3 are plotted in Figure 14.4.[16]

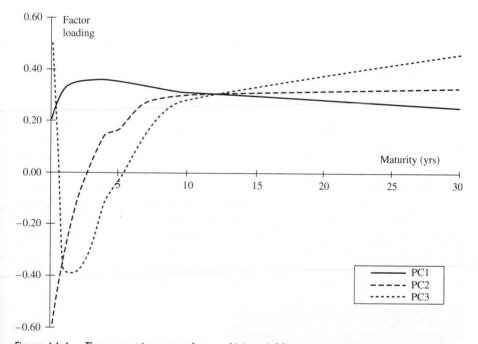

Figure 14.4   Three most important factors driving yield curve movements.

---

[16]Similar results to those described here, as far as the nature of the factors and the amount of the total risk they account for, are obtained when a principal components analysis is used to explain the movements in almost any yield curve in any country.

Using Principal Components Analysis to Calculate VaR

To illustrate how a principal components analysis can be used to calculate VaR, suppose we have a portfolio with the exposures shown in Table 14.5 to interest rate moves. A one basis change in the one-year rate causes the portfolio value to increase by $10 million; a one basis point change in the two-year rate causes it to increase by $4 million; and so on. We use the first two factors to model rate moves. (As mentioned in the preceding, this captures over 90% of the uncertainty in rate moves.) Using the data in Table 14.3, our exposure to the first factor (measured in millions of dollars per factor score basis point) is

$$10 \times 0.32 + 4 \times 0.35 - 8 \times 0.36 - 7 \times 0.36 + 2 \times 0.36 = -0.08$$

and our exposure to the second factor is

$$10 \times (-0.32) + 4 \times (-0.10) - 8 \times 0.02 - 7 \times 0.14 + 2 \times 0.17 = -4.40$$

Suppose that f_1 and f_2 are the factor scores (measured in basis points). The change in the portfolio value is, to a good approximation, given by

$$\Delta P = -0.08 f_1 - 4.40 f_2$$

The factor scores are uncorrelated and have the standard deviations in Table 14.4. The standard deviation of ΔP is, therefore,

$$\sqrt{0.08^2 \times 17.49^2 + 4.40^2 \times 6.05^2} = 26.66$$

The 1-day 99% VaR is, therefore, $26.66 \times 2.33 = 62.12$. Note that the data in Table 14.5 are such that we have very little exposure to the first factor and significant exposure to the second factor. Using only one factor would significantly understate VaR. (See Problem 14.12.) The duration-based analysis in section 14.4 would also significantly understate VaR as it considers only parallel shifts in the yield curve.

Principal components analyses can in theory be used for market variables other than interest rates. Suppose that a financial institution has exposures to a number of different stock indices. A principal components analysis can be used to identify factors describing movements in the indices and the most important of these can be used to replace the market indices in a VaR analysis. How effective a principal components analysis is for a group of market variables depends on how closely correlated they are.

As explained earlier in the chapter, VaR is usually calculated by relating the actual changes in a portfolio to proportional changes in market variables (the Δx_i's). A

Table 14.5	Change in Portfolio Value for a 1 Basis Point Rate Move ($ Millions)			
1 yr rate	*2 yr rate*	*3 yr rate*	*4 yr rate*	*5 yr rate*
+10	+4	−8	−7	+2

principal components analysis is, therefore, often carried out on proportional changes in market variables rather than their actual changes. This leads to some of the Δx_i's being replaced by factor scores in the analyses given earlier in the chapter.

SUMMARY

A value at risk (VaR) calculation is aimed at making a statement of the form "We are X percent certain that we will not lose more than V dollars in the next N days." The variable V is the VaR, X is the confidence level, and N is the time horizon.

The calculation of VaR is greatly simplified if two assumptions can be made:

1. The change in the value of the portfolio (ΔP) is linearly dependent on the proportional changes in the market variables (i.e., Δx_i's).

2. The Δx_i's are normally distributed.

The probability distribution of ΔP is then normal, and there are analytic formulas for relating the standard deviation of ΔP to the volatilities and correlations of the underlying market variables. The VaR can be calculated from well-known properties of the normal distribution.

When a portfolio includes options, ΔP is not linearly related to the Δx_i's. From a knowledge of the gamma of the portfolio, we can derive an approximate quadratic relationship between ΔP and the Δx_i's. This enables us to calculate moments of the probability distribution of ΔP and use the Cornish–Fisher expansion to calculate the percentile of the distribution corresponding to VaR.

Another approach to calculating VaR for a portfolio that includes options is Monte Carlo simulation. It involves repeatedly sampling from the probability distributions of the Δx_i's to calculate a probability distribution for ΔP. The value of ΔP corresponding to a particular set of Δx_i's can be obtained by either revaluing the portfolio or using the quadratic approximation.

An alternative to assuming that the Δx_i's are normal is to base the VaR estimate on a simulation that uses historical data. This approach involves creating a database consisting of the daily movements in all market variables over a period of time. The first simulation trial assumes that the percentage changes in each market variable are the same as those on the first day covered by the database; the second simulation trial assumes that the percentage changes are the same as those on the second day; and so on. The change in the portfolio value, ΔP, is calculated for each simulation trial and the VaR is calculated as the appropriate percentile of the probability distribution of ΔP.

Interest rates can be handled in a number of ways in a VaR analysis. The duration-based approach assumes that all shifts in a yield curve are parallel. Cash flow mapping schemes use zero-coupon bonds with standard maturities as the market variables. The actual exposures in a portfolio are mapped into exposures to these bonds. A principal components analysis defines a relatively small number of factors (i.e., shifts in the yield curve) that account for a high percentage of interest rate uncertainty. Exposures to individual interest rates are replaced by exposures to the factors.

SUGGESTIONS FOR FURTHER READING

Ahn, D., J. Boudoukh, M. Richardson, and R. F. Whitelaw. "Optimal Risk Management Using Options," *Journal of Finance,* 54, 1 (February 1999), 359–75.

Boudoukh, J., M. Richardson, and R. Whitelaw. "The Best of Both Worlds," *RISK,* (May 1998), 64–67.

Dowd, K. *Beyond Value at Risk: The New Science of Risk Management.* New York: John Wiley and Sons, 1998.

Duffie, D., and J. Pan. "An Overview of Value at Risk," *Journal of Derivatives,* 4, 3 (Spring 1997), 7–49.

Embrechts, P., C. Kluppelberg, and T. Mikosch. *Modeling Extremal Events for Insurance and Finance,* Springer, 1997.

Frye, J. "Principals of Risk: Finding VAR through Factor-Based Interest Rate Scenarios." In *VAR: Understanding and Applying Value at Risk.* London: Risk Publications, 1997, 275–288.

Hendricks, D. "Evaluation of Value-at-Risk Models Using Historical Data," *Economic Policy Review,* Federal Reserve Bank of New York, 2 (April 1996), 39–69.

Hopper, G. "Value at Risk: A New Methodology for Measuring Portfolio Risk," *Business Review,* Federal Reserve Bank of Philadelphia, (July–August 1996), 19–29.

Hull, J. C., and A. White. "Value at Risk when Daily Changes in Market Variables are not Normally Distributed," *Journal of Derivatives,* 5, 3 (Spring 1998), 9–19.

Hull, J. C., and A. White. "Incorporating Volatility Updating into the Historical Simulation Method for Value-at-Risk," *Journal of Risk,* 1, 1 (1998).

Jackson, P., D. J. Maude, and W. Perraudin. "Bank Capital and Value at Risk," *Journal of Derivatives* 4, 3 (Spring 1997), 73–90.

Jamshidian, F., and Y. Zhu. "Scenario Simulation Model: Theory and Methodology," *Finance and Stochastics,* 1 (1997), 43–67.

Jorion, P. *Value at Risk: The New Benchmark for Controlling Market Risk.* Chicago: Irwin, 1997.

J. P. Morgan. *RiskMetrics Technical Manual,* New York: J. P. Morgan Bank, 1995.

Risk Publications. "Value at Risk," *RISK* supplement, (June 1996).

QUESTIONS AND PROBLEMS
(ANSWERS IN SOLUTIONS MANUAL)

14.1. Consider a position consisting of a $100,000 investment in asset A and a $100,000 investment in asset B. Assume that the daily volatilities of both assets are 1% and that the coefficient of correlation between their returns is 0.3. What is the 5-day 95% value at risk for the portfolio?

14.2. A company has a position in bonds worth $4 million. The modified duration of the portfolio is 3.7 years. Assume that only parallel shifts in the yield curve can take place and that the yield volatility (measured as the standard deviation of the size of the shift in one day) is 0.09%. Estimate the 20-day 90% VaR for the portfolio using the duration model.

14.3. A financial institution owns a portfolio of options on the U.S. dollar-sterling exchange rate. The delta of the portfolio is 56.0. The current exchange rate is 1.5000. Derive an approximate linear relationship between the change in the portfolio value and the proportional change in the exchange rate. If the daily volatility of the exchange rate is 0.7%, estimate the 10-day 99% VaR.

14.4. Suppose you know that the gamma of the portfolio in the previous question is 16.2. How does this change your estimate of the relationship between the change in the portfolio value and the proportional change in the exchange rate? Calculate a new 10-day 99% VaR based on estimates of the first two moments of the change in the portfolio value.

14.5. Suppose that the daily change in the value of a portfolio is, to a good approximation, linearly dependent on two factors calculated from a principal components analysis. The delta of a portfolio with respect to the first factor is 6 and the delta with respect to the second factor is −4. The standard deviations of the factors are 20 and 8, respectively. What is the 5-day 90% VaR?

14.6. Suppose a company has a portfolio consisting of positions in stocks, bonds, foreign exchange, and commodities. Assume there are no derivatives. Explain the assumptions underlying (a) the linear model and (b) the historical simulation model for calculating VaR.

14.7. Explain how an interest rate swap is mapped into a portfolio of zero-coupon bonds with standard maturities for the purposes of a VaR calculation.

14.8. Explain why the linear model can provide only approximate estimates of VaR for a portfolio containing options.

14.9. Verify that the 0.3-year zero-coupon bond in the cash-flow mapping example in section 14.4 is mapped in a $37,397 position in a three-month bond and a $11,793 position in a six-month bond.

14.10. Suppose that the 5-year rate is 6%, the seven year rate is 7% (both expressed with annual compounding), the daily volatility of a 5-year zero-coupon bond is 0.5%, and the daily volatility of a 7-year zero-coupon bond is 0.58%. The correlation between daily returns on the two bonds is 0.6. Map a cash flow of $1,000 received at time 6.5 years into a position in a five-year bond and a position in a seven-year bond. What cash flows in five and seven years are equivalent to the 6.5-year cash flow?

14.11. A company has entered into a six-month forward contract to buy £1 million for $1.5 million. The daily volatility of a six-month zero-coupon sterling bond (when its price is translated to dollars) is 0.06% and the daily volatility of a six-month zero-coupon dollar bond is 0.05%. The correlation between returns from the two bonds is 0.8. The current exchange rate is 1.53. Calculate the standard deviation of the change in the dollar value of the forward contract in one day. What is the 10-day 99% VaR? Assume that the six-month interest rate in both sterling and dollars is 5% per annum with continuous compounding.

14.12. The text calculates a VaR estimate for the example in Table 14.5 assuming two factors. How does the estimate change if you assume (a) one factor and (b) three factors.

14.13. A bank has a portfolio of options on an asset. The delta of the options is −30 and the gamma is −5. Explain how these numbers can be interpreted. The asset price is 20 and its volatility is 1% per day. Using the quadratic model calculate the first three moments of the change in the portfolio value. Calculate a 1-day 99% VaR using (a) the first two moments and (b) the first three moments.

14.14. Suppose that in Problem 14.13 the vega of the portfolio is −2 per 1% change in the annual volatility. Derive a model relating the change in the portfolio value in one day to delta, gamma, and vega. Explain without doing detailed calculations how you would use the model to calculate a VaR estimate.

ASSIGNMENT QUESTIONS

14.15. Consider a position consisting of a $300,000 investment in gold and a $500,000 investment in silver. Suppose that the daily volatilities of these two assets are 1.8% and 1.2%, respectively, and that the coefficient of correlation between their returns is 0.6. What is the 10-day 97.5% value at risk for the portfolio? By how much does diversification reduce the VaR?

14.16. Consider a portfolio of options on a single asset. Suppose that the delta of the portfolio is 12, the value of the asset is $10, and the daily volatility of the asset is 2%. Estimate the 1-day 95% VaR for the portfolio.

14.17. Suppose that the gamma of the portfolio in Problem 14.16 is −2.6. Derive a quadratic relationship between the change in the portfolio value and the proportional change in the underlying asset price in one day.
(a) Calculate the first three moments of the change in the portfolio value.
(b) Using the first two moments and assuming that the change in the portfolio is normally distributed, calculate the 1-day 95% VaR for the portfolio.
(c) Use the third moment and the Cornish–Fisher expansion to revise your answer to (b).

14.18. A company has a long position in a two-year bond and a three-year bond as well as a short position in a five-year bond. Each bond has a principal of $100 and pays a 5% coupon annually. Calculate the company's exposure to the one-year, two-year, three-year, four-year, and five-year rates. Use the data in Tables 14.3 and 14.4 to calculate a 20-day 95% VaR on the assumption that rate changes are explained by (a) one factor, (b) two factors, and (c) three factors.

14.19. A bank has written a call option on one stock and a put option on another stock. For the first option the stock price is 50, the strike price is 51, the volatility is 28% per annum, and the time to maturity is nine months. For the second option the stock price is 20, the strike price is 19, the volatility is 25% per annum, and the time to maturity is one year. Neither stock pays a dividend, the risk-free rate is 6% per annum, and the correlation between stock price returns is 0.4. Calculate a 10-day 99% VaR
(a) Using only delta.

(b) Using delta, gamma, and the first two moments of the change in the portfolio value.

(c) Using delta, gamma, and the first three moments of the change in the portfolio value.

(d) Using the partial simulation approach.

(e) Using the full simulation approach.

APPENDIX 14A

Use of the Cornish–Fisher Expansion to Estimate VaR

As shown in equation (14.11), we can approximate ΔP for a portfolio containing options as

$$\Delta P = \sum_{i=1}^{n} \alpha_i \Delta x_i + \sum_{i=1}^{n} \sum_{j=1}^{n} \beta_{ij} \Delta x_i \Delta x_j \qquad (16A.1)$$

Define σ_{ij} as the covariance between variable i and j:

$$\sigma_{ij} = \rho_{ij} \sigma_i \sigma_j$$

It can be shown that when the Δx_i are multivariate normal

$$E(\Delta P) = \sum_{i,j} \beta_{ij} \sigma_{ij}$$

$$E[(\Delta P)^2] = \sum_{i,j} \alpha_i \alpha_j \sigma_{ij} + \sum_{i,j,k,l} \beta_{ij} \beta_{kl} (\sigma_{ij} \sigma_{kl} + \sigma_{ik} \sigma_{jl} + \sigma_{il} \sigma_{jk})$$

$$E[(\Delta P)^3] = 3 \sum_{i,j,k,l} \alpha_i \alpha_j \beta_{kl} (\sigma_{ij} \sigma_{kl} + \sigma_{ik} \sigma_{jl} + \sigma_{il} \sigma_{jk}) + \sum_{i_1,i_2,i_3,i_4,i_5,i_6} \beta_{i_1 i_2} \beta_{i_3 i_4} \beta_{i_5 i_6} Q$$

The variable, Q, consists of fifteen terms of the form $\sigma_{k_1 k_2} \sigma_{k_3 k_4} \sigma_{k_5 k_6}$ where the k_1, k_2, k_3, k_4, k_5, and k_6 are permutations of i_1, i_2, i_3, i_4, i_5, and i_6.

Define μ_P and σ_P as the mean and standard deviation of ΔP so that

$$\mu_P = E(\Delta P)$$
$$\sigma_P^2 = E[(\Delta P)^2] - [E(\Delta P)]^2$$

The skewness of the probability distribution of ΔP, ξ_P, is defined as

$$\xi_P = \frac{1}{\sigma_P^3} E[(\Delta P - \mu_P)^3] = \frac{E[(\Delta P)^3] - 3E[(\Delta P)^2]\mu_P + 2\mu_P^3}{\sigma_P^3}$$

Using the first three moments of ΔP, the Cornish–Fisher expansion estimates the q-percentile of the distribution of ΔP as

$$\mu_P + w_q \sigma_P$$

where

$$w_q = z_q + \frac{1}{6}(z_q^2 - 1)\xi_P$$

and z_q is q-percentile of the standard normal distribution $\phi(0, 1)$.

Example 14.3   Suppose that for a certain portfolio we calculate $\mu_P = -0.2$, $\sigma_P = 2.2$, and $\xi_P = -0.4$. If we assume that the probability distribution of ΔP is normal, one percentile of the probability distribution of ΔP is

$$-0.2 - 2.33 \times 2.2 = -5.326$$

In other words, we are 99% certain that

$$\Delta P > -5.326$$

When we use the Cornish–Fisher expansion to adjust for skewness and set $q = 0.01$, we obtain

$$w_q = -2.33 - \frac{1}{6}(2.33^2 - 1) \times 0.4 = -2.625$$

so that one percentile of the distribution is

$$-0.2 - 2.625 \times 2.2 = -5.976$$

Taking account of skewness, therefore, changes the VaR from 5.326 to 5.976.

CHAPTER

15

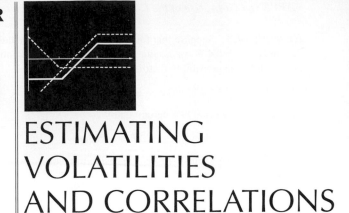

ESTIMATING
VOLATILITIES
AND CORRELATIONS

This chapter explains ways that historical data can be used to produce estimates of the current levels of volatilities and correlations, as well as forecasts of the future values of these variables. The chapter is relevant to both the calculation of value at risk and the valuation of derivatives. When calculating value at risk, we are most interested in the current levels of volatilities and correlations because we are assessing possible changes in the value of a portfolio over a very short period of time. When valuing derivatives, forecasts of volatilities and correlations over the whole life of the derivative are usually required.

The chapter considers models with imposing names such as exponentially weighted moving average (EWMA), autoregressive conditional heteroscedasticity (ARCH), and generalized autoregressive conditional heteroscedasticity (GARCH). The distinctive feature of the models is that they recognize that volatilities and correlations are not constant. During some periods, a particular volatility or correlation may be relatively low whereas during other periods it may be relatively high. The models attempt to keep track of the variations in the volatility or correlation through time.

15.1   ESTIMATING VOLATILITY

Define σ_n as the volatility of a market variable on day n, as estimated at the end of day $n - 1$. The square of the volatility on day n, σ_n^2, is the *variance rate*.

The standard approach to estimating σ_n from historical data was described in section 11.3. Suppose that the value of the market variable at the end of day i is S_i. The variable u_i is defined as the continuously compounded return during day i (between the end of day $i - 1$ and the end of day i):

$$u_i = \ln \frac{S_i}{S_{i-1}}$$

An unbiased estimate of the variance rate per day, σ_n^2, using the most recent m observations on the u_i is

$$\sigma_n^2 = \frac{1}{m-1} \sum_{i=1}^{m} (u_{n-i} - \bar{u})^2 \tag{15.1}$$

where $\bar{u}$ is the mean of the u_i's:

$$\bar{u} = \frac{1}{m} \sum_{i=1}^{m} u_{n-i}$$

For the purposes of calculating VaR, the formula in equation (15.1) is usually changed in a number of ways:

1. u_i is defined as the proportional change in the market variable between the end of day $i - 1$ and the end of day i so that:[1]

$$u_i = \frac{S_i - S_{i-1}}{S_{i-1}} \tag{15.2}$$

2. $\bar{u}$ is assumed to be zero.[2]
3. $m - 1$ is replaced by m.[3]

These three changes make very little difference to the variance estimates that are calculated. The formula for variance rate becomes

$$\sigma_n^2 = \frac{1}{m} \sum_{i=1}^{m} u_{n-i}^2 \tag{15.3}$$

where u_i is given by equation (15.2).[4]

Weighting Schemes

Equation (15.3) gives equal weight to all u_i^2's. Given that the objective is to monitor the current level of volatility, it is appropriate to give more weight to recent data. A model that does this is

$$\sigma_n^2 = \sum_{i=1}^{m} \alpha_i u_{n-i}^2 \tag{15.4}$$

---

[1] This is consistent with the point made in section 14.1 about the way that volatility is defined for the purposes of VaR calculations.

[2] As explained in section 14.2, this assumption usually has very little effect on estimates of the variance because the expected change in a variable in one day is very small when compared with the standard deviation of changes. As an alternative to the assumption we can define u_i as the realized return minus the expected return on day i.

[3] Replacing $m - 1$ by m moves us from an unbiased estimate of the variance to a maximum likelihood estimate. Maximum likelihood estimates are discussed later in the chapter.

[4] Note that the u's in this chapter play the same role as the Δx's in chapter 14. Both are daily proportional changes in market variables. In the case of the u's, the subscripts count observations made on different days on the same market variable. In the case of the Δx's, they count observations made on the same day on different market variables. The use of subscripts for σ is similarly different between the two chapters. In this chapter, the subscripts refer to days; in chapter 14 they referred to market variables.

The variable α_i is the amount of weight given to the observation i days ago. The α's are positive. Because we wish to give less weight to older observations, $\alpha_i < \alpha_j$ when $i > j$. The weights must sum to unity so that:

$$\sum_{i=1}^{m} \alpha_i = 1$$

An extension of the idea in equation (15.4) is to assume that there is a long-run average volatility and that this should be given some weight. This leads to a model that takes the form

$$\sigma_n^2 = \gamma V + \sum_{i=1}^{m} \alpha_i u_{n-i}^2 \tag{15.5}$$

where V is the long-run volatility and γ is the weight assigned to V. Because the weights must sum to unity:

$$\gamma + \sum_{i=1}^{m} \alpha_i = 1$$

This is known as an ARCH(m) model. It was first suggested by Engle.[5] The estimate of the variance is based on a long-run average variance and m observations. The older an observation, the less weight it is given. Defining $\omega = \gamma V$, the model in equation (15.5) can be written

$$\sigma_n^2 = \omega + \sum_{i=1}^{m} \alpha_i u_{n-i}^2 \tag{15.6}$$

This is the version of the model that is used when parameters are estimated.

In the next two sections we discuss two important approaches to monitoring volatility using the ideas in equations (15.4) and (15.5).

15.2   THE EXPONENTIALLY WEIGHTED MOVING AVERAGE MODEL

The exponentially weighted moving average (EWMA) model is a particular case of the model in equation (15.4) where the weights, α_i, decrease exponentially as we move back through time. Specifically, $\alpha_{i+1} = \lambda \alpha_i$ where λ is a constant between zero and one.

It turns out that this weighting scheme leads to a particularly simple formula for updating volatility estimates. The formula is

$$\sigma_n^2 = \lambda \sigma_{n-1}^2 + (1 - \lambda) u_{n-1}^2 \tag{15.7}$$

---

[5] See R. Engle, "Autoregressive Conditional Heteroscedasticity with Estimates of the Variance of UK Inflation," *Econometrica*, 50 (1982), 987–1008.

The estimate, σ_n, of the volatility for day n (made at the end of day $n-1$) is calculated from σ_{n-1} (the estimate that was made one day ago of the volatility for day $n-1$) and u_{n-1} (the most recent observation on changes in the market variable).

To understand why equation (15.7) corresponds to weights that decrease exponentially, we substitute for σ_{n-1}^2 to get

$$\sigma_n^2 = \lambda[\lambda\sigma_{n-2}^2 + (1-\lambda)u_{n-2}^2] + (1-\lambda)u_{n-1}^2$$

or

$$\sigma_n^2 = (1-\lambda)(u_{n-1}^2 + \lambda u_{n-2}^2) + \lambda^2\sigma_{n-2}^2$$

Substituting in a similar way for σ_{n-2}^2 gives

$$\sigma_n^2 = (1-\lambda)(u_{n-1}^2 + \lambda u_{n-2}^2 + \lambda^2 u_{n-3}^2) + \lambda^3\sigma_{n-3}^2$$

Continuing in this way, we see that

$$\sigma_n^2 = (1-\lambda)\sum_{i=1}^{m} \lambda^{i-1}u_{n-i}^2 + \lambda^m\sigma_0^2$$

For a large m, the term $\lambda^m\sigma_0^2$ is sufficiently small to be ignored so that equation (15.7) is the same as equation (15.4) with $\alpha_i = (1-\lambda)\lambda^{i-1}$. The weights for the u_i's decline at rate λ as we move back through time. Each weight is λ times the previous weight.

> **Example 15.1** Suppose that λ is 0.90, the volatility estimated for day $n-1$ is 1% per day, and the proportional change in the market variable during day $n-1$ is 2%. This means that $\sigma_{n-1}^2 = 0.01^2 = 0.0001$ and $u_{n-1}^2 = 0.02^2 = 0.0004$. Equation (15.7) gives
>
> $$\sigma_n^2 = 0.9 \times 0.0001 + 0.1 \times 0.0004 = 0.00013$$
>
> The estimate of the volatility for day n, σ_n, is, therefore, $\sqrt{0.00013}$ or 1.14% per day. Note that the expected value of u_{n-1}^2 is σ_{n-1}^2 or 0.0001. In this example, the realized value of u_{n-1}^2 is greater than the expected value, and as a result our volatility estimate increases. If the realized value of u_{n-1}^2 had been less than its expected value, our estimate of the volatility would have decreased.

The EWMA approach has the attractive feature that relatively little data need to be stored. At any given time, we need to remember only the current estimate of the variance rate and the most recent observation on the value of the market variable. When we get a new observation on the value of the market variable, we calculate a new u^2 and use equation (15.7) to update our estimate of the variance rate. The old estimate of the variance rate and the old value of the market variable can then be discarded.

The EWMA approach is designed to track changes in the volatility. Suppose there is a big move in the market variable on day $n-1$ so that u_{n-1}^2 is large. From equation (15.7) this causes σ_n, our estimate of the daily volatility for day n, to move upward. The value of λ governs how responsive the estimate of the daily volatility is to the most recent observations on the u_i's. A low value of λ leads to a great deal of weight being given to the u_{n-1}^2 when σ_n is calculated. In this case, the estimates produced for the volatility on successive days are themselves highly volatile. A high value of λ (i.e., a value close to 1.0) produces estimates of the daily volatility that respond relatively slowly to new information provided by the u_i^2.

J. P. Morgan uses the EWMA model with $\lambda = 0.94$ for updating daily volatility estimates in its RiskMetrics database.[6] The company found that, across a range of different market variables, this value of λ gives forecasts of the variance rate that come closest to the realized variance rate.[7] The realized variance rate on a particular day was calculated as an equally weighted average of the u_i^2 on the subsequent 25 days.

15.3   THE GARCH (1, 1) MODEL

We now move on to discuss what is known as the GARCH (1,1) model proposed by Bollerslev in 1986.[8] The difference between the GARCH (1,1) model and the EWMA model is analogous to the difference between equation (15.4) and equation (15.5). In GARCH (1,1), σ_n^2 is calculated from a long-run average variance rate, V, as well as from σ_{n-1} and u_{n-1}. The equation for GARCH (1,1) is

$$\sigma_n^2 = \gamma V + \alpha u_{n-1}^2 + \beta \sigma_{n-1}^2 \tag{15.8}$$

where γ is the weight assigned to V, α is the weight assigned to u_{n-1}^2, and β is the weight assigned to σ_{n-1}^2. Because the weights must sum to one:

$$\gamma + \alpha + \beta = 1$$

The EWMA model is a particular case of GARCH (1,1) where $\gamma = 0$, $\alpha = 1 - \lambda$, and $\beta = \lambda$.

The "(1,1)" in GARCH (1,1) indicates that σ_n^2 is based on the most recent observation of u^2 and the most recent estimate of the variance rate. The more general GARCH (p, q) model calculates σ_n^2 from the most recent p observations on u^2 and the most recent q estimates of the variance rate.[9] GARCH (1,1) is by far the most popular of the GARCH models.

---

[6]It is worth noting that the J. P. Morgan RiskMetrics database uses a different definition of volatility per day from the standard one. Its definition of volatility is 1.65 times the standard definition. From the tables at the end of this book, $N(-1.65) = 0.05$. Assuming a normal distribution, the RiskMetrics volatility can, therefore, be interpreted as the decline in a market variable that is expected to be exceeded on only 5% of days.

[7]See J. P. Morgan, *RiskMetrics Monitor*, Fourth Quarter, 1995. We will explain an alternative (maximum likelihood) approach to estimating parameters later in the chapter.

[8]See T. Bollerslev, "Generalized Autoregressive Conditional Heteroscedasticity," *Journal of Econometrics*, 31 (1986), 307–27.

[9]Other GARCH models have been proposed that incorporate asymmetric news. These models are designed so that σ_n depends on the sign of u_{n-1}. Arguably, the models are more appropriate for equities than GARCH (1,1). The volatility of an equity's price tends to be inversely related to the price so that a negative u_{n-1} has a bigger effect on σ_n than the same positive u_{n-1}. (See chapter 17.) For a discussion of models for handling asymmetric news see D. Nelson, "Conditional Heteroscedasticity and Asset Returns; A New Approach," *Econometrica*, 59 (1990), 347–70 and R.F. Engle and V. Ng, "Measuring and Testing the Impact of News on Volatility," *Journal of Finance*, 48 (1993), 1,749–78.

Setting $\omega = \gamma V$, the GARCH(1,1) model can also be written

$$\sigma_n^2 = \omega + \alpha u_{n-1}^2 + \beta \sigma_{n-1}^2 \qquad (15.9)$$

This is the form of the model that is usually used for the purposes of estimating the parameters. Once ω, α, and β have been estimated, we can calculate γ as $1 - \alpha - \beta$. The long-term variance V can then be calculated as ω/γ. For a stable GARCH (1,1) process we require $\alpha + \beta < 1$. Otherwise the weight applied to the long-term variance is negative.

Example 15.2 Suppose that a GARCH (1,1) model is estimated from daily data as

$$\sigma_n^2 = 0.000002 + 0.13 u_{n-1}^2 + 0.86 \sigma_{n-1}^2$$

This corresponds to $\alpha = 0.13$, $\beta = 0.86$, and $\omega = 0.000002$. Because $\gamma = 1 - \alpha - \beta$, it follows that $\gamma = 0.01$. Because $\omega = \gamma V$, it follows that $V = 0.0002$. In other words, the long-run average variance per day implied by the model is 0.0002. This corresponds to a volatility of $\sqrt{0.0002} = 0.014$ or 1.4% per day.
 Suppose that the estimate of the volatility on day $n - 1$ is 1.6% per day so that $\sigma_{n-1}^2 = 0.016^2 = 0.000256$ and that the proportional change in the market variable on day $n - 1$ is 1% so that $u_{n-1}^2 = 0.01^2 = 0.0001$. Then:

$$\sigma_n^2 = 0.000002 + 0.13 \times 0.0001 + 0.86 \times 0.000256 = 0.00023516$$

The new estimate of the volatility is, therefore, $\sqrt{0.00023516} = 0.0153$ or 1.53% per day.

The Weights

Substituting for σ_{n-1}^2 in equation (15.9) we obtain

$$\sigma_n^2 = \omega + \alpha u_{n-1}^2 + \beta[\omega + \alpha u_{n-2}^2 + \beta \sigma_{n-2}^2]$$

or

$$\sigma_n^2 = \omega + \beta\omega + \alpha u_{n-1}^2 + \alpha\beta u_{n-2}^2 + \beta^2 \sigma_{n-2}^2$$

Substituting for σ_{n-2}^2 we get

$$\sigma_n^2 = \omega + \beta\omega + \beta^2\omega + \alpha u_{n-1}^2 + \alpha\beta u_{n-2}^2 + \alpha\beta^2 u_{n-3}^2 + \beta^3 \sigma_{n-3}^2$$

Continuing in this way, we see that the weight applied to u_{n-i}^2 is $\alpha\beta^{i-1}$. The weights decline exponentially at rate β. The parameter β can be interpreted as a "decay rate." It is similar to λ in the EWMA model. It defines the relative importance of the observations on u's in determining the current variance rate. For example, if $\beta = 0.9$, u_{i-2}^2 is only 90% as important as u_{i-1}^2; u_{i-3}^2 is 81% as important as u_{i-1}; and so on. The GARCH (1,1) model is similar to the EWMA model except that, in addition to assigning weights that decline exponentially to past u^2, it also assigns some weight to the long-run average volatility.

15.4   CHOOSING BETWEEN THE MODELS

In practice, a variance rate exhibits what is known as *mean reversion*. Although it moves around randomly, over time it tends to get pulled back toward some long-run average level. Later in the chapter we will show that the GARCH (1,1) model incorporates mean-reversion whereas the EWMA model does not. The GARCH (1,1) model is, therefore, theoretically more appealing than the EWMA model.

In the next section, we will discuss how best fit parameters ω, α, and β in GARCH (1,1) can be estimated. When the parameter ω is zero, the GARCH (1,1) reduces to EWMA. In circumstances where the best fit value of ω turns out to be negative the GARCH (1,1) model is not stable and it makes sense to switch to the EWMA model.

15.5   MAXIMUM LIKELIHOOD METHODS

It is now appropriate to discuss how the parameters in the models we have been considering are estimated from historical data. The approach used is known as the *maximum likelihood method*. It involves choosing values for the parameters that maximize the chance (or likelihood) of the data occurring.

To illustrate the method, we start with a very simple example. Suppose that we sample ten stocks at random on a certain day and find that the price of one of them declined on that day and the prices of the other nine either remained the same or increased. What is our best estimate of the proportion of all stocks with price declines? The natural answer is 10%. Let us see if this is what the maximum likelihood method gives.

Suppose that the proportion of stocks with price declines is p. The probability that one particular stock declines in price and the other nine do not is $p(1 - p)^9$. Using the maximum likelihood approach, the best estimate of p is the one that maximizes $p(1 - p)^9$. Differentiating this expression with respect to p and setting the result equal to zero, we find that $p = 0.1$ maximizes the expression. This shows that the maximum likelihood estimate of p is 10% as expected.

Estimating a Constant Variance

As our next example of maximum likelihood methods, we consider the problem of estimating a variance from m observations when the underlying distribution is normal and the variance is assumed to be constant. We assume that the observations are $u_1, u_2, \ldots, u_m$ and that the mean of the underlying distribution is zero. Denote the variance by v. The probability density for the ith observation, u_i, is the probability density function for a normally distributed variable with mean zero and variance v:

$$\frac{1}{\sqrt{2\pi v}} \exp\left(\frac{-u_i^2}{2v}\right)$$

The probability density of the m observations occurring in the order that they are observed is

$$\prod_{i=1}^{m} \left[\frac{1}{\sqrt{2\pi v}} \exp\left(\frac{-u_i^2}{2v} \right) \right] \tag{15.10}$$

Using the maximum likelihood method, the best estimate of v is the value that maximizes this expression.

Maximizing an expression is equivalent to maximizing the logarithm of the expression. Taking logarithms of the expression in equation (15.10) and ignoring constant multiplicative factors, it can be seen that we wish to maximize

$$\sum_{i=1}^{m} \left[-\ln(v) - \frac{u_i^2}{v} \right] \tag{15.11}$$

or

$$-m \ln(v) - \sum_{i=1}^{m} \frac{u_i^2}{v}$$

Differentiating this expression with respect to v and setting the result equation to zero, we see that the maximum likelihood estimate of v is[10]

$$v = \frac{1}{m} \sum_{i=1}^{m} u_i^2$$

Extension to Estimate Parameters in a Volatility Updating Scheme

We now suppose that the variance is subject to a volatility updating scheme such as GARCH (1,1). Define $v_i = \sigma_i^2$ as the variance estimated for day i. We assume that the probability distribution of u_i conditional on the variance is normal. A similar analysis to the one just given shows that the expression we wish to maximize is

$$\prod_{i=1}^{m} \left[\frac{1}{\sqrt{2\pi v_i}} \exp\left(\frac{-u_i^2}{2v_i} \right) \right]$$

Taking logarithms we see that this is equivalent to maximizing

$$\sum_{i=1}^{m} \left[-\ln(v_i) - \frac{u_i^2}{v_i} \right] \tag{15.12}$$

This is the same as the expression in equation (15.11), except that v is replaced by v_i. We search iteratively to find the parameters in the model that maximize the expression in equation (15.12).

The spreadsheet in Table 15.1 indicates how the calculations could be organized for the GARCH (1,1) model. The table analyzes data on the Japanese yen exchange rate between January 6, 1988, and August 15, 1997. The numbers in the table are based on trial estimates of the three GARCH (1,1) parameters: ω, α, and β. The first

---

[10]This confirms the point made in footnote 3.

Table 15.1   Estimation of Parameters in GARCH(1,1) Model

Date	Day i	S_i	u_i	$v_i = \sigma_i^2$	$-\ln(v_i) - u_i^2/v_i$
06-Jan-88	1	0.007728			
07-Jan-88	2	0.007779	0.006599		
08-Jan-88	3	0.007746	−0.004242	0.00004355	9.6283
11-Jan-88	4	0.007816	0.009037	0.00004198	8.1329
12-Jan-88	5	0.007837	0.002687	0.00004455	9.8568
13-Jan-88	6	0.007924	0.011101	0.00004220	7.1529
...	...	...	...	...	...
...	...	...	...	...	...
13-Aug-97	2421	0.008643	0.003374	0.00007626	9.3321
14-Aug-97	2422	0.008493	−0.017309	0.00007092	5.3294
15-Aug-97	2423	0.008495	0.000144	0.00008417	9.3824
					22,063.5763

Trial estimates of GARCH parameters

ω	α	β
0.00000176	0.0626	0.8976

column in the table records the date. The second column counts the days. The third column shows the exchange rate, S_i, at the end of day i. The fourth column shows the proportional change in the exchange rate between the end of day $i - 1$ and the end of day i. This is $u_i = (S_i - S_{i-1})/S_{i-1}$. The fifth column shows the estimate of the variance rate, $v_i = \sigma_i^2$, for day i made at the end of day $i - 1$. On day three, we start things off by setting the variance equal to u_2^2. On subsequent days equation (15.9) is used. The sixth column tabulates the likelihood measure, $-\ln(v_i) - u_i^2/v_i$. The values in the fifth and sixth columns are based on the current trial estimates of ω, α, and β. We are interested in choosing ω, α, and β to maximize the sum of the numbers in the sixth column. This involves an interative search procedure.[11]

In our example, the optimal values of the parameters turn out to be

$$\omega = 0.00000176$$

$$\alpha = 0.0626$$

$$\beta = 0.8976$$

and the maximum value of the function in equation (15.12) is 22,063.5763. The numbers shown in Table 15.1 were calculated on the final iteration of the search for the optimal ω, α, and β.

---

[11] A general purpose algorithm such as Solver in Microsoft's Excel is liable to provide a local rather than global maximum of the likelihood function. A special purpose algorithm, such as Levenberg–Marquardt, should ideally be used. See W. H. Press, B. P. Flannery, S. A. Teukolsky, and W. T. Vetterling, *Numerical Recipes in C: The Art of Scientific Computing*, Cambridge University Press, 1988.

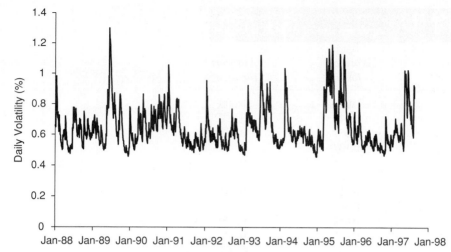

Figure 15.1   Daily volatility of the yen–USD exchange rate, 1987–97.

The long-term variance rate, V, in our example is

$$\frac{\omega}{1 - \alpha - \beta} = \frac{0.00000176}{0.0398} = 0.00004422$$

The long-term volatility is $\sqrt{0.00004422}$ or 0.665% per day.

Figure 15.1 shows the way the volatility for the Japanese yen changed over the 10 year period covered by the data. Most of the time, the volatility was between 0.4% and 0.8% per day, but volatilities over 1% were experienced during some periods.

An alternative, more robust approach to estimating parameters in GARCH (1,1) is known as _variance targeting_.[12] This involves setting the long-run average variance rate, V, equal to the sample variance calculated from the data (or to some other value that is believed to be reasonable.) The value of ω then equals $V(1 - \alpha - \beta)$ and only two parameters have to be estimated. For the data in Table 15.1 the sample variance is 0.00004341, which gives a daily volatility of 0.659%. Setting V equal to the sample variance, the values of α and β that maximize the objective function in equation (15.12) are 0.0607 and 0.8990, respectively. The value of the objective function is 22,063.5274, only marginally below the value of 22,063.5763 obtained using the earlier procedure.[13]

When the EWMA model is used, the estimation procedure is relatively simple. We set $\omega = 0, \alpha = 1 - \lambda$, and $\beta = \lambda$, and only one parameter has to be estimated. In the data in Table 15.1, the value of λ that maximizes the objective function in equation (15.12) is 0.9686 and the value of the objective function is 21,995.8377.

---

[12] See R. Engle and J. Mezrich, "GARCH for Groups," *RISK*, August 1996, 36–40.

[13] The Solver routine in Microsoft's Excel seems to work fine for estimating the optimal parameters when variance targeting is used.

Table 15.2	Autocorrelations Before and After the Use of a GARCH Model	
Time Lag	*Autocorr for u_i^2*	*Autocorr for u_i^2/σ_i^2*
1	0.072	0.000
2	0.041	−0.010
3	0.057	0.005
4	0.107	0.000
5	0.075	0.011
6	0.066	0.008
7	0.019	−0.034
8	0.085	0.015
9	0.054	0.009
10	0.030	−0.022
11	0.038	−0.004
12	0.038	−0.021
13	0.057	−0.002
14	0.040	0.004
15	0.007	−0.026

How Good Is the Model?

The assumption underlying a GARCH model is that volatility changes with the passage of time. During some periods volatility is relatively high; during other periods it is relatively low. To put this another way, when u_i^2 is high there is a tendency for $u_{i+1}^2, u_{i+2}^2, \ldots$ to be high; when u_i^2 is low there is a tendency for $u_{i+1}^2, u_{i+2}^2, \ldots$ to be low. We can test how true this is by examining the autocorrelation structure of the u_i^2.

why?

Let us assume that the u_i^2 do exhibit autocorrelation. If a GARCH model is working well it should remove the autocorrelation. We can test whether it has done this by considering the autocorrelation structure for the variables u_i^2/σ_i^2. If these show very little autocorrelation, our model for σ_i has succeeded in explaining autocorrelations in the u_i^2.

Table 15.2 shows results for the yen–dollar exchange rate data referred to earlier. The first column shows the lags considered when the autocorrelation is calculated. The second column shows autocorrelations for u_i^2; the third column shows autocorrelations for u_i^2/σ_i^2.[14] The table shows that the autocorrelations are positive for u_i^2 for all lags between 1 and 15. In the case of u_i^2/σ_i^2, some of the autocorrelations are positive and some are negative. They are all much smaller in magnitude than the autocorrelations for u_i^2.

The GARCH model appears to have done a good job in explaining the data. For a more scientific test we can use what is known as the Ljung–Box statistic. If a certain

---

[14]For a series x_i, the autocorrelation with a lag of k is the coefficient of correlation between x_i and x_{i+k}.

series has m observations the Ljung–Box statistic is

$$m \sum_{k=1}^{K} w_k \eta_k^2$$

where η_k is the autocorrelation for a lag of k and

$$w_k = \frac{m-2}{m-k}$$

For $k = 15$ zero autocorrelation can be rejected with 95% confidence when the Ljung–Box statistic is greater than 25.

From Table 15.2, the Ljung–Box Statistic for the u_i^2 series is about 123. This is strong evidence of autocorrelation. For the u_i^2/σ_i^2 series the Ljung–Box statistic is 8.2, suggesting that the autocorrelation has been largely removed by the GARCH model.

15.6 USING GARCH (1,1) TO FORECAST FUTURE VOLATILITY

Substituting $\gamma = 1 - \alpha - \beta$ in equation (15.8), the variance rate estimated for day n is

$$\sigma_n^2 = (1 - \alpha - \beta)V + \alpha u_{n-1}^2 + \beta \sigma_{n-1}^2$$

so that

$$\sigma_n^2 - V = \alpha(u_{n-1}^2 - V) + \beta(\sigma_{n-1}^2 - V)$$

On day $n + k$ in the future we have

$$\sigma_{n+k}^2 - V = \alpha(u_{n+k-1}^2 - V) + \beta(\sigma_{n+k-1}^2 - V)$$

The expected value of u_{n+k-1}^2 is σ_{n+k-1}^2. Hence

$$E[\sigma_{n+k}^2 - V] = (\alpha + \beta)E[\sigma_{n+k-1}^2 - V]$$

where E denotes expected value. Using this equation repeatedly yields

$$E[\sigma_{n+k}^2 - V] = (\alpha + \beta)^k(\sigma_n^2 - V)$$

or

$$E[\sigma_{n+k}^2] = V + (\alpha + \beta)^k(\sigma_n^2 - V) \tag{15.13}$$

In the EWMA model, $\alpha + \beta = 1$ and equation (15.13) shows that the expected future variance rate equals the current variance rate. When $\alpha + \beta < 1$, the final term in the equation becomes progressively smaller as k increases. Figure 15.2 shows the expected path followed by the variance rate for situations where the current variance rate is different from V. The variance rate exhibits *mean reversion* with a *reversion level* of V and a *reversion rate* of $1 - \alpha - \beta$. Our forecast of the future variance

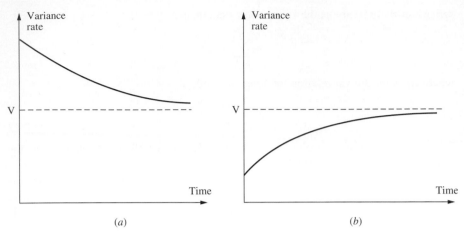

Figure 15.2   Expected path for the variance rate when (a) current variance rate is above long-term variance rate and (b) current variance rate is below long-term variance rate.

rate tends towards V as we look further and further ahead. This analysis emphasizes the point that we must have $\alpha + \beta < 1$ for a stable GARCH (1,1) process. When $\alpha + \beta > 1$, the weight given to the long-term average variance is negative and the process is "mean fleeing" rather than "mean reverting". As mentioned previously, models where the maximum likelihood estimates of α and β are such that $\alpha + \beta > 1$ should be rejected in favor of the EWMA model.

In the yen–dollar exchange rate example considered earlier $\alpha + \beta = 0.9602$ and $V = 0.00004422$. Suppose that the current variance rate per day is 0.00006. (This corresponds to a volatility of 0.77% per day.) In 10 days, the expected variance rate is

$$0.00004422 + 0.9602^{10}(0.00006 - 0.00004422) = 0.00005473$$

The expected volatility per day is 0.74%, which is only marginally below the current volatility of 0.77% per day. However, the expected variance rate in 100 days is

$$0.00004422 + 0.9602^{100}(0.00006 - 0.00004422) = 0.00004449$$

The expected volatility per day is 0.67%, very close to the long-term volatility.

Volatility Term Structures

Consider an option lasting between day n and day $n + N$. We can use equation (15.13) to calculate the expected variance rate during the life of the option as

$$\frac{1}{N} \sum_{k=0}^{N-1} E[\sigma_{n+k}^2] \tag{15.14}$$

The longer the life of the option, the closer this is to V.

As discussed in chapter 17, the market prices of different options on the same asset are often used to calculate a *volatility term structure*. This is the relationship between the implied volatilities of the options and their maturities. Equation (15.14) can be used to estimate a volatility term structure based on the GARCH (1,1) model.

Table 15.3	Yen–Dollar Volatility Term Structure Predicted from GARCH (1,1)				
Option Life (Days)	*10*	*30*	*50*	*100*	*500*
Option volatility (% per annum)	12.03	11.61	11.35	11.01	10.65

The square root of the expression in equation (15.14) is an estimate of the volatility appropriate for valuing the N-day option. The estimated volatility term structure is not usually the same as the actual volatility term structure. However, as we will show, it is often used to predict the way that the actual volatility term structure will respond to volatility changes.

When the current volatility is above the long-term volatility, the GARCH (1,1) model estimates a downward-sloping volatility term structure. When the current volatility is below the long-term volatility, it estimates an upward-sloping volatility term structure. Table 15.3 shows the results of using equation (15.14) to estimate a volatility term structure for options on the yen–dollar exchange rate when the current variance rate is 0.00006. For the purposes of this table, the daily volatilities have been annualized by multiplying them by $\sqrt{252}$.

Impact of Volatility Changes

Table 15.4 forecasts the effect of volatility changes on options of varying maturities. It investigates the effect of a 1% increase in the instantaneous volatility for our yen–dollar exchange rate example. We assume as before that the current variance rate is 0.00006 per day. This corresponds to a daily volatility of 0.7746% and a volatility of $0.7746\sqrt{252} = 12.30\%$ per year. This is an instantaneous volatility. A 1% increase changes the instantaneous volatility to 13.30% per year. The daily volatility becomes 0.84% and the variance rate per day becomes 0.00007016. Applying equation (15.14) to this new situation produces the second row in Table 15.4. The increase in volatility for different maturities is shown in the third row.

Many financial institutions use analyses such as this when determining the exposure of their books to volatility changes. Rather than consider an across-the-board increase of 1% in implied volatilities when calculating vega, they relate the size of the volatility increase that is considered to the maturity of the option. Based on Table 15.4, a 0.86% volatility increase would be considered for a 10-day option, a 0.64% increase for a 30-day option, a 0.48% increase for a 50-day option, and so on.

Table 15.4	Impact of 1% Change in the Instantaneous Volatility Predicted from GARCH (1,1)				
Option Life (Days)	*10*	*30*	*50*	*100*	*500*
Option volatility now (%)	12.03	11.61	11.35	11.01	10.65
Option volatility after change (%)	12.89	12.25	11.83	11.29	10.71
Increase in volatility (%)	0.86	0.64	0.48	0.28	0.06

15.7 CORRELATIONS

The discussion so far has centered on the estimation and forecasting of volatility. As explained in chapter 14, correlations also play a key role in the calculation of VaR. In this section, we indicate how correlation estimates can be updated in a similar way to volatility estimates.

The correlation between two variables X and Y can be defined as

$$\frac{\text{cov}(X, Y)}{\sigma_X \sigma_Y}$$

where σ_X and σ_Y are the standard deviation of X and Y and $\text{cov}(X, Y)$ is the covariance between X and Y. The covariance between X and Y is defined as

$$E[(X - \mu_X)(Y - \mu_Y)]$$

where μ_X and μ_Y are the means of X and Y, and E denotes expected value. Although it is easier to develop intuition about the meaning of a correlation than a covariance, it is covariances that are the fundamental variables of our analysis.[15]

Consider two different market variables, U and V. We define u_i and v_i as the proportional changes in U and V between the end of day $i - 1$ and the end of day i:

$$u_i = \frac{U_i - U_{i-1}}{U_{i-1}} \qquad v_i = \frac{V_i - V_{i-1}}{V_{i-1}}$$

where U_i and V_i are the values of U and V at the end of day i. We also define

$\sigma_{u,n}$: Daily volatility of variable U, estimated for day n.

$\sigma_{v,n}$: Daily volatility of variable V, estimated for day n.

cov_n : Estimate covariance between daily changes in U and V, calculated on day n.

Our estimate of the correlation between U and V on day n is

$$\frac{\text{cov}_n}{\sigma_{u,n} \sigma_{v,n}}$$

Using an equal-weighting scheme and assuming that the means of u_i and v_i are zero, equation (15.3) shows that we can estimate the variance rates of U and V from the most recent m observations as

$$\sigma_{u,n}^2 = \frac{1}{m} \sum_{i=1}^{m} u_{n-i}^2$$

$$\sigma_{v,n}^2 = \frac{1}{m} \sum_{i=1}^{m} v_{n-i}^2$$

---

[15] An analogy here is that variance rates were the fundamental variables for the EWMA and GARCH schemes in the first part of this chapter, even though volatilities are easier to understand.

A similar estimate for the covariance between U and V is

$$\text{cov}_n = \frac{1}{m} \sum_{i=1}^{m} u_{n-i} v_{n-i} \tag{15.15}$$

One alternative is an EWMA model similar to equation (15.7). The formula for updating the covariance estimate is then

$$\text{cov}_n = \lambda \text{cov}_{n-1} + (1 - \lambda) u_{n-1} v_{n-1}$$

A similar analysis to that presented for the EWMA volatility model shows that the weights given to observations on the $u_i v_i$'s decline as we move back through time. The lower the value of λ, the greater the weight that is given to recent observations.

> **Example 15.3** Suppose that $\lambda = 0.95$ and that the estimate of the correlation between two variables U and V on day $n - 1$ is 0.6. Suppose further that the estimate of the volatilities for the U and V on day $n - 1$ are 1% and 2% respectively. From the relationship between correlation and covariance, the estimate of the covariance between the U and V on day $n - 1$ is
>
> $$0.6 \times 0.01 \times 0.02 = 0.00012$$
>
> Suppose that the proportional changes in U and V on day $n - 1$ are 0.5% and 2.5% respectively. The variance and covariance for day n would be updated as follows:
>
> $$\sigma_{u,n}^2 = 0.95 \times 0.01^2 + 0.05 \times 0.005^2 = 0.00009625$$
> $$\sigma_{v,n}^2 = 0.95 \times 0.02^2 + 0.05 \times 0.025^2 = 0.00041125$$
> $$\text{cov}_n = 0.95 \times 0.00012 + 0.05 \times 0.005 \times 0.025 = 0.00012025$$
>
> The new volatility of U is $\sqrt{0.00009625} = 0.981\%$ and the new volatility of V is $\sqrt{0.00041125} = 2.028\%$. The new coefficient of correlation between U and V is
>
> $$\frac{0.00012025}{0.00981 \times 0.02028} = 0.6044$$

GARCH models can also be used for updating covariance estimates and forecasting the future level of covariances. For example, the GARCH (1,1) model for updating a covariance is

$$\text{cov}_n = \omega + \alpha u_{n-1} v_{n-1} + \beta \text{cov}_{n-1}$$

and the long-term average covariance is $\omega/(1 - \alpha - \beta)$. Formulas similar to those in equations (15.13) and (15.14) can be developed for forecasting future covariances and calculating the average covariance during the life of an option.[16]

---

[16] An extension of the ideas in this chapter is to multivariate GARCH models where an entire variance-covariance matrix is updated in a consistent way. See R. Engle and J. Mezrich, "GARCH for Groups," *RISK*, August 1996, 36-40, for a discussion of alternative approaches.

Consistency Condition for Covariances

Once all the variances and covariances have been calculated, a variance-covariance matrix can be constructed. When $i \neq j$, the (i, j) element of this matrix shows the covariance between variable i and variable j. When $i = j$, it shows the variance of variable i.

Not all variance-covariance matrices are internally consistent. The condition for an $N \times N$ variance-covariance matrix, Ω, to be internally consistent is

$$\mathbf{w}^T \Omega \mathbf{w} \geq 0 \tag{15.16}$$

for all $N \times 1$ vectors $\mathbf{w}$ where $\mathbf{w}^T$ is the transpose of $\mathbf{w}$. A matrix that satisfies this property is known as *positive semi-definite*.

To understand why the condition in equation (15.16) must hold, suppose that $\mathbf{w}^T$ is $(w_1, w_2, \ldots, w_n)$. The expression $\mathbf{w}^T \Omega \mathbf{w}$ is the variance of a portfolio consisting of w_i of market variable i. As such, it must be positive or zero.

To ensure that a positive semi-definite matrix is produced, variances and covariances should be calculated consistently. For example, if variances are calculated by giving equal weight to the last m data items, the same should be done for covariances. If variances are updated using an EWMA model with $\lambda = 0.94$, the same should be done for covariances.

An example of a variance-covariance matrix that is not internally consistent is

$$\begin{pmatrix} 1 & 0 & 0.9 \\ 0 & 1 & 0.9 \\ 0.9 & 0.9 & 1 \end{pmatrix}$$

The variance of each variable is 1.0 and so the covariances are also coefficients of correlation. The first variable is highly correlated with the third variable and the second variable is highly correlated with the third variable. However, there is no correlation at all between the first and second variables. This seems strange. When we set $\mathbf{w}$ equal to $(1, 1, -1)$ we find that the condition in equation (15.16) is not satisfied, proving that the matrix is not positive semi-definite.[17]

SUMMARY

Most popular option pricing models, such as Black–Scholes, assume that the volatility of the underlying asset is constant. This assumption is far from perfect. In practice, the volatility of an asset, like the asset's price, is a stochastic variable. Unlike the asset price, it is not directly observable. This chapter has discussed schemes for attempting to keep track of the current level of volatility.

---

[17] It can be shown that the condition for a 3×3 matrix of correlations to be internally consistent is

$$\rho_{12}^2 + \rho_{13}^2 + \rho_{23}^2 - 2\rho_{12}\rho_{13}\rho_{23} \leq 1$$

where ρ_{ij} is the coefficient of correlation between variables i and j.

We define u_i as the proportional change in a market variable between the end of day $i - 1$ and the end of day i. The variance rate of the market variable (that is, the square of its volatility) is calculated as a weighted average of the u_i^2. The key feature of the schemes that have been discussed here is that they do not give equal weight to the observations on the u_i^2. The more recent an observation, the greater the weight assigned to it. In the EWMA model and the GARCH (1,1) model, the weights assigned to observations decrease exponentially as the observations become older. The GARCH (1,1) model differs from the EWMA model in that some weight is also assigned to the long-run average variance rate. Both the EWMA and GARCH (1,1) models have structures that enable forecasts of the future level of variance rate to be produced relatively easily.

Maximum likelihood methods are usually used to estimate parameters in GARCH (1,1) and similar models from historical data. These methods involve using an iterative procedure to determine the parameter values that maximize the chance or likelihood that the historical data will occur. Once its parameters have been determined, a model can be judged by how well it removes autocorrelation from the u_i^2.

For every model that is developed to track variances there is a corresponding model that can be developed to track covariances. The procedures described here can, therefore, be used to update the complete variance-covariance matrix used in value at risk calculations.

SUGGESTIONS FOR FURTHER READING

Bollerslev, T. "Generalized Autoregressive Conditional Heteroscedasticity," *Journal of Econometrics*, 31 (1986), 307–27.

Cumby, R., S. Figlewski, and J. Hasbrook. "Forecasting Volatilities and Correlations with EGARCH Models," *Journal of Derivatives*, 1, 2 (Winter 1993), 51–63.

Engle, R. F. "Autoregressive Conditional Heteroscedasticity with Estimates of the Variance of UK Inflation," *Econometrica*, 50 (1982), 987–1008.

Engle R. F., and J. Mezrich. "Grappling with GARCH," *RISK* (September 1995), 112–17.

Engle, R. F., and J. Mezrich. "GARCH for Groups," *RISK* (August 1996), 36–40.

Engle, R. F., and V. Ng. "Measuring and Testing the Impact of News on Volatility," *Journal of Finance*, 48 (1993), 1,749–78.

Ljung, G. M., and G. E. P. Box. "On a Measure of Lack of Fit in Time Series Models," *Biometrica*, 65 (1978), 297–303.

Nelson D. "Conditional Heteroscedasticity and Asset Returns; A New Approach," *Econometrica*, 59 (1990), 347–70.

Noh, J., R. F. Engle, and A. Kane. "Forecasting Volatility and Option Prices of the S&P 500 Index," *Journal of Derivatives*, 2 (1994), 17–30.

QUESTIONS AND PROBLEMS
(ANSWERS IN SOLUTIONS MANUAL)

15.1. Explain the exponentially weighted moving average (EWMA) model for estimating volatility from historical data.

15.2. What is the difference between the exponentially weighted moving average model and the GARCH (1,1) model for updating volatilities?

15.3. The most recent estimate of the daily volatility of an asset is 1.5% and the price of the asset at the close of trading yesterday was $30.00. The parameter λ in the EWMA model is 0.94. Suppose that the price of the asset at the close of trading today is $30.50. How will this cause the volatility to be updated by the EWMA model?

15.4. A company uses an EWMA model for forecasting volatility. It decides to change the parameter λ from 0.95 to 0.85. Explain the likely impact on the forecasts.

15.5. The volatility of a certain market variable is 30% per annum. Calculate a 99% confidence interval for the size of the proportional daily change in the variable.

15.6. A company uses the GARCH (1,1) model for updating volatility. The three parameters are ω, α and β. Describe the impact of making a small increase in each of the parameters while keeping the others fixed.

15.7. The most recent estimate of the daily volatility of the U.S. dollar–sterling exchange rate is 0.6% and the exchange rate at 4 p.m. yesterday was 1.5000. The parameter λ in the EWMA model is 0.9. Suppose that the exchange rate at 4 p.m. today proves to be 1.4950. How would the estimate of the daily volatility be updated?

15.8. Assume that S&P 500 at close of trading yesterday was 1,040 and the daily volatility of the index was estimated as 1% per day at that time. The parameters in a GARCH (1,1) model are $\omega = 0.000002$, $\alpha = 0.06$, and $\beta = 0.92$. If the level of the index at close of trading today is 1,060, what is the new volatility estimate?

15.9. Suppose that the current daily volatilities of asset A and asset B are 1.6% and 2.5%, respectively. The prices of the assets at close of trading yesterday were $20 and $40 and the estimate of the coefficient of correlation between the returns on the two assets made at that time was 0.25. The parameter λ used in the EWMA model is 0.95.

(a) Calculate the current estimate of the covariance between the assets.

(b) On the assumption that the prices of the assets at close of trading today are $20.5 and $40.5, update the correlation estimate.

15.10. The parameters of a GARCH (1,1) model are estimated as $\omega = 0.000004$, $\alpha = 0.05$, and $\beta = 0.92$. What is the long-run average volatility and what is the equation describing the way that the variance rate reverts to its long-run average? If the current volatility is 20% per year, what is the expected volatility in 20 days?

15.11. Suppose that the current daily volatilities of asset X and asset Y are 1.0% and 1.2%, respectively. The prices of the assets at close of trading yesterday were $30 and $50 and the estimate of the coefficient of correlation between the returns on the two assets made at this time was 0.50. Correlations and volatilities are updated using a GARCH (1,1) model. The estimates of the model's parameters are $\alpha = 0.04$ and $\beta = 0.94$. For the correlation $\omega = 0.000001$; for the volatilities $\omega = 0.000003$. If the prices of the two assets at close of trading today are $31 and $51, how is the correlation estimate updated?

15.12. Suppose that the daily volatility of the FT-SE 100 stock index (measured in pounds sterling) is 1.8% and the daily volatility of the dollar–sterling exchange rate is 0.9%. Suppose further that the correlation between the FT-SE 100 and the dollar–sterling exchange rate is 0.4. What is the volatility of the FT-SE 100 when it is translated to U.S. dollars? Assume that the dollar–sterling exchange rate is expressed as the number of U.S. dollars per pound sterling. (*Hint*: When $Z = XY$, the proportional daily change in Z is approximately equal to the proportional daily change in X plus the proportional daily change in Y.)

15.13. Suppose that in Problem 15.12 the correlation between the S&P 500 Index (measured in dollars) and the FT-SE 100 Index (measured in sterling) is 0.7, the correlation between the S&P 500 index (measured in dollars) and the dollar–sterling exchange rate is 0.3, and the daily volatility of the S&P 500 Index is 1.6%. What is the correlation between the S&P 500 Index (measured in dollars) and the FT-SE 100 Index when it is translated to dollars? (*Hint*: For three variables X, Y, and Z, the covariance between $X + Y$ and Z equals the covariance between X and Z plus the covariance between Y and Z.)

ASSIGNMENT QUESTIONS

15.14. Suppose that the current price of gold at close of trading yesterday was $300 and its volatility was estimated as 1.3% per day. The price at the close of trading today is $298. Update the volatility estimate using
(a) The EWMA model with $\lambda = 0.94$.
(b) The GARCH (1,1) model with $\omega = 0.000002$, $\alpha = 0.04$, and $\beta = 0.94$.

15.15. Suppose that in Problem 15.14 the price of silver at the close of trading yesterday was $8, its volatility was estimated as 1.5% per day, and its correlation with gold was estimated as 0.8. The price of silver at the close of trading today is unchanged at $8. Update the volatility of silver and the correlation between silver and gold using the two models in Problem 15.14. In practice, is the ω parameter likely to be the same for gold and silver?

15.16. An Excel spreadsheet containing 500 days of daily data on a number of different exchange rates and stock indices can be downloaded from the author's Web site: http://www.mgmt.utoronto.ca/~hull. Choose one exchange rate and one stock index. Use the Solver tool in Excel to estimate best fit models for their volatilities, using the GARCH (1,1) variance targeting approach. Set the target variance equal to the sample variance initially, and then try changing the target variance to see if the model can be improved.

CHAPTER

16

NUMERICAL
PROCEDURES

This chapter discusses three numerical procedures that can be used to value derivatives when exact formulas are not available. These involve the use of binomial trees, Monte Carlo simulation, and finite difference methods, respectively. Monte Carlo simulation is used primarily for derivatives where the payoff is dependent on the history of the underlying variable or where there are several underlying variables. Binomial trees and finite difference methods are particularly useful when the holder has early exercise decisions to make prior to maturity. In addition to valuing a derivative, all the procedures can be used to calculate Greek letters such as delta, gamma, and vega.

16.1 BINOMIAL TREES

In chapter 9, we introduced one- and two-step binomial trees for non-dividend-paying stocks and showed how they lead to valuations for European and American options. These trees are very imprecise models of reality and are used only for illustrative purposes. A more realistic model is one that assumes stock price movements are composed of a large number of small binomial movements. This is the assumption that underlies a widely used numerical procedure first proposed by Cox, Ross, and Rubinstein.[1]

Consider the evaluation of an option on a non-dividend-paying stock. We start by dividing the life of the option into a large number of small time intervals of length Δt. We assume that in each time interval the stock price moves from its initial value of S_0 to one of two new values, $S_0 u$ and $S_0 d$. This model is illustrated in Figure 16.1. In general, $u > 1$ and $d < 1$. The movement from S_0 to $S_0 u$ is, therefore, an "up" movement and the movement from S_0 to $S_0 d$ is a "down" movement. The probability of an up movement will be denoted by p. The probability of a down movement is $1 - p$.

---

[1]See J. C. Cox, S. A. Ross, and M. Rubinstein, "Option Pricing: A Simplified Approach," *Journal of Financial Economics*, 7 (October 1979), 229–63.

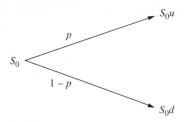

Figure 16.1 Stock price movements in time Δt under the binomial model.

Risk-Neutral Valuation

In chapters 9 and 11, we introduced what is known as the risk-neutral valuation principle. This states that any security dependent on a stock price can be valued on the assumption that the world is risk neutral. It means that for the purposes of valuing an option (or any other derivative), we can assume that:

1. The expected return from all traded securities is the risk-free interest rate.
2. Future cash flows can be valued by discounting their expected values at the risk-free interest rate.

We make use of this result when using a binomial tree. The tree is designed to represent the behavior of a stock price in a risk-neutral world.

Determination of p, u, and d

The parameters p, u, and d must give correct values for the mean and variance of stock price changes during a time interval of length Δt. Because we are working in a risk-neutral world, the expected return from a stock is the risk-free interest rate, r.[2] ①
Hence, the expected value of the stock price at the end of a time interval of length Δt is $Se^{r\Delta t}$, where S is the stock price at the beginning of the time interval. It follows that

$$Se^{r\Delta t} = pSu + (1 - p)Sd \qquad (16.1)$$

or

$$e^{r\Delta t} = pu + (1 - p)d \qquad (16.2)$$

The stochastic process assumed for the stock price implies that the variance of the proportional change in the stock price in a small time interval of length Δt is $\sigma^2 \Delta t$. ②
Because the variance of a variable Q is defined as $E(Q^2) - [E(Q)]^2$, it follows that

$$pu^2 + (1 - p)d^2 - [pu + (1 - p)d]^2 = \sigma^2 \Delta t$$

Substituting from equation (16.2) for p, this reduces to

$$e^{r\Delta t}(u + d) - ud - e^{2r\Delta t} = \sigma^2 \Delta t \qquad (16.3)$$

---

[2]In practice, r is usually set equal to the zero-coupon yield on a bond maturing at the same time as the option. Section 16.4 shows how r can be made a function of time.

Equations (16.2) and (16.3) impose two conditions on p, u, and d. A third condition used by Cox, Ross, and Rubinstein is

③ *combining Tree*

$$u = \frac{1}{d}$$

These three conditions imply

$$p = \frac{a - d}{u - d} \tag{16.4}$$

$$u = e^{\sigma \sqrt{\Delta t}} \tag{16.5}$$

$$d = e^{-\sigma \sqrt{\Delta t}} \tag{16.6}$$

where

$$a = e^{r\Delta t} \tag{16.7}$$

and terms of higher order than Δt are ignored.[3] The variable a is sometimes referred to as the *growth factor*.

Tree of Stock Prices

Figure 16.2 illustrates the complete tree of stock prices that is considered when the binomial model is used. At time zero, the stock price, S_0, is known. At time Δt, there are two possible stock prices, $S_0 u$ and $S_0 d$; at time $2\Delta t$, there are three possible stock prices, $S_0 u^2$, S_0, and $S_0 d^2$; and so on. In general, at time $i\Delta t$, $i + 1$ stock prices are considered. These are

$$S_0 u^j d^{i-j} \qquad j = 0, 1, \ldots, i$$

Note that the relationship $u = 1/d$ is used in computing the stock price at each node of the tree in Figure 16.2. For example, $S_0 u^2 d = S_0 u$. Note also that the tree recombines in the sense that an up movement followed by a down movement leads to the same stock price as a down movement followed by an up movement.

Working Backward through the Tree

Options are evaluated by starting at the end of the tree (time T) and working backward. The value of the option is known at time T. For example, a put option is worth $\max(X - S_T, 0)$ and a call option is worth $\max(S_T - X, 0)$, where S_T is the stock price at time T and X is the strike price. Because a risk-neutral world is being assumed, the value at each node at time $T - \Delta t$ can be calculated as the expected value

---

[3]To see this, we note that equations (16.4) and (16.7) satisfy the condition in equation (16.2) exactly. From Taylor Series expansions, when terms of higher order than Δt are ignored, equation (16.4) implies that $u = 1 + \sigma \sqrt{\Delta t} + \sigma^2 \Delta t$ and equation (16.5) implies that $d = 1 - \sigma \sqrt{\Delta t} + \sigma^2 \Delta t$, with $e^{r\Delta t} = 1 + r\Delta t$ and $e^{2r\Delta t} = 1 + 2r\Delta t$. It follows that equations (16.5) and (16.6) satisfy equation (16.3) when terms of higher order than Δt are ignored.

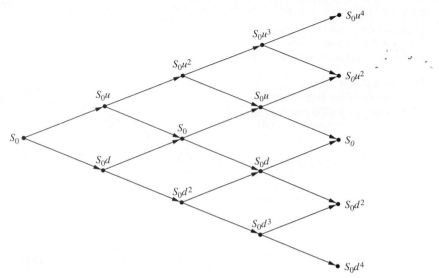

Figure 16.2 Tree used to value a stock option.

at time T discounted at rate r for a time period Δt. Similarly, the value at each node at time $T - 2\Delta t$ can be calculated as the expected value at time $T - \Delta t$ discounted for a time period Δt at rate r, and so on. If the option is American, it is necessary to check at each node to see whether early exercise is preferable to holding the option for a further time period Δt. Eventually, by working back through all the nodes, the value of the option at time zero is obtained.

> **Example 16.1** Consider a five-month American put option on a non-dividend-paying stock when the stock price is $50, the strike price is $50, the risk-free interest rate is 10% per annum, and the volatility is 40% per annum. With our usual notation, this means that $S_0 = 50$, $X = 50$, $r = 0.10$, $\sigma = 0.40$, and $T = 0.4167$. Suppose that we divide the life of the option into five intervals of length one month ($= 0.0833$ year) for the purposes of constructing a binomial tree. Then $\Delta t = 0.0833$ and using equations (16.4) to (16.7),
>
> $$u = e^{\sigma \sqrt{\Delta t}} = 1.1224 \qquad d = e^{-\sigma \sqrt{\Delta t}} = 0.8909$$
>
> $$a = e^{r\Delta t} = 1.0084 \qquad p = \frac{a - d}{u - d} = 0.5073$$
>
> $$1 - p = 0.4927$$
>
> Figure 16.3 shows the binomial tree produced by DerivaGem. At each node there are two numbers. The top one shows the stock price at the node; the lower one shows the value of the option at the node. The probability of an up movement is always 0.5073; the probability of a down movement is always 0.4927.
>
> The stock price at the jth node ($j = 0, 1, \ldots, i$) at time $i\Delta t$ ($i = 0, 1, \ldots, 5$) is calculated as $S_0 u^j d^{i-j}$. For example, the stock price at node A ($i = 4$, $j = 1$) (that is, the second node up at the end of the fourth time step) is $50 \times 1.1224 \times 0.8909^3 = \$39.69$.
>
> The option prices at the final nodes are calculated as max $(X - S_T, 0)$. For example, the option price at node G is $50.00 - 35.36 = 14.64$. The option prices at the

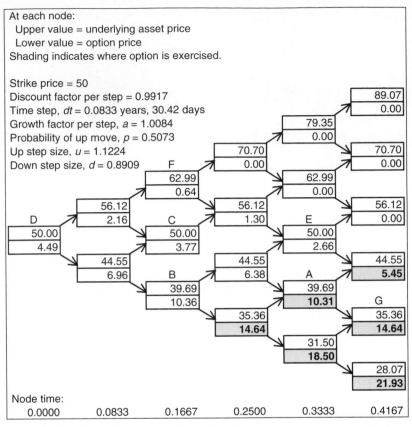

At each node:
  Upper value = underlying asset price
  Lower value = option price
Shading indicates where option is exercised.

Strike price = 50
Discount factor per step = 0.9917
Time step, dt = 0.0833 years, 30.42 days
Growth factor per step, a = 1.0084
Probability of up move, p = 0.5073
Up step size, u = 1.1224
Down step size, d = 0.8909

Node time:
  0.0000   0.0833   0.1667   0.2500   0.3333   0.4167

Figure 16.3   Binomial tree from DerivaGem for American put on non-dividend-paying stock (Example 16.1).

penultimate nodes are calculated from the option prices at the final nodes. First, we assume no exercise of the option at the nodes. This means that the option price is calculated as the present value of the expected option price one time step later. For example, at node E, the option price is calculated as

$$(0.5073 \times 0 + 0.4927 \times 5.45)e^{-0.10 \times 0.0833} = 2.66$$

whereas at node A it is calculated as

$$(0.5073 \times 5.45 + 0.4927 \times 14.64)e^{-0.10 \times 0.0833} = 9.90$$

We then check to see if early exercise is preferable to waiting. At node E, early exercise would give a value for the option of zero because both the stock price and strike price are $50. Clearly it is best to wait. The correct value for the option at node E is, therefore, $2.66. At node A it is a different story. If the option is exercised, it is worth $50.00 − $39.69 or $10.31. This is more than $9.90. If node A is reached, the option should, therefore, be exercised and the correct value for the option at node A is $10.31.

    Option prices at earlier nodes are calculated in a similar way. Note that it is not always best to exercise an option early when it is in the money. Consider node B. If the option is exercised, it is worth $50.00 − $39.69 or $10.31. However, if it is held, it is worth

$$(0.5073 \times 6.38 + 0.4927 \times 14.64)e^{-0.10 \times 0.0833} = 10.36$$

The option should, therefore, not be exercised at this node, and the correct option value at the node is $10.36.

Working back through the tree, we find the value of the option at the initial node to be $4.49. This is our numerical estimate for the option's current value. In practice, a smaller value of Δt, and many more nodes, would be used. DerivaGem shows that with 30, 50, and 100 time steps we get values for the option of 4.263, 4.272, and 4.278.

Expressing the Approach Algebraically

Suppose that the life of an American put option on a non-dividend-paying stock is divided into N subintervals of length Δt. We will refer to the jth node at time $i\Delta t$ as the (i, j) node ($0 \le i \le N, 0 \le j \le i$). Define f_{ij} as the value of the option at the (i, j) node. The stock price at the (i, j) node is $S_0 u^j d^{i-j}$. Because the value of an American put at its expiration date is max $(X − S_T, 0)$, we know that

$$f_{N,j} = \max(X − S_0 u^j d^{N-j}, 0) \qquad j = 0, 1, \ldots, N$$

There is a probability, p, of moving from the (i, j) node at time $i\Delta t$ to the $(i + 1, j + 1)$ node at time $(i + 1)\Delta t$, and a probability $1 − p$ of moving from the (i, j) node at time $i\Delta t$ to the $(i + 1, j)$ node at time $(i + 1)\Delta t$. Assuming no early exercise, risk-neutral valuation gives

$$f_{i,j} = e^{-r\Delta t}[p f_{i+1,j+1} + (1 − p) f_{i+1,j}]$$

for $0 \le i \le N − 1$ and $0 \le j \le i$. When early exercise is taken into account, this value for $f_{i,j}$ must be compared with the option's intrinsic value, and we obtain

$$f_{i,j} = \max\{X − S_0 u^j d^{i-j}, \; e^{-r\Delta t}[p f_{i+1,j+1} + (1 − p) f_{i+1,j}]\}$$

Note that, because the calculations start at time T and work backward, the value at time $i\Delta t$ captures not only the effect of early exercise possibilities at time $i\Delta t$, but also the effect of early exercise at subsequent times. In the limit as Δt tends to zero, an exact value for the American put is obtained. In practice, $N = 30$ usually gives reasonable results.

Estimating Delta and Other Greek Letters

It will be recalled that the delta, Δ, of an option is the rate of change of its price with respect to the underlying stock price. It can be estimated as

$$\Delta = \frac{\Delta f}{\Delta S}$$

where ΔS is a small change in the stock price and Δf is the corresponding small change in the option price. At time Δt we have an estimate, f_{11}, for the option price when the stock price is S_0u; and an estimate, f_{10}, for the option price when the stock price is S_0d. This means that, when $\Delta S = S_0u - S_0d$, the value of Δf is $f_{11} - f_{10}$. An estimate of Δ at time Δt is, therefore:

$$\Delta = \frac{f_{11} - f_{10}}{S_0u - S_0d} \tag{16.8}$$

To determine gamma, Γ, note that we have two estimates of Δ at time $2\Delta t$. When $S = (S_0u^2 + S_0)/2$ (halfway between the second and third node), delta is $(f_{22} - f_{21})/(S_0u^2 - S_0)$; when $S = (S_0 + S_0d^2)/2$ (halfway between the first and second node) delta is $(f_{21} - f_{20})/(S_0 - S_0d^2)$. The difference between the two values of S is h, where

$$h = 0.5(S_0u^2 - S_0d^2)$$

Gamma is the change in delta divided by h:

$$\Gamma = \frac{[(f_{22} - f_{21})/(S_0u^2 - S_0)] - [(f_{21} - f_{20})/(S_0 - S_0d^2)]}{h} \tag{16.9}$$

These procedures provide estimates of delta at time Δt and of gamma at time $2\Delta t$. In practice, they are usually used as estimates of delta and gamma at time zero as well.[4]

A further hedge parameter that can be obtained directly from the tree is theta, Θ. This is the rate of change of the option price with time when all else is kept constant. If the tree starts at time zero, an estimate of theta is

$$\Theta = \frac{f_{21} - f_{00}}{2\Delta t} \tag{16.10}$$

Vega can be calculated by making a small change, $\Delta\sigma$, in the volatility and constructing a new tree to obtain a new value of the option (Δt should be kept the same to minimize error). The estimate of vega is

$$\mathcal{V} = \frac{f^* - f}{\Delta\sigma}$$

where f and f^* are the estimates of the option price from the original and the new tree, respectively. Rho can be calculated similarly.

Example 16.2   Consider again Example 16.1. From Figure 16.3, $f_{1,0} = 6.95$ and $f_{1,1} = 2.15$. Equation (16.8) gives an estimate of delta of

$$\frac{2.16 - 6.96}{56.12 - 44.55} = -0.41$$

From equation (16.9), an estimate of the gamma of the option can be obtained from the values at nodes B, C, and F as

---

[4]If slightly more accuracy is required for delta and gamma, we can start the binomial tree at time $-2\Delta t$ and assume that the stock price is S_0 at this time. This leads to the option price being calculated for three different stock prices at time zero.

$$\frac{[(0.64 - 3.77)/(62.99 - 50.00)] - [(3.77 - 10.36)/(50.00 - 39.69)]}{11.65} = 0.03$$

From equation (16.10), an estimate of the theta of the option can be obtained from the values at nodes D and C as

$$\frac{3.77 - 4.49}{0.1667} = -4.3 \text{ per year}$$

or -0.012 per calendar day. These are, of course, only rough estimates. They become progressively better as the number of time steps on the tree is increased. Using 50 time steps, DerivaGem provides estimates of 0.414, 0.033, and -0.0117 for delta, gamma, and theta respectively.

16.2 USING THE BINOMIAL TREE FOR OPTIONS ON INDICES, CURRENCIES, AND FUTURES CONTRACTS

As shown in section 12.2, the binomial tree approach to valuing options on non-dividend-paying stocks can easily be adapted to valuing American calls and puts on a stock providing a continuous dividend yield at rate q. Because the dividends provide a return of q, the stock price itself must, on average, in a risk-neutral world provide a return of $r - q$.

Hence equation (16.1) becomes:

$$Se^{(r-q)\Delta t} = pSu + (1 - p)Sd$$

so that

$$e^{(r-q)\Delta t} = pu + (1 - p)d$$

Equation (16.3) becomes

$$e^{(r-q)\Delta t}(u + d) - ud - e^{2(r-q)\Delta t} = \sigma^2 \Delta t$$

It can be shown (as in footnote 3) that equations (16.4), (16.5), and (16.6) are still correct (when terms of higher order than Δt are ignored) but with

$$a = e^{(r-q)\Delta t} \tag{16.11}$$

The binomial tree numerical procedure can, therefore, be used exactly as before with this new value of a.

It will be recalled from chapter 12 that stock indices, currencies, and futures contracts can, for the purposes of option evaluation, be considered as stocks paying continuous dividend yields. In the case of a stock index, the relevant dividend yield is the dividend yield on the stock portfolio underlying the index; in the case of a currency, it is the foreign risk-free interest rate; in the case of a futures contract, it is the domestic risk-free interest rate. The binomial tree approach can, therefore, be used to value options on stock indices, currencies, and futures contracts.

Example 16.3   Consider a four-month American call option on index futures where the current futures price is 300, the exercise price is 300, the risk-free interest rate is 8%

per annum, and the volatility of the index is 30% per annum. We divide the life of the option into four 1-month periods for the purposes of constructing the tree. In this case, $F = 300$, $X = 300$, $r = 0.08$, $\sigma = 0.3$, $T = 0.3333$, and $\Delta t = 0.0833$. Because a futures contract is analogous to a stock paying dividends at a continuous rate r, q should be set equal to r in equation (16.11). This gives $a = 1$. The other parameters necessary to construct the tree are

$$u = e^{\sigma \sqrt{\Delta t}} = 1.0905 \qquad d = \frac{1}{u} = 0.9170$$

$$p = \frac{a - d}{u - d} = 0.4784 \qquad 1 - p = 0.5216$$

The tree, as produced by DerivaGem, is shown in Figure 16.4. (The upper number is the futures price; the lower number is the option price.) The estimated value of the option is 19.16. More accuracy is obtained using more steps. With 50 time steps, DerivaGem gives a value of 20.18; with 100 time steps it gives 20.22.)

Example 16.4 Consider a one-year American put option on the British pound. The current exchange rate is 1.6100, the strike price is 1.6000, the U.S. risk-free interest rate

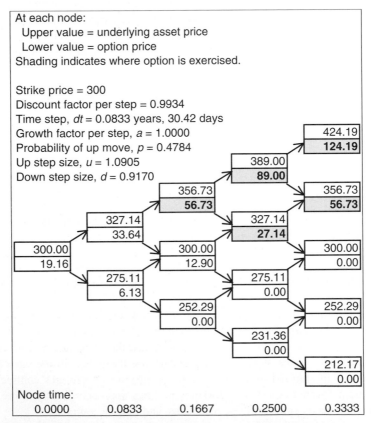

Figure 16.4   Binomial tree produced by DerivaGem for American call option on an index futures contract (Example 16.3).

is 8% per annum, the sterling risk-free interest rate is 9% per annum, and the volatility of the sterling exchange rate is 12% per annum. In this case, $S_0 = 1.61$, $X = 1.60$, $r = 0.08$, $r_f = 0.09$, $\sigma = 0.12$, and $T = 1.0$. We divide the life of the option into four 3-month periods for the purposes of constructing the tree so that $\Delta t = 0.25$. In this case $q = r_f$ and equation (16.11) gives

$$a = e^{(0.08-0.09)\times0.25} = 0.9975$$

The other parameters necessary to construct the tree are

$$u = e^{\sigma\sqrt{\Delta t}} = 1.0618 \qquad d = \frac{1}{u} = 0.9418$$

$$p = \frac{a - d}{u - d} = 0.4642 \qquad 1 - p = 0.5358$$

The tree, as produced by DerivaGem, is shown in Figure 16.5. (The upper number is the exchange rate; the lower number is the option price.) The estimated value of the option is \$0.0710. (With 50 time steps, DerivaGem gives the value of the option as 0.0738; with 100 time steps it also gives 0.0738.)

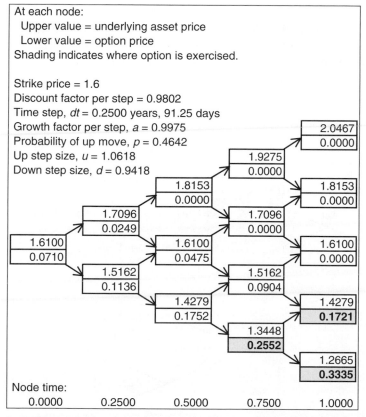

Figure 16.5   Binomial tree produced by DerivaGem for American put option on a currency (Example 16.4).

16.3 BINOMIAL MODEL FOR A DIVIDEND-PAYING STOCK

We now move on to the more tricky issue of how the binomial model can be used for a dividend-paying stock. As in chapter 11, the word *dividend* will, for the purposes of our discussion, be used to refer to the reduction in the stock price on the ex-dividend date as a result of the dividend.

Known Dividend Yield

If it is assumed that there is a single dividend, and the dividend yield (i.e., the dividend as a proportion of the stock price) is known, the tree takes the form shown in Figure 16.6 and can be analyzed in similar manner to that just described. If the time $i\Delta t$ is prior to the stock going ex-dividend, the nodes on the tree correspond to stock prices

$$S_0 u^j d^{i-j} \qquad j = 0, 1, \ldots, i$$

where u and d are defined as in equations (16.5) and (16.6). If the time $i\Delta t$ is after the stock goes ex-dividend, the nodes correspond to stock prices

$$S_0(1 - \delta)u^j d^{i-j} \qquad j = 0, 1, \ldots, i$$

where δ is the dividend yield. Several known dividend yields during the life of an option can be dealt with similarly. If δ_i is the total dividend yield associated with all ex-dividend dates between time zero and time $i\Delta t$, the nodes at time $i\Delta t$ correspond to stock prices

$$S_0(1 - \delta_i)u^j d^{i-j}$$

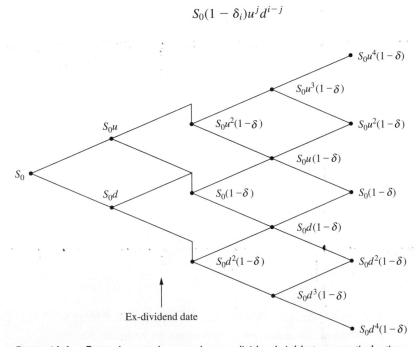

Figure 16.6   Tree when stock pays a known dividend yield at one particular time.

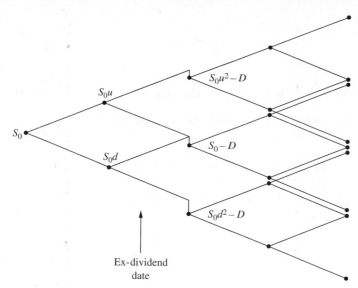

Figure 16.7 Tree when dollar amount of dividend is assumed known and volatility is assumed constant.

Known Dollar Dividend

In some situations, the most realistic assumption is that the dollar amount of the dividend rather than the dividend yield is known in advance. If the volatility of the stock, σ, is assumed constant, the tree then takes the form shown in Figure 16.7. It does not recombine, which means that the number of nodes that have to be evaluated, particularly if there are several dividends, is liable to become very large. Suppose that there is only one dividend, that the ex-dividend date, τ, is between $k\Delta t$ and $(k + 1)\Delta t$, and that the dollar amount of the dividend is D. When $i \leq k$, the nodes on the tree at time $i\Delta t$ correspond to stock prices

$$S_0 u^j d^{i-j} \qquad j = 0, 1, 2, \ldots, i$$

as before. When $i = k + 1$, the nodes on the tree correspond to stock prices

$$S_0 u^j d^{i-j} - D \qquad j = 0, 1, 2, \ldots, i$$

When $i = k + 2$, the nodes on the tree correspond to stock prices

$$(S_0 u^j d^{i-1-j} - D)u \qquad \text{and} \qquad (S_0 u^j d^{i-1-j} - D)d$$

for $j = 0, 1, 2, \ldots, i-1$, so that there are $2i$ rather than $i+1$ nodes. When $i = k+m$, there are $m(k + 2)$ rather than $k + m + 1$ nodes.

The problem can be simplified by assuming, as in the analysis of European options in section 11.12, that the stock price has two components: a part that is uncertain and a part that is the present value of all future dividends during the life of the option. Suppose, as before, that there is only one ex-dividend date, τ, during the life of the option and that $k\Delta t \leq \tau \leq (k + 1)\Delta t$. The value of the uncertain component, S^*, at time $i\Delta t$ is given by

$$S^* = S \qquad \text{when } i\Delta t > \tau$$

and

$$S^* = S - De^{-r(\tau - i\Delta t)} \qquad \text{when } i\Delta t \leq \tau$$

where D is the dividend. Define σ^* as the volatility of S^* and assume that σ^* is constant.[5] The parameters p, u, and d can be calculated from equations (16.4), (16.5), (16.6), and (16.7) with σ replaced by σ^*, and a tree can be constructed in the usual way to model S^*. By adding to the stock price at each node the present value of future dividends (if any), the tree can be converted into another tree that models S. Suppose that S_0^* is the value of S^* at time zero. At time $i\Delta t$, the nodes on this tree correspond to the stock prices

$$S_0^* u^j d^{i-j} + De^{-r(\tau - i\Delta t)} \qquad j = 0, 1, \ldots, i$$

when $i\Delta t < \tau$ and

$$S_0^* u^j d^{i-j} \qquad j = 0, 1, \ldots, i$$

when $i\Delta t > \tau$. This approach, which has the advantage of being consistent with the approach for European options in section 11.12, succeeds in achieving a situation where the tree recombines so that there are $i + 1$ nodes at time $i\Delta t$. It can be generalized in a straightforward way to deal with the situation where there are several dividends.

Example 16.5   Consider a five-month put option on a stock that is expected to pay a single dividend of $2.06 during the life of the option. The initial stock price is $52, the strike price is $50, the risk-free interest rate is 10% per annum, the volatility is 40% per annum, and the ex-dividend date is in $3\frac{1}{2}$ months.

We first construct a tree to model S^*, the stock price less the present value of future dividends during the life of the option. At time zero, the present value of the dividend is

$$2.06e^{-0.2917 \times 0.1} = 2.00$$

The initial value of S^* is, therefore, 50.00. Assuming that the 40% per annum volatility refers to S^*, Figure 16.3 provides a binomial tree for S^*. (S^* has the same initial value and volatility as the stock price that Figure 16.3 was based upon.) Adding the present value of the dividend at each node leads to Figure 16.8, which is a binomial model for S. The probabilities at each node are, as in Figure 16.3, 0.5073 for an up movement and 0.4927 for a down movement. Working back through the tree in the usual way gives the option price as $4.44. (Using 50 time steps, DerivaGem gives a value for the option of 4.202; using 100 time steps it gives 4.212.)

---

[5] In theory σ^* is slightly greater than σ, the volatility of S. In practice, no distinction is usually made between the two.

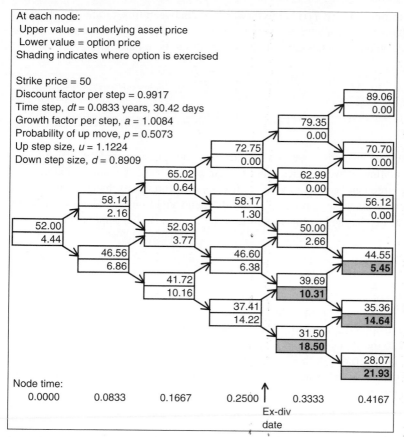

At each node:
 Upper value = underlying asset price
 Lower value = option price
 Shading indicates where option is exercised

Strike price = 50
Discount factor per step = 0.9917
Time step, dt = 0.0833 years, 30.42 days
Growth factor per step, a = 1.0084
Probability of up move, p = 0.5073
Up step size, u = 1.1224
Down step size, d = 0.8909

Node time:
| 0.0000 | 0.0833 | 0.1667 | 0.2500 | 0.3333 | 0.4167 |

Ex-div
date

Figure 16.8 Tree produced by DerivaGem for Example 16.5.

16.4 EXTENSIONS OF THE BASIC TREE APPROACH

In chapter 18 we describe how tree approaches can be extended to handle barrier options, options dependent on two underlying variables, and some types of path-dependent derivatives. Here we cover two relatively minor extensions of the basic methodology.

Time-Dependent Interest Rates

The usual assumption when American options are being valued is that interest rates are constant. When the term structure is steeply upward or downward sloping, this may not be a satisfactory assumption. It is more appropriate to assume that the interest rate for a future period of length Δt equals the current forward interest rate for that period. We can accommodate this assumption by setting

$$a = e^{f(t)\Delta t}$$

(16.12)

for nodes at time t where $f(t)$ is the forward rate between times t and $t + \Delta t$. This does not change the geometry of the tree because u and d do not depend on a. The probabilities on the branches emanating from nodes at time t are:[6]

$$p = \frac{e^{f(t)\Delta t} - d}{u - d}$$

$$1 - p = \frac{u - e^{f(t)\Delta t}}{u - d}$$

The rest of the way that we use the tree is the same as before, except that when discounting between times t and $t + \Delta t$ we use $f(t)$. A similar modification of the basic tree can be used to value index options, foreign exchange options, and futures options. In these applications, the dividend yield on an index or a foreign risk-free rate can be made a function of time by using a similar approach to that just described.

Control Variate Technique

A technique known as the *control variate technique* can be used for the evaluation of an American option.[7] This involves using the same tree to calculate both the value of the American option, f_A, and the value of the corresponding European option, f_E. We also calculate the Black–Scholes price of the European option, f_{BS}. The error given by the tree in the pricing of the European option is assumed equal to that given by the tree in the pricing of the American option. This gives the estimate of the price of the American option to be

$$f_A + f_{BS} - f_E$$

To illustrate this approach, Figure 16.9 values the option in Figure 16.3 on the assumption that it is European. The price obtained is \$4.32. From the Black–Scholes formula, the true European price of the option is \$4.08. The estimate of the American price in Figure 16.3 is \$4.49. The control variate estimate of the American price is, therefore,

$$4.49 + 4.08 - 4.32 = 4.25$$

A good estimate of the American price, calculated using 100 steps, is 4.278. The control variate approach does, therefore, produce a considerable improvement over the basic tree estimate of 4.48 in this case.

The control variate technique in effect involves using the tree to calculate the difference between the European and the American price rather than the American price itself. We give a further application of a control variate technique when we discuss Monte Carlo simulation later in the chapter.

---

[6] For a sufficiently large number of time steps, these probabilities are always positive.

[7] See J. Hull and A. White, "The Use of the Control Variate Technique in Option Pricing," *Journal of Financial and Quantitative Analysis*, 23 (September 1988), 237–51.

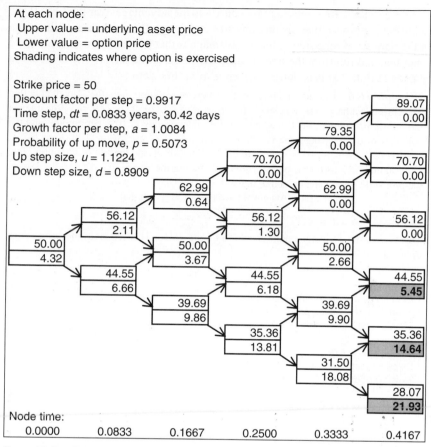

At each node:
 Upper value = underlying asset price
 Lower value = option price
 Shading indicates where option is exercised

Strike price = 50
Discount factor per step = 0.9917
Time step, *dt* = 0.0833 years, 30.42 days
Growth factor per step, *a* = 1.0084
Probability of up move, *p* = 0.5073
Up step size, *u* = 1.1224
Down step size, *d* = 0.8909

Node time:
 0.0000   0.0833   0.1667   0.2500   0.3333   0.4167

Figure 16.9   Tree, as produced by DerivaGem, for European version of option in Figure 16.3. At each node, the upper number is the stock price, and the lower number is the option price.

16.5   ALTERNATIVE PROCEDURES FOR CONSTRUCTING TREES

The original Cox, Ross, and Rubinstein approach is not the only way of building a binomial tree. Instead of imposing the assumption $u = 1/d$ on equations (16.2) and (16.3), we can set $p = 0.5$. A solution to the equations when terms of higher order than Δt are ignored is then

$$u = e^{(r - \sigma^2/2)\Delta t + \sigma\sqrt{\Delta t}}$$

$$d = e^{(r - \sigma^2/2)\Delta t - \sigma\sqrt{\Delta t}}$$

When the stock provides a continuous dividend yield at rate q, the variable r becomes $r - q$ in these formulas. This allows trees with $p = 0.5$ to be built for options on indices, foreign exchange, and futures.

This alternative tree-building procedure has the advantage over the Cox, Ross, and Rubinstein approach that the probabilities are always 0.5 regardless of the value of σ or the number of time steps.[8] Its disadvantage is that it is not as easy to calculate delta, gamma, and rho from the tree because the value of the underlying asset at the central node at time $2\Delta t$ is no longer the same as at time zero.

Example 16.6   Consider a nine-month American call option on the Canadian dollar. The current exchange rate is 0.7900, the strike price is 0.7950, the U.S. risk-free interest rate is 6% per annum, the Canadian risk-free interest rate is 10% per annum, and the volatility of the exchange rate is 4% per annum. In this case, $S_0 = 0.79$, $X = 0.795$, $r = 0.06$, $r_f = 0.10$, $\sigma = 0.04$, and $T = 0.75$. We divide the life of the option into three-month periods for the purposes of constructing the tree so that $\Delta t = 0.25$. We set the probabilities on each branch to 0.5 and

$$u = e^{(0.06-0.10-0.0016/2)0.25+0.04\sqrt{0.25}} = 1.0098$$

$$d = e^{(0.06-0.10-0.0016/2)0.25-0.04\sqrt{0.25}} = 0.9703$$

The tree for the exchange rate is shown in Figure 16.10. The tree gives the value of the option as $0.0026.

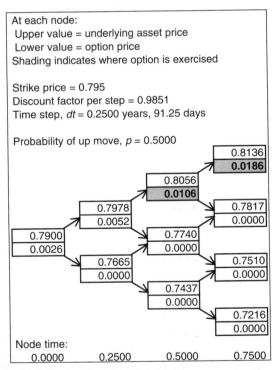

At each node:
 Upper value = underlying asset price
 Lower value = option price
 Shading indicates where option is exercised

Strike price = 0.795
Discount factor per step = 0.9851
Time step, dt = 0.2500 years, 91.25 days

Probability of up move, p = 0.5000

			0.8136
			0.0186
		0.8056	
		0.0106	
	0.7978		0.7817
	0.0052		0.0000
0.7900		0.7740	
0.0026		0.0000	
	0.7665		0.7510
	0.0000		0.0000
		0.7437	
		0.0000	
			0.7216
			0.0000

Node time:
   0.0000   0.2500   0.5000   0.7500

Figure 16.10   Binomial tree for American call option on the Canadian dollar. At each node, uppermost number is spot exchange rate, and the lower number is option price. All probabilities are 0.5.

---

[8] In the unusual situation that time steps are so large that $\sigma < |(r-q)\sqrt{\Delta t}|$ the Cox, Ross, and Rubinstein tree gives negative probabilities. The alternative procedure described here does not have this drawback.

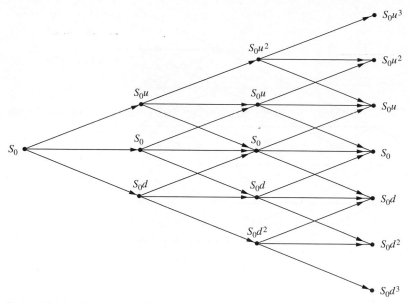

Figure 16.11 Trinomial stock price tree.

Trinomial Trees

Trinomial trees can be used as an alternative to binomial trees. The general form of the tree is as shown in Figure 16.11. Suppose that p_u, p_m, and p_d are the probabilities of up, middle, and down movements at each node and Δt is the length of the time step. For a non-dividend-paying stock, parameter values that match the mean and standard deviation of price changes when terms of higher order than Δt are ignored are

$$u = e^{\sigma \sqrt{3\Delta t}}$$

$$d = \frac{1}{u}$$

$$p_d = -\sqrt{\frac{\Delta t}{12\sigma^2}} \left(r - \frac{\sigma^2}{2} \right) + \frac{1}{6}$$

$$p_m = \frac{2}{3}$$

$$p_u = \sqrt{\frac{\Delta t}{12\sigma^2}} \left(r - \frac{\sigma^2}{2} \right) + \frac{1}{6}$$

For a stock paying a continuous dividend at rate q, we replace r by $r - q$ in these equations. Calculations for a trinomial tree are analogous to those for a binomial tree. The trinomial tree approach proves to be equivalent to the explicit finite difference method, which will be described in section 16.8.

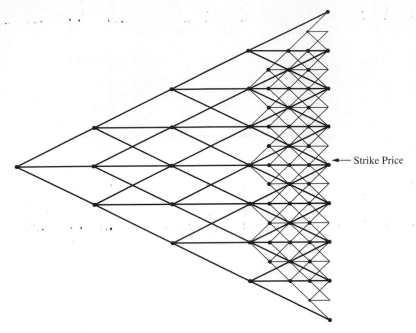

Figure 16.12   Adaptive mesh model for American-style option.

The Adaptive Mesh Model

Figlewski and Gao have proposed a method, which they call the *Adaptive Mesh Model*, for building trees where a high resolution (small Δt) tree is grafted onto a low resolution (large Δt) tree.[9] It turns out that, for an American option, we need high resolution close to the strike price and close to maturity. Figure 16.12 indicates how this can be achieved. In this figure, a trinomial tree with a time step of $\Delta t/4$ has been grafted on to a trinomial tree with a time step of Δt. The calculation of probabilities on branches and the rollback procedure is analogous to that for a regular tree. The tree in Figure 16.12 leads to a significant improvement in numerical efficiency over a regular binomial or trinomial tree.

16.6   MONTE CARLO SIMULATION

We now move on to discuss Monte Carlo simulation. This uses the risk-neutral valuation result. The expected payoff in a risk-neutral world is calculated using a sampling procedure. It is then discounted at the risk-free interest rate.

---

[9]See S. Figlewski and B. Gao, "The Adaptive Mesh Model: A New Approach to Efficient Option Pricing," *Journal of Financial Economics*, forthcoming.

Consider a derivative dependent on a single market variable S that provides a payoff at time T. Assuming that interest rates are constant, we can value the derivative as follows:

1. Sample a random path for S in a risk-neutral world.
2. Calculate the payoff from the derivative.
3. Repeat steps one and two to get many sample values of the payoff from the derivative in a risk-neutral world.
4. Calculate the mean of the sample payoffs to get an estimate of the expected payoff in a risk-neutral world.
5. Discount the expected payoff at the risk-free rate to get an estimate of the value of the derivative.

Suppose that the process followed by the underlying market variable in a risk-neutral world is

$$dS = \hat{\mu} S \, dt + \sigma S \, dz \tag{16.13}$$

where dz is a Weiner process, $\hat{\mu}$ is the expected return in a risk-neutral world, and σ is the volatility.[10] To simulate the path followed by S, we divide the life of the derivative into N short intervals of length Δt and approximate equation (16.15) as

$$S(t + \Delta t) - S(t) = \hat{\mu} S(t) \Delta t + \sigma S(t) \epsilon \sqrt{\Delta t} \tag{16.14}$$

where $S(t)$ denotes the value of S at time t, ϵ is a random sample from a normal distribution with mean zero and standard deviation of 1.0. This enables the value of S at time Δt to be calculated from the initial value of S, the value at time $2\Delta t$ to be calculated from the value at time Δt, and so on. An illustration of the procedure is in section 10.4. One simulation trial involves constructing a complete path for S using N random samples from a normal distribution.

In practice, it is usually more accurate to simulate $\ln S$ rather than S. From Ito's lemma the process followed by $\ln S$ is

$$d \ln S = \left(\hat{\mu} - \frac{\sigma^2}{2} \right) dt + \sigma \, dz$$

so that

$$\ln S(t + \Delta t) - \ln S(t) = \left(\hat{\mu} - \frac{\sigma^2}{2} \right) \Delta t + \sigma \epsilon \sqrt{\Delta t}$$

or equivalently

$$S(t + \Delta t) = S(t) \exp \left[\left(\hat{\mu} - \frac{\sigma^2}{2} \right) \Delta t + \sigma \epsilon \sqrt{\Delta t} \right] \tag{16.15}$$

---

[10]If S is the price of a non-dividend-paying stock $\hat{\mu} = r$; if it is an exchange rate $\hat{\mu} = r - r_f$; and so on. Note that the volatility is the same in a risk-neutral world as in the real world as shown in section 9.7.

This equation is used to construct a path for S in a similar way to equation (16.14). Whereas equation (16.14) is true only in the limit as Δt tends to zero, equation (16.15) is exactly true for all Δt.

The advantage of Monte Carlo simulation is that it can be used when the payoff depends on the path followed by the underlying variable S, as well as when it depends only on the final value of S. Payoffs can occur at several times during the life of the derivative rather than all at the end. Any stochastic process for S can be accommodated. As will be shown shortly, the procedure can also be extended to accommodate situations where the payoff from the derivative depends on several underlying market variables. The drawbacks of Monte Carlo simulation are that it is computationally very time consuming and cannot easily handle situations where there are early exercise opportunities.[11]

Derivatives Dependent on Market Variable Observed at a Single Time

When a derivative depends on the value of S at a single time T, it is often not necessary to sample a whole path for S. Instead we can jump straight from the value of S at time zero to its value at time T. When the process in equation (16.13) is assumed,

$$S(T) = S(0) \exp\left[\left(\hat{\mu} - \frac{\sigma^2}{2}\right)T + \sigma\epsilon\sqrt{T}\right]$$

Derivatives Dependent on More than One Market Variable

Consider the situation where the payoff from a derivative depends on n variables, θ_i ($1 \leq i \leq n$). Define s_i as the volatility of θ_i, $\hat{m}_i$ as the expected growth rate of θ_i in a risk-neutral world, and ρ_{ik} as the instantaneous correlation between θ_i and θ_k.[12] As in the single-variable case, the life of the derivative must be divided into N subintervals of length Δt. The discrete version of the process for θ_i is then

$$\theta_i(t + \Delta t) - \theta_i(t) = \hat{m}_i\theta_i(t)\Delta t + s_i\theta_i(t)\epsilon_i\sqrt{\Delta t} \qquad (16.16)$$

where ϵ_i is a random sample from a standard normal distribution. The coefficient of correlation between ϵ_i and ϵ_k is ρ_{ik} for $1 \leq i, k \leq n$. One simulation trial involves obtaining N samples of the ϵ_i ($1 \leq i \leq n$) from a multivariate standardized normal distribution. These are substituted into equation (16.16) to produce simulated paths for each θ_i and enable a sample value for the derivative to be calculated.

---

[11] A number of researchers have suggested ways Monte Carlo simulation can be extended to value American options. See for example M. Broadie, P. Glasseman, and G. Jain, "Enhanced Monte Carlo Estimates for American Option Prices," *Journal of Derivatives*, 5, 1 (Fall 1997), 25–44; and F. Longstaff and E. S. Schwartz, "Valuing American Options by Simulation: A Simple Least Squares Approach," Working Paper #25-98, 1998, Anderson School at UCLA.

[12] The variables s_i, $\hat{m}_i$, and $\rho_{i,k}$ are not necessarily constant; they may depend on the θ_i.

Generating the Random Samples from Normal Distributions

Most programming languages incorporate routines for sampling a random number between zero and one. An approximate sample from a univariate standardized normal distribution can be obtained from the formula

$$\epsilon = \sum_{i=1}^{12} R_i - 6 \tag{16.17}$$

where the R_i are independent random numbers between zero and one ($1 \leq i \leq 12$) and ϵ is the required sample from $\phi(0, 1)$. This approximation is satisfactory for most purposes.

When two correlated samples ϵ_1 and ϵ_2 from standard normal distributions are required, an appropriate procedure is as follows. Independent samples x_1 and x_2 from a univariate standardized normal distribution are obtained as just described. The required samples ϵ_1 and ϵ_2 are then calculated as follows:

$$\epsilon_1 = x_1$$
$$\epsilon_2 = \rho x_1 + x_2 \sqrt{1 - \rho^2}$$

where ρ is the coefficient of correlation.

Consider next the situation where we require n correlated samples from normal distributions where the coefficient of correlation between sample i and sample j is $\rho_{i,j}$. We first sample n independent variables x_i ($1 \leq i \leq n$), from univariate standardized normal distributions. The required samples are ϵ_i ($1 \leq i \leq n$), where

$$\epsilon_i = \sum_{k=1}^{i} \alpha_{ik} x_k$$

For ϵ_i to have the correct variance and the correct correlation with the ϵ_j ($1 \leq j < i$), we must have

$$\sum_{k=1}^{i} \alpha_{ik}^2 = 1$$

and, for all $j < i$,

$$\sum_{k=1}^{j} \alpha_{ik} \alpha_{jk} = \rho_{i,j}$$

The first sample, ϵ_1, is set equal to x_1. These equations for the α's can be solved so that ϵ_2 is calculated from x_1 and x_2; ϵ_3 is calculated from x_1, x_2 and x_3; and so on.[13] The procedure is known as the *Cholesky decomposition*.

Number of Trials

The number of simulation trials carried out depends on the accuracy required. If M independent trials are carried out as described above, it is usual to calculate the standard deviation as well as the mean of the discounted payoffs given by the simulation

---

[13]If the equations for the α's do not have real solutions, the assumed correlation structure is inconsistent, as explained in section 15.7.

trials for the derivative. Denote the mean by μ and the standard deviation by ω. The variable μ is the simulation's estimate of the value of the derivative. The standard error of the estimate is

$$\frac{\omega}{\sqrt{M}}$$

A 95% confidence interval for the price, f, of the derivative is, therefore, given by

$$\mu - \frac{1.96\omega}{\sqrt{M}} < f < \mu + \frac{1.96\omega}{\sqrt{M}}$$

This shows that our uncertainty about the value of the derivative is inversely proportional to the square root of the number of trials. To double the accuracy of a simulation, we must quadruple the number of trials; to increase the accuracy by a factor of 10, the number of trials must increase by a factor of 100; and so on.

Applications

Monte Carlo simulation tends to be numerically more efficient than other procedures when there are three or more stochastic variables. This is because the time taken to carry out a Monte Carlo simulation increases approximately linearly with the number of variables, whereas the time taken for most other procedures increases exponentially with the number of variables. One advantage of Monte Carlo simulation is that it can provide a standard error for the estimates that it makes. It is an approach that can accommodate complex payoffs and complex stochastic processes. It can be used when the payoff depends on some function of the whole path followed by a variable, not just its terminal value. As already noted, a limitation of the Monte Carlo simulation approach is that it can be used only for European-style derivatives.

Calculating the Greek Letters

The Greek letters discussed in chapter 13 can be calculated using Monte Carlo simulation. Suppose that we are interested in the partial derivative of f with q, where f is the value of the derivative and q is the value of an underlying variable or a parameter. First, Monte Carlo simulation is used in the usual way to calculate an estimate, f, for the value of the derivative. A small increase, Δq, is then made in the value of q, and a new value for the derivative, f^*, is calculated. An estimate for the hedge parameter is given by

$$\frac{f^* - f}{\Delta q}$$

In order to minimize to standard error of the estimate of the Greek letter, the number of time intervals, N, the random number streams, and the number of trials, M, should be the same for estimating both f and f^*.

Sampling through a Tree

Instead of implementing Monte Carlo simulation by randomly sampling from the stochastic process for an underlying variable, we can sample paths for the underlying variable using a binomial tree. Suppose we have a binomial tree where the probability of an "up" movement is 0.6. The procedure for sampling a random path through the tree is as follows. At each node, we sample a random number between zero and one. If the number is less than 0.4, we take the down path. If it is greater than 0.4, we take the up path. Once we have a complete path from the initial node to the end of the tree we can calculate a payoff. This completes the first trial. A similar procedure is used to complete more trials. The mean of the payoffs is discounted at the risk-free rate to get an estimate of the value of the derivative.

16.7 VARIANCE REDUCTION PROCEDURES

If the simulation is carried out as described so far, a very large value of M is usually necessary to estimate f with reasonable accuracy. This is very expensive in terms of computation time. In this section, we examine a number of variance reduction procedures that can lead to dramatic savings in computation time.

Antithetic Variable Technique

In the antithetic variable technique, a simulation trial involves calculating two values of the derivative. The first value, f_1, is calculated in the usual way; the second value, f_2, is calculated by changing the sign of all random samples from standard normal distributions. (If ϵ is a sample used to calculate f_1, $-\epsilon$ is the corresponding sample used to calculate f_2.) The sample value of the derivative calculated from a simulation trial is the average of f_1 and f_2. This works well because when one value is above the true value, the other tends to be below, and vice versa.

Denote $\overline{f}$ as the average of f_1 and f_2:

$$\overline{f} = \frac{f_1 + f_2}{2}$$

The final estimate of the value of the derivative is the average of the $\overline{f}$'s. If $\overline{\omega}$ is the standard deviation of the $\overline{f}$'s, and M is the number of simulation trials (i.e., the number of pairs of values calculated), the standard error of the estimate is $\overline{\omega}/\sqrt{M}$. This is generally much less than the standard error calculated using $2M$ random trials.

Control Variate Technique

We have already given one example of the control variate technique in connection with the use of trees to value American options (see section 16.4). The control variate technique is applicable when there are two similar derivatives, A and B. Derivative A is the security under consideration; derivative B is similar to derivative A and has an analytic solution available. Two simulations using the same random number streams and the same Δt are carried out in parallel. The first is used to obtain an estimate, f_A^*, of the value of A; the second is used to obtain an estimate, f_B^*, of the value of B. A better estimate of the value of A, f_A, is then obtained using the formula

$$f_A = f_A^* - f_B^* + f_B \tag{16.18}$$

where f_B is the known true value of B. Hull and White provide an example of the use of the control variate technique when evaluating the effect of stochastic volatility on the price of a European call option.[14] In this case, f_A is the value of the option assuming stochastic volatility and f_B is its value assuming constant volatility. The latter is known analytically.

Importance Sampling

Importance sampling is best explained with an example. Suppose that we wish to calculate the price of a deep-out-of-the-money European call option with strike price X and maturity T. If we sample values for the underlying asset price at time T in the usual way, most of the paths will lead to zero payoff. This is a waste of computation time because the zero-payoff paths contribute very little to the determination of the value of the option. We therefore try to choose only important paths, that is, paths where the stock price is above X at maturity.

Suppose F is the unconditional probability distribution function for the stock price at T and k, the probability of the stock price being greater than X at maturity, is known analytically. Then $G = F/k$ is the probability distribution of the stock price conditional on the stock price being greater than X. To implement importance sampling, we sample from G rather than F. The estimate of the value of the option is the average discounted payoff multiplied by k.

Stratified Sampling

Stratified sampling is a way of sampling from the probability distribution of a market variable at a future time. It involves dividing the distribution into ranges or intervals and sampling from each interval according to its probability. Suppose for example that there are ten equally likely intervals. We choose a sampling scheme that ensures that exactly 10% of our samples are from the first interval; 10% from the second interval; and so on. If a large number of intervals are used, we can regard either the mean or the median value of the variable, conditional on it being in an interval, as a representative value for the interval. When sampling from an interval, we then always pick the representative value. Curran shows results from using this procedure to value both European call options and path-dependent options.[15] In the case of a standard normal distribution when there are n intervals, we can calculate the representative value for the ith interval as

$$N^{-1}\left(\frac{i - 0.5}{n}\right)$$

where N^{-1} is the inverse cumulative normal distribution. For example, when $n = 4$ the representative values corresponding to the four intervals are $N^{-1}(0.125)$,

---

[14]See J. Hull and A. White, "The Pricing of Options on Assets with Stochastic Volatilities," *Journal of Finance*, 42 (June 1987), 281–300.

[15]See M. Curran, "Strata Gems," *RISK*, (March 1994), 70–71.

$N^{-1}(0.375)$, $N^{-1}(0.625)$, $N^{-1}(0.875)$. The function N^{-1} can be calculated iteratively using the approximation to the N given in section 11.8. An alternative approach is suggested by Moro.[16]

Moment Matching

Moment matching involves adjusting the samples taken from a standardized normal distribution so that the first, second, and possibly higher, moments are matched. Suppose that the normal distribution samples used to calculate the change in the value of a particular variable over a particular time period are ϵ_i ($1 \leq i \leq n$). To match the first two moments we calculate the mean of the samples, m, and the standard deviation of the samples, s. We then define adjusted samples y_i ($1 \leq i \leq n$) as

$$y_i = \frac{\epsilon_i - m}{s}$$

These adjusted samples have the correct mean of zero and the correct standard deviation of 1.0. We use the adjusted samples for all calculations.

Moment matching saves computation time, but can lead to memory problems because every number sampled must be stored until the end of the simulation. Moment matching is sometimes termed *quadratic resampling*. It is often used in conjunction with the antithetic variable technique. Because the latter automatically matches all odd moments, the goal of moment matching then becomes that of matching the second moment and, possibly, the fourth moment.

Using Quasi-Random Sequences

A quasi-random sequence (also called a *low-discrepancy* sequence) is a sequence of representative samples from a probability distribution.[17] Descriptions of the use of quasi-random sequences appear in Brotherton-Ratcliffe and Press et al.[18] Quasi-random sequences can have the desirable property that they lead to the standard error of an estimate being proportional to $1/M$ rather than $1/\sqrt{M}$, where M is the sample size.

Quasi-random sampling is similar to stratified sampling. The objective is to sample representative values for the underlying variables. In stratified sampling, it is assumed that we know in advance how many samples will be taken. A quasi-random sampling scheme is more flexible. The samples are taken in such a way that we are always "filling in" gaps between existing samples. At each stage of the simulation, the sampled points are roughly evenly spaced throughout the probability space.

---

[16]See B. Moro, "The Full Monte," *RISK*, (February 1985), 57–58.

[17]The term *quasi-random* is a misnomer. A quasi-random sequence is totally deterministic.

[18]See R. Brotherton-Ratcliffe, "Monte Carlo Motoring," *RISK*, (December 1994), 53–58; W. H. Press, S. A. Teukolsky, W. T. Vetterling, and B. P. Flannery, *Numerical Recipes in C: The Art of Scientific Computing*, 2nd ed. Cambridge: Cambridge University Press, 1992.

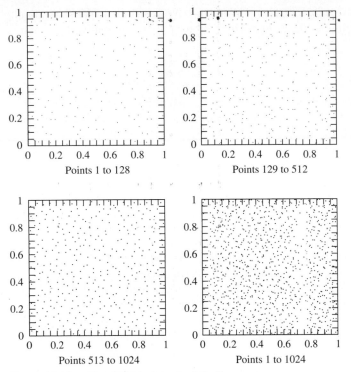

Figure 16.13   First 1024 points of a Sobol' sequence.

Figure 16.13 shows points generated in two dimensions using a procedure suggested by Sobol'.[19] It can be seen that successive points do tend to fill in the gaps left by previous points.

Representative Sampling through a Tree

As explained previously, we can implement Monte Carlo simulation by sampling paths through a tree. In the spirit of stratified sampling, we can choose representative paths through the tree instead of random paths. A set of paths is representative if the proportion of paths going through any given node equals (or is close to) the probability of that node being reached. The construction of representative paths is discussed by Mintz (1997).[20]

The first step is to choose the total number of sample paths. We can then calculate the expected number of sample paths going through each node. (This is the probability of the node being reached times the total number of sample paths.) Sup-

---

[19]See I. M. Sobol', *USSR Computational Mathematics and Mathematical Physics*, 7, 4 (1967), 86–112. A description of Sobol's procedure is in Press et al (1992), *"Numerical Recipes in C: The Art of Scientific Computing."*

[20]See D. Mintz "Less is more" *RISK* 10, 7 (July 1997), 42–45.

pose $u_{i,j}$ is the expected number of sample paths going through node (i, j). Typically the $u_{i,j}$ are not integers. It is necessary to develop an algorithm for the integerization of each $u_{i,j}$ (that is, the decision as to whether each $u_{i,j}$ is rounded up or down). The result of the algorithm should be that the correct number of sample paths leaves the initial node and that the number of sample paths entering each subsequent node equals the number of sample paths leaving the node. Once we have determined the number of sample paths that will pass along each branch, a "sampling without replacement" procedure can be used to define the sample paths.

16.8 FINITE DIFFERENCE METHODS

Finite difference methods value a derivative by solving the differential equation that the derivative satisfies. The differential equation is converted into a set of difference equations, and the difference equations are solved iteratively.

To illustrate the approach, we consider how it might be used to value an American put option on a non-dividend-paying stock. The differential equation that the option must satisfy is from chapter 11

$$\frac{\partial f}{\partial t} + rS\frac{\partial f}{\partial S} + \frac{1}{2}\sigma^2 S^2 \frac{\partial^2 f}{\partial S^2} = rf \qquad (16.19)$$

Suppose that the life of the option is T. We divide this into N equally spaced intervals of length $\Delta t = T/N$. A total of $N + 1$ times are, therefore, considered

$$0, \Delta t, 2\Delta t, \ldots, T$$

Suppose that S_{max} is a stock price sufficiently high that, when it is reached, the put has virtually no value. We define $\Delta S = S_{max}/M$ and consider a total of $M + 1$ equally spaced stock prices:

$$0, \Delta S, 2\Delta S, \ldots, S_{max}$$

The level S_{max} is chosen so that one of these is the current stock price.

The time points and stock price points define a grid consisting of a total of $(M + 1)(N + 1)$ points as shown in Figure 16.14. The (i, j) point on the grid is the point that corresponds to time $i \Delta t$ and stock price $j \Delta S$. We will use the variable $f_{i,j}$ to denote the value of the option at the (i, j) point.

Implicit Finite Difference Method

For an interior point (i, j) on the grid, $\partial f/\partial S$ can be approximated as

$$\frac{\partial f}{\partial S} = \frac{f_{i,j+1} - f_{i,j}}{\Delta S} \qquad (16.20)$$

or as

$$\frac{\partial f}{\partial S} = \frac{f_{i,j} - f_{i,j-1}}{\Delta S} \qquad (16.21)$$

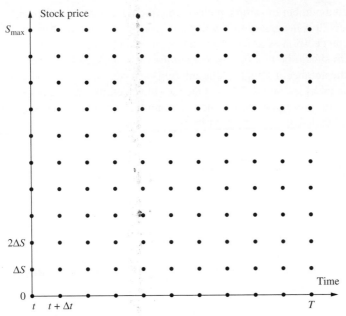

Figure 16.14   Grid for finite difference approach.

Equation (16.20) is known as the *forward difference approximation*; equation (16.21) is known as the *backward difference approximation*. We use a more symmetrical approximation by averaging the two:

$$\frac{\partial f}{\partial S} = \frac{f_{i,j+1} - f_{i,j-1}}{2\,\Delta S} \tag{16.22}$$

For $\partial f / \partial t$ we will use a forward difference approximation so that the value at time $i\,\Delta t$ is related to the value at time $(i + 1)\,\Delta t$:

$$\frac{\partial f}{\partial t} = \frac{f_{i+1,j} - f_{i,j}}{\Delta t} \tag{16.23}$$

The backward difference approximation for $\partial f / \partial S$ at the $(i,\ j)$ point is given by equation (16.21). The backward difference at the $(i,\ j + 1)$ point is

$$\frac{f_{i,j+1} - f_{i,j}}{\Delta S}$$

Hence, a finite difference approximation for $\partial^2 f / \partial S^2$ at the $(i,\ j)$ point is

$$\frac{\partial^2 f}{\partial S^2} = \left(\frac{f_{i,j+1} - f_{i,j}}{\Delta S} - \frac{f_{i,j} - f_{i,j-1}}{\Delta S} \right) \bigg/ \Delta S$$

or

$$\frac{\partial^2 f}{\partial S^2} = \frac{f_{i,j+1} + f_{i,j-1} - 2f_{i,j}}{\Delta S^2} \tag{16.24}$$

Substituting equations (16.22), (16.23), and (16.24) into the differential equation (16.19) and noting that $S = j\Delta S$ gives

$$\frac{f_{i+1,j} - f_{i,j}}{\Delta t} + rj\,\Delta S\frac{f_{i,j+1} - f_{i,j-1}}{2\,\Delta S} + \frac{1}{2}\sigma^2 j^2\,\Delta S^2\frac{f_{i,j+1} + f_{i,j-1} - 2f_{i,j}}{\Delta S^2} = rf_{i,j}$$

for $j = 1, 2, \ldots, M - 1$ and $i = 0, 1, \ldots, N - 1$. Rearranging terms, we obtain

$$a_j f_{i,j-1} + b_j f_{i,j} + c_j f_{i,j+1} = f_{i+1,j} \qquad (16.25)$$

where

$$a_j = \frac{1}{2}rj\,\Delta t - \frac{1}{2}\sigma^2 j^2\,\Delta t$$

$$b_j = 1 + \sigma^2 j^2\,\Delta t + r\,\Delta t$$

$$c_j = -\frac{1}{2}rj\,\Delta t - \frac{1}{2}\sigma^2 j^2\,\Delta t$$

The value of the put at time T is max $[X - S_T,\ 0]$ where S_T is the stock price at time T. Hence,

$$f_{N,j} = \max\,[X - j\,\Delta S,\ 0] \qquad j = 0, 1, \ldots, M \qquad (16.26)$$

The value of the put option when the stock price is zero is X. Hence,

$$f_{i,0} = X \qquad i = 0, 1, \ldots, N \qquad (16.27)$$

We assume that the put option is worth zero when $S = S_{\max}$, so that

$$f_{i,M} = 0 \qquad i = 0, 1, \ldots, N \qquad (16.28)$$

Equations (16.26), (16.27), and (16.28) define the value of the put option along the three edges of the grid in Figure 16.14, where $S = 0$, $S = S_{\max}$, and $t = T$. It remains to use equation (16.25) to arrive at the value of f at all other points. First the points corresponding to time $T - \Delta t$ are tackled. Equation (16.25) with $i = N - 1$ gives:

$$a_j f_{N-1,j-1} + b_j f_{N-1,j} + c_j f_{N-1,j+1} = f_{N,j} \qquad (16.29)$$

for $j = 1, 2, \ldots, M - 1$. The right-hand sides of these equations are known from equation (16.26). Furthermore, from equations (16.27) and (16.28),

$$f_{N-1,0} = X \qquad (16.30)$$
$$f_{N-1,M} = 0 \qquad (16.31)$$

Equations (16.29) are, therefore, $M - 1$ simultaneous equations that can be solved for the $M - 1$ unknowns: $f_{N-1,1}, f_{N-1,2}, \ldots, f_{N-1,M-1}$.[21] After this has been done, each value of $f_{N-1,j}$ is compared with $X - j\Delta S$. If $f_{N-1,j} < X - j\Delta S$, early exercise at

---

[21]This does not involve inverting a matrix. The first equation in (16.29) can be used to express $f_{N-1,2}$ in terms of $f_{N-1,1}$; the second equation can be used to express $f_{N-1,3}$ in terms of $f_{N-1,1}$; and so on. The final equation provides a value for $f_{N-1,1}$, which can then be used to determine the other $f_{N-1,j}$.

time $T - \Delta t$ is optimal and $f_{N-1,j}$ is set equal to $X - j\Delta S$. The nodes corresponding to time $T - 2\Delta t$ are handled in a similar way, and so on. Eventually, $f_{0,1}, f_{0,2}, f_{0,3}, \ldots,$ $f_{0,M-1}$ are obtained. One of these is the option price of interest.

The control variate technique can be used in conjunction with finite difference methods. The same grid is used to value an option that is similar to the one under consideration but for which an analytic valuation is available. Equation (16.18) is then used.

Example 16.7   Table 16.1 shows the result of using the implicit finite difference method as just described for pricing the American put option in Example 16.1. Values of 20, 10, and 5 were chosen for M, N, and ΔS, respectively. Thus, the option price is evaluated at $5 stock price intervals between $0 and $100 and at half-month time intervals throughout the life of the option. The option price given by the grid is $4.07. The same grid gives the price of the corresponding European option as $3.91. The true European price given by the Black–Scholes formula is $4.08. The control variate estimate of the American price is, therefore,

$$4.07 + 4.08 - 3.91 = \$4.24$$

Table 16.1   Grid to Value Option in Example 16.1 Using Implicit Finite Difference Methods

Stock price (dollars)					Time to maturity (months)						
	5	$4\frac{1}{2}$	4	$3\frac{1}{2}$	3	$2\frac{1}{2}$	2	$1\frac{1}{2}$	1	$\frac{1}{2}$	0
100	0.00	0.00	0.00	0.00	0.00	0.00	0.00	0.00	0.00	0.00	0.00
95	0.02	0.02	0.01	0.01	0.00	0.00	0.00	0.00	0.00	0.00	0.00
90	0.05	0.04	0.03	0.02	0.01	0.01	0.00	0.00	0.00	0.00	0.00
85	0.09	0.07	0.05	0.03	0.02	0.01	0.01	0.00	0.00	0.00	0.00
80	0.16	0.12	0.09	0.07	0.04	0.03	0.02	0.01	0.00	0.00	0.00
75	0.27	0.22	0.17	0.13	0.09	0.06	0.03	0.02	0.01	0.00	0.00
70	0.47	0.39	0.32	0.25	0.18	0.13	0.08	0.04	0.02	0.00	0.00
65	0.82	0.71	0.60	0.49	0.38	0.28	0.19	0.11	0.05	0.02	0.00
60	1.42	1.27	1.11	0.95	0.78	0.62	0.45	0.30	0.16	0.05	0.00
55	2.43	2.24	2.05	1.83	1.61	1.36	1.09	0.81	0.51	0.22	0.00
50	4.07	3.88	3.67	3.45	3.19	2.91	2.57	2.17	1.66	0.99	0.00
45	6.58	6.44	6.29	6.13	5.96	5.77	5.57	5.36	5.17	5.02	5.00
40	10.15	10.10	10.05	10.01	10.00	10.00	10.00	10.00	10.00	10.00	10.00
35	15.00	15.00	15.00	15.00	15.00	15.00	15.00	15.00	15.00	15.00	15.00
30	20.00	20.00	20.00	20.00	20.00	20.00	20.00	20.00	20.00	20.00	20.00
25	25.00	25.00	25.00	25.00	25.00	25.00	25.00	25.00	25.00	25.00	25.00
20	30.00	30.00	30.00	30.00	30.00	30.00	30.00	30.00	30.00	30.00	30.00
15	35.00	35.00	35.00	35.00	35.00	35.00	35.00	35.00	35.00	35.00	35.00
10	40.00	40.00	40.00	40.00	40.00	40.00	40.00	40.00	40.00	40.00	40.00
5	45.00	45.00	45.00	45.00	45.00	45.00	45.00	45.00	45.00	45.00	45.00
0	50.00	50.00	50.00	50.00	50.00	50.00	50.00	50.00	50.00	50.00	50.00

Explicit. Finite Difference Method

The implicit finite difference method has the advantage of being very robust. It always converges to the solution of the differential equation as ΔS and Δt approach zero.[22] One of the disadvantages of the implicit finite difference method is that $M - 1$ simultaneous equations have to be solved in order to calculate the $f_{i,j}$'s from the $f_{i+1,j}$'s. The method can be simplified if the values of $\partial f / \partial S$ and $\partial^2 f / \partial S^2$ at point (i, j) on the grid are assumed to be the same as at point $(i + 1, j)$. Equations (16.22) and (16.24) then become

$$\frac{\partial f}{\partial S} = \frac{f_{i+1,j+1} - f_{i+1,j-1}}{2 \Delta S}$$

$$\frac{\partial^2 f}{\partial S^2} = \frac{f_{i+1,j+1} + f_{i+1,j-1} - 2 f_{i+1,j}}{\Delta S^2}$$

The difference equation is

$$\frac{f_{i+1,j} - f_{i,j}}{\Delta t} + rj \Delta S \frac{f_{i+1,j+1} - f_{i+1,j-1}}{2 \Delta S}$$

$$+ \frac{1}{2}\sigma^2 j^2 \Delta S^2 \frac{f_{i+1,j+1} + f_{i+1,j-1} - 2 f_{i+1,j}}{\Delta S^2} = r f_{i,j}$$

or

$$f_{i,j} = a_j^* f_{i+1,j-1} + b_j^* f_{i+1,j} + c_j^* f_{i+1,j+1} \tag{16.32}$$

where

$$a_j^* = \frac{1}{1 + r \Delta t}\left(-\frac{1}{2}rj \Delta t + \frac{1}{2}\sigma^2 j^2 \Delta t\right)$$

$$b_j^* = \frac{1}{1 + r \Delta t}\left(1 - \sigma^2 j^2 \Delta t\right)$$

$$c_j^* = \frac{1}{1 + r \Delta t}\left(\frac{1}{2}rj \Delta t + \frac{1}{2}\sigma^2 j^2 \Delta t\right)$$

This creates what is known as the *explicit finite difference method*.[23] Figure 16.15 shows the difference between the implicit and explicit methods. The implicit method leads to equation (16.25), which gives a relationship between three different values of the option at time $i \Delta t$ (i.e., $f_{i,j-1}$, $f_{i,j}$, and $f_{i,j+1}$) and one value of the option at time $(i + 1) \Delta t$ (i.e., $f_{i+1,j}$). The explicit method leads to equation (16.32), which gives a relationship between one value of the option at time $i \Delta t$ (i.e., $f_{i,j}$) and three different values of the option at time $(i + 1) \Delta t$ (i.e., $f_{i+1,j-1}$, $f_{i+1,j}$, $f_{i+1,j+1}$).

---

[22] A general rule in finite difference methods is that ΔS should be kept proportional to $\sqrt{\Delta t}$ as they approach zero.

[23] We also obtain the explicit finite difference method if we use the backward difference approximation instead of the forward difference approximation for $\partial f / \partial t$.

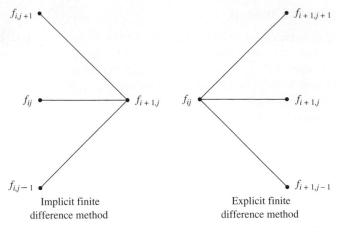

Implicit finite
difference method

Explicit finite
difference method

Figure 16.15   Difference between implicit and explicit finite difference methods.

Example 16.8   Table 16.2 shows the result of using the explicit version of the finite
difference method for pricing the American put option in Example 16.1. As in Example
16.7, values of 20, 10, and 5 were chosen for M, N, and ΔS, respectively. The option
price given by the grid is $4.26.[24]

Change of Variable

It is computationally more efficient to use finite difference methods with $\ln S$ rather
than S as the underlying variable. Define $Z = \ln S$. Equation (16.19) becomes

$$\frac{\partial f}{\partial t} + \left(r - \frac{\sigma^2}{2}\right)\frac{\partial f}{\partial Z} + \frac{1}{2}\sigma^2\frac{\partial^2 f}{\partial Z^2} = rf$$

The grid then evaluates the derivative for equally spaced values of Z rather than
for equally spaced values of S. The difference equation for the implicit method
becomes

$$\frac{f_{i+1,j} - f_{i,j}}{\Delta t} + (r - \sigma^2/2)\frac{f_{i,j+1} - f_{i,j-1}}{2\,\Delta Z} + \frac{1}{2}\sigma^2\frac{f_{i,j+1} + f_{i,j-1} - 2f_{i,j}}{\Delta Z^2} = rf_{i,j}$$

or

$$\alpha_j f_{i,j-1} + \beta_j f_{i,j} + \gamma_j f_{i,j+1} = f_{i+1,j} \tag{16.33}$$

---

[24]The negative numbers and other inconsistencies in the top left-hand part of the grid will be explained
later.

Table 16.2 Grid to Value Option in Example 16.1 Using Explicit Finite Difference Method

Stock price (dollars)	Time to maturity (months)										
	5	$4\frac{1}{2}$	4	$3\frac{1}{2}$	3	$2\frac{1}{2}$	2	$1\frac{1}{2}$	1	$\frac{1}{2}$	0
100	0.00	0.00	0.00	0.00	0.00	0.00	0.00	0.00	0.00	0.00	0.00
95	0.06	0.00	0.00	0.00	0.00	0.00	0.00	0.00	0.00	0.00	0.00
90	−0.11	0.05	0.00	0.00	0.00	0.00	0.00	0.00	0.00	0.00	0.00
85	0.28	−0.05	0.05	0.00	0.00	0.00	0.00	0.00	0.00	0.00	0.00
80	−0.13	0.20	0.00	0.05	0.00	0.00	0.00	0.00	0.00	0.00	0.00
75	0.46	0.06	0.20	0.04	0.06	0.00	0.00	0.00	0.00	0.00	0.00
70	0.32	0.46	0.23	0.25	0.10	0.09	0.00	0.00	0.00	0.00	0.00
65	0.91	0.68	0.63	0.44	0.37	0.21	0.14	0.00	0.00	0.00	0.00
60	1.48	1.37	1.17	1.02	0.81	0.65	0.42	0.27	0.00	0.00	0.00
55	2.59	2.39	2.21	1.99	1.77	1.50	1.24	0.90	0.59	0.00	0.00
50	4.26	4.08	3.89	3.68	3.44	3.18	2.87	2.53	2.07	1.56	0.00
45	6.76	6.61	6.47	6.31	6.15	5.96	5.75	5.50	5.24	5.00	5.00
40	10.28	10.20	10.13	10.06	10.01	10.00	10.00	10.00	10.00	10.00	10.00
35	15.00	15.00	15.00	15.00	15.00	15.00	15.00	15.00	15.00	15.00	15.00
30	20.00	20.00	20.00	20.00	20.00	20.00	20.00	20.00	20.00	20.00	20.00
25	25.00	25.00	25.00	25.00	25.00	25.00	25.00	25.00	25.00	25.00	25.00
20	30.00	30.00	30.00	30.00	30.00	30.00	30.00	30.00	30.00	30.00	30.00
15	35.00	35.00	35.00	35.00	35.00	35.00	35.00	35.00	35.00	35.00	35.00
10	40.00	40.00	40.00	40.00	40.00	40.00	40.00	40.00	40.00	40.00	40.00
5	45.00	45.00	45.00	45.00	45.00	45.00	45.00	45.00	45.00	45.00	45.00
0	50.00	50.00	50.00	50.00	50.00	50.00	50.00	50.00	50.00	50.00	50.00

where

$$\alpha_j = \frac{\Delta t}{2\Delta Z}(r - \sigma^2/2) - \frac{\Delta t}{2\Delta Z^2}\sigma^2$$

$$\beta_j = 1 + \frac{\Delta t}{\Delta Z^2}\sigma^2 + r\Delta t$$

$$\gamma_j = -\frac{\Delta t}{2\Delta Z}(r - \sigma^2/2) - \frac{\Delta t}{2\Delta Z^2}\sigma^2$$

The difference equation for the explicit method becomes

$$\frac{f_{i+1,j} - f_{i,j}}{\Delta t} + (r - \sigma^2/2)\frac{f_{i+1,j+1} - f_{i+1,j-1}}{2\,\Delta Z}$$

$$+ \frac{1}{2}\sigma^2\frac{f_{i+1,j+1} + f_{i+1,j-1} - 2f_{i+1,j}}{\Delta Z^2} = rf_{i,j}$$

or

$$\alpha_j^* f_{i+1,j-1} + \beta_j^* f_{i+1,j} + \gamma_j^* f_{i+1,j+1} = f_{i,j} \tag{16.34}$$

where

$$\alpha_j^* = \frac{1}{1 + r\Delta t}\left[-\frac{\Delta t}{2\Delta}(r - \sigma^2/2) + \frac{\Delta t}{2\Delta Z^2}\sigma^2\right] \tag{16.35}$$

$$\beta_j^* = \frac{1}{1 + r\Delta t}\left[1 - \frac{\Delta t}{\Delta Z^2}\sigma^2\right] \tag{16.36}$$

$$\gamma_j^* = \frac{1}{1 + r\Delta t}\left[\frac{\Delta t}{2\Delta Z}(r - \sigma^2/2) + \frac{\Delta t}{2\Delta Z^2}\sigma^2\right] \tag{16.37}$$

The change of variable approach has the property that α_j, β_j, and γ_j as well as α_j^*, β_j^*, and γ_j^* are independent of j. It can be shown that it is numerically most efficient to set $\Delta Z = \sigma\sqrt{3\Delta t}$.

Relation to Trinomial Tree Approaches

The explicit finite difference method is equivalent to the trinomial tree approach.[25] In the expressions for a_j^*, b_j^*, and c_j^* in equation (16.32), we can interpret terms as follows:

$-\frac{1}{2}rj\,\Delta t + \frac{1}{2}\sigma^2 j^2\,\Delta t$: Probability of stock price decreasing from $j\,\Delta S$ to $(j - 1)\,\Delta S$ in time Δt.

$1 - \sigma^2 j^2\,\Delta t$: Probability of stock price remaining unchanged at $j\,\Delta S$ in time Δt.

$\frac{1}{2}rj\,\Delta t + \frac{1}{2}\sigma^2 j^2\,\Delta t$: Probability of stock price increasing from $j\,\Delta S$ to $(j + 1)\,\Delta S$ in time Δt.

This interpretation is illustrated in Figure 16.16. The three probabilities sum to unity. They give the expected increase in the stock price in time Δt as $rj\,\Delta S\,\Delta t = rS\,\Delta t$. This is the expected increase in a risk-neutral world. For small values of Δt, they also give the variance of the change in the stock price in time Δt as $\sigma^2 j^2\,\Delta S^2\,\Delta t = \sigma^2 S^2\,\Delta t$. This corresponds to the stochastic process followed by S. The value of f at time $i\,\Delta t$ is calculated as the expected value of f at time $(i + 1)\,\Delta t$ in a risk-neutral world discounted at the risk-free rate.

For the explicit version of the finite difference method to work well, the three "probabilities"

$$-\frac{1}{2}rj\,\Delta t + \frac{1}{2}\sigma^2 j^2\,\Delta t$$

$$1 - \sigma^2 j^2\,\Delta t$$

$$\frac{1}{2}rj\,\Delta t + \frac{1}{2}\sigma^2 j^2\,\Delta t$$

---

[25] It can also be shown that the implicit finite difference method is equivalent to a multinomial tree approach where there are $M + 1$ branches emanating from each node.

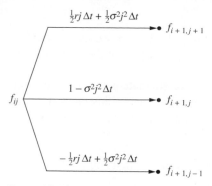

$\frac{1}{2}rj\,\Delta t + \frac{1}{2}\sigma^2 j^2\,\Delta t$

$f_{i+1,j+1}$

$1 - \sigma^2 j^2\,\Delta t$

f_{ij} $f_{i+1,j}$

$-\frac{1}{2}rj\,\Delta t + \frac{1}{2}\sigma^2 j^2\,\Delta t$

$f_{i+1,j-1}$

Figure 16.16 Interpretation of explicit finite difference method as a trinomial tree.

should all be positive. In Example 16.8, $1 - \sigma^2 j^2\,\Delta t$ is negative when $j \geq 13$ (i.e., when $S \geq 65$). This explains the negative option prices and other inconsistencies in the top left-hand part of Table 16.2. This example illustrates the main problem associated with the explicit finite difference method. Because the probabilities in the associated tree may be negative, it does not necessarily produce results that converge to the solution of the differential equation.[26]

When the change-of-variable approach is used [see equations (16.34) to (16.37)], the probability that $Z = \ln S$ will decrease by ΔZ is

$$-\frac{\Delta t}{2\Delta Z}(r - \sigma^2/2) + \frac{\Delta t}{2\Delta Z^2}\sigma^2$$

The probability that it will stay the same is

$$1 - \frac{\Delta t}{\Delta Z^2}\sigma^2$$

The probability that it will increase by ΔZ is

$$\frac{\Delta t}{2\Delta Z}(r - \sigma^2/2) + \frac{\Delta t}{2\Delta Z^2}\sigma^2$$

These movements in Z correspond to the stock price changing from S to $Se^{-\Delta Z}$, S, and $Se^{\Delta Z}$, respectively. If we set $\Delta Z = \sigma\sqrt{3\Delta t}$, the tree and the probabilities are identical to those for the trinomial tree approach discussed in section 16.5.

---

[26] J. Hull and A. White, "Valuing Derivative Securities Using the Explicit Finite Difference Method" *Journal of Financial and Quantitative Analysis*, 25 (March 1990), 87–100, show how this problem can be overcome. In the situation considered here it is sufficient to construct the grid in ln S rather than S to ensure convergence.

Other Finite Difference Methods

Many of the other finite difference methods that have been proposed have some features of the explicit finite difference method and some features of the implicit finite difference method.

In what is known as the *hopscotch method*, we alternate between the explicit and implicit calculations as we move from node to node. This is illustrated in Figure 16.17. At each time we first do all the calculations at the "explicit nodes" in the usual way. We can then deal with the "implicit nodes" without solving a set of simultaneous equations because the values at the adjacent nodes have already been calculated.

The *Crank–Nicholson* scheme is an average of the explicit and implicit methods. For the implicit method, equation (16.25) gives

$$f_{i,j} = a_j f_{i-1,j-1} + b_j f_{i-1,j} + c_j f_{i-1,j+1}$$

For the explicit method, equation (16.32) gives

$$f_{i-1,j} = a_j^* f_{i,j-1} + b_j^* f_{i,j} + c_j^* f_{i,j+1}$$

The Crank–Nicholson method averages these two equations to obtain

$$f_{i,j} + f_{i-1,j} = a_j f_{i-1,j-1} + b_j f_{i-1,j} + c_j f_{i-1,j+1} + a_j^* f_{i,j-1} + b_j^* f_{i,j} + c_j^* f_{i,j+1}$$

Putting

$$g_{i,j} = f_{i,j} - a_j^* f_{i,j-1} - b_j^* f_{i,j} - c_j^* f_{i,j+1}$$

we obtain

$$g_{i,j} = a_j f_{i-1,j-1} + b_j f_{i-1,j} + c_j f_{i-1,j+1} - f_{i-1,j}$$

This shows that implementing the Crank–Nicholson method is similar to implementing the implicit finite difference method. The advantage of the Crank–Nicholson method is that it has faster convergence than either the explicit or implicit method.

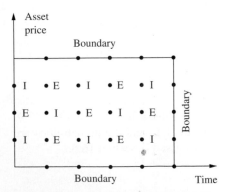

Figure 16.17   The hopscotch method. I indicates node at which implicit calculations are done; E indicates node at which explicit calculations are done.

Applications of Finite Difference Methods

Finite difference methods can be used for the same types of derivative pricing problems as tree approaches. They can handle American-style as well as European-style derivatives but cannot easily be used in situations where the payoff from a derivative depends on the past history of the underlying variable. Finite difference methods can, at the expense of a considerable increase in computer time, be used when there are several state variables. The grid in Figure 16.14 then becomes multidimensional.

The method for calculating Greek letters is similar to that used for trees. Delta, gamma, and theta can be calculated directly from the $f_{i,j}$ values on the grid. For vega, it is necessary to make a small change to volatility and recalculate the value of the derivative using the same grid.

16.9 ANALYTIC APPROXIMATION TO AMERICAN OPTION PRICES

As an alternative to the numerical procedures described thus far, a number of analytic approximations to the valuation of American options have been suggested. The best known of these is a quadratic approximation approach originally suggested by MacMillan and extended by Barone-Adesi and Whaley.[27] It can be used to value American calls and puts on stocks, stock indices, currencies, and futures contracts. It involves estimating the difference, v, between the European option price and the American option price. Because both the European and American option satisfy the same differential equation, v must also satisfy the differential equation. MacMillan, and Barone-Adesi and Whaley show that when an approximation is made, the differential equation can be solved using standard methods. More details on the approach are presented in Appendix 16A.

SUMMARY

We have presented three different numerical procedures for valuing derivatives when no analytic solution is available. These involve the use of trees, Monte Carlo simulation, and finite difference methods.

Binomial trees assume that in each short interval of time, Δt, a stock price either moves up by a proportional amount, u, or down by a proportional amount, d. The sizes of u and d and their associated probabilities are chosen so that the proportional change in the stock price has the correct mean and standard deviation in a risk-neutral world. Derivative prices are calculated by starting at the end of the tree and working

---

[27] See L. W. MacMillan, "Analytic Approximation for the American Put Option," *Advances in Futures and Options Research*, 1 (1986), 119–39; G. Barone-Adesi and R. E. Whaley, "Efficient Analytic Approximation of American Option Values," *Journal of Finance*, 42 (June 1987), 301–20.

backward. For an American option, the value at a node is the greater of the value if it is exercised immediately and the discounted expected value if it is held for a further period of time Δt.

Monte Carlo simulation involves using random numbers to sample many different paths that the variables underlying the derivative could follow in a risk-neutral world. For each path, the payoff is calculated and discounted at the risk-free interest rate. The arithmetic average of the discounted payoffs is the estimated value of the derivative.

Finite difference methods solve the underlying differential equation by converting it to a difference equation. They are similar to tree approaches in that the computations work back from the end of the life of the derivative to the beginning. The explicit method is functionally the same as using a trinomial tree. The implicit finite difference method is more complicated but has the advantage that the user does not have to take any special precautions to ensure convergence.

In practice, the method that is chosen is likely to depend on the characteristics of the derivative being evaluated and the accuracy required. Monte Carlo simulation works forward from the beginning to the end of the life of a security. It can be used for European-style derivatives and can cope with a great deal of complexity as far as the payoffs are concerned. It becomes relatively more efficient as the number of underlying variables increases. Tree approaches and finite difference methods work from the end of the life of a derivative to the beginning and can accommodate American-style as well as European-style derivatives. However, they are very difficult to apply when the payoffs depend on the past history of the state variables as well as on their current values. Also, they are liable to become computationally very time consuming when three or more variables are involved.

SUGGESTIONS FOR FURTHER READING

General

Clewlow, L., and C. Strickland. *Implementing Derivatives Models.* London: John Wiley and Sons, 1998.

On Tree Approaches

Boyle, P. P. "A Lattice Framework for Option Pricing with Two State Variables," *Journal of Financial and Quantitative Analysis*, 23 (March 1988), 1–12.

Broadie, M., and P. Glassman. "A Stochastic Mesh Method for Pricing High-Dimensional American Options," Working Paper, Columbia University, 1997.

Cox, J., S. Ross, and M. Rubinstein. "Option Pricing: A Simplified Approach," *Journal of Financial Economics*, 7 (October 1979), 229–64.

Figlewski, S., and B. Gao. "The Adaptive Mesh Model: A New Approach to Effecient Option Pricing." *Joutnal of Financial Economics*, forthcoming.

Hull, J. C., and A. White. "The Use of the Control Variate Technique in Option Pricing," *Journal of Financial and Quantitative Analysis*, 23 (September 1988), 237–51.

Rendleman, R., and B. Bartter. "Two State Option Pricing," *Journal of Finance*, 34 (1979), 1092–1110.

On Monte Carlo Simulation

Boyle, P. P. "Options: A Monte Carlo Approach," *Journal of Financial Economics*, 4 (1977), 323–38.

Broadie, M., and P. Glasserman. "Estimating Security Prices Using Simulation," *Management Science*, 42, 2 (February 1996), 269–285.

Broadie, M., P. Glasserman, and G. Jain. "Enhanced Monte Carlo Estimates for American Option Prices." *Journal of Derivatives* 5, 1 (Fall 1997), 25–44.

Brotherton-Ratcliffe, R. "Monte Carlo Motoring," *RISK* (December 1994), 53–58.

Curran, M. "Strata Gems," *RISK*, (March 1994), 70–71.

Moro, B. "The Full Monte," *RISK*, (February 1985), 57–58.

Papageorgiou A., and J. Traub. "Beating Monte Carlo," *RISK* (June 1996), 63–65.

Paskov, S. H. "New Methodologies for Valuing Derivatives," in *Mathematics Derivative Securities*, M. A. H. Dempster and S. R. Pliska, eds. Cambridge: Cambridge University Press, 1996.

Press, W. H., S. A. Teukolsky, W. T. Vetterling, and B. P. Flannery. *Numerical Recipes in C: The Art of Scientific Computing*, 2nd ed. Cambridge: Cambridge University Press, 1992.

Sobol', I. M. *USSR Computational Mathematics and Mathematical Physics*, 7, 4 (1967), 86–112.

On Finite Difference Methods

Brennan, M. J., and E. S. Schwartz. "Finite Difference Methods and Jump Processes Arising in the Pricing of Contingent Claims: A Synthesis," *Journal of Financial and Quantitative Analysis*, 13 (September 1978), 462–74.

Brennan, M. J., and E. S. Schwartz. "The Valuation of American Put Options," *Journal of Finance*, 32 (May 1977), 449–62.

Courtadon, G. "A More Accurate Finite Difference Approximation for the Valuation of Options," *Journal of Financial and Quantitative Analysis*, 17 (December 1982), 697–705.

Hull, J. C., and A. White. "Valuing Derivative Securities Using the Explicit Finite Difference Method," *Journal of Financial and Quantitative Analysis*, 25 (March 1990), 87–100.

Schwartz, E. S. "The Valuation of Warrants: Implementing a New Approach," *Journal of Financial Economics*, 4 (1977), 79–94.

Wilmott, P. *Derivatives: The Theory and Practice of Financial Engineering*. Chichester: John Wiley & Sons, 1998.

On Analytic Approximations

Barone-Adesi, G., and R. E. Whaley. "Efficient Analytic Approximation of American Option Values," *Journal of Finance*, 42 (June 1987), 301–20.

Carr, P., R. Jarrow, and R. Myneni. "Alternative Characterizations of American Put Options," *Mathematical Finance*, 2 (1992), 87–106.

Geske, R., and H. E. Johnson. "The American Put Valued Analytically," *Journal of Finance*, 39 (December 1984), 1511–24.

Ho, T.-S., R. S. Stapleton, and M. G. Subrahmanyam. "The Valuation of American options with Stochastic Interest Rates: A Generalization of the Geske-Johnson Technique," *Journal of Finance*, 52, 2 (June 1997), 827–40.

Johnson, H. E. "An Analytic Approximation to the American Put Price," *Journal of Financial and Quantitative Analysis*, 18 (March 1983), 141–48.

MacMillan, L. W. "Analytic Approximation for the American Put Option," *Advances in Futures and Options Research*, 1 (1986), 119–39.

QUESTIONS AND PROBLEMS
(ANSWERS IN SOLUTIONS MANUAL)

16.1. Which of the following can be estimated for an American option by constructing a single binomial tree: delta, gamma, vega, theta, rho?

16.2. Calculate the price of a three-month American put option on a non-dividend-paying stock when the stock price is $60, the strike price is $60, the risk-free interest rate is 10% per annum, and the volatility is 45% per annum. Use a binomial tree with a time interval of one month.

16.3. Explain how the control variate technique is implemented when a tree is used to value American options.

16.4. Calculate the price of a nine-month American call option on corn futures when the current futures price is 198 cents, the strike price is 200 cents, the risk-free interest rate is 8% per annum, and the volatility is 30% per annum. Use a binomial tree with a time interval of three months.

16.5. Consider an option that pays off the amount by which the final stock price exceeds the average stock price achieved during the life of the option. Can this be valued using the binomial tree approach? Explain your answer.

16.6. "For a dividend-paying stock, the tree for the stock price does not recombine; but the tree for the stock price less the present value of future dividends does recombine." Explain this statement.

16.7. Show that the probabilities in a Cox, Ross, and Rubinstein binomial tree are negative when the condition in footnote 8 holds.

16.8. How would you use the binomial tree approach to value an American option on a stock index when the dividend yield on the index is a function of time?

16.9. Explain why the Monte Carlo simulation approach cannot easily be used for American-style derivatives.

16.10. A nine-month American put option on a non-dividend-paying stock has a strike price of $49. The stock price is $50, the risk-free rate is 5% per annum, and the volatility is 30% per annum. Use a three-step binomial tree to calculate the option price.

16.11. Use a three-time-step tree to value a nine-month American call option on wheat futures. The current futures price is 400 cents, the strike price is 420 cents, the risk-free rate is 6%, and the volatility is 35% per annum. Estimate the delta of the option from your tree.

16.12. A three-month American call option on a stock has a strike price of $20. The stock price is $20, the risk-free rate is 3% per annum, and the volatility is 25% per annum. A dividend of $2 is expected in 1.5 months. Use a three-step binomial tree to calculate the option price.

16.13. A one-year American put option on a non-dividend-paying stock has an exercise price of $18. The current stock price is $20, the risk-free interest rate is 15% per annum, and the volatility of the stock price is 40% per annum. Use the DerivaGem software with four 3-month time steps to estimate the value of the option. Display the tree and verify that the option prices at the final and penultimate nodes are correct. Use DerivaGem to value the European version of the option. Use the control variate technique to improve your estimate of the price of the American option.

16.14. A two-month American put option on a stock index has an exercise price of 480. The current level of the index is 484, the risk-free interest rate is 10% per annum, the dividend yield on the index is 3% per annum, and the volatility of the index is 25% per annum. Divide the life of the option into four half-month periods and use the tree approach to estimate the value of the option.

16.15. How can the control variate approach improve the estimate of the delta of an American option when the tree approach is used?

16.16. Suppose that Monte Carlo simulation is being used to evaluate a European call option on a non-dividend-paying stock when the volatility is stochastic. How could the control variate and antithetic variable technique be used to improve numerical efficiency? Explain why it is necessary to calculate six values of the option in each simulation trial when both the control variate and the antithetic variable technique are used.

16.17. Explain how equations (16.25) to (16.28) change when the implicit finite difference method is being used to evaluate an American call option on a currency.

16.18. An American put option on a non-dividend-paying stock has four months to maturity. The exercise price is $21, the stock price is $20, the risk-free rate of interest is 10% per annum, and the volatility is 30% per annum. Use the explicit version of the finite difference approach to value the option. Use stock price intervals of $4 and time intervals of one month.

16.19. Suppose that, as an approximation, it is assumed that the term structure of interest rates is flat for one year and that

$$dr = a(b - r)\, dt + rc\, dz$$

where a, b, and c are known constants; r is the interest rate for maturities up to one year; and dz is a Wiener process. Discuss the problems in using a binomial tree approach to represent movement in r.

16.20. The spot price of copper is $0.60 per pound. Suppose that the futures prices (dollars per pound) are as follows:

3 months	0.59
6 months	0.57
9 months	0.54
12 months	0.50

The volatility of the price of copper is 40% per annum and the risk-free rate is 6% per annum. Use a binomial tree to value an American call option on copper with an exercise price of $0.60 and a time to maturity of one year. Divide the life of the option into four 3-month periods for the purposes of constructing the tree. (Hint: As explained in section 12.7, the futures price of a variable is its expected future price in a risk-neutral world.)

16.21. Use the binomial tree in Problem 16.20 to value a security that pays off x^2 in one year where x is the price of copper.

16.22. When do the boundary conditions for $S = 0$ and $S \longrightarrow \infty$ affect the estimates of derivative prices in the explicit finite difference method?

16.23. How can finite difference methods be used when there are known dividends?

16.24. A company has issued a three-year convertible bond that has a face value of $25 and can be exchanged for two of the company's shares at any time. The company can call the issue forcing conversion when the share price is greater than or equal to $18. Assuming that the company will force conversion at the earliest opportunity, what are the boundary conditions for the price of the convertible? Describe how you would use finite difference methods to value the convertible assuming constant interest rates. Assume there is no risk of the company defaulting.

16.25. Provide formulas that can be used for obtaining three random samples from standard normal distributions when the correlation between sample i and sample j is $\rho_{i,j}$.

ASSIGNMENT QUESTIONS

16.26. An American put option to sell a Swiss franc for dollars has a strike price of $0.80 and a time to maturity of one year. The volatility of the Swiss franc is 10%, the dollar interest rate is 6%, the Swiss franc interest rate is 3%, and the current exchange rate is 0.81. Use a three-time-step tree to value the option. Estimate the delta of the option from your tree.

16.27. A one-year American call option on silver futures has an exercise price of $9.00. The current futures price is $8.50, the risk-free rate of interest is 12% per annum, and the volatility of the futures price is 25% per annum. Use the DerivaGem software with four three-month time steps to estimate the value of the option. Display the tree and verify that the option prices at the final and penultimate nodes are correct. Use DerivaGem to value the European version of the option. Use the control variate technique to improve your estimate of the price of the American option.

16.28. A six-month American call option on a stock is expected to pay dividends of $1 per share at the end of the second month and the fifth month. The current stock price is $30, the exercise price is $34, the risk-free interest rate is 10% per annum, and the volatility of the part of the stock price that will not be used to pay the dividends is 30% per annum. Use the DerivaGem software with the life of the option divided into six time steps to estimate the value of the option. Compare your answer with that given by Black's approximation (see section 11.12).

16.29. The current value of the British pound is $1.60 and the volatility of the pound–dollar exchange rate is 15% per annum. An American call option has an exercise price of $1.62 and a time to maturity of one year. The risk-free rates of interest in the United States and the United Kingdom are 6% per annum and 9% per annum, respectively. Use the explicit finite difference method to value the option. Consider exchange rates at intervals of 0.20 between 0.80 and 2.40 and time intervals of three months.

Analytic Approximation to American Option Prices

Consider an option on a stock providing a continuous dividend yield equal to q. We will denote the difference between the American and European option price by v. Because both the American and the European option prices satisfy the Black–Scholes differential equation, v also does so. Hence,

$$\frac{\partial v}{\partial t} + (r - q)S\frac{\partial v}{\partial S} + \frac{1}{2}\sigma^2 S^2 \frac{\partial^2 v}{\partial S^2} = rv$$

For convenience, we define

$$\tau = T - t$$

$$h(\tau) = 1 - e^{-r\tau}$$

$$\alpha = \frac{2r}{\sigma^2}$$

$$\beta = \frac{2(r - q)}{\sigma^2}$$

We also write, without loss of generality,

$$v = h(\tau)g(S, h)$$

With appropriate substitutions and variable changes, this gives

$$S^2 \frac{\partial^2 g}{\partial S^2} + \beta S\frac{\partial g}{\partial S} - \frac{\alpha}{h}g - (1 - h)\alpha\frac{\partial g}{\partial h} = 0$$

The approximation involves assuming that the final term on the left-hand side is zero, so that

$$S^2 \frac{\partial^2 g}{\partial S^2} + \beta S \frac{\partial g}{\partial S} - \frac{\alpha}{h} g = 0 \qquad (16A.1)$$

The ignored term is generally fairly small. When τ is large, $1 - h$ is close to zero; when τ is small, $\partial g / \partial h$ is close to zero.

The American call and put prices at time t will be denoted by $C(S, t)$ and $P(S, t)$, where S is the stock price, and the corresponding European call and put prices will be denoted by $c(S, t)$ and $p(S, t)$. Equation (16A.1) can be solved using standard techniques. After boundary conditions have been applied, it is found that

$$C(S, t) = \begin{cases} c(S, t) + A_2 \left(\dfrac{S}{S^*} \right)^{\gamma_2} & \text{when } S < S^* \\[2ex] S - X & \text{when } S \geq S^* \end{cases}$$

The variable S^* is the critical price of the stock above which the option should be exercised. It is estimated by solving the equation

$$S^* - X = c(S^*, t) + \left\{ 1 - e^{-q(T-t)} N[d_1(S^*)] \right\} \frac{S^*}{\gamma_2}$$

iteratively. For a put option, the valuation formula is

$$P(S, t) = \begin{cases} p(S, t) + A_1 \left(\dfrac{S}{S^{**}} \right)^{\gamma_1} & \text{when } S > S^{**} \\[2ex] X - S & \text{when } S \leq S^{**} \end{cases}$$

The variable S^{**} is the critical price of the stock below which the option should be exercised. It is estimated by solving the equation

$$X - S^{**} = p(S^{**}, t) - \left\{ 1 - e^{-q(T-t)} N[-d_1(S^{**})] \right\} \frac{S^{**}}{\gamma_1}$$

iteratively. The other variables that have been used here are

$$\gamma_1 = \left[-(\beta - 1) - \sqrt{(\beta - 1)^2 + \frac{4\alpha}{h}} \right] \Big/ 2$$

$$\gamma_2 = \left[-(\beta - 1) + \sqrt{(\beta - 1)^2 + \frac{4\alpha}{h}} \right] \Big/ 2$$

$$A_1 = -\left(\frac{S^{**}}{\gamma_1}\right)\left\{1 - e^{-q(T-t)}N[-d_1(S^{**})]\right\}$$

$$A_2 = \left(\frac{S^*}{\gamma_2}\right)\left\{1 - e^{-q(T-t)}N[d_1(S^*)]\right\}$$

$$d_1(S) = \frac{\ln(S/X) + (r - q + \sigma^2/2)(T - t)}{\sigma\sqrt{T - t}}$$

As pointed out in chapter 12, options on stock indices, currencies, and futures contracts are analogous to options on a stock providing a continuous dividend with the dividend yield constant. Hence the quadratic approximation approach can easily be applied to all of these types of options.

CHAPTER 17

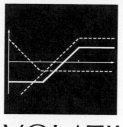

VOLATILITY SMILES AND ALTERNATIVES TO BLACK–SCHOLES

The pricing methods presented in chapters 11, 12, and 16 are often used in conjunction with what are termed "volatility smiles." These recognize that the future probability distribution of the underlying asset may not be lognormal. A volatility smile is a plot of the implied volatility of an option as a function of its strike price.

In this chapter we discuss the volatility smiles used in equity and foreign currency markets. The relationship between a volatility smile and the probability distribution being assumed for the asset price is explained. We also discuss how analysts use volatility term structures and volatility matrices in conjunction with the standard pricing models.

The second part of the chapter covers alternatives to the standard pricing models. These include models where the underlying asset follows a jump process rather than a continuous process and models where the volatility is stochastic. The chapter concludes with a review of some of the empirical research on option pricing.

17.1 PRELIMINARIES

In this section we present some results that follow from put–call parity. With our usual notation, S_0 is the asset price today; X is the exercise price; r is the risk-free interest rate; T is the time to maturity; c is the price of a European call; p is the price of a European put; and q is the dividend yield.

The put–call parity relationship discussed in chapters 7 and 12 is

$$p + S_0 e^{-qT} = c + X e^{-rT} \qquad (17.1)$$

where c and p are the prices of European call and put options with strike price X and maturity T. This relationship is based on a relatively simple arbitrage argument. It does not require any assumption about the future probability distribution of the underlying asset price. It is true both when the asset price distribution is lognormal and when it is not lognormal.

Suppose that, for a particular value of the volatility, p_{bs} and c_{bs} are the values of European put and call options based on the Black–Scholes model. Suppose further

435

that p_{mkt} and c_{mkt} are the market values of these options. Because put–call parity holds for the Black–Scholes model we must have

$$p_{bs} + S_0 e^{-qT} = c_{bs} + Xe^{-rT}$$

Because it also holds for the market prices

$$p_{mkt} + S_0 e^{-qT} = c_{mkt} + Xe^{-rT}$$

Subtracting these two equations

$$p_{bs} - p_{mkt} = c_{bs} - c_{mkt} \tag{17.2}$$

This shows that the dollar pricing error when the Black–Scholes model is used to price a European put option should be exactly the same as the dollar pricing error when it is used to price a European call option with the same strike price and time to maturity.

Suppose that the implied volatility of the put option is 22%. This means that $p_{bs} = p_{mkt}$ when a volatility of 22% is used in the Black–Scholes model. From equation 17.2, it follows that $c_{bs} = c_{mkt}$ when this volatility is used. The implied volatility of the call is, therefore, also 22%. This argument shows that the implied volatility of a European call option is always the same as the implied volatility of a European put option when the two have the same strike price and maturity. To put this another way, for a given strike price and maturity, the correct volatility to use in conjunction with the Black–Scholes model to price a European call should always be the same as that used to price a European put. This is also approximately true for American options. It follows that when analysts refer to a certain relationship between implied volatility and strike price they do not need to state whether they are talking about calls or puts. The relationship is the same for both.

> **Example 17.1**   Suppose that the value of the Australian dollar is $0.60. The risk-free interest rate is 5% in the United States and 10% in Australia. Assume that the market price of a European call option on the Australian dollar with a maturity of one year and a strike price of $0.59 is 0.0236. The DerivaGem software shows that the implied volatility of the call is 14.5%. The put–call parity relation in equation 17.1 applies with q equal to the foreign risk-free rate. For there to be no arbitrage, the price, p, of a European put option with a strike price of $0.59 and maturity of one year should satisfy:
>
> $$p + 0.60e^{-0.10\times1} = 0.0236 + 0.59e^{-0.05\times1}$$
>
> so that $p = 0.0419$. The DerivaGem software shows that, when the put has this price, its implied volatility is also 14.5%. This is as expected.

17.2 FOREIGN CURRENCY OPTIONS

The volatility smile used by traders to price foreign currency options has the general form shown in Figure 17.1. The volatility is lowest for at-the-money options. It becomes progressively higher as an option moves either in the money or out of the money.

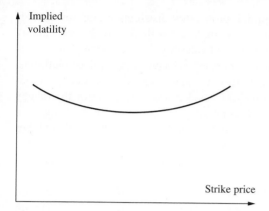

Figure 17.1 Volatility smile for foreign currency options.

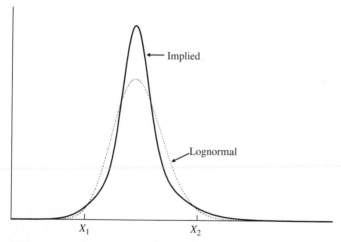

Figure 17.2 Implied distribution and lognormal distribution for foreign currency options.

The volatility smile in Figure 17.1 corresponds to the probability distribution shown by the solid line in Figure 17.2. We will refer to this as the *implied distribution*. A lognormal distribution with the same mean and standard deviation as the implied distribution is shown by the dashed line in Figure 17.2. It can be seen that the implied distribution has fatter tails (that is, more kurtosis) than the lognormal distribution.[1]

To see that Figure 17.1 and 17.2 are consistent with each other, consider first a deep-out-of-the-money call option with a high strike price of X_2. This option pays off only if the exchange rate proves to be above X_2. Figure 17.2 shows that the

---

[1] Note that in addition to having a fatter tail, the implied distribution is more "peaked." Both small and large movements in the exchange rate are more likely than with the lognormal distribution. Intermediate movements are less likely.

probability of this is higher for the implied probability distribution than for the log-normal distribution. We, therefore, expect the implied distribution to give a relatively high price, and therefore relatively high implied volatility, for the option. This is consistent with Figure 17.1 where high-strike-price options have high implied volatilities. (As explained earlier, the same high volatility would be used to price a deep-in-the-money put option with a strike price of X_2.) Consider next a deep-out-of-the-money put option with a low strike price of X_1. This option pays off only if the exchange rate proves to be below X_1. Figure 17.2 shows that the probability of this is also higher for implied probability distribution than for the lognormal distribution. Therefore, we expect the implied distribution to give a relatively high price, and therefore relatively high implied volatility, for this option as well. This is consistent with Figure 17.1 where low-strike-price options have high implied volatilities. (As explained earlier, the same high volatility would be used to price a deep-in-the-money call option with a strike price of X_1.)

Reason for the Smile in Foreign Currency Options

The smile for foreign currency options is consistent with empirical data showing that extreme movements in exchange rates happen more often than the lognormal distribution would predict.

Two of the conditions for an asset price to have a lognormal distribution are

1. The volatility of the asset is constant; and
2. The price of the asset changes smoothly with no jumps.

In practice neither of these conditions is satisfied for an exchange rate. The volatility of an exchange rate is far from constant and exchange rates frequently exhibit jumps.[2] It turns out that the effect of both a nonconstant volatility and jumps is that extreme outcomes become more likely.

The relative impact of jumps and stochastic volatility depends on the time horizon. The percentage impact of a stochastic volatility on prices becomes more pronounced as the maturity of the option is increased, but the volatility smile created by the stochastic volatility usually becomes less pronounced. The percentage impact of jumps on both prices and the volatility smile becomes less pronounced as the maturity of the option is increased. When we look sufficiently far into the future, jumps tend to get "averaged out" so that the stock price distribution when there are jumps is almost indistinguishable from the one obtained when the stock price changes smoothly.

17.3   EQUITY OPTIONS

The volatility smile used by traders to price equity options (both those on individual stocks and those on stock indices) has the general form shown in Figure 17.3. (This is sometimes referred to as a "volatility skew.") The volatility decreases as the strike

---

[2]Often the jumps are in response to the actions of central banks.

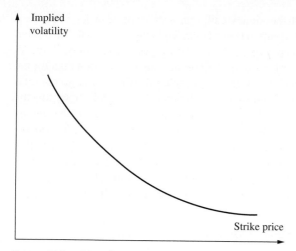

Figure 17.3   Volatility smile for equities.

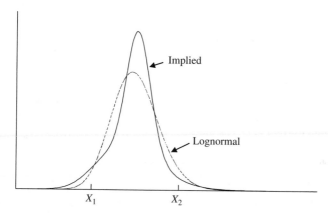

Figure 17.4   Implied distribution and lognormal distribution for equity options.

price increases. The volatility used to price a low strike price option (that is, a deep-out-of-the-money put or a deep-in-the-money call) is significantly higher than that used to price a high-strike-price option (that is, a deep-in-the-money put or a deep-out-of-the-money call).

The volatility smile for equity options corresponds to the implied probability distribution given by the solid line in Figure 17.4. A lognormal distribution with the same mean and standard deviation as the implied distribution is shown by the dotted line. It can be seen that the implied distribution has a fatter left tail and thinner right tail than the lognormal distribution.

To see that Figure 17.3 and 17.4 are consistent with each other, we proceed as for Figures 17.1 and 17.2 and consider options that are deep-out-of-the-money.

From Figure 17.4, a deep-out-of-the-money call with a strike price of X_2 will have a lower price when the implied distribution is used than when the lognormal distribution is used. This is because the option pays off only if the stock price proves to be above X_2 and the probability of this is lower for the implied probability distribution than for the lognormal distribution. We, therefore, expect the implied distribution to give a relatively low price for the option. This is consistent with Figure 17.3 which shows that the option has a relatively low implied volatility. Consider next a deep-out-of-the-money put option with a strike price of X_1. This option pays off only if the stock price proves to be below X_1. Figure 17.4 shows that the probability of this is higher for implied probability distribution than for the lognormal distribution. Therefore, we expect the implied distribution to give a relatively high price for this option. This is consistent with Figure 17.3 which shows that the option has a relatively high implied volatility.

The Reason for the Smile in Equity Options

One possible explanation for the smile in equity options concerns leverage. As a company's equity declines in value, the company's leverage increases. This means that the equity becomes more risky and its volatility increases. As a company's equity increases in value, leverage decreases. The equity then becomes less risky and its volatility decreases. This argument shows that we can expect the volatility of equity to be a decreasing function of price and is consistent with Figures 17.3 and 17.4.

Another explanation concerns what Mark Rubinstein calls "crashophobia." Traders are concerned about the possibility of another crash similar to that experienced in October 1987, and they price options accordingly. This explanation may have some validity. Although the evidence is somewhat mixed, it appears that the implied probability distribution for a stock price has fatter left tails than the probability distribution calculated from empirical data on stock market returns.

17.4   THE VOLATILITY TERM STRUCTURE

In addition to a volatility smile, traders use a volatility term structure when pricing options. This means that the volatility used to price an at-the-money option depends on the maturity of the option. One reason for this was discussed in section 15.6. Volatilities tend to be mean-reverting. If the current volatility is historically low, then there is an expectation that it will increase and so the volatility used for an option should be an increasing function of its maturity. If the current volatility is historically high, there is an expectation that it will decrease and so the volatility used for an option should be a decreasing function of its maturity.

The shape of the volatility smile depends on the option maturity. In most cases, the smile becomes less pronounced as the option maturity increases. Define T as the time to maturity and F_0 as the forward price of the asset. Some traders choose to define the volatility smile as the relationship between implied volatility and

$$\frac{1}{\sqrt{T}} \ln \frac{X}{F_0}$$

rather than as the relationship between the implied volatility and X. The smile is then usually much less dependent on the time to maturity.[3]

17.5 VOLATILITY MATRICES

Volatility matrices combine volatility smiles with the volatility term structure to tabulate the volatilities appropriate for pricing an option with any strike price and any maturity. An example of a volatility matrix that might be used for foreign currency options is shown in Table 17.1.

One dimension of a volatility matrix is strike price; the other is time to maturity. The main body of the matrix shows implied volatilities calculated from the Black–Scholes model. At any given time, some of the entries in the matrix are likely to correspond to options for which reliable market data are available. The volatilities for these options are calculated directly from their market prices and entered into the table. The rest of the matrix is determined using linear interpolation.

When a new option has to be valued, traders look up the appropriate volatility in the table. For example, when valuing a nine-month option with a strike price of 1.05, a trader would interpolate between 13.4 and 14.0 to obtain a volatility of 13.7%. This is the volatility that would be used in the Black–Scholes formula or in the construction of a binomial tree.

Table 17.1   Volatility Matrix

	Strike price				
	0.90	0.95	1.00	1.05	1.10
1 month	14.2	13.0	12.0	13.1	14.5
3 month	14.0	13.0	12.0	13.1	14.2
6 month	14.1	13.3	12.5	13.4	14.3
1 year	14.7	14.0	13.5	14.0	14.8
2 year	15.0	14.4	14.0	14.5	15.1
5 year	14.8	14.6	14.4	14.7	15.0

---

[3]For a discussion of this approach see S. Natenberg *Option Pricing and Volatility: Advanced Trading Strategies and Techniques*, second edition, Chicago: Probus, 1994. The approach makes the assumption that the volatility of an option depends on the number of standard deviations $\ln X$ is away from the mean of $\ln F_0$.

The Role of the Model

How important is the pricing model if traders are prepared to use a different volatility for every deal? It can be argued that an option pricing model is no more than a tool used by traders for understanding the volatility environment and for pricing illiquid securities consistently with the market prices of actively traded securities. If traders stopped using Black–Scholes and switched to another plausible model, the matrix of volatilities would change and the shape of the smile would change. But arguably, the prices quoted in the market would not change appreciably.

17.6 RELAXING THE ASSUMPTIONS IN BLACK–SCHOLES

The assumptions underlying the Black–Scholes formulas are listed in section 11.4. These assumptions can be relaxed in a number of ways. For example, we will show in chapter 19 that the Black–Scholes formulas are correct when interest rates are stochastic if

1. We set the interest rate, r, in Black–Scholes equal to the yield on a zero-coupon bond maturing at the same time as the option.
2. We assume that the risk-neutral probability distribution of the underlying asset price is lognormal at the maturity of the option.

This result can be regarded as an extension of a result produced by Merton in his 1973 paper.[4]

When the volatility is a known function of time, the Black–Scholes formulas are correct with the variance rate, σ^2, replaced by its average value during the remaining life of the option. An indication of how this result can be proved is in Problem 17.8. The result provides some indication as to how volatilities should be adjusted to allow for expected changes in volatility. For example, if the volatility of a stock is expected to rise steadily from 20% to 30% during the life of an option, it is appropriate to use a volatility of about 25% when valuing the option.[5] We implicitly used the result in section 15.6 when discussing how the GARCH (1,1) model can be used to calculate volatility term structures.

---

[4]See R.C. Merton, "Theory of Rational Option Pricing," *Bell Journal of Economics and Management Science,* 4 (Spring 1973), 141–83. Merton assumes that the volatility of the price of the underlying asset and the price of a zero-coupon bond maturing at time T are each, at most, a function of time.

[5]Setting σ^2 equal to the average variance rate during the life of an option is not quite the same as setting σ equal to the average volatility, but in practice there is very little difference between the two. If, in this example, the volatility increases linearly from 20% per annum to 30% per annum, the correct value to use for σ can be shown to be 25.17% per annum.

17.7 ALTERNATIVE MODELS FOR STOCK OPTIONS

For analysts who are uncomfortable with the practice of "massaging" the Black–Scholes model to make it fit observed data in the way described in section 17.5, there are a number of alternative models that can be used for stock options. In this section we discuss three of these.

Compound Option Model

The equity in a levered firm can be viewed as a call option on the value of the firm. To see this, suppose that the value of the firm is V and the face value of outstanding debt is A. Suppose further that all the debt matures at a single time, T^*. If $V < A$ at time T^*, the value of the equity at this time is zero because all the company's assets go to the bondholders. If $V > A$ at time T^*, the value of the equity at this time is $V - A$. Thus, the equity is a European call option on V with maturity T^* and exercise price A.

An option on stock of the firm that expires earlier than T^* can be regarded as an option on an option on V. This is known as a *compound option* and has been analyzed by Geske.[6] The state variable underlying the value of the stock option is the firm value, V, rather than the stock price, S. Geske assumes that σ_V, the volatility of V, is constant and that the amount of debt, A, is also constant. The volatility of S is then negatively correlated with V. When V decreases, leverage increases and the volatility of S increases. When V increases, leverage decreases and the volatility of S decreases. This is consistent with the pattern of implied volatilities observed for equity options (see Figure 17.3).

Geske's formula for pricing a European call option using the compound option model is given in Appendix 17A. It is more complicated than the Black–Scholes formula in that it requires a knowledge of the face value of the debt and the maturity of the debt.

Displaced Diffusion Model

Rubinstein has proposed what is known as a *displaced diffusion model* for stock option pricing.[7] In this model, the firm is assumed to hold two categories of assets: risky assets with a constant volatility, and riskless assets that provide a return, r. There is also assumed to be a certain fixed amount of default-free debt. If α is the initial proportion of assets that are risky and β is the initial debt-to-equity ratio, a key parameter, a, in the model is defined by

$$a = \alpha(1 + \beta)$$

---

[6]See R. Geske, "The Valuation of Compound Options," *Journal of Financial Economics*, 7 (1979), 63–81.
[7]See M. Rubinstein, "Displaced Diffusion Option Pricing," *Journal of Finance*, 38 (March 1983), 213–17.

If $a > 1$, the amount of debt in the displaced diffusion model exceeds the riskless assets. Netting the riskless assets off against the debt, the model becomes very similar to the compound option model and is consistent with the implied volatilities for equity options that are observed in practice. Unlike the compound option model, the displaced diffusion model does not take into account the possibility of default on the debt. In a situation where the value of the assets is less than the face value of the debt, the model assumes that the value of the equity is negative.

If $a < 1$, the amount of debt is less than the amount of riskless assets. The model then has properties that are markedly different from the properties of the compound option model. Netting off the debt against the riskless assets, we can write

$$S = S_A + S_B$$

where S is the stock price, S_A is the value of the risky assets, and S_B is the value of net riskless assets. When S_A increases quickly, S increases and the volatility of S also increases. This is because risky assets have become a proportionately larger part of S. Similarly, when S_A decreases quickly, both S and the volatility of S decrease. It follows that the volatility and stock price are positively correlated. The model, therefore, leads to an implied distribution with a fat right tail and thin left tail (the reverse of that observed in practice).

The formula for pricing a European call option under the displaced diffusion model is given in Appendix 17A. It will be recalled that in valuing options on stocks paying known dividends, we assumed that the stock price can be divided into a riskless component used to pay the dividends and a risky component with a constant volatility. This is a version of the displaced diffusion model with zero debt.

Constant Elasticity of Variance Model

The constant elasticity of variance model was proposed by Cox and Ross.[8] In this model, the stock price has a volatility of $\sigma S^{-\alpha}$ for some α where $0 \leq \alpha \leq 1$.[9] Thus, the volatility decreases as the stock price increases.

The rationale for the constant elasticity of variance model is that all firms have fixed costs that have to be met regardless of the firm's operating performance. When the stock price declines, we can presume that the firm's operating performance has declined and the fixed costs have the effect of increasing volatility. When the stock price increases, the reverse happens and the fixed costs have the effect of decreasing volatility. One type of fixed cost is that arising from financial leverage. In general concept, the constant elasticity of variance model is, therefore, similar to the compound option model. It is consistent with the pattern of implied volatilities observed for equity options (see Figure 17.3).

---

[8]See J. C. Cox and S. A. Ross, "The Valuation of Options for Alternative Stochastic Processes," *Journal of Financial Economics*, 3 (March 1976), 145–66.

[9]More formally, the model for the stock price is

$$dS = \mu S \, dt + \sigma S^{1-\alpha} \, dz$$

The formulas for pricing options under the general constant elasticity of variance model are relatively complicated and are not reproduced in this book. When $\alpha = 1$, the stock price volatility is inversely proportional to the stock price. This gives rise to a simple version of the constant elasticity of variance model known as the *absolute diffusion model*. The formula for pricing a European call under the absolute diffusion model is given in Appendix 17A. The model is easy to apply. Unfortunately, it has a weakness in that it allows stock prices to become negative.

17.8 PRICING MODELS INVOLVING JUMPS

The models considered thus far have involved the asset price changing continuously. In this section we consider two pricing models where the underlying assets exhibit jumps.

The Pure Jump Model

The pure jump model was first suggested by Cox and Ross and elaborated on in a later paper by Cox, Ross, and Rubinstein.[10] The model is illustrated in Figure 17.5. In each small interval of time, Δt, the asset price has a probability $\lambda \, \Delta t$ of moving from S to Su and a probability of $1 - \lambda \, \Delta t$ of moving from S to $Se^{-w\Delta t}$. Most of the time, the asset price declines at rate w. However, occasionally it exhibits jumps equal to $u - 1$ times the current asset price.

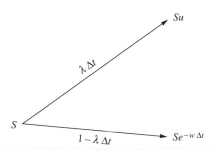

Figure 17.5 Asset price changes under the pure jump model.

---

[10]See J. C. Cox and S. A. Ross, "The Pricing of Options for Jump Processes," Working Paper 2–75, Rodney L. White Center for Financial Research, University of Pennsylvania, April 1975; J. C. Cox, S. A. Ross, and M. Rubinstein, "Option Pricing: A Simplified Approach," *Journal of Financial Economics*, 7 (September 1979), 229–63.

In the limit as $\Delta t \longrightarrow 0$, jumps occur according to a Poisson process at rate λ. The terminal asset price distribution is log-Poisson and the price of a call is as given in Appendix 17A. A pure jump model leads to the situation where the implied distribution has a fat right tail and a thin left tail (the opposite to that observed for equities). Arguably, the model is unrealistic in that jumps can only be positive.

The Jump Diffusion Model

Merton has suggested a model where the asset price has jumps superimposed upon a geometric Brownian motion.[11] Define

μ : Expected return from asset.

λ : Rate at which jumps happen.

k : Average jump size measured as a proportional increase in the asset price.

The proportional jump size is assumed to be drawn from a probability distribution in the model. The average growth rate from the jumps is λk. This means that the expected growth rate provided by the geometric Brownian motion is $\mu - \lambda k$.[12]

The key assumption made by Merton is that the jump component of the asset's return represents nonsystematic risk (i.e., risk not priced in the economy).[13] This means that a Black–Scholes type of portfolio, which eliminates the uncertainty arising from the geometric Brownian motion, must earn the riskless rate. This leads to the pricing formula in Appendix 17A.

The model gives rise to fatter left and right tails than Black–Scholes and is consistent with the implied volatilities observed for currency options. (See section 17.2).

17.9 STOCHASTIC VOLATILITY MODELS

One assumption in Black–Scholes that is clearly not true is the assumption that the volatility is constant. It is interesting, therefore, to compare the prices given by Black–Scholes with the prices given by a model where the volatility follows a stochastic process.

---

[11] See R. C. Merton, "Option Pricing When Underlying Stock Returns Are Discontinuous," *Journal of Financial Economics*, 3 (March 1976), 125–44.

[12] More formally, the model is

$$\frac{dS}{S} = (\mu - \lambda k)\,dt + \sigma\,dz + dq$$

where dz is a Wiener process, dq is the Poisson process generating the jumps, and σ is the volatility of the geometric Brownian motion. The processes dz and dq are assumed to be independent.

[13] This assumption is important because it turns out that we cannot apply risk-neutral valuation to situations where the size of the jump is systematic. For a discussion of this point, see E. Naik and M. Lee, "General Equilibrium Pricing of Options on the Market Portfolios with Discontinuous Returns," *Review of Financial Studies*, 3 (1990), 493–521.

Hull and White consider the following stochastic volatility model for the risk-neutral behavior of a price:

$$\frac{dS}{S} = r\,dt + \sqrt{V}\,dz_S$$

$$dV = a(b - V)\,dt + \xi V^\alpha\,dz_V$$

(17.4)

where a, b, ξ, and α are constant, and dz_S and dz_V are Wiener processes. The variable, V, in this model is the asset's variance rate. This is the square of its volatility. The variance rate has a drift that pulls it back to a level b at rate a. Hull and White compared the price given by this model with the price given by the Black–Scholes model when the variance rate in Black–Scholes is put equal to the expected average variance rate during the life of the option.

Hull and White show that when volatility is stochastic but uncorrelated with the asset price, the price of a European option is the Black–Scholes price integrated over the probability distribution of the average variance rate during the life of the option.[14] Thus a European call price is

$$\int_0^\infty c(\overline{V})g(\overline{V})\,d\overline{V}$$

where $\overline{V}$ is the average value of the variance rate, c is the Black–Scholes price expressed as a function of $\overline{V}$, and g is the probability density function of $\overline{V}$ in a risk-neutral world. They found that Black–Scholes overprices options that are at the money or close to the money, and underprices options that are deep in or deep out of the money. This is consistent with the pattern of implied volatilities observed for currency options. (See section 17.2.)

In the case where the asset price and volatility are correlated, there is no simple result. Option prices can be obtained using Monte Carlo simulation. In the particular case where $\alpha = 0.5$, a series expansion for the option price can be derived.[15] The pattern of implied volatilities obtained when the volatility is negatively correlated with the asset price is similar to that observed for equities. (See section 17.3.)

Chapter 15 discusses exponentially weighted moving average (EWMA) and GARCH (1,1) models. These represent an alterative approach to characterizing a

---

[14]See J. C. Hull and A. White, "The Pricing of Options on Assets with Stochastic Volatilities," *Journal of Finance*, 42 (June 1987), 281–300. This result is independent of the process followed by the variance rate.

[15]For details of this series expansion, see J. C. Hull and A. White, "An Analysis of the Bias in Option Pricing Caused by a Stochastic Volatility," *Advances in Futures and Options Research*, 3 (1988), 27–61. An alternative approach to handling the $\alpha = 0.5$ case is provided by S. L. Heston, "A Closed Form Solution for Options with Stochastic Volatility with Applications to Bonds and Currency Options," *Review of Financial Studies*, 6, 2 (1993), 327–43.

stochastic volatility model. Duan shows that it is possible to use GARCH $(1,1)$ as the basis for an internally consistent option pricing model.[16]

For options that last less than a year, the pricing impact of a stochastic volatility is fairly small in absolute terms (although in percentage terms it can be quite large for deep-out-of-the-money options). It becomes progressively larger as the life of the option increases.

The impact of a stochastic volatility on the performance of delta hedging is generally quite large. This can be tested by carrying out simulations of delta hedging, such as those in section 13.4, assuming first a constant volatility model and second a stochastic volatility model. Delta hedging works far worse when the volatility is stochastic. This emphasizes the point made in chapter 13 that traders should monitor vega as well as delta and gamma.

17.10 EMPIRICAL RESEARCH

A number of problems arise in carrying out empirical research to test the Black–Scholes and other option pricing models.[17] The first problem is that any statistical hypothesis about how options are priced has to be a joint hypothesis to the effect that (1) the option pricing formula is correct and (2) markets are efficient. If the hypothesis is rejected, it may be the case that (1) is untrue, (2) is untrue, or both (1) and (2) are untrue. A second problem is that the stock price volatility is an unobservable variable. One approach is to estimate the volatility from historical stock price data. Alternatively, implied volatilities can be used in some way. A third problem for the researcher is to make sure that data on the stock price and option price are synchronous. For example, if the option is thinly traded, it is not likely to be acceptable to compare closing option prices with closing stock prices. The closing option price might correspond to a trade at 1:00 p.m., whereas the closing stock price corresponds to a trade at 4:00 p.m.

Black and Scholes and Galai have tested whether it is possible to make excess returns above the risk-free rate of interest by buying options that are undervalued by the market (relative to the theoretical price) and selling options that are overvalued by the market (relative to the theoretical price). A riskless delta-neutral portfolio is assumed to be maintained at all times by trading the underlying stocks on a regular basis, as described in chapter 13. Black and Scholes used data from the over-the-counter options market where options are dividend protected. Galai used data from the Chicago Board Options Exchange (CBOE) where options are not protected against the effects of cash dividends. Galai used Black's approximation as described in section 11.12 to incorporate the effect of anticipated dividends into the option price. Both studies showed that, in the absence of transactions costs, significant excess returns over the risk-free rate can be obtained by buying under-

---

[16] See J.-C. Duan, "The GARCH Option Pricing Model," *Mathematical Finance*, vol. 5 (1995), 13–32, and J.-C. Duan, "Cracking the Smile" *RISK*, vol. 9 (December 1996), 55–59.

[17] See the end-of-chapter references for citations to the studies reviewed in this section.

valued options and selling overvalued options. But, it is possible that these excess returns are available only to market makers and that, when transactions costs are considered, they vanish.

A number of researchers have chosen to make no assumptions about the behavior of stock prices and have tested whether arbitrage strategies can be used to make a riskless profit in options markets. Garman provides a very efficient computational procedure for finding any arbitrage possibilities that exist in a given situation. One frequently cited study by Klemkosky and Resnick tests whether the relationship in equation 7.9 is ever violated. It concludes that some small arbitrage profits are possible from using the relationship. These are due mainly to the overpricing of American calls.

Chiras and Manaster carried out a study using CBOE data to compare a weighted implied volatility from options on a stock at a point in time with the volatility calculated from historical data. They found that the former provide a much better forecast of the volatility of the stock price during the life of the option. We can conclude that option traders are using more than just historical data when determining future volatilities. Chiras and Manaster also tested to see whether it was possible to make above-average returns by buying options with low implied volatilities and selling options with high implied volatilities. The strategy showed a profit of 10% per month. The Chiras and Manaster study can be interpreted as providing good support for the Black–Scholes model and showing that the CBOE was inefficient in some respects.

MacBeth and Merville tested the Black–Scholes model using a different approach. They looked at different call options on the same stock at the same time and compared the volatilities implied by the option prices. The stocks chosen were AT&T, Avon, Kodak, Exxon, IBM, and Xerox, and the time period considered was the year 1976. They found that implied volatilities tended to be relatively high for in-the-money options and relatively low for out-of-the-money options. A relatively high implied volatility is indicative of a relatively high option price, and a relatively low implied volatility is indicative of a relatively low option price. Therefore, if it is assumed that Black–Scholes prices at-the-money options correctly, it can be concluded that out-of-the-money (high strike price) call options are overpriced by Black–Scholes and in-the-money (low strike price) call options are underpriced by Black–Scholes. These effects become more pronounced as the time to maturity increases and the degree to which the option is in or out of the money increases. MacBeth and Merville's results are consistent with Figure 17.3. The results were confirmed by Lauterbach and Schultz in a later study concerned with the pricing of warrants.

Rubinstein has done a great deal of research similar to that of MacBeth and Merville. No clear-cut pattern emerged from his early research, but the research in his 1994 paper and joint 1996 paper with Jackwerth gives results consistent with Figure 17.3. Options with low strike prices have much higher volatilites than those with high strike prices. As mentioned previously in the chapter, leverage and the resultant negative correlation between volatility and stock price may partially account for the finding. It is also possible that investors fear a repeat of the crash of 1987.

A number of authors have researched the pricing of options on assets other than stocks. For example, Shastri and Tandon, and Bodurtha and Courtadon have examined the market prices of currency options; in another paper, Shastri and Tandon have examined the market prices of futures options; and Chance has examined the market prices of index options.

In most cases, the mispricing by Black–Scholes is not sufficient to present profitable opportunities to investors when transactions costs and bid–ask spreads are taken into account. When profitable opportunities are searched for, it is important to bear in mind that, even for a market maker, some time must elapse between a profitable opportunity being identified and action being taken. This delay, even if it is only to the next trade, can be sufficient to eliminate the profitable opportunity.

SUMMARY

The Black–Scholes model and its extensions assume that the probability distribution of the stock price at any given future time is lognormal. This assumption is not perfect. The probability distribution of an equity price has a fatter left tail and thinner right tail than the lognormal distribution. The probability of an exchange rate has a fatter right tail and a fatter left tail than the lognormal distribution.

Traders use volatility smiles to allow for nonlognormality. The volatility smile defines the relationship between the implied volatility of an option and its strike price. For equity options, the volatility smile tends to be downward sloping. This means that out-of-the-money puts and in-the-money calls tend to have high implied volatilities wheras out-of-the-money calls and in-the-money puts tend to have low implied volatilities. For foreign currency options, the volatility smile is slightly U-shaped. Deep-out and deep-in-the-money options have higher implied volatilities than at-the-money options.

Often traders use a volatility term structure. The implied volatility of an option then depends on its life. When volatility smiles and volatility term structures are combined they produce a volatility matrix. This defines implied volatility as a function of both the strike price and the time to maturity.

A number of alternatives to the Black–Scholes model have been suggested. These include models where a future volatility of a asset price is uncertain; models where a company's equity is assumed to be an option on its assets; and models where an asset price experiences occasional jumps rather than continuous changes.

SUGGESTIONS FOR FURTHER READING

On Alternative Models

Black, F., "How to Use the Holes in Black–Scholes," *RISK*, (March 1988).

Cox, J. C., and S. A. Ross, "The Valuation of Options for Alternative Stochastic Processes," *Journal of Financial Economics*, 3 (March 1976), 145–66.

Cox, J. C., S. A. Ross, and M. Rubinstein. "Option Pricing: A Simplified Approach," *Journal of Financial Economics*, 7 (September 1979), 229–63.

Derman, E. and I. Kani. "Riding on a Smile," *RISK*, (February 1994), 32–39.

Duan, J.-C. "The GARCH Option Pricing Model," *Mathematical Finance*, vol. 5 (1995), 13–32.

Duan, J.-C. "Cracking the Smile," *RISK*, vol. 9 (December 1996), 55–59.

Dupire, B. "Pricing with a Smile," *RISK*, (February 1994), 18–20.

Geske, R. "The Valuation of Compound Options," *Journal of Financial Economics*, 7 (1979), 63–81.

Heston, S. L. "A Closed Form Solution for Options with Stochastic Volatility with Applications to Bond and Currency Options,"*Review of Financial Studies*, 6, 2 (1993), 327–43.

Hull, J., and A. White. "The Pricing of Options on Assets with Stochastic Volatilities," *Journal of Finance*, 42 (June 1987), 281–300.

Hull, J., and A. White. "An Analysis of the Bias in Option Pricing Caused by a Stochastic Volatility," *Advances in Futures and Options Research* 3 (1988), 27–61.

Merton, R. C. "Option Pricing When Underlying Stock Returns Are Discontinuous," *Journal of Financial Economics*, 3 (March 1976), 125–44.

Merton, R. C. "Theory of Rational Option Pricing," *Bell Journal of Economics and Management Science*, 4 (Spring 1973), 141–83.

Ritchen, P., and R. Trevor, "Pricing Options Under Generalized GARCH and Stochastic Volatility Processes," *Journal of Finance*, 54, 1 (February 1999), 377–402.

Rubinstein, M. "Displaced Diffusion Option Pricing," *Journal of Finance*, 38 (March 1983), 213–17.

Stutzer, M. "A Simple Nonparametric Approach to Derivative Security Valuation," *Journal of Finance*, 51 (December 1996), 1633–52.

On Empirical Research

Bakshi, G., C. Cao, and Z. Chen. "Empirical Performance of Alternative Option Pricing Models," *Journal of Finance*, 52, 5 (December 1997) 2003–49.

Black, F., and M. Scholes. "The Valuation of Option Contracts and a Test of Market Efficiency," *Journal of Finance*, 27 (May 1972), 399–418.

Bodurtha, J. N., and G. R. Courtadon. "Tests of an American Option Pricing Model on the Foreign Currency Options Market," *Journal of Financial and Quantitative Analysis*, 22 (June 1987), 153–68.

Chance, D. M. "Empirical Tests of the Pricing of Index Call Options," *Advances in Futures and Options Research*, 1, pt. A (1986), 141–66.

Chiras, D., and S. Manaster. "The Information Content of Option Prices and a Test of Market Efficiency," *Journal of Financial Economics*, 6 (September 1978), 213–34.

Dumas, B., J. Fleming, and R. E. Whaley. "Implied Volatility Functions: Empirical Tests," *Journal of Finance*, 53, 6 (December 1998), 2059–2106

Galai, D. "Tests of Market Efficiency and the Chicago Board Options Exchange," *Journal of Business*, 50 (April 1977), 167–97.

Harvey, C. R. and R. E. Whaley. "S&P 100 Index Option Volatility," *Journal of Finance*, 46 (1991), 1551–61.

Harvey, C. R., and R. E. Whaley. "Market Volatility Prediction and the Efficiency of the S&P 100 Index Option Market," *Journal of Financial Economics*, 31 (1992) 43–73.

Harvey, C. R., and R. E. Whaley. "Dividends and S&P 100 Index Option Valuations," *Journal of Futures Markets*, 12 (1992), 123–37.

Jackwerth, J. C. and M. Rubinstein. "Recovering Probability Distributions from Option Prices," *Journal of Finance*, 51 (December 1996), 1611–1631.

Klemkosky, R. C., and B. G. Resnick. "Put–Call Parity and Market Efficiency," *Journal of Finance*, 34 (December 1979), 1141–55.

Lauterbach, B. and P. Schultz. "Pricing Warrants: An Empirical Study of the Black–Scholes Model and Its Alternatives," *Journal of Finance*, 4, 4 (September 1990), 1181–1210.

MacBeth, J. D., and L. J. Merville. "An Empirical Examination of the Black–Scholes Call Option Pricing Model," *Journal of Finance*, 34 (December 1979), 1173–86.

Melick, W. R., and C. P. Thomas. "Recovering an Asset's Implied Probability Density Function from Option Prices: An Application to Crude Oil During The Gulf Crisis," *Journal of Financial and Quantitative Analysis*, 32, 1 (March 1997), 91–115.

Rubinstein, M. "Nonparametric Tests of Alternative Option Pricing Models Using All Reported Trades and Quotes on the 30 Most Active CBOE Option Classes from August 23, 1976 through August 31, 1978," *Journal of Finance*, 40 (June 1985), 455–80.

Rubinstein, M. "Implied Binomial Trees," *Journal of Finance*, 49, 3 (July 1994), 771–818.

Shastri, K., and K. Tandon. "An Empirical Test of a Valuation Model for American Options on Futures Contracts," *Journal of Financial and Quantitative Analysis*, 21 (December 1986), 377–92.

Shastri, K., and K. Tandon. "Valuation of Foreign Currency Options: Some Empirical Tests," *Journal of Financial and Quantitative Analysis*, 21 (June 1986), 145–60.

Xu, X., and S. J. Taylor. "The Term Structure of Volatility Implied by Foreign Exchange Options," *Journal of Financial and Quantitative Analysis*, 29 (1994), 57–74.

QUESTIONS AND PROBLEMS
(ANSWERS IN SOLUTIONS MANUAL)

17.1. What pattern of implied volatilities is likely to be observed when
  (a) Both tails of the stock price distribution are thinner than those of the log-normal distribution?
  (b) The right tail is fatter, and the left tail is thinner, than that of a lognormal distribution?

17.2. What pattern of implied volatilities is likely to be observed when the volatility is stochastic and positively correlated to the stock price?

17.3. What pattern of implied volatilities are likely to be caused by jumps in the underlying asset price? Is the pattern likely to be more pronounced for a six-month option than for a three-month option?

17.4. Assume that a stock price follows the compound option model. What pattern would you expect to observe in the implied volatilities?

17.5. Why are the biases (relative to Black–Scholes) for the market prices of in-the-money call options usually similar to the biases for the market prices of out-of-the-money put options?

17.6. A stock price is currently $20. Tomorrow, news is expected to be announced that will either increase the price by $5 or decrease the price by $5. What are the problems in using Black–Scholes to value one-month options on the stock?

17.7. What are the major problems in testing a stock option pricing model empirically?

17.8. At time zero, a stock price is S_0. Suppose that the time interval between 0 and T is divided into two subintervals of length t_1 and t_2. During the first subinterval, the risk-free interest rate and volatility are r_1 and σ_1, respectively. During the second subinterval, they are r_2 and σ_2, respectively. Assume that the world is risk neutral.
  (a) Use the results in chapter 11 to determine the stock price distribution at time T in terms of r_1, r_2, σ_1, σ_2, t_1, t_2, and S_0.
  (b) Suppose that $\bar{r}$ is the average interest rate between time zero and T and that $\overline{V}$ is the average variance rate between times zero and T. What is the stock price distribution as a function of T in terms of $\bar{r}$, $\overline{V}$, T, and S_0?
  (c) What are the results corresponding to (a) and (b) when there are three subintervals with different interest rates and volatilities?
  (d) Show that if the risk-free rate, r, and the volatility, σ, are known functions of time, the stock price distribution at time T in a risk-neutral world is given by equation (11.2) on the assumption that (i) the risk-free rate is constant and equal to the average value of r, and (ii) the variance rate is constant and equal to the average value of σ^2.

17.9. A company has two classes of stock, one voting and one nonvoting. Both pay the same dividends and the voting stock always sells for a 10% premium over the nonvoting stock. If the volatility of the total equity is constant, is the Black–Scholes formula correct for valuing European options on the voting stock? Explain your answer.

17.10. Assume that a stock price follows the jump diffusion model. The Black–Scholes model is used to calculate implied volatilities for call and put options with different exercise prices and different times to maturity. What patterns would you expect to observe in the implied volatilities?

17.11. Repeat Problem 17.10 assuming that the stock price follows a stochastic volatility model with the stock price and its volatility negatively correlated.

17.12. Suppose that a central bank's policy is to allow an exchange rate to fluctuate between 0.97 and 1.03. What pattern of implied volatities for options on the exchange rate would you expect to see?

17.13. Option traders sometimes refer to deep out-of-the-money options as being options on volatility. Why do you think they do this?

ASSIGNMENT QUESTIONS

17.14. A certain stock is selling for $4. Analysts consider the break-up value of the company to be such that the stock price cannot fall below $3 per share. What are the likely differences between the option prices produced by Black–Scholes and option prices in the market? Consider out-of-the-money and in-the-money calls and puts.

17.15. A company is currently awaiting the outcome of a major lawsuit. This is expected to be known within one month. The stock price is currently $20. If the outcome is positive, the stock price is expected to be $24 at the end of one month. If the outcome is negative, it is expected to be $18 at this time. The one-month risk-free interest rate is 8% per annum.
   (a) What is the risk-neutral probability of a positive outcome?
   (b) What are the values of one-month call options with strike prices of $19, $20, $21, $22, and $23?
   (c) Use DerivaGem to calculate a volatility smile for one-month call options.
   (d) Verify that the same volatility smile is obtained for one-month put options.

17.16. A futures price is currently $40. The risk-free interest rate is 5%. Some news is expected tomorrow that will cause the volatility over the next three months to be either 10% or 30%. There is a 60% chance of the first outcome and a 40% chance of the second outcome. Use DerivaGem to calculate a volatility smile for three-month options.

Pricing Formulas for Alternative Models

In this appendix, we present for reference European call option pricing formulas for some of the models considered in the chapter. European put option prices can be obtained from the call prices using put–call parity.

Compound Option Model

The value of a European call on a non-dividend-paying stock is given by

$$c = VM\left(a_1, b_1; \sqrt{\frac{T}{T^*}}\right) - Ae^{-rT^*}M\left(a_2, b_2; \sqrt{\frac{T}{T^*}}\right) - Xe^{-rT}N(a_2)$$

where

$$a_1 = \frac{\ln(V/V^*) + (r + \frac{1}{2}\sigma_V^2)T}{\sigma_V\sqrt{T}}$$

$$b_1 = \frac{\ln(V/A) + (r + \frac{1}{2}\sigma_V^2)T^*}{\sigma_V\sqrt{T^*}}$$

$$a_2 = a_1 - \sigma_V\sqrt{T}$$

$$b_2 = b_1 - \sigma_V\sqrt{T^*}$$

The function $M(a, b; \rho)$ is the cumulative probability in the standardized bivariate normal distribution that the first variable is less than a and the second variable is less than b when the coefficient of correlation between the variables is ρ. A procedure for evaluating it numerically is given in Appendix 11C. The variable V^* is the value of V at time T, that causes the stock price to equal X. This is the value of V that solves

$$X = VN(d_1) - Ae^{-rT^*}N(d_2)$$

where

$$d_1 = \frac{\ln(V/A) + (r + \sigma_V^2/2)T^*}{\sigma_V\sqrt{T^*}}$$

$$d_2 = d_1 - \sigma_V\sqrt{T^*}$$

Other notation is defined in section 17.7.

Displaced Diffusion Model

The price of a European call option on a stock using the displaced diffusion model is

$$c = aS_0 N(d_1) - (X - bS_0)e^{-rT}N(d_2)$$

where

$$d_1 = \frac{\ln[aS_0/(X - bS_0)] + (r - \sigma_R^2/2)T}{\sigma_R \sqrt{T}}$$

$$d_2 = d_1 - \sigma_R \sqrt{T}$$
$$a = \alpha(1 + \beta)$$
$$b = (1 - a)e^{rT}$$

In this formula, α is the initial proportion of the total assets that are risky, β is the initial debt-to-equity ratio, and σ_R is the volatility of the risky assets. If there are known dividends, their value compounded to time T at the risk-free rate should be subtracted from b.

Absolute Diffusion Model

The price of a European call option on a stock using the absolute diffusion model is

$$c = (S_0 - Xe^{-rT})N(y_1) + (S_0 + Xe^{-rT})N(y_2) + v[n(y_1) - n(y_2)]$$

where

$$v = \sigma \sqrt{\frac{1 - e^{-2rT}}{2r}}$$

$$y_1 = \frac{S_0 - Xe^{-rT}}{v}$$

$$y_2 = \frac{-S_0 - Xe^{-rT}}{v}$$

$$n(y) = \frac{1}{\sqrt{2\pi}}e^{-y^2/2}$$

This formula assumes that zero is an absorbing barrier for the stock price.

Pure Jump Model

Using the pure jump model the European call option price is given by

$$c = S_0 \Psi(x; y) - Xe^{-rT}\Psi\left(x, \frac{y}{u}\right)$$

where

$$\Psi(\alpha; \beta) = \sum_{i=\alpha}^{\infty} \frac{e^{-\beta}\beta^i}{i!}$$

$$y = \frac{(r + w)Tu}{u - 1}$$

and x is the smallest nonnegative integer that is greater than

$$\frac{\ln (X/S_0) + wT}{\ln u}$$

Jump Diffusion Model

The simplest form of Merton's jump diffusion model is when the logarithm of the size of the proportional jump has a normal distribution. Assume that the standard deviation of the normal distribution is δ. The European call option price can then be written

$$c = \sum_{n=0}^{\infty} \frac{e^{-\lambda'T}(\lambda'\tau)^n}{n!} f_n$$

where $\lambda' = \lambda(1 + k)$. The variable f_n is the Black–Scholes option price when the instantaneous variance rate is

$$\sigma^2 + \frac{n\delta^2}{T}$$

and the risk-free rate is

$$r - \lambda k + \frac{n\gamma}{T}$$

where $\gamma = \ln (1 + k)$.

EXOTIC OPTIONS

Derivatives with more complicated payoffs than the standard European or American calls and puts are referred to as *exotic options*. Most exotic options trade in the over-the-counter market and have been designed to meet particular needs of corporations.

In this chapter we describe different types of exotic options and discuss their valuation. We assume that the underlying asset is a stock paying a continuous dividend yield at rate q. As discussed in chapter 12, for an option on a stock index we set q equal to the dividend yield on the index; for an option on a currency we set q equal to the foreign risk-free rate; for an option on a futures contract we set q equal to the domestic risk-free rate. Many of the options discussed in this chapter can be valued using the DerivaGem software.

18.1 TYPES OF EXOTIC OPTIONS

In this section, we describe a number of different types of exotic options and present analytic results where they are available. We use a categorization of exotic options similar to that in an excellent series of articles written by Eric Reiner and Mark Rubinstein for *RISK* magazine in 1991 and 1992.

Packages

A *package* is a portfolio consisting of standard European calls, standard European puts, forward contracts, cash, and the underlying asset itself. We discussed a number of different types of packages in chapter 8: bull spreads, bear spreads, butterfly spreads, calendar spreads, straddles, strangles, and so on.

Often a package is structured by traders so that it has zero cost initially. An example is a *range forward contract*.[1] A short range forward contract consists of a long position in a put with a low strike price, X_1, and a short position in a call with a high strike price, X_2. It guarantees that the underlying asset can be sold for a price between X_1 and X_2 at the maturity of the options. A long range forward contract consists of a short position in a put with the low strike price, X_1, and a long position in a call with the high strike price, X_2. It guarantees that the underlying asset can be

---

[1] Other names used for a range forward contract are zero-cost collar, flexible forward, cylinder option, option fence, min–max, and forward band.

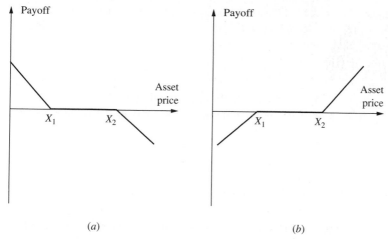

Figure 18.1 Payoffs from (a) short and (b) long range forward contract.

purchased for a price betweeen X_1 and X_2 at the maturity of the options. The price of the call equals the price of the put when the contract is initiated. Figure 18.1 shows the payoff from short and long range forward contracts. As X_1 and X_2 are moved closer to each other, the price that will be received or paid for the asset at maturity becomes more certain. In the limit when $X_1 = X_2$, the range forward contract becomes a regular forward contract.

It is worth noting that any derivative can be converted into a zero-cost product by deferring payment until maturity. Consider a European call option. If c is the cost of the option when payment is made at time zero, then $A = ce^{rT}$ is the cost when payment is made at time T, the maturity of the option. The payoff is then $\max(S_T - X, 0) - A$ or $\max(S_T - X - A, -A)$. When the strike price, X, equals the forward price, other names for a deferred payment option are break forward, Boston option, forward with optional exit, and cancelable forward.

Nonstandard American Options

In a standard American option, exercise can take place at any time during the life of the option and the exercise price is always the same. In practice, the American options that are traded in the over-the-counter market do not always have these standard features.

One type of nonstandard American option is known as a *Bermudan option*. In this, early exercise is restricted to certain dates during the life of the option. An example of a Bermudan option is a bond option that can be exercised only on coupon payment dates.

Other types of nonstandard American options sometimes occur in the warrants issued by a company on its own stock. Sometimes a warrant can be exercised during only part of its life and sometimes the strike price increases with the passage of time. For example, in a seven-year warrant, exercise might be possible during years three to seven with the strike price being $30 during years three and four, $32 during the next two years, and $33 during the final year.

Nonstandard American options can usually be valued using a binomial or trinomial tree in the usual way. At each node the test (if any) for early exercise is adjusted to reflect the terms of the option.

Forward Start Options

Forward start options are options that will start at some time in the future. They are sometimes used in employee incentive schemes. The terms of the options usually specify that they will be at the money at the time they start.

Consider a forward start at-the-money European call option that will start at time T_1 and mature at time T_2. Suppose that the stock price at time zero is S_0 and the stock price at time T_1 is S_1. To value the option, we note from the European option pricing formulas in chapters 11 and 12 that the value of an at-the-money call option is proportional to the stock price. The value of the forward start option at time T_1 is, therefore, cS_1/S_0, where c is the value at time zero of an at-the-money option that lasts for $T_2 - T_1$. Using risk-neutral valuation, the value of the forward start option at time zero is

$$e^{-rT_1}\hat{E}\left[c\frac{S_1}{S_0}\right]$$

where $\hat{E}$ denotes expectations in a risk-neutral world. Because c and S_0 are known and $\hat{E}[S_1] = S_0e^{(r-q)T_1}$, it follows that the value of the forward start option is ce^{-qT_1}. For a non-dividend-paying stock, $q = 0$ and the value of the forward start option is exactly the same as the value of a regular at-the-money option with the same life as the forward start option.

Compound Options

Compound options are options on options. There are four main types of compound options: a call on a call, a put on a call, a call on a put, and a put on a put. Compound options have two strike prices and two exercise dates. Consider, for example, a call on a call. On the first exercise date, T_1, the holder of the compound option is entitled to pay the first strike price, X_1, and receive a call option. The call option gives the holder the right to buy the underlying asset for the second strike price, X_2, on the second exercise date, T_2. The compound option will be exercised on the first exercise date only if the value of the option on that date is greater than the first strike price.

When the usual geometric Brownian motion assumption is made, European-style compound options can be valued analytically in terms of integrals of the bivariate normal distribution.[2] With our usual notation, the value at time zero of a European call option on a call option is

$$S_0e^{-qT_2}M(a_1, b_1; \sqrt{T_1/T_2}) - X_2e^{-rT_2}M(a_2, b_2; \sqrt{T_1/T_2}) - e^{-rT_1}X_1N(a_2)$$

---

[2] See R. Geske, "The Valuation of Compound Options," *Journal of Financial Economics,* 7 (1979), 63–81; M. Rubinstein, "Double Trouble," *RISK,* (December 1991–January 1992), 53–56.

where

$$a_1 = \frac{\ln(S_0/S^*) + (r - q + \sigma^2/2)T_1}{\sigma\sqrt{T_1}} \qquad a_2 = a_1 - \sigma\sqrt{T_1}$$

$$b_1 = \frac{\ln(S_0/X_2) + (r - q + \sigma^2/2)T_2}{\sigma\sqrt{T_2}} \qquad b_2 = b_1 - \sigma\sqrt{T_2}$$

The function, M, is the cumulative bivariate normal distribution function as defined in Appendix 11C. The variable S^* is the stock price at time T_1 for which the option price at time T_1 equals X_1. If the actual stock price is above S^* at time T_1, the first option will be exercised; if it is not above S^*, the option expires worthless.

With similar notation, the value of a European put on a call is

$$X_2 e^{-rT_2} M(-a_2, b_2; -\sqrt{T_1/T_2}) - S_0 e^{-qT_2} M(-a_1, b_1; -\sqrt{T_1/T_2}) + e^{-rT_1} X_1 N(-a_2)$$

The value of a European call on a put is

$$X_2 e^{-rT_2} M(-a_2, -b_2; \sqrt{T_1/T_2}) - S_0 e^{-qT_2} M(-a_1, -b_1; \sqrt{T_1/T_2}) - e^{-rT_1} X_1 N(-a_2)$$

The value of a European put on a put is

$$S_0 e^{-qT_2} M(a_1, -b_1; -\sqrt{T_1/T_2}) - X_2 e^{-rT_2} M(a_2, -b_2; -\sqrt{T_1/T_2}) + e^{-rT_1} X_1 N(a_2)$$

A procedure for computing M is provided in Appendix 11C.

Chooser Options

A *chooser* option (sometimes referred to as an *as you like it* option) has the feature that, after a specified period of time, the holder can choose whether the option is a call or a put. Suppose that the time when the choice is made is T_1. The value of the chooser option at this time is

$$\max(c, p)$$

where c is the value of the call underlying the option and p is the value of the put underlying the option.

If the options underlying the chooser option are both European and have the same strike price, put–call parity can be used to provide a valuation formula. Suppose that S_1 is the stock price at time T_1, X is the strike price, T_2 is the maturity of the options, and r is the risk-free interest rate. Put–call parity implies that

$$\max(c, p) = \max(c, c + Xe^{-r(T_2-T_1)} - S_1 e^{-q(T_2-T_1)})$$
$$= c + e^{-q(T_2-T_1)} \max(0, Xe^{-(r-q)(T_2-T_1)} - S_1)$$

This shows that the chooser option is a package consisting of

1. A call option with strike price X and maturity T_2.
2. $e^{-q(T_2-T_1)}$ put options with strike price $Xe^{-(r-q)(T_2-T_1)}$ and maturity T_1.

As such, it can readily be valued.

More complex chooser options can be defined where the call and the put do not have the same strike price and time to maturity. They are then not packages and have features that are somewhat similar to compound options.

Barrier Options

Barrier options are options where the payoff depends on whether the underlying asset's price reaches a certain level during a certain period of time. In chapter 12, we met one particular type of barrier option: the CAPs that trade on the CBOE. These are options designed so that the payoff cannot exceed $30. This means that a call CAP is exercised automatically on a day when the index reaches a barrier equal to the strike price plus $30; a put CAP is exercised automatically on a day when the index reaches a barrier equal to the strike price less $30.

A number of different types of barrier options regularly trade in the over-the-counter market. They are attractive to some market participants because they are less expensive than the corresponding regular options. These barrier options can be classified as either *knock-out options* or *knock-in options*. A knock-out option ceases to exist when the underlying asset price reaches a certain barrier; a knock-in option comes into existence only when the underlying asset price reaches a barrier.

Equations (12.4) and (12.5) show that the values at time zero of a regular call and put option are

$$c = S_0 e^{-qT} N(d_1) - X e^{-rT} N(d_2)$$
$$p = X e^{-rT} N(-d_2) - S_0 e^{-qT} N(-d_1)$$

where

$$d_1 = \frac{\ln(S_0/X) + (r - q + \sigma^2/2)T}{\sigma \sqrt{T}}$$

and

$$d_2 = \frac{\ln(S_0/X) + (r - q - \sigma^2/2)T}{\sigma \sqrt{T}}$$
$$= d_1 - \sigma \sqrt{T}$$

A *down-and-out call* is one type of knock-out option. It is a regular call option that ceases to exist if the asset price reaches a certain barrier level, H. The barrier level is below the initial stock price. The corresponding knock-in option is a *down-and-in call*. This is a regular call that comes into existence only if the asset price reaches the barrier level.

If H is less than or equal to the strike price, X, the value of a down-and-in call at time zero is given by

$$c_{di} = S_0 e^{-qT} (H/S_0)^{2\lambda} N(y) - X e^{-rT} (H/S_0)^{2\lambda-2} N(y - \sigma \sqrt{T})$$

where

$$\lambda = \frac{r - q + \sigma^2/2}{\sigma^2}$$

$$y = \frac{\ln [H^2/(S_0 X)]}{\sigma \sqrt{T}} + \lambda \sigma \sqrt{T}$$

Because the value of a regular call equals the value of a down-and-in call plus the value of a down-and-out call, the value of a down-and-out call is given by

$$c_{\text{do}} = c - c_{\text{di}}$$

If $H \geq X$, then

$$c_{\text{do}} = S_0 N(x_1) e^{-qT} - X e^{-rT} N(x_1 - \sigma \sqrt{T}) - S_0 e^{-qT} (H/S_0)^{2\lambda} N(y_1)$$
$$+ X e^{-rT} (H/S_0)^{2\lambda - 2} N(y_1 - \sigma \sqrt{T})$$

and

$$c_{\text{di}} = c - c_{\text{do}}$$

where

$$x_1 = \frac{\ln (S_0/H)}{\sigma \sqrt{T}} + \lambda \sigma \sqrt{T}$$

$$y_1 = \frac{\ln (H/S_0)}{\sigma \sqrt{T}} + \lambda \sigma \sqrt{T}$$

An *up-and-out call* is a regular call option that ceases to exist if the asset price reaches a barrier level, H, that is higher than the current asset price. An *up-and-in call* is a regular call option that comes into existence only if the barrier is reached. When H is less than or equal to X, the value of the up-and-out call, c_{uo}, is zero and the value of the up-and-in call, c_{ui}, is c. When H is greater than X,

$$c_{\text{ui}} = S_0 N(x_1) e^{-qT} - X e^{-rT} N(x_1 - \sigma \sqrt{T}) - S_0 e^{-qT} (H/S_0)^{2\lambda} [N(-y) - N(-y_1)]$$
$$+ X e^{-rT} (H/S_0)^{2\lambda - 2} [N(-y + \sigma \sqrt{T}) - N(-y_1 + \sigma \sqrt{T})]$$

and

$$c_{\text{uo}} = c - c_{\text{ui}}$$

Put barrier options are defined similarly to call barrier options. An *up-and-out put* is a put option that ceases to exist when a barrier, H, that is greater than the current stock price is reached. An *up-and-in put* is a put that comes into existence only if the barrier is reached. When the barrier, H, is greater than or equal to the strike price, X, their prices are

$$p_{\text{ui}} = -S_0 e^{-qT} (H/S_0)^{2\lambda} N(-y) + X e^{-rT} (H/S_0)^{2\lambda - 2} N(-y + \sigma \sqrt{T})$$

and

$$p_{uo} = p - p_{ui}$$

When H is less than or equal to X,

$$p_{uo} = -S_0 N(-x_1)e^{-qT} + Xe^{-rT}N(-x_1 + \sigma\sqrt{T}) + S_0 e^{-qT}(H/S_0)^{2\lambda}N(-y_1)$$
$$- Xe^{-rT}(H/S_0)^{2\lambda-2}N(-y_1 + \sigma\sqrt{T})$$

and

$$p_{ui} = p - p_{uo}$$

A *down-and-out put* is a put option that ceases to exist when a barrier less than the current asset price is reached. A *down-and-in put* is a put option that comes into existence only when the barrier is reached. When the barrier is greater than the strike price, $p_{do} = 0$ and $p_{di} = p$. When the barrier is less than the strike price,

$$p_{di} = -S_0 N(-x_1)e^{-qT} + Xe^{-rT}N(-x_1 + \sigma\sqrt{T}) + S_0 e^{-qT}(H/S_0)^{2\lambda}[N(y) - N(y_1)]$$
$$- Xe^{-rT}(H/S_0)^{2\lambda-2}[N(y - \sigma\sqrt{T}) - N(y_1 - \sigma\sqrt{T})]$$

and

$$p_{do} = p - p_{di}$$

All of these valuations make the usual assumption that the probability distribution for the stock price at a future time is lognormal. An important issue for barrier options is the frequency that the stock price, S, is observed for purposes of determining whether the barrier has been reached. The analytic formulas given in this section assume that S is observed continuously. Often, the terms of a contract state that S is observed once a day. For example, in S&P CAPs, S is observed at the close of trading each day. Broadie, Glasserman, and Kou provide a way of adjusting the formulas we have just given for the situation where the price of the underlying is observed discretely.[3] The barrier level, H, is replaced by $He^{0.5826\sigma T/m}$ for an up-and-in or up-and-out option and by $He^{-0.5826\sigma T/m}$ for a down-and-in or down-and-out option, where m is the number of times the stock price is observed (so that T/m is the time interval between observations).

Binary Options

Binary options are options with discontinuous payoffs. A simple example of a binary option is a *cash-or-nothing call*. This pays off nothing if the stock price ends up below the strike price at time T and pays a fixed amount, Q, if it ends up above the strike price. In a risk-neutral world, the probability of the stock price being above the strike price at the maturity of an option is, with our usual notation, $N(d_2)$. The value of a cash-or-nothing call is, therefore, $Qe^{-rT}N(d_2)$. A *cash-or-nothing put* is defined

---

[3] M. Broadie, P. Glasserman, and S. G. Kou, "A Continuity Correction for Discrete Barrier Options," *Mathematical Finance* 7, 4 (October 1997), 325–349.

analogously to a cash-or-nothing call. It pays off Q if the stock price is below the strike price and nothing if it is above the strike price. The value of a cash-or-nothing put is $Qe^{-rT}N(-d_2)$.

Another type of binary option is an *asset-or-nothing call*. This pays off nothing if the underlying stock price ends up below the strike price and pays an amount equal to the stock price itself if it ends up above the strike price. With our usual notation, the value of an asset-or-nothing call is $S_0e^{-qT}N(d_1)$. An *asset-or-nothing put* pays off nothing if the underlying stock price ends up above the strike price and an amount equal to the stock price if it it ends up below the strike price. The value of an asset-or-nothing put is $S_0e^{-qT}N(-d_1)$.

A regular European call option is equivalent to a long position in an asset-or-nothing call and a short position in a cash-or-nothing call where the cash payoff on the cash-or-nothing call equals the strike price. Similarly, a regular European put option is equivalent to a long position in a cash-or-nothing put and a short position in an asset-or-nothing put where the cash payoff on the cash-or-nothing put equals the strike price.

Lookback Options

The payoffs from lookback options depend on the maximum or minimum stock price reached during the life of the option. The payoff from a European-style lookback call is the amount that the final stock price exceeds the minimum stock price achieved during the life of the option. The payoff from a European-style lookback put is the amount by which the maximum stock price achieved during the life of the option exceeds the final stock price.

Valuation formulas have been produced for European lookbacks.[4] The value of a European lookback call at time zero is

$$S_0e^{-qT}N(a_1) - S_0e^{-qT}\frac{\sigma^2}{2(r-q)}N(-a_1) - S_{\min}e^{-rT}\left[N(a_2) - \frac{\sigma^2}{2(r-q)}e^{Y_1}N(-a_3)\right]$$

where

$$a_1 = \frac{\ln(S_0/S_{\min}) + (r - q + \sigma^2/2)T}{\sigma\sqrt{T}}$$

$$a_2 = a_1 - \sigma\sqrt{T}$$

$$a_3 = \frac{\ln(S_0/S_{\min}) + (-r + q + \sigma^2/2)T}{\sigma\sqrt{T}}$$

$$Y_1 = -\frac{2(r - q - \sigma^2/2)\ln(S_0/S_{\min})}{\sigma^2}$$

---

[4]See B. Goldman, H. Sosin, and M. A. Gatto, "Path-Dependent Options: Buy at the Low, Sell at the High," *Journal of Finance*, 34 (December 1979), 1111–27.; M. Garman, "Recollection in Tranquility," *RISK*, (March 1989), 16–19.

and S_{min} is the minimum stock price achieved to date. (If the lookback has just been originated, $S_{min} = S_0$.)

The value of a European lookback put is

$$S_{max}e^{-rT}\left[N(b_1) - \frac{\sigma^2}{2(r-q)}e^{Y_2}N(-b_3)\right] + S_0e^{-qT}\frac{\sigma^2}{2(r-q)}N(-b_2) - S_0e^{-qT}N(b_2)$$

where

$$b_1 = \frac{\ln(S_{max}/S_0) + (-r + q + \sigma^2/2)T}{\sigma\sqrt{T}}$$

$$b_2 = b_1 - \sigma\sqrt{T}$$

$$b_3 = \frac{\ln(S_{max}/S_0) + (r - q - \sigma^2/2)T}{\sigma\sqrt{T}}$$

$$Y_2 = \frac{2(r - q - \sigma^2/2)\ln(S_{max}/S_0)}{\sigma^2}$$

and S_{max} is the maximum stock price achieved to date. (If the lookback has just been originated, $S_{max} = S_0$.)

> **Example 18.1**   Consider a newly issued lookback put on a non-dividend-paying stock where the stock price is 50, the stock price volatility is 40% per annum, the risk-free rate is 10% per annum, and the time to maturity is three months. In this case $S_{max} = 50$, $S_0 = 50, r = 0.1, q = 0, \sigma = 0.4$, and $T = 0.25$. From the formulas just given, $b_1 = -0.025, b_2 = -0.225, b_3 = 0.025$, and $Y_2 = 0$, so that the value of the lookback put is 7.79. A newly issued lookback call on the same stock is worth 8.04.

A lookback call is a way that the holder can buy the underlying asset at the lowest price achieved during the life of the option. Similarly, a lookback put is a way that the holder can sell the underlying asset at the highest price achieved during the life of the option. The underlying asset in a lookback option is often a commodity. As with barrier options, the value of a lookback option is liable to be sensitive to the frequency that the asset price is observed for the purposes of computing the maximum or minimum. The formulas above assume that the asset price is observed continuously. Broadie, Glasserman, and Kou provide a way of adjusting the formulas we have just given for the situation where the asset price is observed discretely.[5]

Shout Options

A *shout option* is a European option where the holder can "shout" to the writer at one time during its life. At the end of the life of the option, the option holder receives either the usual payoff from a European option or the intrinsic value at the time of the shout, whichever is greater. Suppose the strike price is $50 and the holder of a call

---

[5]M. Broadie, P. Glasserman, and S. G. Kou, "Connecting Discrete and Continuous Path-Dependent Options" *Finance and Stochastics* 2 (1998) pp 1–28.

shouts when the price of the underlying asset is $60. If the final asset price is less than $60 the holder receives a payoff of $10. If it is greater than $60, the holder receives the excess of the asset price over $50.

A shout option has some of the same features as a lookback option, but is considerably less expensive. It can be valued by noting that if the option is shouted at a time, τ, when the asset price is S_τ the payoff from the option is

$$\max(0, S_T - S_\tau) + (S_\tau - X)$$

where, as usual, X is the strike price and S_T is the asset price at time T. The value at time τ if the option is shouted is, therefore, the present value of $S_\tau - X$ plus the average strike call pays off max (0, $S_T - S_{ave}$)value of a European option with strike price S_τ. The latter can be calculated using Black–Scholes formulas.

We value a shout option by constructing a binomial or trinomial tree for the nderlying asset in the usual way. As we roll back through the tree, we calculate at each node the value of the option if we shout and the value if we do not shout. The option's price at the node is the greater of the two. The procedure for valuing a shout option is, therefore, very similar to the procedure for valuing a regular American option.

Asian Options

Asian options are options where the payoff depends on the average price of the underlying asset during at least some part of the life of the option. The payoff from an *average price call* is $\max(0, S_{ave} - X)$ and that from an *average price put* is $\max(0, X - S_{ave})$, where S_{ave} is the average value of the underlying asset calculated over a predetermined averaging period. Average price options are less expensive than regular options and are arguably more appropriate than regular options for meeting some of the needs of corporate treasurers. Suppose that a U.S. corporate treasurer expects to receive a cash flow of 100 million Australian dollars spread evenly over the next year from the company's Australian subsidiary. The treasurer is likely to be interested in an option that guarantees that the average exchange rate realized during the year is above some level. An average price put option can achieve this more effectively than regular put options.

Another type of Asian option is an average strike option. An *average strike call* pays off $\max(0, S_T - S_{ave})$ and an *average strike put* pays off $\max(0, S_{ave} - S_T)$. Average strike options can guarantee that the average price paid for an asset in frequent trading over a period of time is not greater than the final price. Alternatively, it can guarantee that the average price received for an asset in frequent trading over a period of time is not less than the final price.

If the underlying asset price, S, is assumed to be lognormally distributed and S_{ave} is a geometric average of the S's, analytic formulas are available for valuing European average price options.[6] This is because the geometric average of a set of

---

[6] See A. Kemna and A. Vorst, "A Pricing Method for Options Based on Average Asset Values," *Journal of Banking and Finance,* 14 (March 1990), 113–29.

lognormally distributed variables is also lognormal. Consider a newly issued option that will provide a payoff at time T based on the geometric average calculated between time zero and time T. In a risk-neutral world, it can be shown that the probability distribution of the geometric average of a stock price over a certain period is the same as that of the stock price at the end of the period if the stock's expected growth rate is set equal to $(r - q - \sigma^2/6)/2$ (rather than $r - q$) and its volatility is set equal to $\sigma/\sqrt{3}$ (rather than σ). The geometric average price option can, therefore, be treated like a regular option with the volatility set equal to $\sigma/\sqrt{3}$ and the dividend yield equal to

$$r - \frac{1}{2}\left(r - q - \frac{\sigma^2}{6}\right) = \frac{1}{2}\left(r + q + \frac{\sigma^2}{6}\right)$$

When, as is nearly always the case, Asian options are defined in terms of arithmetic averages, exact analytic pricing formulas are not available. This is because the distribution of the arithmetic average of a set of lognormal distributions does not have analytically tractable properties. However, the distribution is approximately lognormal and this leads to a good analytic approximation for valuing average price options. We calculate the first two moments of the probability distribution of the arithmetic average in a risk-neutral world exactly and then assume that this distribution is lognormal.[7]

Consider a newly issued Asian option that provides a payoff at time T based on the arithmetic average between time zero and time T. The first moment, M_1, and second moment, M_2, of the average in a risk-neutral world can be shown to be

$$M_1 = \frac{e^{(r-q)T} - 1}{(r - q)T} S_0$$

and

$$M_2 = \frac{2e^{[2(r-q)+\sigma^2]T} S_0^2}{(r - q + \sigma^2)(2r - 2q + \sigma^2)T^2} + \frac{2S_0^2}{(r - q)T^2}\left[\frac{1}{2(r - q) + \sigma^2} - \frac{e^{(r-q)T}}{r - q + \sigma^2}\right]$$

If we assume that the average stock price is lognormal, we can regard an option on the average as like an option on a futures contract and use equations (12.17) and (12.18) with

$$F_0 = M_1 \tag{18.1}$$

and

$$\sigma^2 = \frac{1}{T} \ln\left(\frac{M_2}{M_1^2}\right) \tag{18.2}$$

---

[7] See S. M. Turnbull and L. M. Wakeman, "A Quick Algorithm for Pricing European Average Options," *Journal of Financial and Quantitative Analysis*, 26 (September 1991), 377–89.

Example 18.2 Consider a newly issued average price call option on a non-dividend-paying stock where the stock price is 50, the strike price is 50, the stock price volatility is 40% per annum, the risk-free rate is 10% per annum, and the time to maturity is one year. In this case, $S_0 = 50$, $X = 50$, $r = 0.1$, $q = 0$, $\sigma = 0.4$, and $T = 1$. If the average is a geometric average, we can value the option as a regular option with the volatility equal to $0.4/\sqrt{3}$, or 23.09%, and dividend yield equal to $(0.1 + 0.4^2/6)/2$, or 6.33%. The value of the option is 5.13. If the average is an arithmetic average, we first calculate $M_1 = 52.59$ and $M_2 = 2922.76$. When we assume the average is lognormal, the option has the same value as an option on a futures contract. From equations (18.1) and (18.2), $F_0 = 52.59$ and $\sigma = 23.54\%$. DerivaGem gives the value of the option as 5.62.

The formulas just given for M_1 and M_2 assume that the average is calculated from continuous observations on the stock price. Appendix 18A shows how M_1 and M_2 can be obtained when the average is calculated from observations on the stock price at discrete points in time.

We can modify the analysis to accommodate the situation where the option is not newly issued and some prices used to determine the average have already been observed. Suppose that the averaging period is composed of a period of length t_1 over which prices have already been observed and a future period of length t_2 (the remaining life of the option). Suppose that the average stock price during the first time period is $\bar{S}$. The payoff from an average price call is

$$\max\left(\frac{\bar{S}t_1 + S_{ave}t_2}{t_1 + t_2} - X,\ 0\right)$$

where S_{ave} is the average stock price during the remaining part of the averaging period. This is the same as

$$\frac{t_2}{t_1 + t_2}\max\left(S_{ave} - X^*,\ 0\right)$$

where

$$X^* = \frac{t_1 + t_2}{t_2}X - \frac{t_1}{t_2}\bar{S}$$

When $X^* > 0$, the option can be valued in the same way as a newly issued Asian option provided that we change the strike price from X to X^* and multiply the result by $t_2/(t_1 + t_2)$. When $X^* < 0$ the option is certain to be exercised and can be valued as a forward contract. The value is

$$\frac{t_2}{t_1 + t_2}[S_0 e^{-q_A t_2} - X^* e^{-r t_2}]$$

Options to Exchange One Asset for Another

Options to exchange one asset for another (sometimes referred to as *exchange options*) arise in various contexts. An option to buy yen with Australian dollars is, from the point of view of a U.S. investor, an option to exchange one foreign currency asset for another foreign currency asset. A stock tender offer is an option to exchange shares in one stock for shares in another stock.

Consider a European option to give up an asset worth U_T at time T and receive in return an asset worth V_T. The payoff from the option is

$$\max\,(V_T - U_T,\, 0)$$

A formula for valuing this option was first produced by Margrabe.[8] Suppose that the asset prices U and V both follow geometric Brownian motion with volatilities σ_U and σ_V. Suppose further that the instantaneous correlation between U and V is ρ, and the yields provided by U and V are q_U and q_V, respectively. The value of the option at time zero is

$$V_0 e^{-q_V T} N(d_1) - U_0 e^{-q_U T} N(d_2) \tag{18.3}$$

where

$$d_1 = \frac{\ln\,(V_0/U_0) + (q_U - q_V + \hat{\sigma}^2/2)T}{\hat{\sigma}\,\sqrt{T}}$$

$$d_2 = d_1 - \hat{\sigma}\,\sqrt{T}$$

$$\hat{\sigma} = \sqrt{\sigma_U^2 + \sigma_V^2 - 2\rho\sigma_U\sigma_V}$$

and U_0 and V_0 are the values of U and V at time zero.

This result will be proved in section 19.7. It is interesting to note that equation (18.3) is independent of the risk-free rate r. This is because, as r increases, the growth rate of both asset prices in a risk-neutral world increases, but this is exactly offset by an increase in the discount rate. The variable $\hat{\sigma}$ is the volatility of V/U. Comparisons with equation (12.4) show that the option price is the same as the price of U_0 European call options on an asset worth V/U when the strike price is 1.0, the risk-free interest rate is q_U, and the dividend yield on the asset is q_V. Mark Rubinstein shows that the American version of this option can be characterized similarly for valuation purposes.[9] It can be regarded as U_0 American options to buy an asset worth V/U for 1.0 when the risk-free interest rate is q_U and the dividend yield on the asset is q_V. The option can, therefore, be valued as described in chapter 16 using a binomial tree.

It is worth noting that an option to obtain the better or worse of two assets can be regarded as a position in one of the assets combined with an option to exchange it for the other asset:

$$\min\,(U_T,\, V_T) = V_T - \max\,(V_T - U_T,\, 0)$$
$$\max\,(U_T,\, V_T) = U_T + \max\,(V_T - U_T,\, 0)$$

---

[8] See W. Margrabe, "The Value of an Option to Exchange One Asset for Another." *Journal of Finance,* 33 (March 1978), 177–86.

[9] See M. Rubinstein, "One for Another," *RISK,* (July–August), 1991, 30–32.

Options Involving Several Assets

Options involving two or more risky assets are sometimes referred to as *rainbow options*. One example is the bond futures contract traded on the CBOT described in chapter 4. The party with the short position is allowed to choose between a large number of different bonds when making delivery. Another example is a LIBOR–Contingent FX option. This is a foreign currency option whose payoff occurs only if a prespecified interest rate is within a certain range at maturity.

Basket Options

A *basket option* is an option where the payoff is dependent on the value of a portfolio (or basket) of assets. The assets are usually either individual stocks or stock indices or currencies. A European basket option can be valued with Monte Carlo simulation by assuming that the assets follow correlated geometric Brownian motion processes. A much faster approach is to calculate the first two moments of the basket at the maturity of the option in a risk-neutral world, and then assume that the value of the basket is lognormally distributed at that time. The option can be regarded as an option on a futures contract with the parameters shown in equations (18.1) and (18.2). Appendix 18A shows how the moments of the value of the basket at a future time can be calculated from the volatilities of, and correlations between, the assets.

18.2 PATH-DEPENDENT DERIVATIVES

A path-dependent derivative (or history-dependent derivative) is a derivative where the payoff depends on the the path followed by the price of the underlying asset, not just its final value. Asian options and lookback options are examples of path-dependent derivatives. As explained in the section 18.1, the payoff from an Asian option depends on the average price of the underlying asset; the payoff from a lookback option depends on its maximum or minimum price. One approach to valuing path-dependent options when analytic results are not available is Monte Carlo simulation as discussed in chapter 16. A sample value of the derivative can be calculated by sampling a random path for the underlying asset in a risk-neutral world, calculating the payoff, and discounting the payoff at the risk-free interest rate. An estimate of the value of the derivative is found by obtaining many sample values of the derivative and calculating their mean.

The main problem with using Monte Carlo simulation to value path-dependent derivatives is that the computation time necessary to achieve the required level of accuracy can be unacceptably high. Also, American-style path-dependent derivatives (that is, path-dependent derivatives where one side has exercise opportunities or other decisions to make) cannot easily be handled. In this section, we show how the binomial tree methods presented in chapter 16 can be extended to cope with some path-

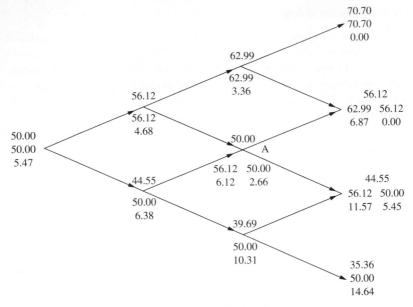

Figure 18.2   Tree for valuing an American lookback option.

dependent derivatives.[10] The procedure can handle American-style path-dependent derivatives and is computationally more efficient than Monte Carlo simulation for European-style path-dependent derivatives.

For the procedure to work, two conditions must be satisfied:

1. The payoff from the derivative must depend on a single function, F, of the path followed by the underlying asset.

2. It must be possible to calculate the value of F at time $\tau + \Delta t$ from the value of F at time τ and the value of the underlying asset at time $\tau + \Delta t$.

Illustration Using Lookback Options

As a first illustration of the procedure, we consider an American lookback put option on a non-dividend-paying stock.[11] If exercised at time τ, this pays off the amount by which the maximum stock price between time 0 and time τ exceeds the current stock price. We suppose that the initial stock price is $50, the stock price volatility is 40% per annum, the risk-free interest rate is 10% per annum, the total life of the option is three months, and that stock price movements are represented by a three-step binomial tree. Using the notation of chapter 16, this means that $S_0 = 50$, $\sigma = 0.4$, $r = 0.10$, $\Delta t = 0.08333$, $u = 1.1224$, $d = 0.8909$, $a = 1.0084$, and $p = 0.5073$.

The tree is shown in Figure 18.2. The top number at each node is the stock price. The next level of numbers at each node shows the possible maximum stock

---

[10]This approach was suggested in J. Hull and A. White, "Efficient Procedures for Valuing European and American Path-Dependent Options," *Journal of Derivatives*, (Fall 1993), 21–31.

[11]This example is used as a first illustration of the general procedure for handling path dependence. We give a more efficient approach to valuing American lookback options in the next section.

prices achievable on paths leading to the node. The final level of numbers shows the values of the derivative corresponding to each of the possible maximum stock prices.

The values of the derivative at the final nodes of the tree are calculated as the maximum stock price minus the actual stock price. To illustrate the rollback procedure, suppose that we are at node A, where the stock price is $50. The maximum stock price achieved thus far is either 56.12 or 50. Consider first the situation where it is equal to 50. If there is an up movement, the maximum stock price becomes 56.12 and the value of the derivative is zero. If there is a down movement, the maximum stock price stays at 50 and the value of the derivative is 5.45. Assuming no early exercise, the value of the derivative at A when the maximum achieved so far is 50 is, therefore,

$$(0 \times 0.5073 + 5.45 \times 0.4927)e^{-0.1 \times 0.08333} = 2.66$$

Clearly, it is not worth exercising at node A in these circumstances because the payoff from doing so is zero. A similar calculation for the situation where the maximum value at node A is 56.12 gives the value of the derivative at node A, without early exercise, to be

$$(0 \times 0.5073 + 11.57 \times 0.4927)e^{-0.1 \times 0.08333} = 5.65$$

In this case, early exercise gives a value of 6.12 and is the optimal strategy. Rolling back through the tree in the way we have indicated gives the value of the American lookback as $5.47.

Generalization

The approach just described is computationally feasible when the number of alternative values of the path function, F, at each node does not grow too fast as the number of time steps is increased. The example we used, a lookback option, presents no problems because the number of alternative values for the maximum asset price at a node in a binomial tree with n time steps is never greater than n.

Luckily, the approach can be extended to cope with situations where there are a very large number of different possible values of the path function at each node. The basic idea is as follows. At a node, we carry out calculations for a small number of representative values of F. When the value of the derivative is required for other values of the path function, we calculate it from the known values using interpolation.

The first stage is to work forward through the tree establishing the maximum and minimum values of the path function at each node. Assuming the value of the path function at time $\tau + \Delta t$ depends only on the value of the path function at time τ and the value of the underlying variable at time $\tau + \Delta t$, the maximum and minimum values of the path function for the nodes at time $\tau + \Delta t$ can be calculated in a straightforward way from those for the nodes at time τ. The second stage is to choose representative values of the path function at each node. There are a number of approaches. A simple rule is to choose the representative values as the maximum value, the minimum value, and a number of other values that are equally spaced between the maximum and the minimum. As we roll back through the tree, we value the derivative for each of representative values of the path function.

We illustrate the nature of the calculation by considering the problem of valuing the average price call option considered in Example 18.2. We consider the case where

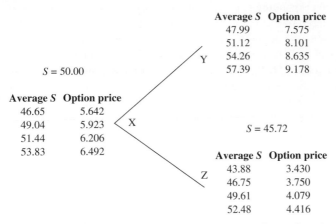

$S = 54.68$

Average S	Option price
47.99	7.575
51.12	8.101
54.26	8.635
57.39	9.178

$S = 50.00$

Average S	Option price
46.65	5.642
49.04	5.923
51.44	6.206
53.83	6.492

$S = 45.72$

Average S	Option price
43.88	3.430
46.75	3.750
49.61	4.079
52.48	4.416

Figure 18.3   Part of tree for valuing option on the arithmetic average.

the payoff depends on the arithmetic average stock price. The initial stock price is 50, the strike price is 50, the risk-free interest rate is 10%, the stock price volatility is 40%, the time to maturity is one year. We use a tree with 20 time steps. The parameters describing the binomial tree parameters are $\Delta t = 0.05$, $u = 1.0936$, $d = 0.9144$, $p = 0.5056$, and $1 - p = 0.4944$. The path function is the arithmetic average of the stock price.

Figure 18.3 shows the calculations that are carried out in one small part of the tree. Node X is the central node at time 0.2 year (at the end of the fourth time step). Nodes Y and Z are the two nodes at time 0.25 year that are reachable from node X. The stock price at node X is 50. Forward induction shows that the maximum average stock price achievable in reaching node X is 53.83. The minimum is 46.65. (We include both the initial and final stock prices when calculating the average.) From node X, we branch to one of the two nodes, Y and Z. At node Y, the stock price is 54.68 and the bounds for the average are 47.99 and 57.39. At node Z, the stock price is 45.72 and the bounds for the average stock price are 43.88 and 52.48.

Suppose that we have chosen the representative values of the average to be four equally spaced values at each node. This means that at node X, we consider the averages 46.65, 49.04, 51.44, and 53.83. At node Y, we consider the averages 47.99, 51.12, 54.26, and 57.39. At node Z, we consider the averages 43.88, 46.75, 49.61, and 52.48. We assume that backward induction has already been used to calculate the value of the option for each of the alternative values of the average at nodes Y and Z. The values are shown in Figure 18.3. For example, at node Y when the average is 51.12, the value of the option is 8.101.

Consider the calculations at node X for the case where the average is 51.44. If the stock price moves up to node Y, the new average will be

$$\frac{5 \times 51.44 + 54.68}{6} = 51.98$$

The value of the derivative at node Y for this average can be found by interpolating between the values when the average is 51.12 and when it is 54.26. It is

$$\frac{(51.98 - 51.12) \times 8.635 + (54.26 - 51.98) \times 8.101}{54.26 - 51.12} = 8.247$$

Similarly, if the stock price moves down to node Z, the new average will be

$$\frac{5 \times 51.44 + 45.72}{6} = 50.49$$

and by interpolation the value of the derivative is 4.182.

The value of the derivative at node X when the average is 51.44 is, therefore,

$$(0.5056 \times 8.247 + 0.4944 \times 4.182)e^{-0.1 \times 0.05} = 6.206$$

The other values at node X are calculated similarly. Once the values at all nodes at time 0.2 year have been calculated, we can move on to the nodes at time 0.15 year.

The value given by the full tree for the option at time zero is 7.17. As the number of time steps and the number of averages considered at each node is increased, the value of the option converges to the correct answer. With 60 time steps and 100 averages at each node, the value of the option is 5.58. The analytic approximation for the value of the option calculated in Example 18.2 is 5.62.

A key advantage of the method described here is that it can handle American options. The calculations are as we have described them except that we test for early exercise at each node for each of the alternative values of the path function at the node. (In practice, the early exercise decision is liable to depend on both the value of the path function and the value of the underlying asset.) Consider the American version of the average price call considered here. The value calculated using the 20-step tree and four averages at each node is 7.77; with 60 time steps and 100 averages, the value is 6.17.

The approach just described can be used in a wide range of different situations. The two conditions that must be satisfied were listed at the beginning of this section. Efficiency is improved somewhat if quadratic rather than linear interpolation is used at each node.

18.3 LOOKBACK OPTIONS

A number of researchers have suggested an interesting and instructive approach to valuing lookback options.[12] To illustrate it, we again consider the American-style lookback put in Figure 18.2. When exercised, this provides a payoff equal to the excess of the maximum stock price over the current stock price. We define $F(t)$ as the

---

[12]The approach was proposed by E. Reiner in a lecture at Berkeley. It is also suggested in S. Babbs, "Binomial Valuation of Lookback Options," Working paper, Midland Global Markets, 1992; and T. H. F. Cheuk and T. C. F. Vorst, "Lookback Options and the Observation Frequency: A Binomial Approach," Working Paper, Erasmus University, Rotterdam.

maximum stock price achieved up to time T and set

$$Y(t) = \frac{F(t)}{S(t)}$$

We next use the Cox, Ross, and Rubinstein tree for the stock price to produce a tree for Y. Initially, $Y = 1$ because $F = S$ at time zero. If there is an up movement in S during the first time step, both F and S increase by a proportional amount u and $Y = 1$. If there is a down movement in S during the first time step, F stays the same, so that $Y = 1/d = u$. Continuing with these types of arguments, we produce the tree shown in Figure 18.4 for Y. (Note that in this example $u = 1.1224$, $d = 0.8909$, $a = 1.0084$, and $p = 0.5073$). The rules defining the geometry of the tree are

1. When $Y = 1$ at time t, it is either u or 1 at time $t + \Delta t$.
2. When $Y = u^m$ at time t for $m \geq 1$, it is either u^{m+1} or u^{m-1} at time $t + \Delta t$.

An up movement in Y corresponds to a down movement in the stock price, and vice versa. The probability of an up movement in Y is, therefore, always $1 - p$ and the probability of a down movement in Y is always p.

We use the tree to value the American lookback option in units of the stock price rather than in dollars. In dollars, the payoff from the option is

$$SY - S$$

In stock price units, the payoff from the option, therefore, is

$$Y - 1$$

We roll back through the tree in the usual way, valuing a derivative that provides this payoff except that we adjust for the differences in the stock price (i.e., the unit of measurement) at the nodes. If $f_{i,j}$ is the value of the lookback at the jth node at time $i\Delta t$ and $Y_{i,j}$ is the value of Y at this node, the rollback procedure gives

$$f_{i,j} = \max\{Y_{i,j} - 1, \, e^{-r\Delta t}[(1 - p)f_{i+1,j+1}d + pf_{i+1,j-1}u]\}$$

when $j \geq 1$. Note that $f_{i+1,j+1}$ is multiplied by d and $f_{i+1,j-1}$ is multiplied by u in this equation. This takes into account that the stock price at node (i, j) is the unit of measurement. The stock price at node $(i + 1, j + 1)$, which is the unit of measurement for $f_{i+1,j+1}$, is d times the stock price at node (i, j) and the stock price at node $(i + 1, j - 1)$, which is the unit of measurement for $f_{i+1,j-1}$, is u times the stock price at node (i, j). Similarly, when $j = 0$ the rollback procedure gives

$$f_{i,j} = \max\{Y_{i,j} - 1, \, e^{-r\Delta t}[(1 - p)f_{i+1,j+1}d + pf_{i+1,j}u]\}$$

The calculations for our example are shown in Figure 18.4. The tree estimates the value of the option at time zero (in stock price units) as 0.1094. This means that the dollar value of the option is $0.1094 \times 50 = 5.47$. This is the same as the value calculated from the tree in Figure 18.2. For a given number of time steps, the two procedures are equivalent. The advantage of the procedure described here is that it considerably reduces the number of computations.

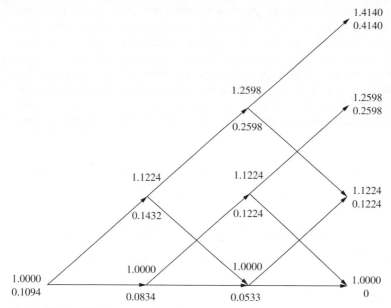

Figure 18.4   Efficient procedure for valuing an American-style lookback option.

The value of the option given by the tree in Figure 18.4, when it is European, is 5.26. The exact value of the European option, as shown in Example 18.1, is 7.79. The value given by the tree converges slowly to this as the number of time steps is increased. For example, with 100, 500, 1,000, and 5,000 time steps the values given by the tree for the European option in our example are 7.24, 7.54, 7.61, and 7.71.

18.4   BARRIER OPTIONS

Earlier in this chapter we presented analytic results for standard barrier options. Here we consider the numerical procedures that can be used for these types of options when there are no analytic results.

In principle, a barrier option can be valued using the binomial and trinomial trees discussed in chapter 16. Consider an American down-and-out option. We can value this in the same way as a regular American option except that, when we encounter a node below the barrier, we set the value of the option equal to zero.

Unfortunately, convergence is very slow when this approach is used. A large number of time steps are required to obtain a reasonably accurate result. The reason for this is that the barrier being assumed by the tree is different from the true barrier.[13]

---

[13] See P. P. Boyle and S. H. Lau, "Bumping Up Against the Barrier with the Binomial Method," *Journal of Derivatives* 1, 4 (Summer 1994), 6–14, for a discussion of this.

Define the *inner barrier* as the barrier formed by nodes just on the inside of the true barrier (i.e., closer to the center of the tree) and *the outer barrier* as the barrier formed by nodes just outside the true barrier (i.e., farther away from the center of the tree). Figure 18.5 shows the inner and outer barrier for a trinomial tree on the assumption that the true barrier is horizontal. Figure 18.6 does the same for a binomial tree. The usual tree calculations implicitly assume that the outer barrier is the true barrier because the barrier conditions are first used at nodes on this barrier. When the time step is Δt, the vertical spacing between the nodes is of order $\sqrt{\Delta t}$. This means that errors created by the difference between the true barrier and the outer barrier also tend to be of order $\sqrt{\Delta t}$.

We now present three alternative approaches for overcoming this problem. For all three approaches, it turns out to be more efficient to use a trinomial tree rather than a binomial tree.

Positioning Nodes on the Barriers

Suppose that there are two horizontal barriers, H_1 and H_2, with $H_1 > H_2$ and that the underlying stock price follows geometric Brownian motion. In a trinomial tree, there are three possible movements in the asset's price at each node: up by a proportional amount u; stay the same; and down by a proportional amount d where $d = 1/u$. We

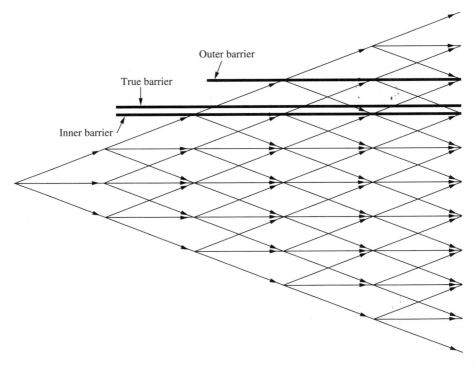

Figure 18.5 Barriers assumed by trinomial trees.

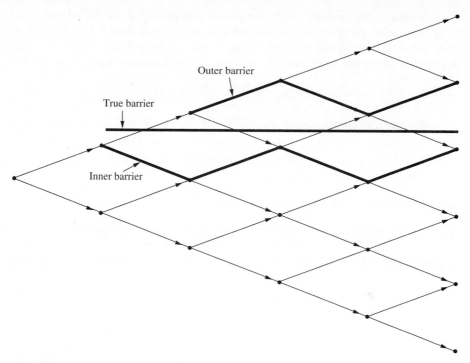

Figure 18.6 Barriers assumed by binomial trees.

can always choose u so that nodes lie on both barriers. The condition that must be satisfied by u is

$$H_2 = H_1 u^N$$

or

$$\ln H_2 = \ln H_1 + N \ln u$$

for some integer N.

When discussing trinomial trees in section 16.5, the value suggested for u was $e^{\sigma \sqrt{3\Delta t}}$ so that $\ln u = \sigma \sqrt{3\Delta t}$. In the situation considered here, a good rule is to choose $\ln u$ to be as close as possible to this value, consistent with the condition given above. This means that we set

$$\ln u = \frac{\ln H_2 - \ln H_1}{N}$$

where

$$N = \text{int} \left[\frac{\ln H_2 - \ln H_1}{\sigma \sqrt{3\Delta t}} + 0.5 \right]$$

Normally, the trinomial stock price tree is constructed so that the central node is the initial stock price. In this case, the stock price at the first node is the initial stock price. After that we choose the central node of the tree to be $H_1 u^M$, where M is the integer that makes this quantity as close as possible to the initial stock price; that is,

$$M = \text{int} \left[\frac{\ln S_0 - \ln H_1}{\ln u} + 0.5 \right]$$

This leads to a tree of the form shown in Figure 18.7. The probabilities on all branches of the tree are chosen, as usual, to match the first two moments of the stochastic process followed by the asset price. The approach works well except when the initial asset price is close to a barrier.

Adjusting for Nodes Not Lying on Barriers

An alternative procedure for coping with barriers is to make no changes to the tree and adjust the rollback procedure.[14] The first step is to calculate an inner barrier and an outer barrier, as described earlier. We then roll back through the tree, calculating

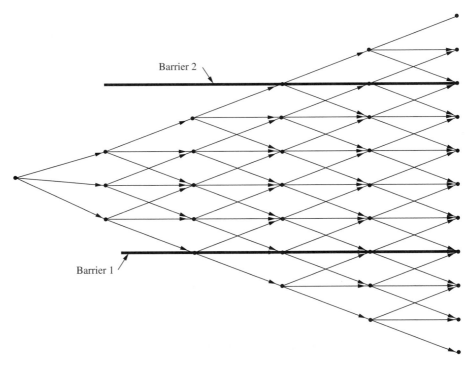

Figure 18.7   Tree with nodes lying on each of two barriers.

[14]The procedure we describe here is similar to that in E. Derman, I. Kani, D. Ergener, and I Bardhan, "Enhanced Numerical Methods for Options with Barriers," Working Paper, Goldman Sachs, (May 1995).

two values of the derivative on the nodes that form the inner barrier. The first of these values is obtained by assuming that the inner barrier is correct; the second is obtained by assuming that the outer barrier is correct. A final estimate for the value of the derivative on the inner barrier is then obtained by interpolating between these two values. Suppose that at time $i\Delta t$, the true barrier is 0.2 from the inner barrier and 0.6 from the outer barrier. Suppose further that the value of the derivative on the inner barrier is 0 if the inner barrier is assumed to be correct and 1.6 if the outer barrier is assumed to be correct. The interpolated value on the inner barrier is 0.4. Once we have obtained a value for the derivative at all nodes on all inner barriers, we can roll back through the tree to obtain the initial value of the derivative in the usual way.

For a single horizontal barrier, this approach is equivalent to the following:

1. Calculate the price of the derivative on the assumption that the inner barrier is the true barrier.
2. Calculate the value of the derivative on the assumption that the outer barrier is the true barrier.
3. Interpolate between the two prices.

The method can be generalized to situations where there is more than one barrier and to situations where the barriers are nonhorizontal.

The Adaptive Mesh Model

Possibly the best method for handling barrier options is the adaptive mesh model, introduced in chapter 16 in connection with the valuation of regular American options. The idea behind the model is that computational efficiency can be improved by grafting a high resolution tree onto a low resolution tree to achieve a more detailed modeling of the asset price in the regions of the tree where it is needed most.[15]

To value a regular American option, it proves useful to have a high resolution tree near maturity in the region around the strike price (See Figure 16.12). To value a barrier option, it is useful to have a high resolution tree close to the barrier. Figure 18.8 illustrates the design of the tree. The geometry of the tree is arranged so that nodes lie on the barrier. The probabilities on branches are chosen, as usual, to match the first two moments of the process followed by the underlying asset.

Figlewski and Gao compared their approach to the first approach described in this section and found that it leads to significant improvements in computational efficiency—particularly when the initial asset price is close to the barrier.

---

[15] See S. Figlewski and B. Gao, "The Adaptive Mesh Model: A New Approach to Efficient Option Pricing," *Journal of Financial Economics*, (forthcoming).

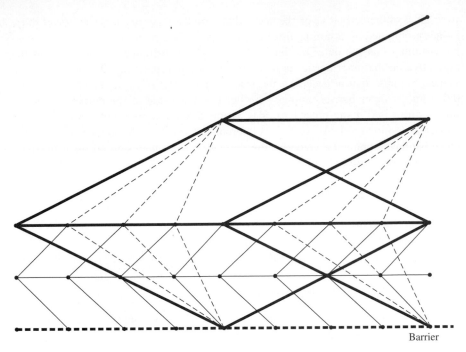

Figure 18.8   The adaptive mesh model used to value barrier options.

18.5   OPTIONS ON TWO CORRELATED ASSETS

Another tricky numerical problem is that of valuing options dependent on two assets whose prices are correlated. (These are sometimes referred to as *rainbow options.*) A number of alternative approaches have been suggested. Three of these approaches are presented in this section.

Transforming Variables

It is relatively easy to construct a tree in three dimensions to represent the movements of two *uncorrelated* variables. The procedure is as follows. First, we construct a two-dimensional tree for each variable. We then combine these trees into a single three-dimensional tree. The probabilities on the branches of the three-dimensional tree are the product of the corresponding probabilities on the two-dimensional trees. Suppose, for example, that the variables are stock prices, S_1 and S_2. Each can be represented in two dimensions by a Cox, Ross, and Rubinstein binomial tree. Assume that S_1 has a probability p_1 of moving up by a proportional amount u_1 and a probability $1 - p_1$ of moving down by a proportional amount d_1. Suppose further that S_2 has a probability p_2 of moving up by a proportional amount u_2 and a probability $1 - p_2$ of moving down by a proportional amount d_2. In the three-dimensional tree there are four branches emanating from each node. The probabilities are

$$p_1 p_2: S_1 \text{ increases}; S_2 \text{ increases}.$$
$$p_1(1 - p_2): S_1 \text{ increases}; S_2 \text{ decreases}.$$
$$(1 - p_1)p_2: S_1 \text{ decreases}; S_2 \text{ increases}.$$
$$(1 - p_1)(1 - p_2): S_1 \text{ decreases}; S_2 \text{ decreases}.$$

Consider next the situation where S_1 and S_2 are correlated. We suppose that the risk-neutral processes are:

$$dS_1 = (r - q_1)S_1 \, dt + \sigma_1 S_1 \, dz_1$$
$$dS_2 = (r - q_2)S_2 \, dt + \sigma_2 S_2 \, dz_2$$

and the instantaneous correlation between the Wiener processes, dz_1 and dz_2, is ρ. This means that

$$d \ln S_1 = (r - q_1 - \sigma_1^2/2) \, dt + \sigma_1 \, dz_1$$
$$d \ln S_2 = (r - q_2 - \sigma_2^2/2) \, dt + \sigma_2 \, dz_2$$

We define two new uncorrelated variables,[16]

$$x_1 = \sigma_2 \ln S_1 + \sigma_1 \ln S_2 \qquad x_2 = \sigma_2 \ln S_1 - \sigma_1 \ln S_2$$

These variables follow the processes

$$dx_1 = [\sigma_2(r - q_1 - \sigma_1^2/2) + \sigma_1(r - q_2 - \sigma_2^2/2)] \, dt + \sigma_1 \sigma_2 \sqrt{2(1 + \rho)} \, dz_A$$
$$dx_2 = [\sigma_2(r - q_1 - \sigma_1^2/2) - \sigma_1(r - q_2 - \sigma_2^2/2)] \, dt + \sigma_1 \sigma_2 \sqrt{2(1 - \rho)} \, dz_B$$

where dz_A and dz_B are uncorrelated Wiener processes.

The variables x_1 and x_2 can be modeled using two separate binomial trees. In time Δt, x_i has a probability p_i of increasing by h_i and a probability $1 - p_i$ of decreasing by h_i. The variables h_i and p_i are chosen so that the tree gives correct values for the first two moments of the distribution of x_1 and x_2. Because they are uncorrelated, the two trees can be combined into a single three-dimensional tree, as already described.

At each node of the tree, S_1 and S_2 can be calculated from x_1 and x_2 using the inverse relationships

$$S_1 = \exp\left[\frac{x_1 + x_2}{2\sigma_2}\right]$$

$$S_2 = \exp\left[\frac{x_1 - x_2}{2\sigma_1}\right]$$

The procedure for rolling back through a three-dimensional tree to value a derivative is analogous to that for a two-dimensional tree.

---

[16]This idea was suggested in J. Hull and A. White, "Valuing Derivative Securities Using the Explicit Finite Difference Method," *Journal of Financial and Quantitative Analysis,* 25 (1990), 87–100.

Using a Nonrectangular Tree

Rubinstein has suggested a way of building a three-dimensional tree for two correlated stock prices by using a nonrectangular arrangement of the nodes.[17] From a node
(S_1, S_2) where the first stock price is S_1 and the second stock price is S_2, we have a
0.25 chance of moving to each of the following:

$$(S_1 u_1, S_2 A)$$
$$(S_1 u_1, S_2 B)$$
$$(S_1 d_1, S_2 C)$$
$$(S_2 d_1, S_2 D)$$

where

$$u_1 = \exp\left[(r - q_1 - \sigma_1^2/2)\Delta t + \sigma_1 \sqrt{\Delta t}\right]$$
$$d_1 = \exp\left[(r - q_1 - \sigma_1^2/2)\Delta t - \sigma_1 \sqrt{\Delta t}\right]$$
$$A = \exp\left[r - q_2 - \sigma_2^2/2 + \sigma_2 \sqrt{\Delta t}(\rho + \sqrt{1 - \rho^2})\right]$$
$$B = \exp\left[r - q_2 - \sigma_2^2/2 + \sigma_2 \sqrt{\Delta t}(\rho - \sqrt{1 - \rho^2})\right]$$
$$C = \exp\left[r - q_2 - \sigma_2^2/2 - \sigma_2 \sqrt{\Delta t}(\rho - \sqrt{1 - \rho^2})\right]$$
$$D = \exp\left[r - q_2 - \sigma_2^2/2 - \sigma_2 \sqrt{\Delta t}(\rho + \sqrt{1 - \rho^2})\right]$$

When the correlation is zero, this method is equivalent to constructing separate trees
for S_1 and S_2 using the alternative binomial tree construction method in section 16.5.

Adjusting the Probabilities

A third approach to building a three-dimensional tree for S_1 and S_2 involves first
assuming no correlation and then adjusting the probabilities at each node to reflect
the correlation.[18] We use the alternative binomial tree construction method for each
of S_1 and S_2 in Section 16.5. This method has the property that all probabilities are
0.5. When the two binomial trees are combined on the assumption that there is no
correlation, the probabilities are as follows.

	S_1-move	
S_2-move	*Down*	*Up*
Up	0.25	0.25
Down	0.25	0.25

---

[17] See M. Rubinstein, "Return to Oz," *RISK*, (November 1994), 67–70.

[18] This approach was suggested in the context of interest rate trees in J. Hull and A. White, "Numerical Procedures for Implementing Term Structure Models II: Two-Factor Models," *Journal of Derivatives*, (Winter
1994), 37–48.

When we adjust these probabilities to reflect the correlation they become

	S_1-*move*	
S_2-*move*	*Down*	*Up*
Up	$0.25(1 - \rho)$	$0.25(1 + \rho)$
Down	$0.25(1 + \rho)$	$0.25(1 - \rho)$

18.6 IMPLIED TREES

In chapter 17 we discussed the volatility smiles that are commonly used when European and American options are valued. A key issue for traders is how the volatility smile should be incorporated into the pricing of exotic options. Unfortunately, there is no simple way of deducing the volatility appropriate for pricing an exotic option from the volatility smile used for regular options. This is because an exotic option is liable to depend on quite different aspects of the future probability distribution of an asset price than a regular option.

A common approach to valuing exotic options is to replace the usual model:

$$dS = (r - q)S\,dt + \sigma S\,dz$$

by

$$dS = [r(t) - q(t)]S\,dt + \sigma(S, t)S\,dz$$

where $r(t)$ is the instantaneous forward interest rate for a contract maturing at time t and $q(t)$ is the dividend yield, both functions of time. The volatility $\sigma(S, t)$ is a function of both S and t and is chosen so that the model provides a perfect fit to both the volatility smile and the volatility term structure. Dupire, and Andersen and Brotherton-Ratcliffe show that $\sigma(S, t)$ can be calculated analytically:[19]

$$[\sigma(X, t)]^2 = 2\frac{\partial c/\partial t + q(t)c + X[r(t) - q(t)]\partial c/\partial X}{X^2(\partial^2 c/\partial X^2)} \qquad (18.4)$$

where $c(X, t)$ is the price of a European call option with strike price X and maturity t. If a sufficiently large number of European call prices are available in the market, this equation can be used to estimate the $\sigma(S, t)$ function.

Andersen and Brotherton-Ratcliffe implement the model by using equation (18.4) in conjunction with the implicit finite difference method. An alternative approach, known as the *implied tree* methodology, is suggested by Derman and Kani,

---

[19]See B. Dupire, "Pricing with a Smile," *RISK*, 7 (February 1994), 18–20; L. B. G Andersen and R. Brotherton-Ratcliffe "The Equity Option Volatility Smile: An Implicit Finite Difference Approach," *Journal of Computation Finance*, vol 1, no. 2 (Winter 1997/98), 5–37. Dupire considers the case where r and q are zero; Andersen and Brotherton-Ratcliffe consider the more general situation.

and Rubinstein.[20] This involves constructing a tree for the asset price that is consistent with option prices in the market. We will now describe the Derman–Kani version of the implied tree approach.

An implied tree is a binomial tree where a forward induction procedure is used to determine the positions of the nodes at the end of each time step and the probabilities on the branches. As in the case of the regular binomial tree, we branch from the jth node at time $(n - 1)\Delta t$ to either the $(j + 1)$th node or the jth node at time $n\Delta t$. To understand the approach, note that there are $n + 1$ nodes at time $n\Delta t$.[21] Assume that the tree has already been constructed up to time $(n - 1)\Delta t$. The next step involves:

1. Choosing the positions of the $n + 1$ nodes at time $n\Delta t$.
2. Choosing the n "up" probabilities on the branches between times $(n - 1)\Delta t$ and $n\Delta t$. (The "down" probabilities are 1 minus the "up" probabilities.)

These choices provide $2n + 1$ degrees of freedom.

The interest rate for the period between $(n - 1)\Delta t$ and $n\Delta t$ is set equal to the forward rate. The expected return from the asset at each of the nodes at time $(n - 1)\Delta t$ must equal this interest rate. This uses up n degrees of freedom. The tree is also constructed to ensure that n European-style options maturing at time $n\Delta t$ are priced correctly. These options have strike prices equal to the stock prices at the nodes at time $(n - 1)\Delta t$.[22] This uses up an additional n degrees of freedom. The final degree of freedom is used up in ensuring that the center of the tree equals today's stock price.

The requirements just mentioned lead to $2n + 1$ equations in $2n + 1$ unknowns. By solving the equations, the construction of the tree is advanced by one time step. One problem with the approach is that negative probabilities do sometimes arise. When a particular probability turns out to be negative, it is necessary to introduce a rule to override the option price responsible for the negative probability.

The approaches outlined in this section have the advantage that they lead to exotic options being priced consistently with actively traded regular options. Their main disadvantage is that we may be pushing a one-factor model too far. The underlying model matches the volatility smile and volatility term structure observed in the market today. However, it implies a volatility smile and volatility term structure that will be observed at future times. The latter may be quite different from those observed in the market today. Caution should, therefore, be exercised when using an implied tree to price instruments that are dependent on the volatility as observed at a future time.[23]

---

[20] See E. Derman and I. Kani, "The Volatility Smile and Its Implied Tree," *Quantitative Strategies Publications,* Goldman Sachs, (January 1994); E. Derman and I. Kani, "Riding on a Smile," *RISK,* (February 1994), 32–39; M. Rubinstein, "Implied Binomial Trees" *Journal of Finance,* 49, 3 (July 1994), 771–818.

[21] The brief description of the implied tree methodology here is based on the work of E. Derman and I. Kani.

[22] In practice, it is necessary to interpolate between the implied volatilities of actively traded options to determine implied volatilities for the options used in the tree construction. These implied volatilities are then converted into option prices using Black–Scholes.

[23] Examples of such deals are forward start options and compound options.

18.7 HEDGING ISSUES

Before trading an exotic option, it is important for a financial institution to assess not only how it should be priced, but also the difficulties that are likely to be experienced in hedging it. The general approach described in chapter 13 involving the monitoring of delta, gamma, vega, and so on, can be used.

Some exotic options are easier to hedge using the underlying asset than the corresponding plain vanilla option. An example is an average price option where the averaging period is the whole life of the option and the underlying asset is a stock price. As time passes, we observe more of the stock prices that will be used in calculating the final average. This means that our uncertainty about the payoff decreases with the passage of time. As a result, the option becomes progressively easier to hedge. In the final few days, the delta of the option always approaches zero because price movements during this time have very little impact on the payoff.

Barrier options can, in certain circumstances, be significantly more difficult to hedge than regular options. Consider a down-and-out call option on a currency when the exchange rate is 0.0005 above the barrier. If the barrier is hit, the option is worth nothing. If the barrier is not hit, the option may prove to be quite valuable. The delta of the option is discontinuous at the barrier and hedging using conventional techniques is difficult. The approach in the following section is often more appropriate.

18.8 STATIC OPTIONS REPLICATION

Hedging an option position involves replicating the opposite position. The procedures described in chapter 13 involve what is sometimes referred to as *dynamic options replication*. They require the position in the hedging assets to be rebalanced frequently and can be quite expensive because of the transaction costs involved.

An alternative approach that can sometimes be used to hedge a position in exotic options is *static options replication*.[24] This involves searching for a portfolio of actively traded options that approximately replicate the option position. Shorting this portfolio provides the hedge. The basic principle underlying static options replication is as follows. If two portfolios are worth the same on a certain boundary, they are also worth the same at all interior points of the boundary.

Consider as an example a nine-month up-and-out call option on a non-dividend-paying stock where the stock price is 50, the strike price is 50, the barrier is 60, the risk-free interest rate is 10% per annum, and the volatility is 30% per annum. Suppose that $f(S, t)$ is the value of the option at time t for a stock price of S. We can use any boundary in (S, t) space for the purposes of producing the replicating portfolio. A convenient one to choose is shown in Figure 18.9. It is defined by $S = 60$ and

---

[24]See E. Derman, D. Ergener, and I. Kani, "Static Options Replication," *Journal of Derivatives* 2, 4 (Summer 1995), 78–95.

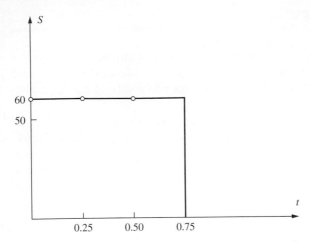

Figure 18.9   Boundary points used for static options replication example.

$t = 0.75$. The values of the up-and-out option on the boundary are given by

$$f(S, 0.75) = \max(S - 50, 0) \qquad \text{when } S < 60$$
$$f(60, t) = 0 \qquad \text{when } 0 \le t \le 0.75$$

There are many ways that we can approximately match these boundary values using regular options. The natural instrument to match the first boundary is a regular nine-month European call option with a strike price of 50. The first instrument introduced into the replicating portfolio is, therefore, likely to be one unit of this option. (We refer to this option as option A) One way of proceeding is as follows. We divide the life of the option into a number of time steps and choose options that satisfy the second boundary condition at the beginning of each time step.

Suppose that we choose time steps of three months. The next instrument we choose should lead to the second boundary being matched at $t = 0.5$. In other words, it should lead to the value of the complete replicating portfolio being zero when $t = 0.5$ and $S = 60$. The option should have the property that it has zero value on the first boundary because this has already been matched. One possibility is a regular nine-month European call option with a strike price of 60. (We will refer to this as option B) Black–Scholes formulas show that this is worth 4.33 at the six-month point when $S = 60$. They also show that the position in option A is worth 11.54 at this point. The position we require in option B is, therefore, $-11.54/4.33 = -2.66$.

We next move on to matching the second boundary condition at $t = 0.25$. The option used should have the property that it has zero value on all boundaries that have been matched thus far. One possibility is a regular six-month European call option with a strike price of 60. (We refer to this as option C.) This is worth 4.33 at the three-month point when $S = 60$. Our position in options A and B is worth -4.21 at this point. The position we require in option C is, therefore, $4.21/4.33 = 0.97$.

Table 18.1	The Portfolio of European Call Options Used to Replicate an Up-and-Out Option			
Option number	*Strike price*	*Maturity (years)*	*Position*	*Initial value*
A	50	0.75	1.00	+6.99
B	60	0.75	−2.66	−8.21
C	60	0.50	0.97	+1.78
D	60	0.25	0.28	+0.17

Finally, we match the second boundary condition at $t = 0$. For this we use a regular three-month European option with a strike price of 60. (We refer to this as option D.) Similarly to the above, our position in option D is calculated to be 0.28.

The portfolio chosen is summarized in Table 18.1. It is worth 0.73 initially (that is, at time zero when the stock price is 50). This compares with 0.31 given by the analytic formula for the up-and-out call earlier in this chapter. The replicating portfolio is not exactly the same as the up-and-out option because it matches the latter at only three points on the second boundary. If we use the same scheme, but match at 18 points on the second boundary (using options that mature every half month), the value of the replicating portfolio reduces to 0.38. If 100 points are matched, the value reduces further to 0.32.

To hedge a derivative, we short the portfolio that replicates its boundary conditions. This has the advantage over delta hedging that it does not require frequent rebalancing. The static replication approach can be used for a wide range of derivatives. The user has a great deal of flexibility in choosing the boundary that is to be matched and the options that are to be used. The portfolio must be unwound when any part of the boundary is reached.

SUMMARY

Exotic options are options with rules governing the payoff that are more complicated than standard options. We have discussed 13 different types of exotic options: packages, nonstandard American options, forward start options, compound options, chooser options, barrier options, binary options, lookback options, shout options, Asian options, options to exchange one asset for another, options involving several assets, and basket options. Some of these can be valued using straightforward extensions of the procedures that we have developed for European and American calls and puts; some can be valued analytically, but using much more complicated formulas than those for regular European calls and puts; and some require special numerical procedures.

The natural technique to use for valuing path-dependent options is Monte Carlo simulation. This has the disadvantage that it is fairly slow and unable to handle American-style derivatives easily. Luckily, trees can be used to value many types of path-dependent derivatives. The approach is to choose representative values for the underlying path function at each node of the tree and calculate the value of the derivative for each alternative value of the path function as we roll back through the tree.

Lookback options can be handled more easily than other path-dependent options. Instead of constructing a tree to represent movements in the stock price, we construct a tree to represent movements in a variable that is the maximum (or minimum) stock price divided by the actual stock price. The option is then valued in stock price units rather than in dollars.

Asian options can be valued by approximating the probability distribution of the average asset price as a lognormal distribution. The lognormal distribution is fitted to the first two moments of the distribution of the average. The latter can be calculated analytically.

Trees can be used to value many types of barrier options, but the convergence of the option value to the correct value as the number of time steps is increased tends to be slow. One approach for improving convergence is to arrange the geometry of the tree so that nodes always lie on the barriers. Another is to use an interpolation scheme to adjust for the possibility that the barrier being assumed by the tree is different from the true barrier. A third method is to design the tree that provides a finer representation of movements in the underlying asset price near the barrier.

One way of valuing options dependent on the prices of two correlated assets is to apply a transformation to the asset price to create two new uncorrelated variables. These two variables are each modeled with trees and the trees are then combined to form a single three-dimensional tree. At each node of the tree, the inverse of the transformation gives the asset prices. A second approach is to arrange the positions of nodes on the three-dimensional tree to reflect the correlation. A third approach is to start with a tree that assumes no correlation between the variables and then adjust the probabilities on the tree to reflect the correlation.

Exotic options are sometimes valued by constructing a one-factor model for the underlying asset price that is consistent with the volatility smile and volatility term structure observed for regular options. This is an attempt to ensure that the prices of exotic options are consistent with the prices of regular options.

Some exotic options are easier to hedge than the corresponding regular options; others are more difficult. In general, Asian options are easier to hedge because the payoff becomes progressively more certain as we approach maturity. Barrier options can be more difficult to hedge because delta is liable to be discontinuous at the barrier. One approach to hedging an exotic option, known as static options replication, is to find a portfolio of regular options whose value matches the value of the exotic option on some boundary. The exotic option is hedged by shorting this portfolio.

SUGGESTIONS FOR FURTHER READING

Andersen, L. B. G., and R. Brotherton-Ratcliffe. "The Equity Option Volatility Smile: An Implicit Finite Difference Approach," *Journal of Computational Finance,* vol. 1, no. 2 (Winter 1997/98), 3–37.

Boyle, P. P., J. Evnine, and S. Gibbs. "Numerical Evaluation of Multivariate Contingent Claims," *Review of Financial Studies,* 2, 2 (1989), 241–50.

Boyle, P. P., and S. H. Lau. "Bumping Up Against the Barrier with the Binomial Method," *Journal of Derivatives,* 1, 4 (Summer 1994), 6–14.

Broadie, M., P. Glasserman, and S. G. Kou. "A Continuity Correction for Discrete Barrier Options," *Mathematical Finance* 7, 4 (October 1997), 325–349.

Broadie M., P. Glasserman, and S. G. Kou. "Connecting Discrete and Continuous Path-Dependent Options," *Finance and Stochastics,* 2 (1998), 1–28.

Clewlow, L., and C. Strickland. *Exotic Options: The State of the Art.* London: Thomson Business Press, 1997.

Conze, A., and R. Viswanathan. "Path Dependent Options: The Case of Lookback Options," *Journal of Finance,* 46 (1991), 1893–1907.

Curran, M. "Beyond Average Intelligence," *RISK,* (October 1992), 60–62.

Derman, E., D. Ergener, and I. Kani. "Static Options Replication," *Journal of Derivatives,* 2, 4 (Summer 1995), 78–95.

Derman, E., I. Kani, and N. Chriss. "Implied Trinomial Trees of the Volatility Smile," *Journal of Derivatives,* 3, 4 (Summer 1996), 7–22.

Garman, M. "Recollection in Tranquility," *RISK,* (March 1989), 16–19.

Geske, R. "The Valuation of Compound Options," *Journal of Financial Economics,* 7 (1979), 63–81.

Goldman, B., H. Sosin, and M. A. Gatto. "Path Dependent Options: Buy at the Low, Sell at the High," *Journal of Finance,* 34 (December 1979), 1111–27.

Hudson, M. "The Value of Going Out," *RISK,* (March 1991), 29–33.

Hull, J., and A. White. "Efficient Procedures for Valuing European and American Path-Dependent Options," *Journal of Derivatives,* (Fall 1993), 21–31.

Hull, J., and A. White. "Finding the Keys," *RISK,* (September 1993), 109–112.

Johnson, H. "Options on the Maximum and Minimum of Several Assets," *Journal of Financial and Quantitative Analysis,* 22, 3 (September 1987), 277–83.

Kemna, A., and A. Vorst. "A Pricing Method for Options Based on Average Asset Values," *Journal of Banking and Finance,* 14 (March 1990), 113–29.

Levy, E. "Pricing European Average Rate Currency Options," *Journal of International Money and Finance,* 11 (1992), 474–91.

Levy, E., and S. M. Turnbull. "Average Intelligence," *RISK,* (February 1992), 53–59.

Margrabe, W. "The Value of an Option to Exchange One Asset for Another," *Journal of Finance,* 33 (March 1978), 177–86.

Milevsky, M. A., and S. E. Posner. "Asian Options: The Sum of Lognormals and the Reciprocal Gamma Distribution," *Journal of Financial and Quanitative Analysis,* 33, 3 (September 1998), 409–22.

Ritchken, P., L. Sankarasubramanian, and A. M. Vijh. "The Valuation of Path Dependent Contracts on the Average," *Management Science,* 39 (1993), 1202–13.

Richken, P. "On Pricing Barrier Options," *Journal of Derivatives,* 3, 2 (Winter 1995), 19–28.

Rubinstein, M., and E. Reiner. "Breaking Down the Barriers," *RISK,* (September 1991), 28–35.

Rubinstein, M. "Double Trouble," *RISK,* (December 1991–January 1992), 53–56.

Rubinstein, M. "One for Another," *RISK,* (July–August 1991), 30–32.

Rubinstein, M. "Options for the Undecided," *RISK,* (April 1991), 70–73.

Rubinstein, M. "Pay Now, Choose Later," *RISK,* (February 1991), 44–47.

Rubinstein, M. "Somewhere Over the Rainbow," *RISK,* (November 1991), 63–66.

Rubinstein, M. "Two in One," *RISK,* (May 1991), 49.

Rubinstein, M., and E. Reiner. "Unscrambling the Binary Code," *RISK,* (October 1991), 75–83.

Stulz, R. "Options on the Minimum or Maximum of Two Assets," *Journal of Financial Economics,* 10 (1982), 161–85.

Turnbull, S. M., and L. M. Wakeman. "A Quick Algorithm for Pricing European Average Options," *Journal of Financial and Quantitative Analysis,* 26 (September 1991), 377–89.

QUESTIONS AND PROBLEMS
(ANSWERS IN SOLUTIONS MANUAL)

18.1. Explain the difference between a forward start option and a chooser option.

18.2. Describe the payoff from a portfolio consisting of a lookback call and a lookback put with the same maturity.

18.3. Consider a chooser option where the holder has the right to choose between a European call and a European put at any time during a two-year period. The maturity dates and strike prices for the calls and puts are the same regardless of when the choice is made. Is it ever optimal to make the choice before the end of the two-year period? Explain your answer.

18.4. Suppose that c_1 and p_1 are the prices of a European average price call and a European average price put with strike X and maturity T, c_2 and p_2 are the prices of a European average strike call and European average strike put with maturity T, and c_3 and p_3 are the prices of a regular European call and a regular European put with strike price X and maturity T. Show that

$$c_1 + c_2 - c_3 = p_1 + p_2 - p_3$$

18.5. The text derives a decomposition of a particular type of chooser option into a call maturing at time t_2 and a put maturing at time t_1. Derive an alternative decomposition into a call maturing at time t_1 and a put maturing at time t_2.

18.6. Section 18.1 gives two formulas for a down-and-out call. The first applies to the situation where the barrier, H, is less than or equal to the strike price, X. The second applies to the situation where $H \geq X$. Show that the two formulas are the same when $H = X$.

18.7. Explain why a down-and-out put is worth zero when the barrier is greater than the strike price.

18.8. Use a three-time-step tree to value an American lookback call option on a currency when the initial exchange rate is 1.6, the domestic risk-free rate is 5% per annum, the foreign risk-free interest rate is 8% per annum, the exchange rate volatility is 15%, and the time to maturity is 18 months. Use the approach in section 18.2.

18.9. Repeat Problem 18.8 using the approach in section 18.3.

18.10. Use a three-time-step tree to value an American put option on the geometric average of the price of a non-dividend-paying stock when the stock price is $40, the strike price is $40, the risk-free interest rate is 10% per annum, the volatility is 35% per annum, and the time to maturity is three months. The geometric average is measured from today until the option matures.

18.11. Suppose that the strike price of an American call option on a non-dividend-paying stock grows at rate g. Show that if g is less than the risk-free rate, r, it is never optimal to exercise the call early.

18.12. How can the value of a forward start put option on a non-dividend-paying stock be calculated if it is agreed that the strike price will be 10% greater than the stock price at the time the option starts?

18.13. If a stock price follows geometric Brownian motion, what process does $A(t)$ follow where $A(t)$ is the arithmetic average stock price between time zero and time t?

18.14. Explain why delta hedging is easier for Asian options than for regular options.

18.15. Calculate the price of a one-year European option to give up 100 ounces of silver in exchange for one ounce of gold. The current prices of gold and silver are $380 and $4, respectively; the risk-free interest rate is 10% per annum; the volatility of each commodity price is 20%; and the correlation between the two prices is 0.7. Ignore storage costs.

18.16. Is a European down-and-out option on an asset worth the same as a European down-and-out option on the asset's futures price for a futures contract maturing at the same time as the option?

18.17. (a) What put–call parity relationship exists between the price of a European call on a call and a European put on a call? Show that the formulas given in the text satisfy the relationship.

(b) What put–call parity relationship exists between the price of a European call on a put and a European put on a put? Show that the formulas given in the text satisfy the relationship.

18.18. Does a lookback call become more valuable or less valuable as we increase the frequency with which we observe the asset price in calculating the minimum?

18.19. Does a down-and-out call become more valuable or less valuable as we increase the frequency with which we observe the asset price in determining whether the barrier has been crossed? What is the answer to the same question for a down-and-in call?

18.20. Explain why a regular European call option is the sum of a down-and-out European call and a down-and-in European call. Is the same true for American call options?

18.21. What is the value of a derivative that pays off $100 in six months if the S&P 500 index is greater than 1000 and zero otherwise? Assume that the current level of the index is 960, the risk-free rate is 8% per annum, the dividend yield on the index is 3% per annum, and the volatility of the index is 20%.

18.22. In a three-month down-and-out call option on silver futures, the strike price is $20 per ounce and the barrier is $18. The current futures price is $19, the risk-free interest rate is 5%, and the volatility of silver futures is 40% per annum. Explain how the option works and calculate its value. What is the value of a regular call option on silver futures with the same terms? What is the value of a down-and-in call option on silver futures with the same terms?

18.23. A new European-style lookback call option on a stock index has a maturity of nine months. The current level of the index is 400, the risk-free rate is 6% per annum, the dividend yield on the index is 4% per annum, and the volatility of the index is 20%. Use the approach in section 18.4 to value the option and compare your answer to the result given by DerivaGem using the analytic valuation formula.

18.24. Estimate the value of a new six-month European-style average price call option on a non-dividend-paying stock. The initial stock price is $30, the strike price is $30, the risk-free interest rate is 5%, and the stock price volatility is 30%.

ASSIGNMENT QUESTIONS

18.25. What is the value in dollars of a derivative that pays off £10,000 in one year provided that the dollar–sterling exchange rate is greater than 1.5000 at that time? The current exchange rate is 1.4800. The dollar and sterling interest rates are 4% and 8% per annum respectively. The volatility of the exchange rate is 12% per annum.

18.26. Consider an up-and-out barrier call option on a non-dividend-paying stock when the stock price is 50, the strike price is 50, the volatility is 30%, the risk-free rate is 5%, the time to maturity is one year, and the barrier at $80. Use the software to value the option and graph the relationship between (a) the option price and the stock price, (b) the option price and the time to maturity, and (c) the option price and the volatility. Provide an intuitive explanation for the results you get. Show that delta, theta, and vega for an up-and-out barrier call option can be either positive or negative.

18.27. Consider a down-and-out call option on a foreign currency. The initial exchange rate is 0.90, the time to maturity is two years, the strike price is 1.00, the barrier is 0.80, the domestic risk-free interest rate is 5%, the foreign risk-free interest rate is 6%, and the volatility is 25% per annum. Use the DerivaGem software to explore alternative static option replication strategies.

Calculation of the First Two Moments of Arithmetic Averages and Baskets

Consider first the problem of calculating the first two moments of the value of a basket of assets at a future time, T, in a risk-neutral world. The price of each asset in the basket is assumed to be lognormal. Define

n: The number of assets.

S_i: The value of the ith asset at time T.

F_i: The forward price of the ith asset for a contract maturing at time T.[25]

σ_i: The volatility of the ith asset between time zero and time T.

ρ_{ij}: Correlation between returns from the ith and jth asset.

P: Value of basket at time T.

M_1: First moment of P in a risk-neutral world.

M_2: Second moment of P in a risk-neutral world.

Because $P = \sum_{i=1}^{n} S_i$ and $\hat{E}(S_i) = F_i$, where $\hat{E}$ denotes expectations in a risk-neutral world, it follows that

$$M_1 = \sum_{i=1}^{n} F_i$$

Also,

$$P^2 = \sum_{i=1}^{n} \sum_{j=1}^{n} S_i S_j$$

From the properties of lognormal distributions

$$\hat{E}(S_i S_j) = F_i F_j e^{\rho_{ij} \sigma_i \sigma_j T}$$

Hence

$$M_2 = \sum_{i=1}^{n} \sum_{j=1}^{n} F_i F_j e^{\rho_{ij} \sigma_i \sigma_j T}$$

We now move on to the related problem of calculating the first two moments of the arithmetic average price of an asset in a risk-neutral world when the average

---

[25] Strictly speaking, F_i should be the futures price rather than the forward price. In practice analysts usually assume no difference between the two when calculating moments.

is calculated from discrete observations. Suppose that the asset price is observed at times T_i ($1 \leq i \leq m$). We redefine variables as follows:

S_i: The value of the asset at time T_i.

F_i: The forward price of the asset for a contract maturing at time T_i.

σ_i: The implied volatility for an option on the asset with maturity T_i.

ρ_{ij}: Correlation between return on asset up to time T_i and the return on the asset up to time T_j.

P: Value of the arithmetic average.

M_1: First moment of P in a risk-neutral world.

M_2: Second moment of P in a risk-neutral world.

As before

$$M_1 = \sum_{i=1}^{m} F_i,$$

Also

$$P^2 = \sum_{i=1}^{m} \sum_{j=1}^{m} S_i S_j$$

In this case

$$\hat{E}(S_i S_j) = F_i F_j e^{\rho_{ij} \sigma_i \sigma_j \sqrt{T_i T_j}}$$

It can be shown that when $i < j$

$$\rho_{ij} = \frac{\sigma_i \sqrt{T_i}}{\sigma_j \sqrt{T_j}}$$

so that

$$\hat{E}(S_i S_j) = F_i F_j e^{\sigma_i^2 T_i}$$

and

$$M_2 = \sum_{i=1}^{m} F_i^2 e^{\sigma_i^2 T_i} + 2 \sum_{i<j} F_i F_j e^{\sigma_i^2 T_i}$$

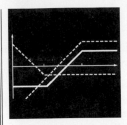

CHAPTER

19

EXTENSIONS OF THE THEORETICAL FRAMEWORK FOR PRICING DERIVATIVES: MARTINGALES AND MEASURES

This chapter extends the risk-neutral valuation arguments presented in chapters 9 and 11. We first define a parameter known as the *market price of risk* and show that the excess return over the risk-free interest rate earned by any derivative is linearly related to the market prices of risk of the stochastic variables underlying the derivative. In the traditional risk-neutral world, the market price of risk for all variables is zero. The chapter explains that derivatives can be correctly valued by assuming values for the market price of risk other than zero. We explain the role of *martingales* and *measures* in derivatives' valuation and introduce a concept known as *forward-risk neutrality*. This material is essential for full understanding of the standard market models, presented in chapter 20, for pricing the most common interest rate derivatives.

19.1 THE MARKET PRICE OF RISK

Here we consider the properties of derivatives dependent on the value of a single variable, θ. We will assume that the process followed by θ is

$$\frac{d\theta}{\theta} = m\,dt + s\,dz \tag{19.1}$$

where dz is a Wiener process. The parameters m and s are the expected growth rate in θ and the volatility of θ, respectively. We assume that they depend only on θ and time, t. The variable θ need not be the price of an investment asset. It could be something as far removed from financial markets as the temperature in the center of New Orleans.

Suppose that f_1 and f_2 are the prices of two derivatives dependent only on θ and t. These could be options or other instruments that provide a payoff equal to some function of θ at some future time. We assume that during the time period under consideration f_1 and f_2 provide no income.[1]

Suppose that the processes followed by f_1 and f_2 are

$$\frac{df_1}{f_1} = \mu_1\,dt + \sigma_1\,dz$$

and

$$\frac{df_2}{f_2} = \mu_2\,dt + \sigma_2\,dz$$

where μ_1, μ_2, σ_1, and σ_2 are functions of θ and t. The dz is the same Wiener process as in equation (19.1) because this is the only source of the uncertainty in their prices. The discrete versions of the processes are

$$\Delta f_1 = \mu_1 f_1\,\Delta t + \sigma_1 f_1\,\Delta z \tag{19.2}$$
$$\Delta f_2 = \mu_2 f_2\,\Delta t + \sigma_2 f_2\,\Delta z \tag{19.3}$$

We can eliminate the Δz by forming an instantaneously riskless portfolio consisting of $\sigma_2 f_2$ of the first derivative and $-\sigma_1 f_1$ of the second derivative. If Π is the value of the portfolio,

$$\Pi = (\sigma_2 f_2)f_1 - (\sigma_1 f_1)f_2 \tag{19.4}$$

and

$$\Delta\Pi = \sigma_2 f_2\,\Delta f_1 - \sigma_1 f_1\,\Delta f_2$$

Substituting from equations (19.2) and (19.3), this becomes

$$\Delta\Pi = (\mu_1\sigma_2 f_1 f_2 - \mu_2\sigma_1 f_1 f_2)\,\Delta t \tag{19.5}$$

Because the portfolio is instantaneously riskless, it must earn the risk-free rate. Hence

$$\Delta\Pi = r\Pi\,\Delta t$$

Substituting into this equation from equations (19.4) and (19.5) gives

$$\mu_1\sigma_2 - \mu_2\sigma_1 = r\sigma_2 - r\sigma_1$$

or

$$\frac{\mu_1 - r}{\sigma_1} = \frac{\mu_2 - r}{\sigma_2} \tag{19.6}$$

---

[1]The analysis can be extended to derivatives that provide income. See Problem 19.9.

Define λ as the value of each side in equation (19.6), so that

$$\frac{\mu_1 - r}{\sigma_1} = \frac{\mu_2 - r}{\sigma_2} = \lambda$$

Dropping subscripts, we have shown that if f is the price of a derivative dependent only on θ and t with

$$\frac{df}{f} = \mu\, dt + \sigma\, dz \tag{19.7}$$

then

$$\frac{\mu - r}{\sigma} = \lambda \tag{19.8}$$

The parameter λ is known as the *market price of risk* of θ. It may be dependent on both θ and t, but it is not dependent on the nature of the derivative f. At any given time, $(\mu - r)/\sigma$ must be the same for all derivatives that are dependent only on θ and t.

It is worth noting that σ, which we are referring to as the volatility of f, is defined as the coefficient of dz in equation (19.7). It can be either positive or negative. If s, the volatility of θ, is positive and f is positively related to θ (so that $\partial f/\partial\theta$ is positive), σ is positive. But if f is negatively related to θ, then σ is negative. The volatility of f, as it is traditionally defined, is $|\sigma|$.

The market price of risk of θ measures the trade-offs between risk and return that are made for securities dependent on θ. Equation (19.8) can be written

$$\mu - r = \lambda\sigma \tag{19.9}$$

For an intuitive understanding of this equation, we note that the variable σ can be loosely interpreted as the quantity of θ-risk present in f. On the right-hand side of the equation we are, therefore, multiplying the quantity of θ-risk by the price of θ-risk. The left-hand side is the expected return in excess of the risk-free interest rate that is required to compensate for this risk. Equation (19.9) is analogous to the capital asset pricing model, which relates the expected excess return on a stock to its risk.

In chapter 3, we distinguished between investment assets and consumption assets. An investment asset is an asset that is bought or sold purely for investment purposes by a significant number of investors. It can be used as part of a trading strategy to set up a riskless portfolio. Consumption assets are held primarily for consumption and cannot be used in this way. If the variable θ is the price of an investment asset, it must be true that

$$\frac{m - r}{s} = \lambda$$

But, if θ is the price of a consumption asset, this relationship is not, in general, true.

Example 19.1   Consider a derivative whose price is positively related to the price of oil and depends on no other stochastic variables. Suppose that it provides an expected return of 12% per annum and has a volatility of 20% per annum. Assume that the risk-free interest rate is 8% per annum. It follows that the market price of risk of oil is

$$\frac{0.12 - 0.08}{0.2} = 0.2$$

Note that oil is a consumption asset rather than an investment asset. Therefore, its market price of risk cannot be calculated from equation (19.8) by setting μ equal to the expected return from an investment in oil and σ equal to the volatility of oil prices.

Example 19.2 Consider two securities, both of which are positively dependent on the 90-day interest rate. Suppose that the first one has an expected return of 3% per annum and a volatility of 20% per annum, and the second one has a volatility of 30% per annum. Assume that the instantaneous risk-free rate of interest is 6% per annum. The market price of interest rate risk is, using the return and volatility for the first security,

$$\frac{0.03 - 0.06}{0.2} = -0.15$$

From a rearrangement of equation (19.9), the expected return from the second security is, therefore,

$$0.06 - 0.15 \times 0.3 = 0.015$$

or 1.5% per annum.

Differential Equation

Because f is a function of θ and t, the process followed by f can be expressed in terms of the process followed by θ using Ito's lemma. [See equation (10.14).] The parameters μ and σ in equation (19.7) are given by

$$\mu f = m\theta \frac{\partial f}{\partial \theta} + \frac{\partial f}{\partial t} + \frac{1}{2}s^2\theta^2\frac{\partial^2 f}{\partial \theta^2}$$

and

$$\sigma f = s\theta \frac{\partial f}{\partial \theta}$$

Substituting these into equation (19.9), we obtain the following differential equation that must be satisfied by f:

$$\frac{\partial f}{\partial t} + \theta\frac{\partial f}{\partial \theta}(m - \lambda s) + \frac{1}{2}s^2\theta^2\frac{\partial^2 f}{\partial \theta^2} = rf \qquad (19.10)$$

Equation (19.10) is structurally very similar to the Black–Scholes differential equation (11.15). As we would expect, it is exactly the same as the Black–Scholes differential equation when θ is S, the price of a non-dividend paying stock. This is because θ is then the price of an investment asset and from equation (19.9) must satisfy $m - r = \lambda s$ so that the second term in equation (19.10) becomes

$$r\theta \frac{\partial f}{\partial \theta}$$

Comparing equation (19.10) with equation (12A.4) we see that the differential equation for a derivative dependent on θ is the same as that for an asset providing a dividend yield equal to q where $q = r - m + \lambda s$. This observation leads to a way of extending the traditional risk-neutral valuation result so that it applies when the variables underlying a derivative are not the prices of traded securities.

Extension of Traditional Risk-Neutral Valuation

Any solution to equation (12A.4) for S is a solution to (19.10) for θ, and vice versa, when the substitution

$$q = r - m + \lambda s$$

is made. As explained in section 12.2, we know how to solve (12A.4) using risk-neutral valuation. This involves setting the expected growth rate of S equal to $r - q$ and discounting expected payoffs at the risk-free interest rate. It follows that we can solve equation (19.10) by setting the expected growth of θ equal to

$$r - (r - m + \lambda s) = m - \lambda s$$

and discounting expected payoffs at the risk-free interest rate.

One approach to valuing a derivative dependent on θ is, therefore, to reduce the expected growth rate of θ by λs, from m to $m - \lambda s$, and then behave as though the world is risk neutral. The risk-neutral valuation result in chapter 11 is a particular case of this more general result. To see this, suppose that θ is the price of a non-dividend-paying stock. From equation (19.9),

$$m - r = \lambda s$$

or

$$m - \lambda s = r$$

shows that changing the expected growth rate of θ to $m - \lambda s$ is the same as setting the return from the stock equal to the risk-free rate of interest.

> **Example 19.3**   The current price of copper is 80 cents per pound and the risk-free interest rate is 5% per annum. The expected growth rate in the price of copper is 2% per annum and its volatility is 20% per annum. The market price of the risk associated with copper is 0.5. Assume that a contract is traded that allows the holder to receive 1,000 pounds of copper at no cost in six months' time. In this case, $m = 0.02$, $\lambda = 0.5$, and $s = 0.2$. The expected growth rate of the price of copper in a risk-neutral world is
>
> $$m - \lambda s = 0.02 - 0.5 \times 0.2 = -0.08$$
>
> or -8% per annum. The expected payoff from the contract in a risk-neutral world is, therefore,
>
> $$1,000 \times 0.80e^{-0.08 \times 0.5} = 768.63$$
>
> Discounting for six months at 5% per annum, we estimate the current value of the contract to be $749.65.

It is worth noting that our extension of the risk-neutral valuation argument is more subtle than it first appears. When θ is not the price of an investment asset, the risk-neutral valuation argument does not necessarily tell us anything about what would happen in a risk-neutral world. It simply states that changing the expected growth rate of θ from m to $m - \lambda s$ and then behaving as though the world is risk neutral gives the correct values for derivatives.[2] For convenience, however, we will refer to a world where expected growth rates are changed from m to $m - \lambda s$ as a risk-neutral world.

19.2 DERIVATIVES DEPENDENT ON SEVERAL STATE VARIABLES

Appendices 19A and 19B extend the results in section 19.1 to derivatives whose prices depend on several underlying variables. Appendix 19A provides a version of Ito's lemma that covers functions of several variables. Appendix 19B uses this result to derive a differential equation that must be satisfied by a derivative dependent on n underlying variables.

Suppose that n variables, $\theta_1, \theta_2, \ldots, \theta_n$, follow stochastic processes of the form

$$\frac{d\theta_i}{\theta_i} = m_i \, dt + s_i \, dz_i \tag{19.11}$$

for $i = 1, 2, \ldots, n$, where the dz_i are Wiener processes. The parameters m_i and s_i are expected growth rates and volatilities and may be functions of the θ_i and time. Appendix 19A shows that the process for the price, f, of a security that is dependent on the θ_i has the form

$$\frac{df}{f} = \mu \, dt + \sum_{i=1}^{n} \sigma_i \, dz_i \tag{19.12}$$

In this equation, μ is the expected return from the security and $\sigma_i \, dz_i$ is the component of the risk of this return attributable to θ_i.

Appendix 19B shows that

$$\mu - r = \sum_{i=1}^{n} \lambda_i \sigma_i \tag{19.13}$$

---

[2]To illustrate this point, suppose that θ is the temperature in the center of New Orleans. The process followed by θ clearly does not depend on the risk preferences (at least, not the risk preferences of human beings), but it is possible that there is a non-zero market price of risk associated with this variable because of the relationship between temperatures and agricultural production. We might, therefore, have to adjust the drift of the process when valuing derivatives dependent on θ.

where λ_i is the market price of risk for θ_i. This equation relates the expected excess return that investors require on the security to the λ_i and σ_i. The term $\lambda_i \sigma_i$ measures the extent that the excess return required by investors on a security is affected by the dependence of the security on θ_i. If $\lambda_i \sigma_i = 0$, there is no effect; if $\lambda_i \sigma_i > 0$, investors require a higher return to compensate them for the risk arising from θ_i; if $\lambda_i \sigma_i < 0$, the dependence of the security on θ_i causes investors to require a lower return than would otherwise be the case. The $\lambda_i \sigma_i < 0$ situation occurs when the variable has the effect of reducing rather than increasing the risks in the portfolio of a typical investor.

> **Example 19.4**   A stock price depends on three underlying variables: the price of oil, the price of gold, and the performance of a stock index. Suppose that the market prices of risk for these variables are 0.2, -0.1, and 0.4, respectively. Suppose also that the σ_i factors in equation (19.12) corresponding to the three variables have been estimated as 0.05, 0.1, and 0.15, respectively. The excess return on the stock over the risk-free rate is
>
> $$0.2 \times 0.05 - 0.1 \times 0.1 + 0.4 \times 0.15 = 0.06$$
>
> or 6.0% per annum. If variables other than those considered affect f, this result is still true provided that the market price of risk for each of these other variables is zero.

Equation (19.13) is closely related to arbitrage pricing theory developed by Stephen Ross in 1976.[3] The continuous-time version of the capital asset pricing model (CAPM) can be regarded as a particular case of the equation. CAPM argues that an investor requires excess returns to compensate for any risk that is correlated to the risk in the return from the stock market, but requires no excess return for other risks. Risks that are correlated with the return from the stock market are referred to as *systematic*; other risks are referred to as *nonsystematic*. If CAPM is true, λ_i is proportional to the correlation between changes in θ_i and the return from the market. When θ_i is uncorrelated with the return from the market, λ_i is zero.

Traditional Risk-Neutral Valuation with Several Underlying Variables

Our risk-neutral valuation arguments in section 19.1 concerning differential equation (19.10) can be extended to cover the more general differential equation (19B.11) in Appendix 19B. A derivative can always be valued as if the world were risk neutral, provided that the expected growth rate of each underlying variable is assumed to be $m_i - \lambda_i s_i$ rather than m_i. The volatility of the variables and the coefficient of correlation between variables are not changed. This result was first developed by Cox, Ingersoll, and Ross and represents an important extension to the basic risk-neutral valuation argument.[4]

---

[3]See S. A. Ross, "The Arbitrage Theory of Capital Asset Pricing," *Journal of Economic Theory*, 13 (December 1976), 343–62.

[4]See lemma 4 in J. C. Cox, J. E. Ingersoll, and S. A. Ross, "An Intertemporal General Equilibrium Model of Asset Prices," *Econometrica*, 53 (1985), 363–84.

Suppose that a derivative dependent on θ_i ($1 \le i \le n$) provides a payoff at time T. To value the derivative, it is necessary to set the expected growth rate of each θ_i equal to $m_i - \lambda_i s_i$ keeping the volatility of each θ_i equal to s_i, and the instantaneous correlation between θ_i and θ_k equal to ρ_{ik} for all i and k. The value of the derivative is then the expected payoff discounted to the present at the risk-free rate of interest. Thus the value at time zero of a security that pays off f_T at time T is given by

$$e^{-rT} \hat{E}(f_T) \tag{19.14}$$

where $\hat{E}$ denotes expected value in a risk-neutral world (i.e., a world where the growth rate in θ_i is $m_i - \lambda_i s_i$).

If r is a stochastic variable, it is treated in the same way as the other θ_i's. The growth rate (or proportional drift rate) in r is, for the purposes of all calculations, reduced by $\lambda_r s_r$, where λ_r is the market price of the risk associated with r, and s_r is the volatility of r.[5] To value a derivative, it is necessary to calculate the expected payoff in a risk-neutral world conditional on the particular path followed by r. This expected payoff is then discounted at the average value of r on the path and the expected value is taken over all possible paths. Thus, the value at time zero of a derivative that pays off f_T at time T is given by

$$\hat{E}[e^{-\bar{r}T} f_T] \tag{19.15}$$

where $\bar{r}$ is the average risk-free interest rate between time zero and time T. This result will be proved more formally later in the chapter.

Equations (19.14) and (19.15) are true when the payoff, f_T, is some function of the paths followed by the underlying variables as well as when the payoff depends only on the final values of the variables. In the former situation, f is termed a *path-dependent derivative*. A number of types of path-dependent securities were discussed in chapter 18.

Example 19.5   Consider a security that pays off $100 at time T if the price of stock A is above X_A and the price of stock B is above X_B. We assume that prices of the two stocks are uncorrelated and that no dividends are paid. Using risk-neutral valuation, the value of the security at time zero is $100 Q_A Q_B e^{-rT}$, where Q_A is the probability of stock A's price being above X_A at time T in a risk-neutral world and Q_B is the probability of stock B's price being above X_B at time T in a risk-neutral world. It can be shown that

$$Q_A = N \left[\frac{\ln(S_A/X_A) + (r - \sigma_A^2/2)T}{\sigma_A \sqrt{T}} \right]$$

$$Q_B = N \left[\frac{\ln(S_B/X_B) + (r - \sigma_B^2/2)T}{\sigma_B \sqrt{T}} \right]$$

where S_A and S_B are the prices of stock A and stock B at time zero, and σ_A and σ_B are the volatilities of stock A and stock B.

---

[5]The parameter λ_r is negative. (This is because increases in interest rates tend to be associated with decreases in stock prices, bond prices, and the prices of other investment assets.) The growth rate of an interest rate is, therefore, higher in a risk-neutral world than in the real world.

19.3   DERIVATIVES DEPENDENT ON COMMODITY PRICES

The main problem in applying the theory we have presented thus far, when there is a variable that is not the price of a traded security, is in the estimation of its market price of risk. It turns out that we can use futures markets to finess this problem in the case of variables that are commodity prices.

From equation (12.12) the expected future price of the commodity in a risk-neutral world is its futures price. If we assume that the growth rate in the commodity price is dependent solely on time and that the volatility of the commodity price is constant, it follows that the risk-neutral process for the commodity price has the form[6]

$$\frac{dS}{S} = \mu(t)\,dt + \sigma\,dz \tag{19.16}$$

where

$$\mu(t) = \frac{\partial}{\partial t}[\ln F(t)]$$

and $F(t)$ is the futures price for a contract with maturity t.

Example 19.6   Suppose that the futures prices of live cattle at the end of July 1999, are as follows:

August 1999	62.20
October 1999	60.60
December 1999	62.70
February 2000	63.37
April 2000	64.42
June 2000	64.40

These can be used to estimate the expected growth rate in live cattle prices in a risk-neutral world. For example, the expected growth rate in live cattle prices between October and December 1999, in a risk-neutral world is

$$\ln\frac{62.70}{60.60} = 0.034$$

or 3.4% with continuous compounding. On an annualized basis, this is 20.4% per annum. As a simple illustration of the value of a derivative, consider one that will pay off at the end of July 2000, an amount equal to the average price of live cattle during the preceding year. As an approximation, the average price of live cattle during the previous year in a risk-neutral world is the average of the six futures prices just given (i.e., it is 62.95 cents). Assuming that the risk-free rate of interest is 10% per annum, the value of the derivative is,

$$62.95e^{-0.1} = 56.96 \text{ cents}$$

---

[6]Note that this is not the only process that can be assumed for commodity prices. Commodity prices are sometimes assumed to be mean reverting. In this case models analogous to those presented in chapter 21 can be used.

As mentioned in chapter 16, the standard binomial tree techniques can be adapted to cope with a time dependent expected growth rate. We can, therefore, use these procedures to model the behavior of commodity prices in a risk-neutral world when the model in equation (19.16) is assumed.

Convenience Yields

The convenience yield for a commodity was introduced in chapter 3. It is a measure of the benefits realized from ownership of the physical commodity that are not realized by the holders of a futures contract. If y is the convenience yield and u is the storage cost, the results in chapter 3 show that the commodity behaves like an investment asset that provides a return equal to $y - u$. In a risk-neutral world its growth is, therefore,

$$r - (y - u) = r - y + u$$

The convenience yield of a commodity can be related to its market price of risk. From the analysis in the first part of the chapter, the expected growth of the commodity price in a risk-neutral world is $m - \lambda s$, where m is its expected growth in the real world, s its volatility, and λ is its market price of risk. It follows that

$$m - \lambda s = r - y + u$$

or

$$y = r + u - m + \lambda s$$

19.4   MARTINGALES AND MEASURES

In the following sections we explain the role of martingales in the valuation of derivatives. We first develop results for the case where there is just one stochastic variable and then extend them to many stochastic variables. As a first step, we explain what is meant by a "martingale" and a "measure".

Martingales

A martingale is a zero-drift stochastic process. A variable, θ, follows a martingale if its process has the form

$$d\theta = \sigma\, dz$$

where dz is a Wiener process and σ is a variable that may itself be stochastic. A martingale has the convenient property that its expected value at any future time is equal to its value today. This means that

$$E(\theta_T) = \theta_0$$

where θ_0 and θ_T are the values of θ at times zero and T respectively. To understand this result we note that, over a very small time interval, the change in θ is normally distributed with zero mean. It follows that over many small time intervals the mean change in θ must also be zero. As a result, the expected value of θ at any future time must be its current value.

Measures

Up to now we have considered processes followed by variables in only two worlds: the real world and the risk-neutral world. Consider, for example, the variable f in section 19.1. Its process in the real world is

$$df = \mu f\,dt + \sigma f\,dz$$

and in a risk-neutral world this becomes

$$df = rf\,dt + \sigma f\,dz$$

The risk-neutral world is a world where the market price of risk is zero, whereas in the real world the market price of risk is given by equation (19.8):

$$\lambda = \frac{\mu - r}{\sigma}$$

By making other assumptions about the market price of risk we define other worlds that are internally consistent. In a world where the market price of risk is λ^*, the expected growth rate μ^* of the process followed by f satisfies

$$\lambda^* = \frac{\mu^* - r}{\sigma}$$

or

$$\mu^* = r + \lambda^*\sigma$$

so that

$$df = (r + \lambda^*\sigma)\,dt + \sigma\,dz \tag{19.17}$$

The market price of risk of a variable determines the growth rates of all securities dependent on the variable. As we move from one market price of risk to another, the expected growth rates of security prices change, but their volatilities remain the same. This was illustrated in section 9.7. Choosing a particular market price of risk is also referred to as defining the *probability measure*.

Equivalent Martingale Measures

Suppose that f and g are the prices of traded securities dependent on a single source of uncertainty. We assume that the securities provide no income during the time period under consideration.[7] We define

$$\theta = \frac{f}{g}$$

---

[7] Problem 19.10 extends the analysis to situations where the securities provide income.

The variable θ is the relative price of f with respect to g. It can be thought of as measuring the price of f in units of g rather than dollars. The security price g is referred to as the *numeraire*.

The *equivalent martingale measure* result shows that, when there are no arbitrage opportunities, θ is a martingale for some choice of the market price of risk. What is more, for a given numeraire security g, the same choice of the market price of risk makes θ a martingale for all securities f. This choice of the market price of risk is the volatility of g. In other words, when the market price of risk is set equal to the volatility of g, f/g is a martingale for all security prices f.

To prove this result, we suppose that the volatilities of f and g are σ_f and σ_g. From equation (19.17), in a world where the market price of risk is σ_g:

$$df = (r + \sigma_g \sigma_f)f \, dt + \sigma_f f \, dz$$

$$dg = (r + \sigma_g^2)g \, dt + \sigma_g g \, dz$$

Using Ito's lemma:

$$d \ln f = (r + \sigma_g \sigma_f - \sigma_f^2/2) \, dt + \sigma_f \, dz$$

$$d \ln g = (r + \sigma_g^2/2) \, dt + \sigma_g \, dz$$

so that

$$d(\ln f - \ln g) = (\sigma_g \sigma_f - \sigma_f^2/2 - \sigma_g^2/2) \, dt + (\sigma_f - \sigma_g) \, dz$$

or

$$d \left(\ln \frac{f}{g} \right) = -\frac{(\sigma_f - \sigma_g)^2}{2} \, dt + (\sigma_f - \sigma_g) \, dz$$

Using Ito's lemma to determine the process for f/g from the process for $\ln (f/g)$ we obtain

$$d \left(\frac{f}{g} \right) = (\sigma_f - \sigma_g) \frac{f}{g} \, dz \qquad (19.18)$$

showing that f/g is a martingale.

This provides the required result. We refer to a world where the market price of risk is σ_g as a world that is *forward risk neutral* with respect to g.

Because f/g is a martingale in a world that is forward risk neutral with respect to g, it follows that

$$\frac{f_0}{g_0} = E_g \left(\frac{f_T}{g_T} \right)$$

or

$$f_0 = g_0 E_g \left(\frac{f_T}{g_T} \right) \qquad (19.19)$$

where E_g denotes expectations in a world that is forward risk neutral with respect to g.

19.5   ALTERNATIVE CHOICES FOR THE NUMERAIRE

We present a number of examples of the equivalent martingale measure result here. The first example shows that it is consistent with the traditional risk-neutral valuation result we have used up to now. The other examples prepare the way for the valuation of bond options, interest-rate caps, and swap options in chapter 20.

Money Market Account as the Numeraire

The dollar money market account is a security that is worth $1 at time zero and earns the instantaneous risk-free rate, r, at any given time.[8] The variable r may be stochastic. If we set g equal to the money market account, it grows at rate r, so that

$$dg = rg\,dt \qquad (19.20)$$

The volatility of g is zero. The world that is forward risk neutral with respect to g is, therefore, a world where the market price of risk is zero (that is, the traditional risk-neutral world). It follows from equation (19.19), that

$$f_0 = g_0\hat{E}\left(\frac{f_T}{g_T}\right) \qquad (19.21)$$

where $\hat{E}$ denotes expectations in the usual risk-neutral world.

In this case $g_0 = 1$ and

$$g_T = e^{\int_0^T r\,dt}$$

so that equation (19.21) reduces to

$$f_0 = \hat{E}\left(e^{-\int_0^T r\,dt}f_T\right) \qquad (19.22)$$

or

$$f_0 = \hat{E}\left(e^{-\bar{r}T}f_T\right) \qquad (19.23)$$

This provides a proof of equation (19.15). When the short-term interest rate r is assumed to be constant, equation (19.23) reduces to

$$f_0 = e^{-rT}\hat{E}(f_T)$$

or the risk-neutral valuation relationship we used in earlier chapters.

---

[8]The money account is the limit as Δt approaches zero of the following security. For the first short period of time of length Δt, it is invested at the initial Δt period rate; at time Δt, it is reinvested for a further period of time Δt at the new Δt period rate; at time $2\Delta t$, it is again reinvested for a further period of time Δt at the new Δt period rate; and so on. The money market accounts in other currencies are defined analogously to the dollar money market account.

To summarize, we have shown that using the money market account as the numeraire is equivalent to using traditional risk-neutral valuation arguments.

Zero-Coupon Bond Price as the Numeraire

Define $P(t, T)$ as the price at time t of a zero-coupon bond that pays off \$1 at time T. We now explore the implications of setting g equal to $P(t, T)$. We use E_T to denote expectations in a world that is forward risk neutral with respect to $P(t, T)$. Because $g_T = P(T, T) = 1$ and $g_0 = P(0, T)$, equation (19.19) gives

$$f_0 = P(0, T)E_T[f_T] \tag{19.24}$$

Notice the difference between equations (19.24) and (19.23). In equation (19.23), the discounting is inside the expectations operator. In equation (19.24) the discounting, as represented by the $P(0, T)$ term, is outside the expectations operator. By using a world that is forward risk neutral with respect to $P(t, T)$, we considerably simplify things for a security that provides a payoff solely at time T.

Define F as the forward price of f for a contract maturing at time T. Simple arbitrage arguments similar to those in chapter 3 show that

$$F = \frac{f_0}{P(0, T)} \tag{19.25}$$

Equations (19.24) and (19.25) jointly imply that

$$F = E_T[f_T] \tag{19.26}$$

showing that, in a world that is forward risk neutral with respect to $P(t, T)$, the forward price of f is its expected future spot price. (This can be contrasted with the traditional risk-neutral world where the expected future spot price of a variable is its futures price.)

Equation (19.24) shows that we can value any security that provides a payoff at time T by calculating its expected payoff in a world that is forward risk neutral with respect to a bond maturing at time T and discounting at the risk-free rate for maturity T. Equation (19.26) shows that it is correct to assume that the expected value of the underlying asset equals its forward value when computing the expected payoff. These results will be critical to our understanding of the standard market model for bond options in the next chapter.

Interest Rates When a Bond Price Is the Numeraire

For our next result, we define $R(t, T_1, T_2)$ as the forward interest rate as seen at time t for the period between T_1 and T_2 expressed with a compounding period of $T_2 - T_1$. The forward price, as seen at time t, of a zero-coupon bond lasting between times T_1 and T_2 is

$$\frac{P(t, T_2)}{P(t, T_1)}$$

Because a forward interest rate is the interest rate implied by the corresponding forward bond price it follows that

$$\frac{1}{[1 + (T_2 - T_1)R(t, T_1, T_2)]} = \frac{P(t, T_2)}{P(t, T_1)}$$

so that

$$R(t, T_1, T_2) = \frac{1}{T_2 - T_1}\left[\frac{P(t, T_1)}{P(t, T_2)} - 1\right]$$

or

$$R(t, T_1, T_2) = \frac{1}{T_2 - T_1}\left[\frac{P(t, T_1) - P(t, T_2)}{P(t, T_2)}\right]$$

Setting

$$f = \frac{1}{T_2 - T_1}[P(t, T_1) - P(t, T_2)]$$

and $g = P(t, T_2)$, the equivalent martingale measure result shows that $R(t, T_1, T_2)$ is a martingale in a world that is forward risk neutral with respect to $P(t, T_2)$. This means that

$$R(0, T_1, T_2) = E_2[R(T_1, T_1, T_2)] \tag{19.27}$$

where E_2 denotes expectations in a world that is forward risk neutral with respect to $P(t, T_2)$.

We have shown that the forward interest rate equals the expected future interest rate in a world that is forward risk neutral with respect to a zero-coupon bond maturing at time T_2. This result, when combined with the result in equation (19.24), will be critical to our understanding of the standard market model for interest-rate caps in the next chapter.

Annuity Factor as the Numeraire

For our next application of equivalent martingale measure arguments we consider a swap starting at time T_n with payment dates at times $T_{n+1}, T_{n+2}, \ldots, T_{N+1}$. Assume that the principal underlying the swap is \$1. Suppose that the forward swap rate (i.e., the interest rate on the fixed side that makes the swap have a value of zero) is $S_{n,N}(t)$. The value of the fixed side of the swap is

$$S_{n,N}(t)A_{n,N}(t)$$

where

$$A_{n,N}(t) = \sum_{i=n}^{N}(T_{i+1} - T_i)P(t, T_{i+1})$$

We showed in chapter 5 that, when the principal is added to the payment on the last payment date swap, the value of the floating side of the swap on the initiation date equals the underlying principal. In the context of our present example, this result shows that, if we add \$1 at time T_{N+1}, the floating side is worth \$1 at time T_n. The value of \$1 received at time T_{N+1} is $P(t, T_{N+1})$. The value of \$1 at time T_n is $P(t, T_n)$. The value of the floating side is, therefore,

$$P(t, T_n) - P(t, T_{N+1})$$

Equating the values of the fixed and floating sides when the swap rate is $S_{n,N}(t)$ we obtain

$$S_{n,N}(t)A_{n,N}(t) = P(t, T_n) - P(t, T_{N+1})$$

or

$$S_{n,N}(t) = \frac{P(t, T_n) - P(t, T_{N+1})}{A_{n,N}(t)}$$

We can apply the equivalent martingale measure result by setting f equal to $P(t, T_n) - P(t, T_{N+1})$ and g equal to $A_{n,N}(t)$. This leads to

$$S_{n,N}(t) = E_A[S_{n,N}(T)] \tag{19.28}$$

where E_A denotes expectations in a world that is forward risk neutral with respect to $A_{n,N}(t)$. In a world that is forward risk neutral with respect to $A_{n,N}(t)$ the expected future swap rate is, therefore, the current swap rate.

For any security, f, the result in equation (19.19) shows

$$f_0 = A_{n,N}(t)E_A\left[\frac{f_T}{A_{n,N}(T)}\right] \tag{19.29}$$

This result, when combined with the result in equation (19.28), will be critical to our understanding of the standard market model for swap options in the next chapter.

19.6 EXTENSION TO MULTIPLE INDEPENDENT FACTORS

The results presented in sections 19.4 and 19.5 can be extended to cover the situation when there are many factors. Assume that there are n independent factors and that the processes for f and g in the usual risk-neutral world are

$$df = r_f\, dt + \sum_{i=1}^{n} \sigma_{f,i} f\, dz_i$$

and

$$dg = r_g\, dt + \sum_{i=1}^{n} \sigma_{g,i} g\, dz_i$$

As shown in section 19.2, we can define other worlds that are internally consistent by setting

$$df = \left[r + \sum_{i=1}^{n} \lambda_i^* \sigma_{f,i} \right] f \, dt + \sum_{i=1}^{n} \sigma_{f,i} f \, dz_i$$

and

$$dg = \left[r + \sum_{i=1}^{n} \lambda_i^* \sigma_{g,i} \right] g \, dt + \sum_{i=1}^{n} \sigma_{g,i} g \, dz_i$$

where the λ_i^* $(1 \leq i \leq n)$ are the n market prices of risk.

We define a world that is forward risk neutral with respect to g as a world where $\lambda_i^* = \sigma_{g,i}$. It can be shown from Ito's lemma, using the fact that the dz_i are uncorrelated, that the process followed by f/g in this world has zero drift. The rest of the results in the last two sections [from equation (19.19) onward] are still true.

19.7   APPLICATIONS

In this section we provide two applications of the forward risk-neutral valuation argument. Several others are in chapter 20.

The Black–Scholes Result

We can use forward risk-neutral arguments to extend the Black–Scholes result to situations where interest rates are stochastic. Consider a European call option maturing at time T on a non-dividend-paying stock. From equation (19.24) the call option's price is given by

$$c = P(0, T) E_T [\max (S_T - X, 0)] \tag{19.30}$$

where S_T is the stock price at time T, X is the strike price, and E_T denotes expectations in a world that is forward risk neutral with respect to a zero-coupon bond maturing at time T. Define R as the zero rate for maturity T so that

$$P(0, T) = e^{-RT}$$

and equation (19.30) becomes

$$c = e^{-RT} E_T [\max (S_T - X, 0)] \tag{19.31}$$

If we assume that S_T is lognormal in the forward risk neutral world we are considering with the standard deviation of $\ln (S_T)$ equal to s, Appendix 11A shows that

$$E_T [\max (S_T - X, 0)] = E_T (S_T) N(d_1) - X N(d_2) \tag{19.32}$$

where

$$d_1 = \frac{\ln [E_T(S_T)/X] + s^2/2}{s}$$

and

$$d_2 = \frac{\ln [E_T(S_T)/X] - s^2/2}{s}$$

From equation (19.26), $E_T(S_T)$ is the forward stock price for a contract maturing at time T. Hence

$$E_T(S_T) = S_0 e^{RT} \tag{19.33}$$

Equations (19.32) and (19.33) give

$$c = S_0 N(d_1) - X e^{-RT} N(d_2)$$

where

$$d_1 = \frac{\ln [S_0/X] + RT + s^2/2}{s}$$

and

$$d_2 = \frac{\ln [S_0/X] + RT - s^2/2}{s}$$

If the stock price volatility σ is defined so that $\sigma \sqrt{T} = s$, the expressions for d_1 and d_2 become

$$d_1 = \frac{\ln [S_0/X] + (R + \sigma^2/2)T}{\sigma \sqrt{T}}$$

and

$$d_2 = \frac{\ln [S_0/X] + (R - \sigma^2/2)T}{\sigma \sqrt{T}}$$

showing that the call price is given by the Black–Scholes formula with r replaced by R. Similar results can be produced for European put options.

Option to Exchange One Asset for Another

Consider next an option to exchange an investment asset worth U for an investment asset worth V. This has already been discussed in section 18.1. As in section 18.1, we suppose that the volatilities of U and V are σ_U and σ_V and the coefficient of correlation between them is ρ.

Suppose first that the assets provide no income. We choose the numeraire security g to be U. Setting $f = V$ in equation (19.19) we obtain

$$V_0 = U_0 E_U \left(\frac{V_T}{U_T} \right) \tag{19.34}$$

where E_U denotes expectations in a world that is forward risk neutral with respect to U.

Next we set f in equation (19.19) as the value the option under consideration so that $f_T = \max(V_T - U_T, 0)$. It follows that

$$f_0 = U_0 E_U \left[\frac{\max(V_T - U_T, 0)}{U_T} \right]$$

or

$$f_0 = U_0 E_U \left[\max \left(\frac{V_T}{U_T} - 1, 0 \right) \right] \qquad (19.35)$$

The volatility of V/U is $\hat{\sigma}$ where

$$\hat{\sigma} = \sigma_U^2 + \sigma_V^2 - 2\rho\sigma_U\sigma_V$$

From Appendix 11A, equation (19.35) becomes

$$f_0 = U_0 \left[E_U \left(\frac{V_T}{U_T} \right) N(d_1) - N(d_2) \right]$$

where

$$d_1 = \frac{\ln(V_0/U_0) + \hat{\sigma}^2 T/2}{\hat{\sigma}\sqrt{T}}$$

and

$$d_2 = d_1 - \hat{\sigma}\sqrt{T}$$

Substituting from equation (19.34) this becomes

$$f_0 = V_0 N(d_1) - U_0 N(d_2) \qquad (19.36)$$

Problem 19.10 shows that when f and g provide income at rate q_f and q_g equation (19.19) becomes

$$f_0 = g_0 e^{(q_f - q_g)T} E_g \left(\frac{f_T}{g_T} \right)$$

This means that equations (19.34) and (19.35) become

$$E_U \left(\frac{V_T}{U_T} \right) = e^{(q_U - q_V)T} \frac{V_0}{U_0}$$

and

$$f_0 = e^{-q_U T} U_0 E_U \left[\max \left(\frac{V_T}{U_T} - 1, 0 \right) \right]$$

and equation (19.36) becomes

$$f_0 = e^{-q_V T} V_0 N(d_1) - e^{-q_U T} U_0 N(d_2)$$

with d_1 and d_2 being redefined as

$$d_1 = \frac{\ln(V_0/U_0) + (q_U - q_V + \hat{\sigma}^2/2)T}{\hat{\sigma}\sqrt{T}}$$

and

$$d_2 = d_1 - \hat{\sigma}\sqrt{T}$$

This is the result given in equation (18.3).

19.8 CHANGE OF NUMERAIRE

In this section we consider the impact of a change in numeraire on the process followed by a market variable. In a world that is forward risk neutral with respect to g, the process followed by a traded security f is

$$df = \left[r + \sum_{i=1}^{n} \sigma_{g,i}\sigma_{f,i}\right]f\,dt + \sum_{i=1}^{n} \sigma_{f,i}f\,dz_i$$

Similarly, in a world that is forward risk neutral with respect to another security h the process followed by f is

$$df = \left[r + \sum_{i=1}^{n} \sigma_{h,i}\sigma_{f,i}\right]f\,dt + \sum_{i=1}^{n} \sigma_{f,i}f\,dz_i$$

where $\sigma_{h,i}$ is the ith component of the volatility of h.

The effect of moving from a world that is forward risk neutral with respect to g to one that is forward risk neutral with respect to h (that is, of changing the numeraire from g to h) is, therefore, to increase the expected growth rate of the price of any traded security f by

$$\sum_{i=1}^{n}(\sigma_{h,i} - \sigma_{g,i})\sigma_{f,i}$$

Consider next a variable, v, that is a function of the prices of traded securities. (The variable, v, is not necessarily the price of a traded security itself.) Define $\sigma_{v,i}$ as the ith component of the volatility of v. From Ito's lemma in Appendix 19A we can calculate what happens to the process followed by v when there is a change in numeraire causing the expected growth rate of the underlying traded securities to change. It turns out that the expected growth rate of v responds to a change in numeraire in the same way as the expected growth rate of the prices of traded securities. (See Problem 10.6 for the situation where there is only one stochastic variable.) It increases by

$$\alpha_v = \sum_{i=1}^{n}(\sigma_{h,i} - \sigma_{g,i})\sigma_{v,i} \tag{19.37}$$

Define $q = f/g$. We will refer to this as the *numeraire ratio*. The term $\sigma_{h,i} - \sigma_{g,i}$ is the ith component volatility of q. Because we are assuming the components are independent, equation (19.37) becomes

$$\alpha_v = \rho \sigma_v \sigma_q \qquad (19.38)$$

where σ_v is the total volatility of v, σ_q is the total volatility of q, and ρ is the instantaneous correlation between v and q.[9]

This is a surprisingly simple result. The adjustment to the expected growth rate of a variable, v, when we change from one numeraire to another is the instantaneous covariance between the proportional change in v and proportional change in the numeraire ratio. We will apply the result to quantos in this chapter and to what are termed timing adjustments in chapter 20.

19.9 QUANTOS

A *quanto* or *cross-currency derivative* is an instrument where two currencies are involved. The payoff is defined in terms of a variable that is measured in one of the currencies and the payoff is made the other currency. One example of a quanto is the CME futures contract on the Nikkei mentioned in section 3.7. The market variable underlying this contract is the Nikkei 225 index (which is measured in yen), but the contract is settled in U.S. dollars.

Consider a quanto that provides a payoff in currency X at time T. We assume that the payoff depends on the value of a variable, V, that is observed in currency Y at time T. Define

$F(t)$: Forward value of V at time t for a contract denominated in currency Y and maturing at time T

V_T: Value of V at time T

$P_X(t, T)$: Value at time t in currency X of a zero-coupon bond paying off 1 unit of currency X at time T

$P_Y(t, T)$: Value at time t in currency X of a zero-coupon bond paying off 1 unit of currency Y at time T

$E_X(\cdot)$: Expectation at time zero in a world that is forward risk neutral with respect to $P_X(t, T)$

$E_Y(\cdot)$: Expectation at time zero in a world that is forward risk neutral with respect to $P_Y(t, T)$

$G(t)$: Forward exchange rate (number of units of currency Y that equal one unit of currency X) for a contract maturing at time T

σ_F: Volatility of $F(t)$

σ_G: Volatility of $G(t)$

ρ: Instantaneous correlation between $F(t)$ and $G(t)$

S_T: Spot exchange rate at time $T [= G(T)]$

---

[9]The total volatility of a variable can be calculated as the square root of the sum of the squares of its component volatilities.

In equation (19.19) we can set $g = P_Y(t, T)$ and f equal to the price of a security, measured in currency X, that pays off V_T units of currency Y at time T. Then $f_T = V_T/S_T$ and $g_T = 1/S_T$ so that $f_0 = P_Y(0, T)E_Y(V_T)$. For there to be no arbitrage $F(0) = f_0/P_Y(0, T)$. Hence

$$E_Y(V_T) = F(0)$$

To value the derivative we require $E_X(V_T)$. The variable $G(t)$ is given by

$$G(t) = \frac{P_X(t, T)}{P_Y(t, T)}$$

It is the numeraire ratio when we move from the $P_Y(t, T)$ world to the $P_X(t, T)$ world.
From equation (19.38), the expected growth rate of $F(t)$, when we move from the $P_Y(t, T)$ world to the $P_X(t, T)$ world, increases by

$$\rho\sigma_F\sigma_G$$

It follows that it is approximately true that

$$E_X[F(T)] = E_Y[F(T)]e^{\rho\sigma_F\sigma_G T}$$

or because $V_T = F(T)$ and $E_Y(V_T) = F(0)$

$$E_X(V_T) = F(0)e^{\rho\sigma_F\sigma_G T} \tag{19.39}$$

This relationship is in turn approximately the same as

$$E_X[V_T] = F(0)(1 + \rho\sigma_F\sigma_G T) \tag{19.40}$$

Example 19.7   Suppose that the current value of the Nikkei stock index for a one-year contract is 15,000 yen, the one-year dollar risk-free rate is 5%, the one-year yen risk-free rate is 2%, and the yen dividend yield is 1%. The forward price of the Nikkei for a contract denominated in yen can be calculated in the usual way from equation (3.12) as

$$15,000e^{(0.02-0.01)\times 1} = 15,150.75$$

Suppose that the volatility of the one-year forward price of the index is 20%, the volatility of the one-year forward yen per dollar exchange rate is 12%, and the correlation of the one-year forward Nikkei with the one-year forward exchange rate is 0.3. In this case $F(0) = 15,150.75$, $\sigma_F = 0.20$, $\sigma_G = 0.12$, and $\rho = 0.3$. From equation (19.39), the expected value of the Nikkei in a world that is forward risk neutral with respect to a dollar bond maturing in one year is

$$15,150.75e^{0.3\times 0.2\times 0.12\times 1} = 15,260.23.39$$

This is the forward price of the Nikkei for a contract that provides a payoff in dollars rather than yen. (As an approximation, it is also the futures price of such a contract.)

Differential Swaps

A *differential swap*, sometimes referred to as a *diff swap*, is an interest rate swap where a floating interest rate is observed in one currency and applied to a principal in another currency. Suppose that we observe the LIBOR rate for the period between T^*

and T in currency Y and apply it to a principal of L in currency X with the payment taking place at time T. Define R as the forward interest rate between T^* and T in currency Y. An analysis similar to that just given shows that the value of the payment is

$$P_X(0, T)R_0\tau L e^{\rho\sigma_G\sigma_R T^*}$$

where $\tau = T - T^*$, R_0 is value of R today, σ_R is the volatility of R, ρ is the correlation between R and G, and other variables are defined as above.

Using Traditional Risk-Neutral Measures

The forward risk-neutral measure we have been using works well when payoffs occur at only one time. In other situations it is sometimes more appropriate to use the traditional risk-neutral measures. Suppose we know the process followed by a variable, V in the traditional currency Y risk-neutral world and we wish to estimate its process in the traditional currency X risk-neutral world. Define

  S: Spot exchange rate (units of Y per unit of X)
  σ_S: Volatility of S
  σ_V: Volatility of V
  ρ: Instantaneous correlation between S and V

In this case, the change of numeraire is from the money market account in currency Y to the money market account in currency X (with both money market accounts being denominated in currency X). As indicated by equation (19.20), each money market account has a stochastic growth rate, but zero volatility. It can be shown from Ito's lemma that the volatility of the numeraire ratio is σ_S. The change of numeraire, therefore, involves increasing the expected growth rate of V by

$$\rho\sigma_V\sigma_S$$

The market price of risk changes from zero to $\rho\sigma_S$.

> **Example 19.8**   The current level of the S&P 500 is 1,200 and a two-year American-style option on the index provides, in pounds sterling, the excess of the index level over the strike price. The risk-free rates in sterling and dollars are both constant at 5% and 3%, respectively, the correlation between the dollars-per-sterling exchange rate and the S&P 500 is 0.2, the volatility of the S&P 500 is 25%, and the volatility of the exchange rate is 12%. The dividend yield on the S&P 500 is 1.5%. We can value this option by constructing a binomial tree in the S&P 500 using as the numeraire the money market account in the U.K. (that is, using the traditional risk-neutral as seen from the perspective of a U.K. investor). We have just shown that the change in numeraire leads to an increase in the expected growth rate of
>
> $$0.2 \times 0.25 \times 0.12 = 0.006$$
>
> or 0.6%. Increasing the expected growth rate by 0.6% is the same as reducing the dividend yield to $1.5\% - 0.6\% = 0.9\%$. The parameters for the binomial tree are, therefore, $S = 1,200$, $X = 1,200$, $r = 0.03$, $q = 0.009$, $\sigma = 0.25$, and $T = 2$. Using 100 time steps DerivaGem gives the value of the option as £144.57.

19.10   SIEGEL'S PARADOX

An interesting application of the results in the last two sections is to what has become known as *Siegel's Paradox*. Consider two currencies, X and Y. Define S as the number of units of currency Y per unit of currency X. Because an exchange rate behaves like a stock paying a continuous dividend yield equal to the foreign risk-free interest rate, the risk-neutral process for S is

$$dS = (r_Y - r_X)S\,dt + \sigma_S S\,dz \qquad (19.41)$$

where r_X and r_Y are the interest rates (assumed constant) in currencies X and Y.

From Ito's lemma, equation (19.41) implies that the process for $1/S$ is

$$d(1/S) = (r_X - r_Y + \sigma_S^2)(1/S)\,dt - \sigma_S(1/S)\,dz \qquad (19.42)$$

This leads to what is known as *Siegel's paradox*. Because the expected growth rate of S is $r_Y - r_X$, symmetry suggests that the expected growth rate of $1/S$ should be $r_X - r_Y$. It appears to be a paradox that the expected growth rate in equation (19.42) is $r_X - r_Y + \sigma_S^2$ rather than $r_X - r_Y$.

To understand Siegel's Paradox, it is necessary to appreciate that equation (19.41) is the risk-neutral process for S in a world where the numeraire is the money market account in currency Y. Equation (19.42), because it is deduced from equation (19.41), therefore gives the risk-neutral process for $1/S$ when this is the numeraire. Because $1/S$ is the number of units of X per unit of Y, to be symmetrical we should measure its process in a world where the numeraire is the money market account in currency X. The previous section shows that when we change numeraires, from the money market account in currency Y to the money market account in currency X, the growth rate of $1/S$, increases by $\rho \sigma_V \sigma_S$ where $V = 1/S$ and ρ is the correlation between S and $1/S$. In this case, $\rho = -1$ and $\sigma_V = \sigma_S$. It follows that the change of numeraire causes the growth rate of $1/S$ to increase by $-\sigma_S^2$. From equation (19.42) the growth rate of $1/S$ in a world where the numeraire is the money market account in currency X rather than currency Y is, therefore,

$$d(1/S) = (r_X - r_Y)(1/S)\,dt - \sigma_S(1/S)\,dz \qquad (19.43)$$

This is symmetrical with the process for S in equation (19.41).

SUMMARY

The market price of risk of a variable defines the trade offs between risk and return for traded securities dependent on the variable. When there is one underlying variable, a derivative's excess return over the risk-free rate equals the market price of risk multiplied by the variable's volatility. When there are many underlying variables, the excess return is the sum of the market price of risk multiplied by the volatility for each variable.

A powerful tool in the valuation of derivatives is risk-neutral valuation, introduced in chapters 9 and 11. The principle of risk-neutral valuation shows that, if we assume that the world is risk neutral when valuing derivatives, we get the right answer—not just in a risk-neutral world, but in all other worlds as well. In the traditional risk-neutral world, the market price of risk of all variables is zero. Furthermore, the expected price of any asset in this world is its futures price.

In this chapter, we have extended the principle of risk-neutral valuation. We have shown that, when interest rates are stochastic, there are many interesting and useful alternatives to the traditional risk-neutral world. When there is only one stochastic variable, a world is defined as forward risk neutral with respect to a security price if the market price of risk for the variable is set equal to the volatility of the security price. A similar definition applies when there are many stochastic variables. We have shown that in a world that is forward risk neutral with respect to a security price g, f/g is a martingale for all other security prices f. A martingale is a zero drift stochastic process. Any variable following a martingale has the simplifying property that its expected value at any future time equals its value today. It turns out that by appropriately choosing the numeraire security, g, we can simplify the valuation of many interest rate dependent derivatives.

We will make use of these results in chapters 20 and 22.

SUGGESTIONS FOR FURTHER READING

Baxter, M. and A. Rennie. *Financial Calculus*. Cambridge: Cambridge University Press 1996.

Cox J. C., J. E. Ingersoll, and S. A. Ross. "An Intertemporal General Equilibrium Model of Asset Prices," *Econometrica*, 53 (1985), 363–84.

Duffie, D. *Dynamic Asset Pricing Theory*. Princeton: Princeton University Press 1992.

Garman, M. "A General Theory of Asset Valuation Under Diffusion State Processes," Working Paper 50, University of California, Berkeley, 1976.

Harrison, J. M., and D. M. Kreps. "Martingales and Arbitrage in Multiperiod Securities Markets," *Journal of Economic Theory*, 20 (1979), 381–408.

Harrison, J. M., and S. R. Pliska. "Martingales and Stochastic Integrals in the Theory of Continuous Trading," *Stochastic Processes and Their Applications*, 11 (1981), 215–260.

Hull, J. C., and A. White. "An Overview of the Pricing of Contingent Claims," *Canadian Journal of Administrative Sciences*, 5 (September 1988), 55–61.

Jamshidian, F. "Corralling Quantos," *RISK*, (March 1994), 71–75.

Reiner, E. "Quanto Mechanics," *RISK*, (March 1992) 59–63.

Sundaram, R. K. "Equivalent Martingale Measures: An Expository Note," *Journal of Derivatives*, 5, 1 (Fall 1997), 85–98.

QUESTIONS AND PROBLEMS
(ANSWERS IN THE SOLUTIONS MANUAL)

19.1. How is the market price of risk defined for a variable that is not the price of an investment asset?

19.2. Suppose that the market price of risk for gold is zero. If the storage costs are 1% per annum and the risk-free rate of interest is 6% per annum, what is the expected growth rate in the price of gold?

19.3. A security's price is positively dependent on two variables: the price of copper and the yen–dollar exchange rate. Suppose that the market price of risk for these variables is 0.5 and 0.1, respectively. If the price of copper were held fixed, the volatility of the security would be 8% per annum; if the yen–dollar exchange rate were held fixed, the volatility of the security would be 12% per annum. The risk-free interest rate is 7% per annum. What is the expected rate of return from the security? If the two variables are uncorrelated with each other, what is the volatility of the security?

19.4. An oil company is set up solely for the purpose of exploring for oil in a certain small area of Texas. Its value depends primarily on two stochastic variables: the price of oil and the quantity of proven oil reserves. Discuss whether the market price of risk for the second of these two variables is likely to be positive, negative, or zero.

19.5. Deduce the differential equation for a derivative dependent on the prices of two non-dividend-paying traded securities by forming a riskless portfolio consisting of the derivative and the two traded securities. Verify that the differential equation is the same as the one given in equation (19B.11).

19.6. The convenience yield for soybean oil is 5% per annum, the storage costs are 1% per annum, the risk-free interest rate is 6% per annum, and the expected growth in the price of soybean oil is zero. What is the relationship between the six-month futures price and the expected price in six months?

19.7. The market price of risk for copper is 0.5, the volatility of copper prices is 20% per annum, the spot price is 80 cents per pound, and the six-month futures price is 75 cents per pound. What is the expected percentage growth rate in copper prices over the next six months?

19.8. Suppose that an interest rate, x, follows the process

$$dx = a(x_0 - x)\,dt + c\,\sqrt{x}\,dz$$

where a, x_0, and c are positive constants. Suppose further that the market price of risk for x is λ. What is the process for r in the traditional risk-neutral world?

19.9. Repeat the analysis in section 19.1 for the situation where the security f provides income at rate q. What is the relationship between expected growth rate and volatility for f? What is the differential equation satisfied by f? (*Hint*: Form a new security, f^* that provides no income by assuming that all the income from f is reinvested in f.)

19.10. Show that when f and g provide income at rates q_f and q_g respectively, equation (19.19) becomes

$$f_0 = g_0 e^{(q_f - q_g)T} E_g \left(\frac{f_T}{g_T} \right)$$

(*Hint*: Form new securities f^* and g^* that provide no income by assuming that all the income from f is reinvested in f and all the income in g is reinvested in g.)

19.11. Consider a commodity with constant volatility, σ, and an expected growth rate that is a function solely of time. Show that in the traditional risk-neutral world,

$$\ln S_T \sim \phi \left[\ln F(T) - \frac{\sigma^2}{2} T, \sigma \sqrt{T} \right]$$

where S_T is the value of the commodity at time T and $F(t)$ is the futures price at time zero for a contract maturing at time t.

19.12. "The expected future value of an interest rate in a risk-neutral world is greater than it is in the real world." What does this statement imply about the market price of risk for (a) an interest rate and (b) a bond price. Do you think the statement is likely to be true? Give reasons.

19.13. The variable S is an investment asset providing income at rate q measured in currency A. It follows the process

$$dS = \mu_S S\, dt + \sigma_S S\, dz$$

in the real world. Defining new variables as necessary, give the process followed by S, and the corresponding market price of risk, in

(a) A world that is the traditional risk neutral world for currency A.

(b) A world that is the traditional risk neutral world for currency B.

(c) A world that is forward risk neutral with respect to a zero-coupon currency A bond maturing at time T.

(d) A world that is forward risk neutral with respect to a zero-coupon currency B bond maturing at time T.

19.14. A call option provides a payoff at time T of max $(S_T - X, 0)$ yen, where S_T is the dollar price of gold at time T and X is the strike price. Assuming that the storage costs of gold are zero and defining other variables as necessary, calculate the value of the contract.

19.15. Suppose that the Toronto 35 index of Canadian stocks currently stands at 400. The Canadian dollar is currently worth 0.70 U.S. dollars. The risk-free interest rates in Canada and the U.S. are constant at 6% and 4%, respectively. The dividend yield on the index is 2%. Define Q as the number of Canadian dollars per U.S dollar and S as the value of the index. The volatility of S is 20%, the volatility of Q is 6%, and the correlation between S and Q is 0.4. Use DerivaGem to determine the value of a two-year American-style call option on the index if

(a) It pays off in Canadian dollars the amount by which the index exceeds 400.
(b) It pays off in U.S. dollars the amount by which the index exceeds 400.

ASSIGNMENT QUESTIONS

19.16. A security pays off $S_1 S_2$ at time T, where S_1 is the level of the S&P 500 index and S_2 is the price of oil. Assume that both S_1 and S_2 follow geometric Brownian motion and are uncorrelated. Defining other variables as necessary, calculate the value of the security at time zero.

19.17. Suppose that the price of a zero-coupon bond maturing at time T follows the process

$$dP(t, T) = \mu_P P(t, T) dt + \sigma_P P(t, T) dz$$

and the price of a derivative dependent on the bond follows the process

$$df = \mu_f f \, dt + \sigma_f f \, dz$$

Assume only one source of uncertainty and that f provides no income.

(a) What is the forward price, F, of f for a contract maturing at time T?

(b) What is the process followed by F in a world that is forward risk neutral with respect to $P(t, T)$?

(c) What is the process followed by F in the traditional risk-neutral world?

(d) What is the process followed by f in a world that is forward risk neutral with respect to a bond maturing at time T^* where $T^* \neq T$? Assume that σ_P^* is the volatility of this bond.

19.18. Consider an instrument that will pay off S dollars in two years where S is the value of the Nikkei index. The index is currently 20,000. The dollar–yen exchange rate (yen per dollar) is 100. The correlation between the exchange rate and the index is 0.3 and the dividend yield on the index is 1% per annum. The volatility of the Nikkei index is 20% and the volatility of the yen–dollar exchange rate is 12%. The interest rates (assumed constant) in the U.S. and Japan are 4% and 2%, respectively.

(a) What is the value of the instrument?

(b) Suppose that the exchange rate at some point during the life of the instrument is Q and the level of the index is S. Show that a U.S. investor can create a portfolio that changes in value by approximately ΔS dollar when the index $F(0) = \$15, 150.75$, $\sigma_F = 0.20$, σ_g changes in value by ΔS yen by investing S dollars in the Nikkei (so that the investment equals Q times the Nikkei) and shorting SQ yen.

(c) Confirm that this is correct by supposing that the index changes from 20,000 to 20,050 and the exchange rate changes from 100 to 99.7.

(d) How would you hedge the instrument under consideration?

APPENDIX 19A

Generalization of Ito's Lemma

Ito's lemma, as presented in Appendix 10A, provides the process followed by a function of a single stochastic variable. Here we present a generalized version of Ito's lemma for the process followed by a function of several stochastic variables.

Suppose that a function, f, depends on the n variables $x_1, x_2, \ldots, x_n$ and time, t. Suppose further that x_i follows an Ito process with instantaneous drift a_i and instantaneous variance b_i^2 ($1 \le i \le n$), that is,

$$dx_i = a_i \, dt + b_i \, dz_i \tag{19A.1}$$

where dz_i is a Wiener process ($1 \le i \le n$). Each a_i and b_i may be any function of all the x_i's and t. A Taylor series expansion of f gives

$$\Delta f = \sum_i \frac{\partial f}{\partial x_i} \Delta x_i + \frac{\partial f}{\partial t} \Delta t + \frac{1}{2} \sum_i \sum_j \frac{\partial^2 f}{\partial x_i \partial x_j} \Delta x_i \Delta x_j + \frac{1}{2} \sum_j \frac{\partial^2 f}{\partial x_i \partial t} \Delta x_i \Delta t + \cdots \tag{19A.2}$$

Equation (19A.1) can be discretized as

$$\Delta x_i = a_i \Delta t + b_i \epsilon_i \sqrt{\Delta t}$$

where ϵ_i is a random sample from a standardized normal distribution. The correlation, ρ_{ij}, between dz_i and dz_j is defined as the correlation between ϵ_i and ϵ_j. In Appendix 10A it was argued that

$$\lim_{\Delta t \to 0} \Delta x_i^2 = b_i^2 \, dt$$

Similarly,

$$\lim_{\Delta t \to 0} \Delta x_i \Delta x_j = b_i b_j \rho_{ij} \, dt$$

As $\Delta t \to 0$, the first three terms in the expansion of Δf in equation (19A.2) are of order Δt. All other terms are of higher order. Hence

$$df = \sum_i \frac{\partial f}{\partial x_i} \, dx_i + \frac{\partial f}{\partial t} \, dt + \frac{1}{2} \sum_i \sum_j \frac{\partial^2 f}{\partial x_i \partial x_j} b_i b_j \rho_{ij} \, dt$$

This is the generalized version of Ito's lemma. Substituting for dx_i from equation (19A.1) gives

$$df = \left(\sum_i \frac{\partial f}{\partial x_i} a_i + \frac{\partial f}{\partial t} + \frac{1}{2} \sum_i \sum_j \frac{\partial^2 f}{\partial x_i \partial x_j} b_i b_j \rho_{ij} \right) dt + \sum_i \frac{\partial f}{\partial x_i} b_i \, dz_i \tag{19A.3}$$

Derivation of the General Differential Equation Satisfied by Derivatives

Consider a certain derivative security that depends on n state variables and time, t. We make the assumption that there are a total of at least $n + 1$ traded securities (including the one under consideration) whose prices depend on some or all of the n state variables. In practice, this is not unduly restrictive. The traded securities may be options with different strike prices and exercise dates, forward contracts, bonds, stocks, and so on. We assume that no dividends or other income is paid by the $n + 1$ traded securities.[10] Other assumptions are similar to those made in chapter 11:

1. The short selling of securities with full use of proceeds is permitted.
2. There are no transactions costs and taxes.
3. All securities are perfectly divisible.
4. There are no riskless arbitrage opportunities.
5. Security trading is continuous.

The n state variables are assumed to follow continuous-time Ito diffusion processes. We denote the ith state variable by θ_i ($1 \le i \le n$) and suppose that

$$d\theta_i = m_i \theta_i \, dt + s_i \theta_i \, dz_i \tag{19B.1}$$

where dz_i is a Wiener process and the parameters, m_i and s_i, are the expected growth rate in θ_i and the volatility of θ_i. The m_i and s_i can be functions of any of the n state variables and time. Other notation used is as follows:

ρ_{ik}: Correlation between dz_i and dz_k ($1 \le i, k \le n$).

f_j: Price of the jth traded security ($1 \le j \le n + 1$).

r: Instantaneous (i.e., very short-term) risk-free rate.

One of the f_j is the price of the security under consideration. The short-term risk-free rate, r, may be one of the n state variables.

Because the $n + 1$ traded securities are all dependent on the θ_i, it follows from Ito's lemma in Appendix 19A that the f_j follow diffusion processes:

$$df_j = \mu_j f_j \, dt + \sum_i \sigma_{ij} f_j \, dz_i \tag{19B.2}$$

---

[10]This is not restrictive. A non-dividend-paying security can always be obtained from a dividend-paying security by reinvesting the dividends in the security.

where

$$\mu_j f_j = \frac{\partial f_j}{\partial t} + \sum_i \frac{\partial f_j}{\partial \theta_i} m_i \theta_i + \frac{1}{2} \sum_{i,k} \rho_{ik} s_i s_k \theta_i \theta_k \frac{\partial^2 f_j}{\partial \theta_i \partial \theta_k} \tag{19B.3}$$

$$\sigma_{ij} f_j = \frac{\partial f_j}{\partial \theta_i} s_i \theta_i \tag{19B.4}$$

In these equations, μ_j is the instantaneous mean rate of return provided by f_j and σ_{ij} is the component of the instantaneous standard deviation of the rate of return provided by f_j that may be attributed to the θ_i.

Because there are $n + 1$ traded securities and n Wiener processes in equation (19B.2), it is possible to form an instantaneously riskless portfolio, Π, using the securities. Define k_j as the amount of the jth security in the portfolio, so that

$$\Pi = \sum_j k_j f_j \tag{19B.5}$$

The k_j must be chosen so that the stochastic components of the returns from the securities are eliminated. From equation (19B.2) this means that

$$\sum_j k_j \sigma_{ij} f_j = 0 \tag{19B.6}$$

for $1 \le i \le n$. The return from the portfolio is then given by

$$d\Pi = \sum_j k_j \mu_j f_j \, dt$$

The cost of setting up the portfolio is $\sum_j k_j f_j$. If there are no arbitrage opportunities, the portfolio must earn the risk-free interest rate, so that

$$\sum_j k_j \mu_j f_j = r \sum_j k_j f_j \tag{19B.7}$$

or

$$\sum_j k_j f_j (\mu_j - r) = 0 \tag{19B.8}$$

Equations (19B.6) and (19B.8) can be regarded as $n+1$ homogeneous linear equations in the k_j's. The k_j's are not all zero. From a well-known theorem in linear algebra, equations (19B.6) and (19B.8) can be consistent only if

$$f_j(\mu_j - r) = \sum_i \lambda_i \sigma_{ij} f_j \tag{19B.9}$$

or

$$\mu_j - r = \sum_i \lambda_i \sigma_{ij} \tag{19B.10}$$

for some λ_i $(1 \leq i \leq n)$ that are dependent only on the state variables and time. This proves the result in equation (19.13).

Substituting from equations (19B.3) and (19B.4) into equation (19B.9), we obtain

$$\frac{\partial f_j}{\partial t} + \sum_i \frac{\partial f_j}{\partial \theta_i} m_i \theta_i + \frac{1}{2} \sum_{i,k} \rho_{ik} s_i s_k \theta_i \theta_k \frac{\partial^2 f_j}{\partial \theta_i \partial \theta_k} - r f_j = \sum_i \lambda_i \frac{\partial f_j}{\partial \theta_i} s_i \theta_i$$

that reduces to

$$\frac{\partial f_j}{\partial t} + \sum_i \theta_i \frac{\partial f_j}{\partial \theta_i} (m_i - \lambda_i s_i) + \frac{1}{2} \sum_{i,k} \rho_{ik} s_i s_k \theta_i \theta_k \frac{\partial^2 f_j}{\partial \theta_i \partial \theta_k} = r f_j$$

Dropping the subscripts to f, we deduce that any security whose price, f, is contingent on the state variables θ_i $(1 \leq i \leq n)$ and time, t, satisfies the second-order differential equation

$$\frac{\partial f}{\partial t} + \sum_i \theta_i \frac{\partial f}{\partial \theta_i} (m_i - \lambda_i s_i) + \frac{1}{2} \sum_{i,k} \rho_{ik} s_i s_k \theta_i \theta_k \frac{\partial^2 f}{\partial \theta_i \partial \theta_k} = r f \quad (19B.11)$$

The particular derivative security that is obtained is determined by the boundary conditions that are imposed on equation (19B.11).

CHAPTER

20

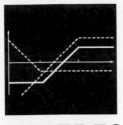

INTEREST RATE DERIVATIVES: THE STANDARD MARKET MODELS

Interest rate derivatives are instruments whose payoffs are dependent in some way on the level of interest rates. In the 1980s and 1990s, the volume of trading in interest rate derivatives in both the over-the-counter and exchange-traded markets increased very quickly. Many new products were developed to meet particular needs of end users. A key challenge for derivatives traders is to find good, robust procedures for pricing and hedging these products.

Interest rate derivatives are more difficult to value than equity and foreign exchange derivatives. There are a number of reasons for this:

1. The behavior of an individual interest rate is more complicated than that of a stock price or exchange rate.

2. For the valuation of many products, it is necessary to develop a model describing the behavior of the entire yield curve.

3. The volatilities of different points on the yield curve are different.

4. Interest rates are used for discounting as well as for defining the payoff from the derivative.

In this chapter we look at the three most popular over-the-counter interest rate option products: bond options, interest rate caps/floors, and swap options. We explain the standard market models for valuing these products and use material from chapter 19 to show that the models are internally consistent. We also consider how some types of nonstandard swaps are valued. As explained in chapter 5, plain vanilla interest rate swaps can be valued by calculating the relevant forward interest rates and assuming that this is not necessarily the correct approach for nonstandard swaps.

530

20.1 BLACK'S MODEL

Since the Black–Scholes model was first published in 1973, it has become a very popular tool. As explained in chapter 12, the model has been extended so that it can be used to value options on foreign exchange, options on indices, and options on futures contracts. Traders have become very comfortable with both the lognormal assumption that underlies the model and the volatility measure that describes uncertainty. It is not surprising that there have been attempts to extend the model so that it covers interest rate derivatives.

In the following few sections we will discuss three of the most popular interest rate derivatives (bond options, interest rate caps, and swap options) and describe how the lognormal assumption underlying the Black–Scholes model can be used to value these instruments. The model we will use is usually referred to as Black's model because the formulas are similar to those in the model suggested by Fischer Black for valuing options on commodity futures. (See section 12.8).

Here we review Black's model and show that it provides a flexible framework for valuing a wide range of European options.

Using Black's Model to Price European Options

Consider a European call option on a variable whose value is V. Define:

T: Maturity date of the option.

F: Forward price of V for a contract with maturity T.

F_0: Value of F at time zero.

X: Strike price of the option.

$P(t, T)$: Price at time t of a zero-coupon bond paying \$1 at time T.

V_T: Value of V at time T.

σ: Volatility of F.

Black's model calculates the expected payoff from the option assuming

1. V_T has a lognormal distribution with the standard deviation of $\ln V_T$ equal to $\sigma \sqrt{T}$.
2. The expected value of V_T is F_0.

It then discounts the expected payoff at the T-year risk-free rate by multiplying by $P(0, T)$.

The payoff from the option is max $(V_T - X, 0)$ at time T. As shown in Appendix 11A, the lognormal assumption implies that the expected payoff is

$$E(V_T)N(d_1) - XN(d_2)$$

where $E(V_T)$ is the expected value of V_T and

$$d_1 = \frac{\ln[E(V_T)/X] + \sigma^2 T/2}{\sigma \sqrt{T}}$$

$$d_2 = \frac{\ln[E(V_T)/X] - \sigma^2 T/2}{\sigma \sqrt{T}} = d_1 - \sigma \sqrt{T}$$

Because we are assuming that $E(V_T) = F_0$, the value of the option is

$$c = P(0, T)[F_0 N(d_1) - X N(d_2)] \tag{20.1}$$

where

$$d_1 = \frac{\ln (F_0/X) + \sigma^2 T/2}{\sigma \sqrt{T}}$$

$$d_2 = \frac{\ln (F_0/X) - \sigma^2 T/2}{\sigma \sqrt{T}} = d_1 - \sigma \sqrt{T}$$

Similarly the value, p, of the corresponding put option is given by

$$p = P(0, T)[X N(-d_2) - F_0 N(-d_1)] \tag{20.2}$$

We can extend Black's model to allow for the situation where the payoff is calculated from the value of the variable V at time T, but the payoff is actually made at some later time T^*. The expected payoff is discounted from time T^* instead of time T so that equations 20.1 and 20.2 become

$$c = P(0, T^*)[F_0 N(d_1) - X N(d_2)] \tag{20.3}$$

$$p = P(0, T^*)[X N(-d_2) - F_0 N(-d_1)] \tag{20.4}$$

where

$$d_1 = \frac{\ln (F_0/X) + \sigma^2 T/2}{\sigma \sqrt{T}}$$

$$d_2 = \frac{\ln (F_0/X) - \sigma^2 T/2}{\sigma \sqrt{T}} = d_1 - \sigma \sqrt{T}$$

An important feature of Black's model is that we do not have to assume geometric Brownian motion for the evolution of either V or F. All that we require is that V_T be lognormal at time T. The parameter, σ, is usually referred to as the volatility of the F or the forward volatility of V. However, its only role is to define the standard deviation of $\ln V_T$ by means of the relationship

$$\text{Standard Deviation of } \ln V_T = \sigma \sqrt{T}$$

The volatility parameter does not necessarily say anything about the standard deviation of $\ln V$ at times other than time T.

Validity of Black's Model

It is easy to see that Black's model is appropriate when interest rates are assumed to be either constant or deterministic. In this case, as explained in chapter 3, the forward price of V equal its futures price. It follows from equation (12.12) that the expected value of V in the traditional risk-neutral world is its forward value.[1] Black's model is,

---

[1] Using the terminology of section 19.5, the traditional risk-neutral world is the world where the numeraire is the money market account.

therefore, a straightforward application of the traditional risk-neutral valuation principle, outlined in chapters 9 and 11.

When interest rates are stochastic Black's model appears to involve two approximations:

1. The expected value of V_T is assumed to equal its forward price, F_0. As just noted, in the traditional risk-neutral world, the expected value of V_T equals its futures price. The forward price and the futures price are not the same when interest rates are stochastic.

2. The stochastic behavior of interest rates is not taken into account in the way the discounting is done.

As we apply Black's model to bond options, caps/floors, and swap options, we will use the results in section 19.5 to show that these two assumptions have exactly offsetting effects. Black's model, when used to value these instruments, does, therefore, have a sound theoretical basis.

20.2 BOND OPTIONS

A bond option is an option to buy or sell a particular bond by a certain date for a particular price. In addition to trading in the over-the-counter market, bond options are frequently embedded in bonds when they are issued to make them more attractive to either the issuer or potential purchasers.

Embedded Bond Options

One example of a bond with an embedded bond option is a *callable bond*. This is a bond that contains provisions allowing the issuing firm to buy back the bond at a predetermined price at certain times in the future. The holder of such a bond has sold a call option to the issuer. The strike price or call price in the option is the predetermined price that must be paid by the issuer to the holder. Callable bonds cannot usually be called for the first few years of their life. After that, the call price is usually a decreasing function of time. For example, in a 10-year callable bond, there might be no call privileges for the first two years. After that, the issuer might have the right to buy the bond back at a price of 110 in years 3 and 4 of its life, at a price of 107.5 in years 5 and 6, at a price of 106 in years 7 and 8, and at a price of 103 in years 9 and 10. The value of the call option is reflected in the quoted yields on bonds. Bonds with call features generally offer higher yields than bonds with no call features.

Another type of bond with an embedded option is a *puttable bond*. This contains provisions that allow the holder to demand early redemption at a predetermined price at certain times in the future. The holder of such a bond has purchased a put option on the bond as well as the bond itself. Because the put option increases the value of the bond to the holder, bonds with put features provide lower yields than bonds with no put features. A simple example of a puttable bond is a 10-year bond where the holder has the right to be repaid at the end of five years. (This is sometimes referred to as a *retractable bond*.)

Loan and deposit instruments also often contain embedded bond options. For example, a five-year fixed rate deposit with a financial institution that can be redeemed without penalty at any time contains an American put option on a bond. (The deposit instrument is a bond that the investor has the right to put back to the financial institution at any time.) Prepayment privileges on loans and mortgages are similarly call options on bonds.

Finally, we note that a loan commitment made by a bank or other financial institution is a put option on a bond. Consider, for example, the situation where a bank quotes a five-year interest rate of 12% per annum to a potential borrower and states that the rate is good for the next two months. The client has, in effect, obtained the right to sell a five-year bond with a 12% coupon to the financial institution for its face value any time within the next two months.

European Bond Options

Many over-the-counter bond options and some embedded bond options are European. We now consider the standard market models used to value European options.

The assumption usually made is that the bond price at the maturity of the option is lognormal. Equations (20.1) and (20.2) can be used to price the option with F_0 equal to the forward bond price. The variable σ is defined so that $\sigma \sqrt{T}$ is the standard deviation of the logarithm of the bond price at the maturity of the option.

A bond is a security that provides a known cash income. From section 3.3, F_0 can be calculated using the formula

$$F_0 = \frac{B_0 - I}{P(0, T)} \tag{20.5}$$

where B_0 is the bond price at time zero and I is the present value of the coupons that will be paid during the life of the option. In this formula, both the spot bond price and the forward bond price are cash prices rather than quoted prices. The relationship between cash and quoted bond prices is explained in section 4.9.

The strike price, X, in equations (20.1) and (20.2) should be the cash strike price. In choosing the correct value for X, the precise terms of the option are, therefore, important. If the strike price is defined as the cash amount that is exchanged for the bond when the option is exercised, X should be put equal to this strike price. If, as is more common, the strike price is the quoted price applicable when the option is exercised, X should be set equal to the strike price plus accrued interest at the expiration date of the option. (As mentioned in chapter 4, traders refer to the quoted price of a bond as the "clean price" and the cash price as the "dirty price.")

> **Example 20.1**   Consider a 10-month European call option on a 9.75-year bond with a face value of $1,000. (When the option matures the bond will have eight years and 11 months remaining.) Suppose that the current cash bond price is $960, the strike price is $1,000, the ten-month risk-free interest rate is 10% per annum, and the volatility of the forward bond price in 10 months is 9% per annum. The bond pays a semiannual coupon of 10% and coupon payments of $50 are expected in three months and nine months. (This means that the accrued interest is $25 and the quoted bond price is $935.) We

suppose that the three-month and nine-month risk-free interest rates are 9.0% and 9.5% per annum, respectively. The present value of the coupon payments is, therefore,

$$50e^{-0.25 \times 0.09} + 50e^{-0.75 \times 0.095} = 95.45$$

or \$95.45. The bond forward price is from equation (20.5) given by

$$F_0 = (960 - 95.45)e^{0.1 \times 0.8333} = 939.68$$

(a) If the strike price is the cash price that would be paid for the bond on exercise, the parameters for equation (20.1) are $F_0 = 939.68$, $X = 1000$, $P(0, T) = e^{-0.1 \times (10/12)} = 0.9200$, $\sigma = 0.09$, and $T = 10/12$. The price of the call option is \$9.49.

(b) If the strike price is the quoted price that would be paid for the bond on exercise, one month's accrued interest must be added to X because the maturity of the option is one month after a coupon date. This produces a value for X of

$$1,000 + 50 \times 0.16667 = 1,008.33$$

The values for the other parameters in equation (20.1) are unchanged (i.e., $F_0 = 939.68$, $P(0, T) = 0.9200$, $\sigma = 0.09$, and $T = 0.8333$). The price of the option is \$7.97.

Figure 20.1 shows how the standard deviation of the logarithm of a bond's price changes with time. The standard deviation is zero today because there is no uncertainty about the bond's price today. It is also zero at the bond's maturity because we know that the bond's price will equal its face value at maturity. Between today and the maturity of the bond, the standard deviation first increases and then decreases. The volatility, σ, that should be used when a European option on the bond is valued is

$$\frac{\text{standard deviation of logarithm of bond price at maturity of option}}{\sqrt{\text{time to maturity of option}}}$$

Figure 20.2 shows a typical pattern for σ as a function of the life of the option. In general, σ declines as the life of the option increases. It also tends to be an increasing function of the life of the underlying bond when the life of the option is held fixed.

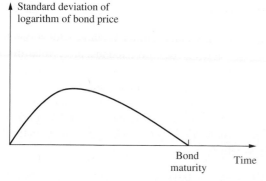

Figure 20.1 Standard deviation of logarithm of bond price as a function of time.

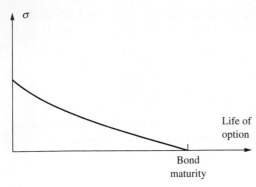

σ

Life of
option

Bond
maturity

Figure 20.2   Variation of volatility, σ, for bond
with life of option.

Yield Volatilities

The volatilities that are quoted for bond options are often forward yield volatilities rather than forward price volatilities. The duration concept, introduced in chapter 4, is used by the market to convert a quoted forward yield volatility into a forward price volatility. Suppose that D is the modified duration of the forward bond underlying the option as defined in section 4.13. The relationship between the change in the bond's price, B, and its yield, y, at the maturity of the option is

$$\frac{\Delta B}{B} \approx -D \, \Delta y$$

or

$$\frac{\Delta B}{B} \approx -Dy\frac{\Delta y}{y}$$

This suggests that the forward price volatility, σ, used in Black's model can be approximately related to the corresponding forward yield volatility, σ_y, using

$$\sigma = Dy_0\sigma_y \tag{20.6}$$

where y_0 is the initial forward yield. When a yield volatility is quoted for a bond option, the implicit assumption is usually that it will be converted to a price volatility using equation (20.6) and that this will then be used in conjunction with equations (20.1) or (20.2) to obtain a price. Suppose that the bond underlying an option will have a modified duration of five years at option maturity, the forward yield is 8% and the forward yield volatility quoted by a broker is 20%. This means that the market price of the option corresponding to the broker quote is the price given by equation (20.1) when the bond's forward price volatility is

$$5 \times 0.08 \times 0.2 = 0.08$$

or 8% per annum.

Theoretical Justification for the Model

In section 19.5, we explored alternatives to the usual risk-neutral valuation assumption for valuing derivatives. One alternative was a world that is forward risk neutral with respect to a zero-coupon bond maturing at time T. We showed that

1. The current value of any security is its expected value at time T in this world multiplied by the price of a zero-coupon bond maturing at time T. (See equation 19.24.)
2. The expected value of any traded security at time T in this world equals its forward price. (See equation 19.26.)

The first of these results shows that the price of a call option with maturity T years on a bond is

$$c = P(0, T)E_T[\max(B_T - X, 0)] \tag{20.7}$$

where B_T is the bond price at time T and E_T denotes expected value in a world that is forward risk neutral with respect to a zero-coupon bond maturing at time T. The second result implies that

$$E_T[B_T] = F_0 \tag{20.8}$$

Assuming the bond price is lognormal with the standard deviation of the logarithm of the bond price equal to $\sigma\sqrt{T}$, Appendix 11A shows that equation (20.7) becomes

$$c = P(0, T)[E_T(B_T)N(d_1) - XN(d_2)]$$

where

$$d_1 = \frac{\ln[E_T(B_T)/X] + \sigma^2 T/2}{\sigma\sqrt{T}}$$

$$d_2 = \frac{\ln[E_T(B_T)/X] - \sigma^2 T/2}{\sigma\sqrt{T}} = d_1 - \sigma\sqrt{T}$$

Using equation (20.8), this reduces to the Black's model formula in equation (20.1). We are entitled to use today's T-year maturity interest rate for discounting providing we also set the expected bond price equal to the forward bond price.

20.3 INTEREST RATE CAPS

A popular interest rate option offered by financial institutions in the over-the-counter market is an *interest rate cap*. Interest rate caps can best be understood by first considering a floating rate note where the interest rate is reset periodically equal to LIBOR. The time between resets is known as the *tenor*. Suppose the tenor is three months. The interest rate on the note for the first three months is the initial three-month LIBOR rate; the interest rate for the next three months is set equal to the three-month LIBOR rate prevailing in the market at the three-month point; and so on.

An interest rate cap is designed to provide insurance against the rate of interest on an underlying floating-rate note rising above a certain level. This level is known as the *cap rate*. Suppose that the principal amount is $10 million, the tenor is three months, the life of the cap is five years, and the cap rate is 8%. (Because the payments are made quarterly, this cap rate is expressed with quarterly compounding.) The cap provides insurance against the interest on the floating rate note rising above 8%. Suppose that on a particular reset date the three-month LIBOR interest rate is 9%. The floating rate note would require

$$0.25 \times 0.09 \times \$10,000,000 = \$225,000$$

of interest to be paid three months later. With a three-month LIBOR rate of 8% the interest payment would be

$$0.25 \times 0.08 \times \$10,000,000 = \$200,000$$

The cap, therefore, provides a payoff of $25,000.[2] Note that the payoff does not occur on the reset date when the 9% is observed. It occurs three months later. This reflects the usual time lag between an interest rate being observed and the corresponding payment being required.

At each reset date during the life of the cap we observe LIBOR. If LIBOR is less than 8%, there is no payoff from the cap three months later. If LIBOR is greater than 8%, the payoff is one quarter of the excess applied to the principal of $10 million. Note that caps are usually defined so that the initial LIBOR rate, even if it is greater than the cap rate, does not lead to a payoff on the first reset date. In our example the cap lasts for five years. There are, therefore, a total of 19 reset dates (at times 0.25, 0.5, 0.75, . . . , 4.75 years) and 19 potential payoffs from the caps (at times 0.50, 0.75, 1.00, . . . , 5.00 years).

The Cap as a Portfolio of Interest Rate Options

Consider a cap with a total life of T, a principal of L, and a cap rate of R_X. Suppose that the reset dates are $t_1, t_2, \ldots, t_n$ and define $t_{n+1} = T$. Define R_k as the interest rate for the period between time t_k and t_{k+1} observed at time t_k ($1 \leq k \leq n$). The cap leads to a payoff at time t_{k+1} ($k = 1, 2, \ldots, n$) of

$$L\delta_k \max(R_k - R_X, 0) \tag{20.9}$$

where $\delta_k = t_{k+1} - t_k$. (Both R_k and R_X are expressed with a compounding frequency equal to the frequency of resets.)

Equation (20.9) is a call option on the LIBOR rate observed at time t_k with the payoff occurring at time t_{k+1}. The cap is a portfolio of n such options. LIBOR rates are observed at times $t_1, t_2, t_3, \ldots, t_n$ and the corresponding payoffs occur at times $t_2, t_3, t_4, \ldots, t_{n+1}$. The n call options underlying the cap are known as *caplets*.

---

[2] This calculation assumes exactly one quarter of a year between reset dates. In practice, the calculation takes account of the exact number of days between reset dates using a specified day count convention.

A Cap as a Portfolio of Bond Options

An interest rate cap can also be characterized as a portfolio of put options on zero-coupon bonds with payoffs on the puts occurring at the time they are calculated. The payoff in equation (20.9) at time t_{k+1} is equivalent to

$$\frac{L\delta_k}{1 + R_k\delta_k} \max (R_k - R_X, 0)$$

at time t_k. A few lines of algebra show that this reduces to

$$\max \left[L - \frac{L(1 + R_X\delta_k)}{1 + \delta_k R_k}, 0 \right] \tag{20.10}$$

The expression

$$\frac{L(1 + R_X\delta_k)}{1 + \delta_k R_k}$$

is the value at time t_k of a zero-coupon bond that pays off $L(1 + R_X\delta_k)$ at time t_{k+1}. The expression in equation (20.10) is, therefore, the payoff from a put option with maturity t_k on a zero-coupon bond with maturity t_{k+1} when the face value of the bond is $L(1 + R_X\delta_k)$ and the strike price is L. It follows that an interest rate cap can be regarded as a portfolio of European put options on zero-coupon bonds.

Floors and Collars

Interest rate floors and interest rate collars (sometimes called floor–ceiling agreements) are defined analogously to caps. A *floor* provides a payoff when the interest rate on the underlying floating-rate note falls below a certain rate. With the notation already introduced, a floor provides a payoff at time t_{k+1} ($k = 1, 2, \ldots, n$) of

$$L\delta_k \max (R_X - R_k, 0)$$

Analogously to an interest rate cap, an interest rate floor is a portfolio of put options on interest rates or a portfolio of call options on zero-coupon bonds. Each of the individual options comprising a floor is known as a *floorlet*. A *collar* is an instrument designed to guarantee that the interest rate on the underlying floating-rate note always lies between two levels. A collar is a combination of a long position in a cap and a short position in a floor. It is usually constructed so that the price of the cap is initially equal to the price of the floor. The cost of entering into the collar is then zero.

There is a put–call parity relationship between the prices of caps and floors. This is

$$\text{cap price} = \text{floor price} + \text{value of swap}$$

In this relationship, the cap and floor have the same strike price, R_X. The swap is an agreement to receive floating and pay a fixed rate of R_X with no exchange of payments on the first reset date.[3] All three instruments have the same life and the same frequency of payments. This result can be seen to be true by noting that a long position in the cap combined with a short position in the floor provides the same cash flows as the swap.

Valuation of Caps and Floors

As shown in equation (20.9), the caplet corresponding to the rate observed at time t_k provides a payoff at time t_{k+1} of

$$L\delta_k \max (R_k - R_X, 0)$$

If the rate R_k is assumed to be lognormal with volatility σ_k, equation (20.3) gives the value of this caplet as

$$L\delta_k P(0, t_{k+1})[F_k N(d_1) - R_X N(d_2)] \tag{20.11}$$

where

$$d_1 = \frac{\ln(F_k/R_X) + \sigma_k^2 t_k/2}{\sigma_k \sqrt{t_k}}$$

$$d_2 = \frac{\ln(F_k/R_X) - \sigma_k^2 t_k/2}{\sigma_k \sqrt{t_k}} = d_1 - \sigma_k \sqrt{t_k}$$

and F_k is the forward rate for the period between time t_k and t_{k+1}. The value of the corresponding floorlet is, from equation (20.4),

$$L\delta_k P(0, t_{k+1})[R_X N(-d_2) - F_k N(-d_1)] \tag{20.12}$$

Note that R_X and F_k are expressed with a compounding frequency equal to the frequency of resets in these equations.

> **Example 20.2**   Consider a contract that caps the interest rate on a $10,000 loan at 8% per annum (with quarterly compounding) for three months starting in one year. This is a caplet and could be one element of a cap. Suppose that the forward interest rate for a three-month period starting in one year is 7% per annum (with quarterly compounding); the current 15-month interest rate is 6.5% per annum (with continuous compounding); and the volatility for the forward three-month rate underlying the caplet is 20% per annum. In equation (20.11), $F_k = 0.07$, $L = 10,000$, $R_X = 0.08$, $\delta_k = 0.25$, $P(0, t_{k+1}) = e^{-0.065 \times 1.25} = 0.9220$, $\sigma_k = 0.20$, and $t_k = 1.0$. Because
>
> $$d_1 = \frac{\ln(0.07/0.08) + 0.2^2/2}{0.20} = -0.5677$$
>
> $$d_2 = d_1 - 0.20 = -0.7677$$

---

[3] Note that swaps are usually structured so that the rate at time zero determines an exchange of payments at the first reset date. As indicated earlier, caps and floors are usually structured so that there is no payoff at the first reset date. This difference explains why we have to exclude the first exchange of payments on the swap.

the caplet price is

$$0.25 \times 10,000 \times 0.9220[0.07N(-0.5677) - 0.08N(-0.7677)] = 5.19$$

or $5.19.

Each caplet of a cap must be valued separately using equation (20.11). One approach is to use a different volatility for each caplet. The volatilities are then referred to as *spot volatilities*.[4] An alternative approach is to use the same volatility for all the caplets comprising any particular cap but to vary this volatility according to the life of the cap. The volatilities used are then referred to as *flat volatilities*. The volatilities quoted in the market are usually flat volatilities. However, many traders like to work with spot volatilities because this allows them to identify underpriced and overpriced caplets. Options on Eurodollar futures are very similar to caplets and the spot volatilities used for caplets on three-month LIBOR are frequently compared with those calculated from the prices of Eurodollar futures options.

Figure 20.3 shows a typical pattern for spot volatilities and flat volatilities as a function of maturity. (In the case of a spot volatility, the maturity is the maturity of a caplet; in the case of a flat volatility, it is the maturity of a cap.) The flat volatilities are akin to cumulative averages of the spot volatilities and, therefore, exhibit less variability. As indicated by Figure 20.3, we usually observe a "hump" in the volatilities. The peak of the hump is at about the two- to three-year point. This hump is observed both when the volatilities are implied from option prices and when they are calculated from historical data. There is no general agreement on the reason for the existence of the hump. One possible explanation is as follows. Rates at the short end of the zero curve are controlled by central banks. By contrast, two- and three-year interest rates are determined to a large extent by the activities of traders. These traders may be over-reacting to the changes they observe in the short rate and causing the volatility of these rates to be higher

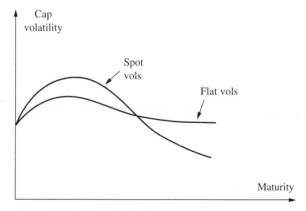

Figure 20.3 The volatility hump.

---

[4]The term *forward volatilities* is sometimes also used to describe these volatilities.

Table 20.1	Typical Broker Volatility Quotes for U.S. Dollar Caps and Floors (Percent Per Annum)			
Life	Cap bid	Cap offer	Floor bid	Floor offer
1 year	18.00	20.00	18.00	20.00
2 year	23.25	24.25	23.75	24.75
3 year	24.00	25.00	24.50	25.50
4 year	23.75	24.75	24.25	25.25
5 year	23.50	24.50	24.00	25.00
7 year	21.75	22.75	22.00	23.00
10 year	20.00	21.00	20.25	21.25

than the volatility of short rates. For maturities beyond two to three years the mean reversion of interest rates, which will be discussed in chapter 21, causes volatilities to decline.

Brokers provide tables of flat implied volatilities for caps and floors. The instruments underlying the quotes are usually at the money. This means that the cap/floor rate equals the swap rate for a swap that has the same payment dates as the cap. Table 20.1 shows typical broker quotes for the U.S. dollar market. The tenor of the cap is three months and the cap life varies from one year to ten years. The data exhibits the type of "hump" shown in Figure 20.3.

Theoretical Justification for the Model

We can show that Black's model for a caplet is internally consistent by considering a world that is forward risk neutral with respect to a zero-coupon bond maturing at time t_{k+1}. The analysis in section 19.5 shows that

1. The current value of any security is its expected value at time t_{k+1} in this world multiplied by the price of a zero-coupon bond maturing at time t_{k+1}. (See equation 19.24.)
2. The expected value of an interest rate lasting between times t_k and t_{k+1} equals the forward interest rate in this world. (See equation 19.27.)

The first of these results shows that, with the notation introduced earlier, the price of a caplet that provides a payoff at time t_{k+1} is

$$L\delta_k P(0, t_{k+1})E_{k+1}[\max(R_k - R_X, 0)]$$

where E_{k+1} denotes expected value in a world that is forward risk neutral with respect to a zero-coupon bond maturing at time t_{k+1}. From Appendix 11A, this becomes

$$L\delta_k P(0, t_{k+1})[E_{k+1}(R_k)N(d_1) - R_X N(d_2)]$$

where

$$d_1 = \frac{\ln\left[E_{k+1}(R_k)/R_X\right] + \sigma_k^2 t_k/2}{\sigma_k\sqrt{t_k}}$$

$$d_2 = \frac{\ln\left[E_{k+1}(R_k)/R_X\right] - \sigma_k^2 t_k/2}{\sigma_k\sqrt{t_k}} = d_1 - \sigma\sqrt{t_k}$$

The second result implies that

$$E_{k+1}[R_k] = F_k$$

Together the results lead to the cap pricing model in equation (20.11). They show that we can discount at the t_{k+1}-maturity interest rate observed in the market today providing we set the expected interest rate equal to the forward interest rate.

20.4 EUROPEAN SWAP OPTIONS

Swap options or *swaptions* are options on interest rate swaps and are another increasingly popular type of interest rate option. They give the holder the right to enter into a certain interest rate swap at a certain time in the future. (The holder does not, of course, have to exercise this right.) Many large financial institutions that offer interest rate swap contracts to their corporate clients are also prepared to sell them swaptions or buy swaptions from them.

To give an example of how a swaption might be used, consider a company that knows that in six months it will enter into a five-year floating-rate loan agreement and knows that it will wish to swap the floating interest payments for fixed interest payments to convert the loan into a fixed-rate loan. (See chapter 5 for a discussion of how swaps can be used in this way.) At a cost, the company could enter into a swaption giving it the right to receive six-month LIBOR and pay a certain fixed rate of interest, say 12% per annum, for a five-year period starting in six months. If the fixed rate exchanged for floating on a regular five-year swap in six months turns out to be less than 12% per annum, the company will choose not to exercise the swaption and will enter into a swap agreement in the usual way. However, if it turns out to be greater than 12% per annum, the company will choose to exercise the swaption and will obtain a swap at more favorable terms than those available in the market.

Swaptions, when used in the way just described, provide companies with a guarantee that the fixed rate of interest they will pay on a loan at some future time will not exceed some level. They are an alternative to forward swaps (sometimes called *deferred swaps*). Forward swaps involve no up-front cost but have the disadvantage of obligating the company to enter into a swap agreement. With a swaption, the company is able to benefit from favorable interest rate movements while acquiring protection from unfavorable interest rate movements. The difference between a swaption and a forward swap is analogous to the difference between an option on foreign exchange and a forward contract on foreign exchange.

Relation to Bond Options

It will be recalled from chapter 5 that an interest rate swap can be regarded as an agreement to exchange a fixed-rate bond for a floating-rate bond. At the start of a swap, the value of the floating-rate bond always equals the principal amount of the swap. A swaption can, therefore, be regarded as an option to exchange a fixed-rate bond for the principal amount of the swap. If a swaption gives the holder the right to pay fixed and receive floating, it is a put option on the fixed-rate bond with strike price equal to the principal. If a swaption gives the holder the right to pay floating and receive fixed, it is a call option on the fixed-rate bond with a strike price equal to the principal.

Valuation of European Swap Options

The swap rate for a particular maturity at a particular time is the fixed rate that would be exchanged for LIBOR in a newly issued swap with that maturity. The model usually used to value a European option on a swap assumes that the relevant swap rate at the maturity of the option is lognormal. Consider a swaption where we have the right to pay a rate R_X and receive LIBOR on a swap that will last n years starting in T years. We suppose that there are m payments per year under the swap and that the principal is L.

Suppose that the swap rate for an n-year swap at the maturity of the swap option is R. (Both R and R_X are expressed with a compounding frequency of m times per year.) By comparing the cash flows on a swap where the fixed rate is R to the cash flows on a swap where the fixed rate is R_X, we see that the payoff from the swaption consists of a series of cash flows equal to

$$\frac{L}{m} \max\left(R - R_X, \, 0\right)$$

The cash flows are received m times per year for the n years of the life of the swap. Suppose that the payment dates are $t_1, t_2, \ldots, t_{mn}$, measured in years from today. (It is approximately true that $t_i = T + \frac{i}{m}$.) Each cash flow is the payoff from a call option on R with strike price R_X.

Using equation (20.3), the value of the cash flow received at time t_i is

$$\frac{L}{m} P(0, t_i)[F_0 N(d_1) - R_X N(d_2)]$$

where

$$d_1 = \frac{\ln\left(F_0/R_X\right) + \sigma^2 T/2}{\sigma\sqrt{T}}$$

$$d_2 = \frac{\ln\left(F_0/R_X\right) - \sigma^2 T/2}{\sigma\sqrt{T}} = d_1 - \sigma\sqrt{T}$$

F_0 is the forward swap rate, and r_i is the continuously compounded zero-coupon interest rate for a maturity of t_i.

The total value of the swaption is

$$\sum_{i=1}^{mn} \frac{L}{m} P(0, t_i)[F_0 N(d_1) - R_X N(d_2)]$$

Defining A as the value of a contract that pays $1/m$ at times t_i ($1 \le i \le mn$), the value of the swaption becomes

$$LA[F_0 N(d_1) - R_X N(d_2)] \tag{20.13}$$

where

$$A = \frac{1}{m} \sum_{i=1}^{mn} P(0, t_i)$$

If the swaption gives the holder the right to receive a fixed rate of R_X instead of paying it, the payoff from the swaption is

$$\frac{L}{m} \max (R_X - R, 0)$$

This is a put option on R. As before, the payoffs are received at times t_i ($1 \le i \le mn$). Equation (20.4) gives the value of the swaption as

$$LA[R_X N(-d_2) - F_0 N(-d_1)] \tag{20.14}$$

Example 20.3 Suppose that the LIBOR yield curve is flat at 6% per annum with continuous compounding. Consider a swaption that gives the holder the right to pay 6.2% in a three-year swap starting in five years. The volatility for the swap rate is 20%. Payments are made semiannually and the principal is $100. In this case

$$A = \frac{1}{2}[e^{-0.06\times5.5} + e^{-0.06\times6} + e^{-0.06\times6.5} + e^{-0.06\times7} + e^{-0.06\times7.5} + e^{-0.06\times8}]$$
$$= 2.0035$$

A rate of 6% per annum with continuous compounding translates into 6.09% with semi-annual compounding. It follows that in this example $F_0 = 0.0609$, $R_X = 0.062$, $T = 5$, $\sigma = 0.2$, so that

$$d_1 = \frac{\ln (0.0609/0.062) + 0.2^2 \times 5/2}{0.2 \sqrt{5}} = 0.1836$$

$$d_2 = d_1 - 0.2 \sqrt{5} = -0.2636$$

From equation (20.13) the value of the swaption is

$$100 \times 2.0035[0.0609 \times N(0.1836) - 0.062 \times N(-0.2636)] = 2.07$$

or $2.07.

Brokers provide tables of implied volatilities for European swap options. The instruments underlying the quotes are usually at the money. This means that the strike swap rate equals the forward swap rate. Table 20.2 shows typical broker quotes provided for the U.S. dollar market. The tenor of the underlying swaps (that is, the frequency of resets on the floating rate) is six months. The life of the option is shown on

Table 20.2 Typical Broker Quotes for U.S. European Swap Options (Mid-Market Volatilities Percent Per Annum)

				Swap length			
Expiration	*1-year*	*2-year*	*3-year*	*4-year*	*5-year*	*7-year*	*10-year*
1 month	17.75	17.75	17.75	17.50	17.00	17.00	16.00
3 month	19.50	19.00	19.00	18.00	17.50	17.00	16.00
6 month	20.00	20.00	19.25	18.50	18.75	17.75	16.75
1 year	22.50	21.75	20.50	20.00	19.50	18.25	16.75
2 year	22.00	22.00	20.75	19.50	19.75	18.25	16.75
3 year	21.50	21.00	20.00	19.25	19.00	17.75	16.50
4 year	20.75	20.25	19.25	18.50	18.25	17.50	16.00
5 year	20.00	19.50	18.50	17.75	17.50	17.00	15.50

the vertical scale. This varies from one month to five years. The life of the underlying swap at the maturity of the option is shown on the horizontal scale. This varies from one year to ten years. The volatilities in the one-year column of the table correspond to instruments that are similar to caps. They exhibit the hump discussed earlier. As we move to the columns corresponding to options on longer-lived swaps, the hump persists but it becomes less pronounced.

Theoretical Justification for the Swap Option Model

We can show that Black's model for swap options is internally consistent by considering a world that is forward risk neutral with respect to the annuity A. The analysis in section 19.5 shows that

1. The current value of any security is the current value of the annuity multiplied by the expected value of

$$\frac{\text{security price at time } T}{\text{value of the annuity at time } T}$$

   in this world. (See equation 19.29.)
2. The expected value of the swap rate at time T in this world equals the forward swap rate. (See equation 19.28.)

The payoff at time T from a swap option where we have the right to pay R_X and receive floating is the value of an annuity times

$$\frac{L}{m} \max [R - R_X, 0]$$

The first result shows that the value of the swaption is

$$LAE_A[\max [R - R_X, 0]]$$

From Appendix 11A this is

$$LA[E_A(R)N(d_1) - R_X N(d_2)]$$

where

$$d_1 = \frac{\ln\left[E_A(R)\big/R_X\right] + \sigma^2 T/2}{\sigma\sqrt{T}}$$

$$d_2 = \frac{\ln\left[E_A(R)\big/R_X\right] - \sigma^2 T/2}{\sigma\sqrt{T}} = d_1 - \sigma\sqrt{T}$$

The second result shows that $E_A(R)$ equals F_0. Taken together, the results lead to the swap option pricing formula in equation (20.13). They show that we are entitled to treat interest rates as constant for the purposes of discounting provided we also set the expected swap rate equal to the forward swap rate.

20.5   GENERALIZATIONS

We have presented three different versions of Black's model: one for bond options, one for caps, and one for swap options. In each case, we have shown that it is theoretically correct to ignore the fact that interest rates are stochastic when discounting, provided we assume that the expected value of the underlying variable is its forward value.

These results can be generalized:

1. Consider any instrument that provides a payoff at time T dependent on the price of a security observed at time T. Its current value is $P(0, T)$ times the expected payoff providing expectations are calculated in a world where the expected value of the underlying security equals its forward price.

2. Consider any instrument that provides a payoff at time T_2 dependent on the T_2-maturity interest rate observed at time T_1. Its current value is $P(0, T_2)$ times the expected payoff providing expectations are calculated in a world where the expected value of the underlying interest rate equals the forward interest rate.

3. Consider any instrument that provides a payoff in the form of an annuity. We suppose that the size of the annuity is determined at time T as a function of the swap rate for an n year swap starting at time T. We also suppose that annuity lasts for n years and payment dates for the annuity are the same as those for the swap. The value of the instrument is A times the expected payoff per year where (a) A is current value of the annuity when payments are at the rate $1 per year and (b) expectations are taken in a world where the expected future swap rate equals the forward swap rate.

The first of these results is a generalization of the European bond option model; the second is a generalization of the cap/floor model; the third is a generalization of the swap option model.

20.6   CONVEXITY ADJUSTMENTS

This section discusses what happens when an instrument provides a payoff at time T dependent on a bond yield calculated at time T.

The forward yield on a bond is defined as the yield calculated from the forward bond price. Suppose that B_T is the price of a bond at time T, y_T is its yield, and the relationship between B_T and y_T is

$$B_T = G(y_T)$$

Define F_0 as the forward bond price at time zero for a contract maturing at time T and y_0 as the forward bond yield at time zero. The definition of a forward bond yield means that:

$$F_0 = G(y_0)$$

The function G is non-linear. This implies that, when the expected future bond price equals the forward bond price (so that we are a world that is forward risk neutral with respect to a zero-coupon bond maturing at time T), the expected future bond yield does not equal the forward bond yield.

This is illustrated in Figure 20.4, which shows the relationship between bond prices and bond yields at time T. For simplicity, we suppose that there are only three possible bond prices, B_1, B_2, and B_3 and they are equally likely. We assume that the bond prices are equally spaced so that $B_2 - B_1 = B_3 - B_2$. The expected bond price is B_2 and we suppose that this is the forward bond price. The bond prices translate into three equally likely bond yields: Y_1, Y_2, and Y_3. The latter are not equally spaced. The variable, Y_2, is the forward bond yield because it is the yield corresponding to the forward bond price. The expected bond yield is the average of Y_1, Y_2, and Y_3 and is clearly greater than Y_2.

Consider now a derivative that provides a payoff dependent on the bond yield at time T. We know from equation (19.24) that it can be valued by (a) calculating the expected payoff in a world that is forward risk neutral with respect to a zero-coupon bond maturing at time T and (b) discounting at the current risk-free rate for maturity T. We know that the expected bond price equals the forward price in the world being considered. We, therefore, need to know the value of the expected bond yield when the expected bond price equals the forward bond price. The analysis in Appendix 20A

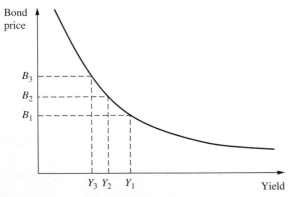

Figure 20.4   Convexity adjustment.

shows that an approximate expression for the required expected bond yield is

$$E_T(y_T) = y_0 - \frac{1}{2} y_0^2 \sigma_y^2 T \frac{G''(y_0)}{G'(y_0)}$$

where G' and G'' denote the first and second partial derivatives of G, E_T denotes expectations in a world that is forward risk neutral with respect to $P(t, T)$, and σ_y is the forward yield volatility. It follows that we can discount expected payoffs at the current risk-free rate for maturity T providing we assume that the expected bond yield is

$$y_0 - \frac{1}{2} y_0^2 \sigma_y^2 T \frac{G''(y_0)}{G'(y_0)}$$

rather than y_0. The difference between the expected bond yield and the forward bond yield:

$$-\frac{1}{2} y_0^2 \sigma_y^2 T \frac{G''(y_0)}{G'(y_0)} \qquad (20.15)$$

is then known as a *convexity adjustment*. It corresponds to the difference between Y_2 and the expected yield in Figure 20.4. (The convexity adjustment is positive because $G'(y_0) < 0$ and $G''(y_0) > 0$.)

Example 20.4 Consider a derivative that provides a payoff in three years equal to the one-year zero-coupon rate (annually compounded) at that time multiplied by $100. Suppose that the zero rate for all maturities is 10% per annum with annual compounding and the volatility of the one year rate in three years is 20%. The payoff is the yield on a one-year bond observed at time three years. The G-function describing the relationship between the bond price and the bond yield at time T is

$$G(y) = \frac{1}{1 + y}$$

so that

$$G'(y) = -\frac{1}{(1 + y)^2}$$

$$G''(y) = \frac{2}{(1 + y)^3}$$

In this case, $y_0 = 0.1$ so that $G'(y_0) = -0.8264$ and $G''(y_0) = 1.5026$. Also $\sigma_y = 0.2$ and $T = 3$. From equation (20.15) the convexity adjustment that must be made to today's forward bond yield is

$$\frac{1}{2} \times 0.1^2 \times 0.2^2 \times 3 \times \frac{1.5026}{0.8264} = 0.00109$$

or 10.9 basis points. $P(0, 3) = e^{-0.1 \times 3} = 0.7408$ and the value of the derivative is, therefore,

$$100 \times 0.10109 \times 0.7408 = 7.60$$

or 7.60. (This compares with a price of 7.51 when no convexity adjustment is made.)

LIBOR-in-Arrears Swap

As explained in chapter 5, a plain vanilla interest rate swap is designed so that the floating rate of interest observed on one payment date is paid on the next payment date. We showed in chapter 5 that it is correct to value the swap by assuming the forward swap rate is realized and then discounting the expected payment using today's zero curve. This is consistent with the second result presented in section 20.5.

An alternative to a plain vanilla swap that is sometimes traded is a *LIBOR-in-arrears swap*. In this, the floating rate paid on a payment date equals the rate observed on the payment date itself. Example 20.4 shows the methodology for valuing a LIBOR-in-arrears swap. Instead of assuming that the interest rate on each reset date equals the forward rate, we assume that it equals the forward rate plus a convexity adjustment.

To derive a general result, we suppose that R is the forward interest rate for the period between time T_1 and T_2. We define $\tau = T_2 - T_1$ and assume that R is measured with a compounding frequency of τ. Define R_0 as the value of R at time zero. When the payoff on a derivative occurs at time T_1 and is dependent on R, the convexity adjustment that must be applied to R_0 is

$$-\frac{1}{2}R_0^2\sigma_R^2T_1\frac{G''(R_0)}{G'(R_0)}$$

where

$$G(y) = \frac{1}{1 + y\tau}$$

and σ_R is the volatility of R. Evaluating $G'(R_0)$ and $G''(R_0)$ the convexity adjustment is

$$\frac{R_0^2\sigma_R^2\tau T_1}{1 + R_0\tau}$$

When a LIBOR-in-arrears swap is valued the interest rate between times T_1 and T_2 should, therefore, be assumed to be

$$R_0 + \frac{R_0^2\sigma_R^2\tau T_1}{1 + R_0\tau} \qquad (20.16)$$

rather than R_0. The required values of σ_R can be estimated from implied caplet volatilities.

> **Example 20.5**   Consider a LIBOR-in-arrears swap with a principal of $100 million where a fixed rate of 5% is received annually and LIBOR is paid. Payments are exchanged at the ends of years 1 to 5. The yield curve is flat at 5% per annum, compounded annually. All caplet volatilities are 22% per annum. The forward rate for each floating payment is 5%. If this were a regular swap rather than an in-arrears swap, its value would be exactly zero. Because it is an in-arrears swap we must make convexity adjustments. In equation (20.16) $R_0 = 0.05$, $\sigma_R = 0.22$, and $\tau = 1$. The convexity adjustment changes the rate observed at time T_1 from 0.05 to
>
> $$0.05 + \frac{0.05^2 \times 0.22^2 \times 1 \times T_1}{1 + 0.05 \times 1} = 0.05 + 0.000105T_1$$

The floating rates for the payments at the ends of years 1, 2, 3, 4, and 5 should therefore be assumed to be 5.0105%, 5.021%, 5.0315%, 5.0420%, and 5.0525%, respectively. The value of the swap is

$$-\frac{10,500}{1.05} - \frac{21,000}{1.05^2} - \frac{31,500}{1.05^3} - \frac{42,000}{1.05^4} - \frac{52,500}{1.05^5}$$

or $-131,947$.

Derivatives with Payoffs Dependent on Swap Rates

Consider next a derivative providing a payoff at time T equal to a swap rate observed at that time. A swap rate is a par yield. For the purposes of calculating a convexity adjustment we make an approximation and assume that the N-year swap rate at time T equals the yield at that time on an N-year bond with a coupon equal to today's forward swap rate. This enables equation (20.15) to be used.

Example 20.6 Consider an instrument that provides a payoff in three years equal to the three-year swap rate at that time multiplied by $100. Suppose that payments are made annually on the swap, the zero rate for all maturities is 12% per annum with annual compounding, the volatility for the three-year forward swap rate in three years (implied from swap option prices) is 22%. We approximate the swap rate as the yield on a 12% bond so that the relevant function $G(y)$ is

$$G(y) = \frac{0.12}{1 + y} + \frac{0.12}{(1 + y)^2} + \frac{1.12}{(1 + y)^3}$$

$$G'(y) = -\frac{0.12}{(1 + y)^2} - \frac{0.24}{(1 + y)^3} - \frac{3.36}{(1 + y)^4}$$

$$G''(y) = \frac{0.24}{(1 + y)^3} + \frac{0.72}{(1 + y)^4} + \frac{13.44}{(1 + y)^5}$$

In this case the forward yield, y_0, is 0.12, so that $G'(y_0) = -2.4018$ and $G''(y_0) = 8.2546$. From equation (20.15) the convexity adjustment is

$$\frac{1}{2} \times 0.12^2 \times 0.22^2 \times 3 \times \frac{8.2546}{2.4018} = 0.0036$$

or 36 basis points. We should, therefore, assume a forward swap rate of 0.1236 ($= 12.36\%$) rather than 0.12 when valuing the instrument. Using risk-neutral valuation, the instrument is worth

$$\frac{100 \times 0.1236}{1.12^3} = 8.80$$

or $8.80. (This compares with a price of 8.54 obtained without any convexity adjustment.)

20.7   TIMING ADJUSTMENTS

In this section we examine the situation where a derivative provides a payoff at time T_2, based on the value of a variable, v, observed at an earlier time T_1. Define:

v_1: Value of v at time T_1

F: Forward value of v for a contract maturing at time T_1

$E_1(v_1)$: Expected value of v_1 in a world that is forward risk-neutral with respect to $P(t, T_1)$

$E_2(v_1)$: Expected value of v_1 in a world that is forward risk-neutral with respect to $P(t, T_2)$

G: Forward price of a zero-coupon bond lasting between T_1 and T_2

R: Forward interest rate for period between T_1 and T_2, expressed with a compounding frequency of m

R_0: Value of R today

σ_F: Volatility of F

σ_G: Volatility of G

σ_R: Volatility of R

ρ: Instantaneous correlation between F and R.

When we move from a world that is forward risk-neutral with respect to $P(t, T_1)$ to one that is forward risk-neutral with respect to $P(t, T_2)$, the numeraire ratio is:

$$G = \frac{P(t, T_2)}{P(t, T_1)}$$

From section 19.8 the growth rate of v increases by

$$\alpha_v = -\rho \sigma_G \sigma_F \tag{20.17}$$

(The minus sign reflects the fact that, because G and R are instantaneously perfectly negatively correlated, the correlation between G and F is $-\rho$.)

Because

$$G = \frac{1}{(1 + R/m)^{m(T_2 - T_1)}}$$

the relationship between the volatility of G and the volatility of R can be calculated from Ito's lemma as

$$\sigma_G = \frac{\sigma_R R (T_2 - T_1)}{1 + R/m}$$

Hence equation (20.17) becomes

$$\alpha_v = -\frac{\rho \sigma_F \sigma_R R (T_2 - T_1)}{1 + R/m}$$

As an approximation we can assume that R remains constant at R_0 to get

$$E_2(v_1) = E_1(v_1) \exp\left[-\frac{\rho\sigma_F\sigma_R R_0 T_1(T_2 - T_1)}{1 + R_0/m}\right] \qquad (20.18)$$

This equation shows how we can adjust the forward value of a variable to allow for a delay between the variable being observed and the payoff being made.

Example 20.7 Consider a derivative that provides a payoff in six years equal to the value of a stock index observed in five years. Suppose that 1,200 is the forward value of the stock index for a contract maturing in five years. Suppose that the volatility of the forward value of the index is 20%, the volatility of the forward interest rate between years five and six is 18%, and the correlation between the two is -0.4. Suppose further that the zero curve is flat at 8% with annual compounding. We apply the results we have just produced to the situation where v is equal to the value of the index, $T_1 = 5$, $T_2 = 6$, $m = 1$, $R_0 = 0.08$, $\rho = -0.4$, $\sigma_F = 0.20$, and $\sigma_R = 0.18$ so that

$$E_2(v_1) = E_1(v_1) \exp\left[-\frac{(-0.4) \times 0.20 \times 0.18 \times 0.08 \times 5 \times 1}{1 + 0.08}\right]$$

or $E_2(v_1) = 1.00535 E_1(v_1)$. From the forward risk-neutral arguments in chapter 19 we know that $E_1(v_1)$ is the forward price of the index, or 1,200. It follows that $E_2(v_T) = 1,200 \times 1.00535 = 1206.42$. The value of the derivative is $1206.36 \times P(0, 6)$. In this case $P(0, 6) = e^{-0.08 \times 6} = 0.6188$ so that the value of the derivative is 746.51.

LIBOR-in-Arrears Swaps Revisited

When the variable v is R, the analysis just given compares the expected interest rate between times T_1 and T_2 in

1. A world that is forward risk neutral with respect to $P(0, T_1)$, and
2. A world that is forward risk neutral with respect to $P(0, T_2)$

We now verify that it gives the same answer as the approach in section 20.6 when used to value LIBOR-in-arrears swaps.

When $v = R$, equation (20.18) becomes

$$E_2(v_1) = E_1(v_1) \exp\left(-\frac{\sigma_R^2 R_0 T_1(T_2 - T_1)}{1 + R_0/m}\right)$$

Define $\tau = T_2 - T_1$. In the situation we are considering the compounding period for R is τ so that $m = 1/\tau$. Also $E_2(v_1) = R_0$ so that

$$E_1(v_1) = R_0 \exp\left(\frac{\sigma_R^2 R_0 \tau T_1}{1 + R_0\tau}\right)$$

Approximating the exponential function, we see that the expected interest rate between times T_1 and T_2 in a world that is forward risk-neutral with respect to a zero-coupon bond maturing at time T_1 is

$$R_0 + \frac{R_0^2 \sigma_R^2 \tau T_1}{1 + R_0 \tau}$$

This is the same result as equation (20.16).

CMS and CMT Swaps

A constant maturity swap (CMS) is an interest rate swap where the floating rate equals the swap rate for a swap with a certain life. For example, the floating payments on a CMS swap might be made every six months at a rate equal to the five-year swap rate. Usually there is a lag so that the payment on a particular payment date is equal to the swap rate observed on the previous payment date. Suppose that the ith payment date is at time t_i and L is the principal. The floating payment at time t_{i+1} is

$$\delta_i L S_i$$

where $\delta_i = t_{i+1} - t_i$ and S_i is the swap rate at time t_i.

    To value the payment on a CMS swap at time t_{i+1}, we must first make a convexity adjustment to calculate the expected swap rate at time t_i in a world that is forward risk neutral with respect to $P(t, t_i)$. (This is similar to what we did in Example 20.5.) We must then make a timing adjustment, changing the numeraire from $P(t, t_i)$ to $P(t, t_{i+1})$, to allow for the fact that the payment is actually made at time t_{i+1}. From equations (20.15) and (20.18), the required expected swap rate in a world that is forward risk neutral with respect to $P(t, t_{i+1})$ is

$$\left[y_0 - \frac{1}{2} y_0^2 \sigma_y^2 t_i \frac{G''(y_0)}{G'(y_0)} \right] \exp\left[-\frac{\delta_i R_0 \rho \sigma_y \sigma_R t_i}{1 + R_0 \delta_i} \right]$$

where y_0 is the forward swap rate at time zero, σ_y is the volatility of the forward swap rate, R_0 is the value at time zero of the forward interest rate between times t_i and t_{i+1}, σ_R is the volatility of this forward interest rate, and ρ is the correlation between the forward swap rate and the forward interest rate. $G(y)$ is the price at time t_i of a bond as a function of its yield, y. The bond pays coupons at rate y_0 and has the same life as the swap. The expressions for the expected swap rate can be approximated as

$$y_0 - \frac{1}{2} y_0^2 \sigma_y^2 t_i \frac{G''(y_0)}{G'(y_0)} - \frac{y_0 \delta_i R_0 \rho \sigma_y \sigma_R t_i}{1 + R_0 \delta_i} \qquad (20.19)$$

In this expression, there are two adjustments to the forward swap rate, y_0. The first is the convexity adjustment; the second is the timing adjustment.

    The volatility σ_y is implied from swap options; the volatility, σ_R is implied from caplet prices; the correlation ρ is the correlation between a relatively short rate and a relatively long rate and is typically about 0.7.

    A constant maturity Treasury swap (CMT swap) works similarly to a CMS swap except that the floating rate is the yield on a Treasury bond with a specified life.

The analysis of a CMT swap is essentially the same as that for a CMS swap with S_i defined as the par yield on a Treasury bond with the specified life.

Example 20.8 Consider a CMS swap where the five-year semiannual swap rate is exchanged for a fixed rate with a payment dependent on a swap rate being made six months after the rate is observed. Assume that the term structure is flat at 5% per annum with semiannual compounding. All options on five-year swaps have 15% volatility and all caplets lasting six months have a 20% implied volatility, and the correlation between the cap rates and swap rates is 0.7. In this case, $y_0 = 0.05, \sigma_y = 0.15, \delta_i = 0.5, R_0 = 0.05, \sigma_R = 0.20$, and

$$G(y) = \sum_{i=1}^{10} \frac{2.5}{(1 + y/2)^i} + \frac{100}{(1 + y/2)^{10}}$$

so that $G'(y_0) = -437.603$ and $G''(y_0) = 2261.23$. Equation (20.19) gives the convexity adjustment as $0.0001453t_i$ and the timing adjustment as $-0.0000256t_i$. The total adjustment is, therefore, $0.0001197t_i$ or 1.197 basis points per year until the swap rate is observed. For example, for the purposes of valuing the CMS swap, the five year swap rate in four years time should be assumed to be 5.045% rather than 5%.

20.8   WHEN IS AN ADJUSTMENT NECESSARY?

We have shown that

1. When the payoff depends on the price of a traded security in a certain currency at time T and is made at time T in the same currency, no adjustment is necessary to the forward price of the security.

2. When the payoff depends on the T_2-maturity interest rate observed at time T_1 in a certain currency and is made at time T_2 in the same currency, no adjustment is necessary to the forward interest rate.

3. When the payoff depends on the swap rate at time T in a certain currency, and is an annuity in the same currency starting at time T, with the annuity payment dates being the swap payment dates, no adjustment is necessary to the forward swap rate.

In each of these cases we can say that the derivative incorporates a natural time lag. When we buy a traded security, we are expected to pay for it immediately. There is no time lag. When we borrow or lend money, we observe the interest rate at one time and the interest is paid (in the same currency) at the maturity of the interest rate. When we enter into a swap, the payments corresponding to the swap rate are made in the form of an annuity. In general, when a derivative is structured so that it incorporates natural time lags, no adjustments to forward rates and prices are required to value the derivative. In other situations, one or more adjustments may be required. Quanto adjustments have been covered in chapter 19. Convexity and timing adjustments have been covered in this chapter.

20.9   ACCRUAL SWAPS

Accrual swaps are swaps where the interest on one side accrues only when the floating reference rate is within a certain range. Sometimes the range remains fixed during the entire life of the swap; sometimes it is reset periodically.

As a simple example of an accrual swap, consider a deal where a fixed rate, Q, is exchanged for three-month LIBOR every quarter. We suppose that the fixed rate accrues only on days when three-month LIBOR is below 8% per annum. Suppose that the principal is L. In a normal swap, the fixed-rate payer would pay QLn_1/n_2 on each payment date where n_1 is the number of business days in the preceding quarter and n_2 is the number of business days in the year. (This assumes that the day count is actual/actual). In an accrual swap, this is changed to QLn_3/n_2, where n_3 is the number of business days in the preceding quarter that the three-month LIBOR was below 8%. The fixed-rate payer saves QL/n_2 on each day when the three-month LIBOR rate is above 8%. The fixed-rate payer's position can, therefore, be considered as equivalent to a regular swap plus a series of binary options, one for each day of the life of the swap. The binary options pay off QL/n_2 when the three-month LIBOR is above 8%.

To generalize, we suppose that the LIBOR cutoff rate (8% in the case just considered) is R_X and that payments are exchanged every δ years. Consider day i during the life of the swap and suppose that t_i is the time until day i. Suppose that the forward LIBOR rate on day i is F_i and its volatility is σ_i. (The latter is estimated from spot caplet volatilities.) Using the usual lognormal assumption, the probability that LIBOR is greater than R_X in a world that is forward risk neutral with respect to a zero-coupon bond maturing at time $t_i + \delta$ is $N(d_2)$, where

$$d_2 = \frac{\ln(F_i/R_X) - \sigma_i^2 t_i/2}{\sigma_i \sqrt{t_i}}$$

The payoff from the binary option is realized at the swap payment date following day i. We suppose that this is at time s_i. The probability that LIBOR is greater than R_X in a world that is forward risk neutral with respect to a zero-coupon bond maturing at time s_i is given by $N(d_2^*)$, where d_2^* is calculated using the same formula as d_2, but with a small timing adjustment to F_i reflecting the difference between time $t_i + \delta$ and time s_i.

The value of the binary option corresponding to day i is

$$\frac{QL}{n_2} P(0, s_i) N(d_2^*)$$

The total value of the binary options is obtained by summing this expression for every day in the life of the swap.[5] The timing adjustment is so small that, in practice, it is frequently ignored.

---

[5] In practice, good results can be obtained by basing calculations on a relatively small number of equally spaced days during the life of the swap.

20.10 SPREAD OPTIONS

Spread options are instruments that provide a payoff dependent on the spread between two interest rates. In some cases, the rates are both calculated from the same yield curve. (An example is the situation where the spread is calculated as three-month LIBOR minus the five-year swap rate.) In other cases, two different yield curves are involved. (An example is the situation where the spread is calculated as the excess of the three-month LIBOR rate over the three-month Treasury bill rate.) To value a spread option, it is necessary to calculate the expected spread in a world that is forward risk neutral with respect to a zero-coupon bond maturing at the time the payoff occurs.

When the spread is always positive, it is sometimes reasonable to assume that it is lognormal at the maturity of the option.[6] Black's model can then be used. Equations (20.1) and (20.2) apply with F_0 equal to the forward value of the spread (adjusted as appropriate for convexity and timing) and $\sigma \sqrt{T}$ equal to the standard deviation of the logarithm of the spread.

When the spread is liable to be positive or negative, one approach is to assume that it is normally distributed, centered on its forward value. Another approach is to assume that each of the two rates used to calculate the spread are lognormal and that there is a correlation between the rates. In the latter case, the expected value of each rate is its forward rate (adjusted as appropriate for convexity and timing). The expected payoff can be calculated using either Monte Carlo simulation or numerical integration.

20.11 HEDGING INTEREST RATE DERIVATIVES

This section discusses how the material on Greek letters in chapter 13 can be extended to cover interest rate derivatives.

In the context of interest rate derivatives, delta risk is the risk associated with a shift in the zero curve. Because there are many ways in which the zero curve can shift, many alternative deltas can be calculated. Some alternatives are:

1. Calculate the impact of a one basis point shift in the zero curve. This is sometimes termed a DV01.
2. Calculate the impact of small changes in the quotes for each of the instruments used to construct the zero curve.
3. Divide the zero curve (or the forward curve) into a number of sections (or buckets). Calculate the impact of shifting the rates in one bucket by one basis point, keeping the rest of the initial term structure unchanged.
4. Carry out a principal components analysis as outlined in section 14.10. Calculate a delta with respect to the first two or three factors. The first delta then measures the

---

[6]An example of a spread that is always positive is the excess of the three-month LIBOR rate over the three-month Treasury bill rate.

impact of a small, approximately parallel, shift in the zero curve; the second delta measures the impact of a small twist in the zero curve; and so on.

In practice, traders tend to prefer the second approach. They argue that the only way the zero curve can change is if the quote for one of the instruments used to compute the zero curve changes. They, therefore, feel that it makes sense to focus on the exposures arising from these instruments.

When several delta measures are calculated, there are many possible gamma measures. Suppose that ten instruments are used to compute the zero curve and that we measure deltas with respect to changes in the quotes for each of these. Gamma is a second partial derivative of the form $\partial^2 \Pi / \partial x_i x_j$ where Π is the portfolio value. We have ten choices for x_i and ten choices for x_j and a total of 55 different gamma measures. This may be more than the trader can handle. One approach is to ignore cross-gammas and focus on the ten partial derivatives where $i = j$. Another is to calculate a single gamma measure as the second partial derivative of the value of the portfolio with respect to a parallel shift in the zero curve. Another is to calculate gamma with respect to the first two factors in a principal components analysis.

The vega of a portfolio of interest rate derivatives measures its exposure to volatility changes. One approach is to calculate the impact on the portfolio of making the same small change to the Black volatilities of all caps and European swap options. However, this assumes that one factor drives all volatilities and is probably too simplistic. A better idea is to carry out a principal components analysis on the volatilities of caps and swap options and calculate vega measures corresponding to the first two or three factors. The first factor proves to be approximately parallel shift in all volatilities; the second is one where short volatilities move in one direction and long volatilities move in the opposite direction.[7]

SUMMARY

Black's model provides a popular approach for valuing European-style interest rate options. The essence of Black's model is that the value of the variable underlying the option is assumed to be lognormal at the maturity of the option. In the case of a European bond option, Black's model assumes that the underlying bond price is lognormal at the option's maturity. For a cap, the model assumes that the interest rate underlying each of the constituent caplets is lognormally distributed. In the case of a swap option, the model assumes that the underlying swap rate is lognormally distributed.

When valuing a plain vanilla swap, it is correct to assume that the expected value of a market variable equals its forward value and then use interest rates observed

---

[7]Term structure models (including those discussed in the next two chapters) are usually calibrated to the prices of caps and European swap options. Vega measures based on changes to the Black volatilities of these instruments can therefore be used in conjunction with term structure models.

in the market today to discount the resulting expected payoff. For other derivatives, it is sometimes necessary to make an adjustment to the forward value of an underlying variable. If the underlying variable is the yield on a bond, a convexity adjustment is usually necessary. If there is a nonstandard time lag between the variable being observed and the payment being made, a timing adjustment is necessary.

Extensions of Black's model can be used to value accrual swaps and spread options. An accrual swap is a swap where interest on one side accrues only when the floating reference rate is within a certain range. A spread option is an option that provides a payoff dependent on the spread between two interest rates.

SUGGESTIONS FOR FURTHER READING

Black, F. "The Pricing of Commodity Contracts," *Journal of Financial Economics*, 3 (March 1976), 167–79.

Brotherton-Ratcliffe, R., and B. Iben. "Yield Curve Applications of Swap Products." In *Advanced Strategies in Financial Risk Management*, R. Schwartz and C. Smith (eds.). New York: New York Institute of Finance, 1993.

Li, A., and V. R. Raghavan. "LIBOR-In-Arrears Swaps," *Journal of Derivatives*, 3, 3 (Spring 1996), 44–48.

QUESTIONS AND PROBLEMS
(ANSWERS IN SOLUTIONS MANUAL)

20.1. A company caps three-month LIBOR at 10% per annum. The principal amount is $20 million. On a reset date, three-month LIBOR is 12% per annum. What payment would this lead to under the cap? When would the payment be made?

20.2. Explain why a swap option can be regarded as a type of bond option.

20.3. Use Black's model to value a one-year European put option on a 10-year bond. Assume that the current value of the bond is $125, the strike price is $110, the one-year interest rate is 10% per annum, the bond's price volatility is 8% per annum, and the present value of the coupons to be paid during the life of the option is $10.

20.4. In the accrual swap discussed in the text, the fixed side accrues only when the floating reference rate lies below a certain level. Discuss how the analysis can be extended to cope with a situation where the fixed side accrues only when the floating reference rate is above one level and below another.

20.5. Explain whether any convexity or timing adjustments are necessary when
   (a) We wish to value a spread option that pays off every quarter the excess (if any) of the five-year swap rate over the three-month LIBOR rate applied to a principal of $100. The payoff occurs 90 days after the rates are observed.
   (b) We wish to value a derivative that pays off every quarter the three-month LIBOR rate minus the three-month Treasury bill rate. The payoff occurs 90 days after the rates are observed.

20.6. Explain carefully how you would use (a) spot volatilities and (b) flat volatilities to value a five-year cap.

20.7. Calculate the price of an option that caps the three-month rate, starting in 15 months time, at 13% (quoted with quarterly compounding) on a principal amount of $1,000. The forward interest rate for the period in question is 12% per annum (quoted with quarterly compounding), the 18-month risk-free interest rate (continuously compounded) is 11.5% per annum, and the volatility of the forward rate is 12% per annum.

20.8. Suppose that an implied price volatility for a five-year option on a bond maturing in ten years (calculated from Black's model) is used to price a nine-year option on the bond. Would you expect the resultant price to be too high or too low? Explain.

20.9. Calculate the value of a four-year European call option on a five-year bond using Black's model. The five-year cash bond price is $105, the cash price of a four-year bond with the same coupon is $102, the strike price is $100, the four-year risk-free interest rate is 10% per annum with continuous compounding, and the volatility for the bond price in four years is 2% per annum.

20.10. What other instrument is the same as a five-year zero-cost collar where the strike price of the cap equals the strike price of the floor? What does the common strike price equal?

20.11. Derive a put–call parity relationship for European bond options.

20.12. Derive a put–call parity relationship for European swap options.

20.13. Explain why there is an arbitrage opportunity if the implied Black (flat) volatility of a cap is different from that of a floor. Do the broker quotes in Table 20.1 present an arbitrage opportunity?

20.14. When a bond's price is lognormal can the bond's yield be negative? Explain your answer.

20.15. Suppose that in Example 20.2 of section 20.3 the payoff occurs after one year (i.e., when the interest rate is observed) rather than in 15 months. What difference does this make to the inputs to Black's models?

20.16. The yield curve is flat at 10% per annum with annual compounding. Calculate the value of an instrument where, in five years' time, the two-year swap rate (with annual compounding) is received and a fixed rate of 10% is paid. Both are applied to a notional principal of $100. Assume that the volatility of the swap rate is 20% per annum. Explain why the value of the instrument is different from zero.

20.17. What difference does it make in Problem 20.16 if the swap rate is observed in five years, but the exchange of payments takes place in (a) six years, and (b) seven years? Assume that the volatilities of all forward rates are 20%. Assume also that the forward swap rate for the period between years five and seven has a correlation of 0.8 with the forward interest rate between years five and six and a correlation of 0.95 with the forward interest rate between years five and seven.

20.18. What is the value of a European swap option that gives the holder the right to enter into a 3-year annual-pay swap in four years where a fixed rate of 5% is paid and LIBOR is received. The swap principal is $10 million. Assume that the yield curve is flat at 5% per annum with annual compounding and the volatility of the swap rate is 20%. Compare your answer to that given by DerivaGem.

20.19. Suppose that the yield, R, on a zero-coupon bond follows the process

$$dR = \mu\, dt + \sigma\, dz$$

where μ and σ are functions of R and t, and dz is a Wiener process. Use Ito's Lemma to show that the volatility of the zero-coupon bond price declines to zero as it approaches maturity.

20.20. The price of a bond at time T, measured in terms of its yield, is $G(y_T)$. Assume geometric Brownian motion for the forward bond yield, y, in a world that is forward risk neutral with respect to a bond maturing at time T. Suppose that the growth rate of the forward bond yield is α and its volatility σ_y.
(a) Use Ito's lemma to calculate the process for the forward bond price, in terms of α, σ_y, y, and $G(y)$.
(b) The forward bond price should follow a martingale in the world considered. Use this fact to calculate an expression for α.
(c) Show that the expression for α is, to a first order of approximation, consistent with equation (20.15).

ASSIGNMENT QUESTIONS

20.21. Consider an eight-month European put option on a Treasury bond that currently has 14.25 years to maturity. The current cash bond price is $910, the exercise price is $900, and the volatility for the bond price is 10% per annum. A coupon of $35 will be paid by the bond in three months. The risk-free interest rate is 8% for all maturities up to one year. Use Black's model to determine the price of the option. Consider both the case where the strike price corresponds to the cash price of the bond and the case where it corresponds to the quoted price.

20.22. Calculate the price of a cap on the three-month LIBOR rate in nine months' time when the principal amount is $1,000. Use Black's model and the following information:
(a) The quoted nine-month Eurodollar futures price = 92. (Ignore the difference between futures and forward rates.)
(b) The interest-rate volatility implied by a nine-month Eurodollar option = 15% per annum.
(c) The current 12-month interest rate with continuous compounding = 7.5% per annum.
(d) The cap rate = 8% per annum.

20.23. Suppose that the LIBOR yield curve is flat at 8% with annual compounding. A swaption gives the holder the right to receive 7.6% in a five-year swap starting in four years. Payments are made annually. The volatility for the swap rate is 25% per annum and the principal is $1 million. Use Black's model to price the swaption. Compare your answer to that given by DerivaGem.

20.24. Suppose that the LIBOR yield curve is flat at 8% (with continuous compounding). The payoff from a derivative occurs in four years. It is equal to the five-year rate minus the two-year rate at this time, applied to a principal of $100, with both rates being continuously compounded. (The payoff can be positive or negative.) Calculate the value of the derivative. Assume that the volatility for all rates is 25%. What difference does it make if the payoff occurs in five years instead of four years? Assume all rates are perfectly correlated.

20.25. Suppose that the payoff from a derivative will occur in ten years and will equal the three-year U.S. dollar swap rate for a semiannual-pay swap observed at that time applied to a certain principal. Assume that the yield curve is flat at 8% (semiannually compounded) per annum in dollars and 3% (semiannually compounded) in yen. The forward swap rate volatility is 18%, the volatility of the ten year "yen per dollar" forward exchange rate is 12%, and the correlation between this exchange rate and U.S. dollar interest rates is 0.25.

   (a) What is the value of the derivative if the swap rate is applied to a principal of $100 million so that the payoff is in dollars?

   (b) What is its value of the derivative if the swap rate is applied to a principal of 100 million yen so that the payoff is in yen?

20.26. The payoff from a derivative will occur in 8 years. It will equal the average of the one-year interest rates observed at times 5, 6, 7, and 8 years applied to a principal of $1,000. The yield curve is flat at 6% with annual compounding and the volatilities of all rates are 16%. Assume perfect correlation between all rates. What is the value of the derivative?

APPENDIX 20A

Proof of the Convexity Adjustment Formula

This appendix calculates a convexity adjustment for forward bond yields. Suppose that the payoff from a derivative at time T depends on a bond yield observed at that time. Define:

> y_0: Forward bond yield observed today for a forward contract with maturity T.
> y_T: Bond yield at time T.
> B_T: Price of the bond at time T.
> σ_y: Volatility of the forward bond yield.

We suppose that

$$B_T = G(y_T)$$

Expanding $G(y_T)$ in a Taylor series about $y_T = y_0$ yields the following approximation

$$B_T = G(y_0) + (y_T - y_0)G'(y_0) + 0.5(y_T - y_0)^2 G''(y_0)$$

where G' and G'' are the first and second partial derivatives of G. Taking expectations in a world that is forward risk neutral with respect to a zero-coupon bond maturing at time T

$$E_T(B_T) = G(y_0) + E_T(y_T - y_0)G'(y_0) + \frac{1}{2}E_T[(y_T - y_0)^2]G''(y_0)$$

where E_T denotes expectations in this world. The expression $G(y_0)$ is, by definition, the forward bond price. Also, because of the particular world we are working in, $E_T(B_T)$ equals the forward bond price. Hence $E_T(B_T) = G(y_0)$ so that

$$E_T(y_T - y_0)G'(y_0) + \frac{1}{2}E_T[(y_T - y_0)^2]G''(y_0) = 0$$

The expression $E_T[(y_T - y_0)^2]$ is approximately $\sigma_y^2 y_0^2 T$. Hence it is approximately true that

$$E_T(y_T) = y_0 - \frac{1}{2}y_0^2\sigma_y^2 T \frac{G''(y_0)}{G'(y_0)}$$

This shows that, to obtain the expected bond yield in a world that is forward risk neutral with respect to a zero-coupon bond maturing at time T, we should add

$$-\frac{1}{2}y_0^2\sigma_y^2 T \frac{G''(y_0)}{G'(y_0)}$$

to the forward bond yield. This is the result in equation (20.15).

INTEREST RATE DERIVATIVES: MODELS OF THE SHORT RATE

The models for pricing interest rate options presented in chapter 20 make the assumption that the probability distribution of an interest rate, a bond price, or some other variable at a future point in time is lognormal. They are widely used for valuing instruments such as caps, European bond options, and European swap options. However, they have limitations. They do not provide a description of the stochastic behavior of interest rates and bond prices. Consequently, they cannot be used for valuing interest rate derivatives such as American-style swap options, callable bonds, and structured notes.

This chapter and the next discuss alternative approaches for overcoming these limitations. These involve building what is known as a *term structure model*. This is a model describing the evolution of the yield curve through time. In this chapter we focus on term structure models that are constructed by specifying the behavior of the short term interest rate, r.

21.1 EQUILIBRIUM MODELS

Equilibrium models usually start with assumptions about economic variables and derive a process for the short rate, r. They then explore what the process for r implies about bond prices and option prices. The short rate, r, at time t is the rate that applies to an infinitesimally short period of time at time t. It is sometimes referred to as the *instantaneous short rate*. It is not the process for r in the real world that matters. Bond prices, option prices, and other derivative prices depend only on the process followed by r in a risk-neutral world. The risk-neutral world we consider here will be the traditional risk-neutral world where, in a very short time period between t and $t + \Delta t$, investors earn on average $r(t)\Delta t$. All processes for r that we present will be processes in this risk-neutral world.

564

From equation (19.15), the value at time t of an interest-rate derivative that provides a payoff of f_T at time T is

$$\hat{E}\left[e^{-\bar{r}(T-t)}f_T\right] \tag{21.1}$$

where $\bar{r}$ is the average value of r in the time interval between t and T, and $\hat{E}$ denotes expected value in the traditional risk-neutral world.

As usual, we define $P(t, T)$ as the price at time t of a zero-coupon bond that pays off \$1 at time T. From equation (21.1),

$$P(t, T) = \hat{E}\left[e^{-\bar{r}(T-t)}\right] \tag{21.2}$$

If $R(t, T)$ is the continuously compounded interest rate at time t for a term of $T - t$,

$$P(t, T) = e^{-R(t,T)(T-t)} \tag{21.3}$$

so that

$$R(t, T) = -\frac{1}{T-t}\ln P(t, T) \tag{21.4}$$

and from equation (21.2),

$$R(t, T) = -\frac{1}{T-t}\ln \hat{E}\left[e^{-\bar{r}(T-t)}\right] \tag{21.5}$$

This equation enables the term structure of interest rates at any given time to be obtained from the value of r at that time and the risk-neutral process for r. It shows that once we have fully defined the process for r, we have fully defined everything about the initial term structure and its evolution through time.

21.2 ONE-FACTOR EQUILIBRIUM MODELS

In a one-factor equilibrium model, the process for r involves only one source of uncertainty. Usually the short rate can be described in a risk-neutral world by an Ito process of the form

$$dr = m(r)\,dt + s(r)\,dz$$

The instantaneous drift, m, and instantaneous standard deviation, s, are assumed to be functions of r, but are independent of time. The assumption of a single factor is not as restrictive as it might appear. A one-factor model implies that all rates move in the same direction over any short time interval, but not that they all move by the same amount. It does not, as is sometimes supposed, imply that the term structure always has the same shape. A fairly rich pattern of term structures can occur under a one-factor model.

The next three sections consider three one-factor equilibrium models:

$$m(r) = \mu r; \; s(r) = \sigma r \qquad \text{(Rendleman and Bartter model).}$$
$$m(r) = a(b - r); \; s(r) = \sigma \qquad \text{(Vasicek model).}$$
$$m(r) = a(b - r); \; s(r) = \sigma \sqrt{r} \qquad \text{(Cox, Ingersoll, and Ross model).}$$

21.3   THE RENDLEMAN AND BARTTER MODEL

In Rendleman and Bartter's model, the risk-neutral process for r is[1]

$$dr = \mu r \, dt + \sigma r \, dz$$

where μ and σ are constants. This means that r follows geometric Brownian motion. The process for r is of the same type as that assumed for a stock price in chapter 10. It can be represented using a binomial tree similar to the one used for stocks in chapter 16.[2]

Mean Reversion

Rendleman and Bartter's assumption that the short-term interest rate behaves like a stock price is less than ideal. One important difference between interest rates and stock prices is that interest rates appear to be pulled back to some long-run average level over time. This phenomenon is known as *mean reversion*. When r is high, mean reversion tends to cause it to have a negative drift; when r is low, mean reversion tends to cause it to have a positive drift. Mean reversion is illustrated in Figure 21.1. The Rendleman and Bartter model does not incorporate mean reversion.

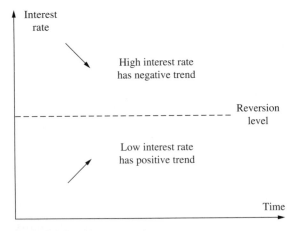

Figure 21.1   Mean reversion.

---

[1]See R. Rendleman and B. Bartter, "The Pricing of Options on Debt Securities," *Journal of Financial and Quantitative Analysis*, 15 (March 1980), 11–24.
[2]The way that the interest rate tree is used is explained later in the chapter.

There are compelling economic arguments in favor of mean reversion. When rates are high, the economy tends to slow down and borrowers require less funds. As a result, rates decline. When rates are low, there tends to be a high demand for funds on the part of borrowers and rates tend to rise.

21.4 THE VASICEK MODEL

In Vasicek's model, the risk-neutral process for r is

$$dr = a(b - r)\, dt + \sigma\, dz$$

where a, b, and σ are constants.[3] This model incorporates mean reversion. The short rate is pulled to a level b at rate a. Superimposed upon this "pull" is a normally distributed stochastic term $\sigma\, dz$.

Vasicek shows that equation (21.2) can be used to obtain the following expression for the price at time t of a zero-coupon bond that pays \$1 at time T:

$$P(t, T) = A(t, T)e^{-B(t,T)r(t)} \tag{21.6}$$

In this equation $r(t)$ is the value of r at time t,

$$B(t, T) = \frac{1 - e^{-a(T-t)}}{a} \tag{21.7}$$

and

$$A(t, T) = \exp\left[\frac{(B(t, T) - T + t)(a^2 b - \sigma^2/2)}{a^2} - \frac{\sigma^2 B(t, T)^2}{4a}\right] \tag{21.8}$$

When $a = 0$, $B(t, T) = T - t$, and $A(t, T) = \exp[\sigma^2(T - t)^3/6]$.

Using equation (21.4) yields

$$R(t, T) = -\frac{1}{T - t}\ln A(t, T) + \frac{1}{T - t}B(t, T)r(t) \tag{21.9}$$

showing that the entire term structure can be determined as a function of $r(t)$ once a, b, and σ are chosen. The shape can be upward sloping, downward sloping, or slightly "humped" (see Figure 21.2). Equation (21.9) shows that $R(t, T)$ is linearly dependent on $r(t)$.

Valuing European Options on Zero-Coupon Bonds

Jamshidian has shown that options on zero-coupon bonds can be valued using Vasicek's model.[4] The price at time zero of a European call option maturing at time T

---

[3] See O. A. Vasicek, "An Equilibrium Characterization of the Term Structure," *Journal of Financial Economics*, 5 (1977), 177–88.

[4] See F. Jamshidian, "An Exact Bond Option Pricing Formula," *Journal of Finance*, 44 (March 1989), 205–9.

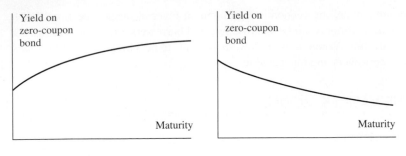

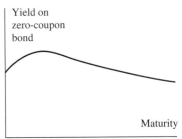

Figure 21.2   Possible shapes of term structure when Vasicek's model is used.

on a zero-coupon bond with principal L is

$$LP(0, s)N(h) - XP(0, T)N(h - \sigma_P) \qquad (21.10)$$

where L is the bond principal, s is the bond maturity,

$$h = \frac{1}{\sigma_P} \ln \frac{LP(0, s)}{P(0, T)X} + \frac{\sigma_P}{2}$$

$$\sigma_P = \frac{\sigma}{a}[1 - e^{-a(s-T)}]\sqrt{\frac{1 - e^{-2aT}}{2a}}$$

and X is the strike price. The price of a European put option on the bond is

$$XP(0, T)N(-h + \sigma_P) - LP(0, s)N(-h) \qquad (21.11)$$

When $a = 0$, $\sigma_P = \sigma(s - T)\sqrt{T}$.

Valuing European Options on Coupon-bearing Bonds

Jamshidian also shows that the prices of options on coupon-bearing bonds can be obtained from the prices of options on zero-coupon bonds in a one-factor model, such as Vasicek's, where all rates are positively related to r. Consider a European call option with exercise price X and maturity T on a coupon-bearing bond. Suppose that the bond provides a total of n cash flows after the option matures. Let the ith cash flow be c_i and occur at time s_i ($1 \leq i \leq n$; $s_i > T$). Define:

> r_X: Value of the short rate, r, at time T that causes the coupon-bearing bond price to equal the strike price.
>
> X_i: Value at time T of a zero-coupon bond paying off \$1 at time s_i when $r = r_X$.

When bond prices are known analytically as a function of r (as they are in Vasicek's model), r_X can be obtained very quickly using an iterative procedure such as the Newton–Raphson method, explained in footnote 2 of chapter 4.

The variable $P(T, s_i)$ is the price at time T of a zero-coupon bond paying \$1 at time s_i. The payoff from the option is, therefore,

$$\max\left[0, \sum_{i=1}^{n} c_i P(T, s_i) - X\right]$$

Because all rates are increasing functions of r, all bond prices are decreasing functions of r. This means that the coupon-bearing bond is worth more than X at time T and should be exercised if, and only if, $r < r_X$. Furthermore, the zero-coupon bond maturing at time s_i underlying the coupon-bearing bond is worth more than $c_i X_i$ at time T if, and only if, $r < r_X$. It follows that the payoff from the option is

$$\sum_{i=1}^{n} c_i \max[0, \ P(T, s_i) - X_i]$$

This shows that the option on the coupon-bearing bond is the sum of n options on the underlying zero-coupon bonds. A similar argument applies to European put options on coupon-bearing bonds.

Example 21.1 Suppose that $a = 0.1$, $b = 0.1$, and $\sigma = 0.02$ in Vasicek's model with the initial value of the short rate being 10% per annum. Consider a three-year European put option with a strike price of \$98 on a bond that will mature in five years. Suppose that the bond has a principal of \$100 and pays a coupon of \$5 every six months. At the end of three years, the bond can be regarded as the sum of four zero-coupon bonds. If the short-term interest rate is r at the end of the three years, the value of the bond is, from equation (21.6),

$$5A(3, 3.5)e^{-B(3,3.5)r} + 5A(3, 4)e^{-B(3,4)r} + 5A(3, 4.5)e^{-B(3,4.5)r} + 105A(3, 5)e^{-B(3,5)r}$$

Using the expressions for $A(t, T)$ and $B(t, T)$ in equations (21.7) and (21.8), this becomes

$$5 \times 0.9988e^{-0.4877r} + 5 \times 0.9952e^{-0.9516r} + 5 \times 0.9895e^{-1.3929r} + 105 \times 0.9819e^{-1.8127r}$$

To apply Jamshidian's procedure, we must find r_X, the value of r for which this bond price equals the strike price of 98. An iterative procedure shows that $r_X = 0.10952$. When r has this value, the values of the four zero-coupon bonds underlying the coupon-bearing bond are 4.734, 4.484, 4.248, and 84.535. The option on the coupon-bearing bond is, therefore, the sum of four options on zero-coupon bonds:

1. A three-year option with strike price 4.734 on a 3.5-year zero-coupon bond with a principal of 5.
2. A three-year option with strike price 4.484 on a four-year zero-coupon bond with a principal of 5.
3. A three-year option with strike price 4.248 on a 4.5-year zero-coupon bond with a principal of 5.
4. A three-year option with strike price 84.535 on a five-year zero-coupon bond with a principal of 105.

To illustrate the pricing of these options, consider the fourth. From equation (21.6), $P(0, 3) = 0.7419$ and $P(0, 5) = 0.6101$. Also, $\sigma_P = 0.05445$, $h = 0.4161$, $L = 105$, and $X = 84.535$. Equation (21.11) gives the value of the option as 0.8085. Similarly, the values of the first, second, and third options are, respectively, 0.0125, 0.0228, and 0.0314. The value of the option under consideration is, therefore, $0.0125 + 0.0228 + 0.0314 + 0.8085 = 0.8752$.

21.5 THE COX, INGERSOLL, AND ROSS MODEL

In Vasicek's model the short-term interest rate, r, can become negative. Cox, Ingersoll, and Ross have proposed an alternative model where rates are always non-negative.[5] The risk-neutral process for r in their model is

$$dr = a(b - r)\,dt + \sigma\,\sqrt{r}\,dz$$

This has the same mean-reverting drift as Vasicek, but the standard deviation is proportional to $\sqrt{r}$. This means that as the short-term interest rate increases, its standard deviation increases.

Cox, Ingersoll, and Ross show that in their model, bond prices have the same general form as in Vasicek's model:

$$P(t, T) = A(t, T)e^{-B(t,T)r}$$

but the functions $B(t, T)$ and $A(t, T)$ are different:

$$B(t, T) = \frac{2(e^{\gamma(T-t)} - 1)}{(\gamma + a)(e^{\gamma(T-t)} - 1) + 2\gamma}$$

and

$$A(t, T) = \left[\frac{2\gamma e^{(a+\gamma)(T-t)/2}}{(\gamma + a)(e^{\gamma(T-t)} - 1) + 2\gamma} \right]^{2ab/\sigma^2}$$

with $\gamma = \sqrt{a^2 + 2\sigma^2}$. As in the case of Vasicek's model, upward-sloping, downward-sloping, and slightly humped yield curves are possible. The long rate, $R(t, T)$, is linearly dependent on $r(t)$. This means that the value of $r(t)$ determines the level of the term structure at time t. The general shape of the term structure at time t is independent of $r(t)$, but does depend on t.

Cox, Ingersoll, and Ross provide formulas for European call and put options on zero-coupon bonds. These involve integrals of the noncentral chi-square distribution. European options on coupon-bearing bonds can be valued using Jamshidian's approach in a similar way to that described for Vasicek's model.

---

[5] See J. C. Cox, J. E. Ingersoll, and S. A. Ross, "A Theory of the Term Structure of Interest Rates," *Econometrica*, 53 (1985), 385–407.

21.6 TWO-FACTOR EQUILIBRIUM MODELS

A number of researchers have investigated the properties of two-factor equilibrium models. For example, Brennan and Schwartz have developed a model where the process for the short rate reverts to a long rate, which in turn follows a stochastic process.[6] The long rate is chosen as the yield on a perpetual bond that pays $1 per year. Because the yield on this bond is the reciprocal of its price, Ito's lemma can be used to calculate the process followed by the yield from the process followed by the price of the bond. The bond is a traded security. This simplifies the analysis because we know that the expected growth rate of its price in a risk-neutral world must be the risk-free interest rate minus its yield.

Another two-factor model, proposed by Longstaff and Schwartz, starts with a general equilibrium model of the economy and derives a term structure model where there is stochastic volatility.[7] The model proves to be analytically quite tractable.

21.7 NO-ARBITRAGE MODELS

The disadvantage of the equilibrium models presented in the preceding sections is that they do not automatically fit today's term structure. By choosing the parameters judiciously, they can be made to provide an approximate fit to many of the term structures that are encountered in practice. But the fit is not usually an exact one and, in some cases, there are significant errors. Most traders find this unsatisfactory. Not unreasonably, they argue that they have very little confidence in the price of a bond option when the model does not price the underlying bond correctly. A 1% error in the price of the underlying bond may lead to a 25% error in an option price.

A *no-arbitrage model* is a model designed to be exactly consistent with today's term structure of interest rates. The difference between an equilibrium and a no-arbitrage model is as follows. In an equilibrium model, today's term structure of interest rates is an output. In a no-arbitrage model, today's term structure of interest rates is an input.

In an equilibrium model, the drift of the short rate (that is, the coefficient of *dt*) is not usually a function of time. In a no-arbitrage model, the drift is, in general, dependent on time. This is because the shape of the initial zero-curve governs the average path taken by the short rate in the future in a no-arbitrage model. If the term structure is upward sloping, *r* will, on average, increase in a risk-neutral world; if the term structure is downward sloping, *r* will, on average, decrease in a

---

[6]See M. J. Brennan and E. S. Schwartz, "A Continuous Time Approach to Pricing Bonds," *Journal of Banking and Finance*, 3 (July 1979), 133–55; M. J. Brennan and E. S. Schwartz, "An Equilibrium Model of Bond Pricing and a Test of Market Efficiency," *Journal of Financial and Quantitative Analysis*, 21, 3 (September 1982), 301–29.

[7]See F. A. Longstaff and E. S. Schwartz, "Interest Rate Volatility and the Term Structure: A Two Factor General Equilibrium Model," *Journal of Finance*, 47, 4 (September 1992), 1259–82.

risk-neutral world; if the term structure first decreases and then increases, the expected path has a negative slope initially and a positive slope later; and so on.

It turns out that some equilibrium models can be converted to no-arbitrage models by including a function of time in the drift of the short rate.

21.8   THE HO AND LEE MODEL

Ho and Lee proposed the first no-arbitrage model of the term structure in 1986.[8] They presented the model in the form of a binomial tree of bond prices with two parameters: the short-rate standard deviation and the market price of risk of the short rate. It has since been shown that the continuous-time limit of the model is

$$dr = \theta(t)\,dt + \sigma\,dz \tag{21.12}$$

where σ, the instantaneous standard deviation of the short rate, is constant and $\theta(t)$ is a function of time chosen to ensure that the model fits the initial term structure. The variable $\theta(t)$ defines the average direction that r moves at time t. This is independent of the level of r. Interestingly, Ho and Lee's parameter that concerns the market price of risk proves to be irrelevant when the model is used to price interest rate derivatives. This is analogous to risk preferences being irrelevant in the pricing of stock options.

The variable $\theta(t)$ can be calculated analytically. It is

$$\theta(t) = F_t(0, t) + \sigma^2 t \tag{21.13}$$

where the $F(0, t)$ is the instantaneous forward rate for a maturity t as seen at time zero and the subscript t denotes a partial derivative with respect to t. As an approximation, $\theta(t)$ equals $= F_t(0, t)$. This means that the average direction that the short rate will be moving in the future is approximately equal to the slope of the instantaneous forward curve. The Ho and Lee model is illustrated in Figure 21.3. The slope of the forward curve defines the average direction that the short rate is moving at any given time. Superimposed on this slope is the normally distributed random outcome.

In the Ho and Lee model, zero-coupon bonds and European options on zero-coupon bonds can be valued analytically. The expression for the price of a zero-coupon bond at time t in terms of the short rate is

$$P(t, T) = A(t, T)e^{-r(t)(T-t)} \tag{21.14}$$

where

$$\ln A(t, T) = \ln \frac{P(0, T)}{P(0, t)} - (T - t)\frac{\partial \ln P(0, t)}{\partial t} - \frac{1}{2}\sigma^2 t(T - t)^2$$

In these equations, time zero is today. Times t and T are general times in the future with $T \geq t$. These equations, therefore, define the price of a zero-coupon bond at a

---

[8]See T. S. Y. Ho and S.-B. Lee, "Term Structure Movements and Pricing Interest Rate Contingent Claims," *Journal of Finance*, 41 (December 1986), 1011–29.

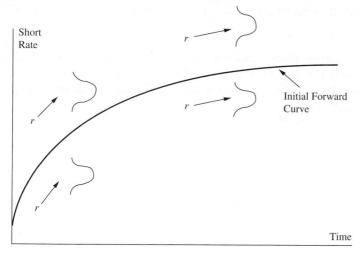

Figure 21.3   The Ho and Lee model.

future time t in terms of the short rate at time t and the prices of bonds today. The latter can be calculated from today's term structure.

For the remainder of the chapter, we will denote the Δt-period interest rate at time t by $R(t)$ or just R. From equation (21.14) we can show that

$$P(t, T) = \hat{A}(t, T)e^{-R(t)(T-t)} \tag{21.15}$$

where

$$\ln \hat{A}(t, T) = \ln \frac{P(0, T)}{P(0, t)} - \frac{T - t}{\Delta t} \ln \frac{P(0, t + \Delta t)}{P(0, t)} - \frac{1}{2}\sigma^2 t(T - t)[(T - t) - \Delta t] \tag{21.16}$$

In practice, we usually compute bond prices in terms of R rather than r and so equation (21.15) is more useful than equation (21.14). Equations (21.15) and (21.16) involve only bond prices at time zero, not partial derivatives of these prices. They demonstrate that we do not require the initial zero curve to be differentiable in applications of the model.

The price at time zero of a call option that matures at time T on a zero-coupon bond maturing at time s is

$$LP(0, s)N(h) - XP(0, T)N(h - \sigma_P)$$

where L is the principal of the bond, X is its strike price,

$$h = \frac{1}{\sigma_P} \ln \frac{LP(0, s)}{P(0, T)X} + \frac{\sigma_P}{2}$$

and

$$\sigma_P = \sigma(s - T)\sqrt{T}$$

The price of a put option on the bond is

$$XP(0, T)N(-h + \sigma_P) - LP(0, s)N(-h)$$

This is essentially the same as Black's model for pricing bond options in section 20.2. The bond price volatility is $\sigma \sqrt{s - T}$ and the standard deviation of the logarithm of the bond price at time T is σ_P. As explained in section 20.3, an interest rate cap or floor can be expressed as a portfolio of options on zero-coupon bonds. It can, therefore, be valued analytically using the Ho–Lee model.

The Ho and Lee model is an analytically tractable no-arbitrage model. It is easy to apply and provides an exact fit to the current term structure of interest rates. One disadvantage of the model is that it gives the user very little flexibility in choosing the volatility structure. All spot and forward rates have the same standard deviation. A related disadvantage of the model is that it has no mean reversion. Equation (21.12) shows that, regardless of how high or low interest rates are at a particular point in time, the average direction in which interest rates move over the next short period of time is always the same.

21.9   THE HULL AND WHITE MODEL

In a paper published in 1990, Hull and White explored extensions of the Vasicek model that provide an exact fit to the initial term structure.[9] One version of the extended Vasicek model that they consider is

$$dr = (\theta(t) - ar) \, dt + \sigma \, dz \qquad (21.17)$$

or

$$dr = a \left[\frac{\theta(t)}{a} - r \right] dt + \sigma \, dz$$

where a and σ are constants. This is known as the Hull–White model. It can be characterized as the Ho and Lee model with mean reversion at rate a. Alternatively, it can be characterized as the Vasicek model with a time-dependent reversion level. At time t the short rate reverts to $\theta(t)/a$ at rate a. The Ho and Lee model is a particular case of the Hull–White model with $a = 0$.

The model has the same amount of analytic tractability as Ho and Lee. The $\theta(t)$ function can be calculated from the initial term structure:

$$\theta(t) = F_t(0, t) + aF(0, t) + \frac{\sigma^2}{2a}(1 - e^{-2at}) \qquad (21.18)$$

The last term in this equation is usually fairly small. If we ignore it, the equation implies that the drift of the process for r at time t is $F_t(0, t) + a[F(0, t) - r]$. This shows that, on average, r approximately follows the slope of the initial instantaneous

[9] See J. Hull and A. White, "Pricing Interest Rate Derivative Securities," *Review of Financial Studies*, 3, 4 (1990), 573–92.

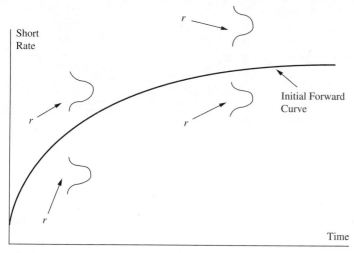

Figure 21.4   The Hull and White model.

forward rate curve. When it deviates from that curve, it reverts back to it at rate a. The model is illustrated in Figure 21.4.

Bond prices at time t in the Hull–White model are given by

$$P(t, T) = A(t, T)e^{-B(t,T)r(t)} \tag{21.19}$$

where

$$B(t, T) = \frac{1 - e^{-a(T-t)}}{a} \tag{21.20}$$

and

$$\ln A(t, T) = \ln \frac{P(0, T)}{P(0, t)} - B(t, T)\frac{\partial \ln P(0, t)}{\partial t} - \frac{1}{4a^3}\sigma^2(e^{-aT} - e^{-at})^2(e^{2at} - 1) \tag{21.21}$$

Equations (21.19), (21.20), and (21.21) define the price of a zero-coupon bond at a future time t in terms of the short rate at time t and the prices of bonds today. The latter can be calculated from today's term structure.

As in the case of the Ho and Lee model, it is more relevant to consider $P(t, T)$ in terms of $R(t)$, the Δt-period rate at time t. We obtain:

$$P(t, T) = \hat{A}(t, T)e^{-\hat{B}(t,T)R(t)} \tag{21.22}$$

where

$$\ln \hat{A}(t, T) = \ln \frac{P(0, T)}{P(0, t)} - \frac{B(t, T)}{B(t, t + \Delta t)} \ln \frac{P(0, t + \Delta t)}{P(0, t)}$$
$$- \frac{\sigma^2}{4a}(1 - e^{-2at})B(t, T)[B(t, T) - B(t, t + \Delta t)] \tag{21.23}$$

$$\hat{B}(t, T) = \frac{B(t, T)}{B(t, t + \Delta t)}\Delta t \tag{21.24}$$

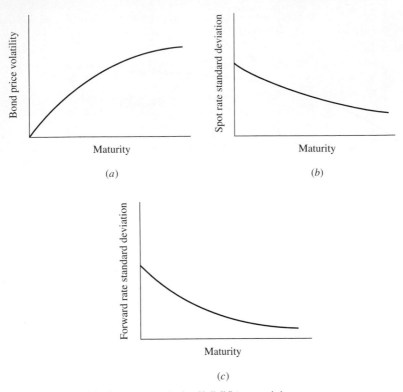

Figure 21.5 Volatility structure in the Hull–White model.

Similarly to the Ho and Lee model, these equations do not require initial zero curve to be differentiable everywhere.

The price at time zero of a call option that matures at time T on a zero-coupon bond maturing at time s is

$$LP(0, s)N(h) - XP(0, T)N(h - \sigma_P) \qquad (21.25)$$

where L is the principal of the bond, X is its strike price,

$$h = \frac{1}{\sigma_P} \ln \frac{LP(0, s)}{P(0, T)X} + \frac{\sigma_P}{2}$$

and

$$\sigma_P = \frac{\sigma}{a}[1 - e^{-a(s-T)}]\sqrt{\frac{1 - e^{-2aT}}{2a}}$$

The price of a put option on the bond is

$$XP(0, T)N(-h + \sigma_P) - LP(0, s)N(-h) \qquad (21.26)$$

These option pricing formulas are the same as those given for the Vasicek model in equations (21.10) and (21.11). They are also equivalent to using Black's model as described in section 20.2. The variable σ_P is the standard deviation of the logarithm of the bond price at time T, and the volatility for the bond used in Black's model is $\sigma_P/\sqrt{T}$. As explained in section 20.3, an interest rate cap or floor can be expressed as a portfolio of options on zero-coupon bonds. It can, therefore, be valued analytically using the Hull–White model.

The volatility structure in the Hull–White model is determined by both σ and a. The model can represent a wider range of volatility structures than Ho and Lee. The volatility at time t of the price of a zero-coupon bond maturing at time T is

$$\frac{\sigma}{a}\left[1 - e^{-a(T-t)}\right]$$

The instantaneous standard deviation at time t of the zero-coupon interest rate maturing at time T is

$$\frac{\sigma}{a(T-t)}\left[1 - e^{-a(T-t)}\right]$$

and the instantaneous standard deviation of the T-maturity instantaneous forward rate is $\sigma e^{-a(T-t)}$. These functions are shown in Figure 21.5. The parameter σ determines the short rate's instantaneous standard deviation. The reversion rate parameter, a, determines the rate at which standard deviations decline with maturity in Figure 21.5b and c. The higher a, the greater the decline. When $a = 0$, the model reduces to Ho and Lee, and zero-coupon bond price volatilities are a linear function of maturity with the instantaneous standard deviations of both spot and forward rates being constant.

21.10 OPTIONS ON COUPON-BEARING BONDS

In section 21.4 we showed how, when the Vasicek equilibrium model is used, we can express an option on a coupon-bearing bond as a portfolio of options on zero-coupon bonds. (See Example 21.1.) This section shows how we can do the same for the Ho–Lee and Hull–White models.

In the case of Vasicek's model, we calculated the value of the short rate, $r = r_X$, for which the coupon-bearing bond price equaled the strike price. We then argued that the option on the coupon-bearing bond was equivalent to a portfolio of options on the zero-coupon bonds comprising the coupon-bearing bond. The strike price of each option is the value of the corresponding zero-coupon bond when $r = r_X$.

We could follow exactly the same procedure for the Ho–Lee and Hull–White models as for the Vasicek model. But it is more convenient to work with the Δt-period rate, R, than with the instantaneous short rate, r. We then never need to calculate partial derivatives of $P(0, t)$ with respect to t.[10] A convenient choice for Δt is the time between the maturity of the option and the first subsequent coupon on the underlying bond.

---

[10]This emphasizes that the initial zero curve does not have to be differentiable to use the Ho–Lee and Hull–White models.

We calculate a value of R for which the coupon-bearing bond's price equals the strike price. Suppose this is R_X. The option on the coupon-bearing bond is equivalent to a portfolio of options on the zero-coupon bonds comprising the coupon-bearing bond. The strike price of each option is the value of the corresponding zero-coupon bond when $R = R_X$.

Example 21.2   Suppose that in the Hull–White model $a = 0.1$ and $\sigma = 0.015$ and we wish to value a 3-month European put option on a 15-month bond that pays a coupon of 12% semiannually. We suppose that both the bond principal and the strike price are 100. The continuously compounded zero rates for maturities of three months, nine months and fifteen months are 9.5%, 10.5%, and 11.5%, respectively. The option under consideration is an option on a portfolio of two zero-coupon bonds. The first zero-coupon bond has a maturity of nine months and a principal of $6. The second zero-coupon bond has a maturity of fifteen months and a principal of $106.

Define R as the value of the six-month rate at the maturity of the option. The value of the first zero-coupon bond underlying the option is $6e^{-R \times 0.5}$. The value of the second zero-coupon bond is, from equation (21.22)

$$106\hat{A}(0.25, 1.25)e^{-\hat{B}(0.25, 1.25)R}$$

where the Δt in equation (21.22) equals 0.5. In this case, $B(0.25, 0.75) = 0.4877$ and $B(0.25, 1.25) = 0.9516$ so that equation (21.24) gives $\hat{B}(0.25, 1.25) = 0.9756$. Also, from equation (21.23), $\hat{A}(0.25, 1.25) = 0.9874$. Let R_X be the value of R for which the coupon-bearing bond price equals the strike price. It follows that

$$6e^{-0.5 \times R_X} + 106\hat{A}(0.25, 1.25)e^{-\hat{B}(0.25, 1.25)R_X} = 100$$

This can be solved using an iterative procedure such as Newton–Raphson to give $R_X = 10.675\%$. When R has this value the zero-coupon bond maturing at time 0.75 is worth 5.68814 and the zero-coupon bond maturing at time 1.25 is worth 94.31186. The option on the coupon-bearing bond is, therefore, equivalent to

1. A European put option with a strike price of 5.68814 on a zero-coupon bond maturing at time 0.75 with a principal of 6; and

2. A European put option with a strike price of 94.31186 on a zero-coupon bond maturing at time 1.25 with a principal of 106.

Equation (21.26) gives the prices of these options as 0.01 and 0.43. The price of the option on the zero-coupon bond is, therefore, 0.44.

As explained in section 20.4 a European swap option can be viewed as an option on a coupon-bearing bond. It can, therefore, be valued analytically using the Ho–Lee or Hull–White model.

21.11   INTEREST RATE TREES

An interest rate tree is a discrete-time representation of the stochastic process for the short rate in much the same way as a stock price tree is a discrete-time representation of the process followed by a stock price. If the time step on the tree is Δt, the rates on the tree are the continuously compounded Δt-period rates. The usual assumption

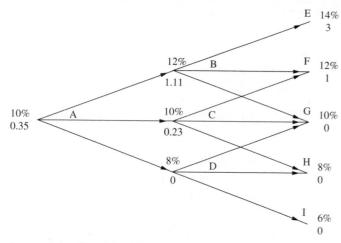

Figure 21.6   Example of the use of trinomial interest rate trees. Upper number at each node is rate; lower number is value of instrument.

when a tree is constructed is that the Δt-period rate, R, follows the same stochastic
process as the instantaneous rate, r, in the corresponding continuous-time model. The
main difference between interest rate trees and stock price trees is in the way that
discounting is done. In a stock price tree, the discount rate is usually assumed to be
the same at each node. In an interest rate tree, the discount rate varies from node to
node.

It often proves to be convenient to use a trinomial rather than a binomial tree
for interest rates. The main advantage of a trinomial tree is that it provides an extra
degree of freedom, making it easier for the tree to represent features of the interest
rate process such as mean reversion. As mentioned in section 16.8, using a trinomial
tree is equivalent to using the explicit finite difference method.

Illustration of Use of Trinomial Trees

To illustrate how trinomial interest rate trees are used to value derivatives, we consider
the simple example shown in Figure 21.6. This is a two-step tree with each time step
equal to one year in length so that $\Delta t = 1$ year. We assume that the up, middle, and
down probabilities are 0.25, 0.50, and 0.25 respectively, at each node. The assumed
Δt-period rate is shown as the upper number at each node.[11]

The tree is used to value a derivative that provides a payoff at the end of the
second time step of

$$\max \left[100(R - 0.11), 0 \right]$$

where R is the Δt-period rate. The calculated value of this derivative is the lower
number at each node. At the final nodes, the value of the derivative equals the payoff.

---

[11] We explain later how the probabilities and rates on an interest rate tree are determined.

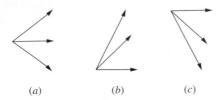

(a)   (b)   (c)

Figure 21.7   Alternative branching methods in a trinomial tree.

For example, at node E, the value is $100 \times (0.14 - 0.11) = 3$. At earlier nodes, the value of the derivative is calculated using the rollback procedure explained in chapter 16. At node B, the one-year interest rate is 12%. This is used for discounting to obtain the value of the derivative at node B from its values at nodes E, F, and G as

$$[0.25 \times 3 + 0.5 \times 1 + 0.25 \times 0]e^{-0.12 \times 1} = 1.11$$

At node C, the one-year interest rate is 10%. This is used for discounting to obtain the value of the derivative at node C as

$$(0.25 \times 1 + 0.5 \times 0 + 0.25 \times 0)e^{-0.1 \times 1} = 0.23$$

At the initial node, A, the interest rate is also 10% and the value of the derivative is

$$(0.25 \times 1.11 + 0.5 \times 0.23 + 0.25 \times 0)e^{-0.1 \times 1} = 0.35$$

Nonstandard Branching

It sometimes proves convenient to modify the standard branching pattern, which is used at all nodes in Figure 21.6. Three alternative branching possibilities are shown in Figure 21.7. The usual branching is shown in Figure 21.7a. It is "up one/straight along/down one." One alternative to this is "up two/up one/straight along," as shown in Figure 21.7b. This proves useful for incorporating mean reversion when interest rates are very low. A third branching pattern shown in Figure 21.7c is "straight along/one down/two down." This is useful for incorporating mean reversion when interest rates are very high. We illustrate the use of different branching patterns in the following section.

21.12   A GENERAL TREE-BUILDING PROCEDURE

Hull and White have proposed a robust two-stage procedure for constructing trinomial trees to represent a wide range of one-factor models.[12] This section first explains how the procedure can be used for the Hull–White model in section 21.9 and then shows how it can be extended to represent other models.

---

[12]See J. Hull and A. White, "Numerical Procedures for Implementing Term Structure Models I: Single Factor Models,"*Journal of Derivatives*, 2, 1 (1994), 7–16; and J. Hull and A. White, "Using Hull–White Interest Rate Trees," *Journal of Derivatives*, (Spring 1996), 26–36.

First Stage

The Hull–White model for the instantaneous short rate r is

$$dr = [\theta(t) - ar]\,dt + \sigma\,dz$$

For the purposes of our initial discussion, we suppose that the time step on the tree is constant and equal to Δt.

We assume that the Δt rate, R, follows the same process as r.

$$dR = [\theta(t) - aR]\,dt + \sigma\,dz$$

Clearly, this is reasonable in the limit as Δt tends to zero. The first stage in building a tree for this model is to construct a tree for a variable R^* that is initially zero and follows the process

$$dR^* = -aR^*\,dt + \sigma\,dz$$

This process is symmetrical about $R^* = 0$. The variable $R^*(t + \Delta t) - R^*(t)$ is normally distributed. If terms of higher order than Δt are ignored, the expected value of $R^*(t + \Delta t) - R^*(t)$ is $-aR^*(t)\Delta t$ and the variance of $R^*(t + \Delta t) - R^*(t)$ is $\sigma^2 \Delta t$.

We define ΔR as the spacing between interest rates on the tree and set

$$\Delta R = \sigma\sqrt{3\Delta t}$$

This proves to be a good choice of ΔR from the viewpoint of error minimization.

Our objective during the first stage is to build a tree similar to that shown in Figure 21.8. To do this, we must resolve which of the three branching methods shown in Figure 21.7 will apply at each node. This will determine the overall geometry of the tree. Once this is done, the branching probabilities must also be calculated.

Define (i, j) as the node where $t = i\Delta t$ and $R^* = j\Delta R$. (The variable i is a positive integer and j is a positive or negative integer.) The branching method used at a node must lead to all three probabilities being positive. Most of the time, the branching in Figure 21.7a is appropriate. When $a > 0$, it is necessary to switch from the branching in Figure 21.7a to the branching in Figure 21.7c for a sufficiently large j. Similarly, it is necessary to switch from the branching in Figure 21.7a to the branching in Figure 21.7b when j is sufficiently negative. Define j_{max} as the value of j where we switch from the Figure 21.7a branching to the Figure 21.7c branching and j_{min} as the value of j where we switch from the Figure 21.7a branching to the Figure 21.7b branching. Hull and White show that probabilities are always positive if we set j_{max} equal to the smallest integer greater than $0.184/(a\Delta t)$ and j_{min} equal to $-j_{max}$.[13]

Define p_u, p_m, and p_d as the probabilities of the highest, middle, and lowest branches emanating from the node. The probabilities are chosen to match the expected change and variance of the change in R^* over the next time interval Δt. The probabilities must also sum to unity. This leads to three equations in the three probabilities.

---

[13] The probabilities are positive for any value of j_{max} between $0.184/(a\Delta t)$ and $0.816/(a\Delta t)$ and for any value of j_{min} between $-0.184/(a\Delta t)$ and $-0.816/(a\Delta t)$. Changing the branching at the first possible node proves to be computationally most efficient.

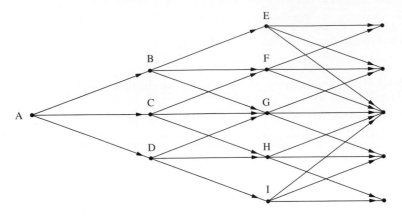

Node	A	B	C	D	E	F	G	H	I
R	0.000%	1.732%	0.000%	−1.732%	3.464%	1.732%	0.000%	−1.732%	−3.464%
p_u	0.1667	0.1217	0.1667	0.2217	0.8867	0.1217	0.1667	0.2217	0.0867
p_m	0.6666	0.6566	0.6666	0.6566	0.0266	0.6566	0.6666	0.6566	0.0266
p_d	0.1667	0.2217	0.1667	0.1217	0.0867	0.2217	0.1667	0.1217	0.8867

Figure 21.8   Tree for R^* in Hull–White model (first stage).

If the branching pattern from node (i, j) is as in Figure 21.7a, the three equations for p_u, p_m, and p_d are

$$p_u\Delta R - p_d\Delta R = -aj\Delta R\Delta t$$
$$p_u\Delta R^2 + p_d\Delta R^2 = \sigma^2\Delta t + a^2 j^2\Delta R^2\Delta t^2$$
$$p_u + p_m + p_d = 1$$

Using $\Delta R^2 = 3\sigma^2\Delta t$, the solution to these equations is:

$$p_u = \frac{1}{6} + \frac{a^2 j^2\Delta t^2 - aj\Delta t}{2}$$

$$p_m = \frac{2}{3} - a^2 j^2\Delta t^2$$

$$p_d = \frac{1}{6} + \frac{a^2 j^2\Delta t^2 + aj\Delta t}{2}$$

Similarly, if the branching has the form shown in Figure 21.7b, the probabilities are

$$p_u = \frac{1}{6} + \frac{a^2 j^2\Delta t^2 + aj\Delta t}{2}$$

$$p_m = -\frac{1}{3} - a^2 j^2\Delta t^2 - 2aj\Delta t$$

$$p_d = \frac{7}{6} + \frac{a^2 j^2\Delta t^2 + 3aj\Delta t}{2}$$

Finally, if the branching has the form shown in Figure 21.7c, the probabilities are

$$p_u = \frac{7}{6} + \frac{a^2 j^2 \Delta t^2 - 3aj\Delta t}{2}$$

$$p_m = -\frac{1}{3} - a^2 j^2 \Delta t^2 + 2aj\Delta t$$

$$p_d = \frac{1}{6} + \frac{a^2 j^2 \Delta t^2 - aj\Delta t}{2}$$

To illustrate the first stage of the tree construction, suppose that $\sigma = 0.01$, $a = 0.1$, and $\Delta t = 1$ year. In this case, $\Delta R = 0.01\sqrt{3} = 0.0173$, j_{max} is set equal to the smallest integer greater than $0.184/0.1$, and $j_{min} = -j_{max}$. This means that $j_{max} = 2$ and $j_{min} = -2$ and the tree is as shown in Figure 21.8. The probabilities on the branches emanating from each node are shown below the tree and are calculated using the equations above for p_u, p_m, and p_d.

Note that the probabilities at each node in Figure 21.8 depend only on j. For example, the probabilities at node B are the same as the probabilities at node F. Furthermore, the tree is symmetrical. The probabilities at node D are the mirror image of the probabilities at node B.

Second Stage

The second stage in the tree construction is to convert the tree for R^* into a tree for R. This is accomplished by displacing the nodes on the R^*-tree so that the initial term structure is exactly matched. Define

$$\alpha(t) = R(t) - R^*(t)$$

Because

$$dR = [\theta(t) - aR]\,dt + \sigma\,dz$$

and

$$dR^* = -aR^*\,dt + \sigma\,dz$$

it follows that

$$d\alpha = [\theta(t) - a\alpha(t)]\,dt$$

If we ignore the distinction between r and R, equation (21.18) shows that the solution to this is

$$\alpha(t) = F(0, t) + \frac{\sigma^2}{2a^2}(1 - e^{-at})^2 \tag{21.27}$$

As a tends to zero this becomes $\alpha(t) = F(0, t) + \sigma^2 t^2/2$.

Equation (21.27) can be used to create a tree for R from the corresponding tree for R^*. The approach is to set the interest rates on the R-tree at time $i\Delta t$ to be equal to the corresponding interest rates on the R^*-tree plus the value of α at time $i\Delta t$ and keeping the probabilities the same.

The tree for R produced using equation (21.27), although satisfactory for most purposes, is not exactly consistent with the initial term structure. An alternative procedure is to calculate the α's iteratively so that the initial term structure is matched exactly. We now explain this approach. It provides a tree-building procedure that can be extended to models where there are no analytic results. Also it is applicable to situations where the initial zero curve is not differentiable everywhere.

Define α_i as $\alpha(i\Delta t)$, the value of R at time $i\Delta t$ on the R-tree minus the corresponding value of R^* at time $i\Delta t$ on the R^*-tree. Define $Q_{i,j}$ as the present value of a security that pays off \$1 if node (i, j) is reached and zero otherwise. The α_i and $Q_{i,j}$ can be calculated using forward induction in such a way that the initial term structure is matched exactly.

Illustration of Second Stage

Suppose that the continuously compounded zero rates in the example in Figure 21.8 are as shown in Table 21.1. The value of $Q_{0,0}$ is 1.0. The value of α_0 is chosen to give the right price for a zero-coupon bond maturing at time Δt. That is, α_0 is set equal to the initial Δt-period interest rate. Because $\Delta t = 1$ in this example, $\alpha_0 = 0.03824$. This defines the position of the initial node on the R-tree in Figure 21.9. The next step is to calculate the values of $Q_{1,1}, Q_{1,0}$, and $Q_{1,-1}$. There is a probability of 0.1667 that the $(1, 1)$ node is reached and the discount rate for the first time step is 3.82%. The value of $Q_{1,1}$ is, therefore, $0.1667e^{-0.0382} = 0.1604$. Similarly, $Q_{1,0} = 0.6417$ and $Q_{1,-1} = 0.1604$.

Once $Q_{1,1}, Q_{1,0}$, and $Q_{1,-1}$ have been calculated, we are in a position to determine α_1. This is chosen to give the right price for a zero-coupon bond maturing at time $2\Delta t$. Because $\Delta R = 0.01732$ and $\Delta t = 1$, the price of this bond as seen at node B is $e^{-(\alpha_1+0.01732)}$. Similarly, the price as seen at node C is $e^{-\alpha_1}$ and the price as seen at node D is $e^{-(\alpha_1-0.01732)}$. The price as seen at the initial node A is, therefore,

$$Q_{1,1}e^{-(\alpha_1+0.01732)} + Q_{1,0}e^{-\alpha_1} + Q_{1,-1}e^{-(\alpha_1-0.01732)} \tag{21.28}$$

From the initial term structure, this bond price should be $e^{-0.04512\times2} = 0.9137$. Substituting for the Q's in equation (21.28), we obtain

$$0.1604e^{-(\alpha_1+0.01732)} + 0.6417e^{-\alpha_1} + 0.1604e^{-(\alpha_1-0.01732)} = 0.9137$$

Table 21.1	Zero Rates for Example
Maturity	**Rate (%)**
0.5	3.430
1.0	3.824
1.5	4.183
2.0	4.512
2.5	4.812
3.0	5.086

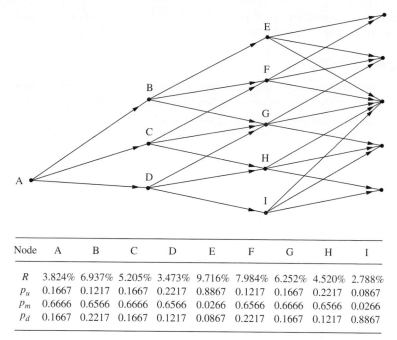

Node	A	B	C	D	E	F	G	H	I
R	3.824%	6.937%	5.205%	3.473%	9.716%	7.984%	6.252%	4.520%	2.788%
p_u	0.1667	0.1217	0.1667	0.2217	0.8867	0.1217	0.1667	0.2217	0.0867
p_m	0.6666	0.6566	0.6666	0.6566	0.0266	0.6566	0.6666	0.6566	0.0266
p_d	0.1667	0.2217	0.1667	0.1217	0.0867	0.2217	0.1667	0.1217	0.8867

Figure 21.9   Tree for *R* in Hull–White model (second stage).

or

$$e^{-\alpha_1}(0.1604e^{-0.01732} + 0.6417 + 0.1604e^{0.01732}) = 0.9137$$

or

$$\alpha_1 = \ln\left[\frac{0.1604e^{-0.01732} + 0.6417 + 0.1604e^{0.01732}}{0.9137}\right] = 0.05205$$

This means that the central node at time Δt in the tree for R corresponds to an interest rate of 5.205%. (See Figure 21.9).

The next step is to calculate $Q_{2,2}$, $Q_{2,1}$, $Q_{2,0}$, $Q_{2,-1}$, and $Q_{2,-2}$. The calculations can be shortened by using previously determined Q values. Consider $Q_{2,1}$ as an example. This is the value of a security that pays off \$1 if node F is reached and zero otherwise. Node F can be reached only from nodes B and C. The interest rates at these nodes are 6.937% and 5.205% respectively. The probabilities associated with the B–F and C–F branches are 0.6566 and 0.1667. The value at node B of a security that pays \$1 at node F is, therefore, $0.6566e^{-0.06937}$. The value at node C is $0.1667e^{-0.05205}$. The variable, $Q_{2,1}$, is $0.6566e^{-0.06937}$ times the present value of \$1 received at node B plus $0.1667e^{-0.05205}$ times the present value of \$1 received at node C; that is:

$$Q_{2,1} = 0.6566e^{-0.06937} \times 0.1604 + 0.1667e^{-0.05205} \times 0.6417 = 0.1998$$

Similarly, $Q_{2,2} = 0.0182$, $Q_{2,0} = 0.4736$, $Q_{2,-1} = 0.2033$, and $Q_{2,-2} = 0.0189$.

The next step in producing the R-tree in Figure 21.9 is to calculate α_2. After that, the $Q_{3,j}$'s can then be computed. We can then calculate α_3; and so on.

Formulas for α's and Q's

To express the approach more formally, we suppose that the $Q_{i,j}$'s have been determined for $i \le m$ $(m \ge 0)$. The next step is to determine α_m so that the tree correctly prices a zero-coupon bond maturing at $(m + 1)\Delta t$. The interest rate at node (m, j) is $\alpha_m + j\Delta R$, so that the price of a zero-coupon bond maturing at time $(m + 1)\Delta t$ is given by

$$P_{m+1} = \sum_{j=-n_m}^{n_m} Q_{m,j} \exp[-(\alpha_m + j\Delta R)\Delta t] \tag{21.29}$$

where n_m is the number of nodes on each side of the central node at time $m\Delta t$. The solution to this equation is

$$\alpha_m = \frac{\ln \sum_{j=-n_m}^{n_m} Q_{m,j} e^{-j\Delta R\Delta t} - \ln P_{m+1}}{\Delta t}$$

Once α_m has been determined, the $Q_{i,j}$ for $i = m + 1$ can be calculated using

$$Q_{m+1,j} = \sum_k Q_{m,k} q(k, j) \exp[-(\alpha_m + k\Delta R)\Delta t]$$

where $q(k, j)$ is the probability of moving from node (m, k) to node $(m + 1, j)$ and the summation is taken over all values of k for which this is nonzero.

Extension to Other Models

The procedure that has just been outlined can be extended to more general models of the form

$$df(r) = [\theta(t) - af(r)] dt + \sigma dz \tag{21.30}$$

This family of models has the property that they can fit any term structure.[14]
As before we assume that the Δt period rate, R, follows the same process as r

$$df(R) = [\theta(t) - af(R)] dt + \sigma dz$$

We start by setting $x = f(R)$ so that

$$dx = [\theta(t) - ax] dt + \sigma dz$$

---

[14]Not all no-arbitrage models have this property. For example, the extended-CIR model, considered by Cox, Ingersoll, and Ross (1985) and Hull and White (1990), which has the form

$$dr = [\theta(t) - ar] dt + \sigma \sqrt{r} dz$$

cannot fit yield curves where the forward rate declines sharply. This is because the process is not well defined when $\theta(t)$ is negative.

The first stage is to build a tree for a variable x^* that follows the same process as x except that $\theta(t) = 0$ and the initial value of x is zero. The procedure here is identical to the procedure already outlined for building a tree such as that in Figure 21.8.

As in Figure 21.9, we then displace the nodes at time $i\Delta t$ by an amount α_i to provide an exact fit to the initial term structure. The equations for determining α_i and $Q_{i,j}$ inductively are slightly different from those for the $f(R) = R$ case. $Q_{0,0} = 1$. Suppose that the $Q_{i,j}$'s have been determined for $i \leq m$ $(m \geq 0)$. The next step is to determine α_m so that the tree correctly prices an $(m + 1)\Delta t$ zero-coupon bond. Define g as the inverse function of f so that the Δt-period interest rate at the jth node at time $m\Delta t$ is

$$g(\alpha_m + j\Delta x)$$

The price of a zero-coupon bond maturing at time $(m + 1)\Delta t$ is given by

$$P_{m+1} = \sum_{j=-n_m}^{n_m} Q_{m,j} \exp\left[-g(\alpha_m + j\Delta x)\Delta t\right] \tag{21.31}$$

This equation can be solved using a numerical procedure such as Newton–Raphson. The value of α when $m = 0$, α_0, is $f[R(0)]$.

Once α_m has been determined, the $Q_{i,j}$ for $i = m + 1$ can be calculated using

$$Q_{m+1,j} = \sum_k Q_{m,k} q(k, j) \exp\left[-g(\alpha_m + k\Delta x)\Delta t\right]$$

where $q(k, j)$ is the probability of moving from node (m, k) to node $(m + 1, j)$ and the summation is taken over all values of k where this is nonzero.

Figure 21.10 shows the results of applying the procedure to the model

$$d \ln(r) = [\theta(t) - a \ln(r)] \, dt + \sigma \, dz$$

when $a = 0.22$, $\sigma = 0.25$, $\Delta t = 0.5$, and the zero rates are as in Table 21.1.

Choosing $f(r)$

The main alternatives when choosing a model of the short rate are $f(r) = r$ and $f(r) = \ln(r)$. These two models appear to perform equally well in fitting market data on actively traded instruments such as caps and European swap options. The main advantage of the $f(r) = r$ model is its analytic tractability. Its main disadvantage is that negative interest rates are possible. In most circumstances, the probability of negative interest rates occurring under the model is very small, but some analysts are reluctant to use a model where there is any chance at all of negative interest rates. The $f(r) = \ln r$ model has no analytic tractability, but has the advantage that it gives no chance at all of negative interest rates. Another advantage is that traders naturally think in terms of σ's arising from a lognormal model rather than σ's arising from a normal model.

There is a problem in choosing a satisfactory model for low-interest-rate countries (for example, Japan at the end of 1998). The normal model is unsatisfactory because, when the initial short rate is low, the probability of negative interest rates in the

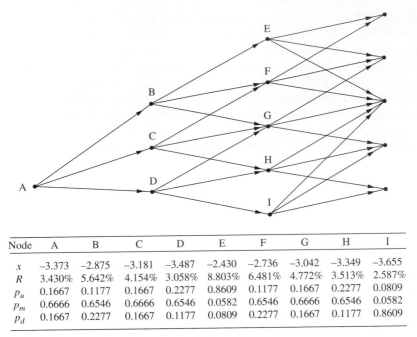

Node	A	B	C	D	E	F	G	H	I
x	−3.373	−2.875	−3.181	−3.487	−2.430	−2.736	−3.042	−3.349	−3.655
R	3.430%	5.642%	4.154%	3.058%	8.803%	6.481%	4.772%	3.513%	2.587%
p_u	0.1667	0.1177	0.1667	0.2277	0.8609	0.1177	0.1667	0.2277	0.0809
p_m	0.6666	0.6546	0.6666	0.6546	0.0582	0.6546	0.6666	0.6546	0.0582
p_d	0.1667	0.2277	0.1667	0.1177	0.0809	0.2277	0.1667	0.1177	0.8609

Figure 21.10   Tree for lognormal model.

future is no longer negligible. The lognormal model is unsatisfactory because the volatility of rates (that is, the σ parameter in the lognormal model) is usually much greater when rates are low than when they are high. (For example, a volatility of 100% might be appropriate when the short rate is less than 1%, and 20% might be appropriate when it is 4% or more.) A model that appears to work well is one where $f(r)$ is chosen so that rates are lognormal for r less than 1% and normal for r greater than 1%.[15]

Using Analytic Results in Conjunction with Trees

When a tree is constructed for the Hull–White model, the analytic results in sections 21.9 and 21.10 can be used to provide the complete term structure and European option prices at each node. It is important to recognize that the interest rate on the tree is the Δt-period rate, R. It is not the instantaneous short rate, r. We should, therefore, calculate bond prices using equation (21.22), not equation (21.19).

> **Example 21.3**   As an example of the use of analytic results, we use the zero rates in Table 21.2. Rates for maturities between those indicated are generated using linear interpolation.

---

[15] See Hull and White, "Taking Rates to the Limit," *RISK*, (December 1997), 168–69.

Table 21.2	DM Zero-Curve, July 8, 1994, with All Rates Continuously Compounded	

Maturity	*Days*	*Rate*
3 days	3	5.01772
1 month	31	4.98284
2 months	62	4.97234
3 months	94	4.96157
6 months	185	4.99058
1 year	367	5.09389
2 years	731	5.79733
3 years	1,096	6.30595
4 years	1,461	6.73464
5 years	1,826	6.94816
6 years	2,194	7.08807
7 years	2,558	7.27527
8 years	2,922	7.30852
9 years	3,287	7.39790
10 years	3,653	7.49015

Data courtesy of A. A. J. Pelsser, ABN Amro.

Table 21.3	Value of a Three-Year Put Option on a Nine-Year Zero-Coupon Bond with a Strike Price of 63 $a = 0.1$ and $\sigma = 0.01$; Zero Curve as in Table 21.1	

Steps	*Tree*	*Analytic*
10	1.8658	1.8093
30	1.8234	1.8093
50	1.8093	1.8093
100	1.8144	1.8093
200	1.8097	1.8093
500	1.8093	1.8093

We will price a three-year ($= 3 \times 365$ day) European put option on a zero-coupon bond that will expire in nine years ($= 9 \times 365$ days). Interest rates are assumed to follow the Hull–White [$f(r) = r$] model. The strike price is 63, $a = 0.1$, and $\sigma = 0.01$. We constructed a three-year tree and calculated zero-coupon bond prices at the final nodes analytically as described in section 21.9. As shown in Table 21.3, the results from the tree are consistent with the analytic price of the option.

This example provides a good test of the implementation of the model because the gradient of the zero curve changes sharply immediately after the expiration of the option. Small errors in the construction and use of the tree are liable to have a big effect on the option values obtained.

Tree for American Bond Options

The DerivaGem software accompanying this book implements the normal and the lognormal model, as well as Black's model, for valuing European bond options, caps/floors, and European swap options. In addition, American-style bond options can be handled. Figure 21.11 shows the tree produced by the software when it is used to value a 1.5-year American call option on a 10-year bond using four time steps and

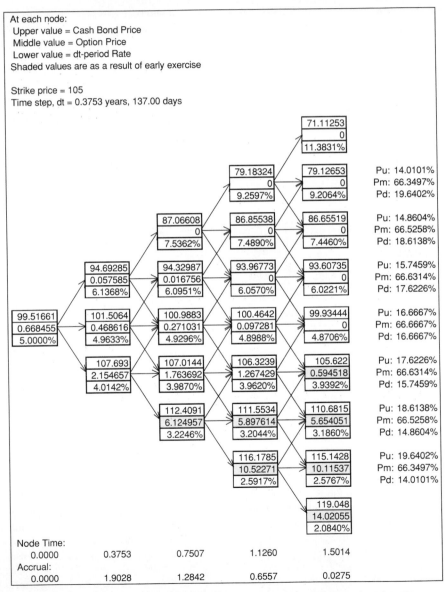

Figure 21.11   Tree, produced by DerivaGem, for valuing an American bond option.

the lognormal model. The parameters used in the lognormal model are $a = 5\%$ and $\sigma = 20\%$. The underlying bond lasts ten years and has a principal of 100 and pays a coupon of 5% per annum semiannually. The yield curve is flat at 5% per annum. The strike price is 105. As explained in section 20.2 the strike price can be a cash strike price or a quoted strike price. In this case it is a quoted strike price. The bond price shown on the tree is the cash bond price. The accrued interest at each node is shown below the tree. The cash strike price is calculated as the quoted strike price plus accrued interest. The quoted bond price is the cash bond price minus accrued interest. The payoff from the option is the cash bond price minus the cash strike price. Equivalently it is the quoted bond price minus the quoted strike price.

The tree gives the price of the option as 0.668. A much larger tree with 100 time steps gives the price of the option as 0.699. Two points should be noted about Figure 21.11:

1. The software measures the time to option maturity in days. When an option maturity of 1.5 years is input, the life of the option is assumed to be 1.5014 years (or 1 year and 183 days).

2. The price of the ten-year bond cannot be computed analytically when the lognormal model is assumed. It is computed numerically by rolling back through a much larger tree than that shown.

Unequal Time Steps

In practice, it is often convenient to construct a tree with unequal time steps. Typically, we want to choose time steps so that nodes lie on certain key dates (for example, payment dates or dates when a Bermudan option can be exercised). We can accommodate unequal time steps as follows. Suppose that the nodes are at times $t_0, t_1, t_2, \ldots, t_n$. When the x^* tree is constructed, the vertical spacing between nodes at time t_{i+1} is set equal to $\sigma\sqrt{3(t_{i+1} - t_i)}$. The branching method is as indicated in Figure 21.12. From any given node at time t_i, we branch to one of three adjacent nodes at time t_{i+1}. Suppose that x_i^* is the value of x^* at time t_i. The central node we branch to at time t_{i+1} is chosen to be the node closest to the expected value of x^*; that is, it is the node closest to $x_i^* - a(t_{i+1} - t_i)x_i^*$. The probabilities are determined so that the mean and standard deviation of the change in x^* are matched. (This involves solving three simultaneous linear equations in the probabilities.) The tree for x is constructed from the tree for x^* as in the constant-time-step case.

21.13   NONSTATIONARY MODELS

The models discussed in the preceding sections have involved only one function of time, $\theta(t)$. Some authors have suggested extending the models by making a or σ (or both) functions of time. For example, in 1990, Hull and White produced analytic results for the model in equation (21.12) when a and σ are both functions of time. Also,

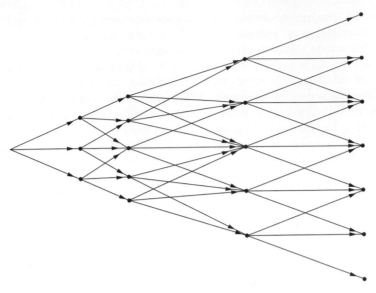

Figure 21.12   Changing the length of the time step.

in 1990, Black, Derman, and Toy suggested a procedure for building a binomial tree that is equivalent to the model[16]

$$d \ln r = \left[\theta(t) + \frac{\sigma'(t)}{\sigma(t)} \ln (r) \right] dt + \sigma(t) \, dz$$

where $\sigma'(t)$ is the partial derivative of σ with respect to t. In 1991, Black and Karasinski suggested a more general model where the reversion rate is decoupled from the volatility[17]

$$d \ln r = \left[\theta(t) - a(t) \ln (r) \right] dt + \sigma(t) \, dz$$

The trinomial tree-building procedure in section 21.12 can be extended to accommodate models such as these where a and σ are known functions of time. As in the constant a and σ case, we first build a tree for x^* where

$$dx^* = -a(t)x^* \, dt + \sigma(t) \, dz$$

The spacing between the nodes at time t_{i+1} is chosen to be

$$\sigma(t_i) \sqrt{3(t_{i+1} - t_i)}$$

[16]See F. Black, E. Derman, and W. Toy, "A One-Factor Model of Interest Rates and Its Application to Treasury Bond Options," *Financial Analysts Journal,* (January–February 1990), 33–39.

[17]See F. Black and P. Karasinski, "Bond and Option Pricing when Short Rates Are Lognormal," *Financial Analysts Journal,* (July–August 1991), 52–59.

From any given node at time t_i, we branch to one of three adjacent nodes at time t_{i+1}. Suppose that x_i^* is the value of x^* at time t_i. The central node we branch to at time t_{i+1} is chosen to be the node closest to the expected value of x^*; that is, it is the node closest to $x_i^* - a(t_i)(t_{i+1} - t_i)x_i^*$. The probabilities are determined similarly to the constant-time-step case, so that the mean and standard deviation of the change in x^* are matched. The tree for x is calculated from the tree for x^* as in the constant a and σ case.

The advantage of making σ or a (or both) functions of time is that the model can be fitted more precisely to the prices of instruments that trade actively in the market. When we use the model to price deals that are fairly similar to actively traded deals we know that it will provide consistent prices. The disadvantage of making a and σ functions of time is that the model has a nonstationary volatility structure. The volatility term structure given by the model in the future is liable to be quite different from that existing in the market today. Caution should be exercised in using the model for pricing instruments that are markedly different from actively traded instruments and for pricing instruments that are dependent on the volatility environment in the future.[18] The point made here is similar to the point we made in connection with implied trees in section 18.6.

21.14 CALIBRATION

Up to now, we have assumed that the volatility parameters a and σ, whether constant or functions of time, are known. We now discuss how they are determined. This is known as calibrating the model.

The volatility parameters are inferred from market data on actively traded options (for example, broker quotes such as those in Tables 20.1 and 20.2). These will be referred to as the *calibrating instruments*. The first stage is to choose a "goodness of fit" measure. Suppose there are n calibrating instruments. One possible goodness of fit measure is

$$\sum_i^n (U_i - V_i)^2$$

where U_i is the market price of the ith calibrating instrument and V_i is the price given by the model for this instrument. Another that gives more weight to short maturity (lesser priced) options is

$$\sum_i^n \frac{(U_i - V_i)^2}{U_i}$$

In both cases, our objective is to minimize the goodness-of-fit measure.

The minimization is accomplished using the Levenberg–Marquardt procedure.[19] When a and σ are constants, the technique is used to determine only two

---

[18]This point is discussed further in J. Hull and A. White, "Using Hull–White Interest Rate Trees," *Journal of Derivatives*, (Spring 1996), 26-36.

[19]For a good description of this procedure see W. H. Press, B. P. Flannery, S. A. Teukolsky, and W. T. Vetterling, *Numerical Recipes in C: The Art of Scientific Computing* (Cambridge: Cambridge University Press, 1988).

parameters. When a and σ are functions of time, it is used to determine more parameters. A convenient way of making a or σ a function of time is to assume a step function. Suppose, for example, we elect to make a constant and σ a function of time. We would choose times $t_1, t_2, \ldots, t_n$ and assume $\sigma(t) = \sigma_0$ for $t \leq t_1$, $\sigma(t) = \sigma_i$ for $t_i < t \leq t_{i+1}$ $(1 \leq i \leq n-1)$, and $\sigma(t) = \sigma_n$ for $t > t_n$. We would use the Levenberg–Marquardt procedure to determine a total of $n + 2$ parameters $a, \sigma_0, \sigma_1, \ldots, \sigma_n$.

The calibrating instruments chosen should be as similar as possible to the instrument being valued. Suppose, for example, that we wish to value a Bermudan-style swap option that lasts five years and can be exercised on any payment date into a swap maturing ten years from today. The most relevant calibrating instruments are 1×9, 2×8, 3×7, 4×6 and 5×5 European swap options. (An $n \times m$ European swap option is an n year option to enter into a swap lasting for m years beyond the maturity of the option.) In the case where there are as many parameters as there are calibrating instruments, the model will provide a perfect fit to the calibrating instruments.

A somewhat different approach to calibration is to use all available calibrating instruments to calculate a "global best fit" constant a and σ parameters. The parameter a is held fixed at its best fit value. The model can then be used in the same way as Black–Scholes. There is a one-to-one relationship between options prices and the σ parameter. The model can be used to convert tables such as Table 20.1 and 20.2 into tables of implied σ's.[20] These tables can be used to assess the σ most appropriate for pricing the instrument under consideration.

These approaches to calibration can be used for any choice of $f(r)$ in the model in equation (21.30). A refinement to the approach is to assume that $f(r)$ is a piecewise linear function and use the Levenberg–Marquardt procedure to determine the parameters of $f(r)$ at the same time as the a and σ parameters.[21]

21.15   HEDGING USING A ONE-FACTOR MODEL

General approaches to hedging a portfolio of interest rate derivatives were outlined in section 20.11. They can be used with the term structure models discussed in this chapter. The calculation of deltas, gammas, and vegas involves making small changes to either the zero curve or the volatilities of calibrating instruments and recomputing the value of the portfolio.

Note that, although we often assume there is one factor when pricing interest rate derivatives, we do not assume only one factor when hedging. For example, the deltas we calculate allow for many different movements in the yield curve, not just

---

[20]Note that in a term structure model the implied σ's are not the same as the implied volatilities calculated from Black's model in Tables 20.1 and 20.2. The procedure for computing implied σ's is as follows. The Black volatilities are converted to prices using Black's model. An iterative procedure is then used to imply the σ parameter in the term structure model from the price.

[21]For a discussion of this, see Hull and White, "Taking Rates to the Limit," *RISK* (December 1997), 168–69.

those that are possible under the model chosen. The practice of taking account of changes that cannot happen under the model considered, as well as those that can, is known as *outside model hedging* and is standard practice for traders.[22] The reality is that relatively simple one-factor models usually give reasonable prices for instruments, but good hedging schemes must explicitly or implicitly assume many factors.

21.16 FORWARD RATES AND FUTURES RATES

In section 4.12 we explained that a convexity adjustment is necessary when a forward interest rate is calculated from a Eurodollar futures price quote.[23] We can derive a theoretical convexity adjustment for either the Ho–Lee or Hull–White model.

Consider a futures contract on the interest rate lasting between times t_1 and t_2. In the Ho–Lee model, the continuously compounded forward rate for the period equals the continuously compounded futures rate minus $\sigma^2 t_1 t_2/2$. A typical value of σ is 0.012. For the Eurodollar futures traded on the CME, $t_2 = t_1 + 0.25$. Typical convexity adjustments that have to be made to the rates given by these contracts when they have maturities of 2, 4, 6, 8, and 10 years are, therefore, 3, 12, 27, 48, and 74 basis points, respectively.

For the Hull–White model, the convexity adjustment that must be subtracted from the continuously compounded futures rate to get the continuously compounded forward rate is

$$\frac{B(t_1, t_2)}{t_2 - t_1}[B(t_1, t_2)(1 - e^{-2at_1}) + 2aB(0, t_1)^2]\frac{\sigma^2}{4a} \tag{21.32}$$

where the B function is as defined in equation (21.20). See Problem 21.21.

> **Example 21.4** Consider the situation where $a = 0.05$ and $\sigma = 0.015$ and we wish to calculate a forward rate when the eight-year Eurodollar futures price is 94. In this case $t_1 = 8, t_2 = 8.25, B(t_1, t_2) = 0.2484, B(0, t_1) = 6.5936$, and the convexity adjustment is
>
> $$\frac{0.2484}{0.25}[0.2484(1 - e^{-2\times0.05\times8}) + 2 \times 0.05 \times 6.5936^2]\frac{0.015^2}{4 \times 0.05} = 0.0050$$
>
> or 0.50%. The futures rate is 6% per annum with quarterly compounding or 5.96% with continuous compounding. The forward rate is, therefore, $5.96 - 0.50 = 5.46\%$ per annum with continuous compounding.

---

[22] A simple example of outside model hedging is in the way that the Black–Scholes model is used. The Black–Scholes model assumes that volatility is constant—but traders regularly calculate vega and hedge against volatility changes.

[23] Note that the term *convexity adjustment* is overworked in derivatives. The convexity adjustment here is quite different from the one talked about in section 20.6.

SUMMARY

The traditional models of the term structure used in finance are known as equilibrium models. These are useful for understanding potential relationships between variables in the economy but have the disadvantage that the initial term structure is an output from the model rather than an input to it. When valuing derivatives, it is important that the model used be consistent with the initial term structure observed in the market. No-arbitrage models are designed to have this property. They take the initial term structure as given and define how it can evolve.

This chapter has provided a description of a number of one-factor no-arbitrage models of the short rate. These are very robust and can be used in conjunction with any set of initial zero rates. The simplest model is the Ho–Lee model. This has the advantage that it is analytically tractable. Its chief disadvantage is that it implies that all rates are equally variable at all times. The Hull–White model is a version of the Ho–Lee model that includes mean reversion. It allows a richer description of the volatility environment while preserving its analytic tractability. Lognormal one-factor models have the advantage that they avoid the possibility of negative interest rates but, unfortunately, they have no analytic tractability.

SUGGESTIONS FOR FURTHER READING

Equilibrium Approaches to Modeling the Term Structure

Brennan, M. J., and E. S. Schwartz. "An Equilibrium Model of Bond Pricing and a Test of Market Efficiency," *Journal of Financial and Quantitative Analysis,* 17, 3 (September 1982), 301–29.

Courtadon, G. "The Pricing of Options on Default-free Bonds," *Journal of Financial and Quantitative Analysis,* 17 (March 1982), 75–100.

Cox, J. C., J. E. Ingersoll, and S. A. Ross. "A Theory of the Term Structure of Interest Rates," *Econometrica,* 53 (1985), 385–407.

Jamshidian, F. "An Exact Bond Option Pricing Formula," *Journal of Finance,* 44 (March 1989), 205–9.

Longstaff, F. A., and E. S. Schwartz. "Interest Rate Volatility and the Term Structure: A Two Factor General Equilibrium Model," *Journal of Finance,* 47, 4 (September 1992), 1259–82.

Rendleman, R., and B. Bartter. "The Pricing of Options on Debt Securities," *Journal of Financial and Quantitative Analysis,* 15 (March 1980), 11–24.

Schaefer, S. M., and E. S. Schwartz. "Time-Dependent Variance and the Pricing of Options," *Journal of Finance,* 42 (December 1987), 1113–28.

Vasicek, O. A. "An Equilibrium Characterization of the Term Structure," *Journal of Financial Economics,* 5 (1977), 177–88.

No-Arbitrage Models

Black, F., E. Derman, and W. Toy. "A One-Factor Model of Interest Rates and Its Application to Treasury Bond Options," *Financial Analysts Journal,* (January–February 1990), 33–39.

Black, F., and P. Karasinski. "Bond and Option Pricing When Short Rates Are Lognormal," *Financial Analysts Journal,* (July–August 1991), 52–59.

Burghardt, G., and B. Hoskins. "A Question of Bias," *RISK* (March 1995), 63-67.

Ho, T. S. Y., and S.-B. Lee. "Term Structure Movements and Pricing Interest Rate Contingent Claims," *Journal of Finance,* 41 (December 1986), 1011–29.

Hull, J., and A. White. "Bond Option Pricing Based on a Model for the Evolution of Bond Prices," *Advances in Futures and Options Research,* 6 (1993), 1–13.

Hull, J., and A. White. "Branching Out," *RISK,* (January 1994), 34–37.

Hull, J., and A. White. "In the Common Interest," *RISK,* (March 1992), 64–68.

Hull, J., and A. White. "Numerical Procedures for Implementing Term Structure Models I: Single-Factor Models,"*Journal of Derivatives,* 2, 1 (Fall 1994), 7–16.

Hull, J., and A. White. "One-Factor Interest Rate Models and the Valuation of Interest Rate Derivative Securities," *Journal of Financial and Quantitative Analysis,* 28 (June 1993), 235–54.

Hull, J., and A. White. "Pricing Interest Rate Derivative Securities," *The Review of Financial Studies,* 3, 4 (1990), 573–92.

Hull, J., and A. White. "Taking Rates to the Limit" *RISK,* (December 1997), 168–9.

Hull, J., and A. White. " The Pricing of Options on Interest Rate Caps and Floors Using the Hull–White Model," *Journal of Financial Engineering,* 2, 3 (1993), 287–96.

Hull, J., and A. White. "Using Hull–White Interest Rate Trees," *Journal of Derivatives,* (Spring 1996), 26–36.

Hull, J., and A. White. "Valuing Derivative Securities Using the Explicit Finite Difference Method," *Journal of Financial and Quantitative Analysis,* 25 (March 1990), 87–100.

Kijima, M., and I. Nagayama. "Efficient Numerical Procedures for the Hull–White Extended Vasicek Model," *Journal of Financial Engineering,* 3 (September–December 1994), 275–92.

Kijima, M., and I. Nagayama. "A Numerical Procedure for the General One-Factor Interest Rate Model," *Journal of Financial Engineering* (December 1996), 317–37.

Li, A., P. Ritchken, and L. Sankarasubramanian. "Lattice Models for Pricing American Interest Rate Claims," *Journal of Finance,* 50, 2 (June 1995), 719–37.

Pelsser, A. A. J. "Efficient Methods for Valuing and Managing Interest Rate and Other Derivative Securities," Ph.D. dissertation, Erasmus University, Rotterdam, 1996.

Rebonato, R. *Interest Rate Option Models,* Chichester: John Wiley & Sons, 1996.

QUESTIONS AND PROBLEMS
(ANSWERS IN SOLUTIONS MANUAL)

21.1. What is the difference between an equilibrium model and a no-arbitrage model?

21.2. If a stock price were mean reverting or followed a path-dependent process there would be market inefficiency. Why is there not a market inefficiency when the short-term interest rate does so?

21.3. Suppose that the short rate is currently 4% and its standard deviation is 1% per annum. What happens to the standard deviation when the short rate increases to 8% in (a) Vasicek's model; (b) Rendleman and Bartter's model; and (c) the Cox, Ingersoll, and Ross model?

21.4. Explain the difference between a one-factor and a two-factor interest rate model.

21.5. Can the approach described in section 21.4 for decomposing an option on a coupon-bearing bond into a portfolio of options on zero-coupon bonds be used in conjunction with a two-factor model? Explain your answer.

21.6. Suppose that $a = 0.1$ and $b = 0.1$ in both the Vasicek and the Cox, Ingersoll, Ross model. In both models, the initial short rate is 10% and the initial standard deviation of the short rate change in a short time Δt is $0.02\sqrt{\Delta t}$. Compare the prices given by the models for a zero-coupon bond that matures in year 10.

21.7. Suppose that $a = 0.1$, $b = 0.08$, and $\sigma = 0.015$ in Vasicek's model with the initial value of the short rate being 5%. Calculate the price of a one-year European call option on a zero-coupon bond with a principal of $100 that matures in three years when the strike price is $87.

21.8. Repeat Problem 21.7 valuing a European put option with a strike of $87. What is the put–call parity relationship between the prices of European call and put options? Show that the put and call option prices satisfy put–call parity in this case.

21.9. Suppose that $a = 0.05$, $b = 0.08$, and $\sigma = 0.015$ in Vasicek's model with the initial short-term interest rate being 6%. Calculate the price of a 2.1-year European call option on a bond that will mature in three years. Suppose that the bond pays a coupon of 5% semiannually. The principal of the bond is 100 and the strike price of the option is 99. The strike price is the cash price (not the quoted price) that will be paid for the bond.

21.10. Use the answer to Problem 21.9 and put–call parity arguments to calculate the price of a put option that has the same terms as the call option in Problem 21.9.

21.11. In the Hull–White model, $a = 0.08$ and $\sigma = 0.01$. Calculate the price of a one-year European call option on a zero-coupon bond that will mature in five years when the term structure is flat at 10%, the principal of the bond is $100, and the strike price is $68.

21.12. Suppose that $a = 0.05$ and $\sigma = 0.015$ in the Hull–White model with the initial term structure being flat at 6% with semiannual compounding. Calculate the price of a 2.1-year European call option on a bond that will mature in three years. Suppose that the bond pays a coupon of 5% per annum semiannually. The principal of the bond is 100 and the strike price of the option is 99. The strike price is the cash price (not the quoted price) that will be paid for the bond.

21.13. Using equation (21.13) and the results in section 21.16, show that the drift rate of the short rate at time t in the Ho and Lee model is $G_t(0, t)$, where $G(t, T)$ is the instantaneous futures rate as seen at time t for a contract maturing at time T and the subscript denotes a partial derivative.

21.14. Using equation (21.18) and the results in section 21.16, show that the drift rate of the short rate at time t in the Hull and White model is $G_t(0, t) + a[G(0, t) - r]$, where $G(t, T)$ is the instantaneous futures rate as seen at time t for a contract maturing at time T and the subscript denotes a partial derivative.

21.15. Suppose that $a = 0.05$, $\sigma = 0.015$, and the term structure is flat at 10%. Construct a trinomial tree for the Hull–White model where there are two time steps, each one year in length.

21.16. Calculate the price of a two-year zero-coupon bond from the tree in Figure 21.6.

21.17. Calculate the price of a two-year zero-coupon bond from the tree in Figure 21.9 and verify that it agrees with the initial term structure.

21.18. Calculate the price of an 18-month zero-coupon bond from the tree in Figure 21.10 and verify that it agrees with the initial term structure.

21.19. Verify that the DerivaGem software gives Figure 21.11 for the example considered. Use the software to calculate the price of the American bond option for the lognormal and normal models when the strike price is 95, 100, and 105. In the case of the normal model, assume that $a = 5\%$ and $\sigma = 1\%$. Discuss the results in the context of the fat tail/thin tail arguments of chapter 17.

21.20. Use the DerivaGem software to value 1×4, 2×3, 3×2, and 4×1 European swap options to receive fixed and pay floating. Assume that the one, two, three, four, and five year interest rates are 6%, 5.5%, 6%, 6.5%, and 7%, respectively. The payment frequency on the swap is semiannual and the fixed rate is 6% per annum with semiannual compounding. Use the Hull–White model with $a = 3\%$ and $\sigma = 1\%$. Calculate the volatility implied by Black's model for each option.

21.21. Use equation (21.32) to calculate an expression for the difference between the instantaneous forward rate and the instantaneous futures rate. Show that it is consistent with equation (21.27).

ASSIGNMENT QUESTIONS

21.22. Construct a trinomial tree for the Ho and Lee model where $\sigma = 0.02$. Suppose that the the initial zero-coupon interest rate for maturities of 0.5, 1.0, and 1.5 years are 7.5%, 8%, and 8.5%. Use two time steps, each six months long. Calculate the value of a zero-coupon bond with a face value of 100 and a remaining life of six months at the ends of the final nodes of the tree. Use the tree to value a one-year European put option with a strike price of 95 on the bond. Compare the price given by your tree with the analytic price given by DerivaGem.

21.23. Suppose that $a = 0.1, \sigma = 0.02$ in the Hull–White model, and a 10-year Euro-dollar futures quote is 92. What is the forward rate for the period between 10.0 years and 10.25 years?

21.24. A trader wishes to compute the price of a one-year American call option on a five-year bond with a face value of 100. The bond pays a coupon of 6% semiannually and the (quoted) strike price of the option is $100. The continuously compounded zero rates for maturities of six months, one year, two years, three years, four years, and five years are 4.5%, 5%, 5.5%, 5.8%, 6.1%, and 6.3%. The best fit reversion rate for either the normal or the lognormal model has been estimated as 5%.

A one-year European call option with a (quoted) strike price of 100 on the bond is actively traded. Its market price is $0.50. The trader decides to use this option for calibration. Use the DerivaGem software with ten time steps to answer the following questions.

(a) Assuming a normal model, imply the σ parameter from the price of the European option.

(b) Use the σ parameter to calculate the price of the option when it is American.

(c) Repeat (a) and (b) for the lognormal model. Show that the model used does not significantly affect the price obtained providing it is calibrated to the known European price.

(d) Display the tree for the normal model and calculate the probability of a negative interest rate occurring.

(e) Display the tree for the lognormal model and verify that the option price is correctly calculated at the node where, with the notation of section 21.12, $i = 9$ and $j = -1$.

CHAPTER 22

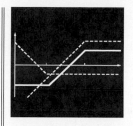

INTEREST RATE DERIVATIVES: MORE ADVANCED MODELS

The interest rate models discussed in chapter 21 are widely used for pricing instruments when the simpler models in chapter 20 are inappropriate. They are easy to implement and, if used carefully, can ensure that most nonstandard interest rate derivatives are priced consistently with actively traded instruments such as interest rate caps, European swap options, and European bond options. Two limitations of the models are

1. They involve only one factor (that is, one source of uncertainty).
2. They do not give the user complete freedom in choosing the volatility structure.

As explained in section 21.13, the models can be made to provide a perfect fit to volatilities observed in the market at time zero, but the user then has no control over the volatilities at subsequent times. Future volatility patterns are liable to be quite different from those observed in the market today.

This chapter discusses multifactor term structure models and presents some general approaches to building term structure models that give the user complete flexibility in specifying the volatility environment (both at time zero and at future times). The models require much more computation time than the models in chapter 21. As a result, they are often used for research and development rather than routine pricing.

This chapter also covers the mortgage-backed security market in the United States and describes how some of the ideas presented in the chapter can be used to price instruments in that market.

22.1 TWO-FACTOR MODELS OF THE SHORT RATE

In recent years there have been a number of attempts to extend the models introduced in chapter 21 so that they involve two or more factors. Examples are Duffie and Kan (1996) and Hull and White (1996).[1] The Hull–White approach involves a similar idea

[1] See D. Duffie and R. Kan, "A Yield-Factor Model of Interest Rates," *Mathematical Finance*, 6, 4 (1996), 379–406; and J. Hull and A. White, "Numerical Procedures for Implementing Term Structure Models II: Two Factor Models," *Journal of Derivatives*, 2, 2 (Winter 1994), 37–48.

to the equilibrium model suggested by Brennan and Schwartz, that was described briefly in section 21.6. It assumes that the risk-neutral process for the short rate, r, is

$$df(r) = [\theta(t) + u - af(r)] dt + \sigma_1 dz_1 \qquad (22.1)$$

where u has an initial value of zero and follows the process

$$du = -bu \, dt + \sigma_2 \, dz_2$$

As in the one-factor models considered in chapter 21, the parameter $\theta(t)$ is chosen to make the model consistent with the initial term structure. The stochastic variable u is a component of the reversion level of r and itself reverts to a level of zero at rate b. The parameters a, b, σ_1, and σ_2 are constants and dz_1 and dz_2 are Wiener processes with instantaneous correlation ρ.

This model provides a richer pattern of term structure movements and a richer pattern of volatility structures than the one-factor models considered in chapter 21. Figure 22.1 shows the forward rate standard deviations that are produced using the model when $f(r) = r$, $a = 1$, $b = 0.1$, $\sigma_1 = 0.01$, $\sigma_2 = 0.0165$, and $\rho = 0.6$. With these parameters, the model exhibits, at all times, a "humped" volatility structure similar to that observed in practice. (See Figure 20.3.) The correlation structure implied by the model is also plausible.

When $f(r) = r$ the model is analytically tractable. The price at time t of a zero-coupon bond that provides a payoff of \$1 at time T is

$$P(t, T) = A(t, T) \exp[-B(t, T)r - C(t, T)u] \qquad (22.2)$$

where

$$B(t, T) = \frac{1}{a}[1 - e^{-a(T-t)}]$$

$$C(t, T) = \frac{1}{a(a - b)} e^{-a(T-t)} - \frac{1}{b(a - b)} e^{-b(T-t)} + \frac{1}{ab}$$

and $A(t, T)$ is as given in Appendix 22A.

The prices, c and p, at time zero of European call and put options on a zero-coupon bond are given by

$$c = LP(0, s)N(h) - XP(0, T)N(h - \sigma_P)$$
$$p = XP(0, T)N(-h + \sigma_P) - LP(0, s)N(-h)$$

where T is the maturity of the option, s is the maturity of the bond, X is the strike price, L is the bond's principal,

$$h = \frac{1}{\sigma_P} \log \frac{LP(0, s)}{P(0, T)X} + \frac{\sigma_P}{2}$$

and σ_P is as given in Appendix 22A. Because this is a two-factor model, an option on a coupon-bearing bond cannot be decomposed into a portfolio of options on zero-coupon bonds as described in section 21.10. However, we can obtain an approximate analytic valuation by calculating the first two moments of the bond price and assuming it is lognormal.

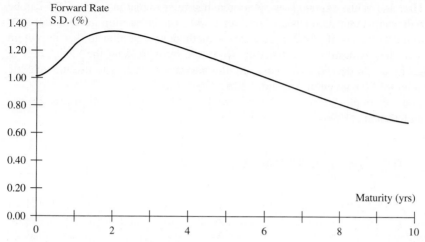

Figure 22.1 Example of volatility term structure that can be produced by the two factor Hull–White model. $f(r) = r$, $a = 1$, $b = 0.1$, $\sigma_1 = 0.01$, $\sigma_2 = 0.0165$, $\rho = 0.6$.

Constructing a Tree

To construct a tree for the model in equation (22.1), we simplify the notation by defining $x = f(r)$ so that

$$dx = [\theta(t) + u - ax] \, dt + \sigma_1 \, dz_1$$

with

$$du = -bu \, dt + \sigma_2 \, dz_2$$

Assuming $a \neq b$ we can eliminate the dependence of the first stochastic variable on the second by defining

$$y = x + \frac{u}{b - a}$$

so that

$$dy = [\theta(t) - ay] \, dt + \sigma_3 \, dz_3$$
$$du = -bu \, dt + \sigma_2 \, dz_2$$

where

$$\sigma_3^2 = \sigma_1^2 + \frac{\sigma_2^2}{(b - a)^2} + \frac{2\rho\sigma_1\sigma_2}{b - a}$$

and dz_3 is a Wiener process. The correlation between dz_2 and dz_3 is

$$\frac{\rho\sigma_1 + \sigma_2/(b - a)}{\sigma_3}$$

Hull and White explain how an approach similar to that in section 18.5 can be used to develop a three-dimensional tree for y and u on the assumption that $\theta(t) = 0$ and the initial values of y and u are zero. A methodology similar to that in section 21.12 can then be used to construct the final tree by increasing the values of y at time $i\Delta t$ by α_i. In the $f(r) = r$ case, an alternative approach is to use the analytic expression for $\theta(t)$, given in Appendix 22A.

Some examples of how the model can be calibrated and used in practice are given in Rebonato (1996).[2]

22.2　THE HEATH, JARROW, AND MORTON APPROACH

We now present some general results on one-factor term structure models and show how they can be extended to situations where there are several factors. We continue to consider the processes followed by variables in the traditional risk-neutral world where investors, on average, earn the risk-free rate in each very short period of time of length Δt.

Notation

We will adopt the following notation:

$P(t, T)$: Price at time t of a zero-coupon bond with principal $1 maturing at time T.

Ω_t: Vector of past and present values of interest rates and bond prices at time t that are relevant for determining bond price volatilities at that time.

$v(t, T, \Omega_t)$: Volatility of $P(t, T)$.

$f(t, T_1, T_2)$: Forward rate as seen at time t for the period between time T_1 and time T_2.

$F(t, T)$: Instantaneous forward rate as seen at time t for a contract maturing at time T.

$r(t)$: Short-term risk-free interest rate at time t.

$dz(t)$: Wiener process driving term structure movements.

The variable $F(t, T)$ is the limit of $f(t, T, T + \Delta t)$ as Δt tends to zero.

Processes for Zero-Coupon Bond Prices and Forward Rates

When we are assuming just one factor, the risk-neutral process for $P(t, T)$ has the form

$$dP(t, T) = r(t)P(t, T)\,dt + v(t, T, \Omega_t)P(t, T)\,dz(t) \qquad (22.3)$$

The expected return is $r(t)$ because a zero-coupon bond is a traded security providing no income. As its argument Ω_t indicates, the volatility, v, can, in the most general form of the model, be any well-behaved function of past and present interest

---

[2] See R. Rebonato, *Interest Rate Option Models*, (2nd Ed., Chichester, England: John Wiley and Sons, 1998) pp. 306–8.

rates and bond prices. Because a bond's price volatility declines to zero at maturity, we must have[3]

$$v(t, t, \Omega_t) = 0$$

From equation (4.1), the forward rate, $f(t, T_1, T_2)$, can be related to zero-coupon bond prices as follows:

$$f(t, T_1, T_2) = \frac{\ln [P(t, T_1)] - \ln [P(t, T_2)]}{T_2 - T_1} \tag{22.4}$$

From equation (22.3) and Ito's lemma,

$$d \ln [P(t, T_1)] = \left[r(t) - \frac{v(t, T_1, \Omega_t)^2}{2} \right] dt + v(t, T_1, \Omega_t) \, dz(t)$$

and

$$d \ln [P(t, T_2)] = \left[r(t) - \frac{v(t, T_2, \Omega_t)^2}{2} \right] dt + v(t, T_2, \Omega_t) \, dz(t)$$

so that

$$df(t, T_1, T_2) = \frac{v(t, T_2, \Omega_t)^2 - v(t, T_1, \Omega_t)^2}{2(T_2 - T_1)} dt + \frac{v(t, T_1, \Omega_t) - v(t, T_2, \Omega_t)}{T_2 - T_1} dz(t) \tag{22.5}$$

Equation (22.5) shows that the risk-neutral process for f depends solely on the v's. It depends on r and the P's only to the extent that the v's themselves depend on these variables.

When we put $T_1 = T$ and $T_2 = T + \Delta T$ in equation (22.5) and then take limits as ΔT tends to zero, $f(t, T_1, T_2)$ becomes $F(t, T)$, the coefficient of $dz(t)$ becomes $v_T(t, T, \Omega_t)$, and the coefficient of dt becomes

$$\frac{1}{2} \frac{\partial [v(t, T, \Omega_t)^2]}{\partial T} = v(t, T, \Omega_t) v_T(t, T, \Omega_t)$$

where the subscript denotes a partial derivative. It follows that

$$dF(t, T) = v(t, T, \Omega_t) v_T(t, T, \Omega_t) \, dt - v_T(t, T, \Omega_t) \, dz(t) \tag{22.6}$$

Once the function $v(t, T, \Omega_t)$ has been specified, the risk-neutral processes for the $F(t, T)$'s are known. The $v(t, T, \Omega_t)$'s are, therefore, sufficient to define fully a one-factor interest rate model.

Equation (22.6) shows that there is a link between the drift and standard deviation of an instantaneous forward rate. Heath, Jarrow, and Morton (HJM) were the first

---

[3]The $v(t, t, \Omega_t) = 0$ condition is equivalent to the assumption that all discount bonds have finite drifts at all times. If the volatility of the bond does not decline to zero at maturity, an infinite drift may be necessary to ensure that the bond's price equals its face value at maturity.

to point this out.[4] Integrating $v_T(t, \tau, \Omega_t)$ between $\tau = t$ and $\tau = T$, we obtain

$$v(t, T, \Omega_t) - v(t, t, \Omega_t) = \int_t^T v_T(t, \tau, \Omega_t) \, d\tau$$

Because $v(t, t, \Omega_t) = 0$, this becomes

$$v(t, T, \Omega_t) = \int_t^T v_T(t, \tau, \Omega_t) \, d\tau$$

If $m(t, T, \Omega_t)$ and $s(t, T, \Omega_t)$ are the instantaneous drift and standard deviation of $F(t, T)$ so that

$$dF(t, T) = m(t, T, \Omega_t) \, dt + s(t, T, \Omega_t) \, dz$$

it follows from equation (22.6) that

$$m(t, T, \Omega_t) = s(t, T, \Omega_t) \int_t^T s(t, \tau, \Omega_t) \, d\tau \tag{22.7}$$

The Process for the Short Rate

We now consider the relationship between the models we have developed in this section and the models of the short rate considered in chapter 21. Consider the one-factor continuous time model for forward rates in equation (22.6). Because

$$F(t, t) = F(0, t) + \int_0^t dF(\tau, t)$$

and $r(t) = F(t, t)$, it follows from equation (22.6) that

$$r(t) = F(0, t) + \int_0^t v(\tau, t, \Omega_\tau) v_t(\tau, t, \Omega_\tau) \, d\tau + \int_0^t v_t(\tau, t, \Omega_\tau) \, dz(\tau) \tag{22.8}$$

Differentiating with respect to t and using $v(t, t, \Omega_t) = 0$ it follows that[5]

$$dr(t) = F_t(0, t) \, dt + \left\{ \int_0^t [v(\tau, t, \Omega_\tau) v_{tt}(\tau, t, \Omega_\tau) + v_t(\tau, t, \Omega_\tau)^2] d\tau \right\} \, dt$$

$$\tag{22.9}$$

$$+ \left\{ \int_0^t v_{tt}(\tau, t, \Omega_\tau) \, dz(\tau) \right\} \, dt + [v_t(\tau, t, \Omega_\tau)|_{\tau = t}] \, dz(t)$$

It is interesting to examine the terms on the right-hand side of this equation. The first and fourth terms are straightforward. The first term shows that one component of the drift in r is the slope of the initial forward rate curve. The fourth term shows that

---

[4]See D. Heath, R. Jarrow, and A. Morton, "Bond Pricing and the Term Structure of Interest Rates; A New Methodology," *Econometrica*, 60, 1 (1992), 77–105.

[5]The stochastic calculus in this equation may be unfamiliar to some readers. To interpret what is going on, we can replace integral signs with summation signs and d's with Δ's. For example, $\int_0^t v(\tau, t, \Omega_\tau) v_t(\tau, t, \Omega_\tau) \, d\tau$ becomes $\sum_{i=1}^n v(i\Delta t, t, \Omega_i) v_t(i\Delta t, t, \Omega_i) \Delta t$, where $\Delta t = t/n$.

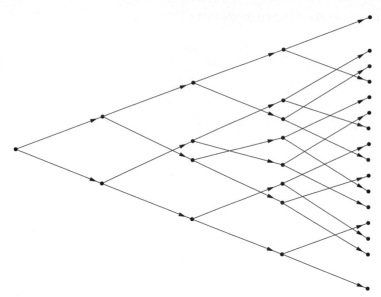

Figure 22.2   A nonrecombining tree such as that arising from the general
HJM model.

the instantaneous standard deviation of r is $v_t(\tau, t, \Omega_\tau)|_{\tau=t}$. The second and third terms
are more complicated, particularly when v is stochastic. The second term depends on
the history of v because it involves $v(\tau, t, \Omega_\tau)$ when $\tau < t$. The third term depends
on the history of both v and dz.

The second and third terms are liable to cause the process for r to be non-
Markov. The drift of r between time t and $t + \Delta t$ is liable to depend not only on
the value of r at time t, but also on the history of r prior to time t. This means that
when we attempt to construct a tree for r it is nonrecombining as shown in Figure
22.2. An up movement followed by a down movement does not lead to the same node
as a down movement followed by an up movement.

This highlights the key problem in implementing a general HJM model. When
we construct a tree representing term structure movements, it is usually nonrecombining. Assuming the model has one factor and the tree is binomial as in Figure 22.2,
there are 2^n nodes after n time steps. If the model has two factors, the tree must be
constructed in three dimensions and there are then 4^n nodes after n time steps. For
$n = 30$, the number of terminal nodes in a one-factor model is, therefore, about 10^9;
in a two-factor model it is about 10^{18}.

The Discrete Version of the Model

We now move on to consider a discrete version of the HJM model. We examine the
process followed by Δt-period forward rates rather than instantaneous forward rates.
Define $m_{i,j}$ and $s_{i,j}$ as the drift and standard deviation of the forward rate for the period
between times $j\Delta t$ and $(j + 1)\Delta t$ as seen at time $i\Delta t$. This means that

$$df(t, j\Delta t, j\Delta t + \Delta t) = m_{i,j}\, dt + s_{i,j}\, dz$$

when $t = i\Delta t$. From equation (22.5) it follows that

$$m_{i,j} = \frac{v_{i,j+1}^2 - v_{i,j}^2}{2\Delta t}$$

$$s_{i,j} = \frac{v_{i,j+1} - v_{i,j}}{\Delta t}$$

where $v_{i,j}$ is the value of $v(t, T, \Omega_t)$ when $t = i\Delta t$ and $T = j\Delta t$. Because $v_{i,i} = 0$, these equations lead to the result

$$\sum_{j=i}^{k} m_{i,j} = \frac{1}{2}\Delta t \left(\sum_{j=i}^{k} s_{i,j} \right)^2 \qquad (22.10)$$

Setting $k = i$ allows $m_{i,i}$ to be calculated from $s_{i,i}$; setting $k = i + 1$ then allows $m_{i,i+1}$ to be calculated from $m_{i,i}$, $s_{i,i}$, and $s_{i,i+1}$; and so on.

Extension to Several Factors

The HJM result can be extended to the situation where there are several independent factors. Suppose that

$$dF(t, T) = m(t, T, \Omega_t)\, dt + \sum_{k} s_k(t, T, \Omega_t)\, dz_k$$

A similar analysis to that just given shows that

$$m(t, T, \Omega_t) = \sum_{k} s_k(t, T, \Omega_t) \int_{t}^{T} s_k(t, \tau, \Omega_t)\, d\tau \qquad (22.11)$$

HJM have proposed a two-factor lognormal model for forward rates

$$dF(t, T) = m(t, T, \Omega_t)\, dt + \sigma_1(t, T)F(t, T)\, dz_1 + \sigma_2(t, T)F(t, T)\, dz_2 \quad (22.12)$$

where dz_1 and dz_2 are uncorrelated, and σ_1 and σ_2 are functions only of $T - t$. The σ_1 and σ_2 functions can (with some difficulty) be estimated from market data. Alternatively, statistical techniques such as principal components analysis can be used to estimate them from historical data. The principal components analysis technique was explained in connection with value at risk in section 14.10. Typical results for a principal components analysis on interest rates were presented in Table 14.3, Table 14.4, and Figure 14.4. The $\sigma_1(t, T)F(t, T)\, dz_1$ term in equation (22.12) corresponds to the most important factor and gives a roughly parallel shift in the forward curve. The $\sigma_2(t, T)F(t, T)$ term corresponds to the second most important factor. It creates a twist in the forward curve by causing short and long rates to move in opposite directions. In any short period of time, the change in the yield curve given by equation (22.12) is a combination of a parallel shift and a twist.

Monte Carlo Simulation Implementation of HJM

Monte Carlo simulation can be used to implement a general HJM model. It is a useful (if somewhat slow) tool for testing the effect of different volatility structures on European option prices. One of its limitations is that it cannot easily be used for American-style options.

The time over which the simulation is to be carried out is divided into n intervals of length Δt. The simulation can then be carried out by discretizing the process for forward rates. In the one-factor case, the continuous-time stochastic process

$$dF(t, T) = m(t, T, \Omega_t)\,dt + s(t, T, \Omega_t)\,dz$$

for the forward rate becomes

$$F_{i+1,j} - F_{i,j} = m_{i,j}\Delta t + s_{i,j}\epsilon\sqrt{\Delta t} \tag{22.13}$$

where $F_{i,j}$ is $f(i\Delta t, j\Delta t, j\Delta t + \Delta t)$; that is, $F_{i,j}$ is the forward rate as seen at time $i\Delta t$ for the period between $j\Delta t$ and $(j+1)\Delta t$. The variable ϵ is a random sample from a unit normal distribution, and $m_{i,j}$ and $s_{i,j}$ are the values of $m(t, T, \Omega_t)$ and $s(t, T, \Omega_t)$ when $t = i\Delta t$ and $T = j\Delta t$. The values of the $m_{i,j}$'s can be calculated from the $s_{i,j}$'s using equation (22.7), but better results are achieved if the discrete-time result in equation (22.10) is used.

Arguably the best approach is to model bond prices. This avoids the problems of calculating the $m_{i,j}$'s altogether. At time $i\Delta t$, we store the prices of bonds that have maturities $j\Delta t$ for $i + 1 \leq j \leq n$. Equation (22.3)

$$\frac{dP(t, T)}{P(t, T)} = r(t)\,dt + v(t, T, \Omega_t)\,dz$$

becomes

$$\frac{P_{i+1,j} - P_{i,j}}{P_{i,j}} = \frac{1}{P_{i,i+1}} - 1 + v_{i,j}\epsilon\sqrt{\Delta t}$$

or

$$P_{i+1,j} = P_{i,j}\left(\frac{1}{P_{i,i+1}} + v_{i,j}\epsilon\sqrt{\Delta t}\right) \tag{22.14}$$

where $P_{i,j}$ is the price at time $i\Delta t$ of a bond maturing at time $j\Delta t$.

Extensions of these approaches can accommodate several factors.

22.3 THE LIBOR MARKET MODEL

One of the drawbacks of the HJM model is that it involves instantaneous forward rates—and these are not directly observable in the market. Another is that it is not easy to calibrate it to prices of actively traded instruments such as caps. An alternative model, proposed by Brace, Gatarek, and Musiela (BGM); Jamshidian; and Miltersen, Sandmann, and Sondermann overcomes this problem.[6] It is known as the *LIBOR market model* or the *BGM model*. It is expressed in terms of the forward rates that trade's are used to working with and is constructed so that it is automatically consistent with cap prices.

The Model

Consider a cap with reset dates $t_1, t_2, \ldots, t_n$ and a final payment date t_{n+1}. Define $t_0 = 0$, $\delta_k = t_{k+1} - t_k$ $(0 \leq k \leq n)$, and

$F_k(t)$: Forward rate between times t_k and t_{k+1} as seen at time t, expressed with a compounding period of δ_k

$m(t)$: Index for the next reset date at time t. This means that $m(t)$ is the smallest integer such that $t \leq t_{m(t)}$.

$\zeta_k(t)$: Volatility of $F_k(t)$ at time t.

$v_k(t)$: Volatility of the zero-coupon bond price, $P(t, t_k)$, at time t.

Initially, we will assume that there is only one factor. In a world that is forward risk neutral with respect to $P(t, t_{k+1})$, $F_k(t)$ is a martingale and follows the process

$$dF_k(t) = \zeta_k(t)F_k(t)\,dz \tag{22.15}$$

where dz is a Wiener process.

In practice, it is often most convenient to value interest rate derivatives by working in a world that is always forward risk-neutral with respect to a bond maturing at the next reset date. We refer to this as a *rolling forward risk-neutral world*.[7] In this world we can discount from time t_{k+1} to time t_k using the zero rate observed at time t_k for a maturity t_{k+1}. We do not have to worry about what happens to interest rates between times t_k and t_{k+1}.

The rolling forward risk-neutral world is a world that is forward risk neutral with respect to the bond price, $P[t, t_{m(t)}]$. Equation (22.15) gives the process followed by $F_k(t)$ in a world that is forward risk neutral with respect to $P(t, t_{k+1})$. From section 19.8, it follows that the process followed by $F_k(t)$ in the rolling forward risk-neutral world is

$$dF_k(t) = \zeta_k(t)[v_{m(t)}(t) - v_{k+1}(t)]\,dt + \zeta_k(t)F_k(t)\,dz \tag{22.16}$$

The relationship between forward rates and bond prices is

$$\frac{P(t, t_i)}{P(t, t_{i+1})} = 1 + \delta_i F_i(t)$$

---

[6]See A. Brace, D. Gatarek, and M. Musiela, "The Market Model of Interest Rate Dynamics," *Mathematical Finance*, 7, 2 (1997), pp. 127–55; F. Jamshidian, "LIBOR and Swap Market Models and Measures," *Finance and Stochastics*, 1 (1997) 293-330; and K. Milterson, K. Sandmann, and D. Sondermann, "Closed Form Solutions for Term Structure Derivatives with Log Normal Interest Rates." *Journal of Finance*, 52, 1 (March 1997), 409–30.

[7]In the terminology of section 19.6 this world corresponds to using a "rolling CD" as the numeraire. A rolling CD is one where we start with $1, buy a bond maturing at time t_1, reinvest the proceeds at time t_1 in a bond maturing at time t_2, reinvest the proceeds at time t_2 in a bond maturing at time t_3, and so on.

Using this in conjunction with Ito's lemma leads to

$$v_i(t) - v_{i+1}(t) = \frac{\delta_i F_i(t) \zeta_i(t)}{1 + \delta_i F_i(t)} \tag{22.17}$$

so that from equation (22.16) the process followed by $F_k(t)$ in the rolling forward risk-neutral world is

$$\frac{dF_k(t)}{F_k(t)} = \sum_{i=m(t)}^{k} \frac{\delta_i F_i(t) \zeta_i(t) \zeta_k(t)}{1 + \delta_i F_i(t)} dt + \zeta_k(t) dz \tag{22.18}$$

The HJM result in equation (22.7) is the limiting case of this as the δ_i tend to zero. (See Problem 22.7.)

Forward Rate Volatilities

We now simplify the model by assuming that $\zeta_k(t)$ is a function only of the number of accrual periods between the next reset date and time t_k. Define Λ_i as the value of $\zeta_k(t)$ when there are i such accrual periods. This means that $\zeta_k(t) = \Lambda_{k-m(t)}$.

The Λ_i can be estimated from the volatilities used to value caplets in Black's model (that is, from the spot volatilities in Figure 20.3). Suppose that σ_k is the Black volatility for the caplet that corresponds to the period between times t_k and t_{k+1}. Equating variances we must have:

$$\sigma_k^2 t_k = \sum_{i=1}^{k} \Lambda_{k-i}^2 \delta_{i-1} \tag{22.19}$$

This equation can be used to obtain the Λ's iteratively.

Example 22.1 Assume that the δ_i are all equal and the Black caplet spot volatilities for the first three caplets are 24%, 22%, and 20%. This means that $\Lambda_0 = 24\%$. Because

$$\Lambda_0^2 + \Lambda_1^2 = 2 \times 0.22^2$$

Λ_1 is 19.80%. Also, because

$$\Lambda_0^2 + \Lambda_1^2 + \Lambda_2^2 = 3 \times 0.20^2$$

Λ_2 is 15.23%.

Example 22.2 A more realistic example is provided by the data in Table 22.1 on the caplet volatilities in the U.K. on February 3, 1995. Notice that the caplet spot volatilities

Table 22.1[a] **Volatility Data; Accrual Period = 1 year**

Year, k	1	2	3	4	5	6	7	8	9	10
σ_k (%)	15.50	18.25	17.91	17.74	17.27	16.79	16.30	16.01	15.76	15.54
Λ_{k-1} (%)	15.50	20.64	17.21	17.22	15.25	14.15	12.98	13.81	13.60	13.40

[a] *Source:* Data on U.K. interest rate volatilities in A. Brace, D. Gatarek, and M. Musiela, "The Market Model of Interest Rate Dynamics," *Mathematical Finance*, 7, 2 (1997), pp. 127–55.

exhibit the hump discussed in section 20.3 and the hump is more pronounced for the Λ's.

Implementation of the Model

The cap market model can be implemented using Monte Carlo simulation. Expressed in terms of the Λ_i's equation (22.18) is

$$\frac{dF_k}{F_k} = \sum_{i=m(t)}^{k} \frac{\delta_i F_i \Lambda_{i-m(t)} \Lambda_{k-m(t)}}{1 + \delta_i F_i} \, dt + \Lambda_{k-m(t)} \, dz \tag{22.20}$$

or

$$d \ln F_k = \left[\sum_{i=m(t)}^{k} \frac{\delta_i F_i \Lambda_{i-m(t)} \Lambda_{k-m(t)}}{1 + \delta_i F_i} - \frac{(\Lambda_{k-m(t)})^2}{2} \right] dt + \Lambda_{k-m(t)} \, dz \tag{22.21}$$

As an approximation we can assume that the drift of $\ln F_k$ is constant between times t_i and t_{i+1}. Then

$$F_k(t_{j+1}) = F_k(t_j) \exp \left[\left(\sum_{i=j}^{k} \frac{\delta_i F_i(t_j) \Lambda_{i-j} \Lambda_{k-j}}{1 + \delta_i F_i(t_j)} - \frac{\Lambda_{k-j}^2}{2} \right) \delta_j + \Lambda_{k-j} \epsilon \sqrt{\delta_j} \right] \tag{22.22}$$

where ϵ is a random sample from a normal distribution with mean equal to zero and standard deviation equal to one.

Extension to Several Factors

The LIBOR market model can be extended to incorporate several independent factors. Suppose that there are p factors and $\zeta_{k,q}$ is the component of the volatility of $F_k(t)$ attributable to the qth factor. Equation (22.18) becomes

$$\frac{dF_k(t)}{F_k(t)} = \sum_{i=m(t)}^{k} \frac{\delta_i F_i(t) \sum_{q=1}^{p} \zeta_{i,q}(t) \zeta_{k,q}(t)}{1 + \delta_i F_i(t)} \, dt + \sum_{q=1}^{p} \zeta_{k,q}(t) \, dz_q \tag{22.23}$$

Define $\Lambda_{i,q}$ as the qth component of the volatility when there are i accrual periods between the next reset date and the maturity of the forward contract. Equation (22.22) then becomes

$$F_k(t_{j+1}) = F_k(t_j) \exp \left[\left(\sum_{i=j}^{k} \frac{\delta_i F_i(t_j) \sum_{q=1}^{p} \Lambda_{i-j,q} \Lambda_{k-j,q}}{1 + \delta_i F_i(t_j)} - \frac{\sum_{q=1}^{p} \Lambda_{k-j,q}^2}{2} \right) \delta_j \right.$$

$$\left. + \sum_{q=1}^{p} \Lambda_{k-j,q} \epsilon_q \sqrt{\delta_j} \right] \tag{22.24}$$

where the ϵ_q are random samples from a normal distribution with mean equal to zero and standard deviation equal to one.

We can test equation (22.22) or (22.24) by using it to value caplets and comparing the prices to those given by Black's model. Each Monte Carlo trial consists of using the equation to generate a path for each forward rate in the rolling forward risk-neutral world. The value of $F_k(t_k)$ is the realized rate for the time period between t_k and t_{k+1} and enables the caplet payoff at time t_{k+1} to be calculated. This payoff is discounted back to time zero, one accrual period at a time. The caplet value is the average of the discounted payoffs.

The values obtained from Equations (22.22) and (22.24) are found to be not significantly different from those given by Black's model. This is true even when the accrual periods are one year in length and a very large number of trials are used.[8] This suggests that the assumption that the drifts of forward rates between reset dates are constant is a reasonable one.

Ratchet Caps, Sticky Caps, and Flexi Caps

The LIBOR market model can be used to value some types of nonstandard caps. Ratchet caps and sticky caps incorporate rules for determining how the cap rate for each caplet is set. In a *ratchet cap*, it equals the LIBOR rate at the previous reset date plus a spread. In a *sticky cap*, it equals the previous capped rate plus a spread. Suppose that the cap rate at time t_k is X_k, the LIBOR rate at time t_k is R_k, and the spread is s. In a ratchet cap, $X_{k+1} = R_k + s$. In a sticky cap, $X_{k+1} = \min(R_k, X_k) + s$.

Tables 22.2 and 22.3 provide valuations of a ratchet cap and sticky cap using the LIBOR market model with one, two, and three factors. The principal is \$100. The term structure is assumed to be flat at 5% per annum and the caplet volatilities are as in Table 22.1. The interest rate is reset annually. The spread is 25 basis points. Tables 22.4 and 22.5 show how the volatility was split into components when two- and three-factor models were used. This split is roughly consistent with the results of the principal components analysis in section 14.10. The results are based on 100,000 Monte Carlo simulations incorporating the antithetic variable technique described in section 16.7. The standard error of each price is about 0.001.

A third type of nonstandard cap is a *flexi-cap*. This is like a regular cap except that there is a limit on the total number of caplets that can be exercised. Consider an annual-pay flexi-cap when the principal is \$100, the term structure is flat at 5%, and the cap volatilities are as in Tables 22.1, 22.4, and 22.5. Suppose that all in-the-money caplets are exercised up to a maximum of five. With one, two, and three factors, the LIBOR market model gives the price of the instrument as 3.43, 3.58, and 3.61, respectively.

It is interesting to note that the prices of all three types of nonstandard caps are dependent on the number of factors. This is because they are all dependent on the joint behavior of two or more forward rates.

Extensions of the Model

The LIBOR market model is not exactly consistent with the standard market model for valuing European swap options—but it can be calibrated very closely to the prices

---

[8] An exception is when the cap volatilities are very high.

Table 22.2   Valuation of Ratchet Caplets

Caplet No.	One Factor	Two Factors	Three Factors
1	0.196	0.194	0.195
2	0.207	0.207	0.209
3	0.201	0.205	0.210
4	0.194	0.198	0.205
5	0.187	0.193	0.201
6	0.180	0.189	0.193
7	0.172	0.180	0.188
8	0.167	0.174	0.182
9	0.160	0.168	0.175
10	0.153	0.162	0.169

Table 22.3   Valuation of Sticky Caplets

Caplet No.	One Factor	Two Factors	Three Factors
1	0.196	0.194	0.195
2	0.336	0.334	0.336
3	0.412	0.413	0.418
4	0.458	0.462	0.472
5	0.484	0.492	0.506
6	0.498	0.512	0.524
7	0.502	0.520	0.533
8	0.501	0.523	0.537
9	0.497	0.523	0.537
10	0.488	0.519	0.534

Table 22.4   Volatility Components in Two-Factor Model

Year, k	1	2	3	4	5	6	7	8	9	10
$\Lambda_{k-1,1}$ (%)	14.10	19.52	16.78	17.11	15.25	14.06	12.65	13.06	12.36	11.63
$\Lambda_{k-1,2}$ (%)	−6.45	−6.70	−3.84	−1.96	0.00	1.61	2.89	4.48	5.65	6.65
Total Vol (%)	15.50	20.64	17.21	17.22	15.25	14.15	12.98	13.81	13.60	13.40

Table 22.5   Volatility Components in Three-Factor Model

Year, k	1	2	3	4	5	6	7	8	9	10
$\Lambda_{k-1,1}$ (%)	13.65	19.28	16.72	16.98	14.85	13.95	12.61	12.90	11.97	10.97
$\Lambda_{k-1,2}$ (%)	−6.62	−7.02	−4.06	−2.06	0.00	1.69	3.06	4.70	5.81	6.66
$\Lambda_{k-1,3}$ (%)	3.19	2.25	0.00	−1.98	−3.47	−1.63	0.00	1.51	2.80	3.84
Total Vol (%)	15.50	20.64	17.21	17.22	15.25	14.15	12.98	13.81	13.60	13.40

given by the model. This means that it can be used to price nonstandard swap options consistently with the market prices of European swap options.

A popular swap option product is a Bermudan swap option,which can be exercised on any of a number of different payment dates of the underlying swap. Bermudan swap options are difficult to value using the LIBOR market model because they are American-style options and the LIBOR market model relies on Monte Carlo simulation. However, some research in the late 1990s has suggested ways in which the LIBOR market model can cope with Bermudan swap options.[9]

The LIBOR market model is usually based on the volatilities of at-the-money caps. An important question is whether in-the-money and out-of-the-money caplets are priced using the same volatility as at-the-money caplets. The answer appears to be that there is a volatility skew similar to that observed for equity options (see Figure 17.3). The implied volatility is a decreasing function of the cap rate. This has led Andersen and Andreasen to suggest an extension of the LIBOR market model based on a constant elasticity of variance process for forward rates.[10]

22.4 MORTGAGE-BACKED SECURITIES

One application of the models presented in this chapter is to the mortgage-backed security (MBS) market in the United States. A mortgage-backed security is created when a financial institution decides to sell part of its residential mortgage portfolio to investors. The mortgages sold are put into a pool and investors acquire a stake in the pool by buying units. The units are known as mortgage-backed securities. A secondary market is usually created for the units so that investors can sell them to other investors as desired. An investor who owns units representing X percent of a certain pool is entitled to X percent of the principal and interest cash flows received from the mortgages in the pool.

The mortgages in a pool are generally guaranteed by a government-related agency such as the Government National Mortgage Association (GNMA) or the Federal National Mortgage Association (FNMA) so that investors are protected against defaults. This makes an MBS sound like a regular fixed-income security issued by the government. In fact, there is a critical difference between an MBS and a regular fixed-income investment. This difference is that the mortgages in an MBS pool have prepayment privileges. These prepayment privileges can be quite valuable to the householder. In the United States, mortgages typically last for 25 years and can be prepaid at any time. This means that the householder has a 25-year American-style option to put the mortgage back to the lender at its face value.

---

[9]See L. Andersen, "A Simple Approach to the Pricing of Bermudan Swaptions in the Multi-Factor LIBOR Market Model," Working Paper, 1998, Gen Re Financial Products, New York; M. Broadie and P. Glasserman, "A Stochastic Mesh Method for Pricing High Dimensional American Options," Working Paper, Columbia University, New York; and F. Longstaff and E. Schwartz, "Valuing American Options by Simulation: A Simple Least Squares Approach," Working Paper # 25-98, 1998, Andersen School at UCLA.

[10]See L. Andersen and J. Andreasen, "Volatility Skews and Extensions of the LIBOR Market Model," Working Paper, 1997, Gen Re Financial Products, New York.

In practice, prepayments on mortgages occur for a variety of reasons. Sometimes interest rates have fallen and the owner of the house decides to refinance at a lower rate of interest. On other occasions, a mortgage is prepaid simply because the house is being sold. A critical element in valuing an MBS is the determination of what is known as the *prepayment function*. This is a function describing expected prepayments on the underlying pool of mortgages at a time *t* in terms of the yield curve at time *t* and other relevant variables.

A prepayment function is very unreliable as a predictor of actual prepayment experience for an individual mortgage. When many similar mortgage loans are combined in the same pool, there is a "law of large numbers" effect at work and prepayments can be predicted more accurately from an analysis of historical data. As mentioned, prepayments are not always motivated by pure interest rate considerations. Nevertheless, there is a tendency for prepayments to be more likely when interest rates are low than when they are high. This means that investors require a higher rate of interest on an MBS than on other fixed-income securities to compensate for the prepayment options they have written.

Collateralized Mortgage Obligations

The MBSs we have described so far are sometimes referred to as *pass-throughs*. All investors receive the same return and bear the same prepayment risk. Not all mortgage-backed securities work in this way. In a *collateralized mortgage obligation* (CMO) the investors are divided into a number of classes and rules are developed for determining how principal repayments are channeled to different classes.

As an example of a CMO, consider an MBS where investors are divided into three classes: class A, class B, and class C. All the principal repayments (both those that are scheduled and those that are prepayments) are channeled to class A investors until investors in this class have been completely paid off. Principal repayments are then channeled to class B investors until these investors have been completely paid off. Finally, principal repayments are channeled to class C investors. In this situation, class A investors bear the most prepayment risk. The class A securities can be expected to last for a shorter time than the class B securities, and these, in turn, can be expected to last less long than the class C securities.

The objective of this type of structure is to create classes of securities that are more attractive to institutional investors than those created by the simpler pass-through MBS. The prepayment risks assumed by the different classes depend on the par value in each class. For example, class C bears very little prepayment risk if the par values in classes A, B, and C are 400, 300, and 100, respectively. Class C bears rather more prepayment risk in the situation where the par values in the classes are 100, 200, and 500.

IOs and POs

In what is known as a *stripped MBS*, principal payments are separated from interest payments. All principal payments are channeled to one class of security, known as a *principal only* (PO). All interest payments are channeled to another class of security known as an *interest only* (IO). Both IOs and POs are risky investments. As prepayment rates increase, a PO becomes more valuable and an IO becomes less valuable. As prepayment rates decrease, the reverse happens. In a PO, a fixed amount of principal is returned to the investor, but the timing is uncertain. A high rate of prepayments on the underlying pool leads to the principal being received early (which is, of course, good news for the holder of the PO). A low rate of prepayments on the underlying pool delays the return of the principal and reduces the yield provided by the PO. In the case of an IO, the total of the cash flows received by the investor is uncertain. The higher the rate of prepayments, the lower the total cash flows received by the investor, and vice versa.

Valuing Mortgage-Backed Securities

Mortgage-backed securities are usually valued using Monte Carlo simulation. Either the HJM or LIBOR market models can be used to simulate the behavior of interest rates month by month throughout the life of an MBS. [See equations (22.13), (22.22), and (22.24).] Consider what happens on one simulation trial. Each month expected prepayments are calculated from the current yield curve and the history of yield curve movements. These prepayments determine the expected cash flows to the holder of the MBS and the cash flows are discounted to time zero to obtain a sample value for the MBS. An estimate of the value of the MBS is the average of the sample values over many simulation trials.

Option Adjusted Spread

A critical input to any term structure model is the initial zero-coupon yield curve. This is a curve, generated in the way described in chapter 4, providing the relationship between yield and maturity for zero-coupon bonds that have no embedded options.

In addition to calculating theoretical prices for mortgage-backed securities and other bonds with embedded options, traders also like to compute what is known as the *option-adjusted spread* (OAS). This is a measure of the spread over the yields on government Treasury bonds provided by the instrument when all options have been taken into account.

To calculate an OAS for an instrument, it is first priced using the zero-coupon government Treasury curve as the input to the pricing model. The price of the instrument given by the model is compared to the price in the market. A series of iterations is then used to determine the parallel shift to the input Treasury curve that causes the model price to be equal to the market price. This parallel shift is the OAS.

To illustrate the nature of the calculations, suppose that the market price is $102.00 and that the price calculated using the Treasury curve is $103.27. As a first trial we might choose to try a 60-basis-point parallel shift to the Treasury zero curve. Suppose that this gives a price of $101.20 for the instrument. This is less than the market price of $102.00 and means that a parallel shift somewhere between 0 and 60 basis points will lead to the model price being equal to the market price. We could use linear interpolation to calculate

$$60 \times \frac{103.27 - 102.00}{103.27 - 101.20} = 36.81$$

or 36.81 basis points as the next trial shift. Suppose that this gives a price of $101.95. This indicates that the OAS is slightly less than 36.81 basis points. Linear interpolation suggests that the next trial shift be

$$36.81 \times \frac{103.27 - 102.00}{103.27 - 101.95} = 35.41$$

or 35.41 basis points; and so on.

SUMMARY

We have covered a number of advanced models for valuing interest rate derivatives. In the two-factor Hull–White model, the short rate reverts to a level dependent on another stochastic variable. This stochastic variable, in turn, reverts to zero. Unlike the models considered in chapter 21, this model can give a permanent "humped" volatility term structure. By this we mean that the volatility term structure is humped, not just at time zero, but at all future times as well.

The HJM and LIBOR market (BGM) models provide approaches that give the user complete freedom in choosing the volatility term structure. The LIBOR market model has two key advantages over the HJM model. First, it is developed in terms of the forward rates that determine the pricing of caps, rather than in terms of instantaneous forward rates. Second, it does not need to be calibrated because it is developed in such a way that it is automatically consistent with cap prices. The HJM and LIBOR market models both have the serious disadvantage that they cannot be represented as recombining trees. In practice, this means that they must be implemented using Monte Carlo simulation.

The mortgage-backed security market in the United States has given birth to many exotic interest rate derivatives: CMOs, IOs, POs, and so on. These instruments provide cash flows to the holder that depend on the prepayments on a pool of mortgages. These prepayments depend on, among other things, the level of interest rates. Because they are heavily path dependent, mortgage-backed securities usually have to be valued using Monte Carlo simulation. These are, therefore, ideal candidates for applications of the HJM and LIBOR market models.

SUGGESTIONS FOR FURTHER READING

Amin, K., and A. Morton. "Implied Volatility Functions in Arbitrage-Free Term Structure Models," *Journal of Financial Economics,* 35 (1994), 141–80.

Andersen, L. "A Simple Approach to the Pricing of Bermudan Swaptions in the Multi-Factor LIBOR Market Model." Working Paper, Gen Re Financial Products, New York, 1998.

Brace, A., D. Gatarek, and M. Musiela. "The Market Model of Interest Rate Dynamics," *Mathematical Finance,* 7, 2 (1997), 127–55.

Buhler, W., M. Ulrig-Homburg, U. Walter, and T. Weber. "An Empirical Comparison of Forward Rate and Spot-Rate Models for Valuing Interest Rate Options," *Journal of Finance,* 54, 1 (February 1999), 269–305

Carverhill, A. "When Is the Short Rate Markovian," *Mathematical Finance,* 4 (1994), 305–12.

Cheyette, O. "Term Structure Dynamics and Mortgage Valuation," *Journal of Fixed Income,* (March 1992), 28–41.

Duffie, D., and R. Kan. "A Yield-Factor Model of Interest Rates," *Mathematical Finance,* 6, 4 (1996), 379–406.

Heath, D., R. Jarrow, and A. Morton. "Bond Pricing and the Term Structure of Interest Rates: A Discrete Time Approximation," *Journal of Financial and Quantitative Analysis,* 25, 4 (December 1990), 419–40.

Heath, D., R. Jarrow, and A. Morton. "Bond Pricing and the Term Structure of the Interest Rates: A New Methodology," *Econometrica,* 60, 1 (1992), 77–105.

Heath, D., R. Jarrow, A. Morton, and M. Spindel. "Easier Done Than Said," *RISK,* (May 1993), 77-80.

Hull, J., and A. White. "Bond Option Pricing Based on a Model for the Evolution of Bond Prices," *Advances in Futures and Options Research,* 6 (1993), 1–13.

Hull, J., and A. White. "Numerical Procedures for Implementing Term Structure Models II: Two-Factor Models,"*Journal of Derivatives,* 2, 2 (Winter 1994), 37–48.

Inui, K., and M. Kijima. "A Markovian Framework in Multi-Factor Heath, Jarrow, and Morton Models," *Journal of Financial and Quantitative Analysis,* 33, 3 (September 1998), 423–40.

Jamshidian, F. "LIBOR and Swap Market Models and Measures," *Finance and Stochastics,* 1 (1997), 293–330.

Jarrow, R. A. *Modeling Fixed Income Securities and Interest Rate Options.* New York: McGraw–Hill, 1995.

Jarrow, R. A., and S. M. Turnbull. "Delta, Gamma, and Bucket Hedging of Interest Rate Derivatives," *Applied Mathematical Finance,* 1 (1994), 21–48.

Jeffrey, A. "Single Factor Heath–Jarrow–Morton Term Structure Models Based on Markov Spot Interest Rate Dynamics," *Journal of Financial and Quantitative Analysis,* 30 (1995), 619–42.

Miltersen, K., K. Sandmann, and D. Sondermann. "Closed Form Solutions for Term Structure Derivatives with Log Normal Interest Rates," *Journal of Finance,* 52, 1 (March 1997), 409–30.

Rebonato, R. *Interest Rate Option Models.* 2nd Ed, Chichester, England: John Wiley & Sons, 1998.

Ritchken, P., and L. Sankarasubramanian. "Volatility Structures of Forward Rates and the Dynamics of the Term Structure," *Mathematical Finance,* 5 (1995), 55–72.

QUESTIONS AND PROBLEMS
(ANSWERS IN SOLUTIONS MANUAL)

22.1. For the model in section 22.1 when $f(r) = r$,
   (a) What is the process followed by the bond price $P(t, T)$ in the traditional risk-neutral world?
   (b) What is the process followed by this bond's yield in this risk-neutral world?
   (c) For the parameters in Figure 22.1, what is the instantaneous correlation between the three-month and ten-year zero rates?

22.2. Explain the difference between a Markov and a non-Markov model of the short rate.

22.3. Show from equation (22.9) that if the instantaneous forward rate $F(t, T)$ in the HJM model has a constant standard deviation, the process for r is the same as in the Ho–Lee model.

22.4. Show that equations (21.17) and (21.18) are consistent with equations (22.8) and (22.9) when $s(t, T) = \sigma e^{-a(T-t)}$.

22.5. It can be shown that in a one-factor model where the bond price volatility $v(t, T, \Omega_t)$ is a function only of t and T, the process for r is Markov, if and only if, $v(t, T)$ has the form $x(t)[y(T) - y(t)]$. Use equations (22.8) and (22.9) to show that when $v(t, T)$ has this form the process for r is Markov.

22.6. Provide an intuitive explanation of why a ratchet cap increases in value as the number of factors increases.

22.7. Show that equation (22.18) reduces to (22.7) as the δ_i tend to zero.

22.8. Explain why a sticky cap is more expensive than a similar ratchet cap.

22.9. Explain why IOs and POs have opposite sensitivities to the rate of prepayments.

22.10. "An option adjusted spread is analogous to the yield on a bond." Explain this statement.

ASSIGNMENT QUESTIONS

22.11. In an annual-pay cap the Black volatilities for caplets with maturities one, two, three, and five years are 18%, 20%, 22%, and 20%, respectively. Estimate the volatility of a one-year forward rate when the time to maturity is (a) zero to one year, (b) one to two years, (c) two to three years, and (d) three to five years. Assume that the zero curve is flat at 5% per annum (annually compounded). Use DerivaGem to estimate flat volatilities for two-, three-, four-, five-, and six-year caps.

22.12. In the flexi-cap considered in section 22.3 the holder is obligated to exercise the first N in-the-money caplets. After that no further caplets can be exercised. (In the example $N = 5$.) Two other ways that flexi-caps are sometimes defined are:
   (a) The holder can choose whether any caplet is exercised, but there is a limit of N on the total number of caplets that can be exercised.
   (b) Once the holder chooses to exercise a caplet all subsequent in-the-money caplets must be exercised up to a maximum of N.
   Discuss the problems in valuing these types of flexi-caps. Of the three types of flexi-caps, which would you expect to be most expensive? Which would you expect to be least expensive?

The $A(t, T)$, σ_P, and $\theta(t)$ Functions in the Two-Factor Hull–White Model

In this appendix, we provide some of the analytic results for the two-factor Hull–White model discussed in section 22.1 when $f(r) = r$.

The $A(t, T)$ function is

$$\log A(t, T) = \log \frac{P(0, T)}{P(0, t)} + B(t, T)F(0, t) - \eta$$

where

$$\eta = \frac{\sigma_1^2}{4a}(1 - e^{-2at})B(t, T)^2 - \rho\sigma_1\sigma_2[B(0, t)C(0, t)B(t, T) + \gamma_4 - \gamma_2]$$

$$- \frac{1}{2}\sigma_2^2[C(0, t)^2 B(t, T) + \gamma_6 - \gamma_5]$$

$$\gamma_1 = \frac{e^{-(a+b)T}[e^{(a+b)t} - 1]}{(a + b)(a - b)} - \frac{e^{-2aT}(e^{2at} - 1)}{2a(a - b)}$$

$$\gamma_2 = \frac{1}{ab}\left[\gamma_1 + C(t, T) - C(0, T) + \frac{1}{2}B(t, T)^2 - \frac{1}{2}B(0, T)^2 + \frac{t}{a} - \frac{e^{-a(T-t)} - e^{-aT}}{a^2}\right]$$

$$\gamma_3 = -\frac{e^{-(a+b)t} - 1}{(a - b)(a + b)} + \frac{e^{-2at} - 1}{2a(a - b)}$$

$$\gamma_4 = \frac{1}{ab}\left[\gamma_3 - C(0, t) - \frac{1}{2}B(0, t)^2 + \frac{t}{a} + \frac{e^{-at} - 1}{a^2}\right]$$

$$\gamma_5 = \frac{1}{b}\left[\frac{1}{2}C(t, T)^2 - \frac{1}{2}C(0, T)^2 + \gamma_2\right]$$

$$\gamma_6 = \frac{1}{b}\left[\gamma_4 - \frac{1}{2}C(0, t)^2\right]$$

where the $B(t, T)$ and $C(t, T)$ functions are as in section 22.1 and $F(t, T)$ is the instantaneous forward rate at time t for maturity T.

The volatility function, σ_P, is

$$\sigma_P^2 = \int_0^t \{\sigma_1^2[B(\tau, T) - B(\tau, t)]^2 + \sigma_2^2[C(\tau, T) - C(\tau, t)]^2$$

$$+ 2\rho\sigma_1\sigma_2[B(\tau, T) - B(\tau, t)][C(\tau, T) - C(\tau, t)]\} \, d\tau$$

This shows that σ_P^2 has three components. Define

$$U = \frac{1}{a(a - b)}[e^{-aT} - e^{-at}]$$

and

$$V = \frac{1}{b(a - b)}[e^{-bT} - e^{-bt}]$$

The first component of σ_P^2 is

$$\frac{\sigma_1^2}{2a}B(t, T)^2(1 - e^{-2at})$$

The second is

$$\sigma_2^2\left[\frac{U^2}{2a}(e^{2at} - 1) + \frac{V^2}{2b}(e^{2bt} - 1) - 2\frac{UV}{a + b}(e^{(a+b)t} - 1)\right]$$

The third is

$$\frac{2\rho\sigma_1\sigma_2}{a}(e^{-at} - e^{-aT})\left[\frac{U}{2a}(e^{2at} - 1) - \frac{V}{a + b}(e^{(a+b)t} - 1)\right]$$

Finally, the $\theta(t)$ function is

$$\theta(t) = F_t(0, t) + aF(0, t) + \phi_t(0, t) + a\phi(0, t)$$

where the subscript denotes a partial derivative and

$$\phi(t, T) = \frac{1}{2}\sigma_1^2 B(t, T)^2 + \frac{1}{2}\sigma_2^2 C(t, T)^2 + \rho\sigma_1\sigma_2 B(t, T)C(t, T)$$

CHAPTER 23

CREDIT RISK

When valuing a derivative, it is customary to assume that there is no risk of default. For an exchange-traded option, this assumption is usually a reasonable one because most exchanges have been very successful in organizing trading to ensure that their contracts are always honored. Unfortunately, the no-default assumption is far less defensible in the over-the-counter market. This market has grown very fast since the mid-1980s. As a result, the quantification and management of credit risk has become an increasingly important activity for financial engineers.

Managing credit risk is particularly important in banks and other financial institutions. Regulators specify a minimum level of capital that banks are required to keep to reflect the credit risks they are bearing.[1] At one time, they did this by specifying minimum levels for balance sheet ratios such as equity to debt. This approach became inappropriate in the late 1980s because derivatives such as swaps and options, which do not appear on the balance sheet, had begun to account for a significant proportion of the total credit risk. Regulators now use a formula for determining credit risk capital that reflects both on- and off-balance sheet contracts.

Analysts must consider many aspects of credit risk. One problem is to determine how the prices of contracts should be adjusted to reflect the risk that the counterparty might default. We know that a bond issued by a company with a good credit rating sells for a higher price than a similar bond issued by a company with a poor credit rating because there is less chance of a default. For the same reason, a swap entered into with a company that has a good credit rating should be worth more than a similar contract entered into with a company that has a poor credit rating. Financial institutions must ensure that their bid–offer spreads on derivatives are large enough to provide compensation for possible defaults. It is a common practice to categorize credit risks as either acceptable or unacceptable and then to price all acceptable credit risks in much the same way. It seems likely that this will change as methods for quantifying credit risk become more widely accepted.

Analysts must also carry out scenario analyses to make worst-case credit loss estimates. In chapter 14 we discussed how value at risk (VaR) provides an estimate of a worst-case loss arising from movements in market variables. Many companies are now also calculating what is known as a credit VaR. This is a measure designed to answer a question that takes the form: "What is the credit loss that we are 99%

---

[1] This capital is in addition to the capital, mentioned in chapter 14, that banks are required to keep for market risk.

623

confident will not be exceeded in the next year?". It is possible that bank regulators will, in the future, base credit risk capital on a credit VaR measure.

The 1990s saw the birth of the market for credit derivatives. These instruments allow companies to manage their credit risks in a way that was not possible before. They allow a company to either purchase insurance against a particular credit risk or exchange one credit risk for another. They can be very effective in achieving credit risk reductions through diversification.

In this chapter, we examine all the aspects of credit risk that have just been mentioned. We start by considering ways that the credit risk on bonds can be quantified. We then discuss the impact of credit risk on the pricing of options and swaps. After that, we move on to cover the calculation of credit VaR, credit derivatives, and the pricing of convertibles.

23.1   THE PROBABILITY OF DEFAULT AND EXPECTED LOSSES

This section examines alternatives for estimating the probability that a counter-party will default between two future times, and expected losses from defaults between the times. There are three approaches. The first is based on bond prices; the second uses historical data; and the third uses equity prices.

Using Bond Prices

Rating agencies such as Moody's and S&P are in the business of providing ratings describing the creditworthiness of bonds. Using the S&P system, the best rating is AAA. Bonds with this rating are considered to have almost no chance of defaulting. The next best rating is AA. Following that comes A, BBB, BB, B, and CCC. Only bonds with ratings of BBB or above are considered to be investment grade.[2]

Bond traders have developed procedures for taking credit risk into account when pricing corporate bonds. They collect market data on actively traded bonds to calculate a generic zero-coupon yield curve for each credit rating category. (See chapter 4 for a description of how zero-coupon yields can be calculated from coupon-bearing bond yields using the bootstrap method.) These zero-coupon yield curves are then used to value other bonds. Figure 23.1 shows a typical pattern for the spread over Treasuries for zero-coupon bonds of different maturity.

We will use the data in Table 23.1 to show how bond yields can be related to default losses. The table shows that zero-coupon Treasury interest rates are assumed to be 5% for all maturities. The zero-coupon interest rates on corporate bonds range from 5.25% for a one-year maturity to 5.95% for a five-year maturity. We assume that

---

[2]The Moody's ratings corresponding to S&P's AAA, AA, A, BBB, BB, B, and CCC are Aaa, Aa, A, Baa, Ba, B, and Caa, respectively.

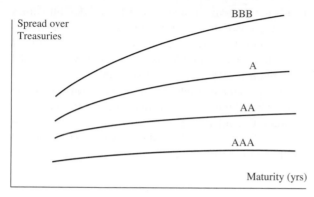

Figure 23.1 Spread over Treasuries for zero-coupon bonds.

Table 23.1 Zero-coupon Yields on Treasury Bonds and on Bonds Issued by a Corporation

Maturity (years)	Treasury zero rate (%)	Corp bond zero rate (%)	Expected default loss (% of no-default value)
1	5.00	5.25	0.2497
2	5.00	5.50	0.9950
3	5.00	5.70	2.0781
4	5.00	5.85	3.3428
5	5.00	5.95	4.6390

the higher yields on the corporate bonds are entirely compensation for possible losses from default. This means that:

Value of Treasury bond − value of corporate bond = present value of cost of defaults

The value of a one-year Treasury bond with a principal of 100 is $100e^{-0.05}$, or 95.1229. The value of a similar corporate bond is $100e^{-0.0525} = 94.8854$. The present value of the loss from defaults on the corporate bond is, therefore, $95.1229 - 94.8854 = 0.2375$. This means that we expect $0.2375/95.1229 = 0.2497\%$ of the no-default value of the corporate bond to be lost from defaults.

Consider next a two-year bond. The value of a two-year Treasury bond with a principal of 100 is $100e^{-0.05 \times 2} = 90.4837$. The value of a similar corporate bond is $100e^{-0.055 \times 2} = 89.5834$. The present value of the expected loss from defaults on the two-year corporate bond is $90.4837 - 89.5834 = 0.9003$. We, therefore, expect $0.9003/90.4937 = 0.9950\%$ of the no-default value of the two-year corporate bond to be lost from defaults.

These results and those for other maturities are shown in the final column of Table 23.1. The bonds in Table 23.1 are assumed to rank equally in the event of default. A further assumption we make is that, in the event of a default by the company, all holders of equal-ranking bonds get the same proportion of the no-default values of their bonds. This means that if there is a default in year two and the holder of a three-year bond realizes 60% of the no-default value of the bond, the same is true of the holder of a four- or five-year bond. This assumption does not exactly correspond to the way bankruptcy laws work, but it is reasonable approximation.

Armed with this assumption, we can use Table 23.1 to make estimates of the proportion of the initial no-default value of the bond expected to be lost from defaults during different periods in the future. Consider the two-year zero-coupon bond. The expected loss in the first year is 0.2497% of the bond's no-default value. The expected loss in the first two years is 0.9950% of the bond's no-default value. The expected loss during the second year, as seen at time zero, is $0.9950 - 0.2497 = 0.7453\%$ of its no-default value.

We now introduce some notation. Define

$h(T_1, T_2)$: Expected proportion of the no-default value of the bond lost through defaults between times T_1 and T_2, as seen at time zero.

$y(T)$: Yield on a zero-coupon corporate bond maturing at time T.

$y^*(T)$: Yield on a zero-coupon Treasury bond maturing at time T.

$P(T)$: Price of a zero-coupon corporate bond with a principal of \$1 maturing at time T.

$P^*(T)$: Price of a zero-coupon Treasury bond with a principal of \$1 maturing at time T.

As in the example in Table 23.1, we assume that the higher yield on corporate bonds is entirely compensation for defaults. This means that

$$h(0, T) = \frac{P^*(T) - P(T)}{P^*(T)} \tag{23.1}$$

Because

$$P(T) = e^{-y(T)T}$$

and

$$P^*(T) = e^{-y^*(T)T}$$

this expression for $h(0, T)$ can be written

$$h(0, T) = \frac{e^{-y^*(T)T} - e^{-y(T)T}}{e^{-y^*(T)T}} = 1 - e^{-[y(T)-y^*(T)]T} \tag{23.2}$$

Because

$$h(T_1, T_2) = h(0, T_2) - h(0, T_1) \tag{23.3}$$

it follows from equation (23.2) that

$$h(T_1, T_2) = e^{-[y(T_1)-y^*(T_1)]T_1} - e^{-[y(T_2)-y^*(T_2)]T_2}$$

Example 23.1 Suppose that the spreads over Treasuries for 5-year and 10-year BBB-rated zero coupon bonds are 130 and 170 basis points, respectively. From equation (23.2)

$$h(0, 5) = 1 - e^{-0.013 \times 5} = 0.0629$$
$$h(0, 10) = 1 - e^{-0.017 \times 10} = 0.1563$$

It follows from equation (23.3) that

$$h(5, 10) = 0.1563 - 0.0629 = 0.0934$$

The expected loss from defaults on a BBB-rated bond between years 5 and 10, as seen at time zero, is 9.34% of the no-default value of the bond.

Using Historical Data

We now consider the actual losses experienced by bond holders from defaults in the past. Table 23.2 is typical of the data produced by rating agencies. It shows the default experience of companies that started with a certain credit rating. For example, a bond issue with an initial credit rating of BBB has a 0.18% chance of defaulting by the end of the first year, a 0.44% chance of defaulting by the end of the second year, and so on. The probability of a bond defaulting during a particular year can be calculated from the table. For example, the probability of a BBB-rated bond defaulting during the second year is $0.44 - 0.18 = 0.26\%$.

It is interesting to note that, for bonds with good credit ratings, the probability of default in a year tends to be an increasing function of time. For bonds with a poor credit rating, the reverse is often true. In Table 23.2, the probabilities, as seen at time zero, of a AA bond defaulting during year one, two, three, four, and five are 0.00%, 0.02%, 0.10%, 0.13%, and 0.18%, respectively. The corresponding probabilities for a CCC bond are 19.79%, 7.13%, 4.71%, 4.34%, and 4.18%.[3] For a bond with a good

Table 23.2 Average Cumulative Default Rates (%)

Term (yrs)	1	2	3	4	5	7	10	15
AAA	0.00	0.00	0.07	0.15	0.24	0.66	1.40	1.40
AA	0.00	0.02	0.12	0.25	0.43	0.89	1.29	1.48
A	0.06	0.16	0.27	0.44	0.67	1.12	2.17	3.00
BBB	0.18	0.44	0.72	1.27	1.78	2.99	4.34	4.70
BB	1.06	3.48	6.12	8.68	10.97	14.46	17.73	19.91
B	5.20	11.00	15.95	19.40	21.88	25.14	29.02	30.65
CCC	19.79	26.92	31.63	35.97	40.15	42.64	45.10	45.10

Source: S&P CreditWeek, April 15, 1996.

---

[3]Note that, as an alternative measure, we can calculate the probability of defaulting in a year conditional on no earlier default. This is sometimes termed the *hazard rate*. The hazard rate for year n is $p_n/(1 - c_n)$ where p_n is the unconditional probability of default in year n and c_n is the cumulative probability of default up to year n. In the case of the CCC company the hazard rates in the five years are 19.79%, 8.89%, 6.44%, 6.35%, and 6.53% respectively.

credit rating, some time must usually elapse for the fortunes of the issuer to decline to such an extent that a default happens. For a bond with a poor credit rating, the next year or two may be critical. If the issuer survives this period, its probability of default per year can be expected to decline.

There are some anomalies in the data in Table 23.2. For example, the cumulative probability of a AA-rated bond defaulting during a ten year period is 1.29%—less than the 1.40% figure for a AAA-rated bond. Analysts often smooth the data to eliminate these types of anomalies before using it for forecasting.

A default by the issuer does not usually lead to a 100% loss for a bond holder. The size of the loss usually depends on how the bond ranks relative to other claims against the assets of the issuer. Table 23.3 shows statistics on the recovery rates for different categories of bonds. The average recovery rate for senior secured debt is 53.8% while that for junior subordinated debt is only 17.09%.

Bond Prices vs Historical Default Experience

The default probabilities in Table 23.2 are significantly less than we would expect from an analysis of bond prices. Consider, for example, bonds that have an A-rating at the time of issue. Table 23.2 shows that these have a probability of 0.67% of defaulting during a five-year period following the rating. From Table 23.3, a conservative estimate of the recovery rate is 30%. This means that we can expect a loss from defaults over the five years of $0.7 \times 0.67 = 0.47\%$. An analysis based on bond prices gives a quite different result. Five-year A-rated bonds typically yield at least 50 basis points more than similar Treasury bonds. From equation (23.2), this means we expect to lose at least

$$1 - e^{-0.005 \times 5} = 0.0247$$

or 2.47% of the bond's value during a five-year period. Bond prices appear to forecast losses over five times as great as historical data.

There is a similar discrepancy for estimates of future default probabilities. Using bond prices, the probability of default during the five years is $0.0247/0.7 =$

Table 23.3   Recovery Rates on Corporate Bonds

Class	Mean (%)	Standard deviation (%)
Senior Secured	53.80	26.86
Senior Unsecured	51.13	25.45
Senior Subordinated	38.52	23.81
Subordinated	32.74	20.18
Junior Subordinated	17.09	10.90

Source: L. V. Carty and D. Lieberman, "Corporate bond defaults and default rates, 1938–1995," *Moody's Investors Service, Global Credit Research*, (January 1996).

3.53%. This is over five times as great as the 0.67% probability estimated from historical data.

Altman was one of the first researchers to examine the discrepancy.[4] He showed that, even after taking account of the impact of defaults, an investor could expect significantly higher returns from investing in corporate bonds than from investing in Treasury bonds. As the credit rating of the corporate bonds declined, the excess return over Treasuries increased.

One possible reason for the discrepancy between bond prices and default experience is that bond traders may be making allowances for the possibility of depression scenarios that are much worse than those seen during the time period covered by the historical data used to produce tables such as Table 23.2. It is also possible that part of the higher return on corporate bonds is compensation for their lower liquidity than Treasury bonds.

The Risk-Neutral World vs the Real World

There is an important theoretical reason for the discrepancy between the 3.53% estimate of the probability of default calculated from bond prices and historical default experience and the 0.67% estimate calculated from historical data. The 3.53% probability of default is calculated from the fact that the corporate bond is worth 2.47% less than the Treasury bond and there is a 30% recovery rate. The analysis implicitly assumes that

(i) The expected cash flow from the corporate bond at the end of five years is 2.47% less than the expected cash flow from the Treasury bond at the end of the five years; and

(ii) The discount rates appropriate for the two cash flows are the same.

This must be the case in a risk-neutral world; that is a world where the expected return required by all investors on all investments is the risk-free interest rate. It is not necessarily the case in other worlds. The 3.53% estimate is therefore the probability of default in a risk-neutral world.

The 0.67% estimate of the probability of default from historical data is an estimate of what will happen in the real world. It is 2.86% lower than the corresponding estimate in the real world. Factoring in a recovery rate of 30%, we see that in the real world an investor can expect to earn about 200 basis points more than in the risk-free world. The investor has this higher expected return because defaults have a lower probability in the real world than in the risk-neutral world.

A 200 basis point difference over five years translates into 40 basis points per year. Arguably this is a reasonable compensation for the systematic risk of A-rated corporate bonds. The excess return of the market over the risk-free rate is about 5%. The example we have been using is consistent with the corporate bond having a beta of

---

[4]See, for example, E. I. Altman, "Measuring Corporate Bond Mortality and Performance," *Journal of Finance*, 44 (1989), 902–22.

about 0.08. An apparently large discrepancy between bond prices, therefore, translates into a relatively small adjustment to expected returns for risk.[5]

This explanation of the difference between estimates calculated from bond prices and those calculated from historical data is consistent with the pattern of Altman's results, mentioned earlier. As the credit rating of a bond declines, it becomes more similar to equity and its beta increases. As a result, the excess of the expected return required by investors over the risk-free rate also increases.

At this stage it is natural to ask whether we should use real-world or risk-neutral default probabilities in the analysis of credit risk. The answer depends on the purpose of the analysis. When valuing credit derivatives or estimating the impact of default risk on the pricing of derivatives we should use risk-neutral default probabilities. This is because we are likely to be implicitly or explicitly using risk-neutral valuation in our analysis. When carrying out scenario analyses to calculate potential future losses from defaults we should use real-world default probabilities.

Using Equity Prices: Merton's Model

The approaches we have examined thus far for estimating a company's probability of default have relied on the company's credit rating. Unfortunately, credit ratings are revised relatively infrequently. This has led some analysts to argue that equity prices can provide more up-to-date estimates of default probabilities.

In 1974, Merton examined a model where a company's equity is an option on the assets of the company.[6] Suppose, for simplicity, that a firm has one zero-coupon bond outstanding and that the bond matures at time T. Define

V_0: Value of company's assets today.
V_T: Value of company's assets at time T.
E_0: Value of company's equity today.
E_T: Value of company's equity at time T.
D: Amount of debt interest and principal due to be repaid at time T.
σ_V: Volatility of assets.
σ_E: Volatility of equity.

If $V_T < D$, it is (at least in theory) rational for the company to default on the debt at time T. The value of the equity is then zero. If $V_T > D$, the company should make the debt repayment at time T and the value of the equity at this time is $V_T - D$. Merton's model, therefore, gives the value of the firm's equity at time T as

$$E_T = \max(V_T - D, 0)$$

This shows that the equity is a call option on the value of the assets with a strike price equal to the repayment required on the debt. The Black–Scholes formula gives the

---

[5]Note that it is important to distinguish between the promised return on a corporate bond, which is its yield, and the expected return, which takes into account expected losses.

[6]See R. Merton, "On the Pricing of Corporate Debt: The Risk Structure of Interest Rates," *Journal of Finance*, 29 (1974), 449–470.

value of the equity today as

$$E_0 = V_0 N(d_1) - De^{-rT} N(d_2) \tag{23.4}$$

where

$$d_1 = \frac{\ln V_0/D + (r + \sigma_V^2/2)T}{\sigma_V \sqrt{T}}$$

and

$$d_2 = d_1 - \sigma_V \sqrt{T}$$

The value of the debt today is $V_0 - E_0$.

The risk-neutral probability that the company will default on the debt is $N(-d_2)$. To calculate this we require V_0 and σ_V. Neither of these are directly observable.[7] However, we can observe E_0. This means that equation (4) provides one condition that must be satisfied by V_0 and σ_V. We can also estimate σ_E. From Ito's lemma

$$\sigma_E E_0 = \frac{\partial E}{\partial V} \sigma_V V_0$$

or

$$\sigma_E E_0 = N(d_1) \sigma_V V_0 \tag{23.5}$$

This provides another equation that must be satisfied by V_0 and σ_V. Equations (23.4) and (23.5) provide a pair of simultaneous equations that can be solved for V_0 and σ_V.

> **Example 23.2** The value of a company's equity is $3 million and the volatility of the equity is 80%. The debt that will have to be paid in one year is $10 million. The risk-free rate is 5% per annum. In this case $E_0 = 3$, $\sigma_E = 0.80$, $r = 0.05$, $T = 1$, and $D = 10$. Solving equations (23.4) and (23.5) iteratively yields $V_0 = 12.40$ and $\sigma_V = 0.2123$. The parameter, d_2 is 1.1408 so that the probability of default is $N(-d_2) = 0.127$ or 12.7%. The market value of the debt is $V_0 - E_0$ or 9.40. The present value of the promised payment on the debt is $10e^{-0.05 \times 1} = 9.51$. The expected loss on the debt is therefore $(9.51 - 9.40)/9.51$ or about 1.2% of its no-default value. Comparing this with the probability of default gives the expected recovery in the event of a default as $(12.7 - 1.2)/12.7$ or about 91%.

Up to now, we have assumed that all of the company's debt is repayable at one time. In practice, debt repayments are likely to be required at a number of different times. This makes the model relating V_0 and E_0 more complicated than equation (23.4), but in principle, it is still possible to use an option pricing approach to obtain estimates of V_0 and σ_V. The probability of the company defaulting at different times in the future can then be estimated.

---

[7]The market value of the assets is the market value of the equity plus the market value of debt and similar obligations. Although we can usually estimate the face value of the debt obligations, we do not usually know their market value.

How well do the default probabilities produced by Merton's model agree with historical default experience? The answer is that there is a significant difference between the two. However, Crosbie reports that there is a good empirical relationship between a variable he defines as "distance to default" and the actual default probability.[8] The distance to default is $(V0 - D)/(V0\sigma_V)$. The variable $V0\sigma_V$ is approximately equal to the size of a one standard deviation move in $V0$. The distance to default is, therefore, an approximate measure of the number of standard deviations between the current value of the assets of the company, $V0$, and the amount owed, $D0$. It implicitly assumes that the change in $V0$ is normally distributed.[9]

Crosbie's results suggest that Merton's model can be used to provide an index of the probability of default risk. Whether it is an index of the actual probability of default or the risk-neutral probability of default depends on how the calibration is done. If the output from Merton's model is calibrated to bond prices, the result is an estimate of the risk-neutral probability of default. If it is calibrated to historical default experience the result is an estimate of the real-world probability of default.

23.2 ADJUSTING THE PRICES OF DERIVATIVES TO REFLECT COUNTERPARTY DEFAULT RISK

We now discuss how credit risk can be taken into account when pricing derivatives. Bond traders have, for many years, known how to take default risk into account when pricing bonds. It is natural to try and base the credit-risk calculation for derivatives on prices observed in the bond market.

The Independence Assumption

When defaults are possible, there are two groups of variables affecting the value of a derivative to a financial institution:

1. The variables affecting its value in a no-default world.
2. The variables affecting the occurrence of defaults by the counterparty and the percentage recovery made in the event of a default.

We assume that the variables in the first group are independent of the variables in the second group. We refer to this as the *independence assumption*. It has been made

---

[8]See P. Crosbie, "Modeling Default Risk." In *Credit Derivatives: Trading & Management of Credit & Default Risk*. S. Das, ed. Singapore: John Wiley and Sons, 1998. A company KMV in California has pioneered the implementation of the ideas behind Merton's model using the distance-to-default measure.

[9]A measure based on the usual lognormal assumption for future values of the company's assets is

$$\frac{1}{\sigma_V} \ln \frac{V_0}{D}$$

by a number of researchers including Hull and White, and Jarrow and Turnbull.[10] It is an assumption that makes an otherwise intractable problem quite manageable.

The independence assumption is not, of course, perfectly true. The market variables that are used to determine the no-default price of a derivative do have an impact on the fortunes of a company and the chance that it will have to file for bankruptcy. However, given the sophisticated systems used by many companies to hedge market risks, the impact is not as great as is sometimes supposed. At the very least, the independence assumption provides a good starting point. In particular cases where the assumption is clearly inappropriate, a trader can use judgment to adjust the assessment of the impact credit risk upward or downward.

Contracts That Are Assets

Suppose that company X has entered into a contract with counterparty Y that will provide a payoff at time T. We first consider the case where the contract is, in all circumstances, an asset to company X and a liability to the counterparty. The contract could, for example, be an option where company X is long and the counterparty is short. Define

f : Value of the contract to company X, taking account of the possibility of a default by the counterparty.

f^* : Value of a similar default-free contract.

Consider a bond maturing at time T that will rank equally with the derivative in the event of a default.[11] As in section 23.1, we define $h(0, T)$ as the expected proportion of no-default value of the bond that will be lost because of defaults between times 0 and T.

The relationship between f and f^* is

$$\frac{f^* - f}{f^*} = h(0, T) \tag{23.6}$$

This equation states that the expected proportional loss on the contract is the same as that on a zero-coupon bond. The reasoning behind the equation is as follows. Because the bond and the contract rank equally, the proportion of the no-default value of the bond that is lost when a default happens equals the proportion of the no-default value of the derivative that is lost. The independence assumption implies that there is no reason to suppose that the value of either the bond or the contract is particularly high or particularly low when a default happens. The overall expected proportional losses on the two contracts should, therefore, be the same.

---

[10] See J. Hull and A. White, "The Impact of Default Risk on the Prices of Options and Other Derivative Securities," *Journal of Banking and Finance*, 19, 2 (May 1995), 299–322; J. Hull and A. White, "The Price of Default," *RISK*, (September 1992), 101-3; R. A. Jarrow and S. M. Turnbull, "Pricing Derivatives on Financial Securities Subject to Credit Risk" *Journal of Finance*, 50 (March 1995), 53–85.

[11] Derivatives such as options usually rank equally with unsecured bonds in the event of a default.

From equation (23.2)

$$h(0, T) = 1 - e^{-[y(T) - y^*(T)]T}$$

Equation (23.6), therefore, implies

$$f = f^* e^{-[y(T) - y^*(T)]T} \tag{23.7}$$

In these equations, $y(T)$ is the zero-coupon yield on a T-year zero-coupon bond, issued by the counterparty and ranking equally with the contract under consideration, and $y^*(T)$ is the zero-coupon yield on a similar Treasury bond. The simple adjustment for credit risk in equation (23.7) is appropriate for all contracts that promise a non-negative payoff at one particular point in time.

> ***Example 23.3***   Consider a 2-year over-the-counter option with a default-free value of $3. Suppose that a 2-year bond issued by the option writer that ranks equal to the option in the event of a default yields 150 basis points over similar Treasury issues. Default risk has the effect of reducing the option price to
>
> $$3e^{-0.015 \times 2} = 2.911$$
>
> or by about 3%.

Interpretation of the Adjustment

Equation (23.7) shows that we can calculate f by applying a discount rate of $y - y^*$ to f^*. Because f^* is itself obtained by discounting the expected payoff in a risk-neutral world at y^*, it follows that f can be calculated by discounting the expected payoff in a risk-neutral world at $y^* + (y - y^*) = y$. One interpretation of equation (23.7) is, therefore, that we should use the "risky" discount rate, y, instead of the risk-free discount rate, y^*, when discounting payoffs from a derivative contract.

Note that the risk-free interest rate enters into the valuation of a derivative in two ways. It is used to define the expected return from the underlying asset in a risk-neutral world, and it is used to discount the expected payoff. We should change the risk-free rate to the risky rate for discounting purposes, but not when determining expected returns in a risk-neutral world. For example, when using a binomial tree the growth rate of the underlying asset should be the risk-free rate, but we should use the risky rate for discounting as we work back through the tree.

American Options

The impact of default risk on contracts, such as American options, where the holder has early exercise decisions is more tricky. This is because the option holder's decision on early exercise may be influenced by new information, received during the life of the option, on the fortunes of the option writer. An example may help to illustrate the point here. Suppose that company X sells a one-year American call option on a non-dividend-paying stock to company Y and that during the following six months company X experiences a series of large, well-publicized loan losses. Normally, the option would not be exercised early. But if the option is somewhat in the money at the end of the six months, company Y might choose to exercise the option at this time rather than wait and risk company X being liquidated before the option matures.

The proportional impact of default risk on the price of an American option is less than that for a similar European option. This is because early exercise shortens the life of an American option, making a loss from defaults less likely. Another general result is that American options subject to default risk are always exercised earlier than similar no-default options. As the example just considered shows, options such as calls on non-dividend-paying stocks, that are never exercised early in a no-default world, should sometimes be exercised early when there is default risk.

Definition of Exposure

As a preliminary to considering the impact of default risk on other types of contracts, we introduce the notion of the exposure on a contract.

Consider a company, X, that has entered into a transaction with a counterparty, Y. We define the company's exposure as the total amount it could lose if the counterparty failed to honor its obligations. This loss is measured relative to the position the company would be in if there were no possibility of default.

When the transaction entered into by company X involves the purchase of a corporate bond issued by Y, company X's exposure is the no-default value of the bond. In other words, it is the value of a Treasury bond with the same maturity and paying the same coupon as the corporate bond. When the transaction involves the purchase of an option from the counterparty, company X's exposure is the no-default value of the option.

When the transaction involves the sale of an option to the counterparty, company X's exposure is zero. This is because the option is an asset to the counterparty. If the counterparty gets into financial difficulties and files for bankruptcy, the option will presumably be sold by the liquidator to another party. This should lead to neither a loss nor a gain to company X.

A more interesting situation is where the transaction is a swap or a forward contract. As we saw in chapters 3 and 5, this type of contract can become either an asset or a liability to company X. If Y gets into financial difficulties when a contract has a positive value to Y and a negative value to X, it is reasonable to assume that the contract will be sold to another party or be taken over by the liquidator in such a way that there is no significant change in company X's position. On the other hand, if Y gets into financial difficulties when the contract has a negative value to Y and a positive value to X, it may default on the contract and company X is then liable to take a loss equal to the positive value it has in the contract.

The general situation is illustrated in Figure 23.2. The financial institution's exposure on a contract, at any given time, is an optionlike function of the no-default value of the contract. Expressed algebraically, the exposure is

$$\max (V, \, 0)$$

where V is the no-default value of the contract to the financial institution.

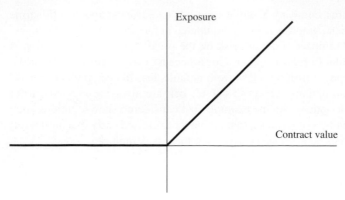

Figure 23.2   Exposure as a function of contract value.

Contracts That can be Assets or Liabilities

We are now in a position to consider the impact of default risk on contracts such as swaps and forward contracts that can become either assets or liabilities. As before, we define f as the value of the contract taking into account the possible defaults, and f^* as the no-default value of the contract. For simplicity, suppose that defaults can occur only at times $t_1, t_2, \ldots, t_n$. We assume that we have data on bonds that rank equally with the contract in the event of a default.[12]

Define u_i as the present value of the expected loss at time t_i as a proportion of the no-default value. Because defaults can occur only at times $t_1, t_2, \ldots, t_n$, it follows that

$$u_1 = h(0, t_1)$$
$$u_2 = h(t_1, t_2)$$
$$u_3 = h(t_2, t_3)$$

and so on. In general,

$$u_i = h(t_{i-1}, t_i) \qquad (23.8)$$

for $1 < i \leq n$.

Define v_i as the value, at time zero, of a derivative that pays off the exposure at time t_i, that is, a derivative that pays off max $(f^*, 0)$ at time t_i. The independence assumption implies that the present value of the expected loss from defaults at time t_i is equal to the present value of the expected exposure at time t_i multiplied by the

---

[12]To keep the analysis simple, we assume that we are in a situation where our counterparty may default, but there is no chance that we ourselves will default. The model can be extended to cover the situation where either party may default. See J. Hull and A. White, "The Impact of Default Risk on the Prices of Options and Other Derivative Securities," *Journal of Banking and Finance*, 19, 2 (May 1995), 299–322.

expected proportional loss at this time. This is $u_i v_i$. The present value of all losses from defaults is, therefore, given by

$$f^* - f = \sum_{i=1}^{n} u_i v_i \tag{23.9}$$

Currency Swap Example

To illustrate the use of equation (23.9), suppose that a financial institution enters into a fixed-for-fixed foreign currency swap with a counterparty where it receives interest in dollars and pays interest in sterling. Principals are exchanged at the end of the life of the swap. Suppose that the swap details are as follows:

Life of swap: five years.

Frequency of payments: annual.

Sterling interest exchanged: 10% per annum (compounded annually).

Dollar interest exchanged: 5% per annum (compounded annually).

Sterling principal: £50 million.

Dollar principal: $100 million.

Initial exchange rate: 2.0000.

Volatility of exchange rate: 15%.

We suppose that the sterling yield curve is flat at 10% per annum (annually compounded) and the dollar yield curve is flat at 5% per annum (annually compounded) with both interest rates constant. We also suppose that one-, two-, three-, four-, and five-year unsecured zero-coupon bonds issued by the counterparty have yields that are spreads of 25, 50, 70, 85, and 95 basis points above the corresponding riskless rate.

We assume that defaults can occur only on payment dates (i.e., just before payments are due to be exchanged). This means that $n = 5$, $t_1 = 1$, $t_2 = 2$, $t_3 = 3$, $t_4 = 4$, and $t_5 = 5$. Because interest rates are assumed constant, we know that the value of the sterling bond underlying the swap at each possible default time is 55 million pounds. Similarly, the value of the dollar bond underlying the swap at each possible default time is 105 million dollars. The value of the swap at time t_i in millions of dollars is, therefore,

$$105 - 55S(t_i)$$

where $S(t)$ is the dollar–sterling exchange rate at time t.

The variable v_i is the value of a derivative that pays off

$$\max[105 - 55S(t_i), 0] = 55 \max\left[\frac{105}{55} - S(t_i), 0\right]$$

millions of dollars at time t_i. This is 55 times the value of a foreign currency put option with strike price of $105/55 = 1.90909$. The initial exchange rate is 2.0000, the domestic interest rate is 5% with annual compounding (or 4.879% with continuous compounding), the foreign risk-free rate is 10% with annual compounding (or 9.531% with continuous compounding), the exchange rate volatility is 15%, and the time to maturity is t_i. The v_i can, therefore, be obtained from equation (11.7) or by using the software DerivaGem. For example, when $t_i = 3$, the value of the option is 0.246403 so that $v_3 = 55 \times 0.246403 = 13.5522$.

The spreads over Treasuries in this example are the same as those in Table 23.1. The u_i's can, therefore, be calculated from the last column in Table 23.1. For example, $u_3 = 0.020781 - 0.009950 = 0.010831$.

Table 23.4 shows the full set of u_i's and v_i's for this example and the calculation of the cost of default. The total cost of defaults is 0.6834 million dollars or 0.6834% of the principal. Table 23.5 shows a similar set of calculations for the situation where the financial institution is paying dollars and receiving sterling. In this case, v_i is the price of a foreign currency call option maturing at time t_i. Table 23.5 shows that the expected cost of defaults is 0.2404 million dollars or 0.2404% of the principal.

This example illustrates the general rule that a financial institution has more default risk when it is receiving a low interest rate currency and paying a high interest rate currency than the other way round. The reason is that the high interest rate currency is expected to depreciate relative to the low interest rate currency causing

Table 23.4   Cost of Defaults in Millions of Dollars on a Currency Swap with a Corporation When Dollars are Received and Sterling is Paid

Maturity, t_i	u_i	v_i	$u_i v_i$
1	0.002497	5.9785	0.0149
2	0.007453	10.2140	0.0761
3	0.010831	13.5522	0.1468
4	0.012647	16.2692	0.2058
5	0.012962	18.4967	0.2398
Total			0.6834

Table 23.5   Cost of Defaults in Millions of Dollars on a Currency Swap with a Corporation When Dollars are Paid and Sterling is Received

Maturity, t_i	u_i	v_i	$u_i v_i$
1	0.002497	5.9785	0.0149
2	0.007453	5.8850	0.0439
3	0.010831	5.4939	0.0595
4	0.012647	5.0169	0.0634
5	0.012962	4.5278	0.0587
Total			0.2404

the low interest rate bond underlying the swap to appreciate in value relative to the high interest rate bond.

The total cost of defaults on a matched pair of swaps with two counterparties that have the same credit rating is $0.6834 + 0.2404 = 0.9238$ million dollars or about 0.924% of the principal. Using a discount rate of 5% per annum, this is equivalent to payments of about 0.21 million dollars per year for five years. Because the principal is 100 million dollars, 0.21 million dollars is 21 basis points. We have, therefore, shown that the financial institution should seek a bid–offer spread of about 21 basis points on a matched pair of currency swaps to compensate for credit risk when the exchange rate volatility is 15%.[13]

Interest Rate Swaps vs Currency Swaps

The impact of default risk on interest rate swaps is considerably less than that on currency swaps. Using similar data to that for the currency swap, the required total spread for a matched pair of interest rate swaps is about 2 basis points. Figure 23.3 compares the expected exposure on a matched pair of offsetting interest rate swaps with the expected exposure on a matched pair of offsetting currency swaps. The expected exposure on a matched pair of interest rate swaps starts at zero, increases, and then decreases to zero. By contrast, the expected exposure on a matched pair of currency swaps increases steadily with the passage of time.[14]

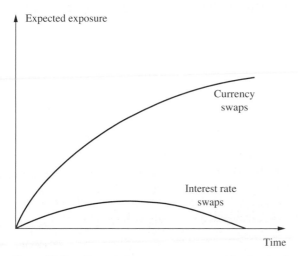

Figure 23.3   Expected exposure on a matched pair of interest rate swaps and a matched pair of currency swaps.

---

[13]The total cost of defaults, and, therefore, the required bid–offer spread, on a matched pair of currency swaps is relatively insensitive to the interest rates in the two currencies, but the way that the cost is split between the swaps does depend on the interest rates.

[14]This is largely because of the impact of the final exchange of principal in the currency swap. Occasionally, currency swaps are negotiated without the final exchange of principal to reduce credit risk.

Netting

Most derivatives contracts written by a financial institution state that if a counterparty defaults on one contract with the financial institution, it must default on all outstanding contracts with the financial institution. This has led banks to argue that when exposures are calculated and credit risk is quantified, a contract with a negative value should be allowed to offset a contract with a positive value if the counterparty is the same in both cases. This procedure is known as *netting*. In many jurisdictions there are now legal precedents that provide financial institutions and their regulators with some assurance that netting will happen in the event of a default.

Consider all the contracts that a bank has with a particular counterparty. Without netting, the bank's exposure at a future time is the payoff from a portfolio of options on the contracts. With netting, it is the payoff from an option on the portfolio of contracts. The latter is never greater than, and is often considerably less than, the former. Without netting, the expected cost of defaults is given by using equation (23.9) for each contract and summing the results. With netting, the expected cost of defaults is given by single application of equation (23.9) with v_i defined as the value of an option that provides a payoff equal to the net exposure on all contracts with the counterparty.

To take account of netting when pricing a new contract with an existing counterparty, it is necessary to calculate the incremental expected cost of credit losses. This involves calculating the expected cost of defaults with and without the contract. Sometimes netting can lead to a negative incremental expected cost of defaults for a new contract with an existing counterparty. This is likely to be the case when the contract has the effect of offsetting the market risk in contracts already outstanding with the counterparty.

Reducing Exposure to Credit Risk

In practice, there are a number of ways that a financial institution can attempt to reduce credit risk. For example:

1. It can set credit limits for every counterparty. The credit limit is usually a limit on the total exposure of the financial institution to the counterparty. Traders are denied the authority to enter into a new trade with the counterparty if it would lead to the credit limit being exceeded.

2. It can ask the counterparty to post collateral and agree that the amount of collateral posted will be adjusted periodically to reflect the value of the derivatives contract to the counterparty. Ideally, the collateral should be at least equal to the financial institution's exposure at any given time. This type of collateralization is similar to the margin requirements of futures exchanges and, if implemented carefully, can eliminate virtually all credit risk. It requires the two parties to agree on a valuation model for the contract and to agree to a rate of interest paid on the collateral. Sometimes collateral is posted by both sides and is held by a third party.

3. It can design the payoffs on contracts to reduce credit risk. Consider, for example, a financial institution wishing to buy an option from a counterparty low credit rating. It might insist on a zero-cost package that involves the option premium being paid in arrears. This reduces the company's exposure arising from the option position.

4. It can include what are termed *downgrade triggers* in the contract. These state that if the credit rating of the counterparty falls below a certain level, say A, the contract is closed out using a predetermined formula with one side paying a cash amount to the other side. Downgrade triggers lead to a significant reduction in credit risk, but they do not completely eliminate all credit risk. If there is a big jump in the credit rating of the counterparty, say from A to Default, in a short period of time the financial institution may still suffer a credit loss.

To evaluate the incremental impact of a new derivatives contract on the present value of expected credit losses in the presence of netting, collateralization, and credit triggers typically involves carrying out a Monte Carlo simulation to determine expected future exposures with and without the new contract. The Monte Carlo simulation must track the collateral posted by the counterparty and the credit rating of the counterparty.

23.3 CREDIT VALUE AT RISK

The analysis presented in section 23.2 was concerned with calculating the present value of expected credit losses on a contract or a portfolio of contracts. This is useful for pricing purposes. For risk management purposes, however, financial institutions are interested in calculating a complete probability distribution for the credit losses. They define a credit value at risk measure similarly to the value at risk measure in chapter 14. The credit VaR answers the question: What credit loss is such that we are $X\%$ certain it will not be exceeded in time T?

Credit losses are experienced not only when a counterparty defaults. If a counterparty's credit rating reduces from, say, A to BBB, a loss is taken if all outstanding contracts with the counterparty are revalued to reflect the new rating. This section sketches out two alternative approaches to calculating credit VaR. The first is aimed at quantifying the probability distribution of the losses arising solely from counterparty defaults. The second is aimed at quantifying the probability distribution of losses arising from both credit rating changes and defaults. In the long run, the two types of losses should be the same, but in the short run they may be different. Note that we are interested in the real-world probabilities of default when calculating credit VaR. It is, therefore, appropriate to base default probabilities on historical data rather than bond prices.

Credit VaR Based On Defaults

Our first approach is based on a methodology proposed by Credit Suisse Financial Products in 1997.[15] It utilizes ideas that are well established in the insurance industry.

Suppose that a financial institution has N counterparties and the probability of default by counterparty i in time T is p_i. Assuming that default events are independent, the expected number of defaults for the whole portfolio is $\mu = \sum_{i=1}^{N} p_i$.

---

[15]See Credit Suisse Financial Products, "Credit Risk Management Framework," (October, 1997).

Assuming that the p_i are small, the probability of n defaults is given by the Poisson distribution as

$$\frac{e^{-\mu}\mu^n}{n!}$$

This can be combined with a probability distribution for the losses experienced on a single default to obtain a probability distribution for total default losses. From this, the credit VaR can be calculated.

The probability distribution for the losses from a single default is difficult to obtain exactly. As an approximation, we can look at the current probability distribution of our exposures to counterparties and adjust this according to historical recovery rates.

In practice, default rates vary significantly from year to year. To account for this, we can assume a probability distribution for the default rates based on historical data. One approach is to assume that the proportional effect of year-to-year changes on all default probabilities is the same and construct a probability distribution for μ. Another approach is to categorize counterparties (for example, by country or industry) and to assume that the proportional effect of year-to-year changes on default probabilities is the same within each category.

Monte Carlo simulation can be used to produce the VaR estimate.[16] Each trial of the Monte Carlo simulation proceeds as follows:

1. Sample an expected default rate for each category.
2. Sample a number of defaults for each category.
3. Sample a loss for each default.
4. Calculate total loss.

The effect of assuming a probability distribution for default rates in the way just described is to build in correlations between the losses from different counterparties. This makes the model much more realistic. It also has the effect of making the probability distribution of total default losses positively skewed as indicated in Figure 23.4.

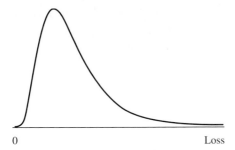

0   Loss

Figure 23.4   Probability distribution of default losses.

---

[16]Credit Suisse Financial Products provide analytic results that can be used as an alternative to Monte Carlo simulation.

Credit VaR Based On Defaults and Credit Rating Changes

We now move on to consider how a credit VaR that accounts for both defaults and credit rating changes can be calculated. Data on credit rating changes is shown in Table 23.6. This table shows the percentage probability of a company moving from one rating to another during a one-year period. For example, a company that starts with a BBB credit rating has an 86.93% chance of still being a BBB at the end of one year.[17] It has a 0.18% chance of defaulting during the year, a 5.30% chance of dropping to BB, and so on. Appendix 23A shows how a table such as Table 23.6 can be used to calculate transition probabilities for time periods other than one year.

We can estimate a probability distribution of credit losses by simulating credit rating changes for each counterparty.[18] Suppose we are interested in determining the probability distribution of losses over a one-year period. On each simulation trial, we sample to determine the credit rating changes of all counterparties throughout the year. We also sample changes in the relevant market variables. We revalue our outstanding contracts to determine the total of credit losses from defaults and credit rating changes.[19]

This approach is clearly more complicated to implement than the approach described earlier where only default events are modeled. The advantage is that the precise terms of outstanding contracts can—at least in theory—be incorporated. Suppose, for example, that a particular contract with an A-rated counterparty includes a downgrade trigger stating that the contract is closed out whenever the counterparty's credit

Table 23.6   One-Year Transition Matrix of Percentage Probabilities

Initial rating	Rating at year-end							
	AAA	*AA*	*A*	*BBB*	*BB*	*B*	*CCC*	*Default*
AAA	90.81	8.33	0.68	0.06	0.12	0.00	0.00	0.00
AA	0.70	90.65	7.79	0.64	0.06	0.14	0.02	0.00
A	0.09	2.27	91.05	5.52	0.74	0.26	0.01	0.06
BBB	0.02	0.33	5.95	86.93	5.30	1.17	0.12	0.18
BB	0.03	0.14	0.67	7.73	80.53	8.84	1.00	1.06
B	0.00	0.11	0.24	0.43	6.48	83.46	4.07	5.20
CCC	0.22	0.00	0.22	1.30	2.38	11.24	64.86	19.79
Default	0.00	0.00	0.00	0.00	0.00	0.00	0.00	100.00

Source: Standard & Poor's Credit week, April 15, 1996. (Numbers are adjusted for the removal of the "not rated " category used by S&P.)

---

[17] A credit rating is in theory an attribute of a bond rather than a company. For the purpose of the present discussion we ignore this distinction.

[18] This is the approach used by J. P. Morgan in their CreditMetrics system.

[19] We determine losses from credit rating changes by valuing the contract at the end of the year with (i) the credit rating at the beginning of the year and (ii) the credit rating at the end of the year. The credit loss is the difference between the two.

rating drops to BBB or lower. The simulation could monitor credit rating changes on a month-to-month basis to take this into account. It would incorporate the condition that a loss occurs only if the credit rating changes directly from A to default.

In sampling to determine credit losses, the credit rating changes for different counterparties should not be assumed to be independent. CreditMetrics suggests a scheme where the correlation between the rating changes for two counterparties is determined from the correlation between their equity prices.

23.4   CREDIT DERIVATIVES

One way of managing credit risk is by using what are termed *credit derivatives*. A credit derivative can be defined as a contract where the payoffs depend partly upon the creditworthiness of one or more commercial or sovereign entities. This section describes three of the most common types of credit derivatives.

Credit Default Swap

A credit default swap is a contract where company A has the right to sell a bond issued by company C for its face value to company B in the event that there is a default on the bond. In return, company A makes periodic payments to company B. Usually credit default swaps are settled by delivery of the bonds, but sometimes they are settled in cash. A cash-settled contract might state the value of the bond after default is to be determined by polling dealers. Alternatively, its terms might incorporate a fixed recovery rate such as 50%.

It is fairly easy to price—at least approximately—plain vanilla credit default swaps such as the one just described. This is because we know that the payoff per annum from assuming a particular bond's credit risk is equal to the excess return on the bond over the risk-free rate. Consider a newly issued credit default swap where company A pays Q dollars per year to company B. Company A has the right to sell to company B a particular bond (the "reference bond") with a face value of $100 for $100 if there is a default on the bond at any time during its life. Company B is receiving Q dollars per year in return for bearing the default risk on the bond. Arbitrage arguments show that Q should be approximately equal to the excess yield on the bond over the risk-free rate. For example, if the bond yield is 90 basis points greater than the risk-free rate, $Q = 90$ cents. If Q is less than 90 cents, company A can improve on the Treasury return by buying the reference bond and entering into the contract. If Q is greater than 90 cents, company B will find it profitable to short the reference bond and enter into the contract.

This analysis is approximate in that it assumes that at the time of default, the no-default value of the bond is $100. It also ignores the credit risk of company B. In other words, it ignores the possibility that the seller of the default insurance may itself default. The latter has a significant effect on the value of a credit default swap when there is a tendency for companies B and C to default at the same time.

Credit default swaps can be used to transfer credit risk from one company to another. Consider a situation where a financial institution has reached its internal credit limit with one particular corporate client. This means that it is so heavily exposed to the client that further lending is considered to be unwise. It can get around this problem and continue to lend to the client (thereby maintaining its relationship with the client) by entering into a credit default swap where the reference bond is a bond issued by the client. The party on the other side of the credit default swap might be another financial institution with little or no exposure to the client. Alternatively, it could be an investor prepared to accept the underlying credit risk.

An interesting point about credit default swaps is that, if they are settled by delivering the underlying bond, their very existence may drive up the price of the underlying bond in the event of a default.[20] Consider the situation where there are a large number of credit default swaps dependent on the same underlying reference bond. In the event of default, there will be many companies trying to buy the bond so that they can resell it for its face value. This will have the effect of driving up the price of the bond and lowering the payoff from the credit derivative.

Total Return Swap

In a total return swap, the return from one asset or group of assets is swapped for the return on another. Consider again the financial institution that has reached its internal credit limit with a certain corporate client. Instead of a credit default swap, it could choose a total return swap where the total returns from a bond issued by the client are swapped for either LIBOR or some other return. In the absence of counterparty credit risk, the value of a total return swap is the difference between the values of the assets generating the returns on each side of the swap. A total return swap is normally structured so that it is worth zero initially.

Total return swaps enable financial institutions to achieve diversification by swapping one type of exposure for another. Consider two banks, A and B. Bank A is located in Texas and is primarily concerned with lending to the oil industry. Bank B is located in Michigan and is primarily concerned with lending to automotive manufacturers and their suppliers. It would make sense for company A to swap the returns on some of its loans to oil companies for the returns on company B's loans to automotive companies. A total return swap enables it to do this without an exchange of assets.

Credit Spread Options

A credit spread option is an option on the spread between the yields earned on two assets. The option provides a payoff whenever the spread exceeds some level (the strike spread). Consider an investor with an investment in dollar denominated bonds issued by Brazil. The investor could purchase an option that pays off whenever the yield on the bonds exceeds the yield on U.S. Treasuries by 500 basis points. The payoff could be calculated as the difference between the value of the bond with a 500 basis point spread and the market value of the bond. This option would limit the investor's exposure to the underlying sovereign credit.

---

[20]For a discussion of this, see *The Economist*, July 18, 1998, p. 67.

23.5   VALUATION OF CONVERTIBLE BONDS

Credit risk plays an important role in the valuation of convertible bonds. These are bonds issued by a company where the holder has the option to exchange the bonds for the company's stock at certain times in the future. The exchange ratio (i.e., the amount of stock obtained in exchange for one bond) may be a function of time. The bonds are usually callable. This means that the issuer has the right to buy back the bonds. The price at which the bonds can be bought back (the call price) is also often a function of time. The holder has the right to convert the bonds once they have been called. The call feature is, therefore, often a way of forcing conversion earlier than the holder would otherwise choose.

One approach to valuing a convertible bond is to construct a tree in the usual way to represent the behavior of the company's stock price. The life of the tree should be set equal to the life of the convertible bond. The value of the convertible at the final nodes of the tree can be calculated based on any conversion options that the holder has at that time. We then roll back through the tree. At nodes where the terms of the instrument allow conversion we test whether conversion is optimal. We also test whether the position of the issuer can be improved by calling the bonds. If so, we assume that the bonds are called and retest whether conversion is optimal. This is equivalent to setting the value at a node equal to

$$\max\left[\min\left(Q_1, Q_2\right), Q_3\right]$$

where Q_1 is the value given by the rollback (assuming that the bond is neither converted nor called at the node), Q_2 is the call price, and Q_3 is the value if conversion takes place.

One complication is the choice of the discount rate used in conjunction with the tree. Suppose first that the convertible is certain to remain a bond. It is then appropriate to use a "risky" discount rate that reflects the credit risk of the issuer. This leads to the value of the convertible being correctly calculated as the market value of a regular nonconvertible bond. Suppose next that the bond is certain to be converted. It is then appropriate to use the risk-free interest rate as the discount rate. The value of the bond is then correctly calculated as the value of the equity underlying the bond.

In practice, we are usually uncertain as to whether the bond will be converted. We, therefore, arrange the calculations so that the value of the bond at each node is divided into two components: a component that arises from situations where the bond ultimately ends up as equity and a component that arises from situations where the bond ends up a debt. We apply a risk-free discount rate to the first component and a "risky" discount rate for the second component.[21]

Example 23.4   As a simple example of the procedure for valuing convertibles, consider a nine-month zero-coupon bond issued by company XYZ with a face value of

---

[21]This approach is formalized in K. Tsiveriotis and C. Fernandes, "Valuing Convertible Bonds with Credit Risk," *Journal of Fixed Income*, vol. 8, no. 2 (Sept 1998), 95–102.

$100. Suppose that it can be exchanged for two shares of company XYZ's stock at any time during the nine months. Assume also that it is callable for $115 at any time. The initial stock price is $50, its volatility is 30% per annum, and there are no dividends. The risk-free yield curve will be assumed to be flat at 10% per annum. The "risky" yield curve corresponding to bonds issued by company XYZ will be assumed to be flat at 15%. Figure 23.5 shows the stock price tree that can be used to value this convertible. The top number at each node is the stock price; the second number is the component of the bond's value arising from situations where it ultimately becomes equity; the third number is the component of the bond's value arising from situations where it ultimately becomes debt; the fourth number is the total value of the bond. The tree parameters are $u = 1.1618$, $d = 0.8607$, $a = 1.0253$, and $p = 0.5467$. At the final nodes, the convertible is worth $\max(100, 2S_T)$. At node G, the numbers show that the stock price is 78.42, the value of the bond is 156.84 and all of this value arises from situations where the bond ends up as equity. At node I, the stock price is 43.04, the value of the convertible is 100, and all of this arises from situations where it ends up as debt.

As we roll back through the tree, we test whether conversion is optimal and whether the bond should be called. At node D, rollback gives the value of the equity component of the convertible as

$$(0.5467 \times 156.84 + 0.4533 \times 116.18)e^{-0.1 \times 0.25} = 134.98$$

The value of the debt component is zero. Calling or converting the bond does not change its value since it is already essentially equity. At node F, the equity component of the convertible is zero and the debt component is worth $100e^{-0.15 \times 0.25}$ or 96.32. Node E is

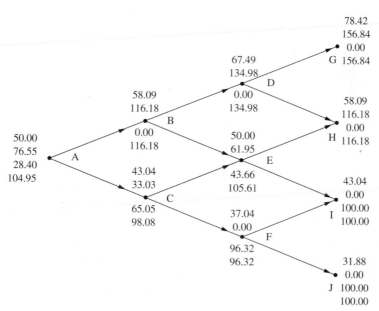

Figure 23.5 Tree for valuing convertible.

more interesting. The equity component of the convertible is worth

$$(0.5467 \times 116.18 + 0.4533 \times 0)e^{-0.1 \times 0.25} = 61.95$$

The debt component is worth

$$(0.5467 \times 0 + 0.4533 \times 100)e^{-0.15 \times 0.25} = 43.66$$

The total value of the bond is $61.95 + 43.66 = 105.61$. Clearly, the bond should be neither converted nor called.

At node B, the equity component of the convertible is worth

$$(0.5467 \times 134.98 + 0.4533 \times 61.95)e^{-0.1 \times 0.25} = 98.28$$

and the debt component is worth

$$(0.5467 \times 0 + 0.4533 \times 43.66)e^{-0.15 \times 0.25} = 19.06$$

The total value of the bond is $98.28 + 19.06 = 117.34$. It is optimal for the issuer to call the bond at node B because this will cause immediate conversion and lead to the value of the bond being reduced to $2 \times 58.09 = 116.18$ at the node. The numbers at node B recognize that this will happen. The bond is worth 116.18, all of it equity, at node B. Continuing in this way, the value of the convertible at the initial node, A, is 104.95. If the bond had no conversion or call option, its value would be

$$100e^{-0.15 \times 0.75} = 89.36.$$

The value of the conversion option (net of the issuer's call option) is, therefore, $104.95 - 89.36 = 15.59$.

When dividends on the equity or interest on the debt is paid, they must be taken into account. At each node, we first assume that the bond is debt. We include in the debt component of the value of the bond the present value of any interest payable on the bond in the next time step. Then, when testing whether the bond should be converted, we take into account the present value of any dividends that will be received during the next time step.

The calculations can be made more precise by allowing the risk-free and "risky" rates to be time dependent and equal to the relevant forward rates. The tree is then built as indicated in section 16.4. Cash flows between time t and $t + \Delta t$ are discounted at the appropriate forward rate applicable to the period between t and $t + \Delta t$.

SUMMARY

As the volume of trading in over-the-counter markets has increased, it has become important for analysts to take potential default losses into account in the pricing and risk management of derivatives. This chapter presents some of the ways that this can be done.

If we are prepared to assume that the variables concerned with defaults are independent of the variables determining the value of a derivative in a no-default world, the impact of defaults on the derivative can be derived from the impact of defaults on bonds. In the case of contracts that are unambiguously assets, default risk is taken into account by increasing the interest rate used for discounting. In the case of contracts that can become assets or liabilities, a more complicated analysis is required.

A credit VaR measure can be defined as the credit loss that, with a certain probability, will not be exceeded during a certain time period. The credit VaR can be defined to take into account only losses arising from defaults. Alternatively, it can be defined so that it reflects the impact of both defaults and credit rating changes.

Credit derivatives provide ways that companies can manage their credit exposures and achieve the benefits of diversification. They allow credit risks to be transferred from one company to another without the underlying assets themselves changing hands.

Convertible bonds are bonds that can be converted to the issuer's equity according to prespecified terms. Credit risk has to be considered in the valuation of a convertible bond. This is because, if the bond is not converted, the promised payments on the bond are subject to credit risk. One procedure for valuing convertible bonds is to calculate the component of the value attributable to the fact that the bond may end up as equity separately from the component of the value attributable to the fact that the bond may end up as debt.

SUGGESTIONS FOR FURTHER READING

Altman, E. I. "Measuring Corporate Bond Mortality and Performance." *Journal of Finance*, 44 (1989), 902–22.

Bank for International Settlements. "Proposals for International Convergence of Capital Adequacy Standards." July 1988.

Cooper, I., and A. Mello. "The Default Risk of Swaps," *Journal of Finance*, 46 (1991), 597–620.

Credit Suisse Financial Products. "Credit Risk Management Framework," October 1997.

Das, S. *Credit Derivatives: Trading & Management of Credit & Default Risk*. Singapore: John Wiley and Sons, 1998.

Duffie, D., and M. Huang. "Swap Rates and Credit Quality," *Journal of Finance*, 51, 3 (July 1996), 921–49.

Goldman Sachs. "Valuing Convertible Bonds as Derivatives." Quantitative Strategies Research Notes, Goldman Sachs, November 1994.

Group of Thirty. "Derivatives: Practices and Principles." Washington, D.C., 1993.

Hull, J. "Assessing Credit Risk in a Financial Institution's Off-Balance Sheet Commitments." *Journal of Financial and Quantitative Analysis,* 24 (1989), 489–501.

Hull, J., and A. White. "The Impact of Default Risk on the Prices of Options and Other Derivative Securities," *Journal of Banking and Finance,* 19, 2 (May 1995), 299–322.

Hull, J., and A. White. "The Price of Default," *RISK* (September 1992), 101–3.

Jarrow, R. A., and S. M. Turnbull. "Pricing Options on Derivative Securities Subject to Credit Risk," *Journal of Finance,* 50 (1995), 53–85.

Jarrow, R. A., D. Lando, and S. M. Turnbull. "A Markov model for the term structure of credit spreads," *Review of Financial Studies,* 10 (1997), 481–523.

Johnson, H., and R. Stulz. "The Pricing of Options Under Default Risk," *Journal of Finance,* 42 (1987), 267–80.

Jonkhart, M. J. L. "On the Term Structure of Interest Rates and the Risk of Default: An Analytical Approach," *Journal of Banking and Finance,* 3 (1979), 253–62.

J. P. Morgan. "CreditMetrics Technical Document." (April 1997).

Litterman, R., and T. Iben. "Corporate Bond Valuation and the Term Structure of Credit Spreads." *Journal of Portfolio Management,* (Spring 1991), 52–64.

Merton, R. C. "On the Pricing of Corporate Debt: The Risk Structure of Interest Rates," *Journal of Finance,* 2 (1974), 449–70.

Rodriguez, R. J. "Default Risk, Yield Spreads, and Time to Maturity," *Journal of Financial and Quantitative Analysis,* 23 (1988), 111–17.

Tavakoli, J. M. *Credit Derivatives: A Guide to Instruments and Applications.* New York: John Wiley and Sons, 1998.

Tsiveriotis, K., and C. Fernandes. "Valuing Convertible Bonds with Credit Risk," *Journal of Fixed Income,* vol. 8, no. 2 (September 1998), 95–102.

Yawitz, J. B., K. J. Maloney, and L. H. Ederington. "Taxes, Default Risk, and Yield Spreads," *Journal of Finance,* 4 (1985), 1127-40.

QUESTIONS AND PROBLEMS
(ANSWERS IN THE SOLUTIONS MANUAL)

23.1. Suppose that the spread between the yield on a three-year zero-coupon corporate bond and the yield on a similar Treasury bond is 50 basis points. The corresponding spread for six-year bonds is 80 basis points. What proportion of the no-default value of the six-year corporate bond do we expect to lose between years three and six?

23.2. Suppose that the spread between the yield on a three-year zero-coupon riskless bond and a three-year zero-coupon bond issued by a corporation is 1%. By how much does Black–Scholes overstate the value of a three-year option sold by the corporation?

23.3. "A long forward contract subject to credit risk is a combination of a short position in a no-default put and a long position in a call subject to credit risk." Explain this statement.

23.4. Explain why the credit exposure on a matched pair of forward contracts resembles a straddle.

23.5. Explain why the impact of credit risk on a matched pair of interest rate swaps tends to be less than that on a matched pair of currency swaps.

23.6. "When a bank is negotiating currency swaps, it should try to ensure that it is receiving the lower interest rate currency from a company with a low credit risk." Explain.

23.7. Does put–call parity hold when there is default risk? Explain your answer.

23.8. Explain how total return swaps are used in credit risk management.

23.9. A company wishes to construct a credit default swap where the underlying reference bond lasts six years and has a yield of 120 basis points above Treasuries. Explain how the credit swap could be structured and priced. What assumptions are you making in your pricing? Do the assumptions tend to overstate or understate the value of the credit default swap?

23.10. Suppose that a financial institution has entered into a swap dependent on the sterling interest rate with counterparty X and an exactly offsetting swap with counterparty Y. Which of the following statements are true and which are false?
   (a) The total present value of the cost of defaults is the sum of the present value of the cost of defaults on the contract with X plus the present value of the cost of defaults on the contract with Y.
   (b) The expected exposure in one year on both contracts is the sum of the expected exposure on the contract with X and the expected exposure on the contract with Y.
   (c) The 95% upper confidence limit for the exposure in one year on both contracts is the sum of the 95% upper confidence limit for the exposure in one year on the contract with X and the 95% upper confidence limit for the exposure in one year on the contract with Y.
   Explain your answers.

23.11. "When netting is allowed, the incremental effect of a new derivative transaction on total expected default costs with a particular counterparty can be negative." Explain this statement.

23.12. In Figure 23.1 the gradient of the curve for BBBs is much steeper than that for AAAs. Show that this is consistent with the explanation given in chapter 5 for the comparative advantage argument concerning interest rate swaps.

23.13. A company enters into a one-year forward contract to sell $100 for AUD150. The contract is initially at the money. In other words, the forward exchange rate is 1.50. The one-year dollar risk-free rate of interest is 5% per annum. The one-year dollar rate of interest that the counterparty can borrow is 6% per annum.

The exchange rate volatility is 12% per annum. What is the present value of the cost of defaults on the contract? Assume that defaults are recognized only at the end of the life of the contract.

23.14. Suppose that in Problem 23.13, the six-month forward rate is also 1.50 and the six-month dollar risk-free interest rate is 5% per annum. Suppose further that the six-month dollar rate of interest that the counterparty can borrow is 5.5% per annum. What is the present value of the cost of defaults assuming that defaults can occur either at the six-month point or at the one-year point? (If a default occurs at the six-month point, the company's potential loss is the market value of the contract.)

23.15. Consider an 18-month zero-coupon bond with a face value of $100 that can be converted into five shares of the company's stock at any time during its life. Suppose that the current share price is $20, no dividends are paid on the stock, the risk-free rate for all maturities is 6% per annum with continuous compounding, and the share price volatility is 25% per annum. Assume that the yield on non-convertible bonds issued by the company is 10% per annum for all maturities. The bond is callable at $110. Use a three-time-step tree to calculate the value of the bond. What is the value of the conversion option net of the issuer's call option?

ASSIGNMENT QUESTIONS

23.16. Suppose that the one-, two-, three-, four-, and five-year interest rates are 4%, 4.8%, 5.3%, 5.5%, and 5.6%, respectively. The volatility of all swap rates is 20%. A bank has entered into an annual-pay swap with a counterparty where the fixed rate exchanged for floating is 5.705%. The notational principal is $100 million. The spreads over Treasuries for one-, two-, three-, four-, and five-year bonds issued by the counterparty are 20, 40, 55, 65, and 75 basis points, respectively. Assume that defaults can occur only on payment dates and ignore any losses arising from payments that are due to be exchanged on the date of default. Use the DerivaGem software to answer the following questions

(a) What is the expected loss from defaults on a five-year swap where the bank receives fixed?

(b) What is the expected loss from defaults on a five-year swap where the bank receives floating? Explain why your answer here is higher than your answer to part (a).

(c) Estimate the spread required by the bank on a matched pair of interest rate swaps to compensate for credit risk.

(d) What difficulties are there in modifying your analysis to allow for losses arising from payments due to be made on the day of default?

23.17. Explain carefully the distinction between real-world and risk-neutral default probabilities. Which is higher? A bank enters into a credit derivative where it agrees to pay $100 at the end of one year if a certain company's credit rating falls from A to BBB or lower during the year. The one-year risk-free rate is 5%. Using Table 23.6, estimate a value for the derivative. What assumptions are you making? Do they tend to overstate or understate the value of the derivative?

23.18. The value of a company's equity is $4 million and the volatility of its equity is 60%. The debt that will have to be repaid in two years is $15 million. The risk-free interest rate is 6% per annum. Use Merton's model to estimate the expected loss from default, the probability of default, and the recovery rate in the event of default. Explain why Merton's model gives a high recovery rate. (*Hint:* The Solver function in Excel can be used for this question.)

23.19. A three-year convertible bond with a face value of $100 has been issued by company ABC. It pays a coupon of $5 at the end of each year. It can be converted into ABC's equity at the end of the first year or at the end of the second year. At the end of the first year, it can be exchanged for 3.6 shares immediately after the coupon date. At the end of the second year it can be exchanged for 3.5 shares immediately after the coupon date. The current stock price is $25 and the stock price volatility is 25%. No dividends are paid on the stock. The risk-free interest rate is 5% with continuous compounding. The yield on bonds issued by ABC is 7% with continuous compounding.

(a) Use a three-step tree to calculate the value of the bond.

(b) How much is the conversion option worth?

(c) What difference does it make to the value of the bond and the value of the conversion option if the bond is callable any time within the first two years for $115?

(d) Explain how your analysis would change if there were a dividend payment of $1 on the equity at the six month, 18-month, and 30-month points.

APPENDIX 23A

Manipulation of the Matrices of Credit Rating Changes

Suppose that $\mathbf{A}$ is an $N \times N$ matrix of credit rating changes in one year. This is a matrix such as the one shown in Table 18.6. The matrix of credit rating changes in m years is $\mathbf{A}^m$. This can be readily calculated using the normal rules for matrix multiplication.

The matrix corresponding to a shorter period than one year, say six months or one month is more difficult to compute. We first use standard routines to calculate eigenvectors $\mathbf{x}_i, \mathbf{x}_2, \ldots, \mathbf{x}_N$ and the corresponding eigenvalues $\lambda_1, \lambda_2, \ldots, \lambda_N$. These have the property that

$$\mathbf{A}\mathbf{x}_i = \lambda\mathbf{x}_i$$

Define $\mathbf{X}$ as a matrix whose ith row is $\mathbf{x}_i$ and $\mathbf{\Lambda}$ as a diagonal matrix where the ith diagonal element is λ_i. A standard result in matrix algebra shows that

$$\mathbf{A} = \mathbf{X}^{-1}\mathbf{\Lambda}\mathbf{X}$$

From this it is easy to see that the nth root of A is

$$\mathbf{X}^{-1}\mathbf{\Lambda}^*\mathbf{X}$$

where $\mathbf{\Lambda}^*$ is a diagonal matrix where the ith diagonal element is $\lambda_i^{1/n}$.

Glossary
of Notation

The following is a guide to the main ways that symbols are used in this book. Symbols that appear in one small part of the book may not be listed here, but are always defined when they are first used.

a Growth factor per step of an underlying variable in a risk-neutral world in a binomial model during time Δt. For example, when the underlying variable is a non-dividend-paying stock $a = e^{r\Delta t}$; when it is a currency, $a = e^{(r-r_f)\Delta t}$; and so on. The variable a is also used in chapter 10 as the drift rate in a generalized Wiener process. In chapter 21, it is the reversion rate in an interest rate process.

b In chapter 10, b^2 is the variance rate in a generalized Wiener process. In chapter 21, b is the reversion level in an interest rate process.

B Coupon-bearing bond price.

c Price of a European call option. It is also used in chapter 4 to denote a bond's coupon.

C Price of an American call option. It is also used in chapter 4 to denote convexity.

d_1, d_2 Parameters in option pricing formulas. See, for example, equations (11.20), (12.4), and (12.17).

d Proportional down movement in a binomial model. If $d = 0.9$, value of variable moves to 90% of its previous value when there is a down movement.

dz Wiener process.

D In chapter 7, D is the present value of dividends on a stock. In chapter 4, D is used to denote duration.

D_i The ith cash dividend payment.

$E(\cdot)$ Expected value of a variable.

$\hat{E}(\cdot)$ Expected value of a variable in a risk-neutral world.

f Value of a derivative. f_T is the value of a derivative at time T and f_0 is the value of a derivative at time zero. f_i is used on occasion to denote the value of the ith derivative.

f_u Value of derivative if an up movement occurs.

f_d Value of derivative if a down movement occurs.

F Forward or futures price at a general time t.

F_0 Forward or futures price at time zero.

F_T Forward or futures price at time T.

$F(t, T)$ Instantaneous forward interest rate as seen at time t for a contract with maturity T.

h Hedge ratio in chapter 2. The variable, h^*, is the optimal hedge ratio.

$h(T_1, T_2)$ Expected proportion of no-default value lost through defaults between times T_1 and T_2.

H Barrier level in a barrier option.

I Present value of income on a security.

K Delivery price in a forward contract.

L Principal amount in an interest rate derivatives contract.

$m(t, T)$ Drift of the instantaneous forward rate, $F(t, T)$, in chapter 22.

$M(x, y, \rho)$ Cumulative probability in a bivariate normal distribution that the first variable is less than x and the second variable is less than y when the coefficient of correlation between variables is ρ.

$N(x)$ Cumulative probability that a variable with a standardized normal distribution is less than x. A standardized normal distribution has a mean of zero and standard deviation of 1.0. Thus $N(0) = 0.5$.

p This is used in two important ways. The first is as the value of a European put option (e.g., in chapter 11). The second is as the probability of an up movement in binomial models (e.g., in chapter 16).

P Value of an American put option. In chapters 3 and 14, P denotes a portfolio value.

$P(t, T)$ The price at time t of a zero-coupon bond maturing at time T.

q Dividend yield rate. In chapter 9, q denotes the probability of an up movement in the real world. (This can be contrasted with p that is the probability of an up movement in the risk-neutral world.)

r Risk-free interest rate. Sometimes (e.g., chapters 3, 7, and 8) it is the rate applicable between times 0 and T and sometimes (e.g., chapter 21) it is the instantaneous (i.e., very short term) risk-free interest rate.

r_f Instantaneous risk-free interest rate in a foreign country.

$\bar{r}$ Average instantaneous risk-free rate of interest during the life of a derivative.

R In chapter 21, this is the Δt-period rate and should be distinguished from r, which is the instantaneous risk-free rate.

$R(t, T)$ Risk-free interest rate at time t for an investment maturing at time T.

$s(t, T)$ Standard deviation of the instantaneous forward rate, $F(t, T)$, in chapter 22.

S Price of asset underlying a derivative at a general time t. In different parts of the book, S is used to refer to the price of a currency, the price of a stock, the price of a stock index, and the price of a commodity.

S_T Value of S at time T.

S_0 Value of S at time zero.

t A future point in time.

T Time at maturity of a derivative.

u Proportional up movement in a binomial model. For example, $u = 1.2$ indicates that the variable increases by 20% when an up movement occurs. The symbol u is also used to denote the storage costs per unit time as a proportion of the price of an asset in chapter 3.

u_i In chapters 11 and 15, this denotes the return provided on an asset between observation $i - 1$ and observation i.

$v(t, T)$ In chapter 22, this denotes the volatility of the zero-coupon bond price $P(t, T)$.

$\mathcal{V}$ Vega of a derivative or a portfolio of derivatives.

X Strike price of an option.

y Usually denotes a bond's yield. In chapters 3 and 19, it denotes the convenience yield.

β In chapters 3 and 12, this denotes the capital asset pricing model's beta parameter.

Γ Gamma of a derivative or a portfolio of derivatives. A lowercase gamma, γ, is used to denote the gamma of a portfolio in chapter 14.

Δ Delta of a derivative or a portfolio of derivatives. A lowercase delta, δ, is used to denote the delta of a portfolio in chapter 14.

Δx Small change in x for any variable x.

ϵ Random sample from a standardized normal distribution.

η Continuously compounded return on a stock.

μ Expected return on an asset.

θ In chapter 19 this is the value of a variable that is not necessarily the price of a traded security.

Θ Theta of a derivative or portfolio of derivatives.

Π Value of a portfolio of derivatives.

ρ Coefficient of correlation.

σ Usually this is the volatility of an asset (i.e., $\sigma \sqrt{\Delta t}$ is the standard deviation of proportional changes in the asset's price in time Δt). Note that in chapter 2, σ_F and σ_S are the standard deviation of S and F at hedge maturity. Also, in the Hull–White and Ho–Lee models (chapter 21), σ is the instantaneous standard deviation (not the volatility) of the short rate.

σ_i In chapter 14, this is the volatility of the ith asset. In chapter 15, it is the volatility of a particular asset on day i.

σ_P Standard deviation (not volatility) of a portfolio in chapter 14.

$\phi(m, s)$ Normal distribution with mean m and standard deviation s.

Glossary
of Terms

Accrual Swap An interest rate swap where interest on one side accrues only when a certain condition is met.

Accrued Interest The interest earned on a bond since the last coupon payment date.

Adaptive Mesh Model A model developed by Figlewski and Gao that grafts a high resolution tree onto a low resolution tree so that there is more detailed modeling of the asset price in critical regions.

American Option An option that can be exercised at any time during its life.

Amortizing Swap A swap where the notional principal decreases in a predetermined way as time passes.

Arbitrage A trading strategy that takes advantage of two or more securities being mispriced relative to each other.

Arbitrageur An individual engaging in arbitrage.

Asian Option An option with a payoff dependent on the average price of the underlying asset during a specified period.

Ask Price The price that a dealer is offering to sell an asset.

Asked Price See ask price.

Asset-or-nothing Call Option An option that provides a payoff equal to the asset price if the asset price is above the strike price and zero otherwise.

Asset-or-nothing Put Option An option that provides a payoff equal to the asset price if the asset price is below the strike price and zero otherwise.

As-you-like-it Option See chooser option.

At-the-money Option An option in which the strike price equals the price of the underlying asset.

Average Price Call Option An option giving a payoff equal to the greater of zero and the amount by which the average price of the asset exceeds the strike price.

Average Price Put Option An option giving a payoff equal to the greater of zero and the amount by which the strike price exceeds the average price of the asset.

Average Strike Option An option that provides a payoff dependent on the difference between the final asset price and the average asset price.

Back Testing Testing a value-at-risk or other model using historical data.

Backwards Induction A procedure for working from the end of a tree to its beginning in order to value an option.

Barrier Option An option whose payoff depends on whether the path of the underlying asset has reached a barrier (i.e., a certain pre-determined level).

Basis The difference between the spot price and the futures price of a commodity.

Basis Point When used to describe an interest rate, a basis point is one hundredth of one percent ($= 0.01$ percent).

Basis Risk The risk to a hedger arising from uncertainty about the basis at a future time.

Basket Option An option that provides a payoff dependent on the value of a portfolio of assets.

Bear Spread A short position in a put option with strike price X_1, combined with a long position in a put option with strike price X_2 where $X_2 > X_1$. (A bear spread can also be created with call options.)

Bermudan Option An option that can be exercised on specified dates during its life.

Beta A measure of the systematic risk of an asset.

Bid–ask Spread The amount by which the ask price exceeds the bid price.

Bid–offer Spread See bid–ask spread.

Bid Price The price that a dealer is prepared to pay for an asset.

Binary Option An option with a discontinuous payoff; for example, a cash-or-nothing option or an asset-or-nothing option.

Binomial Model A model where the price of an asset is monitored over successive short periods of time. In each short period it is assumed that only two price movements are possible.

Binomial Tree A tree that represents how an asset price can evolve under the binomial model.

Bivariate Normal distribution A distribution for two correlated variables, each of which is normal.

Black's Approximation An approximate procedure developed by Fischer Black for valuing a call option on a dividend-paying stock.

Black's Model An extension of the Black–Scholes model for valuing European options on futures contracts.

Black–Scholes Model A model for pricing European options on stocks, developed by Fischer Black, Myron Scholes, and Robert Merton.

Board Broker The individual who handles limit orders in some exchanges. The board broker makes information on outstanding limit orders available to other traders.

Bond Option An option where a bond is the underlying asset.

Bootstrap Method A procedure for calculating the zero-coupon yield curve from market data.

Boston Option See deferred payment option.

Break Forward See deferred payment option.

Bull Spread A long position in a call with strike price X_1 combined with a short position in a call with strike price X_2, where $X_2 > X_1$. (A bull spread can also be created with put options.)

Butterfly Spread A position that is created by taking a long position in a call with strike price X_1, a long position in a call with strike price X_3, and a short position in two calls with strike price X_2, where $X_3 > X_2 > X_1$ and $X_2 = 0.5(X_1 + X_3)$. (A butterfly spread can also be created with put options.)

Calendar Spread A position that is created by taking a long position in a call option that matures at one time and a short position in a similar call option that matures at a different time. (A calendar spread can also be created using put options.)

Calibration A method for implying volatility parameters from the prices of actively traded options.

Callable Bond A bond containing provisions that allow the issuer to buy it back at a predetermined price at certain times during its life.

Call Option An option to buy an asset at a certain price by a certain date.

Cap See interest rate cap.

Capital Asset Pricing Model A model relating the expected return on an asset to its beta.

Caplet One component of an interest rate cap.

Cap Rate The rate determining payoffs in an interest rate cap.

Cash Flow Mapping A procedure for representing an instrument as a portfolio of zero-coupon bonds for the purpose of calculating value at risk.

Cash-or-nothing Call Option An option that provides a fixed predetermined payoff if the final asset price is above the strike price and zero otherwise.

Cash-or-nothing Put Option An option that provides a fixed predetermined payoff if the final asset price is below the strike price and zero otherwise.

Cash Settlement A procedure for settling a futures contract in cash rather than by delivering the underlying asset.

Cheapest-to-deliver Bond The bond that is cheapest to deliver in the Chicago Board of Trade bond futures contract.

Cholesky Decomposition A method of sampling from a multivariate normal distribution.

Chooser Option An option where the holder has the right to choose whether it is a call or a put at some point during its life.

Class of Options See option class.

Clean Price of Bond The quoted price of a bond. The cash price paid for the bond (or dirty price) is calculated by adding the accrued interest to the clean price.

Clearinghouse A firm that guarantees the performance of the parties in an exchange-traded derivatives transaction. (Also referred to as a clearing corporation.)

Clearing Margin A margin posted by a member of a clearinghouse.

Collar See interest rate collar.

Collateralized Mortgage Obligation (CMO) A mortgage-backed security where investors are divided into classes and there are rules for determining how principal repayments are channeled to the classes.

Combination A position involving both calls and puts on the same underlying asset.

Commission Brokers Individuals who execute trades for other people and charge a commission for doing so.

Commodity Futures Trading Commission A body that regulates trading in futures contracts in the United States.

Commodity Swap A swap where cash flows depend on the price of a commodity.

Compounding Frequency This defines how an interest rate is measured.

Compound Option An option on an option.

Compound Option Model A model that treats the equity of a company as an option on the company's assets.

Constant Maturity Swap A swap where a swap rate is exchanged for either a fixed rate or a floating rate on each payment date.

Constant Maturity Treasury Swap A swap where the yield on a Treasury bond is exchanged for either a fixed rate or a floating rate on each payment date.

Consumption Asset An asset held for consumption rather than investment.

Contango A situation where the futures price is above the expected future spot price.

Continuous Compounding A way of quoting interest rates. It is the limit as the assumed compounding interval is made smaller and smaller.

Control Variate Technique A technique that can sometimes be used for improving the accuracy of a numerical procedure.

Convenience Yield A measure of the benefits from ownership of an asset that are not obtained by the holder of a long futures contract on the asset.

Conversion Factor A factor used to determine the number of bonds that must be delivered in the Chicago Board of Trade bond futures contract.

Convertible Bond A corporate bond that can be converted into a predetermined amount of the company's equity at certain times during its life.

Convexity A measure of the curvature in the relationship between bond prices and bond yields.

Convexity Adjustment An overworked term. For example, it can refer to the adjustment necessary to convert a futures interest rate to a forward interest rate. It can also refer to the adjust-

ment to a forward rate that is sometimes necessary when Black's model is used.

Cornish–Fisher Expansion An approximate relationship between the fractiles of a probability distribution and its moments.

Cost of Carry The storage costs plus the cost of financing an asset minus the income earned on the asset.

Counterparty The opposite side in a financial transaction.

Coupon Interest payment made on a bond.

Covered Call A short position in a call option on an asset combined with a long position in the asset.

Credit Default Swap An instrument that gives the holder the right to sell a bond for its face value in the event of a default by the issuer.

Credit Derivative A derivative whose payoff depends on the creditworthiness of one or more entities.

Credit Rating A measure of the creditworthiness of a bond issue.

Credit Risk The risk that a loss will be experienced because of a default by the counterparty in a derivatives transaction.

Credit Transition Matrix A table showing the probability that a company will move from one credit rating to another during a certain period of time.

Credit Value at Risk The credit loss that will not be exceeded at some specified confidence level.

Cumulative Distribution Function The probability that a variable will be less than x as a function of x.

Currency Swap A swap where interest and principal in one currency are exchanged for interest and principal in another currency.

Day Count A convention for quoting interest rates.

Day Trade A trade that is entered into and closed out on the same day.

Deferred Payment Option An option where the price paid is deferred until the end of the option's life.

Deferred Swap An agreement to enter into a swap at some time in the future. Also called a forward swap.

Delta The rate of change of the price of a derivative with the price of the underlying asset.

Delta Hedging A hedging scheme that is designed to make the price of a portfolio of derivatives insensitive to small changes in the price of the underlying asset.

Delta-neutral Portfolio A portfolio with a delta of zero so that there is no sensitivity to small changes in the price of the underlying asset.

Derivative An instrument whose price depends on, or is derived from, the price of another asset.

Diagonal Spread A position in two calls where both the strike prices and times to maturity are different. (A diagonal spread can also be created with put options.)

Differential Swap A swap where a floating rate in one currency is exchanged for a floating rate in another currency and both rates are applied to the same principal.

Discount Bond See zero-coupon bond.

Discount Instrument An instrument, such as a Treasury bill, that provides no coupons.

Discount Rate The annualized dollar return on a Treasury bill or similar instrument expressed as a percentage of the final face value.

Dividend A cash payment made to the owner of a stock.

Dividend Yield The dividend as a percentage of the stock price.

Down-and-in Option An option that comes into existence when the price of the underlying asset declines to a prespecified level.

Down-and-out Option An option that ceases to exist when the price of the underlying asset declines to a prespecified level.

Downgrade Trigger A clause in a contract that states that the contract will be terminated with a cash settlement if the credit rating of one side falls below a certain level.

Drift Rate The average increase per unit of time in a stochastic variable.

Duration A measure of the average life of a bond. It is also an approximation to the ratio of the proportional change in the bond price to the absolute change in its yield.

Duration Matching A procedure for matching the durations of assets and liabilities in a financial institution.

Dynamic Hedging A procedure for hedging an option position by periodically changing the position held in the underlying assets. The objective is usually to maintain a delta-neutral position.

Early Exercise An exercise prior to the maturity date.

Efficient Market Hypothesis A hypothesis that asset prices reflect relevant information.

Embedded Option An option that is an inseparable part of another instrument.

Empirical Research Research based on historical market data.

Equilibrium Model A model for the behavior of interest rates derived from a model of the economy.

Equity Swap A swap where the return on an equity portfolio is exchanged for either a fixed or a floating rate of interest.

Eurocurrency A currency that is outside the formal control of the issuing country's monetary authorities.

Eurodollar A dollar held in a bank outside the United States.

Eurodollar Futures Contract A futures contract written on a Eurodollar deposit.

Eurodollar Interest Rate The interest rate on a Eurodollar deposit.

European Option An option that can be exercised only at the end of its life.

EWMA Exponentially weighted moving average.

Exchange Option An option to exchange one asset for another.

Ex-dividend Date When a dividend is declared, an ex-dividend date is specified. Investors who own shares of the stock up to the ex-dividend date receive the dividend.

Executive Stock Option A stock option issued by a company on its own stock and given to its executives as part of their remuneration.

Exercise Price The price at which the underlying asset may be bought or sold in an option contract. (Also called the strike price.)

Exotic Option A nonstandard option.

Expectations Theory The theory that forward interest rates equal expected future spot interest rates.

Expected Value of a Variable The average value of the variable obtained by weighting the alternative values by their probabilities.

Expiration Date The end of life of a contract.

Explicit Finite Difference Method A method for valuing a derivative by solving the underlying differential equation. The value of the derivative at time t is related to three values at time $t + \Delta t$. It is essentially the same as the trinomial tree method.

Exponentially Weighted Moving Average Model A model where exponential weighting is used to provide forecasts for a variable from historical data. It is sometimes applied to the variance rate in value at risk calculations.

Exponential Weighting A weighting scheme where the weight given to an observation depends on how recent it is. The weight given to an observation t time periods ago is λ times the weight given to an obsevation $t - 1$ time periods ago where $\lambda < 1$.

Exposure The maximum loss from default by a counterparty.

Extendable Bond A bond whose life can be extended at the option of the holder.

Extendable Swap A swap whose life can be extended at the option of one side to the contract.

Factor Analysis An analysis aimed at finding a small number of factors that describe most of the variation in a large number of correlated variables. (Similar to a principal components analysis.)

FASB Financial Accounting Standards Board.

Financial Intermediary A bank or other financial institution that facilitates the flow of funds between different entities in the economy.

Finite Difference Method A method for solving a differential equation.

Flat Volatility The name given to volatility used to price a cap when the same volatility is used for each caplet.

Flex Option An option traded on an exchange with terms that are different from the standard options traded by the exchange.

Floor See interest rate floor.

Floor-ceiling Agreement See collar.

Floorlet One component of a floor.

Floor Rate The rate in an interest rate floor agreement.

Foreign Currency Option An option on a foreign exchange rate.

Forward Contract A contract that obligates the holder to buy or sell an asset for a predetermined delivery price at a predetermined future time.

Forward Exchange Rate The forward price of one unit of a foreign currency.

Forward Interest Rate The interest rate for a future period of time implied by the rates prevailing in the market today.

Forward Price The delivery price in a forward contract that causes the contract to be worth zero.

Forward Rate Agreement (FRA) An agreement that a certain interest rate will apply to a certain principal amount for a certain time period in the future.

Forward Risk-Neutral World A world is forward risk-neutral with respect to a certain asset when the market price of risk equals the volatility of that asset.

Forward Start Option An option designed so that it will be at-the-money at some time in the future.

Forward Swap See deferred swap.

Futures Contract A contract that obligates the holder to buy or sell an asset at a predetermined delivery price during a specified future time period. The contract is marked to market daily.

Futures Option An option on a futures contract.

Futures Price The delivery price currently applicable to a futures contract.

Gamma The rate of change of delta with respect to the asset price.

Gamma-neutral Portfolio A portfolio with a gamma of zero.

GARCH Model A model for forecasting volatility where the variance rate follows a mean-reverting process.

Generalized Wiener Process A stochastic process where the change in a variable in each short time period of length Δt has a normal distribution with mean and variance, both proportional to Δt.

Geometric Average The nth root of the product of n numbers.

Geometric Brownian Motion A stochastic process often assumed for asset prices where the logarithm of the underlying variable follows a generalized Wiener process.

Greeks Hedge parameters such as delta, gamma, vega, theta, and rho.

Hedge A trade designed to reduce risk.

Hedger An individual who enters into hedging trades.

Hedge Ratio A ratio of the size of a position in a hedging instrument to the size of the position being hedged.

Historical Simulation A simulation based on historical data.

Historic Volatility A volatility estimated from historical data.

Implicit Finite Difference Method A method for valuing a derivative by solving the underlying differential equation. The value of the derivative at time $t + \Delta t$ is related to three values at time t.

Implied Distribution A distribution for a future asset price implied from option prices.

Implied Repo Rate The repo rate implied from the price of a Treasury bill and a Treasury bill futures price.

Implied Tree A tree describing the movements of an asset price that is constructed to be consistent with observed option prices.

Implied Volatility Volatility implied from an option price using the Black–Scholes or a similar model.

Index Amortizing Swap See indexed principal swap.

Index Arbitrage An arbitrage involving a position in the stocks comprising a stock index and a position in a futures contract on the stock index.

Indexed Principal Swap A swap where the principal declines over time. The reduction in the principal on a payment date depends on the level of interest rates.

Index Futures A futures contract on a stock index or other index.

Index Option An option contract on a stock index or other index.

Initial Margin The cash required from a futures trader at the time of the trade.

Interest-rate Cap An option that provides a payoff when a specified interest rate is above a certain level. The interest rate is a floating rate that is reset periodically.

Interest-rate Collar A combination of an interest-rate cap and an interest-rate floor.

Interest-rate Derivative A derivative whose payoffs are dependent on future interest rates.

Interest-rate Floor An option that provides a payoff when an interest rate is below a certain level. The interest rate is a floating rate that is reset periodically.

Interest-rate Option An option where the payoff is dependent on the level of interest rates.

Interest-rate Swap An exchange of a fixed rate of interest on a certain notional principal for a floating rate of interest on the same notional principal.

In-the-money Option Either (a) a call option where the asset price is greater than the strike price or (b) a put option where the asset price is less than the strike price.

Intrinsic Value For a call option, this is the greater of the excess of the asset price over the strike price and zero. For a put option, it is the greater of the excess of the strike price over the asset price and zero.

Inverted Market A market where futures prices decrease with maturity.

Investment Asset An asset held by at least some individuals for investment purposes.

IO (Interest Only) A mortgage-backed security where the holder receives only interest cash flows on the underlying mortgage pool.

Ito Process A stochastic process where the change in a variable during each short period of time of length Δt has a normal distribution. The mean and variance of the distribution are proportional to Δt and are not necessarily constant.

Ito's Lemma A result that enables the stochastic process for a function of a variable to be calculated from the stochastic process for the variable itself.

Kappa See vega.

Kurtosis A measure of the fatness of the tails of a distribution.

Lambda See vega.

LEAPS Long-term equity anticipation securities. These are relatively long-term options on individual stocks or stock indices.

LIBID London interbank bid rate. The rate bid by banks on Eurocurrency deposits (i.e., the rate at which a bank is willing to borrow from other banks).

LIBOR London interbank offer rate. The rate offered by banks on Eurocurrency deposits (i.e., the rate at which a bank is willing to lend to other banks).

LIBOR Curve LIBOR zero-coupon interest rates as a function of maturity.

Limit Move The maximum price move permitted by the exchange in a single trading session.

Limit Order An order that can be executed only at a specified price or one more favorable to the investor.

Liquidity Preference Theory A theory leading to the conclusion that forward interest rates are above expected future spot interest rates.

Liquidity Premium The amount that forward interest rates exceed expected future spot interest rates.

Locals Individuals on the floor of an exchange who trade for their own accounts, rather than for someone else.

Lognormal Distribution A variable has a lognormal distribution when the logarithm of the variable has a normal distribution.

Long Hedge A hedge involving a long futures position.

Long Position A position involving the purchase of an asset.

Lookback Option An option whose payoff is dependent on the maximum or minimum of the asset price achieved during a certain period.

Low Discrepancy Sequence See quasi-random sequence.

Maintenance Margin When the balance in a trader's margin account falls below the maintenance margin level, the trader receives a margin call requiring the account to be topped up to the initial margin level.

Margin The cash balance (or security deposit) required from a futures or options trader.

Margin Call A request for extra margin when the balance in the margin account falls below the maintenance margin level.

Market Maker A trader who is willing to quote both bid and offer prices for an asset.

Market Model A model most commonly used by traders.

Market Price of Risk A measure of the trade-offs investors make between risk and return.

Market Segmentation Theory A theory that short interest rates are determined independently of long interest rates by the market.

Marking to Market The practice of revaluing an instrument to reflect the current values of the relevant market variables.

Markov Process A stochastic process where the behavior of the variable over a short period of time depends solely on the value of the variable at the beginning of the period, not on its past history.

Martingale A zero-drift stochastic process.

Maturity Date The end of the life of a contract.

Maximum Likelihood Method A method for choosing the values of parameters by maximizing the probability of a set of observations occurring.

Mean Reversion The tendency of a market variable (such as an interest rate) to revert back to some long-run average level.

Measure Sometimes also called a probability measure, it defines the market price of risk.

Modified Duration A modification to the standard duration measure so that it more accurately describes the relationship between proportional changes in a bond price and absolute changes in its yield. The modification takes account of the compounding frequency with which the yield is quoted.

Money Market Account An investment that is initially equal to $1 and, at time t, increases at the very short-term risk-free interest rate prevailing at that time.

Monte Carlo Simulation A procedure for randomly sampling changes in market variables in order to value a derivative.

Mortgage-Backed Security A security that entitles the owner to a share in the cash flows realized from a pool of mortgages.

Naked Position A short position in a call option that is not combined with a long position in the underlying asset.

Netting The ability to offset contracts with positive and negative values in the event of a default by a counterparty.

Newton–Raphson Method An iterative procedure for solving nonlinear equations.

No-arbitrage Assumption The assumption that there are no arbitrage opportunities in market prices.

No-arbitrage Interest Rate Model A model for the behavior of interest rates that is exactly consistent with the initial term structure of interest rates.

Nonstationary Model A model where the volatility parameters are a function of time.

Nonsystematic Risk Risk that can be diversified away.

Normal Backwardation A situation where the futures price is below the expected future spot price.

Normal Distribution The standard bell-shaped distribution of statistics.

Normal Market A market where futures prices increase with maturity.

Notional Principal The principal used to calculate payments in an interest-rate swap. The principal is "notional" because it is neither paid nor received.

Numerical Procedure A method of valuing an option when no formula is available.

OCC Options Clearing Corporation. See clearinghouse.

Offer Price See ask price.

Open Interest The total number of long positions outstanding in a futures contract (equals the total number of short positions).

Option The right to buy or sell an asset.

Option-Adjusted Spread The spread over the Treasury curve that makes the theoretical price of an interest rate derivative equal to the market price.

Option Class All options of the same type (call or put) on a particular stock.

Option Series All options of a certain class with the same strike price and expiration date.

Order Book official See board broker.

Out-of-the-money Option Either (a) a call option where the asset price is less than the strike price or (b) a put option where the asset price is greater than the strike price.

Over-the-counter Market Market where traders deal by phone. The traders are usually financial institutions, corporations, and fund managers.

Package A derivative that is a portfolio of standard calls and puts, possibly combined with a position in forward contracts and the asset itself.

Parallel Shift A movement in the yield curve where each point on the curve changes by the same amount.

Par Value The principal amount of a bond.

Par Yield The coupon on a bond that makes its price equal the principal.

Path-dependent Option An option whose payoff depends on the whole path followed by the underlying variable—not just its final value.

Payoff The cash realized by the holder of an option or other derivative at the end of its life.

Plain Vanilla A term used to describe a standard deal.

PO (Principal Only) A mortgage-backed security where the holder receives only principal cash flows on the underlying mortgage pool.

Poisson Process A process describing a situation where events happen at random. The probability of an event in time Δt is $\lambda \Delta t$ where λ is the intensity of the process.

Portfolio Immunization Making a portfolio relatively insensitive to interest rates.

Portfolio Insurance Entering into trades to ensure that the value of a portfolio will not fall below a certain level.

Position Limit The maximum position a trader (or group of traders acting together) is allowed to hold.

Premium The price of an option.

Prepayment Function A function estimating the prepayment of principal on a portfolio of mortgages in terms of other variables.

Principal The par or face value of a debt instrument.

Principal Components Analysis An analysis aimed at finding a small number of factors that describe most of the variation in a large number of correlated variables. (Similar to a factor analysis.)

Program Trading A procedure where trades are automatically generated by a computer and transmitted to the trading floor of an exchange.

Protective Put A put option combined with a long position in the underlying asset.

Pull-to-Par The reversion of a bond's price to its par value at maturity.

Put–call Parity The relationship between the price of a European call option and the price of a European put option when they have the same strike price and maturity date.

Put Option An option to sell an asset for a certain price by a certain date.

Puttable Bond A bond where the holder has the right to sell it back to the issuer at certain predetermined times for a predetermined price.

Puttable Swap A swap where one side has the right to terminate early.

Quanto A derivative where the payoff is defined by variables associated with one currency but is paid in another currency.

Quasi–random Sequences Sequences of numbers used in a Monte Carlo simulation that are representative of alternative outcomes rather than random.

Rainbow Option An option whose payoff is dependent on two or more underlying variables.

Range-forward Contract The combination of a long call and short put or the combination of a short call and long put.

Rebalancing The process of adjusting a trading position periodically. Usually the purpose is to maintain delta neutrality.

Repo (Repurchase agreement) A procedure for borrowing money by selling securities to a counterparty and agreeing to buy them back later at a slightly higher price.

Repo Rate The rate of interest in a repo transaction.

Reset Date A date in a swap or cap or floor when the floating rate for the next period is set.

Reversion Level The level to which the value of a market variable (e.g., an interest rate) tends to revert.

Rho The rate of change of the price of a derivative with the interest rate.

Rights Issue An issue to existing shareholders of a security giving them the right to buy new shares at a certain price.

Risk-free Rate The rate of interest that can be earned without assuming any risks.

Risk-neutral Valuation The valuation of an option or other derivative assuming the world is risk neutral. Risk-neutral valuation gives the correct price for a derivative in all worlds, not just in a risk-neutral world.

Risk-neutral World A world where investors are assumed to require no extra return on average for bearing risks.

Roll Back See backwards induction.

Scalper A trader who holds positions for a very short period of time.

Scenario Analysis An analysis of the effects of possible alternative future movements in market variables on the value of a portfolio.

SEC Securities and Exchange Commission.

Settlement Price The average of the prices that a contract trades for immediately before the bell signaling the close of trading for a day. It is used in mark-to-market calculations.

Short Hedge A hedge where a short futures position is taken.

Short Position A position assumed when traders sell shares that they do not own.

Short Rate The interest rate applying for a very short period of time.

Short Selling Selling in the market shares that have been borrowed from another investor.

Shout Option An option where the holder has the right to lock in a minimum value for the payoff at one time during its life.

Sigma See vega.

Simulation See Monte Carlo simulation.

Specialist An individual responsible for managing limit orders on some exchanges. The specialist does not make the information on outstanding limit orders available to other traders.

Spot Interest Rate See zero-coupon interest rate.

Spot Price The price for immediate delivery.

Spot Volatilities The volatilities used to price a cap when a different volatility is used for each caplet.

Spread Option An option where the payoff is dependent on the difference between two market variables.

Spread Transaction A position in two or more options of the same type.

Static Hedge A hedge that does not have to be changed once it is initiated.

Static Options Replication A procedure for hedging a portfolio that involves finding another portfolio of approximately equal value on some boundary.

Step-up Swap A swap where the principal increases over time in a predetermined way.

Stochastic Process An equation describing the probabilistic behavior of a stochastic variable.

Stochastic Variable A variable whose future value is uncertain.

Stock Dividend A dividend paid in the form of additional shares.

Stock Index An index monitoring the value of a portfolio of stocks.

Stock Index Futures Futures on a stock index.

Stock Index Option An option on a stock index.

Stock Option An option on a stock.

Stock Split The conversion of each existing share into more than one new share.

Stop Order See stop-loss order.

Storage Costs The costs of storing a commodity.

Straddle A long position in a call and a put with the same strike price.

Strangle A long position in a call and a put with different strike prices.

Strap A long position in two call options and one put option with the same strike price.

Stress Testing Testing of the impact of extreme market moves on the value of a portfolio.

Strike Price The price at which the asset may be bought or sold in an option contract. (Also called the exercise price.)

Strip A long position in one call option and two put options with the same strike price.

Swap An agreement to exchange cash flows in the future according to a prearranged formula.

Swap Rate The fixed rate in an interest rate swap that causes the swap to have a value of zero.

Swaption An option to enter into an interest rate swap where a specified fixed rate is exchanged for floating.

Synthetic Option An option created by trading the underlying asset.

Systematic Risk Risk that cannot be diversified away.

Terminal Value The value at maturity.

Term Structure of Interest Rates The relationship between interest rates and their maturities.

Theta The rate of change of the price of an option or other derivative with the passage of time.

Time Decay See theta.

Time Value The value of an option arising from the time left to maturity (equals an option's price minus its intrinsic value).

Total Return Swap A swap of the return on one portfolio of assets for the return on another portfolio of assets.

Transactions Costs The cost of carrying out a trade (commisions plus the difference between the price obtained and the midpoint of the bid–offer spread).

Treasury Bill A short-term non-coupon-bearing instrument issued by the government to finance its debt.

Treasury Bill Futures A futures contract on a Treasury bill.

Treasury Bond A long-term coupon-bearing instrument issued by the government to finance its debt.

Treasury Bond Futures A futures contract on Treasury bonds.

Treasury Note See Treasury bond. (Treasury notes have maturities of less than 10 years.)

Treasury Note Futures A futures contract on Treasury notes.

Tree The representation of the evolution of the value of a market variable for the purposes of valuing an option or other derivative.

Trinomial Tree A tree where there are three branches emanating from each node. It is used in the same way as a binomial tree for valuing derivatives.

Triple Witching Hour A term given to the time when stock index futures, stock index options, and options on stock index futures all expire together.

Underlying Variable A variable that the price of an option or other derivative depends on.

Unsystematic Risk See nonsystematic risk.

Up-and-in Option An option that comes into existence when the price of the underlying asset increases to a prespecified level.

Up-and-out Option An option that ceases to exist when the price of the underlying asset increases to a prespecified level.

Uptick An increase in price.

Value at Risk A loss that will not be exceeded at some specified confidence level.

Variance-covariance Matrix A matrix showing variances of, and covariances between, a number of different market variables.

Variance Rate The square of volatility.

Variance Reduction Procedures Procedures for reducing the error in a Monte Carlo simulation.

Variation Margin An extra margin required to bring the balance in a margin account up to the initial margin when there is a margin call.

Vega The rate of change in the price of an option or other derivative with volatility.

Vega-neutral Portfolio A portfolio with a vega of zero.

Volatility A measure of the uncertainty of the return realized on an asset.

Volatility Matrix A table showing the variation of implied volatilities with strike price and time to maturity.

Volatility Skew A term used to describe the volatility smile when it is nonsymmetrical.

Volatility Smile The variation of implied volatility with strike price.

Volatility Term Structure The variation of implied volatility with time to maturity.

Warrant An option issued by a company or a financial institution. Call warrants are frequently issued by companies on their own stock.

Wiener Process A stochastic process where the change in a variable during each short period of time of length Δt has a normal distribution with a mean equal to zero and a variance equal to Δt.

Wild Card Play The right to deliver on a futures contract at the closing price for a period of time after the close of trading.

Writing an Option Selling an option.

Yield A return provided by an instrument.

Yield Curve See term structure.

Zero-Coupon Interest Rate The interest rate that would be earned on a bond that provides no coupons.

Zero-Coupon Yield Curve A plot of the zero-coupon interest rate against time to maturity.

Zero-Curve See zero-coupon yield curve.

Zero Rate See zero-coupon interest rate.

DerivaGem
Software

The software accompanying this text is DerivaGem for Excel, Version 1.2. It requires Excel Version 7.0 or later. The software consists of three files: Dg_95.xls, Dg_addin.xla, and HW_DG_v12.dll. To install the software you should create a directory entitled DerivaGem and load the first two files into the directory. HW_DG_v12.dll should be loaded into the Windows\System directory. Note that it is not uncommon for Windows Explorer to be set up so that *.dll files are not displayed. To change the setting so that the *.dll file can be seen, click *View*, followed by *Options*, followed by *Show All Files*.

Updates to the software can be downloaded from the author's Web site:

http://www.mgmt.utoronto.ca/~hull

Features of the Software

The software consists of three Excel worksheets. The first is used to carry out computations for stock options, currency options, index options, and futures options; the second is used for European and American bond options; the third is used for caps, floors, and European swap options.

The software produces prices, Greek letters, and implied volatilities for a wide range of different instruments. It displays charts showing the way that option prices and the Greek letters depend on inputs. It also displays binomial and trinomial trees showing how the computations are carried out.

General Operation

To use the software, you should choose a worksheet and click on the appropriate buttons to select Option Type, Underlying Type, and so on. You should then enter the parameters for the option you are considering, hit *Enter* on your keyboard, and click on *Calculate*. DerivaGem will then display the price or implied volatility for the option you are considering together with Greek letters. If the price has been calculated from a tree, and you are using the first or second worksheet, you can then click on *Display Tree* to see the tree. Sample displays of the tree are in Figures 16.3, 16.4, 16.5, 16.8, 16.9, and 21.11. Many different charts can be displayed in all three worksheets. To display a chart you must first choose the variable you require on the vertical axis, the variable you require on the horizontal axis, and the range of values to be considered on the horizontal axis. Following that, you should hit *Enter* on your keyboard and then click on *Draw Graph*.

672

Note that whenever the values in one or more cells are changed it is necessary to hit *Enter* on your keyboard before clicking on one of the buttons.

Options On Stocks, Currencies, Indices, and Futures

Worksheet 1 is used for options on stocks, currencies, indices, and futures. To use it, you should first select the Underlying Type (Equity, Currency, Index, or Futures). You should then select the Option Type (Analytic European, Binomial European, Binomial American, Asian,[1] Barrier Up and In, Barrier Up and Out, Barrier Down and In, Barrier Down and Out, Binary Cash or Nothing, Binary Asset or Nothing, Chooser, Compound Option on Call, Compound Option on Put, or Lookback.) You should then enter the data on the underlying asset and data on the option. Note that all interest rates are expressed with continuous compounding.

In the case of European and American equity options, a table pops up allowing you to enter dividends. Enter the time of each ex-dividend date (in years) in the first column and the amount of the dividend in the second column. Dividends must be entered in chronological order.

You must click on buttons to choose whether the option is a call or a put and whether you wish to calculate an implied volatility. If you do wish to calculate an implied volatility, the option price should be entered in the cell labeled Price.

Once all the data has been entered you should hit *Enter* on your keyboard and click on *Calculate*. If Implied Volatility was selected, DerivaGem displays the implied volatility in the Volatility (% per year) cell. If Implied Volatility was not selected, it uses the volatility you entered in this cell and displays the option price in the Price cell.

Once the calculations have been completed, the tree (if used) can be inspected and charts can be displayed.

When Analytic European is selected, DerivaGem uses the equations in chapters 11 and 12 to calculate prices and the equations in chapter 13 to calculate Greek letters. When Binomial European or Binomial American is selected, a binomial tree is constructed as described in sections 16.1 to 16.3. When an exotic option is selected, the equations in chapter 18 are used. For American options and exotic options, Greek letters are computed by perturbing the inputs.

The input data are largely self explanatory. In the case of an Asian option, the Current Average is the average price since inception. If the Asian option is new (time since inception equals zero) then the Current Average cell is irrelevant and can be left blank. In the case of a Lookback Option, the Minimum to Date is used when a Call is valued and the Maximum to Date is used when a Put is valued. For a new deal, these should be set equal to the current price of the underlying asset.

Bond Options

Worksheet 2 is used for European and American options on bonds. You should first select a pricing model (Black European, Normal Analytic European, Normal-Tree European, Normal American, Lognormal European, or Lognormal American). You

---

[1]Note that there is a bug in the valuation of Asian options in Version 1.2 of the software. This has been corrected in subsequent versions available from the author's website.

should then enter the Bond Data and the Option Data. The coupon is the rate paid per year and the frequency of payments can be selected as Quarterly, Semi-Annual, or Annual. The zero-coupon yield curve is entered in the table labeled Term Structure. Enter maturities (measured in years) in the first column and the corresponding continuously compounded rates in the second column. The maturities should be entered in chronological order. DerivaGem assumes a piecewise linear zero-curve similar to that in Figure 4.1. Note that, when valuing interest rate derivatives, DerivaGem rounds all times to the nearest whole number of days.

When all data have been entered, hit *Enter* on your keyboard. The quoted bond price per \$100 of Principal is displayed when the calculations are complete. You should indicate whether the option is a call or a put, and whether the strike price is a quoted (clean) strike price or a cash (dirty) strike price. (See Example 20.1 in section 20.2 for a discussion of this.) Note that the strike price is entered as the price per \$100 of principal. You should indicate whether you are considering a call or a put option and whether you wish to calculate an implied volatility. If you select implied volatility and the normal model or lognormal model is used, DerivaGem implies the short rate volatility keeping the reversion rate fixed.

Once all the inputs are complete, you should hit *Enter* on your keyboard and click *Calculate*. After that, the tree (if used) can be inspected and charts can be displayed. Note that the tree displayed lasts until the end of the life of the option. DerivaGem uses a much larger tree in its computations to value the underlying bond.

Note that when Black's model is selected, DerivaGem uses the equations in section 20.1 and the procedure in section 20.2 for converting the input yield volatility into a price volatility. When the Normal-Analytic European model is selected, it uses the equations in sections 21.8 and 21.9. When the other models are used, it follows the tree-building procedure in sections 21.11 and 21.12.

Swap Options and Caps

Worksheet 3 is used for caps and swap options. You should first select the Option Type (Swap Option or Cap/Floor) and Pricing Model (Black, Normal European, or Normal American). You should then enter data on the option you are considering. The Settlement Frequency indicates the frequency of payments and can be Annual, Semi-Annual, Quarterly, or Monthly. The software calculates payment dates by working backwards from the end of the life of the cap or swap option. The initial accrual period may be a nonstandard length between 0.5 and 1.5 times a normal accrual period. The software can be used to imply either a volatility or a cap rate/swap rate from the price. When a normal model or a lognormal model is used, DerivaGem implies the short rate volatility keeping the reversion rate fixed. The zero-coupon yield curve is entered in the table labeled Term Structure. Enter maturities (measured in years) in the first column and the corresponding continuously compounded rates in the second column. The maturities should be entered in chronological order. DerivaGem assumes a piecewise linear zero curve similar to that in Figure 4.1.

Once all the inputs are complete, you should click *Calculate*. After that, charts can be displayed.

Note that when Black's model is used, DerivaGem uses the equations in sections 20.3 and 20.4. When the other models are used, it follows the tree-building procedure in sections 21.11 to 21.12.

Greek Letters

In Worksheet 1, the Greek letters are calculated as follows.

Delta: Change in option price per dollar increase in underlying asset.
Gamma: Change in delta per dollar increase in underlying asset.
Vega: Change in option price per 1% increase in volatility (e.g., volatility increases from 20% to 21%).
Rho: Change in option price per 1% increase in interest rate (e.g., interest rate increases from 5% to 6%).
Theta: Change in option price per calendar day passing.

In worksheets 2 and 3, the Greek letters are calculated as follows:

DV01: Change in option price per one basis point upward parallel shift in the zero-curve.
Gamma01: Change in DV01 per one basis point upward parallel shift in the zero-curve, multiplied by 100.
Vega: Change in option price when volatility parameter increases by 1% (e.g., volatility increases from 20% to 21%).

MAJOR EXCHANGES TRADING FUTURES AND OPTIONS

Agrarische Termijnmarkt Amsterdam	ATA
American Stock Exchange	AMEX
Australian Options Market	AOM
Beijing Commodity Exchange	BCE
Belgian Futures & Options Exchange	BELFOX
Bolsa de Mercadorias y Futuros, Brazil	BM&F
Chicago Board of Trade	CBOT
Chicago Board Options Exchange	CBOE
Chicago Mercantile Exchange	CME
Coffee, Sugar & Cocoa Exchange, New York	CSCE
Commodity Exchange, New York	COMEX
Copenhagen Stock Exchange	FUTOP
Deutsche Termin Börse, Germany	DTB
European Options Exchange	EOE
Financiële Termijnmarkt Amsterdam	FTA
Finnish Options Market	FOM
Hong Kong Futures Exchange	HKFE
International Petroleum Exchange, London	IPE
Irish Futures & Options Exchange	IFOX
Kansas City Board of Trade	KCBT
Kobe Rubber Exchange	KRE
Kuala Lumpur Commodity Exchange	KLCE
London Commodity Exchange	LCE
London International Financial Futures & Options Exchange	LIFFE
London Metal Exchange	LME
London Securities and Derivatives Exchange	OMLX
Manila International Futures Exchange	MIFE
Marché à Terme International de France	MATIF
Marché des Options Négociables de Paris	MONEP
MEFF Renta Fija and Variable, Spain	MEFF
Mercado de Futuros y Opciones S.A., Argentina	MERFOX
MidAmerica Commodity Exchange	MidAm

676

Minneapolis Grain Exchange	MGE
Montreal Exchange	ME
New York Cotton Exchange	NYCE
New York Futures Exchange	NYFE
New York Mercantile Exchange	NYMEX
New York Stock Exchange	NYSE
New Zealand Futures & Options Exchange	NZFOE
Osaka Grain Exchange	OGE
Osaka Securities Exchange	OSA
Oslo Stock Exchange	OSLO
ÖTOB Aktiengesellschaft Austria	ÖTOB
Pacific Stock Exchange	PSE
Philadelphia Stock Exchange	PHLX
Singapore International Monetary Exchange	SIMEX
South Africa Futures Exchange	SAFEX
Stockholm Options Market	OM
Swiss Options & Financial Futures Exchange	SOFFEX
Sydney Futures Exchange	SFE
Tel Aviv Stock Exchange	TASE
Tokyo Commodity Exchange	TOCOM
Tokyo Grain Exchange	TGE
Tokyo International Financial Futures Exchange	TIFFE
Toronto Stock Exchange	TSE
Vancouver Stock Exchange	VSE
Winnipeg Commodity Exchange	WCE

This table shows values of $N(x)$ for $x \leq 0$. The table should be used with interpolation. For example,

$$N(-0.1234) = N(-0.12) - 0.34[N(-0.12) - N(-0.13)]$$
$$= 0.4522 - 0.34 \times (0.4522 - 0.4483)$$
$$= 0.4509$$

x	0.00	0.01	0.02	0.03	0.04	0.05	0.06	0.07	0.08	0.09
-0.0	0.5000	0.4960	0.4920	0.4880	0.4840	0.4801	0.4761	0.4721	0.4681	0.4641
-0.1	0.4602	0.4562	0.4522	0.4483	0.4443	0.4404	0.4364	0.4325	0.4286	0.4247
-0.2	0.4207	0.4168	0.4129	0.4090	0.4052	0.4013	0.3974	0.3936	0.3897	0.3859
-0.3	0.3821	0.3783	0.3745	0.3707	0.3669	0.3632	0.3594	0.3557	0.3520	0.3483
-0.4	0.3446	0.3409	0.3372	0.3336	0.3300	0.3264	0.3228	0.3192	0.3156	0.3121
-0.5	0.3085	0.3050	0.3015	0.2981	0.2946	0.2912	0.2877	0.2843	0.2810	0.2776
-0.6	0.2743	0.2709	0.2676	0.2643	0.2611	0.2578	0.2546	0.2514	0.2483	0.2451
-0.7	0.2420	0.2389	0.2358	0.2327	0.2296	0.2266	0.2236	0.2206	0.2177	0.2148
-0.8	0.2119	0.2090	0.2061	0.2033	0.2005	0.1977	0.1949	0.1922	0.1894	0.1867
-0.9	0.1841	0.1814	0.1788	0.1762	0.1736	0.1711	0.1685	0.1660	0.1635	0.1611
-1.0	0.1587	0.1562	0.1539	0.1515	0.1492	0.1469	0.1446	0.1423	0.1401	0.1379
-1.1	0.1357	0.1335	0.1314	0.1292	0.1271	0.1251	0.1230	0.1210	0.1190	0.1170
-1.2	0.1151	0.1131	0.1112	0.1093	0.1075	0.1056	0.1038	0.1020	0.1003	0.0985
-1.3	0.0968	0.0951	0.0934	0.0918	0.0901	0.0885	0.0869	0.0853	0.0838	0.0823
-1.4	0.0808	0.0793	0.0778	0.0764	0.0749	0.0735	0.0721	0.0708	0.0694	0.0681
-1.5	0.0668	0.0655	0.0643	0.0630	0.0618	0.0606	0.0594	0.0582	0.0571	0.0559
-1.6	0.0548	0.0537	0.0526	0.0516	0.0505	0.0495	0.0485	0.0475	0.0465	0.0455
-1.7	0.0446	0.0436	0.0427	0.0418	0.0409	0.0401	0.0392	0.0384	0.0375	0.0367
-1.8	0.0359	0.0351	0.0344	0.0336	0.0329	0.0322	0.0314	0.0307	0.0301	0.0294
-1.9	0.0287	0.0281	0.0274	0.0268	0.0262	0.0256	0.0250	0.0244	0.0239	0.0233
-2.0	0.0228	0.0222	0.0217	0.0212	0.0207	0.0202	0.0197	0.0192	0.0188	0.0183
-2.1	0.0179	0.0174	0.0170	0.0166	0.0162	0.0158	0.0154	0.0150	0.0146	0.0143
-2.2	0.0139	0.0136	0.0132	0.0129	0.0125	0.0122	0.0119	0.0116	0.0113	0.0110
-2.3	0.0107	0.0104	0.0102	0.0099	0.0096	0.0094	0.0091	0.0089	0.0087	0.0084
-2.4	0.0082	0.0080	0.0078	0.0075	0.0073	0.0071	0.0069	0.0068	0.0066	0.0064
-2.5	0.0062	0.0060	0.0059	0.0057	0.0055	0.0054	0.0052	0.0051	0.0049	0.0048
-2.6	0.0047	0.0045	0.0044	0.0043	0.0041	0.0040	0.0039	0.0038	0.0037	0.0036
-2.7	0.0035	0.0034	0.0033	0.0032	0.0031	0.0030	0.0029	0.0028	0.0027	0.0026
-2.8	0.0026	0.0025	0.0024	0.0023	0.0023	0.0022	0.0021	0.0021	0.0020	0.0019
-2.9	0.0019	0.0018	0.0018	0.0017	0.0016	0.0016	0.0015	0.0015	0.0014	0.0014
-3.0	0.0014	0.0013	0.0013	0.0012	0.0012	0.0011	0.0011	0.0011	0.0010	0.0010
-3.1	0.0010	0.0009	0.0009	0.0009	0.0008	0.0008	0.0008	0.0008	0.0007	0.0007
-3.2	0.0007	0.0007	0.0006	0.0006	0.0006	0.0006	0.0006	0.0005	0.0005	0.0005
-3.3	0.0005	0.0005	0.0005	0.0004	0.0004	0.0004	0.0004	0.0004	0.0004	0.0003
-3.4	0.0003	0.0003	0.0003	0.0003	0.0003	0.0003	0.0003	0.0003	0.0003	0.0002
-3.5	0.0002	0.0002	0.0002	0.0002	0.0002	0.0002	0.0002	0.0002	0.0002	0.0002
-3.6	0.0002	0.0002	0.0001	0.0001	0.0001	0.0001	0.0001	0.0001	0.0001	0.0001
-3.7	0.0001	0.0001	0.0001	0.0001	0.0001	0.0001	0.0001	0.0001	0.0001	0.0001
-3.8	0.0001	0.0001	0.0001	0.0001	0.0001	0.0001	0.0001	0.0001	0.0001	0.0001
-3.9	0.0000	0.0000	0.0000	0.0000	0.0000	0.0000	0.0000	0.0000	0.0000	0.0000
-4.0	0.0000	0.0000	0.0000	0.0000	0.0000	0.0000	0.0000	0.0000	0.0000	0.0000

This table shows values of $N(x)$ for $x \geq 0$. The table should be used with interpolation. For example,

$$N(0.6278) = N(0.62) + 0.78[N(0.63) - N(0.62)]$$
$$= 0.7324 + 0.78 \times (0.7357 - 0.7324)$$
$$= 0.7350$$

x	0.00	0.01	0.02	0.03	0.04	0.05	0.06	0.07	0.08	0.09
0.0	0.5000	0.5040	0.5080	0.5120	0.5160	0.5199	0.5239	0.5279	0.5319	0.5359
0.1	0.5398	0.5438	0.5478	0.5517	0.5557	0.5596	0.5636	0.5675	0.5714	0.5753
0.2	0.5793	0.5832	0.5871	0.5910	0.5948	0.5987	0.6026	0.6064	0.6103	0.6141
0.3	0.6179	0.6217	0.6255	0.6293	0.6331	0.6368	0.6406	0.6443	0.6480	0.6517
0.4	0.6554	0.6591	0.6628	0.6664	0.6700	0.6736	0.6772	0.6808	0.6844	0.6879
0.5	0.6915	0.6950	0.6985	0.7019	0.7054	0.7088	0.7123	0.7157	0.7190	0.7224
0.6	0.7257	0.7291	0.7324	0.7357	0.7389	0.7422	0.7454	0.7486	0.7517	0.7549
0.7	0.7580	0.7611	0.7642	0.7673	0.7704	0.7734	0.7764	0.7794	0.7823	0.7852
0.8	0.7881	0.7910	0.7939	0.7967	0.7995	0.8023	0.8051	0.8078	0.8106	0.8133
0.9	0.8159	0.8186	0.8212	0.8238	0.8264	0.8289	0.8315	0.8340	0.8365	0.8389
1.0	0.8413	0.8438	0.8461	0.8485	0.8508	0.8531	0.8554	0.8577	0.8599	0.8621
1.1	0.8643	0.8665	0.8686	0.8708	0.8729	0.8749	0.8770	0.8790	0.8810	0.8830
1.2	0.8849	0.8869	0.8888	0.8907	0.8925	0.8944	0.8962	0.8980	0.8997	0.9015
1.3	0.9032	0.9049	0.9066	0.9082	0.9099	0.9115	0.9131	0.9147	0.9162	0.9177
1.4	0.9192	0.9207	0.9222	0.9236	0.9251	0.9265	0.9279	0.9292	0.9306	0.9319
1.5	0.9332	0.9345	0.9357	0.9370	0.9382	0.9394	0.9406	0.9418	0.9429	0.9441
1.6	0.9452	0.9463	0.9474	0.9484	0.9495	0.9505	0.9515	0.9525	0.9535	0.9545
1.7	0.9554	0.9564	0.9573	0.9582	0.9591	0.9599	0.9608	0.9616	0.9625	0.9633
1.8	0.9641	0.9649	0.9656	0.9664	0.9671	0.9678	0.9686	0.9693	0.9699	0.9706
1.9	0.9713	0.9719	0.9726	0.9732	0.9738	0.9744	0.9750	0.9756	0.9761	0.9767
2.0	0.9772	0.9778	0.9783	0.9788	0.9793	0.9798	0.9803	0.9808	0.9812	0.9817
2.1	0.9821	0.9826	0.9830	0.9834	0.9838	0.9842	0.9846	0.9850	0.9854	0.9857
2.2	0.9861	0.9864	0.9868	0.9871	0.9875	0.9878	0.9881	0.9884	0.9887	0.9890
2.3	0.9893	0.9896	0.9898	0.9901	0.9904	0.9906	0.9909	0.9911	0.9913	0.9916
2.4	0.9918	0.9920	0.9922	0.9925	0.9927	0.9929	0.9931	0.9932	0.9934	0.9936
2.5	0.9938	0.9940	0.9941	0.9943	0.9945	0.9946	0.9948	0.9949	0.9951	0.9952
2.6	0.9953	0.9955	0.9956	0.9957	0.9959	0.9960	0.9961	0.9962	0.9963	0.9964
2.7	0.9965	0.9966	0.9967	0.9968	0.9969	0.9970	0.9971	0.9972	0.9973	0.9974
2.8	0.9974	0.9975	0.9976	0.9977	0.9977	0.9978	0.9979	0.9979	0.9980	0.9981
2.9	0.9981	0.9982	0.9982	0.9983	0.9984	0.9984	0.9985	0.9985	0.9986	0.9986
3.0	0.9986	0.9987	0.9987	0.9988	0.9988	0.9989	0.9989	0.9989	0.9990	0.9990
3.1	0.9990	0.9991	0.9991	0.9991	0.9992	0.9992	0.9992	0.9992	0.9993	0.9993
3.2	0.9993	0.9993	0.9994	0.9994	0.9994	0.9994	0.9994	0.9995	0.9995	0.9995
3.3	0.9995	0.9995	0.9995	0.9996	0.9996	0.9996	0.9996	0.9996	0.9996	0.9997
3.4	0.9997	0.9997	0.9997	0.9997	0.9997	0.9997	0.9997	0.9997	0.9997	0.9998
3.5	0.9998	0.9998	0.9998	0.9998	0.9998	0.9998	0.9998	0.9998	0.9998	0.9998
3.6	0.9998	0.9998	0.9999	0.9999	0.9999	0.9999	0.9999	0.9999	0.9999	0.9999
3.7	0.9999	0.9999	0.9999	0.9999	0.9999	0.9999	0.9999	0.9999	0.9999	0.9999
3.8	0.9999	0.9999	0.9999	0.9999	0.9999	0.9999	0.9999	0.9999	0.9999	0.9999
3.9	1.0000	1.0000	1.0000	1.0000	1.0000	1.0000	1.0000	1.0000	1.0000	1.0000
4.0	1.0000	1.0000	1.0000	1.0000	1.0000	1.0000	1.0000	1.0000	1.0000	1.0000

Author Index

680

Subject Index

G

P

T

Derivagem to accompany Hull's Options, Futures, and Other Derivatives, 4/e